Work Motivation in Organizational Behavior

Craig C. Pinder

University of British Columbia

Prentice Hall, Upper Saddle River, New Jersey 07458

Senior Editor: David Shafer
Assistant Editor: Lisamarie Brassini
Editor-in-Chief: Natalie Anderson
Editorial Assistant: Christopher Stogdill
Marketing Manager: Tammy Wederbrand
Production Editor: Judith Leale
Managing Editor: Dee Josephson
Manufacturing Buyer: Diane Peirano
Manufacturing Supervisor: Arnold Vila
Manufacturing Manager: Vincent Scelta
Cover Design: Wendy Alling Judy

Library of Congress Cataloging-in-Publication Data

Pinder, Craig C.
    Work motivation in organizational behavior / Craig C. Pinder.
       p. cm.
    Includes bibliographical references and index.
    ISBN 0-02-395622-4
    1. Employee motivation. 2. Organizational behavior. I. Title.
HF5549.5.M63P56   1997
658.3'14—DC21   97-30764
                                            CIP

Prentice-Hall International (UK) Limited,London
Prentice-Hall of Australia Pty. Limited, Sydney
Prentice-Hall Canada Inc., Toronto
Prentice-Hall Hispanoamericana, S.A., Mexico
Prentice-Hall of India Private Limited, New Delhi
Prentice-Hall of Japan, Inc., Tokyo
Pearson Education Asia Pte. Ltd., Singapore
Editora Prentice-Hall do Brasil, Ltda., Rio de Janeiro

Printed in the United States of America

10 9 8 7 6 5 4 3 2

Brief Contents

Contents

v

Preface

This book is about why people work. It is a critical compilation of the social scientific literature about the nature of work, the origins of people's desire to work, and the emotional, attitudinal, social, and economic consequences of their work. This is not a book intended to instruct managers or supervisors about how to motivate employees—rather it is an examination of what is currently known about the nature, the origins, and the consequences of human work activity at the end of the twentieth century. Readers with applied interests should find the book informative but will not find simple prescriptions for motivating other people.

My interest in work motivation originated 30 years ago when I was a teenager who planned to go to law school, become a politician and, ultimately, become the prime minister of Canada. All of those lofty career goals changed when I reflected on the emotional aspects of the work I had been doing in grocery stores, on garbage trucks and street-cleaning gangs, and in the offices of the City of Vancouver's personnel department. In those various summer and part-time jobs, I witnessed how work can be a source of joy, pride, and satisfaction for people and how it can also be a daily source of dread, anger, and misery. I had witnessed for years the efforts of my parents to provide my family with a decent standard of living: Doing so required my father to moonlight during much of his career as a letter carrier and my mother to work evening shifts sorting mail or working in grocery stores. By the age of 20, I developed an intellectual curiosity and personal sympathy with regard to the meaning and significance of work and work organizations in the lives of working people. Law school lost its luster and organizational psychology captured my attention. I have subsequently invested more than 26 years in the organizational sciences in order to understand and to help others to understand the meaning and significance of work to human beings. This purpose has been the central mission of my professional life. I have tried to reflect these personal and emotional origins of my interest in work motivation throughout the book, and, at the same time, provide a dispassionate assessment of the theory and research on the subject. Academic books can often be sterile and too cerebral to convey the human significance of the topics they cover. Accordingly, I have tried as much as I can to reveal the emotional dimensions of working and work motivation while providing what is intended to be a hard-nosed analysis of the social science that pertains to it.

Many friends, students, and colleagues have been generous with their advice and assistance as I researched and prepared this manuscript. Kai Lamertz of the University of Toronto and Karen Harlos of the University of Otago provided helpful guidance into and through the burgeoning literature on justice in the workplace. Richard Stackman of the University of Washington offered significant substantive and stylistic suggestions on many of the chapters in their earlier forms. Wilfred Zerbe of the University of Calgary co-authored chapter 12, which deals with Valence-Instrumentality-Expectancy models of work motivation. Professor Jim Russell of the Psychology Department at UBC gave his kind approval to my chapter on emotion and work motivation (chapter 4). I am grateful to all of these folks for their help.

Students of Professor Patricia Smith used early draft versions of many chapters of this book in a course she taught at Berry College in Atlanta, Georgia, nearly three years ago. I thank Pat Smith and her students for their interest, their support, and their commentary on the manuscript as it existed at that time.

I sought and received the advice of several colleagues whose own work on work motivation I admire, specifically on the standing of behaviorism in the organizational sciences. For their opinions on the matter, I thank Jone Pearce and Barry Staw of the University of California; Richard Mowday of the University of Oregon; Judy Komaki of the City University of New York; Gary Latham of the University of Toronto; and Dennis Organ of Indiana University. On the basis of their mixed suggestions, I decided to address the behaviorist model of work motivation and behavior from an historical perspective, attempting to tell the story of the rise and fall of that school of thought, both for its own sake as well as for the sake of offering an example of the history of enquiry in organizational behavior. Special thanks are reserved for Professor Edwin Locke of the University of Maryland who offered considerable support and many critical suggestions as I prepared and finalized the manuscript.

This book borrows from but is intended to go far beyond my earlier book *Work Motivation: Theory, Issues and Applications*. The treatment of topics related to work motivation is broader here than it was in the first book, and, I hope, this book will serve more as a vehicle for the general study of human behavior in work settings than the earlier book.

I dedicate this work with affection to my loving wife and best friend, Pat Pinder.

Craig Pinder
Vancouver, B.C.
June 1997

Part One: Introduction

CHAPTER

Work Motivation, Productivity, and Individual Survival

*The principal object of management should be to secure
the maximum prosperity for the employer, coupled
with the maximum prosperity for each employee.*
—F. W. TAYLOR

The alarm clock rings early on Monday morning. It's cold and rainy outdoors, with a stiff wind that will ensure you get wet on your way to work. You didn't sleep well last night, and the bed sure feels good: warm, cozy, and secure. There are a few cobwebs to clear from your head as well—souvenirs from a weekend of fun, perhaps. Then a thought occurs: "To heck with work today! I don't feel very well, and I haven't missed a day in weeks. Besides, lots of the others seem to be missing from work on Monday mornings, so maybe it's my turn!"

Scenarios like this are familiar to most of us who work or have worked for a living. It's often a challenge not to turn off the alarm, pull up the blankets, and go back to sleep.

The decision whether to get out of bed rests at the core of the issue of work motivation—the central topic of this book. Later, a formal definition of work motivation will be offered, but until then, let's merely think of it as the energy a person expends in relation to work: to get and to keep a job, to perform well at one's job, and perhaps even to create ways of improving how the job is done. Work motivation includes creating a job for one's self or moving to another job. For many people today, work motivation often also means retraining and reentering the workforce after losing a job. Motivating people to get out of bed on mornings such as the one just described (not to mention other days, when there is neither rain nor wind, and the soul and mind are fresh and alert) is one of the principal concerns of managers in any society. The next challenge for managers is to encourage employees to engage themselves mentally and emotionally while they are on the job, because people do not always fully engage in their work roles even when they show up for work (see W. A. Kahn, 1990).

The well-being of most economies depends heavily on the willingness of its citizens to get out of bed, to find jobs or to report to the jobs they already hold, and to perform their work with excellence. In some cases, there is no manager or superior for an employee to report to. In other cases, such an authority figure exists but that person is not concerned with the attendance and punctuality of employees, so motivation must come from within the individual employee. Finally, in more and more cases in recent years, there is not even a job to report to, so the goal of motivated work effort is to find work for remuneration. All these examples are matters of work motivation.

The topic of work motivation is popular in the media, although opinions vary. Newspaper stories or the results of studies attempt to demonstrate that people don't work as hard as they used to or that they work harder, that the desire for leisure is driving out the desire to work and prosper, that today's employees aren't as eager as their ancestors, or that people in other countries are collectively outworking those in North America.[1] A recent article in *The Economist* (1996), for example, claims that the Organization for Economic Cooperation and Development (OECD) found that Americans are working harder and longer hours than had been previously recognized, in part because their study took into account the multiple jobs that many Americans are now working. One reason, reports *The Economist,* is that Americans' tastes for high consumption must be fed, one way or another, so they are working harder and for longer hours. The same study reports, interestingly, that the average number of hours worked in Germany has declined dramatically since the early 1970s. Until recently it was the Japanese, although there are signs that their vaunted work ethic may be eroding (see *The Economist,* 1996; Veale, 1993), perhaps in part because companies there can no longer guarantee lifetime employment and, in addition, often expect lasting devotion and hard work from their employees (see Rifkin, 1995, pp. 185–186). These days it is the Koreans who are frequently seen as the most highly motivated and hard-working.

The case of a woman who quit a well paying civil service job in Ontario in 1993 in order to go on welfare while she planned ways to start her own business is a fascinating example of the importance of work motivation in the minds of the public at large (see *Montreal Gazette,* 1993). Helle Hulgaard had been working as a community relations officer for the Metropolitan Toronto Housing Authority at an annual salary of $41,500. Ms. Hulgaard recognized that although she would lose a few hundred dollars a month in income by quitting her job, the support provided by welfare would be enough for her to get by on, given that she would no longer incur the many costs of holding a regular job: costs such as travel, meals, and day-care expenses for her two children. Considerable hostility was reported by the Canadian media, including allegations that Ms. Hulgaard was lazy and exploiting the social support systems of Canada. At the same time, considerable heat was directed at the premier of Ontario, whose newly elevated tax system had precipitated Hulgaard's decision to quit her job and look for an apparently easier way to survive. Were the allegations of laziness valid and fair? Ms. Hulgaard had paid her own way through school, earning a degree in philosophy from York University while working 30 hours a week (*Montreal Gazette,* 1993). All she wanted to do, she said, was to begin a small housecleaning business.

---

[1]Ironically, even on the day the author was polishing the first draft of this chapter for review by outside reviewers (July 24, 1995), an article appeared in Ann Landers' famous column in the *Vancouver Sun* (originating in the *Chicago Tribune*). The heading of the column was "Stop putting the younger generation down—we ARE prepared to work hard." There is no need to elaborate on the contents of the letter to Ms. Landers; the title (P.O.'d in Seattle) speaks well for the author's theme.

Our purpose is neither to judge Ms. Hulgaard nor the fairness of Ontario's taxation system. It is to report one incident in which the public showed keen interest (some of it simple outrage) in the issue of Hulgaard's decision not to work—apparently a matter of high social interest and importance. There are many opinions about work motivation and the work ethic, trends in work motivation, and the importance of a motivated workforce. In a recent review of the field of organizational behavior, O'Reilly (1991) suggested that the topic of work motivation will increase in importance in the next decade to practitioners as increasingly fewer *new* workers enter the workforce.

In part, this book is about the nature of differences among people in their motivation to work: whether for oneself, a small employer, a government agency, or a large multinational conglomerate. It seems that we must, collectively, be willing to put our feet on the floor on cold, rainy mornings such as the one described at the beginning of the chapter and go to work if we are to survive and flourish as individuals and as a safe, comfortable, and stable economic society. Both individually and collectively, we *must* be productive. Yet, as we will see shortly, the productivity mentality that has characterized the concepts of work and working since the beginning of the first industrial revolution may have, ironically, become a portent of the doom of many millions of people while being the indicator of success only for a selected few. What is productivity, then, and how is it related to work motivation? We address these questions in the following sections.

PRODUCTIVITY: A RELATIVE CONCEPT
WITH IRONIC CONSEQUENCES FOR THE FUTURE

The competitive economic edge and subsequent well-being of countries such as Canada, the United States, Sweden, and Switzerland in recent decades has largely been a result of the high comparative levels of productivity in the economies of these countries over the past few generations. High productivity *and comparatively high increases in productivity* have permitted high wages, inexpensive goods and services, abundant public amenities and social services, and a generally high standard of living for all (T. A. Mahoney, 1988; Thurow, 1980). High productivity has long been both a measure of, and a contributing factor to, the quality of life that we enjoy.

T. A. Mahoney (1988) points out that increases in *production* are accomplished through either or both of two means: (1) increased use of production inputs (e.g., capital, land, water resources, and labor), and (2) increased efficiency in the transformation of inputs into usable outputs (such as goods or services). For Mahoney and for most economists, productivity has to do with the second of these two approaches—getting more goods and services for a given or fixed level of input factors. Moreover, productivity has meaning only in relative terms. "There is no ideal level of productivity, and judgements are limited to 'more' or 'less' comparisons" (T. A. Mahoney, 1988, p. 14). Therefore, we can reasonably compare the productivity of a given firm or economy with its own level from an earlier time, and/or we can make comparisons among firms or entire economies for a common period. In its simplest terms, *productivity* is the value of the economic output achieved in an industry or economy per unit of human labor and fixed capital required to attain it. It is a measure of how much work people accomplish at their jobs, divided by the amount of time they spend doing those jobs:

time spent collecting salaries (or wages) and benefits. When the level of economic output per unit of input increases, more people can enjoy more goods and services without causing others to consume less (Rees, 1980).

Economists, business executives, shareholders, and public leaders are concerned continuously with the productivity problem and make both types of comparisons described by T. A. Mahoney (1988). Productivity is measured by a variety of indicators, such as profit, customer satisfaction, reduced costs, or units produced. Productivity ratios, such as return on investment, net earnings per share, and output per employee are other examples. There is no "one best way" to measure productivity: Different types of measures are required for different contexts and purposes. Moreover, regardless of how it is measured, increases in one's productivity over time are universally seen as good, both an increase over someone else's level or one's own increased productivity rate. To repeat, "comparative level and rate of change are the key aspects of productivity measurement" (T. A. Mahoney, 1988, p. 22).

Sometimes the wages, salaries, and benefits paid to a nation's workforce rise faster than the nation's productivity. When we speak of declining productivity, we mean that it is taking comparatively more human labor to accomplish the same amount of economic output as before—fewer goods and services for the same investment as in the past. The consequence, in part, is that the benefits an economy can deliver cost everyone more than in the past—a phenomenon referred to as *cost-push inflation* (Blair, 1975). Some economists (e.g., Malkiel, 1979) see declining productivity (or a failure to increase productivity as much as in other countries) as the most serious threat to the health of the economies of the Western world. The question arises: How well are we in North America doing these days compared with countries with whom we trade and compete?

Table 1-1 presents recent data on the aggregate productivity levels of member countries of the OECD (Organization for Economic and Cooperation and Development). Reported are total factor, labor, and capital productivity for the 21 member countries, over three periods from 1960 to 1995. Of most interest for the current discussion is the right half of the table, which represents the average percentage changes in annual rates of output per employed person in the business sectors of the OECD countries. Clearly, labor productivity increases in Japan and most of the European member countries have outstripped increases in the United States and Canada during the most recent period reported. A study by Denny, Bernstein, Fuss, Nakamura, and Waverman (1992) shows that whereas productivity increases in Japan are higher than those in Canada and the United States, since the slump of the 1980s the annual gains (in the manufacturing sector at least) are not yet back to the levels prior to 1973, when the slowdown began. As discussed below, it is the size of the *changes* in productivity that are of paramount importance.

Productivity is an important issue in the industrial and service sectors (see J. B. Quinn and Baily, 1994) as well as in government (Crane and Jones, 1991), affecting the quality of life enjoyed by all of us. In fact, with a growing proportion of modern economies originating in service (rather than in manufacturing), economists and national income accountants have paid increased attention in recent years to measuring and monitoring comparative productivity levels in the service sectors (e.g., J. B. Quinn and Baily, 1994).

TABLE 1-1 Comparative Productivity Data among OECD Countries
(Percentage Changes at Annual Rates for Three Periods of Time)

	Total Factor Productivity			Labor Productivity		
	1960–73	*1973–79*	*1979–95*	*1960–73*	*1973–79*	*1979–95*
United States	2.5	0.2	0.5	2.6	0.4	0.8
Japan	5.4	1.1	1.2	8.4	2.8	2.2
Germany	2.6	1.8	0.4	4.5	3.1	0.9
France	3.7	1.6	1.5	5.3	2.9	2.2
Italy	4.5	2.0	1.1	6.4	2.8	2.0
United Kingdom	2.6	0.6	1.5	3.9	1.5	2.0
Canada	1.9	0.6	−0.1	2.9	1.5	1.1
Total of countries above	3.3	0.8	0.8	4.5	1.6	1.4
Australia	2.2	1.1	0.8	3.3	2.4	1.4
Austria	3.1	1.0	1.0	5.5	3.0	2.3
Belgium	4.4	1.7	1.4	5.2	2.7	2.2
Denmark	2.3	0.9	1.2	3.9	2.4	2.1
Finland	4.0	1.9	2.5	5.0	3.2	3.5
Greece	2.5	0.7	−0.3	9.0	3.3	0.6
Ireland	4.5	3.4	2.6	5.0	4.0	3.3
Netherlands	3.6	1.7	1.1	4.9	2.6	1.6
Norway	2.0	1.7	−0.1	3.8	3.1	1.5
Portugal	5.4	−0.2	1.6	7.4	0.5	2.4
Spain	3.2	0.8	1.6	6.0	3.2	2.9
Sweden	2.0	0.0	1.1	3.7	1.4	2.0
Switzerland	2.2	−0.2	−0.1	3.3	0.9	0.4

Source: OECD, 1996, *OECD Economic Outlook*. Reproduced with permission of the OECD.

Determinants of Productivity

What determines the level of productivity in an industrial economy? A traditional answer to this question might begin by observing that there are many contributing factors, which we may categorize in two major groups. The first group consists of large-scale factors generally beyond the control of individual managers, executives, corporations, or governments. In fact, as we shall see, some of them may eventually be responsible for an ironic, cataclysmic redefinition of the very nature of human work.

The second group of productivity determinants is potentially much more amenable to control by individual managers in an economy. The central concern of this book is to explore the nature of one of these more manipulable factors: the level of motivation of the workforce and of the individual worker. Before beginning a treatment of the nature and causes of work motivation, however, let's take a brief look at some of the larger-scale determinants of productivity.

Large-Scale Factors

One key determinant of economic productivity is the level of investment made in fixed capital, such as new plants, refineries, office buildings, and other operating sites—places that help to make more efficient the way the work gets done (Freund, 1981). The amazing levels of productivity in postwar Germany and Japan can be explained partially by the new industrial facilities constructed in those nations following 1945, although more recently, other factors have caused low productivity and inflationary pressure in these countries (Bowen, 1979).

Other factors that have contributed to productivity in recent years include successful innovation and the development of new technology, such as the notebook computer used by the author for the writing of much of this book (B. Gold, 1979; Reilly and Fuhr, 1983). But innovation takes investment in research and development activities, and it is notable that some critics of the poor performance of Canada's economy from time to time (e.g., Britton and Gilmour, 1978; McFetridge, 1981) have cited its comparatively low levels of research and development activities as a contributing cause of its productivity problem. We shall return to the role of technology shortly, to present the ironic hypothesis that such innovations may soon bring about a major change in the nature of work as we have known it and necessitate an entirely new mentality about work, working, careers, and work motivation.

Scarcity of many raw materials contributes heavily to the cost of production of goods and services. The quintupling of energy costs in recent years is a major example with which all of us are familiar. According to those economic critics who desire a return to a laissez-faire framework for conducting business, legislation that restricts the natural workings of the marketplace also limits productivity. Guidelines and regulations concerning equal employment opportunity, health and safety, minimum wages, antitrust, and rates that may be charged for services are examples cited by these critics. Although regulations of this type do contribute to the cost of production, it is important to consider the economic (and social) benefits they contribute in return. For example, if the aggregate cost of a regulation is greater than the net value it generates, the regulation might be judged dysfunctional from a strict social and economic perspective.

In short, there are many large-scale economic and political factors that have traditionally been blamed for combining and interacting to restrict productivity, thereby fueling price inflation and compromising the quality of life that is achievable in Western society. These factors are beyond the control of the vast majority of managers and executives in industry. For example, not many chief executives can immediately cause a rollback in government regulations (although a few have tried). Similarly, not many first-line supervisors can initiate major changes in the basic physical design of work plants so as to make their employees significantly more productive. Executives and managers who wish to influence the productivity of the workforce must find alternatives to the means described above. The question becomes: What sources of productivity are there that fall within the grasp of individual employees and employers?

Human Factors in Productivity

There are at least two other major factors that determine the level of productivity in any given organization, industry, or economy which can be influenced (within limits) by executives, managers, and first-line supervisors: the level of ability of people who are assigned to work and the amount of effort these people expend doing that work (J. P. Campbell, R. J. Campbell and Associates, 1988).[2]

Employee Ability   Some critics claim that the postwar workforce is less skillful and less devoted to hard work than were the workforces of earlier times. It is a simple fact of demographics that today's worker is, on average, younger and less experienced than workers of previous generations. But today's average employee is generally better trained and/or educated as well, so it is difficult to make summary statements about the comparative net levels of skill of the employees of various eras. The point is that individual supervisors can sometimes have considerable influence on the level of job-related ability of the people they assign to particular tasks on a daily basis. Training programs, job redesign, and merely making careful person–job matches are means that, within limits, enable supervisors in many work settings to gain leverage on the problem of productivity in their organizations.

Employee Motivation   The second factor over which effective supervisors can often have some control is the level of motivated effort expended by those below them in organizational hierarchies. Motivation is a popular topic that relates directly to all of us, particularly to those of us whose job it is to accomplish organizational goals through the efforts of other people. We generally believe in the importance of a widespread desire to work, and many critics are quick to blame slumps in such a desire for social and (especially) economic decline. In a thoughtful study of the constant importance of work values and the "work ethic," four scholars recently wrote:

> So ingrained is the work ethic as an explanation for the success of the U.S. economy that managers reflexively attribute declines in productivity and increases in worker recalcitrance and discontent to the decline of the work ethic. For example, in analyzing unrest in the workplace in the early 1970's, Deans (1973) observed, "Corporation executives seem no less puzzled than any other Americans as to why young people entering the labor force—even in a time of scarcity—are less enchanted with the so-called Protestant ethic of hard work and upward striving than their parents and grandparents" (pp. 8–9). Thus, it is evident that the tenets of the Protestant work ethic . . . are still taken seriously by managers, scholars and policy makers. They are viewed as central to the development and functioning of capitalism. (Nord, Brief, Atieh, and Doherty, 1988, p. 8)

In both its general connotation and as it relates to work, motivation is a topic about which many people claim to have some degree of knowledge, even expertise. *Motivation* is a buzzword in virtually all work settings and educational institutions.

---

[2]Economists often argue that large-scale factors such as those discussed here are much more important in their impact on productivity than are the human factors discussed throughout the remainder of this book. For example, Freund (1981) believes that capital investment is the most important determinant of productivity and that human factors are far less influential. It is hard to separate the contributions made to productivity by these various factors, but it is important to note that even when they are working side by side in the same factory, plant, or office, different employees produce widely differing amounts of work output. Lawler (1973) has noted, for example, that the ratio of output produced by the best worker to that produced by the poorest worker in many work settings can be 3:1 or greater. Similarly, the average automaker in Japan produces twice as many cars per year as does its U.S. counterpart, using essentially the same production techniques (Weil, 1979). Therefore, it would seem that human factors are, in fact, important determinants of productivity that must be considered (J. P. Campbell, R. J. Campbell and Associates, 1988; O'Toole, 1981).

Folklore on the topic dates back at least as far as the literature on any other managerial topic, and newspapers and magazines regularly feature stories and essays on it. Countless self-help books have been published to provide managers and executives with quick insights into what makes them and their subordinates work (or not work). Airport bookstores are replete with books offering quick fixes of this variety.

But there is also a vast scientific literature on work motivation, the content of which only sometimes relates to the wisdom imparted to managers through the materials they read. Nevertheless, work motivation is one of the most important topics of organizational science; no other issue in the discipline has more significance for our general economic well-being, and few other topics command more attention in the journals and textbooks of the field (Steers and Porter, 1991, pp. xii, 3). Moreover, in view of the intractability of many key determinants of productivity, we can expect work motivation to be at least as important an issue in organizational science and management in the future as it has been in the past, although perhaps for very different reasons (see Pinder, 1984).

What Goes Around Comes Around:
Some Ironic Consequences of High Productivity

A startling hypothesis advanced recently by economists and social critics[3] holds that productivity gained through electronic and information technology has been responsible for the loss of millions of jobs in North America and elsewhere (Bridges, 1994; Rifkin, 1995). In fact, Jeremy Rifkin's shocking book *The End of Work* makes this point vividly: The third industrial revolution, brought on by a combination of high technology and corporate reengineering (see M. Hammer and Champy, 1993), has portended the end of tens of thousands of job categories and caused the unemployment of millions of workers. Both Bridges (1994) and Rifkin (1995) argue convincingly that workers at *all* levels of North American society have been displaced from what were once high-paying, economically secure jobs into positions of unemployment or drastic underemployment. They cite countless economic facts from recent labor history and labor economics to show that we are moving, somehow, into a world in which there are no jobs and very little work for human beings to perform. Global competition has fueled these dynamics, and the social and psychological costs to erstwhile working people everywhere are only now being appreciated. Job categories from the arts, agriculture, the sciences, governments, and private services—work in virtually every level and category of our economies—are vanishing. The jobs that do exist are increasingly temporary, low skilled, low paying, and unfulfilling. Scores of thousands of managers and executives have been laid off. The major exceptions to the universality of the carnage, according to Rifkin (1995), are senior-level executives whose own remunerative standards have skyrocketed, leading inexorably to a bipolarization of society that was perhaps begun by President Reagan's supply-side economics.

Bridges (1994) writes:

> The job is a social artifact, although it is so deeply embodied in our consciousness that most of us have forgotten its artificiality or the fact that most societies since the begin-

---

[3]In fact, many of the startling observations reported in this section are only slightly different from the portents, complaints, and caveats of social critics such as Karl Marx and Friedrich Engels. Although these nineteenth-century socialists are generally given credit for their theoretical contribution, they are given rather short shrift by modern observers such as Bridges (1994) and Rifkin (1995).

ning of time have done just fine without jobs. . . . Before people had jobs, they worked just as hard but on shifting clusters of tasks, in a variety of locations, on a schedule set by the sun, the weather, and the needs of the day. . . . Now the world of work is changing again. The very conditions (mass production and the large organization) that created jobs two hundred years ago are disappearing. . . . Big firms (where most of the good jobs used to be) are 'unbundling' their various activities and farming them out to little firms, who have created or taken over profitable niches. . . . As the conditions that created jobs fade, we lose the need to package work into jobs. No wonder they are disappearing. (pp. viii–ix)

Juxtaposed with these economic and social realities, there is shocking evidence that North Americans, at least those who still have jobs, are working longer and harder than ever (Fassel, 1990; Rifkin, 1995; Schor, 1991). Rifkin (1995) would argue that people are working harder for the sake of gaining or holding onto precious jobs in view of incredible competition from other people living within our borders as well as from people who work hard for low pay in other countries. Although a new world order may evolve in which we will survive without work in the form of jobs and careers as we have known them, in the short and intermediate terms most of us are driven to find work and jobs because whatever the new social and economic order will be, it is not here yet. To the extent that observers and critics such as Bridges (1994) and Rifkin (1995) are correct, mass unemployment and underemployment, layoffs, fear, escalating innovation, and competition will be the primary reasons for high levels of work motivation over the coming decades.

In summary, the necessities of the post–World War II global economic structure have resulted in a revolution of computer-based information technology that has made corporations more efficient, lean, mean, and profitable for those who own them and for the few who work at the top echelons of their administrative structures. These innovations have not resulted in the sort of "trickle-down" benefits that early advocates of technology envisioned. Instead, they have spelled the end of countless jobs and countless careers, reducing substantially the economic well-being of most of us (Rifkin, 1995). Because of these global changes, the very nature of work is changing. Much of it will simply disappear as an economic form of human activity. Consequently, the motivation to work will become even more important than it has been in the past because of fear of economic deprivation, unemployment, substandard health care, and a generally impoverished existence. The doomsday scenarios painted by Bridges (1994), Rifkin (1995), and others are hard to discount because they are well documented. To the extent that these scenarios unfold or are anticipated by large portions of the populace, the competition to attain and hold onto work (whether in the form of jobs or not) will become even more brutal in the future than it has been in the recent (and not-so-recent) past. Until fundamentally new rules and means for survival are found, institutionalized, and perfected to replace work and jobs, people will be very highly motivated to work. The alternatives are few and frightening.

PURPOSE OF THIS BOOK

Our purpose in this book is to examine the current state of knowledge pertaining to work motivation, with a view to estimating just how much is known about this important phenomenon. *This is not a book about how to motivate a workforce,* although the applied implications of the various theories and approaches to motivation will be identified as we come to them.[4] Rather, our purpose is to explore a number of the most viable current theories of work motivation and to consider and evaluate a variety of managerial programs and procedures used to influence work motivation. In making these evaluations, the perspectives of the social scientist and the practicing manager are adopted throughout.

It is important to state at the outset that most of the ideas presented in this book are either theoretical or derived from theory. There are virtually no laws or solid facts pertaining to human behavior, whose complexity most of us are quick to acknowledge in some settings but equally quick to forget when we seek solutions to behavioral problems in other settings. Some of the theories presented contradict one another, either conceptually or in application, which is something that the reader will simply have to accept. Notwithstanding the pithy advice offered by many of those airport paperbacks, there are no simple "quick fixes" that have withstood the scrutiny of social scientists and knowledgeable managers over the long haul. As we will see, many old ideas from social science have appeared and reappeared more than once, usually with new names and buzzwords, since World War II (see chapters 4 and 13, for examples).

In the remaining sections of this chapter we define and examine the meaning of work motivation and key concepts related to it. We will argue that individual managers are generally less able to observe their employees' work motivation than they are to observe their levels of job performance. We begin the discussion by providing a definition of work motivation and delineating a number of features and implications of that definition. We then focus on the meaning of job performance and show why the difference between the two concepts is so important. As we will see, factors other than motivation help determine an employee's level of job performance, one of which is ability. We discuss the nature and significance of work-related ability in a later section.

To begin, then, what is work motivation?

WHAT IS WORK MOTIVATION?

It is only a slight exaggeration to say that there have been almost as many definitions of motivation offered over the years as there have been thinkers who have considered the nature of human behavior (Kleinginna and Kleinginna, 1981, report and categorize 140 definitions). One classic textbook (Atkinson, 1964) deliberately sidesteps the definitional problem until almost 300 pages of material on the topic are presented. Another major textbook (Cofer and Appley, 1964) presents the definitions of a number of scholars without offering a simple definition of its own. Other books (e.g., Korman, 1974; Locke and Latham, 1990a) discuss the issues that motivation is seen as dealing with but do not define the concept.

There are many reasons for the apparent difficulty in defining motivation, although a full treatment of these reasons is beyond our purpose. Suffice it to say that there are paradoxically no singular definitions of motivation because there are so

---

[4]A comprehensive theory about the applied technology of motivating human behavior toward a variety of ends is provided by M. E. Ford (1992).

many aspects of it. There are also many philosophical orientations toward the nature of human beings and about what can be known about people. Some theorists deny the usefulness of the concept altogether, and concentrate primarily on the consequences of behavior as its causes. Some writers view motivation from a strictly physiological perspective while others view human beings as primarily hedonistic, and explain most of human behavior as goal-oriented, seeking only to gain pleasure and avoid pain. Others stress the rationality of people, and consider human behavior to be the result of conscious choice processes. Some thinkers stress unconscious or subconscious factors. The multiplicity of the views on the fundamental nature of human motivation and behavior is reflected in the diversity of chapters found in modern anthologies such as those of Levine (1975) or Petrie (1991). The interested reader is referred to these sources as well as to the works of Atkinson (1964) and Cofer and Appley (1964) for thorough treatments of the historical and philosophical perspectives.

Definition of Work Motivation

Where does this leave the student or manager who wants to learn about motivation and job performance in the workplace? Since the topic of this book is *work motivation, attitudes, and behavior* (as opposed to general human motivation, attitudes, and behavior), a traditional definition will be offered and then used throughout. This definition draws heavily on those of a number of other writers and attempts to provide some balance in the philosophical assumptions that underlie those definitions. The work of M. R. Jones (1995), Locke, Shaw, Saari, and Latham (1981), Steers and Porter (1979), and Vroom (1964) is of particular importance in the following definition:

> *Work motivation* is a set of energetic forces that originate both within as well as beyond an individual's being, to initiate work-related behavior, and to determine its form, direction, intensity, and duration.[5]

Implications of the Definition

A number of features of our definition deserve highlighting. First, it attempts to be both specific enough to relate primarily to work-related behaviors, but general and eclectic enough to avoid many of the basic issues that have divided writers who have concerned themselves with the origins of human behavior, particularly work behavior. For example, it is intended to apply to behaviors such as joining or not joining an organization for employment purposes; being late or on time for work on a given day; obeying or rejecting a supervisor's orders to work harder; accepting or rejecting a directive to relocate to another city; conceiving of better and smarter ways of performing one's job; and even retiring or resigning from an organization. Implicit in the foregoing is that our definition sees work motivation as a middle-range concept (see Merton, 1968; Pinder and Moore, 1980) that purports to deal only with events and phenomena

---

[5]This definition was offered in an earlier review (Pinder, 1984) and is not changed here. Although it was developed with the thinking of a number of earlier theorists in mind, the definition has also been adopted by or been consistent with definitions used by other writers since 1984 (e.g., M. E. Ford, 1992; Landy and Becker, 1987).

of work, careers, and the management of people at work. It does not presume to be a general definition of human motivation that transcends all contexts, such as that of M. E. Ford (1992).

Second, the concept of *force* is central to the definition. This makes it consistent with Vroom's (1964) definition of motivation, without necessarily adopting the cognitive orientation or the elements of decision making that are so important to his theory (see chapter 12 of this book). The notion of force also makes our definition consistent with the hydraulic metaphors found in Freud's work in psychoanalysis. The definition allows for motivation levels to be either weak or strong, varying both between individuals at a particular time as well as within a given individual at different times and under different circumstances.

Our definition states that there is a set of energetic forces, implying the *multiplicity* of needs, drives, instincts, and external factors that have been considered over the years regarding human behavior, without necessarily accepting the primary importance of any of these sources. The idea of force suggests that motivation will manifest itself through effort. In fact, the concepts of effort and motivation are frequently treated as being identical. In other places, effort is used as operationalization of motivation. In this book, effort is treated as a consequence and primary indicator of motivation but not as identical with it.

The definition implies the notion of movement, in recognition of the Latin root of the word *motivation* (*movere,* to move). Recognition of both internal and external origins acknowledges the merits of the philosophical positions of both those who believe in free will and those who believe in determinism (see Joad, 1957, and chapters 7 and 13 of this book). This feature of the definition permits recognition of the importance of characteristics of the work environment that can arouse behavior (such as the nature of the work being performed or the style of leadership being applied), without ruling out certain work behaviors originating primarily from within the employee (such as staying home when ill). More will be said on this critical issue shortly.

Our definition does not stress hedonism as a primary force in work motivation, but it does not rule it out, either. Nor does it preclude consideration of a number of other human traits, such as fear, lust, greed, or jealousy in the context of work behavior. Following on some of his own earlier work with Katerberg (Katerberg and Blau, 1983), G. Blau (1993) has recently examined some of the components of the definition of work motivation to determine whether and how each contributes to job performance. In a study of 115 bank tellers, he operationalized "effort" by observing the tellers on video cameras and then rating the degree to which they were actually working at tasks related to their jobs as opposed to nonwork activities. To assess direction of effort, Blau asked the tellers to indicate the frequency with which they engaged in 20 different legitimate behaviors related to the tellers' jobs. These 20 items were reduced to two factors, financial behaviors and customer behaviors. Next, Blau sought relationships between his effort and direction indicators with two different criteria of job performance, controlling for a variety of other variables that might have confounded or confused the results. The two criteria of performance were (1) raw productivity, the percentage of time on the job the teller actually engaged in one or more of the legitimate activities; and (2) the number of referrals of customers the tellers made for opening new accounts.

G. Blau (1993) found that both effort and direction contributed to performance on the tellers' jobs, although they were more predictive of productivity than of sales referrals. Of particular interest was the finding that aside from individual contributions of effort and direction, an interaction term that combined the two motivational components was also effective for explaining variance in the productivity (dependent) variable.

Studies such as G. Blau's (1993) make a tremendous contribution to our understanding of the nature of work motivation, of the relationships among the components of this tricky construct, and of the relationships between work motivation and other important variables, such as job performance. It is one thing for theorists to posit and postulate the existence of constructs such as work motivation and how it relates to people's lives. It is another matter for researchers such as Blau to go to the field, develop valid measures, and test for the expected relationships among the constructs of interest. More work of this quality will be needed for us to understand fully the empirical qualities of the work motivation construct.

Another element of our definition of work motivation has also received attention in recent years—the *intensity* dimension. Brehm and Self (1989) have made a distinction between *potential motivation* and *motivational arousal*. For them, needs, values, and the person's perceptions about whether effort will result in need satisfaction determine, in a multiplicative way, the amount of motivational effort that is available. This, however, is not a sufficient set of conditions to determine actual arousal of the person. In addition, the person must be engaged in some degree of behavior thought to be instrumental for the sake of meeting the needs in existence. The amount of energy is assumed to be no greater than what is needed to produce the required instrumental behavior. So, when little effort is needed, motivational arousal will be low, no matter how great the need is or how valuable the potential outcome (Brehm and Self, 1989, p. 111). Intensity is then defined as the momentary magnitude of motivational arousal (p. 110). In other words, "potential motivation is created by needs and/or potential outcomes and the expectation that performance of a behavior will affect those needs and outcomes. Motivational arousal occurs, however, only to the extent that the required behavior is difficult, within one's capacity, and is justified by the magnitude of potential motivation. When the difficulty of the instrumental behavior surpasses one's capacities or outweighs the value of the potential gain . . . there will be little or no mobilization of energy. The greater the potential motivation, the greater is the amount of energy that a person will be willing to mobilize" (p. 111). To repeat, intensity is defined as the momentary magnitude of actual motivational arousal, regardless of the potential available.

The *direction* toward which motivated force is focused also appears in the definition. Inclusion of this feature recognizes that it is not sufficient merely to consider the intensity and duration of work motivation. Rather, to understand it fully, one must allow for the specific goals toward which motivated energy is directed (Katerberg and Blau, 1983).

The notion of *duration* implies that goal attainment may be a possible (but not a necessary) outcome of behavior on the job, keeping the definition generally consistent with goal-oriented theorists such as Murray (1938) and Dunnette and Kirchner (1965) and more recent goal theorists such as Locke and Latham (1990a).

Our definition accommodates three of the five behavior patterns identified by Maehr and Braskamp (1986) and Maehr (1987): choice (as it relates to absenteeism behavior), persistence (length of service), and continuing motivation (voluntarily upgrading one's work skills).[6] Similarly, the definition takes into account a variety of work behaviors, described as willingness to cooperate, innovative and spontaneous behavior, prosocial behavior, and, most recently, as personal initiative (Frese, Kring, Soose, and Zempel, 1996), all of which imply working in a way that goes above and beyond the call of duty (see Organ, 1990, for a review).

Another feature of the definition is that it does not imply that motivation is the sole source of human behavior, or that work motivation is the sole source of work behavior per se. Rather, it readily accommodates the fact that forces other than motivation also contribute to human action, both on the job and off. This matter is critical in view of a recent highly critical attack by M. E. Ford (1992) on traditional theories of motivation. Among other claims, Ford (p. 10) has argued that to be of value, the concept of motivation must be limited to account only for the "*psychological* processes in the direction, energization and regulation of behavior pattern." Whereas Ford sees motivation as strictly psychological and separate from other forces such as biology, environmental, and "nonmotivational psychological and behavioral influences," our definition admits the role of many biological factors in energizing and controlling behavior. It also permits the possibility that features of the environment can trigger motivational (even primarily psychological) forces. We differ somewhat with Ford on these counts but do not imply by our definition that all behavior is motivated. Much human activity is nonmotivated, compulsive, and habitual. The definition also accommodates the assumption that not all behavior results from conscious phenomenological states. Instead, as Brody (1980) put it: "Behavior may be influenced by motive states which are not in awareness, and . . . certain motive states will not exert a particular influence on behavior unless they are out of awareness" (p. 156).

But the most important feature of the definition is that it views motivation as an invisible, internal concept, or what may be called a hypothetical construct (MacCorquodale and Meehl, 1948), a concept representing an assumed physical process that is, as yet, unobservable directly. We cannot actually see motivation or measure it directly. Instead, we assume that it exists and rely on the theories to guide us in measuring what they suggest are its manifestations. Hypothetical constructs of this sort abound in psychology (e.g., personality, perceptions, beliefs, attitudes, etc.), as well as in virtually all other sciences at one time or another during their development. Although there are countless examples of hypothetical constructs in the sciences, the reliance on invisible internal processes such as motivation constitutes an important point of controversy. In chapter 14, for example, we discuss a school of thought that rejects the use of such hypothetical constructs in favor of focusing on observable behavior.

In short, the definition offered above is intended to apply to work behaviors of all sorts while avoiding many of the ontological and epistemological issues that have caused debate and confusion. Motivation is an important factor in job performance and human productivity. It is the central concept of interest in this book, and when the term is used in subsequent chapters, it follows the definition provided above.

---

[6]The definition does not, however, fit with two of their categories, "activity level" and "performance," because they are related to performance, not to motivation per se. This is a major distinction that is discussed at length later in the chapter.

HAS WORK MOTIVATION BEEN DECLINING?

Earlier we observed that there are sometimes disagreements, even heated quarrels, between members of different generations over the issue of work motivation. The question becomes: Are today's employees any more or less motivated than those of past times?[7]

Whether for purposes of work motivation per se or because of strong gains in our desire for the material and nonmaterial things that money from work can buy, there is evidence that today's American workers are working longer hours than workers did immediately after World War II (Schor, 1991). The survey of OECD members depicted in Table 1-1 supports the hypothesis that Americans *appear* to be working more than they used to, although the longer hours may reflect only the fact that the survey took into account the hours that people are working on all of their jobs rather than simply on their primary jobs (*The Economist*, 1996).

As we will see, some theories of work motivation rely primarily on factors inside the individual, such as needs, values, and attitudes. Other theories focus on factors external to the individual, seeking explanations that rely on variables such as job design, organizational structures, and the like (Katzell and Thompson, 1990). For the sake of the current discussion, the origins of the desire or necessity to work more and more over the past two decades is a moot point. The point is that as one author puts it, we may be "working ourselves to death" (Fassel, 1992). Now we might ask: Do people, in fact, place greater or less *value* on work and working today than they did "in the old days"?

A popular novel by Coupland (1991) on the values and work-related anxieties of "Generation X" implies that people born in North America during the 1960s see things related to work and careers differently than do older North Americans. The sheer success of the novel implies that it has struck a chord among both Generation X'ers and the baby boomers they abhor. Those of Generation X claim that the work values of preceding generations are of little value to them. This is in part because the benefits of work and traditional careers are not available to them, and will continue not to be, because baby boomers are clogging organizational hierarchies, driving up the prices of consumer goods and services, mortgaging the X'ers' futures by current deficit spending and other transgressions. Yet a cover story in *Maclean's* magazine in October 1996 reported that many previously hard-working Canadians in their fifties and early sixties are "cashing out"—selling their Volvos and downtown condominiums and moving to small hobby farms and country towns, leaving their highly paid, high-stress jobs in favor of slower, more peaceful lifestyles (see M. McDonald, 1996). Maybe these middle-aged people have acquired some of the values usually associated with members of Generation X?

But what do history and the current scientific literature say on the matter? Erikson and Vallas (1990), Nord et al. (1988), and Tausky (1995), among others, have sketched how work values have evolved from the days of the ancient Greek philosophers (when work was viewed as a waste of time), the ancient Hebrew and Roman philosophers and

---

[7]The very existence of this debate might seem peculiar to the reader in view of the analysis and predictions presented earlier pertaining to the disappearance of jobs and the end of human work. The author's view is that although organizational reengineering has displaced millions of employees, removed the necessity for countless jobs, and made work motivation more critical than at any time in recent memory, there remains the issue of whether these economic realities have yet been noticed and appreciated well enough to begin to affect the work aspirations of many individuals, particularly those who may have to face the sort of world without work that may be looming.

theologians (who believed that, in addition to being a waste, work comprised a sort of punishment for original sin), right through to current times, when there are many secular and nonsecular views of work and work values. When measured by such a broad brush, it is clear that work, the meaning of work, and what is of value in work have changed dramatically. The study of work values and the meaning of work must therefore always be placed in the sociohistoric times of the analysis.

There is not a lot of research on the matter, but a recent study by G. W. England (1991) investigated the issue as it pertains to the U.S. workforce. Specifically, comparing data from two matched samples—one gathered in 1982, the other in 1989—he examined the degree of change that had occurred in 41 values related to work. Four general factors underlay the items: (1) the importance and significance of work and working in one's life, (2) the normative beliefs and expectations that people held about their obligations and entitlements at work, (3) the relative importance of achieving various work goals (alternatively called work values, work needs, and incentive preferences), and (4) the bases used by people to decide whether an activity is considered work or nonwork.

The findings of the study were interesting. In such a short period of time as seven years, it was clear that there had been significant shifting of American values related to work. Although no single factor among the 41 studied had altered dramatically, collectively the findings were that Americans had changed their views of work and working. Statistically significant shifts were observed on 21 of the 41 items studied. Economic goals had become more important and "comfort" goals seemed less important. This reflects what England sees as an instrumental reaction to the economic realities during the period between the two studies. Yet the importance of working as a life role declined over the same period. For many people in the second study, work seemed to be less intrinsically valued and more a means to instrumental ends. Finally (and contrary to the general trend of change), people's beliefs about their entitlements and obligations showed virtually no change over the period studied.

England's study is not the final word on the matter, nor should it be accepted as the sole ground for the payment of wagers between parents and their offspring. The study does remind us, however, that values *do* change with time and that values, beliefs, and attitudes regarding work are subject to large-scale movement over relatively short periods of time. We have much more to say later about job attitudes and work values (see chapter 3).

Work Motivation and Job Performance Are Not the Same Thing

One of the most important distinctions that needs to be made early in this book is the difference between job performance and motivation. The difference is much more than a matter of semantics. It is one that has powerful implications for both an understanding and application of the theories and ideas that constitute the remainder of this book. It is a distinction noted by Vroom (1964) and one that has been acknowledged frequently since (see L. L. Cummings and Schwab, 1973; Lawler, 1973; L. W. Porter and Lawler, 1968; Terborg, 1977). What is the difference between the two concepts?

Managers are concerned primarily with the accomplishment of work through other people. They are responsible for seeing to it that others accomplish the work assigned to them. Therefore, a manager is effective when subordinates accomplish their respective work goals. But successful accomplishment of one's work goals is normally the result of interaction among a number of factors, only some of which can be controlled by the employee (such as the amount of effort invested in the task). Another critical factor, for example, is the level of ability the employee possesses to do the particular job assigned. (We return shortly to the issue of ability.) Still other factors are external to the employee, such as the amount of support received from supervisors and from staff.

A massive study of American workers reported by J. Hall (1994) makes the point that most people wish to work and perform well at their jobs but are prevented from doing so by the restrictive practices of their supervisors and limited policies of their companies.[8] Characteristics of the physical work environment, such as the lighting and noise levels, temperature, air quality (Baron, 1994), and the availability of materials needed to perform the job, limit the degree to which employees can convert all of their well-intended efforts into what the organization would call effective job performance. In short, *we can define job performance as the accomplishment of work-related goals regardless of the means of their accomplishment.*[9]

The Importance of the Distinction between Motivation and Performance

When we think of poor employee performance, we implicitly or explicitly assume that some sort of goals exist, having been set either by the individual in question or by some person or group (T. R. Mitchell and O'Reilly, 1983). We also implicitly assume that it is possible to measure performance to see whether the goals have been reached. Therefore, what is judged to be poor performance will depend strongly on who sets the goals, whether there is more than one goal in place at a given time or there are multiple goals, and if there is more than one goal, whether they are mutually exclusive.

Also of importance in considering alleged "poor performance" is the issue of how and when the performance is measured and by whom. Finally, there is the issue of whether the performance is measured in an absolute sense or whether it is measured vis-à-vis performance levels attained by other people, either at present or in the past. Hence *poor performance* can be arbitrary—very much related to the eye of the beholder (T. R. Mitchell and O'Reilly, 1983).

A common mistake made by managers who notice poor job performance by their subordinates is to attempt automatically to remedy the problem as if it were the result of low motivation. For example, a sales manager may notice a slump in the average monthly sales figures (low job performance) for a key salesperson and react by increasing the rate of commission that will be paid to that person for future sales. The manager's reaction is

---

[8]It is interesting to note that a similar observation was published on the basis of large-scale studies decades ago by Likert (1961, pp. 97–103) and others, and that the solutions provided at that time were virtually the same as those offered by J. Hall (1994).

[9]Staw and Boettger (1990) have pointed out that traditional definitions of performance are limited in scope because often it is in the best interests of an employer, an employee, or both, for the individual to deviate from the directives of a predefined task role and alter the nature of the job. They refer to this form of behavior as *task revision* and argue that there are many instances in which rigid adherence to formal tasks and goals is not in the best interest of anyone involved, such as when instructions become inappropriate or outdated, circumstances change, or when new alternatives present themselves. We suspect that such elasticity and innovativeness will become more relevant and important in work settings of the future.

an explicit attempt to increase the sales rep's motivation level, as might be reflected in the degree of effort the rep will spend selling the firm's products. The manager assumes that the person is not trying hard enough for some reason—that the rep has lost interest or has simply become lazy (see T. R. Mitchell, Green, and Wood, 1981).

But in many cases the problem might better be attributed to any (or all) of a number of the types of external factors mentioned above (a superb recent review is provided by Baron, 1994). For instance, it may be that the sales rep is now facing stiffer competition in his sales region from representatives of other companies with superior products to sell; it may be that the rep has lost a few traditionally held accounts and that he is struggling to recapture them; or it may be that he is not fully aware of new company policies reflected in the firm's marketing strategies.

In short, apparent performance problems must be considered from the perspective of the person who alleges that work is not up to standard. We must take into consideration the possibility of outside, situational factors—factors that are, in part at least, beyond the employee's control. Even if the person is the primary source of the difficulty, it can be a mistake to attribute the blame to work motivation problems. To apply strategies that are implicitly (or explicitly) designed to increase motivation levels when motivation is not the problem can result in a self-fulfilling prophesy: The employee responds to the new threats or incentives but still cannot perform up to standard (for the same reasons as before), becomes frustrated, and withdraws. He may ultimately quit trying altogether. (We take a more complete look at the problem of frustration in chapter 8.)

Diagnostic errors of the sort made by our fictitious sales manager are common and easy to make. Parents often make a similar mistake when they notice a decline in the performance of their children in high school or college. Many students find that they can achieve acceptable standards in high school with a certain level of effort, their natural level of mental ability, and a minimum amount of charm. Once in college, these students often find that greater ability is required and/or higher levels of effort are necessary. Charm is usually helpful as well. Parents who attempt to apply motivational strategies to children who simply do not have the native ability, or a sufficient level of acquired skills, are not usually able to help their children perform more effectively. In fact, the sort of pressure that parents can apply in these cases can result in resentment, fear, and withdrawal by the now-frustrated student. The author has known of cases of student suicide which have resulted from this sort of pressure. Like success on most jobs, success in college requires a blend of ingredients, only one of which is motivation; ability is another; and usually a host of other factors function to magnify or attenuate the effects of motivation and ability on successful performance (cf. Baron, 1994).

In short, the point here is this: It can be a serious mistake to assume that poor performance is the result of low motivation. Other factors interact with motivation to determine job performance. One of these is the level of the person's ability to do the task in question. Let's take a look at what is meant by the term *ability*.

Ability in the Workplace

As the preceding examples have suggested, employee ability is an important factor in effective job performance. Some psychologists have argued that ability is more important than motivation to job performance (e.g., Dunnette, 1972). A person might be highly motivated to lift a heavy weight from the floor onto a table but may not have the physical strength (a type of ability) to do it. The result: high motivation, no ability, no performance.

Defining Ability

But what is ability? We run into almost as much difficulty finding a simple definition for ability as we did when we sought to define motivation. The reason for the difficulty this time seems to be that the word ability includes and represents a number of other concepts, such as skill and aptitude. In its simplest form, we might define ability as a person's capacity to accomplish tasks, controlling for the person's level of motivation to attempt those tasks. But this merely begs the question by substituting *capacity* for *ability*. One author defines ability in terms of the performance that people can achieve on tests designed to assess ability (Cronbach, 1970). In other words, ability is what ability tests measure. The circularity is not very helpful.

One way to approach the problem is to define *ability* by looking at definitions of those things that, collectively, constitute ability. One of these is *aptitude*, defined by the *Oxford English Dictionary* (1961, Vol. 1) as "natural capacity, endowment, or ability; talent for any pursuit." We can dodge the circularity in this definition by focusing on two of its key terms: *natural* and *talent*. This suggests that aptitude consists of the innate part of ability, or that which seems to develop naturally, without explicit training, an example being spatial intelligence.

Another element of aptitude is *skill* (Dunnette, 1976a), defined by the *Oxford English Dictionary* (1961, Vol. 9) as the "capability of accomplishing something with precision and certainty; practical knowledge in combination with ability; cleverness, expertness." (The reader should be developing a sense of appreciation for the difficulty in defining these terms independent of one another!) The essence of skill is the capacity or capability resulting from raw, natural aptitude (as defined above) as well as from the capability that people gain through both explicit training and development of their aptitudes. Development of this sort can be deliberate and active, or it can occur passively as a person grows and learns (see chapter 14). We are left with a definition that is similar, but not identical, to that reached by Lawler (1973): Ability is an aggregation of natural aptitude plus the capacity to behave which results from the application of training and experience to one's aptitude. That is,

$$\text{ability} = \text{aptitude} + \text{aptitude (training and experience)}$$

Defined as such, ability subsumes common concepts such as wisdom, sagacity, and competence—words we often hear attributed to people in work settings. The point is that natural talent and skill developed over time are major determinants of effective job performance. Highly motivated people working at jobs for which they lack the necessary ability are not generally capable of performing the job.

Types of Ability

There are many forms of human ability. Guilford (1967) claims that *there may be as many as 120 distinct varieties of basic mental ability alone!* When combined in various proportions with the many sensory and psychomotor abilities that people can have (see Guion, 1965, chap. 10), we are left with virtually an infinite number of possible combinations or sets of abilities that any employee might possess (see McCall, Lombardo, and Morrison, 1988, for a treatment of managerial skills and abilities).

In principle, this seems like an obvious point, but it requires explication because of the tendency of so many of us to make remarks such as "Jones has no skill" or "Smith is incompetent." Regarding skill sets, it is true that some people are more richly endowed than others. But in organizational settings we must ask: "Competent for what?" (see Warr and Conner, 1992). Highly competent people who are assigned to jobs for which their ability sets are not appropriate are generally no more effective in organizations than are people with less impressive ability sets who are assigned to jobs for which they have some of the basic requisite abilities (Dawis and Lofquist, 1984). Hence we appreciate the importance of careful personnel selection, placement, and job design.

The Concept of Job Competence

In recognition of the increasing importance of mental abilities for job performance in many (most?) modern job settings, Warr and Conner (1992) offer a broad definition of what hitherto might have been considered ability but what they refer to as *job competence,* which they define as follows:

> A job competence is a set of behaviors, knowledge, thought processes, and/or attitudes, which are likely to be reflected in job performance that reaches a defined elementary, basic or high-performance standard. Statements about job competence may refer to one or a number of jobs, at one or several job-levels. Measurement of specific types of job competence may be undertaken either in job settings or through observation of behavior in other controlled situations. (p. 99)

Warr and Conner focus attention on the fact that competence may be broad or narrow, relating to merely one task or to a variety of tasks in a large number of job settings. They also stress the critical importance of mental skills, including intelligence, cognitive style, and cognitive complexity for the effective performance of work in today's work settings.

Motivation, Ability, and Job Performance

Empirical studies that have examined the role of ability in task performance have generally tended to affirm and reaffirm its importance, although the exact ways by which it combines with motivation are still not clear. Some early studies suggested an interactive relationship such that high levels of one factor can compensate for low levels of the other (Fleishman, 1958; French, 1957). This view would predict that a person with twice as much ability but only half as much motivation as another person would be of approximately equal effectiveness on the job. Moreover, if either factor were essentially absent (i.e., the person has no ability for the job and/or has no motivation to engage in it), job performance would be negligible. Studies by Locke (1965) and Terborg (1977) support the importance of ability as a determinant of performance but challenge its interactive relationship with motivation. They conclude that it is not necessary for both factors to be at least somewhat operative for performance to result. More recently, Borman, White, Pulakos, and Oppler (1991) and O'Reilly and Chatman (1994) confirmed the role of ability and its interactive effect with motivation in yielding employee performance. On one level, the necessity for both ability and motivation seems obvious. There is now sufficient evidence and impressive theory to put an end to the debate.

The history of industrial and organizational psychology has witnessed the rise and fall of the view that mental ability is the most important form of ability for the performance of most jobs. It makes sense that as less work is done by simple physical strength and more is performed by human beings equipped with technology in various forms, mental capacity is critical (see Herrnstein and Murray, 1994; Warr and Conner, 1992). The argument then shifts to which types of mental ability are most critical. Psychologists have long been interested in the concept of *general intelligence* and the concept of *specific abilities,* and their relative importance. In brief, the question is one of whether a general, overarching level of more specific mental skills is most important for effective human functioning, or whether less broadly focused skills, each of which relates to particular types of problems and issues, best explain human mental competence.

There are impressive bodies of evidence and argument for both sides of the matter. The interested reader is referred to two recent summaries of the debate by Herrnstein and Murray (1994) and Ree, Earles, and Teachout (1994). Our purpose here is not to adopt a position on the debate, merely to draw attention to it. For our purposes it is clear that regardless of how broadly it is considered, mental ability is of major importance in human functioning and in job performance. Hence any analysis of work performance must consider mental ability as well as work motivation, especially when the purpose is to award credit for good work or to ascribe blame for poor performance.

Before leaving our discussion of employee ability and its role in job performance, it is worth noting one type of ability that is especially important in job performance in many organizations. We might refer to this sort of ability as *savoir faire,* or simply "savvy." For college students, savvy is having a feel for which professor's assignments can be turned in late and which stand behind their deadlines. For the junior employees in an organization, savoir faire involves a host of things, such as knowing the clique structure of the work group and knowing the people with whom they should or should not exchange rumors. It is knowing how to read their supervisor's facial expression and the mood of the boss's secretary—it is knowing the ropes. A delightful and highly instructive treatment of these matters–one that can be very useful to the new college graduate—is Ritti's (1994) book.

In brief, both ability and motivation are required by employees to perform most jobs, although the exact form of the relationships among motivation, ability, and performance is not clear. In addition, a myriad of external factors can either enhance or inhibit the impact of motivation and ability—a key point that receives plenty of attention throughout the book. Regardless of the precise nature of this relationship, however, the important point is that not all performance problems in the workplace are a consequence of low levels of motivation to work, so the supervisor or manager in charge must be careful in diagnosing the causes of whatever performance problems are observed. As we will see, there are a host of other factors in most work settings that can either magnify or attenuate the effects on task performance of both motivation and job-related ability. When it is not the problem, tactics to increase motivation may make matters worse for both the individual employee and the organization.

DISPOSITIONS AND/OR SITUATIONS AND CONTEXTS?

We have already noted that a major issue in our consideration of work motivation is whether the force that comprises it originates solely from inside the person in question, or whether outside factors are responsible. Earlier we saw how the debate rages over the predictive power of general intelligence as opposed to the need for specific factors. It appears that general intelligence has considerable capacity to explain job performance in jobs requiring mental skill at least, regardless of the job or the organizational setting involved (Anastasi, 1986; Schmidt and Hunter, 1977, 1984; Schmidt et al., 1993).

On the other hand, this author has argued (Pinder, 1984) the importance of situational factors in an understanding of work motivation. Since then, in fact, there has been a proliferation of thought, research, and theory that addresses this matter directly, and several scholars who have reviewed the organizational literature have repeated the appeal for attention to situational factors and the interaction between them and individual variables (e.g., Cappelli and Sherer, 1991; Mowday and Sutton, 1993; Newton and Keenan, 1991; Schneider, 1983).

Some authors claim that the dispositional/situational issue may be as old as the traditional nature versus nurture debate as it relates to the development of human personality, aptitude, and mental health (T. R. Mitchell and James, 1989). The parallel between the two sets of issues is both interesting and suggestive. In her summary and review of the matter of the relative importance of dispositional and situational factors, Anastasi (1986) concluded that situational factors are more important in determining *personality differences* than they are in determining differences in people's *abilities.* "For example, a person may be quite sociable and outgoing at the office, but rather shy and reserved at social gatherings. Or a student who cheats on examinations may be scrupulously honest in handling money. . . . Individuals exhibit considerable situational specificity in several nonintellective dimensions, such as aggression, social conformity, dependency, rigidity, honesty, and attitudes toward authority" (pp. 9–10).

By comparison, the effectiveness of a person's abilities, especially mental skills, seems to be more consistent *across situations.* In other words, a person with superior intelligence is generally able to apply that gift in many dissimilar task settings. Anastasi (1986) suggests that it is our basic school curriculum and our experiences as young people in formal settings that develop "broadly applicable cognitive skills in the verbal and numerical areas. Personality development, in contrast, occurs under far less uniform conditions. Moreover, in the personality domain, the same response may elicit social consequences that are positively reinforcing in one type of situation and negatively reinforcing in another. The person may thus learn to respond in different ways in different contexts" (p. 10).

Further discussion of this debate is beyond the purpose of this chapter. The interested reader is referred to other authors who have undertaken the task.[10] The position adopted here is interactionist. Theories of work motivation and behavior offer more intellectual muscle and predictive validity when the theorist and the practitioner admit that both sets of factors may be relevant. A dogmatic posture that precludes, a priori, the possibility that either individual traits or environmental conditions are not likely to be relevant is foolish and shortsighted. This issue is raised often throughout this book as we present various theories of work motivation that differ dramatically in terms of the relative emphasis they place on situational, dispositional, and even biological determinants of motivated work behavior and work attitudes.

SUMMARY

In this chapter it has been argued that productivity is an issue of major economic concern in Western civilization. Our ability to live in comparative economic affluence depends, in large measure, on workforce productivity in all sectors of the economy. Many of the most powerful determinants of productivity in any economy are well beyond the influence of individual managers and executives. The levels of motivation and ability of the workforce are two factors that can, within limits, be influenced by enlightened managerial practices. The importance of human productivity in economic well-being is a topic that has been written about and studied many times (e.g., J. P. Campbell, J. R. Campbell and Associates, 1988; McClelland and Winter, 1969; O'Toole, 1981; Thurow, 1980). The purpose of this book is to provide scientifically based treatment of our knowledge of work motivation and its role in job performance, and ultimately, the overall level of productivity in Western economies and the quality of life that we can expect to enjoy.

OUTLINE OF THE BOOK

Now that we have dealt with a few basic concepts and definitions, we can begin the major task of this book, which is to examine current knowledge pertaining to work motivation. A major theme of the book is that what we know about work motivation consists of theory. *Theory* is an aversive word in some quarters, but a failure to recognize that most social and behavioral science knowledge is merely theory can lead to a number of disappointments for the student or manager who tries to utilize this knowledge and who then finds it limited in what it can provide. Therefore, part one concludes with chapter 2, in which we present a framework that illustrates how theories of work motivation are developed. Understanding the framework will be important

---

[10]The author's (Pinder, 1984) was not the first appeal for attention to situational factors in the study of organizational behavior. In fact, many other writers had made similar calls (see Cappelli and Sherer, 1991, for a review). Nevertheless, there does seem to be a resurrection of research, theory, and polemics on the relative impacts of personal (or dispositional) factors (e.g., Arvey and Bouchard, 1994) and situational (e.g., Baron, 1994) factors over the past decade or so. Unfortunately, some of the research has been flawed, adding an element of confusion to the issue (see Newton and Keenan, 1991). Cappelli and Sherer (1991), House, Shane, and Herold (1996), and Mowday and Sutton (1993) provide reviews of the debate.

for comprehending much of the analysis that follows in subsequent chapters, where specific details about current theories of work motivation are presented.

When we speak of human motivation, we necessarily speak about human nature. To understand why people behave the way they do, we must have some understanding of the essential nature of human beings. Therefore, a number of alternative models of human functioning are presented in the six chapters of part two. Chapter 3 provides a groundwork for the presentation of theories of work motivation that examine specific human needs, one at a time, in the five remaining chapters of part two. It will become clear as the book develops that different theories of work motivation rest on entirely different assumptions concerning human nature. The bulk of chapter 3 begins an analysis of work motivation by looking at theories assuming that human beings want things and are driven by sets of basic needs and values. For the most part, we do not address the proposition that much human work is undertaken to provide people with the resources to meet their most basic biological needs: for food, water, and shelter. These lower-level needs are clearly highly important in all human behavior, but we do not spend much space studying them here.[11]

The emotional side of human nature is the focus of chapter 4. We examine a variety of theoretical views of human emotions and emotionality and discuss the resurgence of emotions in behavioral science, paying particular attention to the important yet largely unexplored nature of emotion in current thinking about work motivation.

In chapters 5, 6, and 7 we build on the general concepts of chapter 3 by focusing on a variety of specific human needs that have been shown to be relevant to the study of work motivation. Human needs for intimacy, love, sex, and power are examined, along with a discussion of how these needs may or may not account for aspects of the behavior of people in the workplace. A dominant theme throughout part two is that much of the most interesting behavior in organizations arises from the fact that humans are gregarious, social creatures, who must interact with others of their kind. In chapter 6 we look in depth at human needs for affiliation and esteem. We examine not only the fact that people frequently elect to be around others while working, but that the sheer presence of others can influence perceptions and beliefs about the work and how people behave in the workplace. In chapter 6 we also look at the human need for esteem—to be thought well of by others.

Chapter 7 deals with growth needs and how they are related to the concept of intrinsic motivation. Then, to finish part two, in chapter 8 we explore the meaning and significance of frustration, the phenomenon that occurs when needs are blocked from satisfaction. Taken collectively, chapters 3 through 8 provide a current summary and critique of the hundreds of research-based statements of the role of human needs, particularly socially based human needs, in the workplace. Again: The assumption underlying all of this work is that hypothetical concepts called needs are useful lenses through which to study work motivation; this assumption is relaxed (or replaced) in parts three and four.

Part three consists of five chapters dealing with concepts of work motivation that assume that people's beliefs, attitudes, and intentions are the ultimate determinants of

---

[11]If the doomsday scenarios about the end of jobs and the end of work as we know them come to be as portended by Bridges (1994) and Rifkin (1995), lower-level needs for sheer survival in tough, unending periods of unemployment may take on much greater importance in the motivation to work.

their behavior. Accordingly, in chapter 9 we discuss some of the more popular[12] views of the nature of human beliefs, attitudes, and intentions and provide the basic concepts needed to understand the cognitive theories that follow in chapters 10 through 13. In chapter 10 we examine three types of human beliefs and attitudes that are especially relevant to work motivation. In chapter 11 we focus on human perceptions and beliefs about fairness, justice, and equity and their place in a study of work motivation. This is the largest and most detailed chapter in the book, largely because the author believes that the core concepts contained there (such as perceptions of equity, fairness, and justice) are among the most potent and important forces in the behavior of people at work.

In chapter 12 we examine the popular expectancy-valence models of work motivation, paying special attention to the notion of human agency, the issue of people's beliefs about their capacity to perform particular tasks, and the newer control theory, which takes a similar approach. Chapter 13 deals with the specific nature of human intentions and their role in human goal-setting processes, followed by a treatment of the formal theory of goal setting. We continue with a study of self-regulation processes that are founded at least in part in goal-setting concepts and techniques. Management by objectives, a managerial technique that has its main roots in the theory of goal setting, is the final topic of chapter 13.

Chapter 14 is the sole chapter in part four, where we deal with views of work motivation that to varying degrees among their adherents, deny the importance of the concept altogether, preferring to focus on work *behavior.* The chapter features a historical treatment of the role of behaviorism in psychology, organizational behavior, and work motivation in particular. It concludes with a presentation of the currently popular social cognitive theory and the applied techniques of self-regulation. Theories in this part have in common the feature that they take a learning approach to work motivation.

Part five provides closure to topics related to the human motivation to work. In chapter 15 we present a succinct summary of the most important principles of work motivation that have potential for application by managers. The chapter closes with a short overview of the state of the science pertaining to the study of work motivation and presents a few suggestions for future research and theory.

To begin, then, because most of what follows in the book is theory, in chapter 2 we explain the meaning of theory and show how the theoretical nature of our knowledge of work motivation is an important feature of that knowledge for both the student and the practicing manager.

---

[12]We refer to these selected theories of attitudes here as being among the most popular. To be more precise, the theories that comprise most of the focus are those that have been the most useful and popular to organizational and social psychologists in their study of work motivation. A complete survey of the theory of attitudes is far beyond the scope of this book.

CHAPTER

Methods of Inquiry in Work Motivation Theory and Research

No way of thinking or doing, however ancient, can be trusted without proof.
—H. D. THOREAU

In chapter 1 we argued that managers might benefit from an understanding of human work motivation because such knowledge can help them to contribute to workforce productivity in their respective organizations and, indirectly, to the aggregate level of economic prosperity of the nation. Most managers are aware of the need for some knowledge of employee motivation, and as argued in chapter 3, most managers hold implicit mental models as to "what makes employees tick." In response to the widespread desire for solutions to the problem of employee motivation, many consultants, academics, and businesspeople have developed and promulgated theories of work motivation. Some of these theories have merit, others do not.

The purpose of this chapter is to provide the reader with an understanding of the means by which theories of work motivation are developed and made available to practitioners for application in organizational settings. A model is presented that represents the cyclical process through which research and theory development often proceed as new ideas about work motivation are generated and refined for application. It is important for the reader to understand the nature of this process to appreciate or apply the theoretic notions presented throughout the remainder of this book and in other books dealing with human behavior in organizations. This cyclical process is illustrated through a detailed summary of the development and promulgation of one of the most influential and controversial theories of work motivation, Herzberg's motivator-hygiene theory. Finally, we discuss the general problem of the ways that a practitioner can determine the readiness for application of any theoretical framework that has its roots in behavioral and social science. The issues and concepts introduced in this part of the chapter have relevance for the discussion elsewhere in the book, where various theories and techniques of employee motivation are presented in greater detail.[1]

To begin, let's look at the cycle of events that is typical during the development of most new theories in behavioral science—a cycle that is particularly common in the development of theories of work motivation.

DEVELOPMENT AND ADOPTION OF THEORIES

Where Do Theories Come From?

The knowledge base of most social and behavioral sciences results from a cycle of activities, a cycle that many practitioners are either not aware of or tend to ignore. Our base of knowledge about work motivation is no exception to this cycle, so it is important for the student or manager who wishes to apply these theories to understand the nature of their origins. For the sake of discussion, the cycle is illustrated graphically in Figure 2-1. Although the sequence of events varies to some degree from one case to another, it is common for the cycle to begin with the observation of a problem or a phenomenon of concern to someone (such as a manager or administrator) who is responsible for dealing

FIGURE 2-1   Cycle of Events Leading to Theories of Work Motivation

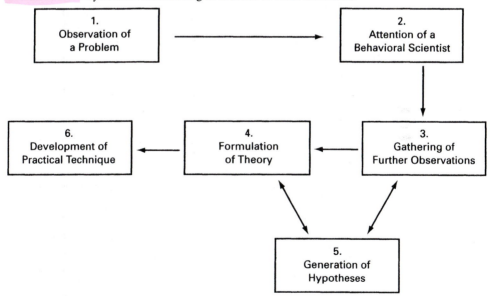

[1]Readers may find that the content of this chapter is different from that in the rest of the book. Those who wish to get to the particular details of the various theories we examine, disregarding the caveats and considerations developed in this chapter, may do so by moving directly to chapter 3. In fact, some readers may find it most useful to do just that and once having acquired a working knowledge of the major tenets and features of the various theories discussed in the book, return to chapter 2. Our suggestion, however, is that the reader carefully work through the points contained in the current chapter, because aside from being of intrinsic importance, they provide an understanding of the approaches and values that we apply in our treatments of the theories and techniques that comprise the rest of the book.

with it [see box (1) in Figure 2-1].[2] Low job performance, absenteeism, tardiness, insubordination, or the occurrence of wildcat strikes are a number of examples that are of particular relevance to us here. At some time or other, the problem may come to the attention of a behavioral scientist, at which stage any of a number of things may occur [see box (2)]. In some cases the scientist may set about to explore the phenomenon of interest, gathering more preliminary observations related to it, relying, sometimes, on only a few more observations [see Eisenhardt, 1989, and box (3) in Figure 2-1]. In other cases, the scientist may already have a number of hypotheses or hunches that can be tested with the data already in hand. Regardless, once a phenomenon comes to the attention of a social or behavioral scientist, a cycle of scientific activity gets under way, leading sooner or later to a formal theory to explain it.

The term *theory* is often viewed with suspicion by practical people, so many academics and consultants avoid using it when dealing with them. Nevertheless, virtually all of our knowledge of business, organizations, and the behavior of people in organizations consists entirely of theory. There are few irrefutable *laws* pertaining to human behavior. This point has a number of important implications for anyone who wishes to permit behavioral science to influence the policies and practices of a manager of human resources. In later sections of the chapter we deal with some of these implications, but since the bulk of the ideas presented in this book consist of or derive from theory, it is important that we define the term and begin to understand it.

What Is a Theory?

As usual, definitions abound, but in this case they tend to converge. One popular definition from a major philosopher of science—one that seems to represent most others—holds that "theories are nets cast to catch what we call 'the world': to rationalize, to explain, and to master it" (Popper, 1968, p. 59). Another, more recent definition, offered by an organizational scholar, defines theory as "a system of constructs and variables in which the constructs are related to each other by propositions and the variables are related to each other by hypotheses" (Bacharach, 1989, p. 498).

Theories are like templates that are fashioned as representations of reality: Sometimes they are accurate reflections of that reality; sometimes they are not. When a theory truly represents the part of reality it purports to represent, it is said to be *valid*. Proposing a theory can be easy; proposing a valid theory can be much more difficult, and proposing a theory that will be truly useful to managers and social scientists requires imagination and nonlinear thinking (Weick, 1989). But validity is not an all-or-nothing phenomenon (nor is it the only criterion by which to assess a theory, as we discuss shortly). Rather, it is possible for some aspects of a theory to be more valid than other aspects. Moreover, as the phenomenon of interest changes, the theory that purports to represent it may become less valid unless it is changed accordingly (see Cronbach, 1975), and the value of any social theory must be assessed in relation to the sociopolitical environment in which it is offered (Nord et al., 1988).

There has recently been considerable debate—some of it colorful and overly heated—in the organizational sciences about the processes of theorizing and about the criteria that one can, or should, use to evaluate a theory. Much of the polemics results

---

[2]It is not always the case that real-world problems are the origins of theories (Ziman, 1987), but we restrict our discussion here to cases in which this is so.

from the fact that participating scholars represent fundamentally opposing philosophical views about human nature, social events, the ontological meaning of "organizations," and the meaning of life in general (Gioia and Pitrie, 1990). Some of the difference is rooted in differing political ideologies (Nehbrass, 1979). A complete discussion of these issues and of the various positions related to them is beyond our scope and purpose here.[3] Rather, we restrict our discussion to a relatively conventional view on the matter: what makes for a good theory (of work motivation).

Criteria for Evaluating Theories of Work Motivation

One author has proposed that the two major bases for evaluating a theory are *falsifiability* and *utility* (Bacharach, 1989). This means that a theory must be constructed such that it is possible for someone to gather (valid) data by observing the phenomenon of interest (e.g., work motivation) and then to demonstrate that the information gathered conflicts in important ways with the tenets of the theory or with hypotheses legitimately derived from the theory. This criterion has been widely popular in the social and physical sciences for many years (see Popper, 1968). The utility criterion implies that the theory should permit us to both explain and predict events with better-than-chance regularity and accuracy.[4] Nevertheless, it is sometimes possible to predict events (such as the likelihood of a wildcat strike), but it is not as easy to explain *why* they happen.

To return to the typical cycle of events portrayed in Figure 2-1, we see that theories result from observations and are intended to make sense of those observations. There is usually a prolonged sequence in which the scientist gathers observations through the conduct of formal research, formulates propositions based on those observations, and then gathers more data to confirm, modify, or reject the propositions. Often, many scientists are involved: Some gather and report data; others criticize the data or the inferences derived from them; still others may be responsible for integrating the ideas of several researchers into a theoretical formulation. The iterative relationship between the collection of observations, the casting of propositions, and the refinement of theory is represented by boxes (4) to (6) of Figure 2-1.

Varieties of Validity

One of the most important criteria applied throughout this book in our comparative assessment of research and theories is *validity*. The validity criterion is a difficult standard to apply. Moreover, there are many varieties of validity (T. D. Cook and Campbell, 1979). The four forms that we adopt for our purposes are internal validity, construct validity, statistical conclusion validity, and external validity. It is important that the reader be basically familiar with all these forms. We provide only an outline of them here; the interested reader is referred to T. D. Cook and Campbell (1979) for complete details.

Internal validity deals with the following question: Do the putative causal variables in a research study really account for the variation we observe in the putative

---

[3]The interested reader is referred to special issues of the *Academy of Management Review* (e.g., October 1989, July 1991, July 1992) for representative treatments of the various positions and the controversies involved.

[4]It also sometimes implies the managerial value of using the theory in applied problems over and above what can be accomplished without the assistance of the theory. We have more to say later in the chapter about this second interpretation of the utility concept.

outcome variables of the research, or are other factors at work that better explain the effects we see on the dependent variables? Sometimes research designs are not careful enough to rule out plausible alternatives to the cause-and-effect relationships that researchers offer at the end of a study to explain their results. For example, assume that a field experiment on work motivation is conducted in the forests of British Columbia into the relationship between reward systems and levels of worker motivation. Two types of pay system are used: one a flat salary system and the other a piece-rate pay plan. Assume that the people studied in the salary group are older and better educated than the people who work under the piece-rate plan. If there are differences in performance between the two groups and the experimenter concludes that, indeed, the piece-rate program produced higher levels of motivation than the salary system did, a critic may challenge these results, saying that they may not be internally valid. Why? The critic can point out that the differences in age and/or education between the two pay groups may both be feasible explanations for the observed performance differences. In other words, the critic may say that the results argue just as strongly that education, or age, or both, are the cause of differences in motivation, not the pay system being used.

The burden of proof is on the researcher: He or she is required to rule out "confounding" factors such as age and education, by whatever means, so that there can be one and only one reasonable explanation for any observed differences in the dependent variable—in this case, the planned independent variable, reward systems. If there are such alternative explanations, there is no reason to think that we have learned anything from this research about the link between pay and motivation (or performance). There are many other generic ways that research can be poorly designed so as to permit *threats to internal validity* (or what we have here called confounds, or alternative explanations) to cast a shadow of doubt on the conclusions of a study (see T. D. Cook and Campbell, 1979, pp. 50–58).

This leads to a second concern: *construct validity*. In the foregoing example, the researcher planned to study the link between pay systems and work motivation but measured "motivation" by performance rates. We saw in chapter 1 that motivation and performance are not the same. So if there are differences between the two pay groups in terms of performance, the researcher would be making a mistake in construct validity by concluding that pay affects motivation: Again, *motivation is not performance*. As a second example of a problem of construct validity, suppose we held a theory that overly strict supervision was a cause of employee aggression. Testing that theory would require distilling this general proposition into testable hypotheses using real-world indicators that reflect both *overly strict supervision* and *employee aggression,* gathering data on both of these sets of indicators, and conducting analyses of the data to determine whether the indicators are related in the way suggested by the theory. Problems abound, however, in finding indicators that are *construct valid*—that represent all of what we mean conceptually by the term *overly strict supervision* and that do not include elements of other constructs as well (Schwab, 1980). Similarly, we would have to find real-world indicators that represent all of what we imply by the term *aggression*—nothing more and nothing less. If these real-world indicators do not meet the test of construct validity (e.g., if we measured employee behavior that really does not represent aggression and/or excluded from our empirical observations supervisory behavior that should have been included under the umbrella of overly strict supervision), any conclusions that we draw at the conceptual level about the validity of the theory will be false. Finally, we would have to design our study so as to validly test our hypothesis that the relationship between supervisory style and aggression was causal and in the direction we anticipated. Again, failure to do so constrains our ability to say that we have validly tested our theory.

Now suppose that the researcher managed to gather data using construct valid measures of both the independent variable (reward system) and the dependent variable (e.g., supervisory reports of employee effort) but failed to find any differences between the effort levels of the two pay groups. The conclusion may be that there is, in fact, no differential effect on motivation by pay systems. On the other hand, a closer look might reveal that the researchers made mistakes in the use of the inferential statistics that they gathered on pay structures (which would be unlikely in this example) and effort levels. There are a number of ways that such *statistical conclusion* errors can be made. The researchers may not have studied enough people in the two pay systems to have had enough *statistical power* to find systematic differences that did in fact exist; or perhaps the variables used to measure the constructs were not measured reliably. The reader is referred to T. D. Cook and Campbell's (1979, especially pp. 39–50) classic treatment of these matters for further explanation and examples.

A fourth validity concern has to do with the generalizability of the results of a study. *External validity* is the issue of the degree to which the results can reasonably be generalized to populations other than the one used in the study, to periods of time other than the present, and to settings other than the one studied. In our pay and motivation example, we would be interested to know whether any results that we might find could be generalized from the forest products industry to mining, fishing, and manufacturing, for example; we would hope that the results gathered today would be of value for planning compensation systems in the future; and we would want to know whether the results of our study would generalize to American and Asian workers. Notice that a study must be internally valid to be externally valid: Before we can safely generalize a finding (such as how pay systems affect work motivation), we must be sure that we actually have an internally valid conclusion to generalize!

We refer to the various forms of validity as we discuss theories and techniques of work motivation throughout the book, especially in chapter 12. Generally, our concern is with internal validity: the issue of whether the conclusions that researchers report are justified given the research design and execution on which those conclusions are based. Our point is this: Validity is a necessary criterion for us to take a theory seriously, yet it is extremely difficult to demonstrate the validity of a theory. In addition, validity is not enough; the theory must be useful and falsifiable. R. Jacques (1992) even proposes that we adopt an "ethic of caring," which would require that we take into account the social conditions of power and authority and would raise questions about whether a theory is likely to be used to strengthen the grip of those who hold power in society or whether the theory may be useful in furthering the cause of disadvantaged groups, such as women and minorities (R. Jacques, 1992, p. 601).

A second point here is that theories ultimately rest on the more or less structured observations of scientists (gathered during their research activities). It stands to reason that mistakes made in the way a problem is formulated or conceived (Weick, 1989), in the way constructs are operationalized, and in the means by which data are collected and analyzed can all result in theories that are less valid (and/or less useful) than they might otherwise be. Although a full treatment of research methodology is not our purpose here, the reader should recognize that faulty scientific methods can lead to inaccurate and useless theories and/or make it difficult to assess the level of validity of extant theories. There are countless ways to err in the research process, some of which are more common than others (see T. D. Cook and Campbell, 1979). Nevertheless, the reader is reminded that virtually all of the ideas concerning work motivation presented in this book consist of or are derived from theory, and the true level of validity of these theories is often open to dispute. Accordingly, managerial techniques rooted in these theories are likely to be of limited value. In fact, they may even be harmful (Pinder, 1977).

In closing this section, we express our support for a view proposed by Fry and Smith (1987, pp. 129–130), who wrote: "The driving force behind our quest for theory, especially theories of organization [and, we would add, work motivation], is the innate need to impose order on unordered experiences, and thereby solve real-world problems that require collective effort. Grounding our theories in everyday problems is all important because it is the logical relation to a problem situation which makes a theory interesting and meaningful, and gives it power to solve existing problems and to illuminate new ones" (Popper, 1976).

In the following section we illustrate the cycle described above and represented in Figure 2-1 by relating the story of the development of one of the most widely known theories of work motivation, proposed nearly 40 years ago by Frederick Herzberg and his colleagues. In addition to illustrating the cycle of activities that commonly occurs in the development of a science, the following section should serve to introduce the first of the major theories of work motivation described in this book. Later in the chapter we discuss the general validity of theories of work motivation and introduce other criteria for theory evaluation that have been applied to the assessment of these theories in recent years.

THE MOTIVATOR-HYGIENE THEORY AS EXAMPLE

On the basis of an exhaustive review of hundreds of early studies of the causes, correlates, and consequences of job attitudes, Herzberg and his colleagues (Herzberg, Mausner, Peterson, and Capwell, 1957) developed the preliminary hypothesis that the factors which cause positive attitudes toward one's job are different from the factors that generate negative job-related attitudes. This hypothesis was revolutionary at the time because it implies that job satisfaction is not simply the opposite of job dissatisfaction, as had commonly been assumed. Instead, the new hypothesis held that feelings of job satisfaction and job dissatisfaction are independent of one another, such that an employee can be happy about some aspects of his job while being unhappy about others. Using the terms shown in Figure 2-1, the problem of interest in this case was employee work attitudes, and the observations that led to the preliminary hypothesis were actually the observations of hundreds of other researchers and behavioral scientists—a much wider and more justifiable base for offering a hypothesis than is usually the case in behavioral science.

Herzberg's Own Research

To test the two-factor concept, Herzberg and his colleagues (Herzberg, Mausner, and Snyderman, 1959) gathered their own original data (observations) from a sample of 203 engineers and accountants who worked for a variety of organizations in the Pittsburgh area. Using a semistructured interview technique (meaning that both the researcher and the interviewee influenced the direction taken during the interview), the researchers asked the employees, one at a time, to think of an occasion when they felt "exceptionally good" or "exceptionally bad" about their jobs. Interviewees were permitted to recall such critical incidents from their current jobs or from any held previously. They recorded two or three incidents of this sort, on average, from each employee. For each incident, detail was requested concerning three things: (1) a description of the objective conditions surrounding and causing the incident, (2) a description of the reasons why the employee felt a particular way at the time of the incident, and (3) a summary of the consequences of the incident for the employee and the job.

Analysis of the Incidents

Once the data in a research project are gathered, they must be analyzed. (As we saw earlier, both the collection and analysis phases of such a project are potentially problematic.) Herzberg and his colleagues broke each interview down into almost 500 separate thought items and then classified these items into categories based on the degree of similarity that appeared among them. Notice that the researchers allowed the nature of the items to determine the categories to emerge from this analysis rather than sorting them into predefined categories. Care was taken to assure that independent researchers could agree on the classification of particular items into the various clusters that resulted. The items were also categorized as having either long- or short-term effects on the employees at the time.

Sixteen separate groups of items, or factors, emerged from this exercise—16 sets of items that were related in one way or another with instances of extremely satisfying or unsatisfying job experiences. The next step was to see whether any of these groups of factors seemed to be more closely associated with instances of positive job attitudes than with instances of negative job attitudes, and similarly, whether certain factors appeared more frequently in stories of negative incidents than in stories of positive job attitudes.

Further detail on the data analysis techniques employed is well beyond the scope of this book; the interested reader is referred to the original report (Herzberg et al., 1959). What is important to the present discussion is a summary of the results, and even more important, the way the results have been interpreted, misinterpreted, and fought over ever since by pro- and anti-Herzberg factions.

The Motivators

In fact, certain patterns did seem to emerge from the data. As had been the researchers' hunch before the data were collected, one set of factors appeared more frequently in stories of positive job attitudes than in stories of negative job attitudes. For example, reports of achievement appeared in 41 percent of the instances of positive job attitudes, making it the single feature most frequently related to job satisfaction experiences. (An example from the study is the case of a marine engineer who described an instance when he succeeded in designing a propeller for a new boat design.) Similarly, recognition appeared in 33 percent of the positive stories; challenging, varied, or interesting work appeared in 26 percent; responsibility appeared in 23 percent; and advancement was an element of fully 20 percent of the stories of high job satisfaction.

On the other hand, 10 of the 16 factors that were identified previously appeared in fewer than 7 percent of the job satisfaction episodes, suggesting, as had been expected, that they were not usually related to job satisfaction experiences. Because the interviewees indicated that the occurrences of these highly favorable periods of job attitudes tended to result in greater job performance, Herzberg labeled these as sources of satisfaction motivators. A number of special features emerged from a close look at the five most frequently mentioned satisfiers/motivators. First, positive stories that featured one of these factors tended to include elements related to one or more of the other four—they seemed to go hand in hand in producing job satisfaction. Further, the researchers noted that compared to the negative feelings, the positive feelings tended to be relatively long-lasting rather than short term in effect. They also tended to be related to aspects of the content of the job and to the personal relationship between the worker and the job. It was eventually determined that these five factors were associated with job satisfaction because they tended to cause feelings of growth and personal development.

The Hygiene Factors

The researchers then looked at the stories that referred to instances of job dissatisfaction and found that the 11 remaining factors revealed in their earlier analysis seemed to appear most frequently in them. Thus, company policy and administration were blamed at least partially for 31 percent of the reported cases of job dissatisfaction. Similarly, unhappy relationships with the employee's supervisor appeared in 20 percent of the stories, and poor interpersonal relations with one's peers was the critical factor in 15 percent of the instances of poor job attitudes. Unhappiness with technical aspects of the employee's supervisor was a critical factor in 20 percent of the stories of low job attitudes, while bad relations with the supervisor on a personal level appeared important in 15 percent of these stories. Two other factors that figured predominantly in the episodes of low job attitudes were poor working conditions and unfriendly relationships with one's peers, which appeared in 11 percent and 8 percent of the stories of dissatisfaction, respectively. Compared to the frequency with which this second set of factors appeared in stories of job dissatisfaction, they were not frequently related to instances of high job attitudes.

Herzberg and his colleagues (1959) named the second set of factors *hygienes* because, analogous to the concept of mental hygiene in psychiatry, these items were seen as necessary, but not sufficient, for healthy adjustment. (In this case, they are necessary for preventing job dissatisfaction but are not capable of generating either job satisfaction or motivated behavior.) The researchers noted a number of features shared among the hygiene factors. First, they all tend to be related to the context of the work—the circumstances within which the person performs the job. (Recall that the motivators were more closely linked to the content of the work.) Second, the hygiene factors tended to be associated with shorter-lasting job experiences than were the motivators. Herzberg (1981) argues that providing decent working conditions and cordial interactions on the job, for example, may serve to move people in the short run, but that their zero point escalates, so that people quickly take these things for granted, and become likely to ask, "What have you done for me lately?" On the other hand, the provision of motivator factors in the employee's work is seen as having a much longer-lasting effect on the individual, resulting in motivation rather than simple movement.

The predominant reason given by the respondents in the original study (Herzberg et al., 1959) to explain why the lack of hygiene factors was associated with dissatisfaction was that their absence tended to cause feelings of being unfairly treated. So whereas the provision of motivators led to feelings of growth and development, a sense of injustice seemed to explain the link between the absence of hygienes and job dissatisfaction.

Overlap among the Factors

There was at least one other important aspect of the hygiene factors noted by Herzberg and his colleagues, a feature that is highly relevant to the controversy sparked by the theory. There were a number of stories of job dissatisfaction that featured elements of some of the motivator factors, especially recognition, work itself, and advancement. For example, failure to receive recognition was said to be the principal cause in 18 percent of the stories of job dissatisfaction. It is important to acknowledge that the researchers recognize these deviations from the basic split in their original book:

> All the basic satisfiers, recognition, achievement, advancement, responsibility, and work itself appeared with significantly greater frequencies in the highs [stories of job satisfaction] than they did in the low sequences of events [stories of job dissatisfaction]. However, some of these factors also appeared with some frequency in the low stories: recognition, 18 percent; work itself, 14 percent; and advancement, 11 percent. Evidently these three satisfiers are not so unidirectional in their effect on job attitudes as the factors that cause job dissatisfaction. From these results it would appear that a better statement of the hypothesis would be that the satisfier factors are much more likely to increase job satisfaction than they would be to decrease job satisfaction but that the factors that relate to job dissatisfaction very infrequently act to increase job satisfaction. (Herzberg et al., 1959, p. 80)

Anyone who has ever worked at a dull or disagreeable job knows from experience that the nature of the work, by itself, can be a very powerful cause of job dissatisfaction, as can instances in which either recognition for accomplishment is hard to come by or in which employees are not advanced at a rate that is deemed fair. Quite clearly, if absent from an employee's job, these motivators can be great sources of frustration and dissatisfaction.

Two issues require highlighting here. The first is a technical point but one with significance for the argument being presented in this chapter: Notice that in their well-intended acknowledgment of the lack of perfect symmetry between the causes of job satisfaction and dissatisfaction, Herzberg and his colleagues indicated the possibility that the three motivators in question could also decrease job satisfaction. The problem lies in the fact that their data, as well as their own theoretical interpretation of data, imply that satisfaction and dissatisfaction are not opposite sides of the same emotion. Instead, they are held to be entirely independent and different from one another—but not opposites[5] (see Bobko, 1985). To be consistent with the rest of the theory, what the caveat should have said about the three common crossovers is that like the major hygiene factors, these motivators are capable of causing job dissatisfaction

---

[5]Later, Herzberg (1966) described how the motivators are responsible for meeting growth needs, whereas the hygienes are needed only to provide basic survival.

(as opposed to decreasing job satisfaction) among people. The difference is important, because it illustrates the ways by which misinterpretations and misunderstandings can arise as a theory is developed and then passed from one researcher to another in the cycle of testing and modification shown in Figure 2-1.

The second point is that although they drew attention to the fact that their data featured these (as well as other) crossovers, both Herzberg and others who followed him seemed to lose sight of this acknowledgment in the original statement of the theory. In popularized interpretations of his own theory, for example, Herzberg himself (1968, 1981) lists his basic motivators as associated with motivation and satisfaction, and his hygienes as causative only of dissatisfaction, failing to mention the reversals in the data that originally gave rise to the theory. In short, these two points illustrate how the refinement of a theory can encounter snags and delays, making the process shown in Figure 2-1 less precise than one might wish it to be.

The Role of Pay

The most ambivalent of the 16 factors found in the stories of satisfaction and dissatisfaction was salary. It appeared in almost as many stories (proportionately) of job satisfaction as it did in stories of dissatisfaction. However, because it was related to more stories of long-term negative attitude shifts than to long-term positive shifts, Herzberg and his team classified salary in the hygiene category.

The Two-Factor Theory in a Nutshell

Briefly, the two-factor theory proposes that human beings have two basic sets of needs and that different elements of the work experience can serve to meet them (Herzberg, 1966). The first set of needs are for *basic survival* or maintenance. They are characterized as being concerned with avoiding pain and discomfort and as providing for primary drives such as sex, thirst, and hunger. The second set of needs are called *growth needs*. They express themselves in attempts by people to become all that they are capable of becoming, by exploring and conquering challenges posed by their environments. (See chapter 7, where the notion of growth needs is discussed in greater detail.) Minimum levels of the hygiene factors (e.g., salary) are necessary for fulfillment of the survival needs, but when they are present, they do not cause feelings of job satisfaction: they merely prevent feelings of job dissatisfaction. Hygienes can be useful motivators, according to the theory, only until the survival needs are somewhat provided for. Then they lose effect.

To produce positive job attitudes and to motivate employees, the theory claims that items originally identified as motivators must be built into all types of jobs. The content of the work rather than the setting in which it is conducted is the important thing. The work must provide opportunities for the employee to achieve, and the person must receive recognition for that achievement. The work should be interesting, provide for advancement, and require responsibility. When jobs are designed according to these principles (or enriched), motivation and positive attitudes will be forthcoming. When these factors are missing, however, no dissatisfaction results, simply an absence of satisfaction. The original study revealed a number of other findings, but those mentioned above are the most important as well as the most controversial and the most relevant for the present discussion.

The Ensuing Controversy

The cycle shown in Figure 2-1 indicates that newly developed theories are usually put to the test of reality either by their original proponents or by others interested in confirming, refining, or refuting them. Accordingly, the motivator-hygiene theory quickly drew a lot of attention. Within a few years, dozens of attempts were made to interpret the theory, develop means of measuring the various factors included in it, and to gather data and compare the results found in the data with predictions that followed from the theory. As is often the case, the results were highly mixed. Some studies seemed to support the two-factor concept, others did not. As evidence accumulated on both sides of the ledger, a dispute between pro- and anti-Herzberg factions developed, generated in part by a number of allegations that Herzberg's results (and therefore the theory itself) could be explained primarily by the methods he and his colleagues used to both gather and analyze the data! This point is crucial. A theory of work motivation is supposed to reflect the true underlying nature of just that—work motivation. Such a theory should not, in fact, be merely an artifact of the methodology used to generate it.

The argument was that the storytelling technique (described above) naturally tended to cause the interviewees to link instances of satisfaction to their own accomplishments, and—not wanting to look bad—caused them to associate instances of negative feelings with factors that were somewhat beyond their control or responsibility. So, for example, it was alleged that the engineers and accountants quite understandably blamed company policies, their supervisors and peers, and other contextual factors for the negative events reported in their stories. This criticism was a serious challenge to the validity of the theory because it cast fundamental doubt on the very meaning of the data. Moreover, the criticism grew in seriousness when it was noted that studies using the Herzberg methodology tended to support the theory, whereas those that used other methods to gather and analyze data tended not to support it (Behling, Labovitz, and Kosmo, 1968).

A complete history of the Herzberg debate is beyond the scope of this book. Interested readers are referred to papers by Bockman (1971), Grigaliunas and Weiner (1974), House and Wigdor (1967), and Whitsett and Winslow (1967) for summaries of the controversy and insight into the many fine points that are involved. Briefly, however, by 1970 enough data had been gathered that cast doubt on the theory for Korman (1971) to conclude that research had "effectively laid the Herzberg theory to rest" (p. 149). Subsequent pronouncements of the demise of the theory have been plentiful. But more than a decade after the two-factor theory was formally proposed, some of its proponents claimed that it was seldom tested fairly, so that the conclusion that it is invalid is itself not well founded (Grigaliunas and Weiner, 1974). For example, these writers argued that virtually none of the studies that were conducted to test the theory used measures of job satisfaction and job dissatisfaction that represented two separate and independent continua, as the theory would demand. Moreover, data are presented that imply that the social desirability explanation for the original data (as discussed above) is not tenable. Grigaliunas and Weiner also pointed out that critics of Herzberg's theory have tended to ignore the substantial evidence that has accumulated to support the theory's prescriptions for job design. In short, these authors believe that it may not be possible to test the theory fairly and that attempts to do so before 1974 failed to provide sufficient grounds to conclude that it is not valid. (One study that employed a methodology that Grigaliunas and Weiner propose—Ondrack [1974]—failed to support the theory.)

Herzberg himself has alleged at times that he has been misinterpreted (e.g., Herzberg, 1976). The problem is that for the self-correcting cycle of scientific activity shown in Figure 2-1 to occur, it is first necessary that the theory in question be interpreted accurately, without biases or nuances that are not founded on the basis of the observations that gave rise to it initially. To the extent that Herzberg and his codefendants are correct in their position that the theory has been misinterpreted and tested with inappropriate instruments, there is no way that anyone—including academics, students, or practitioners—can be sure that the theory has anything to offer to help them understand and/or influence work motivation.

Aside from the allegation that inappropriate instruments have been used to examine the motivator-hygiene theory, it has been demonstrated by N. King (1970) that there have been as many as five different interpretations of the two-factor notion, and that none of these interpretations enjoys much empirical support that cannot be attributed to methodological artifact, as was alleged of the original study. To illustrate, one interpretation suggests that all of the motivator factors combined contribute more to job satisfaction than to job dissatisfaction, and that all hygienes combined contribute more to dissatisfaction than to satisfaction. A different interpretation holds that all motivators combined contribute more to satisfaction than do all hygiene factors combined, and that all hygiene factors combined contribute more to dissatisfaction than do all motivators combined. Remarks made in Herzberg's 1966 book suggest that this is what the theory implies. Regardless, N. King (1970) shows that only studies that used the Herzberg method have been successful at replicating and supporting the theory and that the various interpretations fail, as tested, to provide unequivocal support for the two-factor feature of the theory.

On balance, when we combine all the evidence with all the allegations that the theory has been misinterpreted and that its major concepts have not been assessed properly, we are left not really knowing whether to take the theory itself seriously, let alone whether it should be put into practice in organizational settings. There is support for many of the implications the theory has for enriching jobs to make them more motivating. But the two-factor aspect of the theory—the feature that makes it unique—is not really a necessary element in use of the theory for designing jobs per se. One need only believe that building jobs to provide responsibility, achievement, recognition for achievement, and advancement will make them satisfying and motivating. There is no need to assume that failure to provide these 28 factors will not lead to job dissatisfaction or that the provision of certain hygiene factors in the workplace cannot also be motivating, in the true sense of the word.

Implications of the Herzberg Controversy

Why have we devoted so much attention to the details surrounding development of the two-factor theory and to the controversy it generated? One obvious purpose was to explain the theory, because it remains one of the best known approaches to work motivation among practitioners today, despite the decades of doubt and controversy that have surrounded it.[6] But there are several other reasons for examining it so closely. First, the Herzberg story permits us to illustrate a number of important prob-

---

[6]Very few general textbooks in organizational behavior treat work motivation without discussing the two-factor theory, notwithstanding its dubious validity and all of the controversy we have reviewed here.

lems and issues that relate to the development of new theories in behavioral science as we introduced them earlier in the chapter. In fairness, these problems and issues are certainly not unique to the case of the motivator-hygiene theory; rather, it is the one theory of work motivation that seems to have been exposed to the closest criticism on grounds of methodology.

The foregoing story illustrates the difficulty of developing tools or instruments for assessing hypothetical concepts such as motivation. As was noted both in chapter 1 and earlier in this chapter, we must *infer* the existence of motivated force from the observation of effort or by asking people what is going on inside them. We cannot directly weigh or measure concepts such as attitudes and motivation as we would physical objects (M. A. Hughes, Price, and Marrs, 1986; Schwab, 1980). This means that we must worry about whether our crude proxy measures (such as Herzberg's interview technique) really allow us to measure those things we think we are measuring, nothing more and nothing less. This is the problem of construct validity described earlier (Schwab, 1980), a constant issue in assessing nonphysical entities and a major limitation on our capacity to establish fairly the validity of theories of work motivation.

To make matters worse, we must also worry about the possibility that the measurements we make vary from one time to the next (when in fact we know that the entity being measured has not changed). That is, do our measures fluctuate or are they relatively stable? This is referred to as the problem of *reliability of measurement*. Clearly, we cannot develop or test a theory with instruments that give us inconsistent assessments of the concepts that must be calibrated, yet the stability of measurement in behavioral science when interviews and/or questionnaires are used is usually a problem (Nunnally, 1967).

Further, consider the possibility that the very process of asking people how they feel toward their jobs may itself influence the type of response. Some critics (e.g., Salancik and Pfeffer, 1977, 1978) claim that it is virtually impossible to assess job attitudes without changing those attitudes merely by asking about them. This is referred to as the problem of *reactivity of measurement* (Webb, Campbell, Schwartz, and Sechrest, 1966). It, too, is endemic in behavioral research and figures heavily in the problem of measurement reliability. In the case of Herzberg's research, the allegation that his results could be accounted for by the ego-defense (or social desirability) motives of the interviewees provides an example of how difficult it is to assess attitudes and motives without influencing them simply by asking about them.

The Herzberg example also shows that there are many ways to make observations, and that once a theory has been proposed, there are many ways to test its validity (i.e., to determine whether it actually reflects reality). The story shows how theories are sometimes not tested appropriately, and as a result, may be either confirmed or rejected for the wrong reasons. Hypotheses that are supported by poorly conducted research (when, in fact, they should be rejected) can accumulate, resulting in theories that misrepresent the nature of things. Alternatively, valid hypotheses that do not pass the scientist's test (as a result of poor research) may be ignored and forgotten. The result is that potentially useful knowledge is discredited. The Herzberg case also illustrates what can happen when a theory, once developed, is oversimplified, misinterpreted, or misrepresented. In chapter 3 we see that Maslow's famous theory of needs has suffered similar treatment, as has the currently popular expectancy theory of motivation, discussed in chapter 12. If a new theory is not interpreted accurately, how can its true level of validity be determined and how can either the scientist or the practitioner decide whether it has any value in understanding and/or influencing the world?

In short, the story of the development of Herzberg's theory and the controversies that followed it help to illustrate many of the difficulties involved in the advancement of new theories of work motivation. It helps us understand the potential for error on the part of any new theory that purports to reflect the nature of work motivation. It also suggests that because of difficulties inherent in operationalizing them for testing, certain theories may be more valid than scientists are able to demonstrate, a proposition advanced repeatedly in later chapters. On the other hand, the story shows that as in other sciences, progress in organizational science is a nonlinear affair, such that new theoretical developments can earn widespread attention and influence despite—rather than because of—the quality of the research on which they are based. We hope that the Herzberg story will help the reader understand the necessity for caution on the part of behavioral scientists as they generate new theories. But more important, we hope that the reader with applied interests will learn to be somewhat discriminating and cautious in the adoption of new managerial techniques and programs that are grounded in theoretical ideas that are, in turn, based on more or less rigorous scientific methods of observation, analysis, and interpretation.

APPLYING MOTIVATION THEORY

The preceding analysis raises a number of questions. First, if it is accepted that caution is required in the application of new theories of motivation, how can an enlightened manager know when it is safe or advisable to adopt and begin applying new theories to human resource problems? What criteria or standards are available to suggest that such applications are appropriate? Further, just how valid are our best theories of work motivation? Simple answers to these questions are not possible, but in the following sections we shed some light on the issues involved.

Field Testing versus Commercial Application

When we consider the issue of the application of new theories of motivation in real organizational settings, it is important to keep in mind a distinction between two different types of application. The first type is that done by behavioral scientists, whose purpose is to examine the validity of the new theory in real settings. The second type of application is that conducted by practitioners, who (more or less) assume that the theory being adopted holds some probable value for them in dealing with actual organizational problems.

The first type of application is a necessary step in the appropriate refinement and ultimate scientific adoption of a theory of motivation. Scientists simply cannot determine whether a theory represents reality without comparing it to samples of that reality (Garner, 1972). As we will see in subsequent chapters, some theories (such as equity theory) have shown promising levels of accuracy when tested in contrived artificial settings but have failed to hold up to the scrutiny provided by testing in the field. On the other hand, goal-setting theory (see chapter 13) has benefited considerably by research conducted to examine it in real settings (Latham and Yukl, 1975; Locke and Latham,

1990). In short, application of the first type is advisable and necessary in the development of new theoretic ideas.

But when is application of the second type warranted? In other words, when is it safe and reasonable for a new theoretical idea to be distilled into formalized commercial packages and programs for use by practitioners in their respective organizations? Too frequently it has been the case that new applied motivation-oriented programs, based on behavioral science, have been widely disseminated among practitioners with unrealistic expectations for what they could accomplish (Pinder, 1977; Walter and Pinder, 1980). Two important examples are job enrichment and management-by-objectives (MBO) programs. As we will see later, MBO (which has some of its theoretic underpinnings in the very successful goal-setting theory mentioned above) has failed in most organizations in which it has been installed. Years after so many failures, more complete understanding of the organizational circumstances necessary for it to succeed became understood (Halpern and Osofsky, 1990; Jamieson, 1973). Similarly, only after several years of difficulties with formal job enrichment programs has it been learned what organizational preconditions are necessary for these programs to succeed (see Heckscher, 1988; Oldham and Hackman, 1980; Yorks, 1979). The point here is not that motivation theories have no applied utility, nor is it that they should not be implemented in real organizational settings. Rather, too often the urgency of applied managerial problems, such as employee motivation, has occasioned the premature widespread commercial application of new behavioral science technology in situations where it has not been appropriate and, consequently, where it has failed. Why does this happen?

Managers tend to be practical people who seek practical tools to deal with urgent organizational problems. They tend to process information very quickly, looking for the essential elements of the problems they face as well as of the solutions they consider in their decision making (Mintzberg, 1973). Often, however, managers' preferences for practicality translate into demands for simplicity—managers often seek and expect relatively simple solutions to problems that they openly recognize as complex. They often prefer nuts-and-bolts solutions, stripped of most cautions, caveats, and reservations that might appropriately accompany the advice they seek from others. In response, people with managerial programs (such as motivation-oriented techniques) willingly cater to the managerial preference for simplicity by offering or advocating scientifically based procedures stripped of all the "ifs, ands, and buts" that are justified by the research findings that underlie the procedures. The popular best-seller *The One-Minute Manager* (Blanchard and Johnson, 1981) is a legitimate and highly popular example. This author has sat through countless highly entertaining, yet oversimplified presentations at conferences for human resources practitioners—clever routines offered by witty "motivational experts" and speakers who have offered half-truths, oversimplifications, and simply false assertions about human work behavior. The humor and simplicity of these acts makes them the *sine qua non* of many practitioners' conferences. They do little to enhance the status and reputation of scholars and professors who are serious in the pursuit of knowledge about work motivation and behavior. Our advice here is borrowed from Alfred North Whitehead: "Seek simplicity and distrust it." In short, complex phenomena such as human work motivation are often oversimplified to make them palatable to practical people. Techniques that require unrealistic and oversimplifying assumptions are doomed to be ineffective when installed in complex, real settings.

Costs of Premature Application

Repeated instances of failure of hastily applied behavioral science are costly and unfortunate. Changes implemented on the basis of such techniques can have a profound influence on both the job satisfaction and life satisfaction of people in organizations—especially so for the lower-level participants whose jobs are changed in accordance with the theory being applied. Organizational change is necessary for effectiveness and survival, but changes that are ill advised and inappropriate are disruptive and unfair to those affected (e.g., Pringle and Longenecker, 1982). But premature and ill-advised applications are costly in other ways as well (Pinder, 1977, 1982; Walter and Pinder, 1980). Organizations that adopt programs such as MBO, job enrichment, or flex time (to cite three examples) must invest considerable amounts of money and managerial effort in the installation and operation of these programs. When the programs fail, management groups are justified in investigating the soundness of the advice in which they have invested. In cases where it becomes clear that the technique in question was really not appropriate, disappointment and/or hostility toward behavioral science and behavioral scientists is understandable. Alienation of this sort is unfortunate in view of the absolute necessity for science to interact with practitioners for the sake of solving real problems (Fry and Smith, 1987; Garner, 1972; Pinder, 1982).

If managers and behavioral scientists are mutually dependent on one another in the ways described above, how can a progressive management group decide in favor of formal attempts to install behavioral science–based programs and engage in application of the second type described above? One obvious basis for deciding that a theory is ready and safe for application is the level of scientific validity the theory has demonstrated in research-oriented applications of the first type described above and explained in detail earlier in the chapter.[7] On the other hand, there may be a case against reliance on validity alone, as we see in the following section.

Application: Validity or Marginal Utility?

In response to a paper written by the author (Pinder, 1977), Bobko (1978) has suggested that the absolute level of validity of a theory of motivation is an inappropriate basis for determining whether formal application of that theory is warranted or justified. He argues that managers must make decisions on a day-to-day basis, using implicit theories of human nature and motivation to guide them (see chapter 3 of this volume). The decisions reached on the basis of these implicit, informal theories result in more or less value (or utility) for their respective organizations. Bobko (1978) argues that whether a manager should employ a formal theory or motivation to guide human resource–related decisions should depend on the marginal utility (or extra value) added by application of the theory. (Cronbach and Gleser, 1965, make the same argument with regard to the use of psychological tests for the selection of personnel.)

Bobko's argument is compelling, but as argued elsewhere, the application of his marginal utility criterion for determining whether or not to apply a formal theory of motivation is impractical (Pinder, 1978). To follow Bobko's advice a manager would be required to estimate the base rate of effective motivation-related decisions (or influence attempts) between himself or herself and each employee prior to the application

---

[7]The reader will recall that we also described other, nonscientific criteria for the adoption of theories, such as interest value and the caring ethic. The focus here is on an issue related only to validity per se.

of a particular theory. The manager would then have to estimate the value of decisions (or influence attempts) that are made with the assistance of the particular theory in question and determine whether the value added as a consequence of the advice provided by the theory is sufficient to justify its use. This would be impractical, if not impossible, in view of the many difficulties associated with assessing individual job performance (see Latham and Wexley, 1981) and the fact that a particular supervisor's success would vary from one subordinate to another as well as across time and across circumstances for all employees. Moreover, in view of the complexity of organizational events, it would be very difficult to rule out explanations other than the application of theoretical principles if changes in decision-making effectiveness did seem to occur.

On balance, utility may be a reasonable criterion, in principle, for deciding when a theory is ready for application, but the practical difficulties it poses make it hard to employ. The enlightened manager is left, therefore, with the validity of a new theory as the only "objective" basis for deciding on its formal adoption in practice. This raises the next question we address in this chapter: How valid (and useful) are our major theories of work motivation, and are we capable of knowing the answer?

WORK MOTIVATION THEORY: VALID, UNBIASED, AND VALUE-FREE?

We introduced validity early in this chapter as a basis for evaluating social science theory and research. Now we return to the issue of validity and other criteria that have been applied to the assessment of theories of work motivation, the principal concern of this book. The question of the absolute validity of current work motivation theory is difficult to answer with much certainty, for a variety of reasons. Some of these are a matter of measurement and statistics; others are much more basic, having to do with fundamental issues in the philosophy and sociology of organizational science. We examine the matter, therefore, at several levels.

Measurement Issues

First, the very means by which the concept of motivation itself is measured are limited and problematic. The reader will recall that we defined work motivation as dealing with issues of intensity, direction, and duration; it is, by definition, a multidimensional concept. Typically, however, only the concept of intensity is operationalized for the sake of representing the entire concept. This comprises a problem of construct validity, as we discussed above (see Schwab, 1980). To make matters worse, researchers have typically measured only some of the components of the various theories, applied the various sorts of arithmetic formulas dictated by the theory in question (such as addition or multiplication of component scores), and come up with a total "score" representing the predicted level of motivation for individuals. Then some sort of correlation is conducted between these predicted levels and another outside measure or criterion variable. Often, perhaps usually, the same sort of problem occurs: What is used as the outside criterion, the basis that will be used to validate the theoretical predictions made by the theory?

Sometimes variables such as supervisory ratings are employed. Sometimes individual levels of *performance* are used as the criterion. (In chapter 1 we discussed the error of confusing motivation with performance; they are simply not the same thing.)

Aside from the fact that many of these outside criteria are inappropriate by their very nature, they are frequently subject to measurement problems of their own (such as unreliability). As a result, it can be very difficult to find significant and meaningful correlations between the levels of motivation predicted by the components of a theory (and as measured by the tools of the researcher) and external criteria that are supposed to verify (or validate) the theory under examination. For this reason, many of the theories available to us may in fact be more valid than we as social scientists are capable of demonstrating with our crude tools. Having stated that, we see, generally, that predicted levels of motivation (or at least the effort component of it) explain only minor proportions in the variance of criterion variables and that results are rarely stable from one empirical study to another (Mohr, 1982). Again, it may be that these theories are, in fact, better representations of motivated effort than we can demonstrate, but still, it is hard to tell, for the reasons just outlined.

The Validity and Usefulness of Work Motivation Theories

Just how valid are current theories of work motivation? There have been a number of attempts over the past two decades to answer this question. (See Locke and Latham, 1990a, chap. 2, for one review of these studies.) In most cases the issue addressed is the judged *comparative* value of the theories in question, not their absolute levels per se. The people making the judgments are typically "experts" in the field, and the criteria used are normally comparative validity, utility, and influence in the field. We summarize one of these studies in detail to illustrate the usual procedure.

In 1984, a senior academic industrial psychologist reported a study that examined the importance, validity, and usefulness of 32 established organizational science theories, the most common of which were theories of work motivation (J. B. Miner, 1984). The purpose of the study was to see whether there was any relationship among the three variables of interest. Miner solicited the "importance" ratings from a panel of key journal editors and former journal editors, asking them to nominate theories on the basis of their usefulness in understanding, explaining, and predicting organizational behavior. The nominations were also to take into account whether the theories had clear implications for practice and applications in management settings and whether the theories had generated significant research. (Notice the similarity between the criteria Miner used with his judges and the criteria we discussed earlier in this chapter.) In short, then, independent experts rated the *importance* of theories. The theories that were culled from those nominated in this fashion were then rated by Miner himself on the basis of two other criteria. One was his estimate of the *scientific validity* of each of the theories: that is, whether scientific tests had been carried out on them and had been supportive of some or all of the major tenets of each theory. Miner's third criterion (again, as rated by himself) was one that we discussed earlier in this chapter—the theories' estimated *usefulness,* "the extent to which the theory had contributed applications that could be put to use in practice to achieve stated goals" (J. B. Miner, 1984, p. 297).[8]

Then, using simple statistics of association, Miner examined the relationships among the three rating criteria over the 32 theories of organizational behavior. His findings were interesting:

---

[8]The notion of usefulness was mentioned earlier; we return to a discussion of it toward the end of the chapter.

1. No relationship was found between ratings of importance and scientific validity (despite the fact that his independent raters has been asked to consider validity in their determination of the theories' importance).

2. Similarly, there was no relationship between ratings of importance (by the outside panel) and Miner's own ratings of the theories' usefulness (again despite the fact that usefulness was one criterion the external judges were asked to use to rate importance).

3. There was only a slight relationship between the criteria of validity and usefulness (the two criteria by which Miner judged the theories himself).

4. Of most significance for our discussion here, there was a highly significant clustering of theories of work motivation (as opposed to other areas of management and organizational science) in the high validity/high usefulness cell. In other words, it was the various theories of work motivation that had been disproportionately rated as high in importance by the judges and at the same time rated as high in scientific validity by Miner himself.

Aside from the particulars of the major findings of Miner's study, it is important to remember that the results are in comparative terms only: his work (as well as other studies of the same sort) look only at the comparative value of work motivation theories; they say little or nothing about their *absolute* levels of validity or usefulness.

By now, the reader is probably wondering: Aside from all these considerations, then, which are the most valid theories of work motivation today? We answer this question gradually as we present, discuss, and evaluate the various perspectives throughout the book. But for the curious, we will side for the time being with those reviewers who cite goal-setting theory and social-cognitive theory as probably the most valid theories of work motivation available today. These two theories are presented in chapters 13 and 14, respectively.

The Relevance Criterion

J. B. Miner's (1984) work suggests another criterion for the evaluation of work motivation theory (or any organizational theory). Actually, as discussed by K. W. Thomas and Tymon (1982), the relevance criterion is related more directly to the evaluation of the research on which the theories are based, but nevertheless, their concepts of research relevance have a major bearing on the "value" of the theory that emerges from such research. K. W. Thomas and Tymon (1982) see relevance as consisting of five key components. For them, to be relevant a theory should be:

1. As concerned with generalizability as it is with tight, internal standards of scientific rigor.

2. Focused on problems that managers and administrators actually have to deal with, even if these are not obvious or hard to measure and conceptualize. Researchers have tended to work on problems (or dependent variables) that are tractable or interesting from a scholarly perspective, as opposed to problems that are "real" to the average person regardless of how slippery these problems may be.

3. Capable of being applied and implemented by manipulation of the independent variables contained in the theory.

4. Nonobvious: The theory should offer the practitioner insights that are not readily available by mature common sense or everyday experience.

5. Timely: The theory should be available to deal with problems when the problems are, in fact, problematic, not too late to be of value, after events have run their natural courses.

The Usefulness and Practicality Criteria

Earlier we mentioned that J. B. Miner (1984) assessed theories of organizational behavior on the basis of their usefulness. Since Miner's review, Brief and Dukerich (1991) have taken up the issue of usefulness and have argued that it is not a reasonable or appropriate basis on which to evaluate theories in the organizational sciences. Whereas Miner defined usefulness as "the extent to which the theory had contributed applications that could be put to use in practice to achieve stated goals" (p. 297), Brief and Dukerich (1991) conceive of usefulness as "a theory's prescriptive value in terms of the degree to which it contains actionable solutions to 'real world' problems" (p. 328). They then differentiate between usefulness and *practicality,* which they define as follows:

> A practical theory is an idea generator—it is capable of stimulating practitioners to view their worlds in ways they might not otherwise have. A practical theory can suggest courses of action but, unlike a prescriptive ("useful") theory, it is *not* an advocate of one particular course of action. (p. 341)

Brief and Dukerich put forth a conservative argument embraced by this author (Pinder, 1977). Their argument has many strands, the most important of which for our purposes is that all knowledge in the social and behavioral sciences has limited generalizability; it is bounded by the nature of the people on whom it is founded and by the contexts in which it is generated. They use a specific example from the literature on goal setting—one of the major theories discussed in this book—to illustrate their point. They believe that the best organizational scientists can and should offer is to develop and advance practical theory, not useful theory. They point out that we can never really take into account all the contextual variables that are at play when a research project is undertaken to yield or to test a theory, so to presume to make predictions and prescriptions on the basis of research done in the present or the past is risky. They argue that the best thinking on a matter of organizational behavior at a given point in time may become obsolete with the passage of time and with the further "discovery" of new variables and "boundary conditions" as further research is conducted. Brief and Dukerich believe that the best we can expect from organizational science is description and explanation, but not prediction, and certainly not prescription. They state that "usefulness as a criterion for evaluating organizational behavior theories would appear to be threatened by such failure to expect generalizability or, at least minimally, by the inability to specify a priori, in any certain way, the likelihood that a prescription will hold in a given context. . . . What *might* work is different from saying it either will work or should work in a probabilistic sense" (Brief and Dukerich, 1991, p. 337).

The distinction between *useful* and *practical* is adopted in this book, along with the conservative implications the distinction implies. Again, quoting Brief and Dukerich (1991), "Present theory may be the best we have *to raise people's consciousness,* not to specify particular actions in particular contexts. Since we cannot be sure what specific parts of any theory may be fallible or not, we assert that it is inappropriate to make authoritative statements based on the theory" (p. 346).

A Broader Perspective

Now that we have looked at the views of a number of thinkers on the criteria by which we should evaluate work motivation (and other behavioral and social) theories, we must step back and take a broader perspective by recognizing, as we mentioned earlier, that there are other bases for evaluation, bases that are either ascientific, such as interest value and even beauty, or that recognize that concepts such as relevance and usefulness are socially constructed notions, rooted in the sociology of the times and in the eyes of the beholder.

Social and Ideological Issues

It is important to keep in mind that science (especially social and behavioral science) is a social institution and set of social processes (see Merton, 1973; Mitroff, 1983). This implies that social science is fraught with all or most of the phenomena that characterize social institutions of other sorts, including processes of politics, status and power, tradition, and the like (L. Mayhew, 1971). An implication of this is that as we discussed in chapter 1, it is necessary to keep in mind the social and historical contexts within which any body of research or theory emerges and becomes popular (or unpopular). As social beings, motivation theorists and other social scientists have ideological belief systems, and these ideologies can (and do) influence the perception of what is "good" or "useful." Keeley (1983) observes that "scientific and ethical criteria can complement one another—not *substitute* for one another—in the evaluation of alternative views [regarding organizations and the management of people]. Social science can indicate only whether a model yields good (factual) solutions to specific problems. Ethics, on the other hand, can indicate whether a model yields good (worthwhile) problems to begin with. Although neither scientific nor ethical tests are apt to be conclusive, only if both show reasonably acceptable results should much trust be placed in the *general* validity of a social model" (p. 384).

A specific example of Keeley's (1983) point in the areas related to work motivation was furnished by Nehbrass (1979), who described how an ideological belief in the inherent virtue of human nature has fostered the promulgation of many management techniques, particularly those pertaining to worker participation—techniques that could not otherwise be supported or justified by cold, objective analysis: "The central belief of the ideology in question is a faith in the inherent goodness of humanity. People by nature are [seen as] good but they find themselves in an organizational (and societal) system that often distorts their nature and prevents the goodness from showing. In the face of this dehumanizing organization environment it is the role of the theorists to design new . . . management techniques that will capture the natural worth of workers. Although not always identified as such, the adherents of this belief system could be termed 'humanists' " (p. 427).

Nehbrass (1979) cited scientific reports from that time period which claimed that workers were alienated from their jobs, dissatisfied in massive numbers, and uncommitted to their work. He compared these popular reports with data from surveys at the time that failed to support such conclusions. At the time, quality of work life (QWL) was the management technique in vogue—every decade has one. Proponents of the movement at that time claimed that the North American worker was thoroughly alienated from work and that the "new worker" was rebelling at the lack of variety, autonomy, and challenge that characterized so many of the jobs in the economy at that time. For Nehbrass (1979), such sentiments were the informal, popular signs of the times—the stuff managerial literature was made of—but, he reported, these beliefs were not supported by the scientific evidence of the day that dealt with such matters.

Singling out the case of the argument at that time in favor of participative management, Nehbrass noted how the fervor of the managerial theorizing of the 1960s and 1970s was based largely on dated empirical studies of small groups of boys in contrived laboratory situations 30 years earlier. Nehbrass wrote:

> The impression the reader is intended to come away with is clear: Participation is a *proven* management tool; it is 'extremely motivational' [Carlisle, 1976, p. 478]; it "fosters commitment" [Scanlon, 1973] . . . and it is, indeed, "probably the most widely recognized motivational technique in practice today" [Trewatha and Newport, 1976].
>
> What is surprising about so many discussions of the positive nature of [participative decision making] is that there is no mention of the plethora of research [he cites five studies] that does not support the authors' ideological stance. Practicing managers can find numerous reason for not sharing decision-making authority with subordinates and when they encounter these utopian and one-sided views supported by research that is two and three decades old, it is little wonder that they view academics with scepticism and perhaps a bit of condescension. (1979, pp. 428–429)

Interestingly, the same sort of case has been made throughout the 1980s and 1990s in organizational science by a new generation of scholars who, although using new terminology and research methodology, embrace the same basic beliefs as those expressed by Nehbrass: Science is a social–political process and the knowledge of the day is a socially constructed artifact, subject to change as times change (see *Academy of Management Review,* July 1992; P. L. Berger and Luckman, 1966; Merton, 1973; Nord et al., 1988). But academics and theorists are not alone in the effects that social structures can have on them. Managers and administrators are heavily influenced by the ideologies and prevailing value structures of the times. Managerial programs and techniques cycle into and out of popularity in much the same way as fads and fashions in other arenas of life. Recent decades have seen the ascendancy and decline of such managerial techniques as employee participation, MBO, job enlargement, job enrichment, quality circles, management by walking around, employee empowerment, and organizational reengineering.

To summarize, the prevailing ideological values and belief structures of a given age determine the most appropriate problems to investigate and place boundaries around the nature of scientific enquiry that is imaginable or possible. The same values and beliefs will then heavily influence the nature of the criteria that are used to determine what is deemed to be "good," "useful," or "valid." In fact, they may even foster sentiments in favor of discarding such traditional standards and replacing them with entirely new sets of criteria for the evaluation of theory and social scientific activity (see Brief and Dukerich, 1991; R. Jacques, 1992).

SUMMARY AND A LOOK AHEAD

It has been argued in this chapter that our knowledge of work motivation consists largely of theory and that much or most of that theory is of limited or unknown validity. Moreover, it has been argued that there are risks to the premature application of work motivation theory—risks that can result in costs for the organizations that engage in such premature application, as well as for the future prospect for organizational scientists to contribute to the economic well-being of our economy. In short, work motivation is an important issue, about which our current knowledge is still limited. But that knowledge base is growing, and the purpose of this book is to examine and evaluate it.

In chapter 3 we explore a variety of basic assumptions that underpin current approaches to work motivation and behavior, setting up our subsequent presentations and discussions of the most important current theories available today.

CHAPTER

Human Nature: Needs and Values at Work

*It is a characteristic of man that the more he becomes involved in complexity,
the more he longs for simplicity; the simpler his life becomes, the more
he longs for complexity; the busier he becomes, the stronger is his desire
for leisure; the more leisure he has, the more boredom he feels, the more
his concerns, the more he feels the allure of unconcern, the more his unconcern,
the more he suffers from vacuousness; the more tumultuous
his life, the more he seeks quietude; the more placid his life, the lonelier
he becomes and the more he quests for liveliness.*

—SHIN'LCHI HISAMATSU,
"The Zen Understanding of Man," *The Eastern Buddhist (n.s.), 1*(1), 1965

To some extent, almost all of us harbor beliefs about the nature of human beings, about "what makes people tick." To some extent we all tend to be amateur philosophers and "naive psychologists" (Heider, 1958). In fact, the pursuit and discovery of the basic "essence of man" has occupied thinkers since the days of early philosophy (see Fromm and Xirau, 1968; J. J. Mitchell, 1972) and continues today. It should come as no surprise that philosophers and psychologists have failed to reach unanimity on the issue of human nature. On the other hand, an analysis of many of the attempts made to grapple with the problem reveals that there has been some convergence concerning a number of essential attributes of human beings (where essential attributes are seen as elements common to all people but that do not themselves comprise the essence of humanity per se). The most common of these attributes is rationality. Human beings are commonly thought of as more or less rational beings. Second, there is wide agreement that we are gregarious creatures. We tend, more or less, to exist in the presence of others. A third essential attribute of human beings is that we tend to be producers. Although many lower animals are also producers, only human beings produce according to plans developed in their own minds, and only humans are effective producers of tools, which in turn are used for further production. A final commonly agreed upon attribute is that human beings are symbol-making creatures. We generate, acknowledge, and make use of countless symbols, the most important of which are words (Fromm and Xirau, 1968).

People tend to assess other individuals and behave in their presence according to beliefs they have about their essential characteristics, whether or not the specific set of beliefs they hold matches the set identified above. Nowhere is this more the case than in work and organizational settings (Knowles and Saxberg, 1967; McGregor, 1960; Tead, 1929; Urwick, 1967). To quote McGregor (1960): "Behind every managerial decision or action are assumptions about human nature and human behavior" (p. 33).

This chapter has a number of purposes. The first is to examine a variety of widely held sets of assumptions about human beings that are particularly relevant when we consider work motivation and how it might be influenced. We then discuss two major sets of concepts that have served to help us understand the essential nature of human needs and personal values. As theories of motivation and techniques are presented in later chapters, the reader should bear in mind that each theory is predicated on certain sets of assumptions regarding human nature. Often, the nature of these assumptions is not explicitly recognized by those who advance theories of work motivation or who develop managerial techniques based on their theories (see Sullivan, 1986). Careful consumers of behavioral theories and techniques will allow themselves to be influenced by them only to the extent that the assumptions they make seem appropriate. We begin with a survey of beliefs about the underlying nature of human beings, particularly as they relate to the motivation to work.

THEORY X AND THEORY Y

One of the most insightful and enduring observations ever made by behavioral science concerning work is that of McGregor (1960). McGregor was acutely aware of the pervasiveness of a set of assumptions held by managers and administrators in particular concerning human beings at work. He referred to this set of assumptions as Theory X, the key elements of which are the following:

1. Average human adults are by nature indolent—they work as little as possible.
2. They lack ambition, dislike responsibility, and prefer to be led by other people.
3. They are inherently selfish and indifferent to organizational needs and goals.
4. They are resistant to change, by their very nature.
5. Finally, they are gullible, not very intelligent, and are easily duped by manipulators.

McGregor claimed that the importance of this implicit theory of human nature is that it lies behind much of what we observe in the practice of management. If managers believe that human nature is inherently as described by Theory X, they will formulate policies and utilize motivational and control strategies designed to tame people and coerce work effort from them. The direct result of policies, practices, and procedures of this sort is that they often cause the very behaviors that reinforce managers' beliefs that people are in fact like the Theory X model—a self-fulfilling prophecy of the sort diagrammed in Figure 3-1. Managers caught in this cycle believe that the problem lies in the basic nature of human beings. McGregor recognized that low interest, resentment, embezzling, sabotage, tardiness, and absenteeism are, in fact, commonly ob-

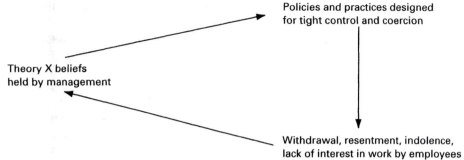

Policies and practices designed
for tight control and coercion

Theory X beliefs
held by management

Withdrawal, resentment, indolence,
lack of interest in work by employees

FIGURE 3-1 The Self-Fulfilling Prophecy of Theory X Assumptions

served in organizations. The wisdom in his analysis lies in his recognition that these be-haviors are frequently *caused* by managerial practices, which, in turn, are based on The-ory X beliefs about human nature: a case of chicken and egg, with powerful implica-tions for the design of motivation and reward systems. In practice, who can blame managers for holding views of the Theory X variety when they regularly observe be-havior that reinforces those beliefs?

McGregor proposed an alternative view of human nature in work organizations which he called, simply, *Theory Y.* The main tenets of Theory Y are:

1. People are not passive by nature. They have become so as a consequence of the way they are usually treated in organizations.

2. People possess, by nature, the potential to develop, assume responsibility, and behave in accordance with organizational goals. Management's responsibility is to recognize these potentials and to make it possible for employees to develop them themselves.

3. To do this, management should structure organizational policies so that human beings can achieve their own goals while pursuing the goals of the organization.

When McGregor put forth his observations four decades ago, he noted how diffi-cult it would be to see Theory X supplanted by Theory Y as the basic model of human nature underlying organizational policies and procedures. Belief systems are very hard to change, especially when the person holding a set of beliefs (such as those of Theory X) constantly observes behaviors that reinforce them. McGregor's pessimism seemed well founded at the time. If he were alive today, one wonders whether he would be any more optimistic. We still see an abundance of time clocks, highly differentiated and boring jobs, close supervisory practices, and "carrot-and-stick" reward systems (e.g., Kohn, 1993). For example, adult employees of a meatpacking plant in Alberta are per-mitted only two authorized breaks to use the washroom. Any more on a given day costs them money. If an employee at the plant wishes to use the toilet more than his or her designated two times, the employee must find the shift supervisor, who records the time the employee is away from the job. That time is deducted from the worker's pay at the person's regular wage rate. Some employees report that they either sneak away from their workstations or "hold" their urges, to avoid being docked pay. Women, par-ticularly, are affected by this policy; there are fewer washrooms for them, so they must take more time overall. As archaic as this policy sounds, it is legal under Alberta law (*Vancouver Sun,* 1994).

Clearly, as employees enter the lower ranks of organizational hierarchies and observe behaviors around them (including their own) that support Theory X views, they naturally tend to believe in Theory X and to accept the organizational structures and policies that are needed to control people—even as these employees are promoted up the ranks. People become socialized to, and take as natural, those practices with which they are familiar. Breaking free to different views of human nature and how organizations should be designed is difficult after so much socialization to Theory X beliefs and methods. The negative view of human nature continues to characterize a considerable amount of managerial behavior and organizational policy, notwithstanding the wide familiarity with McGregor's work among practitioners (J.B. Miner, 1984) and the constant exhortations in management best-sellers to adopt philosophies of a Theory Y nature (e.g., Covey, 1989; Kouzes and Posner, 1995; Pfeffer, 1994). Old habits die hard.

A TYPOLOGY OF HUMAN FUNCTIONING

Walter and Marks (1981) offer a theory of how human beings change and develop. As they note, if you wish to understand something, try changing it (or, to gain an understanding of human beings, try changing them). Drawing from the works of Levy (1970), Maddi (1976), and others, Walter and Marks have compiled a typology (or classification scheme) that summarizes the models of human nature that have been developed and studied by more than 60 behavioral and social scientists. Their typology is especially useful as a means of setting the stage for a presentation of the most popular theories of work motivation because the assumptions about human nature underlying most of these theories correspond with various categories in Walter and Marks' typology. Let's look briefly at the major categories they have identified, emphasizing those most often underlying current theories of work motivation.

First, there are the *fulfillment* models (Maddi, 1976, 1980). Representing these views are the theories of Maslow (1943, 1954) and Rogers (1959). These theories share the notion of human beings as unfolding, as developing their innate potentialities. They see people as experiencing pressure "that leads to the direction of their becoming whatever it is in their inherited nature to be" (Maddi, 1980, p. 90). Different people hold different types of potential on the basis of their unique sets of abilities, interests, and genetic characteristics. In the case of Maslow (1955, 1962), fulfillment motivation is less urgent in the short run as a motivating force behind behavior than are the forces directed at assuring the continued existence of the person—first survival, then fulfillment. We have more to say about Maslow's theory of motivation later in the chapter.

Consistency models of human nature (Maddi, 1980; Walter and Marks, 1981) emphasize "that there is a particular kind of information or emotional experience that is best for persons, and hence, that they will develop personalities which increase the likelihood of interaction with the world such as to get this kind of information or emotional experience" (Maddi, 1980, p. 156). The critical aspect of this set of models is that human nature is the result of people's interactions with their environments rather than the result of inherited attributes of the people themselves (a position similar to that of the philosopher John Locke). These theories are more concerned with consistency among the acts, beliefs, and predispositions that reflect human nature than with understanding the precise nature of the content of those acts, beliefs, and predispositions. They see people as driven to be consistent and to seek circumstances that are compatible with their previous experiences. Korman's (1970, 1976) theory of work motivation is predicated largely on this model of human nature.

The *cognitive–perceptual* models (Levy, 1970; Walter and Marks, 1981) see human beings as information-processing systems. In this view, human behavior results from the interpretation of events in the environment rather than from the strict, objective nature of the events themselves. This model does not deny the existence of an external reality, but views human action as caused by the way in which reality is perceived and understood. Work motivation theories predicated on this assumption of human nature are presented in chapters 8 through 12.

The *learning* models of human functioning are composed primarily of the various brands of behaviorism that were first put forth in the 1940s (see Hull, 1943) and that have since evolved in the work of B. F. Skinner (1953, 1969, 1971). This view avoids recourse to internal states and processes such as those used in cognitive–perceptual models (such as beliefs and expectations). Instead, they tend to see behavior as determined solely by its consequences. Underlying this perspective is Thorndike's (1911) *law of effect,* which states that people will be more likely to do those things which experience has shown to be rewarding. They will be less likely to do things they have found aversive. Behavior is a function of its consequences—period. Application of this model in the form of motivation-oriented programs in organizations is presented in chapters 13 and 14.

The *contextual* models of human nature (Levy, 1970; Walter and Marks, 1981) focus primarily on the social and gregarious aspects of human beings. There are no current theories of work motivation that derive exclusively from this perspective. However, many of the theories treated in this book include social needs and/or social comparison processes as part of more general need-oriented perspectives to work motivation. Finally, although it has not yet been articulated into a theory of work motivation per se, the social information processing approach to job attitudes developed by Salancik and Pfeffer (1978) is entirely consistent with the contextual models of human nature described by Levy (1970) and Walter and Marks (1981), although it also places heavy reliance on the cognitive and perceptual assumptions described above.

Walter and Marks' typology includes two other categories of theory: the conflict and life sciences models. The conflict views share an orientation toward intrapsychic and social conflict, in which life is seen as a process of compromise and balancing. The life science models are biological in nature, drawing most heavily on ethology, sociobiology, and neuroscience. Whereas these three disciplines are active in their own right, they have yet to enter any formal theories of work motivation. The author is also not aware of any theories of work motivation that have their philosophical roots in the conflict model.

Recapitulation

Five of the seven major categories in Walter and Marks' (1981) typology of models of human functioning unlie the many theories of work motivation that have appeared during the past half century. Three of these—the fulfillment model, the cognitive–perceptual model, and the learning model—have been most dominant to date. Although evidence is presented throughout the book concerning the validity of the various motivation theories discussed, it will not be possible to conclude which of the five sets of assumptions concerning human nature is "correct" or most valid. For as Walter and Marks (1981) conclude: "Each of the models of human functioning has [its own] implications . . . when used in combination their explanatory power is increased—the whole is greater than the sum of its parts" (p. 57). Hyland (1988) agrees: "Motivational research is now at a stage when different theories need to be brought together" (p. 650). Later in the book we take a look at Hyland's (1988) suggestion for integrating a number of popular theories.

In later sections of this chapter we examine two major work motivation theories that rest primarily on the fulfillment model of human functioning. Before we do, however, more detail is required about the basic view that human beings are acquisitive, self-fulfilling creatures. In particular, we need to gain an understanding of the exact nature of human needs and values. Let's take a closer look at the fundamental elements underlying this perspective.

NEEDS AND HUMAN BEHAVIOR: "HUMANS ARE WANTING ANIMALS . . ."

The model of human nature implied by this statement (Maslow, 1954, p. 24) has underpinned a great deal of the scientific work by psychologists into the nature of human motivation. It reflects a set of assumptions that whatever else we might be, people are always in need of something, and that much or all of our work behavior (and other forms of conscious behavior) is directed toward the fulfillment of our needs. This raises a question concerning the nature of the energetic force (see chapter 1) that actually constitutes motivation—what is it?

Over the years, psychologists have studied a number of concepts that have represented the essential energetic force that constitutes human motivation. Among the earliest of these concepts was instinct. It was thought that like most animals, people are born with certain inherent behavioral capacities. McDougall (1923) defined an instinct as "an innate disposition which determines the organism to perceive (or pay attention to) any object of a certain class, and to experience in its presence a certain emotional excitement and an impulse to action which find expression in a specific mode of behavior in relation to that object" (p. 110). Instincts were invoked to explain acts of all varieties. But by explaining everything, the concept really explained nothing. Before long there were lengthy lists of instincts attributed to human nature. They were cumbersome, ascientific, and somewhat ludicrous. For example, an early book by Tead (1918) discussed the role of 10 instincts (such as parental, sex, workmanship, and pugnacity) in employee behavior in industry. As we see later in this chapter, some modern critics (e.g., M. E. Ford, 1992) believe that the concept of human needs (and perhaps values as well) is as cumbersome, scientifically vague, and of as little practical use as instincts were deemed to be 50 years earlier.

After publication of the book *Dynamic Psychology* (Woodworth, 1918), the notion of instinct gave way to the concept of *drive* as the explanation for why people do things. According to drive theorists, people have primary and secondary drives. *Primary drives* arise either from deficiencies of substances necessary for survival or from excesses in substances that are harmful to survival. For example, Hull (1943) listed the following primary drives: hunger, thirst, air, temperature regulation, defecation, urination, rest, sleep, activity, sexual intercourse, nest building, care of the young, and avoidance of, or relief from, pain. *Secondary drives* are seen as being learned through association with primary drives. For instance, fear is associated with the pain of bodily injury and itself comes to be learned as a source of energy that can arouse behavior. A detailed treatment of the historical and scientific development of instinct and drive theories is beyond the scope of this book. The interested reader is referred to Atkinson (1964) and Cofer and Appley (1964). Our focus in this chapter is on two other concepts: the meaning and nature of human needs and values, which have been among the most commonly invoked concepts in theories of work behavior.

What Needs Are

Again, we have a problem of definition. The reader is referred to Atkinson (1964) or Cofer and Appley (1964) to gain an appreciation of the multitude of uses and interpretations the concept of need has assumed over the years. For the purposes of this book, Murray's (1938) definition will be adopted because it is most compatible with the need-oriented theories that have been developed to explain work motivation. For Murray, a need is

> a construct (a convenient fiction or hypothetical concept) which stands for a force . . . in the brain region, a force which organizes perception, apperception, intellection, conation and action in such a way as to transform in a certain direction an existing unsatisfying situation. A need is sometimes provoked directly by internal processes of a certain kind . . . but, more frequently (when in a state of readiness) by the occurrence of one of a few commonly effective presses (or features of the environment). . . . Thus, it manifests itself by leading the organism to search for or to avoid encountering, or when encountered, to attend to and respond to certain kinds of press. Each need is characteristically accompanied by a particular feeling or emotion and tends to use certain modes . . . to further its trend. It may be weak or intense, momentary or enduring. But usually it persists and gives rise to a certain course of overt behavior (or fantasy) which changes the initiating circumstance in such a way as to bring about an end situation which stills (appeases or satisfies) the organism. (pp. 123–124)

A number of elements of this definition deserve highlighting. First, notice that like the concepts of instinct, drive, personality, interest, or ambition, a need is a hypothetical entity (recall chapter 1). We cannot assess it directly or determine its color. It has no physical mass, density, or specific gravity. We must infer its existence by indirect means such as by observing the behavior of the person said to have a particular need. Second, notice the use of the "force" metaphor, making it consistent with the definition of work motivation given in chapter 2. The organizing function of needs is something with which most of us are familiar. It underlies the concepts of perceptual vigilance and perceptual defense in psychology (see Zalkind and Costello, 1962). For example, an employee's need state may make her more likely to notice a job opportunity at another organization, an opening that may have existed long before the employee reached the particular need state that she was in when she read the advertisement. The emergence of a need makes a person more likely to notice things that may satisfy the need.

Third, notice the possibility for needs to be induced by characteristics of the environment. In much the same way as seeing an attractive member of the opposite sex may arouse one's sexual needs, for example, being promoted into a job with supervisory responsibilities can arouse an erstwhile dormant need for power in an upwardly mobile employee. A fourth feature of Murray's definition of need is that it helps us understand approach behaviors as well as avoidance behaviors. An example from the work setting is the preferences that employees develop for particular types of jobs and the aversion they have to other jobs.

One very important feature of the definition is that needs are seen as either strong or weak and as either momentary or enduring. Thus, some employees are constantly gregarious and seeking social interaction on the job, whereas for others, working in groups may be less important. People not only differ among themselves but the same person can experience increases and decreases in the strength of various needs. For example, consider the avoidance of further fatigue that motivates certain employee behaviors toward the end of a tedious day in an office setting.

Finally, the definition states that needs give rise to behavior (or fantasy) aimed at reducing the force behind the needs. A number of points need elaboration here. First, not all need-driven, goal-oriented behavior is successful in reaching the goals sought. The result is defined as frustration, a topic discussed in chapter 8. Notice the possible role that fantasy can play, especially when behavior itself is not feasible. At one time or another, most people fantasize about what they would do if they won a lottery. Similarly, many frustrated workers fantasize about the regimes they would administer if, magically, they were promoted to powerful managerial positions.

Throughout the remainder of this book, the term *need* will imply all that is involved in Murray's definition. A solid grasp of that definition and the implications that arise from it will be essential to understanding the rest of the material to be presented, particularly in the remainder of this chapter and in chapters 3 through 8.

The Relationship between Needs and Behavior

Consider the difficulty involved in making inferences about the need(s) that determine a person's behavior. First, most motivated[1] behavior is said to be *overdetermined*, meaning that deliberately or inadvertently, behavior is driven by the force to satisfy more than one need (Maslow, 1954).

For example, an employee may seek a promotion for the sake of meeting several needs (although the person may be more conscious of the importance of some of them when seeking promotion). Second, the same need may be satisfied by any of a variety of acts. So our upwardly aspiring employee may in part be seeking greater satisfaction of esteem needs. Notice that gaining a promotion is one way—but only one way—to meet esteem needs. Volunteer service after hours or becoming president of the employees' union are alternative behaviors that might be employed. In short, there is no one-to-one relationship between the force of a particular need and the type of behavior that one will observe. To complicate matters, there is a common tendency for people to *project* their own need–behavior styles into their interpretations of the behavior

---

[1]We recognize that not all behavior, indeed not all behavior in the workplace, is motivated behavior. Many of the acts that people perform are habitual, impulsive, or compulsive, based on little or no thought or sense of drive (Landy and Becker, 1987).

of others (Zalkind and Costello, 1962). For example, in attempting to infer why their subordinates frequently exaggerate the stress levels of their jobs, supervisors are apt to come to reasonably sound understandings of why they themselves might make such exaggerations.

The importance of all this lies in the difficulties and risks it implies for the application of need theories to an understanding of employee behavior. Remember, we cannot observe needs directly, so we must make inferences about the role of needs in behavior by observing that behavior. This lack of one-to-one correspondence between needs and behavior and the natural tendency to impute our own behavior-motivation styles onto others make explanation very difficult after the fact. It makes precise predictions of employee acts almost impossible, except in cases involving the most simple behaviors (see Bandura, 1977; M. E. Ford, 1992). Yet managers do it all the time, especially those who consciously attempt to "motivate" their employees. Indeed, notwithstanding these problems of explanation and prediction, of scientific imprecision and applied usefulness, the concept of needs seems to have a certain appeal to both scientists and practitioners. Research into needs and reliance on the concept in theories of work motivation have both enjoyed long and popular traditions.

Need Satisfaction

Most people tend to view need satisfaction as the state that a person feels after the tension associated with a need has been removed (such as the pleasurable feeling of a full stomach, for example). In the case of certain needs, however, satisfaction may consist more of the experience one has while in the process of *reducing* the tension (Murray and Kluckhohn, 1953). Again using the example of eating, this principle would suggest that satisfaction consists more of the joy of eating than of the joy of having eaten. Moreover, greater satisfaction seems to occur when more tension is reduced, implying that people may be motivated to deprive themselves of gratification (within safe limits) so as to be able to experience greater subsequent satisfaction from the process of need fulfillment. Sexual foreplay illustrates this principle, as does the notion of skipping lunch to assure that one has a sharp appetite for a special dinner.

In work settings this principle would imply that employee satisfaction results from the process of interacting with one's peers, for example, rather than from having done so. As we will see in chapter 10, job satisfaction has typically been equated with the satisfaction of one's needs on the job, particularly with the experience of having met one's needs. It may be that researchers have overlooked the importance of the fulfillment process itself in their understanding of job satisfaction.

A New Perspective on Satisfaction

Recent experimental work on human emotions has yielded an *emodynamic* view of human satisfaction. We touch on this view again later in the book, notably in chapter 10, where we examine job satisfaction, and again in chapter 14, where we discuss the self-control of human emotions. For our purposes here we simply summarize this new approach (see Salovey, Hsee, and Mayer, 1993, for an extended summary of this perspective). According to the emodynamic view, people experience satisfaction (which is viewed as a set of positive emotions) when they attain higher levels of outcomes (e.g., goods or rewards) than they possessed previously. The rate or *velocity* at which they acquire these additional levels is the key. A person whose pay increases by 30 percent over a period of seven months will experience greater satisfaction than will a person who receives the same increase over a longer period. Eventually though, people become used to their new levels of satisfaction. A person who wins a lottery is much happier immediately after receiving the good news than she is months later. This approach suggests that *changes in the rate of improvement* are also important. If things become better more and more quickly, a person experiences even greater joy.

Now that we have examined the general concepts of need and need satisfaction and have a brief understanding of the emergence of that concept in the recent history of psychology, we discuss some of the most important theories of work motivation—theories that have invoked needs as the concept representing the force behind employee behavior. In the terms of J. P. Campbell, Dunnette, Lawler, and Weick (1970), we will be dealing with the question of what determines work motivation—a question of content (hence these theories are labeled *content* theories). We deal with how and why motivation occurs later (chapters 10 through 14 in particular) when we look at a number of *process* theories.

Maslow's Hierarchical Theory of Needs

The hierarchical theory of human motivation developed by Maslow (1943, 1954, 1968) is the most paradoxical of all the current approaches to work motivation. On the one hand, it is one of the most familiar theories among academics and practitioners (see J. B. Miner, 1984). On the other hand, it is probably the most misunderstood and the most frequently oversimplified and misrepresented. Further, despite its widespread popularity, it is a theory which enjoys very little scientific support and suffers from the same shortcomings of weak explanatory accuracy and negligible predictive power as lamented by M. E. Ford (1992)—but it is popular nevertheless.

Rudiments of the Theory

Maslow's theory holds that there are basically five categories of human needs, and that these needs account for much or most of human behavior but not all of it. The needs vary in their relative prepotency or urgency for survival, arranging themselves in a sort of hierarchy. As the most prepotent needs become reasonably satisfied, the less prepotent ones (referred to as the higher-order needs) become increasingly important in causing behavior.

The most prepotent category of needs in the theory are *physiological* in nature. They function in a homeostatic fashion, such that imbalances or deficiencies in certain physiological substances instigate behavior aimed at restoring the balance by filling the deficiencies. Hunger, sex, and thirst are three examples. The physiological needs correspond closely to the primary drives in the drive theories discussed earlier. According to Maslow, when someone lacks satisfaction of physiological needs, the person becomes obsessed with acquiring whatever is needed to satisfy these needs and thus restore equilibrium. In short, deficiency dominates behavior, and no other need set is more dominating than the physiological needs when unfulfilled. According to Maslow (1954), "if the physiological needs are relatively-well gratified, there then emerges a new set of needs, which we may categorize roughly as the safety needs (security; stability; dependency; protection; freedom from fear, from anxiety and chaos; need for structure, order, law, limits; strength in the protector, and so on)" (p. 39). Next to the physiological needs, the safety needs are the most prepotent determinants of behavior. When unfulfilled, they possess the same sort of potential for dominating behavior as do the physiological needs.

Problems of (Mis)Interpretation

It is worth stopping at this point to consider one of the ways that Maslow's hierarchical theory has been oversimplified and misrepresented. The theory is often interpreted as if all of the force motivating a person's behavior at a given time originates in one and only one need state and that this total domination continues until satisfaction is experienced, at which time that need state somehow shuts off, or goes away, while the next set of needs clicks on to take its place. (This discrete shutting off/clicking on image is fostered by the staircaselike pictures often used in management textbooks to represent the hierarchy.)

Instead, Maslow (1954) saw most behavior as multimotivated or overdetermined (p. 55). Any particular behavior will tend to be the consequence of simultaneous functioning of more than one need, perhaps several. It is a matter of relative deprivation or satisfaction (as stated in the passage quoted above) and relative influence of the various needs in determining behavior. Clearly, when a person faces an emergency such as extreme hunger, desperate thirst, or an onrushing assailant, one need set does dominate until gratification occurs. But once gratification is achieved, that need does not disappear as a factor in behavior. It does, however, account for less of the total force working on the person, because other needs then take on relatively more importance than before. Maslow (1954) wrote: "In actual fact, most members of our society . . . are partially satisfied in all their basic needs and partially unsatisfied . . . at the same time. A . . . realistic description of the hierarchy would be in terms of decreasing percentages of satisfaction as we go up the hierarchy of prepotency. . . . As for the concept of emergence of a new need after satisfaction of the prepotent need, this emergence is not a sudden, salutary phenomenon, but rather a gradual emergence by slow degrees from nothingness" (pp. 53–54).

The author has chosen to quote directly to emphasize that Maslow never intended to portray the emergence of new need states in the crisp, all-or-nothing, lock-step fashion adopted by so many of his interpreters. Human behavior is clearly not that simple, and Maslow never portrayed it as such. Nevertheless, many managers, teachers, parents, counselors, and administrators over the years have demanded simplistic models and streamlined interpretations of Maslow's work. Sadly, many textbook authors and other academics have been more than willing to provide such oversimplifications.

Let's return to the hierarchy.

Love, Esteem, and Self-Actualization

The next most prepotent set of human needs, according to Maslow, are the *love* needs. They take on comparatively more influence in behavior as the physiological and safety needs are reasonably well gratified. The person desires relations with other people and will feel more compelled than before to achieve such relations. Feelings of loneliness, ostracism, rejection, and friendlessness will be experienced much more than before. Maslow (1954) claims that the thwarting of the love needs "is the most commonly found core in cases of maladjustment" (p. 44). A person who suffers frustration of these needs becomes ill, although the illness is mental rather than physical (see Wilmer, 1992). It is important to note that the theory claims that people need both to give and receive love, and that social interactions need not be cordial to satisfy these needs.

The *esteem* needs, the next most prepotent category in Maslow's hierarchy, are grouped into two sets. One set includes desires for strength, achievement, adequacy, mastery and competence, independence, freedom, and a fundamental confidence in facing the world. Gratification of these needs for self-esteem leads to feelings of self-confidence, capability, and worth, whereas frustration of them results in neurotic feelings of weakness, inferiority, and even helplessness. The second subset of esteem needs are for prestige and reputation—the esteem of others. This motivates people to seek recognition, praise, dominance, glory, and the attention of other people. When people fail to achieve these outcomes in sufficient quantity, they suffer the same sort of feelings as result when the need for self-esteem is thwarted.

The esteem needs are seen as less prepotent than the highest set of needs on the hierarchy—the need for *self-actualization*. Maslow himself seems to have given differing interpretations of the meaning of this need (see Maslow, 1943, 1954, with Maslow, 1968), but the clearest and most widely accepted view is that it consists of a requirement to fulfill one's potential, to become that which one is capable of becoming. Amateur athletes who are already well established economically and who have many friends and all the prestige that being world champions has earned for them will still be motivated to continue to improve their performance. Why? Because they feel that they are capable of running faster or jumping higher than they have in the past. The force behind this urge to become even more of what they are capable of becoming is referred to as the need to self-actualize. (Note that some of the lower needs could help explain the athletes' continued striving for further excellence, such as a fear of losing their championship status, the esteem of their admirers, or their contracts for the commercial endorsement of athletic equipment. Remember that most behavior is multiply determined.) The U.S. Army has used a recruitment campaign that includes a catchy jingle: "Be all that you can be—in the Army," an appeal to the self-development and actualizing needs of prospective soldiers.

An important feature of self-actualization needs is that they express themselves in different ways in different people. For example, one person may seek fulfillment through the refinement of musical skills, while another may seek to develop talents as a father. Moreover, the satisfaction of self-actualization needs tends to increase their importance rather than reduce it (Maslow, 1962)—they become somewhat addictive. This is an important difference between self-actualization and the other needs in the hierarchy, all of which are seen as losing their capacity to motivate behavior once they are relatively well fulfilled.

Fine Points of the Theory

With a background now in the primary elements of Maslow's theory, let's look at some of the less frequently recognized features of the theory, features that when dropped lead to many of the misinterpretations and misrepresentations mentioned earlier. First, Maslow recognized that there are many differences among people in the relative prepotency of their needs (although the order described above is held to be the most common). He referred to variations from the basic ordering as *reversals*, and he acknowledged several common varieties. For instance, many people seem to place self-esteem ahead of love, seeking respect rather than affection from others. As another example, some people are innately creative and seem to pursue self-actualization despite the fact that their lower-level needs have not been met (as in the starving artist syndrome). Still others, who have been deprived of social interaction for extended periods, seem to lose the capacity to respond to the affection of others. Maslow (1954, pp. 51–52) notes other reversals, but the point is that the basic hierarchy was never intended to be totally universal and invariant, either across individuals or within the behavioral styles of any one person over time.

Another important point in the theory is that not all behavior is seen as resulting from the force provided by basic needs. Much of human behavior can be determined by forces outside a person (recall Murray's notion of environmental press, discussed earlier). In addition, some behavior is obsessive-compulsive, and some behavior is simply expressive of personality (e.g., the random movements of a child or smiles made by a happy person when alone). In fact, Landy and Becker (1987) suggest that we should consider a sort of continuum, ranging from simple reflexive behavior, to consciously initiated acts, to overlearned or automatic patterns and habits.

A third fine point of the theory is that the needs are seen as neither necessarily conscious or unconscious, but that on the whole, most people are not consciously aware of their needs at the time they behave. This point will be important in subsequent chapters when we discuss the issues of designing jobs and reward systems to match employee needs.

The key factor here is that Maslow's theory, as seemingly well known as it is, is much more complex and much less mechanistic than is implied in many management and human relations textbooks. The importance of acknowledging the details lies in the implications they have for both understanding human behavior and for attempts to influence it. For example, supervisors who assume that their subordinates are constantly conscious of their own needs and are therefore under total control of their acts will probably give them far too much credit or blame for these acts (T.R. Mitchell, Green, and Wood, 1981). Similarly, reward and punishment systems which assume implicitly that employees are motivated by single needs, one at a time ("George is into security needs"), will be misguided and quite ineffective. Finally, assuming that everyone seeks to satisfy their needs according to the same strict order will foster the development of managerial policies that will frustrate as many employees as they will satisfy.

How Valid Is the Theory?

It was stated earlier that Maslow's theory is paradoxical—most people in organizations think they know about it, while many tend to oversimplify it. An additional aspect of the paradox centers on the fact that there has been very little evidence to attest to its scientific validity, and these results have been mixed, at best. In other words, the theory has been popular despite the limited evidence that it is valid. To make things worse, most of the research conducted to test the theory has not been conducted appropriately (V.F. Mitchell and Moudgill, 1976), although most studies that have been done have resulted in negative conclusions (see Huizinga, 1970, for an early, relatively supportive summary with Wahba and Bridwell, 1976).

Some critics have argued that Maslow's theory and, indeed, all theories based on concepts such as needs and instincts are destined to be of only limited value in understanding human behavior. They claim that these theories are capable only of making uncertain, after-the-fact explanations of human action. They are far less capable of making precise predictions of behavior before the fact (see M. E. Ford, 1992). Moreover, these critics argue that a sort of "conceptual confounding" occurs in which, as Ford (1992) put it, "the evidence for a need or instinct [is] identical with the behavior it was designed to explain" (p. 9). This is related to the problem of overdetermination we discussed earlier and to the human tendency to project one's need state onto others when we attempt to explain the needs–behaviors connections of other persons.

These criticisms and shortcomings are hard to refute. Nevertheless, Maslow's theory remains very popular among managers and students of organizational behavior, although there are still very few studies that can legitimately confirm (or refute) it. One attempt used techniques that were more appropriate than most that have been employed (Rauschenberger, Schmitt, and Hunter, 1980) but failed to support the theory. It may be that the dynamics implied by Maslow's theory of needs are too complex to be operationalized and confirmed by scientific research. If this is the case, we may never be able to determine how valid the theory is or—more precisely—which aspects of the theory are valid and which are not.

Modifications of the Hierarchy

Since Maslow's last writings on the subject of his hierarchical theory of needs, there have been at least two modifications of the theory as it relates to work motivation. Both modifications propose a reduction in the number of levels in the hierarchy and converge, accordingly, with the suggestion by Maslow in some of his later work that we might fruitfully consider two basic levels of human needs (Maslow, 1968). One of these modifications (Lawler and Suttle, 1973) resulted from an unsuccessful attempt to support the original five-level theory empirically. Another modification (Alderfer, 1972) resulted from a deliberate attempt to develop and test a model with fewer need levels. Let's examine this second theory, because it is the most comprehensive alternative generated to date.

Existence, Relatedness, and Growth

For the most part, Maslow's theory of human needs was based on induction from his own clinical observations rather than from empirical research conducted in organizational settings as such. Nevertheless, as suggested above, it provided an attractive and intuitively acceptable perspective to writers in the human relations movement of the time (e.g., Argyris, 1957; McGregor, 1960). One of the earliest empirical attempts to generate and test an alternative to Maslow's theory was that of Alderfer (1969, 1972), who proposed an existence, relatedness, and growth (ERG) model of his own. Alderfer's theory has its roots in Maslow's work as well as in the theory and research of a number of earlier psychologists concerned with human motivation.

The theory posits three general categories of human needs. These categories are similar to and partly derived from those in Maslow's model but are not identical. Each of the needs is seen as primary, innate to human nature rather than learned, although learning can increase their strength. The theory concerns itself with the subjective states of need satisfaction and desire and how satisfaction of certain needs influences the strength of the desires of other needs. *Satisfaction* refers to the internal state of a person who has obtained what he is seeking to quell his desires. It is synonymous with getting or fulfilling (Alderfer, 1972, p. 7). *Desire* refers to an internal state that is synonymous with concepts such as want, need strength or intensity, or motive. Let's take a look at the three categories of needs.

Existence Needs

The first set in the model is referred to as the existence needs. They correspond closely to Maslow's physiological needs as well as to those aspects of Maslow's category of security needs that have to do with physical (as opposed to interpersonal) security. Typically, the substances required to satisfy existence needs are concrete in nature. Moreover, these substances are often scarce, such that more satisfaction for one person will tend to result in lower potential satisfaction for others. In work settings, pay and fringe benefits are examples—the more money that is paid to the office staff, the less is available to pay the shop workers. The types of outcomes (such as money) instrumental for gratifying Maslow's physiological needs are basically the same as those required to provide for physical safety; and according to Alderfer, Maslow's physiological and physical safety needs are approximately equal in importance in a person's existence. For example, people who are threatened with physical violence quickly abandon all behaviors that are not intended to provide for their safety. There are logical grounds, at least, for gathering them in a single class.

Relatedness Needs

Similarly, the goals typically sought by people to satisfy what Maslow calls love needs are basically those that are necessary to provide for the need for prestige or for the esteem of others as well as for the interpersonal security needs included in the second level of Maslow's hierarchy. Successful satisfaction of each of these Maslow needs requires interaction with other human beings and the development of meaningful relationships with others. Moreover, each of these three varieties of social needs, on a logical level at least, seems equally important.

The interaction among people needed to satisfy this category of needs, referred to as relatedness needs by Alderfer, does not necessarily have to be positive or cordial. In fact, the expression of hostile feelings toward others is seen as an important aspect of developing meaningful interpersonal relationships. Unlike the zero-sum aspects of the satisfaction of existence needs, relatedness need satisfaction by one person tends to be positively associated with the same sort of satisfaction for others, by virtue of the very nature of social interaction. Therefore, Alderfer's theory combines all of Maslow's need categories pertaining to social interaction into a single class called relatedness needs.

Growth Needs

The third category of needs in Alderfer's model is referred to as the growth needs. They are similar to the needs for self-esteem and self-actualization in Maslow's theory, but not identical. Whereas Maslow saw self-actualization as consisting of the fulfillment of innate potential (a potential that may have a unique form for a given person), Alderfer's growth needs consist of desires to interact successfully with one's environment—to investigate, explore, and master it. As the person's environment changes, so will the expression of growth needs, according to Alderfer. Nevertheless, the highest-level needs on Maslow's hierarchy are similar enough to the needs classed as growth needs by Alderfer (if for no reason other than the fact that self-actualization activities tend to enhance one's self concept) to justify combining them into a single class.[2]

Differences between Maslow and Alderfer

Whereas Maslow posited five major groups of human needs, Alderfer's model is more parsimonious, suggesting only three discrete categories, although the two models often dovetail. Aside from these similarities, however, there are a few key differences between the two theories. For instance, ERG theory holds that all three sets of need are active in all human beings, although the notion of hierarchy and general prepotency found in Maslow (his reversals notwithstanding) is absent in ERG theory. Alderfer's model does not require that a person be satisfied at the level of existence to witness a shift upward in importance from relatedness to growth needs. It would be possible for employees who work under short-term contracts with their employers to derive sufficient satisfaction of their relatedness needs that they could experience an increase in the importance of gaining growth experiences through their work.

Another important feature in ERG theory that does not appear in Maslow's work is what Alderfer refers to as the *frustration regression hypothesis*. As we will see in chapter 8, frustration is defined as a situation in which individuals' behavioral attempts to satisfy their needs are blocked or thwarted (by forces that lie either inside the people themselves or beyond their control). ERG theory posits that failure of a person to satisfy growth needs can result in an increase in the importance of the person's relatedness needs. Similarly, a failure to satisfy one's relatedness needs can result in an increase in the importance of existence needs. In hierarchical terms, these two propositions imply a movement downward in the face of frustration. We have more to say about the causes and consequences of frustration in subsequent chapters.

Initially, Alderfer proposed seven basic propositions that summarized how the satisfaction or frustration of needs at a particular level influence the satisfaction and the strength of desires at that level as well as at other levels. He subjected his theory to a four-year study involving hundreds of research subjects and several different types of organizations. By most standards the research was reasonably well conducted. Some of his original propositions received empirical support, but others did not. Some were revised based on the evidence gathered. The reader is referred to Alderfer (1969, 1972) for more complete detail concerning the total set of propositions both before and after the research was conducted.

Need Hierarchies: Some Conclusions

Is there such a thing as a hierarchy of needs? There is evidence that different needs exist and that they can be measured (Alderfer, 1972; V. F. Mitchell and Moudgill, 1976; D. E. Williams and Page, 1989). There is much less empirical support that these needs vary in their relative importance so consistently across individuals that we can safely

---

[2]The theory of intrinsic motivation advanced by Deci and his colleagues (presented in chapter 7) extends considerably the notion of mastery of one's environment.

speak of a generalizable hierarchy. To do so seems to ignore substantial differences among people at various stages in their lives and careers (see R. Katz, 1980).

Before we abandon the concept of hierarchy altogether, a word of caution is in order. Although it is unwise to advocate a theory unabashedly in the absence of any proof that the theory has empirical validity (recall chapter 2), it is equally irresponsible to abandon a theory that has yielded primarily negative results when those results come from empirical tests that are largely inappropriate or unfair. As stated earlier, it may be that many of the theories presented in this book are, in fact, better representations of the nature of work motivation than organizational researchers are capable of demonstrating. For example, there are countless complex problems associated with developing instruments that are truly appropriate for operationalizing and measuring the various dimensions associated with motivation theories, as well as many more problems involved in appropriate gathering and analyzing of data yielded by these instruments once they are developed (see J. P. Campbell and Pritchard, 1976). In the case of the concept of a hierarchy of human needs, there is some agreement that biologically based needs (such as Alderfer's existence needs) are probably more prepotent than other needs (Lawler and Suttle, 1973), but the nature of any clear cut hierarchical ordering beyond that has not yet been demonstrated. On the other hand, work by R. Katz (1978, 1980) and E. H. Schein (1978), among others, reminds us that there are some predictable patterns among people at various life and career stages in the desires they express on their jobs. It may be that we will eventually be forced to abandon the search for a universal hierarchy of needs and settle for a number of middle-range theories (Landy and Becker, 1987; Pinder and Moore, 1980) that take individual and organizational circumstances more fully into account. We have more to say on this point toward the end of the book.

The Nature of Needs and Their Role in Work Motivation

Locke (1991b, p. 290) has provided a succinct summary of the nature of human needs, a summary that concludes that needs are the basic set of factors underlying human behavior, including human work behavior. In particular, he notes nine features of needs that social science and everyday observation and experience support:

1. Needs operate cyclically; they are never satisfied permanently.
2. Needs can be only partially satisfied habitually, either by choice (e.g., by sleeping) or involuntarily (e.g., by imprisonment).
3. Need frustration is experienced as pain, discomfort, or illness.
4. Different needs signal different degrees of urgency.
5. Needs exist whether or not we are aware of them.
6. People can plan in advance to provide for their needs.
7. A given need can instigate many different behaviors.
8. Any particular act may satisfy more than a single need.
9. Problems such as errors, irrationality, and practical circumstances frequently prevent human acts from resulting in the need satisfaction intended.

Finally, for our purposes here, Locke (1991b) also sees needs as lying at the very base of human and organizational behavior. Needs give rise to and help shape other concepts we discuss in this book, such as values, intentions, and ultimately, action.

LOOKING AHEAD

Before closing our general discussion of human needs and their role in theories of work motivation, it must be repeated that not all approaches to understanding work behavior recognize the importance of these concepts. Specifically, the behavior modification or operant conditioning approach (Komaki, 1986; Luthans and Kreitner, 1975; Mawhinney, 1990; B. F. Skinner, 1953) avoids the use of such "black box" explanations of behavior, relying instead on the circumstances that surround behavior and serve either to encourage or discourage it. The debate between need-oriented theorists and those who focus on other internal concepts (such as values, beliefs, attitudes, and perceptions), on the one hand, and the behaviorists, on the other, constitutes one of the most fundamental controversies in psychology in general and in organizational science in particular. We provide the reader with a representation of both schools of thought in subsequent chapters. We present more focused analyses of a number of needs that are of special interest to an understanding of work motivation in chapters 5 through 7.

VALUES AND WORK MOTIVATION[3]

Related to the tradition that has sought to use human needs as the basis for understanding work behavior is a similar tradition that has focused on human *values*. To consider values in the workplace is to probe the very reasons that people work and why they behave the way they do in their jobs (Posner and Munson, 1979; Sikula, 1971). A person's values lie at the core of his or her conscious career decisions (Judge and Bretz, 1992) and the affective reactions people have to their jobs, defining for us the concepts of job satisfaction and job dissatisfaction (Locke, 1969).

In fact, some studies suggest that merely subscribing to certain values in the course of a career contributes to satisfaction with one's work (Blood, 1969; Merrens and Garrett, 1975).[4] Values and value similarity between managers and their subordinates can also interfere with the legitimacy of day-to-day human resource management, as in the case of the validity of performance ratings made by superiors of their employees (Senger, 1971). In fact, the degree of perceived similarity between one's own values and those of one's leader has been shown to predict a person's satisfaction with the leader (Meglino, Ravlin, and Adkins, 1991). In short, values play a key role in human behavior in general and in the world of work in particular. We turn now to defining values and distinguishing them from needs.

Some Definitions of Values

Although needs and values are related concepts, they are distinct from one another both conceptually and empirically. It is also critical to distinguish between values and *attitudes,* a concept that we examine later in the book. What are values, and how are they related to the human desire to work or not to work? According to Kilmann (1981), values are ob-

---

[3]Much of the material in this section draws on a paper written by Pinder, Stackman, and Connor (1997).

[4]Merrens and Garrett (1975) specifically studied the "Protestant ethic," where "hard and steady work is valued" (p. 125).

jects, qualities, standards, or conditions that satisfy or are perceived to satisfy needs and/or that act as guides to human action. Similarly, Tisdale (1961) defines values as "inferred motivational constructs associated with perceived differences in goal-directed behaviour and indicated by the selection of action-alternatives within social situations" (cited by Kilmann, 1981, p. 940). More recently, Connor and Becker (1994) have defined values as "global beliefs [about desirable end states or modes of behavior] that underlie attitudinal processes. In particular, they serve as the basis for making choices" (p. 68). Hence, conceived of as global beliefs, values are neither attitudes nor behaviors. Instead, values are the very building blocks of the behavior of and choices made by individuals.

In much of the organizational literature dealing with values, the framework and definition advanced by Rokeach (1969) has been particularly popular: "an enduring belief that a specific mode of conduct or end-state of existence is personally and socially preferable to alternative modes of conduct or end-states" (p. 160). For Rokeach and those who have adopted his conception, values entail attention to both means (such as acts) and ends (such as outcomes of various sorts). Examples of *instrumental* values for Rokeach are: ambitious, capable, broadminded, clean, logical, and loving. Examples of his *terminal* values are: a comfortable life, a world of beauty, pleasure, and wisdom (Rokeach, 1973).

Needs versus Values

As we defined them earlier in this chapter, needs represent forces in the brain region and central nervous system (Murray, 1938). These forces, aroused internally or by outside factors, compel a person to search for or avoid certain things thought to be useful to reduce the force(s). (*Press* is a feature of the outside environment that can arouse or strengthen the force of a need, such as a plate of aromatic food presented at a time when a person may or may not otherwise have felt hungry.)

Values enter the picture through their effects on the choices a person makes in selecting among commodities, events, or outcomes to satisfy needs. In fact, Rokeach (1979) claims that values "can be regarded as the cognitive representations of internal 'needs' mediated by external 'presses' (Murray, 1938). Put another way, values may be conceived of as cognitive representations of underlying needs—whether social or antisocial, selfish or altruistic—after they have been transformed to also take into account institutional goals and demands. In this way, all of a person's values, unlike all of a person's needs, are capable of being openly admitted, advocated, exhorted, and defended, to oneself and to others, in a socially sanctioned language" (p. 48). For example, a person may have a strong need for other people's esteem, which he seeks to satisfy by purchasing expensive clothes, cars, and other toys. Such a person would be said to *value* expensive clothes, cars, and other toys, but it could not be said that he needs them per se. A second person, by contrast, might seek to satisfy an equally strong need for esteem through community service and a humble life of spirituality and clean living. The second person may be well able to articulate a desire to provide such service or to live in such a manner but may not be able to identify the needs that underlie these stated values and behaviors. Same need but different instrumental and terminal values.

If we set aside the distinction between needs and values, it is clear that both are critical in understanding work motivation. Most theories in this area assume that people have basic, underlying needs but that it is their values that most directly influence the preferences people express for how they desire to be rewarded (and punished) in the workplace. Similarly, managers who wish to influence, reward, and/or punish employee behavior at work need to be most keenly aware of employee values, because at one level or another, we all share the same ultimate set of needs, to varying degrees.

Attitudes are cognitive and affective *orientations toward specific objects and situations,* as we will see in detail in chapter 9. For values theorists, behavior is the manifestation of a person's fundamental values and corresponding attitudes. The relationships among these concepts are depicted in Figure 3-2.

Terminal and Instrumental Values

Rokeach (1969, 1973) made an important distinction between terminal and instrumental values, as suggested above. Terminal values represent ultimate end goals of existence, such as wisdom, equality, and family security. Instrumental values represent the behavioral means of achieving various end goals, such as being honest, ambitious, or logical (Rokeach and Ball-Rokeach, 1989).

Values versus Work Values

One issue of major contention in the values literature has to do with a distinction between values (in the general sense) and *work values,* a concept that implies the particular set(s) of values that govern employee work behavior in all its forms. Most conceptions and definitions of *work values* per se are consistent with most general definitions of values in the broader sense, but their focus is on work, work behavior, and work-related outcomes (e.g., Wollack, Goodale, Wijting, and Smith, 1971). One typical definition is provided by Pine and Innis (1987), who conceive of work values as "an individual's needs and priorities and consequent personal dispositions and orientations to work roles that have the perceived capacity to satisfy those needs and priorities" (p. 280). A more recent definition of work values is provided by Nord et al. (1988): "We define work values as the end states people desire and feel they ought to be able to realize through working" (p. 2).

The controversy has to do with whether there is any benefit added—such as conceptual clarity, applied insights, or academic usefulness of any sort—in distinguishing between values in general (as Rokeach and his followers do, for instance) and values

FIGURE 3-2   Relationships among Needs, Values, Attitudes, and Behavior

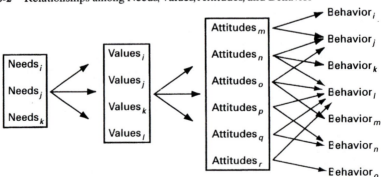

related to the workplace. Critics of the generality distinction claim that work values are, or should be conceived of as, subsets or derivatives of general values and that the distinction is bogus and muddies the water, adding nothing that is really new. The other side argues that finer analysis and understanding of the workplace and of problems and successes in the workplace and in people's careers can be gained by thinking of sets of less general/more specific values that pertain to the world of work. One popular typology of work values includes concepts such as pride in work, activity preference, job involvement, attitudes toward earnings, and upward striving.

The Role of Work Values

The point may be obvious but is probably worth stating nevertheless. The values approach to work motivation assumes that people will pursue through work those things, states, conditions, activities, and outcomes that they value. The job of managing or of motivating someone is, by this view, to arrange jobs, working conditions, and organizational policies in a way that appeals to workers' values. Whether this is possible is an interesting issue. We return to the matter shortly after we examine the question of the stability of human values. If values are not more or less stable, it will be virtually impossible for managers, teachers, parents, and others to influence human behavior by appealing to them.

Do Work Values Change?

Nord et al. (1988) have described how work values (as opposed to values in general) have evolved since the time of the early Greeks, for whom work was seen as a waste of time (such a view is feasible in a society where there are slaves to do the work). Later, Roman and Hebrew philosophers and clergy added to the Greek position the belief that work was a form of atonement necessary for humankind to pay for original sin. Much later, the emergence of the "Protestant work ethic" (Weber, 1930) expounded the virtue of work as "in itself the end of life, ordained as such by God" (p. 159). Clearly, if one stands back to examine the prevailing nature of work values over the millennia, change is abundantly apparent.

But what about value change over shorter periods of time? A study by Inglehart (1981) found that U.S. employee values remained remarkably stable over the 13-year period 1968–1981. The top six and bottom six values in his research did not vary by more than one rank over the period of the study. More recently, G. W. England (1991) has reported the second phase of a large-scale study of values among the U.S. workforce. Specifically, comparing data from two matched samples, one gathered in 1982, the other in 1989, England examined the degree of change that had occurred in over 41 *work values*. Underlying the 41 specific items were four general factors: (1) the importance and significance of work and working in one's life, (2) the normative beliefs and expectations that people hold about their obligations and entitlements at work, (3) the relative importance of achieving various work goals (alternatively called work values, work needs, and incentive preferences), and (4) the bases used by people to decide whether an activity is considered work or nonwork.

England found statistically significant shifts of U.S. work values over the seven years of the study. Although no single factor among the 41 he studied altered dramatically, collectively the findings suggested that economic goals had become more important and "comfort" goals seemed less important, reflecting what England sees as an instrumental reaction to the economic realities during the period between the two studies. Nevertheless, the importance of working as a life role declined over the same period. For many people, work seemed to be less intrinsically valued and more a means to certain ends than it had been previously. Between 1982 and 1989, no significant change was observed in the beliefs that Americans held about their entitlements from employers or about their obligations to the organizations for which they worked.

Value Change at the Individual Level

Studies by Inglehart (1981) and G. W. England (1991) suggest that people's values can and do change, particularly values related to working. Large-scale studies of this sort are interesting, but they fail to shed much light on the dynamics related to the change in individuals' values. Few studies have, in fact, tried to do this. An exception is a fascinating, classic study by Lieberman (1956), which demonstrated how natural changes in workplace roles altered the attitudes of a sample of workers as they moved from rank-and-file jobs into either foreman's or shop steward's positions, and back again.[5] The attitudes in question were the employees' views regarding management and officials of management, their views regarding unions and union officials, their attitudes toward the management-sponsored incentive system, and finally, their attitudes regarding the union-sponsored seniority system. The results of the study, somewhat simplified, can be summarized as follows: The expressed attitudes of the employees studied correlated directly with the roles they occupied at given points in time. As their work roles changed and then changed back again, so did their attitudes (and presumably their work values) in accordance with their roles.

A second, rare, longitudinal study conducted by Armon (1993) adopted an unusual approach based on the concept of moral development (Kohlberg, 1981, 1984). Armon asked 50 people ranging in age from 23 to 70 years, "What is good work?" She followed these people and asked them the same question four times over a 12-year period. Armon found that many of the participants in her sample matured through a five-stage developmental sequence in which what they valued in work became less visceral, less instrumental, and directed more heavily toward the pursuit of higher values, such as ethical conduct, assisting other people, and having a positive impact on the world in general. She also found that those people who did progress toward higher philosophical standards of work values did so through a common developmental sequence, and that there were no differences between the men and women in her sample. In fact, progression through the stages was related to education. Those people who advanced toward less selfish, more worldly values were more highly educated than those who did not. They also tended to have experienced more critical life events—mostly work-related events—that featured ethical problems or dilemmas that had to be dealt with or that required them to address issues of their own self-identity and integrity.

Despite the empirical studies cited here, very little is known about *how* values actually change in individuals, particularly their values about work and working, yet it seems clear that they do change (Connor and Becker, 1994; Pinder et al., 1997). More-

---

[5]We emphasize that Lieberman was studying certain work-related attitudes, not values per se. Values theorists such as Rokeach (1969) and Connor and Becker (1994) would argue that the apparent changes in attitudes were instigated by corresponding changes in values, since values underlie and are consistent with attitudes.

over, we know that many (most?) work organizations attempt to gain varying degrees of control over employees by the standardization of individual values. In fact, recent emphasis on the concept of organizational culture relates to these issues, as academics and practitioners alike have sought to understand and manipulate the homogeneity of individual values in North American workplaces. We examine briefly next the concept of organizational culture as it relates to work motivation and control.

Values and Organizational Culture

Organizational culture consists of the shared beliefs, norms, values, knowledge, and tacit understandings held by members of an organization or organizational subunit (e.g., Frost et al., 1993; Maehr, 1987; Sackman, 1992; Schein, 1985; Schneider, 1990). In fact, values (or shared values) are the very essence of cultures and of organizational cultures in particular (Meglino, Ravlin, and Adkins, 1989; O'Reilly, Chatman, and Caldwell, 1991):

> Research on culture usually begins with a set of values and assumptions. . . . These values, whether conscious or unconscious, typically act as the defining elements around which norms, symbols, rituals and other cultural activities revolve. . . . In this vein, basic values may be thought of as internalized normative beliefs that can guide behaviour. When a social unit's members share values, they may form the basis for social expectations or norms. . . . Thus, researchers who investigate culture by focusing on norms . . . are studying social expectations that are based on underlying values. Others who study culture through rituals, stories, or myths . . . are examining phenotypic outcroppings that reflect underlying beliefs and values. (O'Reilly et al., 1991, pp. 491–492)

To have a "strong culture" implies that there is a high degree of consistency among employees' belief structures, values, and general assumptions about life.[6] "If there is no substantial agreement that a limited set of values is important in a social unit, a strong culture cannot be said to exist" (Meglino, Ravlin, and Adkins, 1989, 1991; O'Reilly et al., 1991, p. 493). What are the benefits of strong organizational culture? There is some evidence that homogeneity among the value structures of organizational actors can be a source of job satisfaction, commitment, job proficiency, and long tenure (see Brown, 1976; O'Reilly et al., 1991; O'Reilly, Caldwell, and Mirable, 1992). Further, value homogeneity among employees enables managers to make better-than-chance predictions about the behaviors of their subordinates when other forms of control, such as rules or direct supervision, are not in place (Adkins, Ravlin, and Meglino, 1992; P. McDonald and Gandz, 1992). By standardizing the premises that organizational members use for information processing and decision making, managers can attain higher degrees of control over their personnel and greater predictability about the ways that employees will behave when not under direct supervision (Pinder et al., 1997).

What about possible benefits for employees? Adkins et al. (1992) have concluded that "value congruence between coworkers serves to make social cues, including information about the importance of exerting effort and seeking to improve quality on the job, as well as the importance of attendance behaviours, more salient. . . . [I]n situations

---

[6]Van Maanen and Kunda (1989) have noted that shared or *appropriate* emotions are also part of an organization's culture and that many organizations stage more or less formal rituals and ceremonies for the sake of teaching employees how to emote "properly." More will be said about this in chapter 4 when we focus directly on the role of emotions in work motivation.

where individuals must work closely together to perform the job, value congruence may facilitate task performance" (p. 15). In short, proponents of strong organizational cultures claim that such cultures can be sources of positive job attitudes for workers and at the same time, powerful managerial control devices in the absence of more direct measures. If the benefits are so great, why aren't all organizations characterized by high value homogeneity?

Consider the story of Levi-Strauss, the world's largest apparel maker (*Business Week,* 1994). Since taking the family business private in 1985, Chairman and CEO Robert D. Haas has tried, with considerable difficulty and only limited success, to introduce and sustain two important workplace values: ethnic diversity and employee empowerment. But the powerful active and passive resistance of other key executives in the company largely thwarted Mr. Haas's attempts. Levi-Strauss learned that the many pragmatic constraints of the world of business, traditional values, and work procedures, when coupled with outright resistance to change, can frustrate even the most powerful, best-intentioned senior executives from pursuing admirable values in business.

Values and the Concept of Fit

How do organizations achieve homogeneity among the values of their employees? There are two basic strategies: to select people who appear to possess the "appropriate" values in the first place and/or to socialize employees, once hired, to conform to a set of value standards that management desires. P. McDonald and Gandz (1992) have concluded that, for the sake of securing managerial control, the optimal strategy is to combine "make-value" with "buy-value" strategies.[7] They report that virtually all the Canadian executives they have interviewed on the matter agree with the importance of value congruity among their employees, and many described a variety of techniques they employed to encourage and reinforce the sharing of common values among their workers.

A U.S. study by Posner and Schmidt (1984) and a Canadian project by P. McDonald and Gandz (1992) have shown how human resource management programs of recruitment, selection, training, counseling, and support systems can create and nurture adherence to key organizational goals. For example, a recent study by Ashforth and Saks (1994) found interesting empirical support for a conceptual model proposed more than a decade ago by Van Maanen and Schein (1979) dealing with the various means by which organizations attempt to "socialize" employees (Ashforth and Saks, 1994). The researchers demonstrated how, to varying degrees, employers used six basic tactics with their new recruits (all recent business school graduates of Concordia University in Montreal) for the sake of making them malleable.

Common institutionalized socialization tactics, conducted in a fixed sequence of steps and with a fixed timetable for completion—rather than a series of idiosyncratic or individualized experiences—were related to lower levels of role innovation (i.e., higher levels of compliance) by the new hirees. The findings also showed that segregating newcomers from existing employees by designating them as initiates also made them more compliant. Also effective was the use of designated, experienced role models as trainers and mentors.

---

[7]Chatman (1991) writes that person–organization fit can be created either by selection (assessments of who the person is when he or she enters the organization) and/or by socialization (how the organization influences the person's values, attitudes, and behaviors during employment). The former is an example of "buy values," the latter, "make values."

Although we have abundant everyday and anecdotal experience with organizational socialization tactics, procedures, and programs, only a few systematic studies such as that by Ashforth and Saks (1994) are known to this author. Army and Marine boot camps, the training sessions and codes of conduct prescribed by strong culture firms such as McDonald's, IBM, and Mary Kay, and even the early weeks in some graduate business programs comprise examples of the anecdotal and everyday experience. Clearly, some employee work values are malleable, and it would appear that the work values of some people are more malleable than those of others.

Later we address the notion of *organizational values* and claim that the term is inappropriate. In the meantime, however, it is worth noting one study that sought to show that higher levels of "personal investment" (i.e., motivation) would result among employees whose personal incentives (or values) matched the rewards and espoused cultural values of an organization than among employees for whom such a match was lower or did not exist. Contrary to expectations, the results showed that a highly salient organizational culture in which goals are clear, a work ethic is emphasized, and employees are evaluated and rewarded for their accomplishments had beneficial effects on the investment levels of most employees. The degree of match between the employee and the company did not seem to matter (Mayberry, 1985, reported by Maehr, 1987).

Before moving along, let us be clear that the notion of congruence or match has at least two interpretations: (1) the degree of similarity among the values of employees, and (2) the degree of fit between employee values and the incentive structure of an organization. At the time of this writing, more work needs to be done on both of these issues before definitive conclusions can be drawn with regard to either question.

The Ethics of a Strong Culture

It appears that most North American employers implicitly assume that they have a right as part of the employment contract to attempt to alter employee values. Similarly, many or most employees seem to share, tacitly at least, that assumption—that the company has a right to alter their values, within limits, in ways that will increase managerial control and employee uniformity and predictability. This is a moral issue that students of work motivation should consider. At some point, a question arises as to the limits of the rights of employers (as well as administrators in organizations such as graduate schools of business) to attempt to socialize, homogenize, deindividuate, and standardize the values and behaviors of managers, workers, clients, and students. Basic questions concerning the limits to the loss of individual rights and freedoms that can reasonably be expected or accepted in the greater context of a free society should be raised.

As discussed earlier, a central element of managerialism[8] has been the development of a shared culture or corporate value system. This feature, Heckscher (1988) observes, is antithetical to some very fundamental beliefs of North American society:

> This aspect is the source of some of the strongest emotions that have been aroused by managerialism. Our society retains a deep suspicion of social values from its historical struggles against religious oppression. The right to believe in whatever we please is one

---

[8]*Managerialism* is an umbrella term used by Heckscher (1988) to refer to a range of managerial techniques that go back decades, most of which have had as their goals increased employee satisfaction and productivity, usually through some form of work redesign or participation scheme.

of our most cherished freedoms. We tend to emphasize impersonal and rational values because they protect us from arbitrary uses of personal power. *Thus any attempt to build shared values arouses suspicion* [emphasis added]. On the other hand, there seems to be an equally deep social longing for the sense of community that has been shattered by bureaucracy, a longing that creates an unresolved tension in many of our institutions. (pp. 95–96)

There may be fundamental ethical issues related to achieving value homogeneity by manipulating employee values and belief structures. Similarly, it is deemed unethical, and in many cases illegal, to *select* employees on the basis of their personal traits, such as gender, race, or age. One might ask why it is ethical, by the same token, for employers to presume to select from among job applicants on the basis of their apparent value structures. It seems that we take for granted that such practices are fair, reasonable, and morally justifiable. Yet as long as a selection device is related to a performance criterion, employers regularly select and reject prospective employees on their apparent values. As in the case of value manipulation after hiring, what are the limits to which an individual's values should be used as a basis to hire, fire, or transfer to a new job at a different location within a company? Is there nothing sacred about a person's values?

To our knowledge, such questions are seldom raised by managers and students of work motivation. Rarely are such practices examined objectively from the point of view of ethics, informed consent, freedom, and human dignity. It is obvious that by their very nature and definition, organizations require control and predictability. But where are the limits, and who is to decide how much managerial control used to "motivate" employees by tampering with (or appealing to) their values is legitimate in a democratic society?

Do Organizations Have Values?

Do organizations have values? The discussion earlier in this chapter may have implied that they do. Certainly, we often hear people speak of organizational values. There are even books published with these words in their titles (e.g., Woodcock and Francis, 1989). In fact, Rokeach, one of the great scholars in the domain of the study of values, wrote the following: "The value concept is an especially powerful one for all the social sciences because it can be meaningfully employed at all levels of social analysis. . . . [I]t is just as meaningful to speak of cultural, societal, institutional, organizational, and group values as it is to speak of individual values. If individual values are socially shared cognitive representations of personal needs and the means for satisfying them, then institutional values are socially shared representations of institutional goals and demands" (1979, p. 50).

It is a logical error many of us make when we anthropomorphize the organizations in which we work and with which we interact. To *anthropomorphize* something is to attribute to it characteristics of individual human beings—organizations are thought and spoken of as having, in a sense, minds, memories, hearts, and other distinguishing properties of *Homo sapiens*. For example, we may hear people speak of "loving" the Air Force or of hoping that Eaton's will remember them when they are due for a raise. When people cry while chopping onions, it is not because they are sorry for inflicting pain on the onions. It is true that organizations are comprised of people and can be defined as systems of interactions and events linking people (D. Katz and Kahn, 1966), but it is a logical error to attribute, other than metaphorically, human properties to aggregations of individuals. Organizations do not have minds, memories, or hearts. Organizations do not possess aspirations, loves, or fears.

The point has been presented elsewhere: "Organizations do not possess values or needs. Rather, key players in organizations, as individual human beings, possess values and needs, and sometimes the most powerful of these people can determine the goals and policies of these organizations in directions that are consistent with their own values and needs" (Pinder et al., 1997, pp. 33–34). In the paper cited earlier, Rokeach (1979) outlined five methods by which institutional values can be measured. Four of these methods require assessment of the value structures of individual "gatekeepers" or "special clients" related to the institutions in question. (The fifth method is to apply content analysis to the instrumental and terminal values reflected in formal documents and publications produced by the institutions for public consumption [1979, pp. 53–54]). Hence, although Rokeach claims that aggregations of people have values, he recognizes that operationally, one must assess the values of key players to make sense of the concept.

There are many problems with these practices. First is the matter of determining whose individual values are to be assessed and then aggregated to yield a composite definition of the organization's values. Second is the issue of how, arithmetically, such values or value profiles (see Connor and Becker, 1975) are to be aggregated. Third, there are the possible ethical problems of (mis)leading lower-level participants and interested outside parties (such as customers, clients, and others) about the "values" of the organization, as if these values possessed the same qualities as those possessed by single persons (e.g., trustworthiness, loyalty, and honesty). Finally, there is a major practical problem here, one that should concern practitioners and scholars alike. We must assume that there is a degree of coherence or agreement among the value structures of the gatekeepers. Modern theorists in organizational culture openly and readily admit that organizations of any size are likely to feature multiple cultures, varying across various functional, ethnic, age, or professional groups, for example. Hence, to portray a single organization as having a strong culture implies that value congruence exists, in abundance, throughout the organization. To the extent that this is not so, then it becomes meaningless to speak of an organization's (singular) culture, and hence, of its values. Therefore, the transporting of an individual-level trait or concept (in this case, values) to a level of analysis higher than that of single individuals is, at best, a metaphorical use of the terms involved. At worst, it is a logical error that will only confound analysis and our study of how organizations work (Pinder et al., 1997).

The case study of Levi-Strauss mentioned earlier illustrates the problem. Mr. Haas was possessed of strong desires to promote values of empowerment, employee involvement, and equal opportunity. Even as the chief executive officer, Mr. Haas was unable to implement policies in accordance with these values, mostly because the values were not really shared by other powerful people in his company and, we suppose, by the simple inertia that usually surrounds radical changes in organizational policies and goals. The key point here is that it is critical to keep individual-level concepts (such as needs and values) focused on and devoted to the understanding of individual-level problems and phenomena, and to create, invoke, and utilize other terms, representing other concepts, to deal with group, organizational, and institutional issues, as appropriate.

What Do Employees Value?

Now that we have examined at length the concepts of employee needs and values and some of the important theoretical and applied issues related to them and to their roles in work motivation, we turn briefly to two questions: What then, *do* North American employees value? What do they seek from their work? Actually, these questions have been the focus over many decades of countless surveys conducted by journalists and social scientists. Often, the focus is on reported *changes* in employee work values (as discussed earlier). One study found that the basic rankings provided by samples of employees taken in 1946, 1981, and 1986 did not change very much. "Interesting work" was ranked highest on all three occasions when various employee subgroups were combined (Kovach, 1987). Often, the focus is specifically on the issue of the relative importance of money vis-à-vis other outcomes. In fact, the revelation that employees value more than merely money and economic security was probably the most socially significant findings of the famous Hawthorne studies, which precipitated the human relations movement of the 1940s (see Roethlisberger and Dickson, 1939). In virtually every study of this variety, money is found not to be the most important motivator for most groups of employees (Kovach, 1987, p. 65).[9]

Sometimes the focus is on international similarities and differences in values. A recent example of this line of inquiry is provided by S. H. Schwartz and Bilsky (1987, 1990) and S. H. Schwartz (1992). These researchers propose that, for example, there are seven distinctly different motivational values which transcend many international boundaries: achievement, enjoyment, maturity, prosocial, restrictive conformity, security, and self-direction (S.H. Schwartz and Bilsky, 1987). Another vein of attention has been on gender differences. Do men and women value the same things from their work? Kovach's (1987) research suggests that there are few significant gender differences these days, although it appears from his work that women may place slightly higher emphasis on "full appreciation of work" than men do and that women also place greater importance on interpersonal relations and communications. A study by Konrad and Langton (1991) tends to support these conclusions. These researchers surveyed a total of 42 empirical studies that were published in the North American management and organizations literature in the late 1980s and early 1990s and found that certain "job outcomes," such as prestige, autonomy, leisure, avoiding pressure, and influence, appear not to be valued differently by men and women. On the other hand, certain other work values (or job preferences, as they call them)--money, advancement, leading others, and taking responsibility for risks—were more or less important to men than to women. They also found that six work-related outcomes were more important to women than to men: achievement, intrinsic job aspects, relationships on the job, working conditions, balancing work and family, and helping others. Interestingly, of the 32 studies Konrad and Langton (1991) surveyed, 17 showed that men placed a higher value on money than women did and no studies reported that women valued money more highly than men.

Before we close our discussion on individual and employee values, we draw attention to a personal expression by Torbert (1994) of what is meant by "good work."

---

[9]The usual exceptions to this rule, not surprisingly, are the younger workforce and those in the lowest remuneration categories.

Good work is one of four personal values that, for him, collectively comprise a good life. In addition to good work, Torbert draws attention to the importance of "good money," good friends, and good ideas. Of these, good ideas are the highest value because, in Torbert's integrated scheme, they are most likely to emerge in the context of good work with good friends, all enabled by the earning of good money. Good work

> means work that invites the development of craft-like skills and judgment (whether in the realm of materials or language). Such work calls for a kind of mastery that is never fully achieved, in the sense that it can thereafter be exercised in a rote, repetitive or mechanical fashion. Instead, good masterwork requires and reflects an active attention by the masterworker at each moment to the interplay between one's own body in action and the material. . . . This active attention integrates knowledge and application. Prior experience and future ideal, disciplined sobriety and spontaneous responsiveness. In short, good work raises the consciousness of the worker. It integrates mind, body, and good health. (Torbert, 1994, p. 61)

Good money does not necessarily means lots of it, according to Torbert's values. Rather, good money is enough money to enable a person to achieve and blend the other three values (good work, good friends, and good ideas). A person who doesn't earn enough to pursue these other values is earning too little money. A person who is driven to make lots of money often must do so at the expense of not attaining good friends, enjoying good work, or pursuing good ideas. Torbert's notions about the good life are provocative, coherent, and clearly the result of many years of existential insight and experience. The reader is urged to read the original essay to get a complete appreciation of this fascinating concept of one person's values, especially as they relate so closely to a person's motivation to work.

The Value of the Values Concept

In their recent review of values and the workplace, Connor and Becker (1994) were quite critical of the state of our collective understanding of individual values. They cite a list of reasons for their assessment, some of which are methodological and many of which sound similar to the sorts of criticisms raised by theorists such as M. E. Ford (1992) of motivation theory based on needs. Connor and Becker (1994) decry the limited capacity of knowledge of a person's values to enable us to predict that person's behavior. They criticize values researchers who use only parts of existing values instruments or rapidly compose their own ad hoc measures. The problems of unreliability that this causes means that there is unknown validity in the measures that are taken, so it becomes impossible for values theorists to accumulate a coherent body of knowledge. Finally, Connor and Becker (1994) argue that researchers frequently neglect to consider values as a feasible set of factors to take into account when trying to understand organizational behavior, even, in some cases, after values data are collected. In short, Connor and Becker (1994) have issued a plea for more and better inclusion of the values concept in our thinking about work organizations. Their cry is acknowledged by this author, who believes that values have, in fact, been ignored, badly conceived of, and poorly measured in the particular context of the study of work motivation. Researchers and theorists in the field could—and should—do better with values.

SUMMARY AND A LOOK AHEAD

The purpose of this chapter was to introduce a number of perspectives on human nature that are relevant to the study of work motivation. The assumptions we make about the essence of human nature affect the ways that employees interact with one another, the ways managers and supervisors treat subordinates, and the nature of organizational policies as well as how they are generated and administered. Finally, the assumptions that students and scholars make about human beings underlie the various theories of work motivation that come from social science (see Sullivan, 1986).

Clearly, there are many, many perspectives that we might have taken to examine human nature, but given the primary focus and topic of this book, in this chapter we focused most heavily on popular views of human nature that feature needs and values. People have been characterized by many popular theories of work motivation to be driven by their needs and guided by their values—in life as well as in their work. By comparison, the emotional side of human functioning has received short shrift. Accordingly, in chapter 4 we encourage a newly developing interest in emotions and emotionality in theory and research dealing with work motivation.

C H A P T E R

Human Nature:
Emotions at Work

Thought is deeper than all speech,
Feeling deeper than all thought;
Souls to souls can never teach
What unto themselves was taught.

—CHRISTOPHER PEARSE CRANCH

Whatever else it may be, work is an emotional experience, a major part of the emotional lives of most people. Strangely, however, emotion has not played an important role in most theories of organizational behavior during the past 30 years, nor has it entered in any significant way into the models and theories of scholars who study work motivation. In fact, George and Brief (1996) have recently pointed out that this author failed to mention emotion in a review of the work motivation literature 15 years ago (Pinder, 1984), as have other reviewers since then (e.g., Kanfer, 1990). We redress that omission here.

It is obvious that *people have feelings at work* and that *they have feelings about their work*. They brag with pride about their work successes and complain about their frustrations at work. Consider the joy people feel when they are promoted or when they succeed in a difficult task at their work. Consider the anger they feel when colleagues or co-workers frustrate their efforts. Consider the envy that many people feel when their peers are rewarded and they are not for work they judge to be of equal value. Consider the fear that people feel when there are rumors about layoffs. Consider the resentment when an employee is disciplined by management for breaking a company rule. Consider the excitement that a person feels when s/he falls in love with an employee in the office or in the factory. By nature, people are emotional creatures, and they take these emotions to work with them. Moreover, many of the emotions that people feel are formed, shaped, and experienced in the workplace.

A BRIEF HISTORY OF EMOTIONS
IN ORGANIZATIONAL SCIENCE

Ironically, some of the earliest theories of organizational behavior (e.g., Barnard, 1938; Likert, 1967; Mayo, 1933; Roethlisberger and Dickson, 1939; W. F. Whyte, 1948) were laced with observations about the emotional side of work and working (Ashforth and Humphrey, 1995). Then emotions seemed to go out of style in North American behavioral science, and the dominant assumption for decades was that cognition is the primary cause of behavior (Derryberry and Tucker, 1994; L. Ross and Nisbett, 1991). Behaviorism also had a period of hegemony (see B. F. Skinner, 1953); there was no room for emotion in understanding the origins of human action in behaviorism (see chapter 14). Then in the mid-1970s, Locke (1976) defined job satisfaction as an *emotional reaction* that people feel after they appraise their jobs vis-à-vis their values (see chapter 12 for more detail). It was a start, but Locke's definition was about all the emotional content in the field, even though the necessity to bring emotion back into organizational theorizing was being acknowledged. For example, Sandelands and Buckner (1989) wrote: "There is a lot to learn about work feelings. Despite a reconnaissance by literally thousands of studies ... the territory of work feelings remains largely uncharted, beyond the frontier. Questions about why people feel as they do when working find superficial answers. It is said that the work is interesting, or challenging, or stressful, or dehumanizing. Or it is said that the match between the worker and work is a good or a bad one. Such answers betray little of the subtle texture and dynamics of the work itself, and even less of the intricate psychology of its apprehension and appreciation" (p. 106).

But the tide has turned: Emotions are now taking on more importance in psychology (see Goleman, 1995, p. xi) and other disciplines. Nobel laureate Herbert Simon (1995) has called for an increased emphasis on "affect" as part of his plan for further advancement of cognitive psychology. Emotions are even being recognized in economics and decision analysis (see Pieters and Van Raaij, 1988). Indeed, Lazarus and Lazarus (1994) claim that human beings are the most emotional animals on earth. People experience emotions such as joy, rage, envy, guilt, passion, love, lust, despair, rejection, and a host of others, originating in parts of the brain other than those associated with thought, reasoning, and deliberation (Damasio, 1994), and they have these experiences while at work and because of their work. Organizational scientists have responded to the call, and research and theory construction is under way in organizational behavior (e.g., George and Brief, 1996; Rafaeli and Sutton, 1987; Weiss and Cropanzano, 1996). Emotions are back in style, and the purpose of this chapter is to explore the role of human emotionality in matters related to work motivation and behavior.

EMOTIONS, MOODS, TEMPERAMENTS, FEELINGS,
AND PREDISPOSITIONS: WHAT ARE THEY?

Emotions

Two leading authorities have recently defined *emotions* as

> complex reactions that engage both our minds and our bodies. These reactions include: a subjective mental state, such as the feeling of anger, anxiety, or love; an impulse to act,

such as fleeing or attacking, whether or not it is expressed overtly; and profound changes in the body, such as increased heart rate or blood pressure. Some of these bodily changes prepare for and sustain coping actions, and others—such as postures, gestures, and facial expressions—communicate to others what we are feeling, or want others to believe we are feeling.

An emotion is a personal life drama, which has to do with the fate of our goals in a particular encounter and our beliefs about ourselves and the world we live in. It is aroused by an appraisal of the personal significance or meaning of what is happening in that encounter. The dramatic plot differs from one emotion to another, each emotion having its own particular story. (Lazarus and Lazarus, 1994, p. 151).

Emotions can be thought of as "communications" to oneself and to others (Oatley and Jenkins, 1992). In this view, they are readouts, some of which are communicative (Buck, 1985), although there are frequently "substantial differences between a person's conscious awareness and behavioral or physiological indications of emotions. Hence communications of emotion, which are picked up from behavioral signs, need not be consciously recognized by the person emitting these signs" (Oatley and Jenkins, 1992, p. 59, summarizing work by Lang, 1988).

Emotions can signal the occurrence of events relevant to important goals. They are changes of action readiness (Frijda, 1986). Emotions are mental states, or processes, that are usually elicited by external events. They are phasic; they have a "defined onset, perhaps rising to one or more peaks of intensity, and a decline" (Oatley and Jenkins, 1992, p. 59, citing work by Fridja, Mesquita, Sonnemans, and van Goozen, 1991). Emotions are determined by the personal meanings we attach to things and events, and hence depend on what is important to us and the things we believe about ourselves and the world.

Emotions often indicate intentions or changes of intentions. They affect other people's actions, tending to set pairs or groups of people into particular modes of interaction (Oatley and Jenkins, 1992). At any moment, an emotion can be experienced internally, behaviorally, and have varying degrees of intensity. They can be registered physiologically or by self-report. Emotions are usually elicited by evaluating events that concern a person's goals or needs. Sometimes these evaluations are innate or subconscious (Oatley and Jenkins, 1992). As noted above in the definition by Lazarus and Lazarus, most emotions usually include a distinctive subjective experience and physiological accompaniments, which Oatley (1992) calls "distinctive phenomenological tones" (p. 20). Thus, sadness feels different from joy or fear; love different from anxiety (although they may go hand in hand). Similarly, emotions are usually also associated with compulsive thoughts and, on many occasions, distinct facial expressions and bodily reactions.

For Oatley (1992) and Fridja (1986) an emotion is a "mental state of readiness for action . . . or a change of readiness" (Oatley, 1992, pp. 19–20) that is usually based on an evaluation of something in a person's life space that affects the person's goals or concerns. Moreover, these evaluations are not necessarily conscious but operate to specify a possible range of actions the person might take to protect personal concerns. For example, when we are frightened, we might consider acts such as fighting, fleeing, or submitting to the source of fear.

Whereas some emotions are thought of as "basic," others are conceived of as blends or mixtures. Ekman and Friesen (1975) cite happiness, surprise, anger, and fear as examples of basic emotions. Oatley's (1992; Oatley and Johnson-Laird, 1987) list of basic emotions is restricted to happiness, sadness, anger, fear, and disgust. An important means for determining whether an emotion is basic is whether the facial expression associated with it is recognized across cultures (Oatley and Johnson-Laird, 1987). In comparison, blended emotions such as wariness may consist mostly of interest and moderate fear (Frijda, 1986). Hence, categorizing emotions can be a problem, and there are, in fact, many different taxonomies of emotions with only some overlap or agreement among theorists regarding which emotions are basic and which are mixes or composites of others (see J. A. Russell, 1991). Nevertheless, eventually we must adopt a taxonomy of emotions that has some degree of apparent academic merit as well as practical utility. We do so shortly.

Of critical importance is the fact that different events may result in different emotions for different people because the events are interpreted differently. For example, a flip comment by a supervisor may generate anger in one employee because of a history of conflict between the supervisor and the employee, whereas the same comment may not be significant to another employee and therefore have no emotional consequence. This lack of one-to-one connection between events and emotional reactions often makes it difficult for outsiders to understand a person's emotional reaction to events such as comments made by others or even to more powerful events such as accidents or deaths.

Emotions as Internal Commodities

In common parlance, many emotions are often *reified*—spoken of and considered as if they are physical entities within people, much as one might contain gallstones, a quart of beer, or even a goldfish (Tavris, 1982). Anger is a good example, as when people say: "She is full of anger" or "Henry was filled with jealousy." One implication of this conception of an emotion is that it is possible, even desirable, for the person *to get the thing out of themselves,* like a badly digesting meal. This raises the issue of voluntary control of our emotions. Some early thinkers, including Charles Darwin, extrapolated their observations of lower animals to the case of human beings. Dogs might be seen or thought of as becoming angry in response to threats or danger—their animalistic response is instinctive. Although Darwin was a brilliant ethologist, he is accused of being a poor psychologist: "[Darwin's] account of anger was oversimplified: someone offends you, so you dislike him; your dislike turns to hatred; brooding over your hatred makes you angry" (Tavris, 1982, p. 33).

Since the days of Darwin (and Freud), there have been schools of thought that people are healthier if they do *get their anger out,* because keeping it bottled up inside is bad for us. These "ventilationists" believe that not expressing our emotions causes pain and interpersonal conflict. They believe that we should openly express anger, love, sympathy, and other emotions openly and honestly—that high blood pressure, ulcers, depression, sexual problems, and substance abuse are probable consequences of withholding the expression of our emotions. As early as the 1960s we heard stories of Japanese companies providing their employees with rubber dummies and baseball bats so that they could give vent to their bottled-up emotions. A leading engineering firm in Calgary has established and furnished a quiet room for similar purposes, a place where emotional employees may go to cry, shout, or merely work through their emotions in private. The room is very popular.

At least one theorist rejects the value of the view that emotions are something locked up inside us, and that processes and devices aimed at "getting them out" are beneficial. She argues that although "such views get people ventilating and agitating . . . they rarely recognize or fix the circumstances that make them angry in the first place. When Aesop's lion roared, no one thought the lion had a hostility complex or a problem with temper control; they knew a net had trapped him. No amount of chanting or shouting or pillow pounding will extricate us from the many nets of modern life" (Tavris, 1982, p. 45). Tavris's point has major implications for the management of many emotions in the workplace, particularly as they relate to frustration. No number of silent rooms, baseball bats, or ersatz supervisors will themselves rectify the dysfunctional policies and practices that give rise to human emotionality in organizations. People may feel better after cathartic sessions of violence, tears, or brooding, but their return to similar circumstances is likely to occasion recurrences of the emotions. The debate about the therapeutic value of expressing one's emotions—anger in particular—and of the possibility of controlling them completely is not resolved. The interested reader is referred to Tice and Baumeister (1993) for a summary of the history and contending positions in that debate. Their summary position is that "anger can be controlled and regulated and channelled to a substantial degree. But it cannot be eliminated" (p. 396).

Human Control of Emotions

More current thinking about human emotions, however, assumes that to varying degrees, emotions can be controlled by and dealt with at the will of and at the time preferred by the person holding the emotions. Thus, although the sequence cited above may be possible, things could happen in reverse just as easily. You hate someone's values, therefore you dislike the person. Your dislike turns to anger and you say or do something to insult the person. This display of anger in turn causes the person to insult you. The point is that a variety of perceptions, events, and attributions may result in anger, or be caused by anger, and some elements of these sequences are well within our control (J. A. Russell, Fernandez-Dols, Manstead, and Wellenkamp, 1994; Tavris, 1982; Tice and Baumeister, 1993). A person may feel angry and express that emotion in countless ways, such as cleaning the house with extra fury, organizing a protest rally, playing racquet ball, engaging in meditation, or simply screaming out loud. Others merely perform a "slow burn": "Human anger is not a biological reflex like the sneeze, nor simply a reactive display designed to ward off enemies. You may become aroused to anger by memories and symbols as well as by real and present dangers, and you can maintain that anger for years. You may even decide retrospectively to get angry, which is 'the more I thought about it, the madder I got' phenomenon" (Tavris, 1982, p. 33).

The tenuous connection between anger and aggression will be of critical importance in chapter 8, where we discuss work frustration and aggression. We return to the particular issue of the control of anger later in this chapter and to the notion of self-regulation of one's emotions and behaviors much later in the book (see chapter 14).

Moods, Temperaments, and Affectivity

When emotional states are enduring and "have no specific objects to which the emotion is directed, they are called *moods*" (Kitayama and Niedenthal, 1994, p. 7; see also Salovey and Mayer, 1990). Moods can begin and last beyond exposure to an event or an agent in a person's life space. Moods tend to persist in the absence of specific events and stimuli (Fridja, 1986, p. 59). "The focus of a mood is broad rather than being centered on a single, narrow goal or event. Acute emotions usually are provoked by some event that sets them going, whereas moods express existential concerns that are apt to be diffuse" (Lazarus and Lazarus, 1994, p. 84). A person may have a general mood of anger or anxiety and carry it around for a period of two or three days, attaching it to all elements of her life. "Behaviorally, moods are configurations of activity that are not centered around an object or event, but in that fleeting manner attach now to this object, then to that; or similar configurations of activity easily evoked by a multitude of relatively insignificant events" (Frijda, 1986, p. 59). In one study of more than 200 sales personnel, for example, it was found that people's moods were negatively related to their absenteeism behavior (George, 1989). So in a sense, moods are not well focused but are generalized feelings that may attach to any and all events and people in a person's life as long as the mood is activated.

By contrast, a *temperament* is defined as a predisposition to an emotion (Oatley and Johnson-Laird, 1987). In other words, if someone has a predisposition toward the emotion of anger, for example, we say that the person "has an angry temperament." Psychologists use the terms *negative* and *positive affectivity* to describe people's characteristic tendencies to view the world either negatively or positively. One might expect that a person who has a basic negative affectivity would not often display a positive temperament or positive affectivity toward life's events. In fact, the two dimensions appear to be independent of one another; most of us are capable of projecting either affective state (George, 1992; Warr, Barter, and Brownbridge, 1983; Watson, Clarke, and Tellegen, 1988). As we will see later in the chapter, many authors believe that possession of a generally positive mood, backed by a characteristically positive affectivity, can be the source of many good things for both individuals and organizations.

Emotions and Feelings

A critical aspect of emotion is that it entails activation (Kitayama and Niedenthal, 1994). An emotional person is activated and prepared to act, depending on the strength of the feelings aroused and the potential objects of the aroused energy. Oatley and Duncan (1992) found that 77 percent of the emotions of happiness, sadness, anger, and fear included a subjective inner feeling of emotion; 77 percent included a bodily sensation; 81 percent came with involuntary thoughts; and 90 percent involved a "consciously recognized action or urge to act emotionally. Most episodes of emotion included all these features, but in some one or several features were absent" (Oatley, 1992, p. 21).

When we emote, we witness one or more bodily stimulations. When we say "love hurts," the expression has more than metaphorical meaning. Similarly, the condition we refer to as having a "broken heart" is actually characterized by pain and aching in one's heart and stomach, often accompanied by sadness and dread that one *feels* at the visceral level. Depending on which of many different philosophical perspectives one has, there are any of a wide number of emotions recognized by various camps. Accordingly, there are many different visceral feelings associated with emotional states, and there is not necessarily a one-to-one correspondence between emotions and their physical symptoms (Crawford, Kippax, Onyx, Gault, and Benton, 1992, p. 34). The emotional feeling associated with the death of a friend may be similar to that associated with the absence of a loved one, even for a temporary period. The first emotion is usually referred to in our culture as grief, but in many ways it is similar to the longing and pining experience related to the absence of a loved one.

Two organizational scholars who helped to renew attention to the role of emotions in the workplace have emphasized the feeling aspect of emotion in their definition:

> Emotions are ineffable feelings of the self-referential sort. They index or signal our current involvements and evaluations. Like sight and hearing, emotion provides a communication channel between the world and its moments and our assessments of just how we are gearing in and out of this perceptual world. They may be intense or subtle, fluctuate wildly or show stability within a narrow band. *What is certain, however, is the fact that we have no scientific or otherwise privileged access to feelings as either states or processes beyond that provided by self-reports. The validity of an emotion for those who feel it is a given, is subject to no known truth test, and is neither right nor wrong.* . . . They are self-referential feelings an actor experiences or, at least, claims to experience in regard to the performances he or she brings to the social world [emphasis added]. (Van Maanen and Kunda, 1989, p. 53)

Sometimes, emotions instigate other emotions and feelings. For example, people who exhibit what they quickly decide are extreme levels of joy and happiness may then immediately express embarrassment for their lack of control. People who catch themselves obviously engaging in extreme displays of pride (e.g., after a conquest) may quickly feel episodes of shame (or of guilt if their pride display offends the vanquished). The sensations of jealousy or envy can often trigger hatred toward those who would take a loved one from us or who possess things we covet. We may even accuse people of being "emotional" as a way of denigrating them, when, in fact, these people may be feeling the same emotion we feel, or are capable of feeling, in similar circumstances. Many men in our culture feel ashamed of their inability to control their spontaneous expressions of "soft" emotions, such as love or sadness, especially when tears confirm the feeling. In short, emotions often come in clusters and sequences, and the many combinations available are often difficult to predict and informative to witness.

Perceptions, Cognitions, and Emotions

An ongoing debate in psychology that has lasted for decades concerns the relationships among what people perceive, what they think and believe, and how they feel. In fact, the basic dualism between thinking and feeling dates back at least as far as Descartes: thinking was thought to be the key activity of the mind, whereas emoting was one of several roles associated with the body (see Damasio, 1994; Goleman, 1995). One issue is whether a person's feelings or emotional state influence what is seen and believed. Another is whether, to have an emotional reaction to agents and events, a person has to perceive and think about events and impinging stimuli or whether emotions can affect a person directly, without being filtered through cognitive processes or accompanying them. Consider a person who is experiencing blockage in attempts to perform well on the job by the unavailability of subordinates. Is this manager likely to experience negative emotions (such as anger) immediately, without a clue as to the causes of employee absences? Or will the manager have to gain some insight, accurate or otherwise, into the motives and circumstances of the staff before emotion occurs?

Some of the earliest and most interesting work on this matter was reported by S. Schacter and Singer (1962) in what is called the *cognition-arousal theory* of emotions. The key hypothesis in this theory is that emotional states result from an interaction of two factors: physiological arousal and cognition about the causes of the arousal. The arousal is perceived of as being emotionally nonspecific; that is, the person merely feels stimulated and immediately becomes prepared to make sense of the cause of the stimulation, but the stimulation itself is experienced initially in the same way for all emotions. Once arousal has occurred, the person seeks clues as to its cause. The theory holds that both arousal and cognitive activity are *necessary* for an emotion such as happiness, fear, or shame to occur, *but they are not sufficient, taken together,* because the person must make the link between the arousal and those features of the environment associated with the arousal. This theory dominated the social psychology of emotion for many years. A review of the empirical support and current status of the theory is provided by H. Leventhal and Tomarken (1986).

Much of the more recent theory and controversy in the field of emotions has its roots in issues raised by cognition-arousal theory. The central issue is whether people can have emotional reactions and, indeed, even behave exclusively on the basis of their emotions, before and without engaging in conscious thought about the circumstances they face. For example, consider a debate by two leading protagonists in an issue of the *American Psychologist* in 1984. One of these theorists, Lazarus (1984), summarized his position as follows: "Cognitive activity is a necessary precondition of emotion because to experience an emotion, people must comprehend—whether in the form of a primary evaluative perception or a highly differentiated symbolic process—that their well-being is implicated in a transaction, for better or worse" (p. 124). Thus, a person would not experience jealousy until realizing that the developing friendship between his sweetheart and the new employee in the office was based on more than business matters. He would have to recognize that there was an amorous interpersonal attraction developing between the two.

More recently, Lazarus (1991) has repeated and expanded his position slightly. He claims that "cognitive activity causally precedes an emotion in the flow of psychological events, and subsequent cognitive activity is also affected by that emotion" (p. 127). For instance, consider a supervisor who is being blocked in attempts to improve the performance of her unit. The frequent absence of her employees is not likely to generate negative emotions (such as anger) until she gains some understanding of the situation. She will seek to determine whether her personnel are deliberately avoiding her (in which case anger is possible), or whether they are overworked and unable to come to her assistance. If it appears that there is some degree of insubordination afoot, the supervisor may immediately become angry and express that anger.[1] In turn, the expressed anger will affect the way the supervisor perceives the subsequent attempts of her staff either to be more available or to continue not to

---

[1]Recall from our earlier discussion that anger may not always arise spontaneously when a person is frustrated or perceives agents or events that are negative or dissatisfying. To varying degrees, anger may be controlled and/or displayed when the circumstances are seen as most beneficial, or suppressed altogether.

be available when needed. On the other hand, if the supervisor perceives that it is a matter of overwork for her team, no emotion, or a different emotion, may be expressed. In fact, such a conclusion might yield positive influences on her beliefs about the value of her staff.

For many years, some people thought of emotions as "drive" variables, similar to hunger, fatigue, and thirst. According to the Lazarus school of thought, the difference between drives (or needs, as we have defined them) and emotions is that the latter require assessment by the person of what is happening. Emotions imply consciousness, an assessment of the situation. So although a person may become more and more thirsty the longer he is without water, an emotion such as fear occurs "only if a person appraises a situation as dangerous or fearful" (Averill, 1982, p. 10). Representing the other side of the debate is Zajonc (1980, 1984). He believes in the "primacy of affect" and its independence from cognition. In his words, "preferences need no inferences." He believes that affect (emotion) can occur before, after, or simultaneously with cognition, and he adopts a slightly different definition of cognition than that of Lazarus. For example, Zajonc believes that it is possible for an employee to have an emotional reaction such as fear in response to the appearance of a supervisor without actually thinking about the supervisor and their relationship.

Much of the debate on the primacy of either emotion or cognition hinges on the difference between the two theories in their definitions of cognition. Zajonc (1984) claims that his position is irreconcilable with that of Lazarus (1984) because of the way Lazarus defines cognition, a definition that Zajonc calls narrow and limited. He argues that it is impossible to refute Lazarus's position, and "all distinctions between cognition, perception, and sensation disappear" (Zajonc, 1984, p. 121). These nuances and the semantics they involve are beyond our purposes here. The interested reader is referred to helpful summaries and critiques of the debate by H. Leventhal and Scherer (1987) and Crawford et al. (1992, chap. 2).

Recent Physiological Evidence on the Debate

Damasio's (1994) and Goleman's (1995) summaries of research on the brain help to clarify some of the central debates related to the primacy issue and the issue of whether emotions help or hinder rational decision making. Goleman (1995) presents many cases of human behavior (often related to parents with children in peril) where the "passions overwhelm reason time and again" (p. 5). He speaks of human beings as having "two minds": a rational mind (which is centered in the cerebral cortex) and an emotional mind, whose functions are centered in other brain regions, such as the *limbic system*. In many or most day-to-day circumstances, the two minds work in harmony, with the emotional mind considering circumstances and the rational mind electing choices from alternatives available to the person for action.

But Goleman (1995) reminds us that from an evolutionary perspective, the emotional mind preceded the cortex. Our species developed the capacity to sense and feel long before we refined the capacity to think and reason. Sociologist Georg Simmel (1950) agreed: "If one arranges the psychological manifestations in a genetic and systematic hierarchy, one will certainly place, at its basis, feeling (though not *all* feelings), rather than intellect. Pleasure and pain, as well as certain instinctive feelings that serve the preservation of the individual and species, have developed prior to all operations with concepts, judgements and conclusions. Thus, the development of the intellect, more than anything else, reveals the lag of the social behind the individual level, whereas the realm of feeling may show the opposite" (pp. 34–35).

Whether it is this primacy in evolutionary history that makes it happen is not clear, but human beings often act on the basis of emotion (after there has been perceptual activity) before the mind enters the decision. Goleman refers to such instances as "emotional highjacking" and offers many examples of cases where people perform extreme acts on the basis of their emotions—acts they regret (or appreciate) later, upon reflection. Goleman cites an incident involving himself as an example. He was fast asleep when he was suddenly wakened by a loud crashing sound in his bedroom. He leaped out of bed and hurried from the room, pausing only once he was outside to peer back in to see that the noise was caused by a stack of boxes that was falling in the corner of the bedroom. Goleman concluded that his flight from the room resulted from a simple connection between his perceptual apparatus (in this case, his hearing) and his amygdala (part of his limbic system). There had not been enough time for his cortex to get into the act until after the fact. He provides many similar stories to make the point that our emotional side can, in emergencies and on occasion, trigger behavior before the mind cuts in, but that human decision making is at its best when both the cognitive and the emotional systems are involved. (See Damasio, 1994, for similar evidence.) We return to this issue shortly.

THE PROTOTYPE APPROACH
TO DEFINING EMOTIONS

Some theorists believe that taking a "classical" approach to defining emotion in general or particular emotions such as love, anger, or fear is not possible (Fehr and Russell, 1991; J. A. Russell, 1991). The classical approach requires that a concept (such as emotions) be defined by articulating all the necessary and sufficient conditions for an object or event to be considered an example of that concept. Using this approach, the boundaries between concepts (e.g., between fear and anger) are clear, and we would have no trouble distinguishing between the two emotions (Fehr and Russell, 1991; J. A. Russell, 1991). But this is not the case, according to Russell and his colleagues, who believe that in practice, the boundaries between emotions are not clear for people. Rather, it is more useful to think of emotions as "prototypes," that is, to think of and define particular emotions in terms of the everyday language and experience of people within a certain culture. The prototype approach considers the boundaries between emotions to be fuzzy rather than crisp and distinct, so that any one emotion may feature a number of characteristics and it is not necessary for all these features to be in place for a set of perceptions, feelings, and actions to be categorized as a particular emotion.

For example, anger may be seen as comprising a sequence of events such as the following. A person is offended by another, after which the person scowls at the offender, then feels internal agitation and tension. Next, the person feels his heart pounding and muscles tensing. Finally, the offended person may (or may not) strike back at the offender. By the prototype approach to emotions, a sequence such as this would be defined as the experience of anger, but not all the elements need to be in place to so qualify.[2] This approach to defining emotions acknowledges that the same "emotion" may not be witnessed the same way from one time to another by the same person, nor in the same way between any two people, because the specific blend of experiences and events may vary somewhat from time to time or between people. It is seen as especially relevant as one moves "downward" from the broad category of emotion (in general) to increasingly specific forms and types of emotions (e.g., down to "anger"), then to even more specific forms, such as rage, wrath, annoyance, and so on (J. A. Russell, 1991).[3] Hence, defining emotions and emotionality is accepted as difficult and somewhat objective by this approach. Yet it is not seen as totally subjective as it is in the subjectivist view.

SOCIALLY CONSTRUCTED EMOTIONS

Another, more recent body of thought claims that we should think of emotions as "*socially-constituted syndromes (transitory social roles)* which include an individual's *appraisal of the situation* and which are *interpreted as passions, rather than as actions*" (Averill, 1982, p. 6). This approach "assumes that any given emotional state is best regarded as an associative network in which specific types of feelings, physiological reactions, motor responses, and thoughts and memories are all interconnected. . . . The linkages tying the various parts of the emotional network vary in strength, and the arousal of any one component is not necessarily accompanied by an arousal of the other subsystems to the same degree. . . . Nevertheless, to the extent that they are linked together, the activation of any one subsystem in the network (or syndrome) will tend to activate the other components with which it is associated" (Berkowitz, 1993a, p. 9). As Averill (1982) puts it, "*no single response, or subset of responses, is a necessary or sufficient condition for the attribution of emotion*" (p. 7).

As the concept applies in medicine, *syndromes* consist of many interrelated symptoms, no one of which itself determines the existence of a particular disease. A relatively new disease that is thought of as a syndrome is fibromyalgia (Ediger, 1991). The major symptoms associated with this syndrome are widespread pain, especially in the joints and muscles, fatigue, morning muscular stiffness, troubled sleep, a propensity to allergies, chest pains, irritable bowels, numbness and tingling, and loss of memory. Any of these symptoms can occur alone, or they can affect a person a few at a time as a result of other diseases or disorders. When they come as a package, however, each with more or less force, they are referred to as a syndrome, with a name that identifies them as a collectivity—fibromyalgia. Similarly, for Averill (1982) and Berkowitz (1993a), emotions are syndromes of reactions.

By defining emotions as socially constituted syndromes, Averill means that people learn, through their own experiences and by observing others, what acts, reactions, facial expressions, and utterances are appropriate, within a given culture, to express

---

[2]This example, cited by J. A. Russell (1991), is attributed to Lakoff's (1987) analysis of anger. Moreover, it bears repeating that anger is an emotion that may or may not emerge or express itself in predictable ways. It may be controlled, deflected, repressed, or channeled in idiosyncratic ways that are hard to predict or to understand (see Tice and Baumeister, 1993).

[3]Fehr and Russell (1991) illustrate how love can be viewed from a prototype perspective.

particular emotions (see Harre, 1986). That is, according to Armon-Jones (1986), "emotions are characterized by attitudes such as beliefs, judgements and desires, the contents of which are not natural, but are determined by the systems of cultural belief, value and moral value of particular communities: 'the capacity to experience either shame or guilt . . . involves cultural knowledge and reasoning conventions' (Coulter, 1979); '. . . our capacity to experience certain emotions is contingent upon our learning to interpret and appraise matters in terms of norms, standards, principles and ends . . . judged desirable . . . or appropriate'" (M. Pritchard, 1976).

For example, when we are angry, we express tenseness, a stern or severe facial expression, and an abrupt manner to those around us. We may also become loud and boisterous, or quiet, withdrawn, and sullen, but whatever combination of reflections we put together, it will have been learned from experiences within our culture as well as those of others. The same emotion may, for example, be expressed by a different combination of signals and affectations in another culture at another time even though the basic emotions are defined as those whose facial manifestations are pan-cultural (Oatley and Johnson-Laird, 1987). To some degree, then, expressing an emotion is playing a role for a short period of time (Sarbin, 1986). The anthology edited by Harre (1986) contains many chapters that illustrate the role of cultural and temporal contexts in our understanding of emotions and their role in human behavior.

Thus, for social constructionists, there are an infinite number of emotions because of the varying social and life events that can interact, all of which are subject to the interpretations of those involved. "In the English language, there are more than 550 concepts that refer more or less directly to emotions. Joy, happiness, delight, awe, wonder, fear, grief, sadness, anger, pride, shame, guilt, surprise, envy are such names for emotions" (Crawford et al., 1992, p. 33).

EMOTIONS, PERCEPTIONS, AND RATIONALITY

A number of myths about emotions bear rejection. One is that emotions are irrational and do not depend on thinking and reasoning (Lazarus and Lazarus, 1994). Nevertheless (or at least to indicate how strongly people feel about the relationship between emotionality and rationality), consider an empirical investigation of Georgetown University students reported by Parrott (1994). He found that when his students were asked to recall a time when they were "emotional" and to describe what it felt like, the most common interpretation provided was that they were "irrational": unable to think clearly, to cope effectively, or to appreciate others' points of view (Parrott, 1994). People seem to think of emotionality and rationality as incompatible. It may simply be a matter of language; that is, what people believe to be states of irrationality may simply be labeled or thought of as states of emotionality, when in other cultures or in other languages the same phenomenological state may not be thought of or defined as "emotional" (see J.A. Russell et al., 1994).

It may have been the pervasiveness of this "myth" that has caused the field to ignore emotions and emotionality to the extent that it has for the past several decades (Ashforth and Humphrey, 1995). So much writing and theorizing about organizations operating under "norms of rationality" (see Thompson, 1967) has affected not only the academic study of work and motivation but the very practice of management. To be rational has been the goal; to be emotional or to be seen as emotional has not been in vogue for many decades. As noted earlier, the venerable Herbert Simon has indicated his belief that even cognitive psychology will now have to embrace emotionality in order to proceed as an academic science (Simon, 1995).

Another myth is that emotionality gets in the way of human adaptation. Emotions are seen as "intimately connected with the fate of our struggles to adapt to life in a world that is not very forgiving of adaptive failure" (Lazarus and Lazurus, 1994, p. 3). For example, in their discussion of the sources of error that can arise when people are taking tests, D. Cooper and Emory (1995, p. 147) state that "respondents may also suffer from temporary factors like fatigue, boredom, *anxiety,* or another distraction; these limit the ability to respond carefully and fully. Hunger, impatience, or *general variations in mood* may also have an impact." Thus, emotions and emotionality are seen as pesky problems that need to be contained and controlled, or they may yield an unreliable assessment of human nature and functioning.[4]

Nevertheless, there is considerable evidence that emotions affect what we *perceive and how well and quickly we perceive things* (see Oatley and Jenkins, 1992, for a summary of the evidence). Thus, people have been found to identify words and emotion-bearing faces more quickly when these words and faces are consistent with the emotions they are experiencing at the time (Niedenthal, Setterlund, and Jones, 1994). Do our emotions influence our capacity to act rationally? Damasio (1994) claims that "there never has been any doubt that, under certain circumstances, emotion disrupts reasoning" (p. 52). Hence people advise one another not to respond immediately to someone who has offended or caused the person injury. "Stay cool," we advise, "sleep on it." This line of thought implies that emotion can only hurt intelligent reasoning. On the other hand, drawing on work that combines neuropsychology and decision analysis, Damasio (1994) argues that reductions in emotions can constitute an equally important source of irrational behavior. As we saw earlier, the actions of certain brain regions are closely related to reasoning and decision making, on the one hand, *and* to human emotional processes, on the other.

Emotionality and Gender

We have suggested that emotions and emotionality are closely linked to culture and to language, making it difficult for us to nail down a pancultural, classically determined definition of emotion. Aside from cultural differences, there is the question of gender differences. Within our Western culture, women are often stereotyped as being more "emotional" than men. This stereotype is problematic for a number of reasons (Fischer, 1994). There is no solid empirical evidence that women experience the most prototypical emotions more often than men do (recall our earlier discussion of the prototype approach to defining emotions). That is, there is no evidence that women are more susceptible than men to anger, happiness, sadness, or disgust. On the other hand, there is some evidence that women may experience certain specific emotions, such as sadness, fear, and uncertainty, more frequently and more intensely than men do (Fischer, 1994). Interestingly, it is the latter class of emotions that is most commonly associated with the "person-on-the-street" concept of emotionality in our culture. "Someone who

---

[4]The author thanks Martin Martens (1995) for bringing D. Cooper and Emory's (1995) statement to his attention.

is sad, crying, or terribly afraid is more likely to be called emotional than a man (or woman) who is angry. An important characteristic that links these so-called 'feminine' emotions is powerlessness: the belief that nothing can be done about the negative situation and that one is helpless. We may *speculate* [emphasis added] that the relatively frequent or intense experience of these emotions by women may also lead them to have knowledge of this domain. On the basis of their larger experience, they may know more about the causes, characteristics, and consequences of these [female] emotions" (Fischer, 1994, pp. 459–460).

There is some evidence that the differences in the ways in which boys and girls are socialized can result in significant differences between men and women in their "emotional expertise" (Fischer, 1994, p. 472). Females in our culture learn to talk about and express emotions more than males do and thus become more familiar with the emotional side of human existence. Men and women may also apply different emotion words (or labels) to the same phenomena because of differences in their early experiences. Whatever differences do exist, however, are not major and should not be overstated. In chapter 8 we will see how gender differences in emotional responses to frustration may be responsible for some of the stereotypes that exist about the effectiveness and suitability of women for managerial jobs. It will be important to keep these developmental, cultural, and linguistic dimensions about the meaning and expression of emotions in mind when we consider people's responses to frustration in the workplace.

Emotional Intelligence

Aside from gender differences, well-educated people with high IQs may or may not be equally competent in dealing with the emotional aspects of their lives. Goleman cites the poor statistical connections between indicators of cognitive skill (e.g., SAT scores, high school grades) in making valid predictions of people's ultimate success in life. In other words, "making it" requires more than simple cognitive intelligence. Goleman (1995) argues that if people are to function effectively with others and to succeed, *emotional intelligence* may be just as important as the more traditional indicators, which are largely cognitive in nature. He defines emotional intelligence as follows: "abilities such as being able to motivate oneself and persist and persist in the face of frustrations; to control impulse and delay gratification; to regulate one's moods and keep distress from swamping the ability to think; to empathize and to hope" (p. 34).

An earlier definition of emotional intelligence is offered by Salovey and Mayer (1990): "the subset of social intelligence that involves the ability to monitor one's own and others' feelings and emotions, to discriminate among them and to use this information to guide one's thinking and actions" (p. 189). For these authors, social intelligence has several dimensions. As we consider these dimensions (or categories), it is worth keeping in mind how the various forms of abilities must contribute to effective performance in most work settings, that is, how possessing or not possessing these skills might make a difference in the way that organizational members get along with one another and are likely to succeed in their careers:

1. *Knowing one's emotions:* self-awareness, recognizing a feeling as it happens
2. *Managing emotions:* handling feelings so they are appropriate in the circumstances; being able to soothe oneself, to shake off gloom, and to generate positive feelings when necessary

3. *Motivating oneself:* being able to energize oneself, to get "into the flow state," to delay gratification and stifle impulsiveness

4. *Recognizing emotions in others:* being empathic, able to sense the feeling states that others are experiencing

5. *Handling relationships:* being able to generate constructive relationships with others, being popular, exerting leadership or support, being able to be a friend

There is no denying the importance of cognitive intelligence in leadership and effective job performance, but the point here is that without minimum levels of these and related emotional abilities, personal effectiveness in work relationships is likely to be attenuated. According to Salovey and Mayer (1990), people with high emotional intelligence may be more creative and better able to plan flexibly, because their periodic mood swings can cause them to "break set" and move their concentration from one issue to another more easily than can people with lower emotional intelligence. People in happy mood states appear to be more successful at creative problem solving and at tasks involving inductive reasoning. People in sadder mood states may be more effective at deductive problem solving, so the capacity to alter one's own emotional state may be a skill that makes some people more creative and productive than others (Salovey, Hsee, and Mayer, 1993). We return to this possibility in chapter 14, where we examine notions of self-regulation more broadly. In short, people who possess high emotional intelligence "can be thought of as having attained at least a limited form of positive mental health. [They] are aware of their own feelings and those of others. They are open to positive and negative aspects of internal experience, are able to label them, and when appropriate, communicate them. Such awareness will often lead to the effective regulation of affect within themselves and others, and so contribute to well being" (Salovey and Mayer, 1990, p. 201).

It seems that most people *believe* that they possess adequate degrees of emotional intelligence and that they can correctly identify emotions in themselves and in others. We tend to assume that we are able to diagnose the emotional events occurring in other people. We believe that we can tell whether they are sad, happy, or fearful, in large part because certain facial and vocal expressions have interpersonal effects that are registered independently of any words spoken (see Oatley and Jenkins, 1992). Despite these beliefs, there is considerable evidence to show that adults differ considerably in terms of these interpersonal sensitivity skills, even though many children do develop them early in life (see Salovey et al., 1993).

Managing One's Emotions

Aside from being in touch with one's emotions and being able more or less accurately to perceive the emotions of others, a major component of emotional intelligence consists of the ability to regulate one's emotions. The simple hedonistic hypothesis that people are happier when they possess more of things they like has been challenged by a series of studies which show that in addition to the possession of desired outcomes, the rates at which we receive such outcomes and the changes that these outcomes imply over our baseline experiences are also critical in determining our satisfaction and pleasure (Salovey et al., 1993). That is, we compare the level of outcomes we have at a given moment with the levels we have had in the past. Positive additions of good things bring pleasure, but after we have grown used to the new level of our circumstances, the pleasure level drops. An employee who receives a sudden 10 percent pay increase may be ecstatic at first, but the joy will probably subside as he grows used to the new level of income. Similarly, when we lose valued commodities, the initial anger tends to diminish with the passing of time. So far, so good: People adapt to their new circumstances more or less readily. In addition, the *faster* things improve, the greater our satisfaction and the happier our mood. If pay increases come quickly, they bring more satisfaction than if they take longer. A person whose house increases in value by $10,000 over a year's time will be happier than a person whose house increases in value by $10,000 over two years (Salovey et al., 1993). So, in addition to positive changes from a baseline position, the rate at which the positive changes occur also makes a difference in our satisfaction (Salovey et al., 1993). Researchers refer to this phenomenon as the *velocity* of change.

There is more. In addition to a high velocity of change, people appear to gain even greater satisfaction when the velocity itself changes from negative to positive. That is, people are happiest when the desired value first decreases and then increases, and they are unhappiest when the velocity changes from positive to negative: "that is, when the desired value first increases and then decreases" (Salovey et al., 1993). We gain most pleasure from watching our favorite sports team win a game after falling behind and then making a valiant comeback to score the winning goal late in the match. By contrast, the pain we feel for our team is especially acute when they blow a lead and lose late in the game.[5] Salovey and his colleagues (1993) conclude: "This dynamic—indeed *emodynamic* view suggests that we are acutely sensitive to the pattern over which outcomes accrue in time, especially to their rate and shifts in that rate" (p. 269). We return to the self-control of emotions in chapter 14, where we examine the broader notion of people's capacity to self-regulate their behavior.

Summary and a Look Ahead

A complete exploration of the current state of research and theory on the matter of the relations between thinking, perceiving, and emoting is well beyond our purpose here. The reason for raising the matter has been to alert the reader not to assume that these processes are separate from or independent of one another. Human behavior, including human work behavior, is generated, directed, and accompanied by a mix of thoughts, feelings, perceptions, habits, and reflexes. Any teacher or manager who attempts to understand the behavior of another person using a strictly cognitive and perceptual orientation will, of necessity, limit the possible depth of understanding that can be attained. Similarly, to rely only on an analysis of another's emotional expressions will limit the analysis that is possible. Having said this, we repeat that the predominant models of psychology over the past many decades have, by and large, ignored the role of emotion in behavior, and that, certainly, most of the research and theorizing on work motivation over that period has been equally limited in its focus.

To this point we have studied a number of definitions of emotions and emotionality and have presented a survey of many of the current (and traditional) points of dis-

---

[5]It is tempting to think of the notions of velocity and increases in velocity in mathematical terms, such as first and second derivatives. In these terms, neohedonism hypothesizes that satisfaction is greatest when both the first and second derivatives of the curve relating a person's level of desired outcome acquisition are both positive, and that dissatisfaction is at its worst when both mathematical terms are negative.

pute among scholars who have considered and written about the nature of emotions in human beings. If we set aside the social constructionist perspective (Crawford et al., 1992; Harre, 1986), however, we find that the remaining more traditional approaches share a number of common elements. For example, there is agreement that emotions involve affect, or feelings, and sometimes these are equated with certain physiological events. There is also agreement that emotions involve cognitions, although there are differing views on the temporal positioning of cognitions in the emotional process. These cognitive elements serve the roles of remembering and/or appraising. Emotions are widely believed to be expressions of inner feelings and to communicate our feelings to others. To varying degrees, there is agreement that emotions can "overcome" us (Crawford et al., 1992, p. 110). In addition, we have seen that different philosophical positions result in different conclusions about whether it is possible to classify emotions into categories, and, if it is possible, how many types of emotions are thought to exist. The social constructionist view claims that there is virtually an infinite number of emotions, so typologies are impossible, even absurd. Of the many views on emotions reviewed above, this author finds the *emotional syndrome* concept of Averill (1982) and Berkowitz (1993a) most useful for our study of work motivation. So, notwithstanding the wisdom of the social constructivists, we will adopt one recently proposed typology of emotions and consider the many ways that emotions may be related to the human motivation to work.

A TYPOLOGY OF EMOTIONS FOR MOTIVATION IN THE WORKPLACE

When we discussed the concepts of instincts and needs in chapter 3, we saw the difficulty of achieving typologies that didn't boil down to tautological lists associated, one to one, with every distinctly possible human act. There is a similar danger when we think of categories of emotions. There are a variety of categorical schemes, or typologies, of emotions, and there are even different approaches to making such typologies (see Frijda, 1986, pp. 72–73, and the debate between J. A. Russell, 1991, and Clore and Ortony, 1991). Moreover, as noted earlier, because of the way they conceive of emotions as formed and enacted by people within unique social and situational settings, social constructionists believe that there are countless emotions. Regardless of the ontological position that one adopts, the author is not aware of any typology of emotions that deals specifically with human work motivation or organizational behavior.

Accordingly, avoiding the intractability of the social constructionist perspective, we draw from a variety of existing typologies found in psychology for the sake of piecing together a list of our own. Many of the emotions to be discussed here come from a list of 15 emotions offered by Lazarus and Lazarus (1994). They begin with three "nasty" emotions: anger, envy, and jealousy. *Anger* occurs over a broad range of intensity, as reflected by the range of nouns used to represent it, such as *rage, fury, wrath, ferocity, indignation,* and *outrage. Hostility* is seen as a predisposition to become angry at someone, although it is not itself an emotion.

Anger can have either positive or negative consequences, although we normally tend to think of the latter. Lazarus and Lazarus (1994) state the following: "The dramatic plot for anger is a *demeaning offence against me or mine.* When we have been slighted, we all have a built-in impulse to retaliate, to extract vengeance for the slight so that our wounded egos can be restored" (p. 20). Thus, anger results from frustration only when the frustrated person believes that the actions of the person who causes the situation are avoidable, deliberate, or arbitrary (Averill, 1982)

Anger is not aggression as such; rather, it is the impulse to aggress. In work settings, anger is one of the primary emotions that accompanies need frustration: the blockage of goal-directed behavior that is intended to satisfy one or more of our needs. In fact, as we will see in chapter 8, the anger that accompanies frustration can be responsible for many acts of aggression, including homicide. Anyone who has been employed for even a short period of time knows that anger is a common emotion experienced in the workplace, because the workplace is usually very central to our lives in general and therefore a forum where our best interests are so often at stake.

Envy is an especially interesting emotion that entails wanting something that someone else has or possesses (Lazarus and Lazarus, 1994, p. 31). The subjective state is a yearning to have or possess the article or item in question. It results from the "negative comparison of oneself with others" (Lazarus and Lazarus, 1994, p. 29). The experience of envy entails both feelings of discontent brought on by another person's superiority (or possession of prized items) and feelings of hostility directed toward the envied person (R. H. Smith, 1991). Envy can be a source of obsession and compulsion or simply a mild, passing phase in which we desire an article of someone's briefly and then forget about it.

People can develop envy over any of a number of things, material or otherwise. Nonmaterial things such as status, education, opportunity, good looks, talent, and youth are examples of traits or characteristics of others that some people covet and envy. To envy is to be human, which is why people often experience a lot of envy in the workplace. In fact, as we will see in detail in chapter 11, people are constantly comparing themselves with others, especially in terms of the relative value of the exchange relationships they have with one another and with their employers. Frequently, of course, an employee will believe that she doesn't have as good a deal as someone else, and a sense of injustice or inequity may develop. R. H. Smith (1991) would argue that the primary emotion that accompanies perceptions and beliefs of injustice is envy. Before we look at envy in the workplace, we examine the third "nasty" emotion, which is related to but somewhat distinct from envy.

Jealousy is similar to envy in many ways, and sometimes the two terms are used synonymously. The critical difference is that envy is a two-person emotion, whereas jealousy "is a three-way triangle in which someone threatens or has taken what we consider ours, most often the affection of a third party" (Lazarus and Lazarus, 1994; Salovey, 1991). Research summarized by Vecchio (1995) suggests that envy is normally accompanied by a sense of inferiority, self-criticism, and a desire to improve (presumably so that the person will become capable of attaining the coveted item). By contrast, jealousy is more likely to be characterized by feelings of suspicion, fear of loss, anger, rejection, and a desire to get even. Envy can exist without jealousy, but jealousy is often accompanied by feelings of envy (Lazarus and Lazarus, 1994; Vecchio, 1995). Van Sommers (1988) summarizes the relationship and the differences between the two emotions by noting that envy is concerned with what we don't have, whereas jealousy concerns what we have but are afraid we might lose.

It would seem that both envy and jealousy would have generally negative effects in the workplace, although it is possible to imagine how each of them might help to mobilize positive reactions: for example, employee coping responses such as taking on more responsibility, developing more realistic assessments of people about whom the jealousy exists, seeking support and collaboration with peers, and so on (Vecchio, 1995). It is clear to this author that envy and jealousy frequently result from unfortunate social relationships in the workplace and, in turn, result in many other unfortunate consequences. For example, envy may cause a person to denigrate the work or status of co-workers. Jealousy (such as of a supervisor) may generate disingenuous behavior, ingratiation, and political behavior that is intended to win the three-way game rather than to pursue legitimate work goals. The reader will readily imagine the difficulties that obsessive envy and jealousy might cause in any social setting, particularly work settings.

Preliminary work reported by Vecchio (1995) reveals that a majority of people with work experience have either encountered envy or jealousy as third parties or have been involved directly as players. To varying degrees, we are all subject to the experience and effects of fundamental human emotions. Nasty emotions are as universal in experience as more pleasant ones. The relevance of envy and jealousy will readily be apparent in many places throughout the book, particularly in chapter 11, where we examine concepts of fairness, equity, and justice.

Although it is not included in Lazarus and Lazarus's (1994) typology, *fear*—defined by Aristotle as a *sense of impending evil* (Frijda, 1986)—is a powerful human emotion witnessed intermittently by all of us (Oatley, 1992). Fear is one of the most important instruments civilizations use to maintain social control. Fear of punishment can be more effective in maintaining or altering behavior than punishment itself (Crawford et al., 1992, p. 92). Naturally, the same dynamics occur in the workplace, so fear frequently plays an important role in human work motivation. In fact, much motivated work behavior is driven by fear: fear of not being able to find a job that one's parents will approve of, fear of not making enough money to sustain a decent living or to pay off one's debts, fear of a supervisor, fear of being revealed as uncommitted to one's company, fear of being fired or laid off, fear of being disciplined or punished for real or alleged violations of company or union rules. Despite the obvious role of fear in work, few, if any, modern theories of work motivation include fear as a factor in explaining human work behavior, so there is little empirical evidence to cite. Nevertheless, we know that many people are driven by fear in many aspects of their work lives.

Fear has been moving nation states to form economic alliances for decades, perhaps for centuries. It is commonplace, even trite, to observe that the world marketplace is getting smaller and that fewer trading blocks with varying arrangements of free trade will characterize the economic and social structure of the decades to come. It seems only a matter of time until the world is divided into three economic–social–military sectors of the sort that George Orwell described in his prophetic novel *1984*. On a global level, fear has compelled nation states to align with each other for the impending competition among these massive economic forces. Not to align with some other state has been portended to result in cataclysm.

Some economists (e.g., Rifkin, 1995) have painted the bleak picture that emerged in recent years regarding the disappearance of jobs and the ultimate elimination of work. Much of the analysis in this book is predicated on the assumed validity of Rifkin's (1995) analysis and others similar to it (e.g., Bridges, 1994). In a world of the sort that these theorists anticipate, fear is likely to become a much more important factor in survival. Certainly, the path to that world will be characterized by a great deal of fear as the processes associated with the elimination of jobs and the end of work come about.

A reader who wishes to get a visceral understanding of the role of fear as a motivator of work behavior should rent and watch such classic movies as *Ben Hur and The Ten Commandments*. Fear and coercion enabled the conquerors of ancient times to enslave and to coerce heavy, dehumanizing, and powerful work energy from countless millions. The system worked: A slave had either to comply with the directives of the managers in charge or suffer the most terrible consequences. The whip and constant supervision under subhuman conditions sufficed for centuries to "motivate" people to work, whether or not they liked the conditions of employment.

The references to ancient slavery and the role of coercion in motivating human work behavior may be viewed as extreme or hyperbolic. They are offered as a dramatic example of how managerial control, backed up by important sanctions to the employees involved, can generate and sustain motivated work behavior. The purpose of this section is to consider the ways by which modern managerial policies and practices extort the same sort of compliant behavior from subordinates in the North American workplace. The whip is no longer used, but the sanctions that relate to fear are still very much in use, and in many work settings, it would appear that the terror, fear, and suffering of underlings differ only by degree, not by type, from the terror, fear, and suffering of the slaves of yore and the slaves emancipated in the United States after the Civil War. Fear is certainly rampant among illegal immigrant laborers and countless people working at minimum wage in sweatshops everywhere. Fear is the predominant emotion that motivates adherence to organizational rules and regulations. By extension, it is the principal emotion instigated when organizational discipline and punishment are administered for rule violation (see chapter 11).

A former premier of the province of British Columbia was once quoted as saying that "all human behavior is motivated by just two things: greed and fear." The author suspects that Premier W. A. C. Bennett was not the originator of this pithy insight because it has appeared in a variety of places. Regardless of its source, however, the point is important. In many ways, people work to acquire wealth, and greed causes the accumulation of as much material wealth by any person as possible. Meanwhile, the person develops mortal fear that someone else will take away that wealth, someone who, in turn, is driven by the forces of his own greed. Like all generalizations, the aphorism oversimplifies reality, but its very existence requires that we consider the powerful forces of fear, envy, and jealousy in human behavior, especially as they are enacted in the workplace.

Anxiety, guilt, and *shame* are three "existential" emotions discussed by Lazarus and Lazarus (1994)—existential in the sense that "the threats on which they are based have to do with meanings and ideas about who we are, our place in the world, life and death, and the quality of our existence" (p. 41). *Anxiety,* which they link with the notion of *fright,* involves our personal security, our personal identity as individuals, as well as concerns about life and death. Symptoms of anxiety are apprehension, unease, concern, worry, and a sense of insecurity. The anxious person has a vague sense that there is something wrong with her life but is uncertain as to what the problem is. She is unable to relax, not knowing if and when harm will befall her and, if it does, what form it will take.

One of the more common sources of anxiety in work settings has to do with changes in work procedures or in one's job. Lazarus and Lazarus (1994) observe: "Anxiety is provoked when the meanings on which we have come to depend are undermined, disrupted or endangered. If the threat to these meanings seems great, and the endangered meanings are fundamental to our being, the resulting anxiety can be intense and constitute an important personal crisis" (p. 47). Consider the anxiety a person faces upon being hired into a new job or being transferred to a new location: new faces, new people, new role expectations, new political structure, few or no work friends (see Louis, 1980; Pinder and Walter, 1984).[6] A great deal of information seeking occurs (Ashford, 1986; Ashford and Cummings, 1983, 1985; D. C. Feldman and Brett, 1983; V. D. Miller and Jablin, 1991), and usually, it is only a matter of time until the newcomer "learns the ropes" at the new job or location, and things work out well. The social support provided by new co-workers and supervisors plays an especially important role until the newcomer adjusts and can become productive (Pinder and Schroeder, 1987).

One recent study found, for example, that newcomers both watched established employees and questioned them to acquire five types of information intended to help assuage the newcomers' anxiety: (1) technical information (about how to perform their jobs); (2) referent information (i.e., information about the demands of their roles and the expectations that people place on them); (3) normative information (about expected behaviors and attitudes); (4) feedback about their performance; and (5) feedback about their acceptability regarding the social, nontask aspects of their behavior at work. The results also showed that positive job attitudes, better job performance, and lower levels of intention to leave the job were related to the amount of information that newcomers sought (E. W. Morrison, 1993).

There are many other work-related and career situations that can generate fear and anxiety among people, the most traumatic of which is job loss or its possibility and the prospect of long-term unemployment (see chapter 11). Part-time and temporary workers face constant, although varying levels of uncertainty about their employment status, never being quite sure how long they will remain employed, or if they lose their current employment, whether and with whom future employment opportunities might arise. In short, anxiety is a universally distributed and experienced emotion, one that plays a central role in the attitudes, feelings, and behavior of people at work.

For Lazarus and Lazarus (1994), *guilt* is similar to anxiety, and may sometimes even be seen as a form of anxiety. They state that "guilt is as much a product of what is going on in our minds as it is about what is happening in our lives" (p. 52). Guilt centers on our moral lapses, fueled by our consciences. "To experience guilt, people must feel that they have transgressed a moral code that has been accepted as part of their own set of values, whether they have or have not done anything wrong—it is the believing that matters" (p. 55). "Guilt feeling is characterized as . . . painful self-evaluation due to some action evaluated negatively and for which action the person holds himself responsible" (Frijda, 1986, p. 201). For example, a person who claims to believe in religious precepts such as the Ten Commandments will experience guilt whenever he believes he has violated one of them. At the societal level, guilt is a useful emotion because it helps restrict socially undesirable behavior. It helps prevent people from breaking laws or moral codes. People who are prone to guilt are generally more honest

---

[6]Martin Martens, currently a doctoral student in my university department, claims that the same emotions are experienced by new doctoral students.

than those who are not, hence may make more dependable and trustworthy employees. In addition, guilt-prone employees are more likely than others to consider how they might have acted differently once they have broken a company rule or norm (see Frijda, 1986, p. 431).

In chapter 8 we will see how frustration at the workplace often results in violent behavior and/or aggressive acts against the organization, such as theft and sabotage. Other things being equal, guilt-prone employees would be less likely to engage in such acts. In fact, the author speculates that susceptibility to feelings of guilt must lie behind much of the loyalty that highly committed employees display toward their employers (see chapter 10). People who are raised to embrace work values such as the "Protestant work ethic" seem especially prone to feeling guilty about work. Fear of guilt feelings may help explain a considerable proportion of their commitment to work in general, in addition to their loyalty to their employers. The author knows of no research to support these conjectures, but they seem plausible. In short, guilt hurts those who experience it but benefits those with whom the guilt-prone person interacts.

What about the emotion we refer to as *shame?* It consists of varying degrees of feelings of mortification, embarrassment, ridiculousness, and/or humiliation (Lazarus and Lazarus, 1994, p. 63). "Shame is caused by some act that should have been left undone (or done so as not to be noticed)" (Frijda, 1986, p. 168). Because it is similar in many ways to guilt, psychologists avoided drawing distinctions between the two emotions until relatively recently.

Like guilt, shame is most likely to be experienced when a person fails to live up to a standard. In the case of shame, the standard may or may not be a widely held or espoused value. The standard arises from the ego-ideal of the person involved. If the person has an image of herself as courageous, street smart, a bold warrior, and tough-minded, acting in ways that violate that ideal may result in shame (the examples are taken from Lazarus and Lazarus, 1994). Ego-ideals are the characterizations we might like to have said about us, or written in our obituaries, after we are dead. Being caught violating our ego-ideal brings us shame, and we tend to hide it. The threat underlying shame is criticism, rejection, or abandonment (H. B. Lewis, 1992, cited by Lazarus and Lazarus, 1994, p. 64). A person who transgresses may feel guilt even if no one is aware of the failure. He may also feel shame when others are aware of the misdeed or when he believes that others are aware.

As we just suggested, one of the common means used to cope with shame is denial. The person merely denies that he has done anything wrong, externalizing the causes for anything that has obviously gone wrong (Lazarus and Lazarus, 1994, p. 66). People who do this will become angry with others who charge them with miscreance and imply that the guilty party is, in fact, guilty. By contrast, guilt is more likely to compel us to seek publicity that will allow us to atone for our sins (p. 64).

How does shame enter our thinking about work motivation? In practical terms, it is so closely related to guilt that many of the ideas we expressed in relation to guilt could also be related to shame. Clearly, small doses of either emotion, or low to moderate tendencies to experience either one of them, may be healthy for any of us. But to be guilt- or shame-ridden is dysfunctional, and people so afflicted are not likely to be able to communicate effectively or be taken seriously by those around them. Large doses and frequent intervals of shame, in particular, are likely to result in mistrust, a lack of trustworthiness, and ineffective work behavior.

Lazarus and Lazarus (1994) discuss a number of emotions that are provoked by unfavorable life conditions, including, hope, sadness, and depression. *Hope* is an emotion that involves promise, expectation, and anticipation. Lazarus and Lazarus (1994, p. 72) describe hope as an "antidote to despair." "Hope may be sustained when there is some possibility that the outcome you wish for might occur, when you have not given up . . . and start despairing" (p. 72). Again: "The personal meaning of hope is that one believes that there is a possibility that things will get better, however, bleak they may seem at the moment" (p. 72). These authors claim that the usual provocation for an emotional experience of hope is an unfavorable life condition whose outcome is uncertain, yet in which there is a chance that there will be a reversal of fate—an increase in the odds that things will improve.

What is the role of hope in work motivation? The question seems almost not worth asking. People hope that they will be able to find jobs after periods of unemployment, they hope that they will be able to improve their relationships with co-workers and superiors, they hope that they will be promoted and/or given a chance to enter programs that will develop their skills, they hope that they will be able to earn enough money and pension funds to be able to retire comfortably. Hope springs eternal in almost all aspects of work for most people. In chapters 12 and 13, where we discuss expectancy-based theories of work motivation and goal setting, respectively, we examine a number of cognitive concepts such as expectancy and self-efficacy whose experience must be accompanied by the emotion of hope. Lest we forget during that discussion, we make the point here: Work motivation is a matter of more than needs, beliefs, cognitive events, and values. Emotions are collateral events that are very human and that provide much of the color of motivation to work. Hope can be a strong emotional factor in work motivation.

Sadness and *depression* are two more emotions that figure largely in the picture of work motivation. Sadness is an emotion that is felt following the loss of something significant that we think cannot be retrieved or restored (Lazarus and Lazarus, 1994, p. 78). Probably the most extreme example comes with the death of a loved one, but the same emotion occurs, to varying degrees, in reaction to the loss of other valued commodities or elements of one's life, such as a job. In chapter 11 we discuss job loss at length, including the emotional and attitudinal reactions of both victims and survivors of job loss, both as it occurs "for cause"—as a matter of dismissal for poor performance, insubordination, or rule violation—or for the sake of downsizing by an organization trying to cut costs.

Grieving is defined by Lazarus and Lazarus (1994) as the process of coping with a loss (p. 79), although they suggest that the concept is used most commonly in reference to loss due to death of a loved one. Nevertheless, organizational downsizing and reengineering result in tremendous losses to millions of people. Sadness has been felt by many people as their hopes have been dashed and they have been faced with serious uncertainty concerning themselves, their careers, and the safety of their dependents.

Depression is defined as emotional but not as a specific emotion itself (Lazarus and Lazarus, 1994, p. 82). Instead, it is a composite of a number of other emotions, including anger, anxiety, and guilt. We know that depression is a serious emotional condition that can result from job loss and unemployment and that can lead to severe consequences, including suicide (Ahlberg, 1986; Ahlberg and Shapiro, 1983–1984).

Remember that there are many different typologies of emotions; the one by Lazarus and Lazarus (1994) generally being followed here is only one of many that might be invoked for an exploration of the feeling side of work motivation and the experiences of people in the workplace. We turn next to a set of emotions that they describe as the "happy" emotions. What is happy about work?

Happiness is a strong emotion that many of us witness through our work and our careers. Like the others, this emotion can vary in intensity and duration. Hence we see a wide range of synonyms for happiness, all the way from terms such as *joyous* and *jubilant* to less extreme feelings such as *carefree* or *amused* (Lazarus and Lazarus, 1994, p. 89). Different things make different people happy, although there are some events that seem to be widespread as sources of happiness, such as when we are paid a compliment, when we are shown that we are loved, when we are promoted, or when we see our loved ones doing well. Happiness can be conceived of as a temporary emotional state and as a more long-term mood which stands for a sort of calculation of how well we are doing in life in general. It is a general assessment of our quality of life (Lazarus and Lazarus, 1994, p. 89).

Work can lead to happiness in many ways. It can result from the sheer experience of working (in which case we would think of the phenomenon referred to as *intrinsic motivation* (see chapter 7). It might result from the joyous interactions we have with the people at work, in which case we think of the gregarious side of our beings and the social needs discussed in chapters 5 and 6). We might find that happiness comes from the satisfaction of our needs for power, sex, or esteem. Lazarus and Lazarus (1994, p. 96) cite evidence that positive, happy moods contribute to our thinking effectiveness as well as to our relationships with other people. We tend to be more considerate and helpful toward others. We feel more inclined to see problems as challenges rather than as hassles, and we are somewhat less inhibited. On the other hand, unhappy moods can make us self-centered and defensive. The point is that work can be a very happy and satisfying experience for people, subject to only minor and infrequent interludes of unhappiness. In fact, national surveys continue to show that most North Americans are, in fact, satisfied with their jobs (see Firebraugh and Harley, 1995; Watson Wyatt Worldwide, 1995). As discussed at length in chapter 10, job and career dissatisfaction can be extremely aversive states that can spill over into the rest of our lives. Interestingly, happiness is one of the few emotions that has been taken seriously in the modern literature on work motivation, figuring into the widely adopted definition of job satisfaction advanced by Locke (1969).

Pride is another (generally) positive human emotion that accompanies work experiences and affects the motivation to work. Pride entails the "enhancement of one's ego-identity by taking credit for a valued object or achievement, either our own or that of someone or of a group with whom we identify—for example, a compatriot, a member of the family, or a social group" (Lazarus, 1991, p. 271). Pride is different from happiness in that pride entails a confirmation of personal worth, a boost to our egos that is missing from the emotion we typically call happiness (Lazarus, 1991, p. 271). Pride (as well as happiness) typically compels us to become expansive and to share the experience with other people. In this way it is somehow the opposite of shame, which compels us to hide from others. As with all emotions, it is the personal meaning that a person attaches to an event that determines whether pride is experienced. The objective truth of a person's circumstances is only part of the picture.

Lazarus and Lazarus (1994) point out that pride is a sort of "competitive" emotion "because it centers on the need to protect and enhance our personal identity" (p. 101).

As a result, pride can sometimes be a negative emotion, because it can amount to stubbornness, preventing people from apologizing for mistakes they make or from forgiving the mistakes made by others. How does pride figure into work motivation? There are a variety of possible roles for pride at work. Pride can be experienced when we receive compliments on our work, or when we perform well and simply know that we did, without the help of praise from outsiders. Pride can be instigated when a person's ability is challenged, doubted, or denigrated. Pride can be hurt when we are disciplined or punished on the job. Pride can be dashed when we are dismissed from our jobs.

We often hear the phrase *pride of workmanship.* The English author John Galsworthy (1867–1933) tells a poignant story of a young man who purchased his boots from a German bootmaker who believed in quality (Galsworthy, 1927). Once when the boy ordered a pair of custom-made boots from the old craftsman, he asked: "Isn't it awfully hard to do, Mr. Gessler?" The older man gave the lad a sudden smile and replied "Id is an Ardt!" The good boots lasted a long time and later the boy returned to the German's shop, only to find that the old man had recently died. The new occupant of the shop reported that the German bootmaker had starved to death because he wouldn't allow anyone else to participate in making boots for his customers, he spent untold hours making each pair, and he simply could not compete with mass producers who easily made a profit at the trade. In response to the competition, the old man simply redoubled his efforts and cut his costs by cutting off the heat in his shop and, ultimately, the nourishment he provided his own body.

Hubris is an extreme form of pride that is not completely justified by one's accomplishments. It can often lead to the downfall of the prideful person. For example, an employee who brags at length about the quality of his work may bring undue attention to the work—attention that reveals that it is flawed.

Love is another (generally) happy emotion that is also conceived of as a need, as we saw in the early part of the chapter. Since we discuss love and intimate relationships in the workplace extensively in chapter 5 we will not go into the matter here. It suffices to note only that love happens frequently in the workplace, as does the heartache that comes with the withdrawal of love and from unrequited love.

Gratitude is an interesting emotion discussed by Lazarus and Lazarus (1994). It is provoked when one receives material help in the form of money, information, assistance, advice, or some other form of social support. It is generally a mildly felt emotion rather than a strong passion. People feel gratitude when others around them provide such resources without apparent personal motive. That is, the motives of the provider must be experienced as selfless or empathic. Gratitude may be experienced when one person performs a job for another at a level above and beyond the call of duty.

Gratitude was a primary emotional rationale lying behind many of the tenets of the old human relations movement. A "law" of that movement has always been that satisfied employees are more productive employees, presumably in part because satisfied employees are grateful to employers who treat them well. We will see that the simple belief linking satisfaction and performance is just that—oversimplified—unless we define the concept of "performance" broadly to include more than just individual productivity (see Brief and Motowidlo, 1986, for a discussion of a variety of "prosocial organizational behaviors," as well as chapter 10). Similarly, gratitude is probably one of the most important emotions that accompanies (and/or causes) loyalty and commitment to an employer. In chapter 10 we discuss organizational commitment at length. It will be good to keep emotions in mind at that point, as well as the more cognitively oriented aspects of organizational commitment.

Many of the devices and rituals that an organization's management can use to build commitment among employees may work because they are effective at generating feelings of gratitude on the part of employees. On the other hand, it follows that such tactics may backfire and result not in gratitude but in cynicism among workers if they believe that the kindnesses of management are *intended* to build commitment (see Isen and Baron, 1991; Van Maanen and Kunda, 1989). A manager may elect not to displace (or "outplace") a worker at a time of economic exigency out of a sense of compassion for the worker, so feelings of gratitude may be in order as long as it is clear that the manager's decision was intended primarily to benefit the worker in question. In such a case it is clear that gratitude on the part of the worker is an understandable and justified emotional reaction that may, in fact, result in redoubled effort and increased loyalty and devotion. Similarly, work above and beyond the call of duty may generate feelings of gratitude in the heart of the manager overseeing the work, because she believes that the extra effort and attention to excellence is offered by the workers as a selfless act, intended to make the manager look good to her superiors. Gratitude would seem to be called for in such cases.

The author's position on the matter is that in times of severe competition and downsizing, gratitude to an employer becomes an especially interesting and complicated matter. It is up to the person to decide on a day-by-day basis whether he chooses to be grateful to any particular co-workers, whether they are peers, superiors, or subordinates. But caution must be exercised if and when a person begins to feel gratitude (or any other emotion) in relation to an organization. The reason for caution is that to emote toward an organization as one would toward a human being is to anthropomorphize the organization—to attribute human qualities to it, qualities that an organization does not possess. It is a mistake to anthropomorphize organizations, to think about and relate to them as if they are human beings with minds, hearts, and memories. Notwithstanding all the recent theory about "organizational memory" (see, e.g., Walsh and Ungson, 1991) and "organizational learning" (see Fiol and Lyles, 1985; Pennings, Barkema, and Douma, 1994; Senge, 1990), it is *individuals* who treat one another well or badly. It is individual people who should be the recipients of our gratitude or our rage in relation to our work experiences. A person who "falls in love" with or becomes angry toward an organization is fooling herself: No organization has a mind, a memory, a conscience, or a heart. Specific individuals within organizations possess these human traits, but it makes no more sense to emote toward an organization than it does toward a piece of iron. The necessary properties of human nature are not contained in an organization per se any more than they are contained in the iron. We say more on this matter in chapter 10.

Lazarus and Lazarus (1994) refer to *compassion* as a "uniquely human emotion" (p. 122). Similar to compassion are concepts such as sympathy, pity, and empathy, although they are not the same. When a person is compassionate, he understands that another human being is suffering and deserves help. Awareness of the plight and suffering of another is what triggers compassion. The emotion is particularly strong when the person doing the emoting has had experiences similar to those of the person perceived to be suffering. Compassion may also be more readily instigated when the person in trouble is someone we love. Things are more complicated when the troubled person is a stranger (Lazarus and Lazarus, 1994).

Earlier in this chapter we discussed the issue of whether cognitions precede emotions or whether emotions can be experienced independently of cognitions. We also noted that in the debate between Lazarus (1984) and Zajonc (1980, 1984) on the matter, the issue may depend primarily on how we define *cognition.* Nevertheless, when we consider compassion as an emotion and its role in instigating human behavior, the question of the primacy of either cognitions or emotions comes to the fore.

The author was recently at a cocktail party when the topic of intervening in emergencies came up. We discussed the case of Deletha Word, the woman whose car hit another car early one Sunday morning in Detroit in September 1995. The occupant of the second car attacked Ms. Word with an iron bar and chased her off a bridge into the Detroit River, where she drowned despite the efforts of two bystanders to save her (Grant and Wark, 1995). The timeliness of the discussion, given the author's writing activities that week, was fortuitous and prompted the question: "If you had been present at that incident, would you have jumped into the river to save the drowning woman strictly on the basis of emotional reaction, or would you have stopped, even for an instant, to consider what was happening and what to do about it?" Eight adults were present, and all eight answered quickly. Six said they would have reacted on the "basis of impulse," "automatically," or on the "basis of instinct." Only two said they would have "stopped to think about it." Of course, we can never be sure whether we would act the way we think we would to a hypothetical situation being described in the warmth of a friend's living room. It would be another matter to be faced with the real thing (see Nisbett and Wilson, 1977). The point is that compassion would have been the primary emotion at work when Lawrence Walker and Orlando Brown actually dove into the river to try to save Ms. Word. The force of that compassion is even more impressive when we consider that both of the "good Samaritans" who made the rescue attempt had recently been in trouble with the law and, on logical grounds alone, may have reasoned that to become involved would expose them to further contact with the police (Grant and Wark, 1995). Compassion is, indeed, a very human emotion.

Examples of the relationship between compassion and work motivation are common. Compassion must enter a person's decision-making process during the early stages of selecting an occupation and pursuing an education to realize that occupation. It is relatively easy to imagine that compassion figures into the decisions that people make to pursue health care, social work, education, law enforcement, and other careers where helping other people is a (or *the*) primary goal. It is less obvious whether compassion affects the choice of other occupations, but it must be operative to some degree inasmuch as economies are based on exchanges of goods and services between parties.

Compassion may also account for many of the instances of *prosocial behavior* we observe in work settings, instances in which people work above and beyond the call of duty in the service of customers and clients (see Organ, 1990). Two studies shed partial light on this possibility. Although these studies did not examine compassion, as such, they did address the role of emotion in prosocial organizational behavior. The first of these studies (Organ and Konovsky, 1989) failed to find a link between employees' "typical mood states" and the occurrence of prosocial acts. The second study (George, 1991) *did* find that when mood was assessed as a transitory state rather than as an ongoing, stable trait, there was a connection between affect and prosocial acts. The author is not aware of any work that addresses the specific effects of compassion (or of any other specific emotion, for that matter) on the willingness or tendency of workers to provide services that exceed the formal expectations of a job. For that matter, we have noted repeatedly the paucity of empirical work that deals with the role of any emotions in work motivation. As we will see shortly, evidence has been collected that supports the idea that positive mood states are beneficial for organizational functioning, largely through the favorable impact they can have on cooperation and communication in the workplace (Isen and Baron, 1991). Finally, compassion may be an emotion that we can develop after having held positions in careers where we see people suffer and experience difficulty. In this sense, compassion may be both a cause and a consequence of our work experiences.

We complete our discussion of Lazarus and Lazarus's (1994) typology of emotions by a look at the emotions that are aroused by *aesthetic experiences* on the job. This final category is different from most of the others we have examined because there is no single emotion related to our contact with beautiful music, good food, a stirring screenplay, or a spectacular sunset. In fact, the particular emotion(s) that is/are aroused after experiencing something aesthetically appealing will depend primarily on the particular meaning the person places on it (much as in the case of other emotional events, but more so in this case). Hence, when we encounter something that is aesthetically appealing, any or many of the other emotions we have listed and discussed above may come into our experiences, either alone or in sequence. Again, the particular emotions felt will vary from person to person as well as within the same person on different occasions, depending on the meaning attributed to the stimulus at any given time. For example, a favorite song may bring joy when it is experienced by a young man when he is in the company of his sweetheart, but the same song may bring heartache and sorrow when he hears it after she has left his life. The meaning depends on the circumstances and people involved.

We have observed the lack of attention by researchers to the emotional aspects of work motivation and organizational behavior. Aesthetic experiences associated with work and motivation are perhaps the least well understood. Sandelands and Buckner (1989) have recently attempted to begin to fill the void by drawing associations between aspects of work and the work process on the one hand and art on the other. They cite literature from history, management, and organizational behavior in an attempt to explore what work feels like to people who perform it. The issue for them is not one of "How do you like your job?"; rather, it is one of "How do you feel when you are on your job?" It is a matter of work feelings rather than of feelings about work (p. 125). For Sandelands and Buckner, aesthetic experience is not antithetical to the experience of everyday work life, with all of its typically practical values and goals. They claim that the practical and the aesthetic can be experienced simultaneously, especially when the work is done well. They cite Henri (1923), who wrote: "Art . . . is the province of every human being. It is simply a question of doing things, anything, well. It is not an outside, extra thing. When the artist is alive in any person, whatever his kind of work may be, he becomes an inventive, searching, daring, self-expressing creature. . . . He does not have to be an artist. He can work in any medium. He simply has to find the gain in the work itself, not outside it" (Henri, 1923, p. 15, cited by Sandelands and Buckner, 1989, p. 118).

Sandelands and Buckner (1989) also argued that the passion for "excellence" that was a popular management theme during the 1980s and early 1990s (see Peters and Waterman, 1982) had an artistic, aesthetic quality. In chapter 7 we explore the meaning of concepts referred to as *intrinsic motivation* and *intrinsic satisfaction*. These are motivational forces and sources of satisfaction that emerge from the performance of work for its own sake. There is an element of play or playfulness related to these concepts that is somewhat distinct from the instrumental satisfactions and emotions that derive from the recognition and rewards from outside sources. There is also a strong element of feeling of control over one's fate and of making things happen according to one's preferences that feels good when we are working (see Deci and Ryan, 1985, and chapters 7 and 13 of this book).

Summary

In the foregoing sections we discussed the possible relationships between a variety of human emotions distilled and listed by Lazarus and Lazarus (1994) and the motivation to work. Many aspects of work and work motivation were brought to bear in the analysis, such as the motivation to seek and hold a job or career, the motivation to start one's own business, the desire to perform one's job well and with excellence and pride, and the notion of performing above and beyond the call of one's formal job requirements. We also considered how emotions can originate in either one's work life or outside of it and then follow the individual from either of these fora to the other. We have seen how emotions may help to cause and explain work motivation and organizational behavior or result from motivated effort and work experience.

    We have acknowledged repeatedly that little has been done to research and build theory regarding emotions and work motivation. Accordingly, much of the foregoing discussion was speculative and hypothetical. The author hopes that it will help to stimulate researchers and theorists to resurrect emotions and emotionality in their own work and to alert managers to pay closer attention to the emotional side of the workplace in their daily practice. The premise has been that work is an emotional part of people's lives. As obvious as that premise appears, we need to pay a lot more attention to it and to the implications that follow from it. In the next section we look briefly at some of the work that has been done in the area of managing emotions in the workplace.

THE BENEFITS OF POSITIVE AFFECT

At this point we can ask why we should be concerned with positive emotional states among employees. The answer lies in the following. There is a growing body of evidence that supports the idea that positive employee emotional states contribute to organizational effectiveness. At a glance, this seems obvious. At a closer look, it is clear that we know very little about *how* positive affect influences work motivation, performance, or organizational effectiveness. Isen and Baron (1991) have reviewed the research evidence on the matter and have concluded that

> positive affect, defined as pleasant feelings induced by commonplace events or circumstances, has been found to exert significant effects on several aspects of social behavior. For example, positive affect usually increases a person's tendency to help others and reduces aggression. Positive affect also facilitates recall of material in memory with a positive tone, increases efficiency in making some types of decisions, broadens the range of material individuals think about in response to stimuli, and promotes innovation and creative problem solving. . . . [This can result in effectiveness at] face-to-face bargaining, preference for various modes of resolving interpersonal conflicts . . . evaluations of ratees, and task perception and satisfaction. (p. 1)

It makes intuitive sense that someone who is basically happy about life is likely to be ready to deal with the difficulties of modern work life.[7] At the minimum, it makes even more sense to expect that someone who is not happy, someone with negative emotions such as guilt, shame, jealousy, and envy, is less likely to be effective on the job and, certainly, less popular as a co-worker, making the relationships of work groups and teams awkward and ineffective. The point here is that people are, by definition, more or less emotional by nature, and these emotions can affect their behavior in life, their motivation to work, and their work behavior. This may seem obvious to a reader in the late 1990s, but in fact, affect, emotion, and the "softer" side of people have generally been neglected in theorizing about work motivation during the past half-century.

For example, it is believed that people who characteristically are emotionally positive tend to be more satisfied with their jobs, more productive in their jobs (T. A. Wright and Staw, 1994),[8] and experience lower rates of burnout (Iverson, Deery, and Erwin, 1994). Aside from satisfaction and productivity, positive affectivity and positive mood may have other work-related benefits. For example, a recent longitudinal Australian study of unionized blue-collar production and assembly workers found that employees who were assessed to have high positive affectivity enjoyed reduced rates of injury on the job a year later. In addition, employees with high rates of negative affectivity experienced increased levels of injury a year after their affectivity was measured (Iverson and Erwin, 1995).

Positive affectivity may even influence work motivation itself. George and Brief (1996) have spelled out in careful and creative detail just *how* this may be so. Many of the details of their thinking are presented in chapter 12 (in the context of valence-instrumentality-expectancy theory). The basic idea is that people who are in positive mood states see things differently from people who are not as upbeat. These differences in perceptions can affect the way people think about their desire to undertake particular jobs, as well as their beliefs about whether they will be able to perform the jobs well.

In addition to their arguments about the possible direct effects of mood on motivation, George and Brief (1992) have also developed a theoretical argument claiming that people with positive mood states in the workplace are more likely to engage in what they call *spontaneous behavior*. This consists of five different forms of prosocial work behavior: helping co-workers, protecting the organization from threats and damage, making constructive suggestions, developing oneself in skills that will benefit the organization and one's career, and spreading goodwill with regard to the organization. As we saw earlier, the evidence from psychology on moods and emotions justifies the arguments and hypotheses advanced by George and Brief (1992, 1996), so it would now seem to be time for many of their insights to be tested directly. The author suspects that direct testing of these and related ideas would prove positive and fruitful.

There does seem to be something of benefit to being a generally positive person when we consider the many good and bad things that can occur at work. We explore the concepts of positive and negative affectivity and their role in job satisfaction in chapter 10.

---

[7]Jennifer Cliff (personal communication, 1996) notes that a degree of healthy skepticism, perhaps even cynicism, is also required for one's success and mental health in modern work organizations. The author agrees with this position.

[8]It is important to note that T. A. Wright and Staw (1994) found a positive relationship between productivity and indicators of *dispositional* positive affect but that there was no relationship between *state* positive attitudes and performance.

THE MANAGEMENT OF EMOTIONS AT WORK

The forced expression of happiness, pleasure, and joy is a job requirement for thousands of employees in many modern work settings, especially those who work in boundary-spanning roles (Rafaeli and Sutton, 1987; Wharton and Erickson, 1993). Using Disneyland as an example, Van Maanen and Kunda (1989) provide colorful detail about how young employees must "put on a happy face" under virtually all circumstances while running the rides at the theme park and serving its visitors on a daily basis. They describe how internal police forces assure that the happy faces are always engaged and that the young people representing the Disney experience are always at their most (apparent) cheerful emotional best. The authors detail how this enforced and contrived joy and effervescence is maintained, guarded, and disciplined. How often or for how long, for example, can a 22-year-old woman express the same uniform joy and vicarious excitement while witnessing families from around the world discovering the thrills of "Pirates of the Caribbean"?

In private-sector businesses, customer satisfaction is the immediate goal. Long-term economic survival is the ultimate goal. Employees who conform to the practices of contrived emotional display are rewarded. Those who do not comply are typically dismissed (see Van Maanen and Kunda, 1989). In fact, many formalized management rituals and events, such as parties, retreats, and picnics, have as their major goal the expression and development of the set of emotions that management wishes workers to adopt. In the case of professional employees, masking of one's emotions is critical, and violations of this norm are patently unprofessional (see Wharton and Erickson, 1993). A matter of managing "organizational culture," these formal functions are intended to teach employees what to emote, as well as when and how to emote (Isen and Baron, 1991; Van Maanen and Kunda, 1989). People who must project one range of emotions in their personal lives and a different range of emotions when they are at work must be especially flexible in order to be effective in their various life roles (Wharton and Erickson, 1993).

A 22-year-old student told the author recently that he was holding down two part-time jobs. During the day he worked for a store that sells hiking gear, clothing, and equipment. It is a sales-driven job in which the clerks are supposed to help customers with friendly sales pitches and helpful, smiling advice about what equipment to buy, how to use it, and so on. After his shift at the store is finished, the student works as a server at a "steak and beer" restaurant noted for its emphasis on suggestion sales, friendly *smiling* service, and close pseudopersonal attention to diners' needs. Says the student: "Some days, I just can't do it. There is only so much you can smile and put on a phony face. Sometimes, I'm actually too tired or bored or pissed off at the world to pretend I am happy, but my jobs both require that I pretend that I am really happy, all the time."

In any other circumstances, such behavior would be called manipulation, intimidation, duplicity, phoniness, even unethical. For our purposes it is often a matter of required work behavior, driven by reward and punishment schedules which assure that all patrons and customers go home happy and harbor desires to return for more of the same (contrived) treatment. The bind that manipulated emotions place on employees who must return to their lives outside the workplace, often facing emotion-management roles and expectations of their own at home, can be pernicious (Wharton and Erickson, 1993). Hochschild (1983) notes that workers in such situations lose more control of their work and of themselves than do most employees. As we will see later in the book, feelings of self-control and self-determination are critical elements of both work motivation and people's self-esteem.

More than a decade ago, Hochschild (1983) coined the term *emotional labor* to represent "the management of feeling to create observable facial and bodily display; emotional labor is sold for a wage and therefore has exchange value" (p. 7). This is the sort of contrived emotion and emotional expression that Van Maanen and Kunda (1989) describe. Hochschild (1983) makes great use of the emotional labor demanded by airline managers of their flight attendants to illustrate the concept. Attendants are told to smile, smile, smile. "Now girls, I want you to go out there and really *smile*. Your smile is your biggest *asset*. I want you to go out there and use it. Smile. *Really* smile. Really *lay it on*" (p. 4). These smiles are not a genuine indicator of the flight attendants' actual beliefs about their jobs or about how they feel with regard to serving passengers. The smiles are *on* the workers, not *of* them (p. 8). Hochschild estimated at that time (in 1983) that approximately one-third of all American workers had jobs that expose them to "substantial" demands for emotional labor and that the proportion is closer to one-half among working American women (p. 11). A more recent estimate claims that "services account for approximately three-fourths of the gross national product and nine out of every ten jobs the economy creates" (Zeithaml, Parasuraman, and Berry, 1990, cited by Wharton, 1993). Hochschild refers to the false presentation of emotions in emotional labor as a *transmutation* of one's emotional system. She discusses at length the individual and social costs of this process when it is conducted widely and regularly. Her complaints concern the loss of people's privacy, their sense of credibility and genuineness vis-à-vis the world, self-concepts, and sense of personal worth. In short, for Hochschild, emotional labor is akin to exploitation and the sort of alienation portended by writers such as Jean-Jacques Rousseau and Karl Marx—not a good thing.

Ten years later, another empirical study of bank employees and health-care workers provided partial support for Hochschild's claims (Wharton, 1993). This survey found greater levels of emotional exhaustion and strain among employees in occupations that Hochschild had classified as high risk than those she had classified as low risk. Wharton (1993) did not find, however, greater levels of emotional exhaustion among workers in emotional-labor job categories who were either women or who had partners at home. In fact, she found that women who perform emotional labor were significantly more satisfied with their jobs than were their male counterparts in similar types of work. Finally, Wharton found that the effects of emotional labor may be somewhat mitigated by the degree of an employee's level of job involvement, autonomy on the job, and capacity to self-monitor.

The major points of this section are the following. Managers and owners realize the importance of expressed positive emotion on the part of their employees. In addition, the proportion of the jobs in our economy in which emotional labor is required is high and growing as North America advances services more and more. There are many philosophical, theoretical, and empirical reasons to believe that performing emotional labor is hard on those who must do it, although there is some evidence that the negative effects vary from person to person. Interestingly, the same managers of emotion who require emotional labor of other people tend to become less able to recognize the true meaning and significance of real, spontaneous emotions expressed by people working for them (Oatley, 1992).

Our discussion of the management of emotions would not be complete without noting that it has been the cultural norm for decades for people to control their (and others') negative feelings and emotions in most contexts, but in organizational contexts in particular. To the same degree that it has been the norm to behave rationally because of the belief that rationality is optimal for decision making, it has been against the norm to express negative feelings such as rage, hatred, and jealousy in the workplace. (It is not acceptable to express positive emotions too vociferously either!) Ashforth and Humphrey (1995) have noted that negative emotionality is generally contained through one or more of four basic methods. First, they describe *neutralizing,* a tactic that relies on emphasizing the virtues of the norms of rationality, as we have described them. This is accomplished through simple socialization processes, bureaucratic procedures, and the use of subtle (or not so subtle) rewards and punishments.

A second tactic is referred to as *buffering* (Ashforth and Humphrey, 1995). The essence of this approach is that emotionality is contained and allowed to appear only in prescribed, well-organized settings and times, such as at office parties, retreats, and the like (see Van Maanen and Kunda, 1989). A third approach used to deal with emotions is what Ashforth and Humphrey (1995) call *prescribing emotion.* This is the method that we discussed at length earlier: People are trained, even required, to express emotion on the job (usually positive affect backed up with a contrived smile).

Finally, organizations and individuals often have to deal with emotion that simply escapes the other constraints listed above. They "normalize" emotionality, recognizing that sometimes emotionality is inevitable and unstoppable (Ashforth and Humphrey, 1995). Hence people are expected to apologize to one another after displaying sufficient lack of control over their emotions. Humor is often used, especially to dispel emotions such as fear. Police officers make jokes about dangerous and frightening situations, and pathologists engage in crude or light remarks in reference to the ghoulish tasks they must perform.

The point here is that the norms of rationality have dominated the desire to be emotional and to express emotionality, especially in the extreme. These norms have resulted in a variety of characteristic managerial and bureaucratic styles and mechanisms to control emotionality, and when it cannot be stopped, to cover it up, rationalize it, or minimize its effects. Management has also developed many tactics to motivate and enforce norms of false or contrived positive emotionality in many industries and job categories where their businesses interface with customers and the community. It seems to the author that these devices for suppressing emotionality where it is not desired and for encouraging it where it is deemed necessary are so common and pervasive and so powerful in effect that we neither notice them nor object to them on a day-by-day basis. Given the power and ubiquity of these emotion management procedures, it is high time that organizational researchers began to pay attention to them.

Emotionality and Partial Inclusion

If we are to begin to admit consideration of emotions and emotionality into our thinking (and feeling) about work motivation, we must bear in mind that people are generally only partially included in their work and in the organizations for which they work (Weick, 1969). In other words, they have lives outside their jobs (although we often suspect that some people have too little life other than that found in their work) and they bring elements of their makeup from the outside with them into the job. A person who holds certain values about life in general will bring those values to work (see our discussion of values and work values earlier in the book). If a person places a strong general emphasis on loyalty, for example, he may be more likely to develop strong commitment to his employer.

People's emotions and moods are evidenced similarly. The emotions that may play significant roles in our motivation to perform well or to quit a job or to join a union or to pursue a romantic relationship with a clerk in the purchasing department do not reside solely within the confines of the work setting. It is important to recognize that emotions (and more so, moods) that we feel on the job can follow outside the job, and vice versa. As George and Brief (1996) put it: "Workers are people too." Therefore, adopting emotions and moods as lenses through which to study or influence human work motivation requires that we take a holistic view of the individual, recognizing that people's perceptions, beliefs, attitudes, intentions, values, needs, and emotions reside and have influence both within and outside the bounds of the work setting (see Wharton and Erickson, 1993).

Locating Emotionality in the Motivation to Work

Our purpose in much of the preceding has been to discuss possible linkages between emotions (and emotionality) and work experience, especially with the motivation to work. To this point, however, the precise role of emotions in motivation has not been located, ordered, or described systematically. Sometimes emotions result from performance that was motivated by other factors, such as intrinsic or extrinsic incentives. Sometimes, emotions seem to serve as a precursor to motivational experiences. Other times, emotions seem to accompany and occur with motivated effort simultaneously. In short, we are lacking firm rules of thumb as to where in the cycles of experience related to the motivation to work emotionality resides.

Some help is offered by Buck (1985), who has argued that

> emotion is a readout mechanism associated with motivation. Emotion is generally defined in terms of subjective experiences or feelings, goal-directed behaviors (attack, flight), expressive behavior (smiling, snarling) and physiological arousal (heart rate increases, sweating). . . . [E]motion has evolved as a readout mechanism carrying information about motivation . . . in a kind of running progress report. . . . Motivation is the *potential* for behavior inherent in the neurochemical structure, and emotion involves the means by which that potential is realized or read out, when activated by challenging stimuli. The relation of motivation and emotion in this view is analogous to the relation of energy and matter in physics: Just as energy is a potential that manifests itself in matter, motivation, as seen here, is a potential that manifests itself in emotion. Thus motivation and emotion are seen to be two sides of the same coin, two aspects of the same process. (p. 396)

Of concern here is the possibility that work motivation theory will find itself in yet another conundrum of the chicken-and-egg variety, similar to the one we discussed earlier in the context of the primacy of cognitions over affect (or vice versa). Notwithstanding this risk, if we wish to include emotions in theory and research, it may be useful at this stage to consider the possible range of "roles" that emotions may play in the work motivation process. If we adapt Buck's (1985) approach, it would seem that emotions and emotionality are virtually omnipresent and become more or less salient as people become more aroused (by their needs, values, or cognitions) by work experiences. Buck's (1985) view also suggests that emotions serve a readout function, providing people with information about the state of motivation to engage in and gain experience from work events.

Carver and Scheier (1990a) have suggested a similar, consistent notion. Adopting a self-regulation perspective (of the sort that we discuss in chapter 14), they suggest that a person's affective state is in part determined by the observation the person makes about his or her progress in pursuit of goals and objectives. The emotions that people experience and display follow from their own assessments of their success at goal accomplishment. To the extent that this is the case, emotions would seem best to be studied at all stages of the motivational sequence. Hence, although the theoretical perspective Carver and Scheier (1990a) adopt is different from that embraced by Buck (1985), the implications for a wide-ranging role for emotionality in work motivation theory seems to result from their approach as well.

The most recent and well-reasoned attempt to locate emotions in the spectrum of workplace experience has been provided by Weiss and Cropanzano (1996). They have developed a conceptual model they call *affective events theory*. Represented here as Figure 4-1, this model shows that people have emotional reactions to work events. These affective responses, in combination with the influence of objective features of the work environment, determine an employee's work attitudes. In addition, affective reactions to work events can result directly in job-related behavior, which, in turn, may also affect work attitudes, although this linkage is not central to the model as it is

FIGURE 4-1 Affective Events Theory

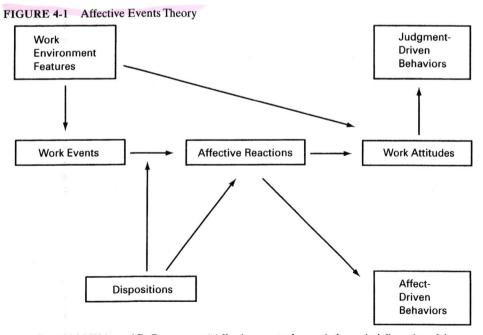

Source: From H. M. Weiss and R. Cropanzano, "Affective events theory: A theoretical discussion of the structure, causes and consequences of affective experiences at work," in B. M. Staw and L. L. Cummings (Eds.), *Research in organizational behavior,* Vol. 18 (Greenwich, CT: JAI Press, 1996). Reprinted with permission.

portrayed in Figure 4-1 (H. M. Weiss, personal communication, July 15, 1997). Weiss and Cropanzano's (1996) model is bound to provide considerable guidance to researchers who wish to pursue the challenge of studying the role(s) of emotions in workplace attitudes and behavior.

The author suggests that future theory building and research that seeks to include emotionality—along with other variables, such as needs, satisfactions, frustration, and the like—should begin with a tolerant stance that will admit emotions to appear in any and all places in causal sequences. Ironically, it may be that emotions are the most ubiquitous category of factors related to work motivation that we can study. They may enter the work motivation process at the beginning, at the end, and throughout the entire cycle.

SUMMARY AND A LOOK AHEAD

We started this chapter by noting that the field of psychology in general has largely ignored the meaning and role of emotions in human behavior. We noted that the organizational sciences in general, as well as work motivation theory in particular, have also been guilty of this omission. However, there has been a promising resurgence of interest in emotion in psychology and a corresponding emergence of interest in organizational behavior and the theory of work motivation (see Fineman, 1993). A major objective of this chapter has been to encourage a renaissance of empirical and theoretical efforts on work motivation that will include—indeed, feature—human emotionality.

In the following three chapters we return our focus to human needs and explore more closely a variety of needs and how they relate to work motivation. In chapter 8 we discuss the causes and consequences of need frustration.

CHAPTER

Power, Love, and Sex at Work

Life is a search after power.
—Ralph Waldo Emerson

O, rank is good, and gold is fair,
And high and low mate ill;
But love has never known a law
Beyond its own sweet will!
—John Greenleaf Whittier

THE NEED FOR POWER
AND THE MOTIVATION TO WORK

Most work organizations provide opportunities for the expression and satisfaction of power motives. Research studies have shown that the power motive is related to behaviors such as the following: seeking political office and other positions of prestige, speaking out and taking risks for the sake of having impact, adopting authoritative (rather than egalitarian) leadership strategies, collecting prestigious possessions, and carving out a personal image of strength, courage, and adventure—all or most of which are possible, to varying degrees at varying times, in work organizations (McAdams, 1988). Work organizations can be rich venues for the satisfaction or frustration of power needs.

Defining Power

What is power? There are many conceptions of power from a wide range of humanities and social sciences. Because the term *power* is used as a descriptor of both persons and positions, we take some care here defining our basic terms. Careful distinctions between power as a need and power as a goal will be necessary for an understanding of the role of power in work motivation, particularly in chapter 8, where we discuss frustration.

117

The most basic and perhaps parsimonious definition comes from Dahl (1957, 1986), who defines *power* as the capacity of one person (or social unit) to change the probability that another person (or social unit) will or will not do something. For example, if an office supervisor's orders result in her work crew spending more time cleaning their desks and work spaces than they spent previously, we would conclude that the supervisor has power over her subordinates and that she has exercised her power successfully. This formulation of power is meant to apply to social units of all levels: individuals, groups, organizations, and even nation-states (1957). Similarly, Winter (1973) defines *social power* as "the ability or capacity of [one person] to produce (consciously or unconsciously) intended effects on the behavior or emotions of another person" (p. 5).

In these definitions, power is a characteristic of a person-in-context, but it is different from the power motive per se. The power motive is a more basic personal trait that transcends contexts and settings. For Winter (1973) the *power motive* is "a disposition to strive for certain kinds of goals, or to be affected by certain kinds of incentives. People who have the power motive, or who strive for power, are trying to bring about a certain state of affairs—they want to feel 'power' or 'more powerful than. . . .' " Power is their goal. Therefore, a person may possess power by virtue of social status, physical prowess, or superior reasoning skills. Whether the person uses that power is another matter. Most critically, whether the person *wants* to attain and retain the power and use it is at issue. A person may be in a position of power but not have a desire or craving for power. Our focus here is on the need for power (or the power motive).

Winter and Stewart (1978) define the power motive as "the quest for power, the desire for power, or the seeking of power (or the subjective feelings associated with power). This motive is not always conscious, nor does it always lead to a single behavior or set of behaviors. . . . Moreover, the power motive may be in conflict with other motives such as affiliation, play, autonomy, or being taken care of" (p. 393). Elsewhere, Winter (1988) has defined the power motive as "a concern for having impact on others, arousing strong emotions in others, or maintaining reputation and prestige" (p. 510). It is possible to think of power as an attribute of certain roles and positions. For much of our purpose in this book, we will do so. The focus in this section is on power as a motivating force, a need that is subject to and characterized by all the aspects of needs described in chapter 3.

Power behavior is another useful concept, but one that must be distinguished from the idea of power motive. Power behavior is any act by one person to attempt to alter or change the behavior or emotions of another person. The danger in confusing the two concepts is that power behavior may be motivated by needs or desires other than power motives (such as a desire to affiliate or make friends). Similarly, we must distinguish between power motivation and *feeling powerful* (Winter and Stewart, 1978, p. 408). People high in the power motive often strive for positions in life that offer formal power, prestige, and symbols of potency. In fact, attaining such positions is often the way a person manages to achieve the end state of a high need for power—feeling powerful! However, there is not necessarily a one-to-one connection between the power motive and the *goal* of formal positions of power, such as political office or a senior executive position. Indeed, the power motive can cause a person to seek feelings of power by means such as alcohol use, drug consumption, exploitation of loved ones, risk taking, or exposing oneself to physical challenges.

We must be clear that a strong power motive usually has the same end goal—feelings of power and influence. However, there are countless ways in which people may attain that psychological feeling that have nothing to do with formal position, status, or authority or with the conquest of others.

Two "Faces" of Power

McClelland (1970, 1975) has distinguished between what he calls two varieties (or two "faces") of power. The first type of power, which he calls *personal power,* is characterized by a desire to dominate and defeat other people. It causes people to behave as if life is a zero-sum game: If I win, you lose. "The imagery is that of the 'law of the jungle' in which the strongest survive by destroying their adversaries" (p. 36). People with this form of power motive are more likely to engage in fights, excessive drinking, and interpersonal dominance. They seek out symbols of prestige to display and announce their personal power motives and accomplishments. They are not interested in the welfare of others. Instead, they use others for their own benefit.

The second variety of power identified by McClelland (1970) is called *socialized power.* "It is aroused by the possibility of winning an election. At the fantasy level it expresses itself in thoughts of exercising power for the benefit of others and by feelings of greater ambivalence about holding power. . . ." (p. 36). People with this form of power motive are more concerned about the possible negative consequences, for others, of their own use of power. They seek office for the sake of serving other people, not for their own self-aggrandizement.

POWER AND EFFECTIVE MANAGEMENT

McClelland (1976) has argued that effective managers are characterized by high levels of the need for power, but that socialized power is most important. Such managers are effective because they use their power to energize and empower those around them. They do not dominate or intimidate; instead, they generate energy and enthusiasm among subordinates for working effectively. They delegate. As opposed to managers who are high in the need for achievement (as we discuss in chapter 7), managers high in socialized power motivation succeed in large part by achieving goals through the actions of other people. Managers high in achievement motivation, on the other hand, get things done themselves. They also have a strong desire for feedback as to how well they are doing, so they often set short-term goals that may or may not be appropriate for the well-being of the company.

One study found that managers who scored high on a self-report measure of need for power also reported lower levels of stress from their work. The explanation provided by the researchers was that the higher levels of power needs among some managers allowed them to deal more effectively with stressors in their environment through the control they attained by their power-seeking behavior. Managers who were lower in reported power needs experienced higher job stress, presumably because they were not able to acquire the same degree of control over their work environments. Interestingly, the same study found no relationship between power needs and stress among the nonmanagers studied (Hendrix and Stahl, 1986).

To summarize: Effective managers, according to McClelland's research, must be motivated by a strong need for power, combined with considerable self-control. This power must be socialized power, not personalized power. These managers must be more driven by a socialized need for power than by a need for achievement or a high need for affiliation. They must be devoted more to the welfare of the organization than to having warm personal relationships with subordinates. They must want to empower other people so that they can get the job done through them rather than by their own direct efforts (McClelland, 1976).

GENDER, LEADERSHIP, AND THE NEED FOR POWER

For many years, nearly all the work done on the power motive was with male samples. Most of what we "knew" about the power motive among women was based on folklore and intuition. We tended to surmise that women were generally lower in power motivation than men. In those cases where women had strong power motivation, it was somehow different from the male variety and was expressed differently among men than among women (Stewart and Chester, 1982). Recently, however, abundant evidence has been accumulated to suggest that there are no systematic gender differences in the ways by which the power motive is aroused, in average levels of the need for power, or in relationships between the need for power and attaining formal social power, power-related careers, and prestige (Winter, 1988). Men and women express their power motives in substantially the same ways. People seeking socially appropriate power (the second of McClelland's two "faces" of power) show no gender differences in styles for seeking, maintaining, or expressing this power need (Winter, 1988).

An interesting issue related to gender differences in the need for power is whether men and women differ in the styles of leadership they employ in the workplace. Just as stereotypes have been developed and maintained about gender differences in the power motive (described above), there is a rich North American tradition in stereotypes about the ways in which men and women lead other people. This stereotype has it that women employ a much less autocratic style than men, featuring instead more of a tendency toward interpersonal and supportive styles. In one study representing this line of thought, a researcher found among a sample of effective women managers a greater tendency than among men to use *transformational* styles, by which they motivated others to transform their own self-interest into the goals of the organization (Rosener, 1990). Although she didn't make reference to McClelland's (1970) distinction between personal and socialized power, Rosener's findings were clearly consistent with the stereotypes about men and women as managers. They provide an interesting parallel between the stereotypes as they pertain to power motives and to leadership styles. The stereotypes about women's leadership styles are entirely consistent with the parallel stereotypes about their power motives, and it would be easy to confound or equate the two concepts. Clearly, leadership positions can serve to satisfy power motives. It is also true that people high in the power motive may be more likely to seek out positions of formal power and authority. But it is a mistake to assume a one-to-one correspondence between power motivation and leadership style. McClelland (1976), among others, has shown that seeking leadership and the expression of leader behavior are driven by more than simple power motives. In addition to the need for power, other motives (e.g., affiliation and achievement) can explain leader behavior and differences in leadership style.

What are the similarities and differences in leadership between men and women, especially in view of the interesting parallels between them in the need for and expression of power? One study investigated possible gender differences in the use of the two varieties of power by managers (Chusmir and Parker, 1984). Consistent with the researchers' hypotheses, the women managers displayed higher overall need for power than did the male managers. Most of the difference between the two groups was found in the socialized power category, where the women showed significantly stronger needs than the men for the "desirable" variety of power. There was no significant difference between the two groups on the less socially desirable form of power from McClelland's dichotomy.

A comprehensive review of the empirical evidence on the matter reveals that male and female leaders are no different from one another on a systematic basis when they are studied in real organizational settings. On the other hand, when researchers have examined the matter in laboratory studies or in hypothetical circumstances in which the participants were not in a leadership context, stereotypic gender differences have been observed. That is, in these two generally contrived research contexts, there has been a tendency for women to be more interpersonally oriented and for men to be somewhat more task oriented in their leadership styles (Eagly and Johnson, 1990). The study by Rosener (1990) that found apparent gender differences is an example of this sort of artifact. Rosener asked people to self-report on their leadership styles rather than actually observing the leaders in action. As Eagly and Johnson (1990) found, Rosener's data suggested that men and women differ as managers in their relative use of interpersonal styles and task orientation (see the debate between Epstein et al., 1991, Rosener, 1990, and others).

USES AND ABUSES OF POWER IN THE WORKPLACE

The human need for power can contribute to the instigation of a variety of behaviors in work organizations. Some can be useful and positive, and others can be intriguing, dangerous, and sometimes dysfunctional. For example, Pfeffer (1981a), Pfeffer and Salancik (1974), and Salancik and Pfeffer (1974) have detailed the many ways that people attempt to accumulate power over those around them by building networks of dependencies. The fundamental strategy is to provide resources of various kinds that co-workers need to pursue their careers and do their jobs. Possessing and distributing such resources can make the recipient dependent on the one who has the resources to dispense, thereby giving the latter bases of power. Power can be useful and put to positive ends. It can also be pernicious and dysfunctional. Kanter (1979) distinguishes between *productive power,* which comes from having open channels to valued organizational resources, and *oppressive power,* derived from these channels being controlled and manipulated. Kanter's two varieties are reminiscent of another dual concept of power offered by McClelland (1970), which we discussed earlier.

The active acquisition of power is usually defined as *political behavior* (see Frost and Hayes, 1979). This label often makes political activity *sound* inherently evil.

Countless popular paperbacks dealing with the art and strategies of organizational politics and power acquisition have been published and sold to North American managers over the years. Whether it is good, evil, or benign, *the need for power* motivates a great deal of organizational behavior that is intended to acquire and maintain power as a commodity, tool, or weapon. In the following sections we examine two forms of behavior, ingratiation and tyranny, that occur frequently in work settings: forms of behavior that can be unpleasant and harmful to those who witness them, yet that are often effective, in the short run at least, for those who engage in them.

Ingratiation

Most of us are aware of the phenomenon called by various names: "brownnosing," "sucking up," and others. Organizational scientists refer to this activity as *ingratiation.* Ingratiation is considered to consist of three types of interrelated acts: (1) self-presentation, (2) opinion conformity, and (3) the enhancement of other people (E. E. Jones, 1964). *Self-presentation* is "behaving in a manner perceived to be appropriate by the target person (i.e., person being ingratiated) or in a manner to which this individual will be attracted" (Ralston, 1985, p. 477). *Opinion conformity* is defined as "expressing an opinion or behaving in a manner that is consistent with the opinions, judgements, or behaviors of the target person" (Ralston, 1985, p. 477). *Other enhancement* "is expressing favorable opinions and evaluations of the target person by the ingratiating individual" (Ralston, 1985, p. 477).

For example, if a subordinate is aware that a superior is constantly trying to lose weight, ingratiation may take the form of a compliment about the superior's "robust build" (Ralston, 1985, p. 477). Wortman and Linsenmeier (1977) add that "the ingratiator tries to behave as though the issue at hand were his only concern, when in fact he is also interested in enhancing himself in the target person's eyes. An ingratiator may seek attraction because he is personally gratified by liking and approval from others, or he may value attraction or positive evaluation not as an end in itself but because it is instrumental to achieving other goals" (p. 134). Ralston (1985) observes that ingratiation has a long history of use, citing the story of Adam, Eve, and the snake. "The bite from an apple in the Garden of Eden resulted from the snake's skillful use of ingratiation for its own self-interests" (p. 477).

An ingratiator may employ a variety of tactics to impress a supervisor. One is simply by doing well on the job. Although it is true that being the star performer may bring on the wrath or indignation of co-workers, bosses generally like subordinates who perform well, including in particular those people who are good organizational citizens (see chapter 10). Probably the most blatant tactic is for the ingratiator to express openly liking or admiration for the target person: "Gee, Boss, I really like your new car!" Simple balance theory from social psychology (Heider, 1958), as well as a considerable amount of evidence, show that if one person (Stanley) believes that another person (Huntley) likes him, then Stanley is probably going to like Huntley. If Stanley has low self-esteem, he may be suspicious of the ingratiation attempt, so it could backfire on Huntley (see Wortman and Linsenmeier, 1977, p. 143). The lesson is that the ingratiator should avoid making statements about the target person that are inconsistent with the target's self-concept. Balance theory also helps to explain why espousing attitudes similar to those of a target person can be successful in getting the target's attention and affection. Similarly, doing favors for a target person can yield positive feelings as long as the helper's intention seems genuine and that she *intended* to be helpful.

Ingratiation may be unsuccessful in situations where the ingratiator's motives are transparent or when the ingratiator generally lacks credibility for other prior reasons. A husband who agrees that his wife's choice of dress for an evening out is terrific has much more credibility if he has a reputation for speaking honestly on earlier occasions when he thought the wife's choice was poor. It follows that a tactic for an ingratiator to employ is to be on record with both positive and negative commentary and opinions, establishing a bank of credibility for occasions when she wants to attempt false flattery. But again, if the ingratiator is in an obvious position of subordination to the target, his motives may be questioned and the attitudinal structuring attempt can backfire (Wortman and Linsenmeier, 1977, p. 161).

Ralston (1985) believes that ingratiatory behavior is influenced as readily by organizational context factors as by the characteristics of the individuals involved. He proposes that autocratic bosses (who tend to make decisions unilaterally and not allow subordinates to exercise their own skills and abilities) are more likely than nonautocratic bosses to produce ingratiatory acts among their workers. He does not propose that democratic bosses will be associated with particularly low levels of such influence attempts, simply that autocracy *will* yield high levels. Ralston also suggests that employees in generally ambiguous task settings, where it is not clear what is expected of them, are most likely to attempt to influence their bosses through ingratiation, especially when the employees want to do well and move ahead in the organization. A third organizational context factor likely to foster ingratiation, according to Ralson (1985), is resource scarcity. When there is scarcity of money for supplies and expenses, raw materials, equipment, information, or access to the attention of one's superior's time and attention, for example, people are likely to use whatever means are available to acquire these resources, including ingratiatory behavior.

In summary, Ralston (1985) hypothesizes that more than simple personality predispositions of organizational actors will determine the use of ingratiation in work organizations. The policies and practices of management may also contribute through the leadership styles used by managers, the degree of uncertainty about the nature of the work, and the level of scarcity of resources needed to get the organization's work accomplished.

Ingratiation is a deliberate attempt by people to misrepresent themselves for the sake of gaining personal advantage. Whether there is anything inherently wrong with such deception is a matter determined by one's values. To the extent that we value integrity and honesty, we cannot condone false presentation of our other values or our beliefs and attitudes in work settings. Most of us know people who spin false praise when it seems to serve their ends. The desire for power and influence can motivate people to misrepresent themselves and undermine a climate of honesty and trust.

Tyranny and Bullying

A quarter of a century ago, Kipnis (1972, p. 33) observed that Hobbes, in *Leviathan*, claimed that "men formed societies as a means of limiting the exploitive consequences of the unequal division of power." Following on this possibility, Kipnis and his colleagues reported two fascinating studies two decades ago which suggest that power may have a corrupting influence on some people (Kipnis, 1972; Kipnis, Castell, Gergen, and Mauch, 1976). On the basis of these two projects, the researchers concluded that the possession and use of power over other people can cause power holders to devalue the worth of the work of less powerful people, to increase their attempts to use their power, to take personal credit for the efforts provided by the less powerful, and to express a preference to keep a social distance from those over whom they use their power.

More recently, the cover story of the October 18, 1993, *Fortune* magazine is entitled "America's Toughest Bosses" (Dumaine, 1993). The story reports on seven American CEOs who were judged to be mean, demanding, sadistic, impossible to satisfy, and at the same time, highly successful—they have "made pots of money" (p. 39). Typically, these tyrannical executives please their shareholders but only a few of the people who must work for them. As long as they survive, the tyrants don't care. They are capricious, vague, and critical. Sometimes, they yell and swear at people. But they get results, at least until they annoy enough of the wrong people and are terminated.

In fact, the *Fortune* article is only one of a number of papers and books that have appeared recently to showcase the extreme exercise of power in work organizations. Books entitled *Corporate Abuse, Bullying at Work,* and *Psycho-Bosses from Hell* have enjoyed considerable commercial success recently. Why is that? Is it because most of us who hold jobs have been subjected to abusive bosses? Is it because many of us desire to confirm that we are not the only bosses who are abusive? Whatever the cause, the popularity of these managerial books suggests that North Americans are once again (or still) acutely interested in the use and abuse of power in organizations. Let's take a brief look at the proposition that the need for power, or the possession of power, or both, can cause people to behave in ways that would otherwise be unacceptable.

In their startling book *Corporate Abuse,* L. Wright and Smye (1996) have summarized a variety of forms of abuse that people suffer in modern organizational settings. They note that some abuse results from strict adherence to bureaucratic norms and rules, while other abuse follows from the "wrenching changes in industrial and economic structures that put an entire company under pressure" (p. 55). These two sources of abuse are common, and frequently beyond the control of any individual: They are natural costs of life in work organizations of the 1990s. Another form of abuse, however, is less innocent and less acceptable. This is the abuse dished out by "bullies," people who flaunt and abuse their administrative power. They exercise authority through the fear they generate in other people. They taunt and ridicule their co-workers, particularly their subordinates. Their "leadership styles" are modeled after that of military commanders such as the style associated in the movies with General George Patton. Citing *Bullying at Work* (A. Adams, 1992), L. Wright and Smye (1996) list a number of ways we can recognize bullies in the workplace. They include acts such as displaying uncontrolled anger, including the use of loud, vulgar language; humiliating other workers, either alone or in public; persistently using sarcasm and criticism, setting impossible deadlines; changing instructions in midstream, making failure for others inevitable; resisting delegation of authority to others; taking credit for other people's work and success; and undermining other people's attempts to get ahead.

Ashforth (1994) has explored the "petty tyrant" syndrome. There may be many personal and situational factors associated with this form of behavior, but a few factors are particularly interesting. Ashforth suggests that some people of this sort may, in fact, be low in self-esteem, using their formal authority as a sort of compensatory device.[1] Petty tyrants often fit a mold that includes authoritarianism and dogmatic belief structures and *Theory X* beliefs about workers (recall chapter 3). They place high importance on conformity and order and low value on treating other people with respect. They have a preference for action and a relatively low tolerance for ambiguity. But petty tyranny may be caused by factors other than a person's personality predispositions. Highly controlling institutional factors such as those found in prisons and many hospitals may give rise to this sort of behavior as well. And, ironically, people who actually have relatively little institutional power may behave tyrannically, lording what power they do have over others around them. For example, a low-level office clerk who keeps the keys to important conference rooms may exhibit a haughty, indifferent style that reminds others who need access to those rooms that *he* determines who gains access and who does not.

What are the effects of petty tyranny? Ashforth (1994) suggests that this sort of style results primarily in bad things for the organization, including the rejection of supervisors by their subordinates; heightened stress among its victims; emotional reactions normally associated with frustration, such as fear, anxiety, and irritation; reactance *against* the directives and preferences of the tyrant (as the victim asserts defiance and self-control); feelings of helplessness and alienation; a reduction in individual initiative; reduced self-esteem; and diminished work performance. Finally, the hostility and aggressive behavior of petty tyrants can undermine work group cohesiveness. As we discussed in the context of Theory X supervisory styles in chapter 3, tyrannical behavior by managers can result in a vicious circle: Employees react with fear, low initiative, and low performance, triggering a continuation or escalation of tyrannical behavior by the manager.

What is the point here? Over the long term, by making life miserable for those around them, bullies are usually not good for the organizations they work for. Although this sort of style *can* achieve short-term results, the longer-term effects on the attitudes, emotions, and withdrawal behavior of other people are usually dysfunctional. The work of Ashforth (1994), L. Wright and Smye (1996), and A. Adams (1992) continues the tradition in organizational science that shows that power *can* corrupt those who hold it in organizational settings. Power may be one of the great motivators, as McClelland and Burnham (1976) observed. It can arouse, direct, sustain, and explain much of the motivated work behavior we observe every day.

Looking Forward

In the foregoing sections we have examined the human need for power. We saw that the word *power* is used to represent both an important human need and one of the most important goals associated with that need: the power to make things happen that otherwise might not. The need for power, the pursuit of power, and the exercise of power are all commonplace in work organizations. They account for many of the good things that occur in work settings as well as many dysfunctional events. People who work in and around organizations ignore power dynamics at their own peril. In the following sections we look at another need that shares a noun with the goal it

---

[1]Petty tyrants can also be people with *high* levels of self-esteem (Ashforth, 1994).

seeks: love. In fact, the two sets of needs—love and power—have many features in common. Ultimately, both represent important determinants of motivated behavior in work settings.

LOVE, SEX, AND WORK MOTIVATION

Maslow (1954) and other need theorists included love as a basic human need. Maslow proposed that if a person's physiological and safety needs are fairly well gratified, "there will emerge the love and affection and belongingness needs. . . . The person will feel keenly, as never before, the absence of friends, or a sweetheart, or a wife, or children. He will hunger for affectionate relationships with people in general, namely, for a place in his group or family, and he will strive with great intensity to achieve his goal. He . . . may even forget that once, when he was hungry, he sneered at love as unreal or unnecessary or unimportant. Now he will feel sharply pangs of loneliness, of ostracism, of rejection, of friendlessness, of ruthlessness" (p. 43). Maslow (1954) claimed that deprivation of the love need early in one's life is frequently associated with neuroses. Unless the condition has progressed so far as to be irreversible, the administration of affection and kindness can be an integral part of treating such neuroses. Healthy adults, he believed, may need less love than maladjusted adults because, presumably, they have already enjoyed enough of it.

More recent work has viewed love as having psychological, biological, social, and physiological dimensions, all of which have demonstrated validity (see A. B. Fisher, 1992; Jankowiak, 1995). Historical analysis of the phenomenon suggests that until recently, Western cultures assumed that only we have been capable of experiencing romantic love (or romantic passion, as some authors call it): "Indeed, it has become axiomatic among Western literati that the experience of romantic passion is a mark of cultural refinement, if not obvious superiority, and that the less cultured 'masses' are incapable of such refinement; lust, yes; romance and love, no. The hidden inference of this assumption may be that romantic love is the prize or reward of true culture" (Jankowiak, 1995, p. 2). Research has shown this is not so. Two anthropologists have found romantic love to be a reality among 146 of 166 cultures investigated (Jankowiak and Fischer, 1992). The way that love is manifested may depend in part on socioecological, political, or economic conditions and the stress that they can cause during a person's childhood (Chisholm, 1995). This multidimensional nature of love makes it unusual among human needs and emotions.

The Many Varieties of Love

The nature and force of love must be one of the most dominant themes in art and literature. Countless people have observed that there are many types of love, although there is little agreement on the issue of how many types there are (see Fehr and Russell, 1991). For example, the British author C. S. Lewis (1960) suggested that there are four main categories or types of human love: affection, friendship, erotic love, and the love of God. Lazarus and Lazarus (1994) distinguish between two types: romantic love and companionate love; sexual intimacy may accompany the former but not the latter. Modern social scientists use a variety of terms to refer to *romantic love,* defining it as "any intense attraction involving the idealization of the other within an erotic context.

The idealization carries with it the desire for intimacy and the pleasurable expectation of enduring for some unknown time into the future" (Jankowiak, 1995, p. 4).

Companionate love features many of the same feelings and emotions as romantic love but is detached from sexual impulses. This category includes the filial love among family members, such as that between parents and their children, as well as the friendship that occurs between people of either the same or opposite genders. Women can have strong loving relationships with other men or women without sexual impulses or implications. According to Lazarus and Lazarus (1994), men in our culture often prefer to speak of their *friendship* for each other rather than their *love* for each other because of their definition of maleness and, presumably, fear of the stigma associated with homosexuality.

Prototypical Love

To this point we have observed several attempts to define two or three broad types of love. We have yet to come to grips with a general definition of love as a concept or phenomenon, for good reason. As we saw in chapter 4, many emotional states defy definition by the classical approach to defining objects and entities. The classical approach requires that we specify a set of necessary and sufficient conditions and characteristics for an object or concept to qualify for a definitional category (J. A. Russell, 1991). Instead of trying in vain to form hard-and-fast distinctions among human emotions, J. A. Russell (1991) and others have advanced the idea of using prototypes: classifying human emotions with fuzzy boundaries on the basis of their resemblance to prototypic examples and instances of a particular emotion. For example, there are variations and "shades of gray" among the various forms of anger, such as annoyance, wrath, rage, and so on.

The reader is referred to chapter 4 for a more thorough treatment of the prototype approach to defining emotions. In this chapter our attention is on *love as a need*, while not denying that it is also an emotion and, for some, an attitude as well (Fehr and Russell, 1991). This approach helps us get around the difficulty of defining love by the classical approach, as was observed by Brehm (1985, p. 90): "Social scientists have had as much trouble defining love as philosophers and poets. We have books on love, theories on love, and research on love. Yet no one has a single, simple definition that is widely accepted by other social scientists."

Perhaps the very elusiveness of the concept is one feature that makes love so fascinating. Regardless, a prototype approach helps us understand the many elements of the phenomenon that people in our culture have in mind when they think about love. Studies conducted at the University of Winnipeg used students to generate all of the types of love they could think of. The students generated an average of 8.69 varieties. As the song says, "Love is a many-splendored thing!" A total of 20 varieties were selected by the researchers on the basis of the student brainstorming. The rank ordering by which students rated each form as "an extremely good example" versus "an extremely poor example" of love is as follows: maternal love, paternal love, friendship, sisterly love, romantic love, brotherly love, familial love, sibling love, affection, committed love, love for humanity, spiritual love, passionate love, Platonic love, self-love, sexual love, patriotic love, love of work,[2] puppy love, and infatuation.

---

[2]Inclusion of work as a commonly held object for love, in the company of other objects such as mothers, fathers, and sisters, is of particular interest to us here.

The researchers conducted a series of further investigations to delineate the ways in which these categories could be clustered into smaller families. Eight different criteria emerged, eight different ways by which it appears that people seem to think of categories of love as more or less similar to one another. One of these criteria was the number of features that each type had in common with other types. A second criterion was the quickness with which the students would respond on a computer by touching either a "T" (for "true") or an "F" (for "false") when each of the 20 varieties of love was flashed on the screen and they were asked if, for example, "infatuation is a type of love."

The complete mapping of the relationships among the various varieties of love studied by Fehr and Russell (1991) is beyond our scope here. The interested reader is referred to the original, very fascinating, research report. Suffice it to say that there are many types of love and that, in our culture, some of these types seem more closely related than others to the core concept of love—whatever that is. There is still plenty of room for philosophers, novelists, and poets to have fun with the concept.

Experiencing Love and Rejection: Love Hurts

The feeling of romantic love is one of tenderness and affection. If it is going well, it features feelings of joy, elation, satisfaction, and even ecstasy. There is a desire to be close to, to touch and embrace, the loved one. The person is seen as special, beautiful, or wonderful in some way or another (Harris, 1995). What we see as beautiful or wonderful is largely culturally determined (Lazarus and Lazarus, 1994). Harris (1995) has identified seven "mind-centered attributes" or "core properties" experienced by people who are in romantic love with one another in most cultural settings: (1) the desire for union or merger, (2) idealization of the beloved person, (3) exclusivity of the relationship, (4) intrusive thinking about the loved one, (5) emotional dependency, (6) a reordering of the individual's goals and priorities, and (7) a strong sense of empathy and concern for the beloved person.

There are some universal differences between men and women in the bases for romantic attraction—differences that can make things interesting as well as difficult and painful from time to time. Women tend to show more interest in men's social status or in understanding a man's character, whereas (it may come as no surprise) men are more immediately attracted by the physical attributes of a woman (Jankowiak, 1995). As a result, women often appear to take longer to develop and to show romantic interest because character and social status usually take longer to gauge than do a person's physical attributes.

Rejection and Unrequited Love

Separation or detachment causes distress and depression (Lazarus and Lazarus, 1994). Having one's love not reciprocated is also very painful and can sometimes cause obsessive behaviors such as stalking the loved one. Doubtless, this form of harassment has existed for as long as people have loved each other romantically, yet stories of the stalking of public figures such as Anne Murray and Madonna capture the attention of both the media and the public at large. Without doubt, it is our capacity to identify with either public icon as victim or with the stalker as the unloved one that fosters our identification with these stories. The pain of unrequited love is as universal as the experiencing of romantic love itself. There is a "Society for the Study of Broken Hearts" in India. This society sets aside May 3 as a special day on which people whose hearts have been broken by unrequited or lost love can commiserate with each other (Jankowiak, 1995).

The frequency of rejection and of the occurrence of love not being mutual are some features of this need that make its manifestation in the work setting difficult. In our culture, love usually results in one of two outcomes: marriage or rejection. Rejection by a lover can be a source of great pain, embarrassment, loss of face and reputation, and inner sorrow. It is definitely a powerful form of frustration (see chapter 8), a natural consequence of which is aggression. People often strike back one way or another at either the source of their frustration or at more convenient targets. Unrequited love in the relatively small world of most workplaces can be awkward not only for those involved but also for people around them. When we turn our attention directly to love and sex in the work setting, the odds and the costs of love breaking down must be kept in mind.

With our focus on motivation in the workplace, the following observation from Maslow (1954) is germane: "[The] feeling of pleasure in contact and in being with, shows itself also in the desire to be together with the loved one as much as possible in as many situations as possible; *in work* [emphasis added], in play, during aesthetic and intellectual pursuits" (p. 182). Thus a person in love can be consumed with the desire to be in the presence of the loved one, perhaps regardless of the context involved. As we describe later, the workplace is both an arena for the establishment of love relationships and a forum for their pursuit and fulfilment.

A Need and an Emotion

Although love can be defined and understood as a need, it is also an emotion. In practice and in theory, it is hard to disentangle one from the other. Lazarus and Lazarus (1994) note that a difficulty in considering love from an emotional perspective is that the passion associated with it "waxes and wanes and cannot be sustained moment by moment over the long haul. Long-term relationships are not conducive to constant passion or the acute emotion of love, but the meanings required for active loving feelings surface from time to time . . . when other considerations in the relationship take a back seat" (p. 112).

The Relationship between Love and Sex Needs

The human need for love is related to, but must be kept distinguished from, the need for sex. Maslow (1954) was one of the first need theorists to discuss the relationship between these two needs. He writes: "One thing that must be stressed at this point is that love is not synonymous with sex. Sex may be studied as a purely physiological need. Ordinarily sexual behavior is multidetermined, that is to say, determined not only by sexual but also by other needs, chief among which are the love and affection needs" (pp. 44–45). Henry Murray, the psychologist whose concept and definition of human needs underlie most of the discussion on needs in this book, defined the *sex need* simply as the need *to form and further an erotic relationship, to have sexual intercourse* (C. S. Hall and Lindzey, 1970, p. 177). There is no mention of love in this definition, making it at least partially supportive of Maslow's perspective on the matter.

Although it is easy to exhort the reader to keep the notions of romantic love and sex disentangled, the close and often-confusing link between the two needs is understandable. Jankowiak (1995) states: "They are organized around different cultural and psychological criteria, which puts them, in several ways, in direct competition with one another, and this competition raises important implications for understanding their origins and manifestations in everyday life" (p. 6). As a result, it appears that most cultures have highlighted the importance of either sexuality or love, but seldom both at the same time. This is especially true of the intellectual history of the Western world, which has repeatedly shown a continuous and pronounced ambivalence toward sexuality and love (Jankowiak, 1995, p. 6). Ovid believed[3] that "love is essentially a sexual behavior sport in which duplicity is used in order that a man might win his way into a woman's heart and subsequently her boudoir" (Murstein, 1988, p. 22). The tight linkage and "direct competition" between them is part of what makes understanding and dealing with amorous relationships in the workplace difficult, as we will see.

Romantic Love and Sex in the Workplace

The workplace is a rich forum for the expression and satisfaction of love and relatedness needs. Many (perhaps most) of us find friendships there and enjoy going to work for the social interaction the workplace provides. The offices and factories in which we work also provide venues where many of us encounter love interests, partners, lovers, or spouses. Although "love in the workplace" and sexual harassment have been popular topics in tabloids and everyday magazines for years, until recently little work had been done on these phenomena by social scientists. The very nature of the topic itself makes it difficult to research. Nevertheless, more scientific work has been done since the mid-1980s. Frequently, the focus in much of this literature has been on the managerial and ethical issues related to dealing with the matter of intimacy in the workplace, especially since many legal cases have emerged because of disciplinary actions and policies intended to restrict natural interpersonal relationships (e.g., *Vancouver Sun*, 1993).

Workplace romances are "relationships that occur between two individuals who work for the same organization and experience enduring erotic or romantic interest in one another that is known to observers" (T. J. Brown and Allgeier, 1996). These relationships may be instigated by more than simple love, however. R. E. Quinn's (1977) early study into the matter concluded that romance at work can help to satisfy as many as three motives: love needs, ego gratification, and job advantage. The needs for love or sex may even be major determinants of a person's decision to work, where to work, which hours to work, and so on. What do we know about this hitherto taboo subject?

According to Mainiero (1989), one of the most active researchers on this topic, a variety of factors make interpersonal attraction, amorous relationships in particular, frequently occur at work. The first is physical proximity. People working in close proximity for extended periods are more likely to become attracted to each other. A recent empirical investigation by Gutek, Cohen, and Konrad (1990) supports this hypothesis. Second, Mainiero (1989) argues that intense task accomplishment also fosters

---

[3]The Roman poet Ovid was a self-styled expert in matters of love and sex. It was his poem entitled *Ars Amatoria* (which is about the art of making love) as well as his alleged knowledge of a scandal involving the Emperor Augustus's daughter that had him exiled to remote territory that is now in Romania.

attraction. She cites the characters in the Hollywood movie *Broadcast News* to illustrate this hypothesis. Working together with high stakes involved can encourage people to cooperate and reciprocate favors, help, assistance, and admiration. Third, similarity between the players also contributes. "Birds of a feather" do seem to flock together (Byrne, 1971). Similarities of interests and pastimes are especially important because they at least provide the prospective couple with a basis for conversation, social comparison, and shared activities.

Traveling together on work assignments is an aid to attraction, in part because it is exciting, requires proximity, and assures that the people involved have at least one thing in common—their destinations. Opportunities to explore possibilities with co-workers are generally safer when one is away from home. Hence, shared travel combines elements of many other factors that Mainiero (1989) identifies. In fact, there is something inherently sexy about travel, she notes. Similarly, during mixed-gender office retreats, employees "get together" during meetings and after hours. Often, the work group travels to a place away from the office and its interruptions. Once on site it is common for formalities to be abandoned temporarily and for people to engage in joint problem-solving sessions for hours at a time, often with those with whom they don't normally work. Games, entertainment, good food, and liquor are frequently provided to promote good feelings and a party atmosphere—largely intended to diminish people's inhibitions. Travel in general and office retreats in particular are fertile occasions for interpersonal and amorous relationships to develop.

Much of the early work on love and sexual relationships in the workplace treated these topics as taboo. It generally seemed in bad taste for people to become intimately involved with co-workers (see Mead, 1980) because of the many risks for the people involved in the relationship. According to one interpretation of Mead's (1980) position, these risks are likely to exist in all intimate relationships at work, whether between mentors and protégés, superiors and subordinates, or between organizational peers (Colwill and Lips, 1988). Relationships can destabilize legitimate working relationships and isolate individuals from their co-workers (see Collins, 1983; M.M. Kennedy, 1992; R.E. Quinn, 1977). The gossip associated with relationships can disrupt work flow and distract people's attention. Real or imagined favoritism can upset norms of fairness of treatment and equity (Mainiero, 1986). Sometimes innocent sexual attraction and activity can lead to serious cases of harassment (discussed below).

A survey conducted on a sample of personnel managers in the United States nearly a decade ago found widespread concern for the issue and a general lack of consensus as to what companies can or should do about love and sex in the workplace (R. Ford and McLaughlin, 1987). Nearly 40 percent of respondents believed that the romantic interests of employees should be of no interest to employers, while 70 percent agreed that "there is really nothing the organization can do to stop romantic attractions between men and women working together" (R. Ford and McLaughlin, 1987). A more recent survey of the same sort (A.B. Fisher, 1994) found a strong continuation of these trends. Nearly three-fourths of the executives polled in the 1994 survey (conducted for *Fortune* magazine) believed that romances between workers are none of the employers' business, although they acknowledged that such relationships can increase the risks of sexual harassment suits against employers.

Other studies of the matter have reached somewhat different, more balanced conclusions (Dullard and Miller, 1988). For example, a study of 1,044 American executives and managers examined three varieties of *nonsexual* interpersonal attraction at work: deep emotional bonds, mutual interest and respect, and willingness to devote time and energy to another person on a strictly voluntary basis (Label, Quinn, St. Clair, and Warfield, 1994). The researchers found that people who were involved in any of these intimate varieties of relationships were more supportive of each other at work, sharing career information, working toward task goals, and providing work-related feedback. They also found that people in such relationships were more committed to their work, their employers, and their spouses. The women in the study reported higher levels of intimacy in their workplace relationships than the men did and that these relationships provided greater amounts of the work-related social support described earlier.

It must be repeated that this study looked only at nonsexual relationships. Nevertheless, the findings were overall much more balanced and less negative than those of earlier studies that reported only bad outcomes from intimacy at work. On the negative side were some of the usual caveats: Romance at work *can* result in non-work-related activities, downtime, gossip, conflicts of interest, and reduced morale among observers who believe that special treatments are accruing to one or the other of the partners.

A recent study of graduate students at an American university found that the marital status of the people involved in an office romance was especially important in determining the reactions of third parties to such affairs (T.J. Brown and Allgeier, 1996). The same study revealed that third parties are more likely to accept office romance if the two parties are of equal status (rather than being in a superior–subordinate relationship), when the affair didn't seem to affect negatively the job performance of the male (the same was not found in relation to the female's job performance) and when the partners behaved "in a professional manner," not flaunting their relationship at work. Students in this study were more accepting of office romances if they had been engaged in one themselves and when they perceived that the motives of the couple were love-oriented rather than driven by ego needs or job leverage (see R.E. Quinn, 1977). Clearly, when people fall in love in work settings, other people around them frequently become aware of the relationship and are likely to form attitudes about them. Whether these attitudes are positive or negative seems to depend on the marital and organizational statuses of the lovers and the blatancy of their amorous acts.

By far the most positive treatments of office romance are provided by Mainiero (1989) and A.B. Fisher (1994). While acknowledging all of the potential risks and cost factors described by earlier students of the topic, Mainiero (1989) identifies an interesting list of potential benefits of romance at work. Some observations are based on her own research; some are inferred from the research of others. Her list of good things that *can* result from romance in the workplace includes the following: energizing of general workplace morale ("love is in the air"); increased motivation and improved attitudes among the particular employees involved; encouragement of creativity and innovation; improved teamwork, communication, and cooperation; enriched personal relationships; and stabilized workforces. The last item is particularly interesting. Permitting married or involved couples to work in the same workplace can help reduce the loss of good employees. Why? Because it can reduce the odds that one member of a couple will seek or accept employment opportunities in other organizations. To leave for greener pastures would entail leaving behind a sweetheart. Interesting: the ties that bind.

Many authorities interviewed by A.B. Fisher (1994) made the same claims about the energizing effects that love can have in the workplace, although the vast majority of executives surveyed in the *Fortune* study believed that office romances can increase the possibility of favoritism or the appearance of it and that they can create "unbusinesslike" appearances. Fisher concludes her analysis with these words: "As the old lifetime employment guarantee fades into history, employees—particularly the best and the brightest ones—are less willing to let a company dictate the terms of their private lives. Even with the divorce rate [as high as it is], a marriage these days is likely to last longer than a job. . . . The 1.5 percent of employers still struggling to wrestle Eros to the ground will find, if they haven't already, that they can no more stamp out sex than they can enforce rules about gossip, daydreaming, or wine with lunch" (p. 144).

More has been written in the past 15 years about the role of intimate and romantic relationships in the workplace. In addition to impressionistic articles found in the public press, there is now growing academic literature on the topic. A more balanced, less dogmatic assessment of the pros and cons of the phenomenon seems to be emerging. Whereas early writings typically rejected romance in the workplace as an inherently harmful and disruptive phenomenon, more recent work reports that benefits can accrue as well. Still, many of the truisms and caveats from the past seem worth keeping in mind.

First, people are inherently sexual by nature and will pursue love and sex wherever they find opportunities to do so. Therefore, dogmatic rules and regulations designed to prevent or to punish such activities are doomed to resistance, subversion, and/or outright failure. Love and sex are simply human needs that seek expression. The second point follows from the first. Management should leave well enough alone unless relationships can be shown to be detrimental to workplace performance. Managers' jobs are to produce goods and services through the efforts of other people. There is not (nor should there be) an inherent right for any manager to interfere with the human dignity and freedom of those who express their humanity in any form. If a romance can be shown to interfere with organizational effectiveness, steps should be taken to change the outcome. The law and some common practice seem to have adopted this principle. It should be enacted in all work settings.

Third, there appear to be more risks in intimate relationships at work when there is an imbalance of power between two people involved. Superior–subordinate relationships seem to be the most risky variety, in large part because these relationships can evolve from romance to harassment. Considering the *apparent* linkage between sex and harassment, we examine the harassment issue next.

What Is Sexual Harassment?

In the United States, sexual harassment "takes place when one person engages in sexual behavior toward another but the other person is unwilling to reciprocate and work rewards are attached to the bargain" (Maniero, 1989, p. 34). In Canada, two forms of sexual harassment are recognized, and both are illegal. The first form, *quid pro quo harassment,* occurs when a sexual act is requested or extorted in exchange for a promotion, pay increase, or other form of work-related outcome. This form of harassment can be either subtle or blatant in its expression, but it amounts to simple extortion in either case. It is both unethical and illegal. The second variety is referred to as *systemic* or *environmental harassment*. It, too, can be either subtle or blatant. It consists of requiring employees to work in an environment that is in some way permeated with sexual innuendo, pictures, themes, or other features. "Girlie calendars" on the wall, jokes with sexual overtones, and verbal or nonverbal overtures that are unwanted by the recipient comprise this second form of harassment. The employing organization is legally responsible for the conduct of its management group and therefore liable in the case of charges brought successfully against the organization by an employee who has been exposed to either form of harassment. The laws in the United States are virtually identical to those in Canada.

Sexual harassment is a power issue, not a matter of love and innocent sexual desire. Simple romance between consenting partners of comparable organizational status levels is a different matter from situations in which one person demands sex or behaves sexually in regard to someone who does not want such attention, particularly when there is a disparity in the power and status levels of the players involved. Managers have had difficulty in the past distinguishing between romance and harassment, in part because the form the latter takes may, on the surface, appear very similar to the former. Companies can clamp down on harassment by promulgating and enforcing policies prohibiting it, but they cannot prevent the occurrence of natural romantic love. Managers are missing the point when they cannot distinguish between the two phenomena. A complete treatment of the causes, consequences, and legal aspects of sexual harassment is beyond the scope of this book. The interested reader is referred to an anthology of papers on the topic by Stockdale (1996).

SUMMARY AND A LOOK AHEAD

In this chapter we have examined two fundamental human needs that comprise two very interesting elements of human nature that can explain significant degrees of behavior of people in work organizations. Of necessity, our treatment was brief. Countless thinkers and observers of the human condition have produced endless insights and observations about both the human need for power and the propensity for people to love each other. Our purpose here has been to reveal some aspects of power and love (and sex) that seem to have particular relevance for a comprehensive understanding of human work motivation. In the following chapter we focus attention on three more categories of human needs that share with power and love the important gregarious nature of our species: the needs for affiliation, self-esteem, and what social scientists now call *social motivation*.

C H A P T E R

Affiliation, Social Motivation, and Self-Esteem at Work

No man is an island.
—John Donne

AFFILIATION AND INTERPERSONAL ATTRACTION
IN THE WORKPLACE

Need theorists such as Maslow (1954) and others have discussed at length the importance of interpersonal relations among human beings for their health and survival (see Battle, 1990; Branden, 1969). People are gregarious creatures by nature and to be and remain healthy, must interact with one another (McAdams, 1988). Although need satisfaction is only one of a number of explanations for social interaction, it is clearly an important one, and some theorists—such as Murray (1938), whose definition of need we have adopted in this book—believe that social interaction may serve to satisfy as many as 10 different needs: abasement, affiliation, aggression, dominance, exhibition, nurturance, order, play, sex, succorance, and understanding.

By definition, work organizations consist of two or more persons, making the possibility for human interaction immediately and inherently possible. Even in the case of single-person companies, the single person must interact with others to permit the business to survive. We take these points as obvious and do not belabor them: The major point here is that work organizations of all sizes are *more or less capable* of providing social interaction between people. Moreover, as we will see in this chapter, there are certain features of many or most organizations that actually compel or motivate their members to affiliate with one another. Finally, work organizations frequently provide numerous opportunities for people to get to know one another on a friendship or more intimate basis. These interpersonal dynamics in the workplace can be addressed and understood from the perspective of need theory, and are so examined in this chapter.

We begin with an examination of the need for affiliation and discuss various ways that affiliative motives are relevant for an understanding of work motivation and organizational behavior. Then we look at the literature on social motivation—the effects that people can have on one another's motivation to perform (even without trying). We examine a number of ways that the mere presence of other people can inadvertently, and without awareness, affect a person's motivation. Finally, we study another social need, the need for esteem, and examine the role that esteem needs play in work motivation.

AFFILIATION MOTIVATION

Consider the following letter that appeared in a national women's magazine:

> My coworkers hate me. Ever since I joined the company three years ago, these cliquish women have treated me like a pariah. At meetings, I'm rarely addressed, and when I speak up, they don't seem to listen. I tell a joke and they roll their eyes, but if someone else tells the same joke, it's hilarious. They all go out for lunch together, buy each other birthday cakes and cards . . . and forget about me. During my down time, I've offered to assist a few of them with their work; that favor has yet to be returned. The rudest thing is, when I'm in the middle of a conversation with an employee from another department, the ring-leader of the group invariably interrupts, ignores me, and talks to the other person as if I'm invisible. I realize we're not at work to socialize, but their nastiness is affecting my morale. I do have a great relationship with my boss, who says the offensive employees are probably jealous because I'm vivacious and talented. From the beginning, he's always advised me to ignore them and focus on doing my job. But how can I do that when we're working in such close quarters? (*Cosmopolitan,* September 1995, p. 48)

A leading scholar in the area of affiliation motivation has written: "The motivation for social contact can be considered a central influence on human behavior" (Hill, 1987a, p. 1008). At one level, Hill's assertion seems obvious, but the poignancy of the statement above helps to emphasize just how important being accepted or rejected by other people is to most of us. In addition, the letter reminds us vividly that emotions are a major manifestation of need states (see Murray, 1938, and chapter 4 of this book) and that these emotions can be powerful, visceral, and very real. This particular case reveals a potent blend of loneliness, bitterness, anxiety, jealousy, and a touch of anger. At some point in our lives, most of us will have occasion to witness the sort of isolation, loneliness, and bitterness expressed in the woman's letter.

What Is the Need for Affiliation?

Henry Murray (1938) originally defined the need for affiliation as follows: "To draw near and enjoyably cooperate or reciprocate with an allied other (an other who resembles the subject or who likes the subject). To please and win affection of a cathected[1] object. To adhere and remain loyal to a friend" (from C. S. Hall and Lindzey, 1957, p. 176). Murray's definition makes sense; it fits with most common, everyday connotations of affiliation.

More recently, Hill (1987a) has suggested that we can gain a better understanding of affiliation motivation if we distinguish among four different subtypes of the motive

---

[1]*Cathexis* is a term from psychoanalytic theory that refers to the "accumulation of mental energy on some particular idea, memory, or line of thought or action" (Drever, 1952, p. 35).

while maintaining an appreciation for the common features they share. Hill proposes that the desire for social contact can originate with one (or more) of four social rewards that may be associated with affiliation, enabling us to differentiate among the following subtypes of the motive: "(1) positive affect or stimulation associated with interpersonal closeness and communion, (2) attention or praise, (3) reduction of negative affect [specifically fear and stress] through social contact, and (4) social comparison" (p. 1008). The first dimension is close in meaning to what we normally refer to as *love* (Buss, 1983). We will not explore this subtype here because it is dealt with at length in chapter 5. However, each of the other three categories of social reward (and corresponding variety of affiliation motive) has implications and value for our study of work motivation.

Attention and Praise

The second social reward Hill (1987a) discusses is the attention and praise that people can provide one another. Work organizations are arenas in which people are constantly evaluating one another and providing praise, criticism, approval and disapproval, and feedback in its various forms (see Ashford, 1993). Although it is true that many people thrive on the feedback *they administer to themselves* (so to speak) as they master tasks and accomplish goals (see Ashford, 1989; Hanser and Muchinsky, 1978; and chapter 7 of this book), the attention and praise that we receive from others, such as peers and supervisors, is also very important for understanding the mechanisms by which affiliation motives are aroused and satisfied. Of course, the feedback that people send and receive in work settings is usually intended to influence the work behavior or performance of another; the primary purpose of the feedback is rarely the satisfaction of affiliation needs, as such. Nevertheless, such feedback may serve other functions, such as satisfying part of people's need for affiliation. Ashford (1993) reports a study in which it was found that regardless of a person's seniority, the feedback provided by the company and supervisor was seen as more important than that emanating from peers and self-assessments.

Positive feedback is a mainstay in the arsenal of tools used in operant conditioning, organizational behavior modification programs, and self-regulation programs in work organizations (see chapter 14). Similarly, the provision of praise and attention is a key component of many current *employee empowerment* programs (see Eylon, 1994; Eylon and Pinder, 1995). Although work settings can be forums for the distribution and receipt of criticism of one's work and one's worth as a person, they are also certainly places where people regularly receive attention and praise, two elements of one of the main social rewards that meet people's need for affiliation (Hill, 1987a).

Reduction of Fear and Stress

Hill (1987a) claims that a third social reward that can stimulate and satisfy the need for affiliation is the reduction in difficulties that people encounter through the provision of support by others. Generally, the literature refers to this form of interaction as dealing with *social support,* which can be defined as "an exchange of resources between at least two individuals perceived by the provider or the recipient to be intended to enhance the well-being of the recipient" (Shumaker and Brownell, 1984, p. 13).

S. Cohen and Wills (1985) have suggested that there are four basic types of resources that one person can provide another in the form of support: emotional, informational, companionship, and instrumental. *Emotional support* (which has also been referred to as *esteem support*) is information provided to a person that s/he is esteemed and accepted. This form of support enhances self-esteem (which we discuss at length later in the chapter) by communicating to others that they are valued for what they are, for their own worth, including any difficulties or personal flaws. *Informational support* is assistance provided to a person to help define, understand, and cope with problems. *Social companionship* is "spending time with others in leisure and recreational activities" (S. Cohen and Wills, 1985, p. 313). It seems to work simply by providing contact and affiliation and by distracting people from their problems and difficulties. The fourth category, *instrumental support,* consists of the provision of financial aid, material resources, and needed services. It can work directly by addressing and removing the other's problems, or it can work by providing the person in difficulty with extra time and reduced pressure for performance.

There has been some debate over the mechanisms by which social support has benefits for people. One position has it that support works only to the extent that it assuages the effects of stress. This is referred to as the *buffering hypothesis:* Support "buffers" the effects of stress. The second position holds that support has beneficial effects on people whether or not they are under stress. This is referred to as the *main-effect hypothesis* (S. Cohen and Wills, 1985). One comprehensive review of the matter concluded that there is empirical support for both positions, depending on the circumstances. In a study of the length of time it took a sample of Canadian managers to "get up to speed" following geographic transfers, Pinder and Schroeder (1987) found that the levels of social support the transferees received from their supervisors and co-workers was critical. In fact, social support had the greatest beneficial influence on the time to job proficiency among those transferred employees whose moves entailed the most radical changes in the work they had to do following their transfers, as opposed to before the transfers.

The concept of *mentoring* is an organizational form of the provision of social support. Mentoring relationships may be formalized, as when a newcomer is assigned to the care and attention of someone who has more experience in the organization, or they may be informal, as when one person helps another out often enough and in sufficiently meaningful ways that the recipient eventually recognizes that, de facto, s/he has been mentored. For Kram (1985), one of the earliest to study and describe formal mentoring relationships in work organizations, mentoring required that the mentor provide all or most of a set of 10 different varieties of service, such as sponsoring, exposure and visibility, role modeling, and personal counseling. Since then Schroeder (1988) has shown that it is not necessary for a person to receive all these forms of support from one other person; it is only necessary that s/he receive them from any of a number of other people. Hence, to enjoy the benefits of mentoring it is not necessary that one have a formally designated mentor. Schroeder's work demonstrated that employees who receive these varieties of support, regardless of the number and nature of the sources, demonstrated higher levels of skill development, promotion success, and other job-related outcomes, such as salary increases and job satisfaction.

Hill (1987b) has shown that different types of support can have different effects on the well-being of people, depending on the strength of their need for affiliation. He collapsed the four varieties of support mentioned above (positive affect, attention and praise, reduction of fear and anxiety, and social comparison) into two basic forms: material and socioemotional. He found that material support was of benefit for all the people included in his study, regardless of their need for affiliation. However, only those people with low affiliative needs benefited from socioemotional support.[2]

Social Comparison

In chapter 4 we discussed the emotions of fear and anxiety. People generally face new work assignments with a certain amount of trepidation (or dread), and these emotions can be very strong. People in strange and uncertain circumstances naturally experience some degree of anxiety, if not fear. One of the ways that we cope with these emotions is to seek the social support of other people; this is no less true on the job than in any other arena of life (see Festinger, 1954, and chapter 11 of this book).

The hypothesis linking social affiliation to the experiencing of anxiety was first offered by S. Schacter and Singer (1962) in a series of clever experiments in which women students were recruited and told that they would be exposed to either mild or severe electric shocks as part of their involvement in the research. The students were then provided alternative ways to wait until the experiment was to begin; the options included staying alone in a room or staying in another room in the presence of other students. The results of the study suggested that those people who were induced into the higher levels of anxiety about what was about to happen to them preferred to be in the company of others, especially, it was found in subsequent research (Schacter and Singer, 1962), other students who were "in the same boat" they were in. On the basis of these studies, social psychologists concluded and have believed for years that "misery loves company" and that "miserable people love miserable company." People affiliate to help reduce anxiety and fear.[3]

Louis (1980a) has described the process of "sense making" in a new career situation: New faces, new roles, new local politics, new supervisors and peers, and new tasks are frequently encountered when a person undergoes a career transition. Clearly, different types of transitions will feature more or less novelty than others (see Louis, 1980b), but entering, leaving, or moving around inside an organization can be stressful and can cause the people involved to seek out the social support and information available from others at the scene. In fact, R. Katz (1980) has suggested that interpersonal needs may be the most critical at the time of career transitions, and that existence and growth-related needs may become salient only after there has been sufficient affiliation for the sake of reducing anxiety and helping those in transition to make sense of what is happening to them and around them (see Festinger, 1954; Pinder and Walter, 1984; S. Schacter and Singer, 1962).

In summary, Hill (1987a) has suggested at least four varieties of social rewards that can be involved in affiliation behaviors: four different, albeit interrelated, types of comfort, enjoyment, and pleasure that can arouse the need for affiliation and then

---

[2]In fact, there was some suggestion from this study that socioemotional support may even have a deleterious effect on the physical health of high-affiliation-need persons.

[3]From time to time, researchers replicate the original S. Schacter and Singer (1962) experiments for the sake of finding different explanations of the results. One such attempt was made by Rofe and Lewin (1988), who sought to demonstrate that a simple utility argument could explain the results—that is, that by affiliating under conditions of high anxiety, it is a matter of practical mutual assistance rather than anxiety through sense making that occurs. Their results were mixed and suggested that there may be gender differences in the phenomenon.

serve to satisfy that need. The strength of the need and the strength of the pleasure that the various rewards provide can vary, of course, as in the case of any need. We examine that issue next.

Intensity of the Affiliation Need and Related Emotions

In chapter 4 we saw that people vary in the degree of intensity with which they experience emotions (Diener, Larsen, Levine, and Emmons, 1985) and that the tendency to experience emotions strongly generalizes across the range of human emotions; similarly, if a person tends to experience some emotions only mildly, s/he probably experiences other emotions only mildly. More recent research has found that affiliation motivation may be related to the strength of people's feelings. In fact, one study showed that the strength of people's emotions is related to all four of the varieties of affiliation motivation that we have just discussed (Hill, 1987a). In other words, it seems that people who experience emotions intensely are more likely to seek higher levels of positive stimulation, emotional support, attention, and social comparison (Blankenstein, Flett, Koledin, and Bortolotto, 1989). In a similar study, Hill (1991) found that people with high needs for affiliation were more likely to seek social support from others than were those with lower levels of affiliation need. Interestingly, neither of these studies found gender differences in the strength of the correlations: Neither the link between affiliation motives and intensity of affect nor that between affiliation motivation and desire for social support was stronger for men than for women (or, as a common stereotype might have it, the other way around). What does this mean? Only that people who tend, by nature, to feel emotions strongly seem more motivated to seek out others with whom they might interact for the sake of getting the optimal level of emotional arousal they desire.

When we discuss the strength of people's motives, we must consider those persons who tend not to be particularly "emotional" as well, and we must also keep in mind that motives and motive strength are only partly responsible for human behavior. In the specific context of affiliation motivation, for example, one study in India found that interpersonal similarity was much stronger than people's need for affiliation in predicting interpersonal attraction (Shaikh and Kanekar, 1994). In other words, needs do, as we have discussed at length, account for a considerable amount of motivated effort, in both work settings and in other settings, but needs are not the sole instigators of action. Rather, needs should be considered only as a class of variables among sets of other factors that can account for human behavior, such as perceived similarity between people in the case of the Indian research (Shaikh and Kanekar, 1994).

Affiliation Motivation and Managerial Effectiveness

Next we can ask about the value to people of having strong affiliation motivation in the context of their work. Some interesting research has recently been devoted to studying managerial and executive needs, including the need for affiliation, and the findings of much of this work have been consistent and of practical importance. One study found that affiliation motivation had virtually no relationship with the financial success of a sample of chief executive officers of top American corporations (Chusmir and Azevedo, 1992). Using the lead researcher's own definition of need for affiliation as "a concern for establishing, maintaining, or restoring positive or love relationships with other persons" (Chusmir, 1985), a negative correlation was in fact expected between the strength of the executives' affiliation needs and business success measures such as sales growth, profits, return on equity, and return on sales. Although no significant negative relationship was found between business performance and affiliation needs of the executives, there were, as predicted, significant positive relationships between the executives' power and achievement needs and patterns of the success indicators.

Findings of this sort are consistent with writings of McClelland and his colleagues, who have developed a *leadership motive profile,* a profile of needs associated with effective leadership. Specifically, the effective leader is most likely to have a strong need for power and what is referred to as *activity inhibition,* a capacity to use power to achieve institutional goals rather than personal goals. At the same time, however, the leadership motive profile is characterized by a *low need for affiliation* (see McClelland and Boyatzis, 1982; McClelland and Burnham, 1976). Finally, strong need for achievement is hypothesized to be related to success in small, entrepreneurial organizations in which the person can be responsible directly for the growth and success of the enterprise, but it is not expected to be a factor in larger organizations where success or failure are determined by many people working in harmony (McClelland and Boyatzis, 1982, p. 738). In their study, Chusmir and Azevedo (1992) reasoned that the need for power can motivate an executive to pursue growth and profits, while a strong need for achievement is likely to induce a concern with immediate growth in sales. Having a strong need for affiliation, however, "is normally not a desirable motive for top-level managers since the effort to please others may get in the way of needed hard decision making" (Chusmir and Azevedo, 1992, p. 610).

House and his colleagues have reported some fascinating research on the personalities of 39 U.S. presidents and the varying degrees of success these presidents have accomplished in office (see House, Spangler, and Woyke, 1991; Spangler and House, 1991). In one analysis they examined the inaugural addresses of the presidents and found that references and imagery related to power, affiliation, and achievement were predictive of their rated success in office, although consistent with prior work on the leadership motive profile, affiliative tendencies were generally related to lower effectiveness (Spangler and House, 1991). Although being affiliative by nature may have helped the presidents to become nominated and elected, once in office it seems that affiliative tendencies have been detrimental. Analysis of the same data set found that amid a number of powerful positive connections between power motivation and activity inhibition, and indicators of presidential success, affiliation motivation was either unrelated or negatively related to all the success criteria studied (House et al., 1991).[4]

The need for affiliation has an interesting role in the current theory and research about employee work motivation, managerial performance, and organizational behavior. It is clear that affiliation motivation is one of the central motives of people as they live with other people and that the workplace can be a rich venue for arousing, directing, satisfying, or thwarting the desire to affiliate. It also seems clear that strong affiliation tendencies may not be instrumental to those who seek positions of power and authority in management because people who like people (too much) may not be very successful at placing the interests of organizations above those of their personal

---

[4]Similarly, achievement motivation was also negatively related to many of the measures of presidential performance, presumably because of the sheer size of the organization the president must manage.

friendships; they may not be capable of making the tough decisions that positions of leadership and authority require for managerial and executive success.

Next we turn to another fascinating feature of the relationships among people in work settings: the ways by which people can influence one another's work motivation and performance without even consciously trying to do so: We explore the phenomena referred to collectively as social motivation.

SOCIAL MOTIVATION AND WORK BEHAVIOR

The ambiguous phrase *social motivation* has emerged and gained some use in the social sciences in recent years. We describe it as "ambiguous" because there is only partial agreement among scholars regarding which social phenomena are included under this rubric (see Brody, 1980; Geen, 1991; Pittman and Heller, 1987; Reykowski, 1982). In fact, one reviewer has implied that the very notion of social motivation may be somewhat redundant, inasmuch as most human motivation and behavior occur within the company of other people and are determined at least in part by the existence of these people in our lives (Reykowski, 1982). Nevertheless, one recent reviewer has offered guidelines, or criteria, for determining which human processes are and are not appropriately seen as social motivation (Geen, 1991, p. 178):

> First, the conditions of social motivation [are] defined as those in which the person is in direct contact with another person or group of persons, such as an audience, a group of co-actors, or a partner in interaction. Second, the effect of the social presence [is] defined as *nondirective* [emphasis added; the social entity does not provide specific cues to the individual about how to act in the situation]. For example, direct social influence, persuasion, or attempts at attitude modification fall outside the . . . definition of a social motivational phenomenon. Third, this socially engendered effect on the individual is considered an intrapsychic state capable of initiating and/or intensifying behavior.

On the basis of the criteria delineated in this definition, Geen (1991) isolated three particular phenomena for study, albeit recognizing that other topics had been considered part of "social motivation" by other authors at other times. Each of these three phenomena—social facilitation, social loafing, and social anxiety—has implications for our study of work motivation, so we examine each in this section.

Social Facilitation

Modern interest in the social facilitation effect was kindled three decades ago by Zajonc (1965). In brief, this effect takes the form of increased task motivation (and often performance) when people work "in the sheer presence of other individuals" (Zajonc, 1965, p. 269), as opposed to working in isolation. The effect was reported to occur over a broad array of activities and over a wide number of animals. Pigs eating, ants working, human beings solving problems: In all cases, performance increases, according to Zajonc, when it is conducted in the presence of others.

Among human beings it is not clear whether the mere presence of others can stimulate heightened motivation or whether the observer in question must be perceived to be in the position of evaluator of the performance for the effect to occur (Geen, 1991).

Regardless, it does seem that the mere presence of others may trigger apprehension about one's performance being negatively evaluated. Moreover, it appears that the degree of the apprehension grows as the perceived status of the group members present grows (Seta, Caisson, Seta, and Wang, 1989). Two explanations that have been offered for the effect are that the person is distracted by the presence of others, or that the person desires to "look good" in front of observers. Either way, it appears that having other people observe us at a task—people who are not part of the task activity themselves—frequently increases the levels of uncertainty and anxiety we experience, and this elevated anxiety, in turn, explains the increase in motivation to perform well (Geen, 1991).

Whereas social facilitation can occur when one person watches another perform a job, the presence of more than one person actually involved in doing the job (as in a team) may work the other way. This seemingly opposite phenomenon is referred to as *social loafing.*

Social Loafing

In 1913, a scholar named Ringelmann observed that individual output in a wide variety of tasks often decreases as the size of the group performing the task increases.[5] As Geen (1991, p. 384) notes: "When a person is a member of a group, subjected to social forces, the impact of those forces on each person in the group is diminished in inverse proportion to the strength (e.g. status, power), immediacy, and number of persons in the group." This social loafing effect (Latane, Williams, and Harkins, 1979) has been observed among task groups working at maze performance, writing, swimming, problem solving, and a host of other activities. In a recent meta-analysis of the phenomenon, Karau and Williams (1993) defined social loafing as "the reduction in motivation and effort when individuals work collectively compared with when they work individually or coactively" (p. 681). Working collectively means that people are working together in the real or imagined presence of others, with whom their inputs will be combined to yield a single product. Working coactively, by contrast, implies that people are working in the real or imagined presence of other people but that their inputs are not pooled or combined to yield a single product. Collective effort seems to foster social loafing, whereas coactive work does not.

Several explanations have been offered for this effect (see Karau and Williams, 1993; J. M. Levine, Resnick, and Higgins, 1993). One early explanation held that there can be a coordination loss, in which the individual efforts of group members interfere with one another. More recent explanations, however, discount the coordination explanation and have offered more psychological reasoning. For example, one study derived an equity explanation: Individuals expended more effort when they were told that their group partners were going to expend more (Jackson and Harkins, 1985). Another explanation looks to the inherent level of interest the participants may have in the task itself. If the task is seen as boring or lacking in fun, people may attempt to "hide in the crowd" (N. L. Kerr and Bruun, 1981) and permit their team members to bear the brunt of the work (see Geen, 1991, pp. 385–386). It appears that social loafing is also likely to occur in settings in which there is no chance of being evaluated for one's individual performance and/or when there is no stated standard for performance. When people are provided with a set of standards that have been established by the performance of

---

[5]The original paper has been discussed and described in detail by Kravitz and Martin (1986).

other people, there may be a desire to see whether one can measure up to those standards, similar to the dynamics lying behind social comparison theory (see chapter 11). N. L. Kerr (1983) has also proposed a *free-rider effect,* which may occur when a person believes that some other member of the group will do the work, solve the puzzle, or whatever, and that *his or her own contributions to the success will not be differentiated from those who actually contributed.*

Geen (1991) summarizes the recent scientific evidence on social loafing: "Social loafing may be due not so much to a group-engendered loss of motivation as to the facilitation of performance decrements motivated by other conditions. For various reasons, individuals may not be motivated to exert effort on a group task. Believing their efforts to be unnecessary, they may be content to let others do the work. They may wish to avoid putting out more than their fair share of effort. The task may be uninteresting. When subjects believe they are safely anonymous in the group, they will, given such low motivation to perform, become loafers" (p. 389). Since Geen's (1991) interpretation of social loafing, a meta-analysis of 78 prior studies conducted by Karau and Williams (1993) concluded that a theoretical model they call the *collective effort model* explains a considerable amount of the phenomenon that earlier researchers had reported. They concluded that social loafing "appears to be moderate in magnitude and generalizable across tasks and subject populations." It occurs "because individuals expect their effort to be less likely to lead to valued outcomes when working collectively than when working coactively" (p. 700).

The collective effort model has its roots in the popular and influential expectancy theory of motivation that we examine in detail in chapter 12. It is necessary to foreshadow that discussion briefly to report an interesting study of how social loafing can be affected by threats of punishment. In a nutshell, the expectancy theory (or theories) of motivation hold that a person's work motivation is maximized to the extent that s/he believes three things: (1) that if the person expends effort at a task, task success is likely; (2) that if task success is achieved, positively valued outcomes will be received; and that (3) negative outcomes such as punishment will be avoided.

J. A. Miles and Greenberg (1993) have reported a study of a high school swimming team of 120 members to demonstrate social loafing and how threats of punishment may reduce its effect. First, they established a standard performance goal for swimming speed that team members found difficult but reasonable. They then had some of the students swim as teams, in relay, in which their performance would be determined by their combined efforts. Other swimmers swam alone. The coaches manipulated the threat of punishment three different ways for poor-performing swimmers: There was a "severe" punishment condition, a "moderate" punishment condition, and a control group in which no punishment would be contingent upon poor swimming performance. (The punishment took the form of extra laps.)

As expected by social learning theory, and consistent with the expectancy theory–based collective effort model, individuals in groups performed worse than individuals performing alone under conditions in which punishment threats were not in place. In other words, "whereas adolescent swimmers attempting to meet a group relay goal time swam slower than comparable individuals attempting to meet an analogous individual goal time, [the] social loafing effect did not occur when the coaches threatened the swimmers with relay laps for failing to meet their goals . . ." (J. A. Miles and Greenberg, 1993, p. 259). The point here is that social loafing is more likely to occur when people believe that they are part of a group effort and that their individual efforts will not be rewarded directly to themselves, or when their restrained effort will not result in direct punishment to themselves. On the other hand, as shown in the swimming example, when reduced effort is expected to result in punishment for the entire team for poor performance, the social loafing effect was reduced, and team members performed as well as they would in working-alone conditions. Pooling appears to bring out social loafing.

Comer (1995) has observed that unlike the case of the swimming experiment, much of the theory of social loafing arises from laboratory experiments conducted with students performing contrived tasks. There is nothing inherently wrong with laboratory research, as long as the phenomena being studied are considered to be independent of the contexts in which they occur (Runkel and McGrath, 1972). In the case of social loafing, however, a key factor is the reality of the evaluations that are made—if any—of individual and group performance. Comer notes that such evaluations and the attributions that people make about success and failure are much more meaningful in real, ongoing work groups than they are in artificial laboratory research groups. Accordingly, she offers a somewhat more complex model of the causes of social loafing than those discussed above. The schematic shown in Figure 6-1 summarizes her model.

A complete description of Comer's (1995) model is beyond the scope of this chapter. The interested reader is referred to the original article. For our purposes here, however, a few important factors deserve attention. One of these is the perception by a group member that the group is not doing well, and that, therefore, s/he has little influence over task performance. This may cause the person not to contribute as heartily as s/he otherwise might contribute to subsequent group performance. (Reduced self-efficacy beliefs would explain this phenomenon.) The same effect might occur, according to Comer (1995), if the person felt that s/he didn't have sufficient task ability, regardless of the apparent success of the group. Persons who believe that they possess comparatively high levels of task ability might engage in "self-effacing" behavior, hoping not to diminish the spirits of others whom they perceive as less competent. Again, Comer's (1995) model deserves to be considered in its original formulation, and field experimentation must yet be conducted to test its validity.

Concepts Similar to Social Loafing

In contrast to Geen's (1991) position and the work of Karau and Williams (1993), Kidwell and Bennett (1993) assert a set of sharp distinctions among definitions of social loafing, *shirking,* and *free riding.* For Kidwell and Bennett (1993):

> In the shirking process, a person can withhold effort for various reasons, such as monitoring difficulties, self-interested behavior, and opportunism. . . . In the social loafing process, a person withholds effort as he or she moves from an individual performing alone to individuals performing in groups of increasing size. Perhaps because a collective task is involved, individuals can hide in a crowd, and their performance becomes less identifiable, and, they believe, more dispensable. . . . In the free riding process, a person withholds effort when invisible public goods [M. Olson, 1965] are involved, and it is rational to reduce effort because the free rider believes he or she can receive the goods by letting others do the work. (p. 430)

In short, according to Kidwell and Bennett (1993), it is important to distinguish among these three categories of phenomena, although collectively, they comprise the *propensity*

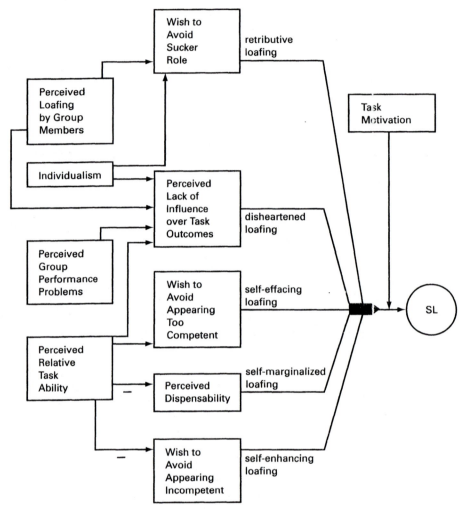

Source: From D. R. Comer, "A model of social loafing in real work groups," *Human Relations, 48,* pp. 647–667 (New York, 1995). Reprinted with permission of Plenum Publishing Corp.

FIGURE 6-1   Social Loafing in Work Groups

to withhold effort. Although the author sides with Kidwell and Bennett on this issue, believing that clarity and precision of constructs is critical, the reader may prefer merely to conclude that the important thing is that for whatever reason(s), people frequently expend less energy while working in groups with other people than they would while working alone.

Social Anxiety

We mentioned earlier that Geen (1991) has identified a third class of social motivation that may be of interest to our study of work motivation and behavior. He refers to this phenomenon as *social anxiety,* the state created in a person when he or she is motivated to make a certain impression on other people but believes that s/he is unable to make that impression (see Geen, 1991; Schlenker and Leary, 1982). It involves that feeling we all experience from time to time, and in varying degrees, of being out of place or of not projecting the kind of attitude, aura, or image that we would optimally elect to project. Public speaking affects many people this way. This author is not aware of any work that examines the effects of social anxiety directly on work motivation, although the concept would seem to have relevance for at least two other dynamics that we have examined in this book: the expression of emotions and the desire to project an image of fairness.

In chapter 4 we discussed at length the concept of emotional labor—the requirement made in many jobs and occupations for us to emit and control certain emotions. Required friendliness, obligatory smiling, and carefully controlled sadness or upset are examples: Many jobs require that we emit or inhibit the expression of emotions. To the extent that a person suffers from social anxiety, the person will harbor self-doubts about his or her capacity to do what is expected. In the terms of expectancy theory (see chapter 12), this would imply that the person would be less likely to undertake such task assignments or to engage in jobs where emotional labor is required.

In chapter 11 we will see that there may be a cultural norm that motivates people to project an image of fairness; that is, that it is generally the case that people prefer to be viewed as fair in their interactions with others rather than unfair, dishonest, or exploitive (see Greenberg, 1990a). Hypothetically at least, it would seem that managers (or even work peers) who experience social anxiety may be quite frustrated in their attempts to generate, instill, and foster an image of fairness in the eyes of others, frustrating their attempts to make friends or to be judged as fair supervisors or honorable people. If Greenberg (1990a) is correct that people in our culture favor a norm for projecting an image of fairness to others about themselves, occupying a job where perceived fairness is critical would be very difficult and discouraging for people who frequently experience social anxiety.

We include the notion of social anxiety for two purposes: first, for the sake of completeness in reporting on Geen's (1991) scholarly typology of social motivation effects, and second, for the sake of stimulating research into the possible or likely relationships between social anxiety and the motivation to engage in work that requires emotional labor.

Summary

In summary, it appears that social motivation effects are very real and that they can have varying degrees of impact on human work motivation and performance. It seems obvious to state that the presence of other people will influence the ways we work, how hard we work, when and where we work, and so on. The central point in the foregoing section is that much or most human work activity is conducted in social settings and it is important to remember that aside from the deliberate attempts of bosses, managers, and peers to influence our work motivation, there can also be subtle, inadvertent, and unconscious social influences as well. In this section of the chapter we have looked briefly at the latter category of social influences: the mechanisms through which human beings subconsciously or unknowingly affect the motivation of one another.

The author feels that more empirical research is required to gain an estimate of the relative strength of social influence effects, in comparison with the more direct and intentional forms of social influence on work in work organizations. The powerful rewards and punishments that people can deliberately apply to one another for influencing work motivation and performance have been studied for years (e.g., Roethlisberger and Dickson, 1939); the results are reported in myriad places dealing with topics such as group dynamics (see the early paper by Roy, 1952), and leadership and supervision (e.g., Bass, 1981). How powerful are the effects of social motivation in relation to the formal and conscious forces? Considerable empirical work needs to be done to provide the answer.

ESTEEM NEEDS, STATUS, AND WORK MOTIVATION

The nature of the work that people do (or do not have to do) has long been a principal basis for the determination and definition of one's social class—of one's comparative status within society as a whole (S. R. Parker, 1981; Pfautz, 1953; Striker, 1988). Among modern thinkers, Karl Marx was probably the most influential adherent to this concept. However, long after the death of Marx and the wane of Marxism, there is still a strong relationship in most cultures between work (or nonwork) and a person's status in the greater scheme of things (see Clegg, 1990).

To bring the concepts of this chapter closer to home, consider the psychological impact of being demoted. Consider the effects of having another employee take over a job or assignment that you were in charge of previously. Consider the effect on a person of being "disciplined" by a supervisor. Consider the effect on a person's emotions of being told that she is no longer deemed able to hold a job or to continue working for an employer. Consider the effects on a person's feelings of watching a rival in an organization being trained, advanced, and promoted ahead of the person who may have thought that she deserved the promotion and the adulation that goes with it. Consider the effects on a person's emotions when a client or a customer degrades or complains about the person's work. Especially consider the impact when a person is berated for a job into which she or he has placed a lot of time, energy, devotion, and care, particularly when comparisons are made between the person's worth and that of another employee.

In chapter 4 we discussed emotions such as pride, envy, and jealousy. These are the things that people take home with them after a day's work in which their work, even their basic integrity and value to the employer has been assailed. It hurts; it really hurts.

Some Key Definitions

The discussion in the following sections could be difficult to understand unless a few concepts and terms are made clear. The *need for esteem* is the central concept in what follows: It is a need of the sort defined in chapter 3. Maslow (1954) claimed that

> all people in our society have a need or desire for a stable, firmly-based, usually high evaluation of themselves, for self respect, or self esteem, and for the esteem of others. These are, first, the desire for strength, for achievement, for adequacy, for mastery and competence, for confidence in the face of the world, and for independence and free-

dom. Second, we have what we may call the desire for reputation or prestige (defining it as respect or esteem from other people), status, fame and glory, dominance, recognition, attention, importance, dignity, or appreciation. . . .

Satisfaction of the self esteem needs leads to feelings of self-confidence, worth, strength, capability, and adequacy, of being useful and necessary in the world. But thwarting of these needs produces feelings of inferiority, of weakness, and of helplessness. (p. 45)

A more recent argument of the thesis that self-esteem is a need has been provided by Locke, McClear, and Knight (1996). They argue that

self-esteem is a profound psychological need. It is impossible for a human being to tolerate the full, conscious conviction that he is fundamentally no good, that is, evil, worthless, inefficacious, without going insane or committing suicide. A person with low self esteem experiences self-doubt, anxiety, self-contempt and ultimately depression. . . . One with high self esteem experiences the serenity that comes from the conviction that he is fundamentally "ok" and not on trial with himself. Self esteem has two closely-related dimensions: efficacy and worth. By efficacy here we mean general efficacy—the ability to deal effectively in principle with life and the world. By worth we mean the conviction that one is morally good. (p. 1)

Whereas we can talk about and define a person's need for esteem, we can also consider his or her level of *self-esteem* as one's perception of his or her own worth (Battle, 1990, p. 22). Self-esteem is a *multifaceted set of beliefs,* one that grows and changes gradually, evolving as the person ages and has experiences with the world. Maslow (1954), among others, viewed self-esteem as a syndrome—an interrelated set of beliefs and attitudes that give rise to limited sets of behaviors. When a person can be influenced to act in certain ways that demand more strength and force, that person's entire belief structure about his worth may improve accordingly (Maslow, 1954).

A child's parents and early life experiences (whether successful or failures) can have a significant impact on the person's self-esteem. Nevertheless, positive self-esteem may sometimes develop *despite* the quality of a child's upbringing. For example, in February 1996, CBC Radio conducted an interview with a woman named Karen who was raised in a series of miserable and sometimes brutal foster homes. Eventually, she was transferred to a family in which her new mother instructed her to call herself "Suzie [Smith]," not the mother's real surname. The young Karen refused and proclaimed that her name was Karen, not Suzie. Years later, when she learned that she had so asserted herself in such a high-risk situation, the adult Karen rejoiced at how noble she thought the youngster had been. She reasoned to herself that if she liked and admired the youngster for having such courage and self-control, she was also proud of herself as an adult. She pursued an education and became a successful professor of English literature.

In many ways, self-esteem is related to the concept of self-determination that underlies so much of what we can call intrinsic motivation (see chapter 7). It is the sum of one's self-confidence and self-respect (Branden, 1969). For Branden, self-esteem is the most important value judgment that a person makes: It is about his or her value vis-à-vis the world (p. 103). Maslow (1954) explains how the satisfaction of esteem needs is central to the social and mental adjustment of people in our society. He points out, however, that the most valuable and most healthy self-esteem is based on the *deserved* respect from other people, rather than from false external fame or unwarranted celebrity. Branden (1969) asserts that the need for self-esteem is so powerful that people who don't really enjoy its satisfaction often engage in faking behavior: They pretend to like themselves and to be more proud of themselves than they really are. Such inauthentic self-esteem is an irrational pretence, maintained by the use of defense mechanisms (such as by rationalizing one's failures or making excuses and attributing defeats to external causes). Branden (1969) states: "Man experiences his desire for self esteem as an urgent imperative, as a basic need. Whether he identifies the issue explicitly or not, he cannot escape the feeling that his estimate of himself is of life-and-death importance" (p. 103).

People with high levels of self-esteem are simply healthier than those with lower levels; they are less anxious and demonstrate fewer symptoms of depression. High self-esteem is associated with higher levels of happiness with life in general. People with high self-esteem engage in fewer self-defeating acts and tend to be far more optimistic about themselves and their opportunities. In short, people *need* to feel good about themselves and to have others respect them and to feel good about them as well. In this chapter we focus on people's beliefs about whether they are able to do their work effectively and to succeed in the work world.

The concept of esteem is internal to a person's need structure—some have stronger needs for esteem than others. The concept of self-esteem is a more cognitive construct, a belief having to do with one's self-worth and how others appraise the person. Now, consider the concept of *status*. Status is not a need, it is a goal (recall chapter 3). The term *need* refers to a force internal to a person. Status is a designation ascribed to a person by other people. A person may have a high need for esteem but may or may not enjoy status. The social setting in which a person exists is the source of her status. As we will see later, status is a socially constructed concept and force that others place on a person. Whereas esteem is a potent, universal need, status is a social designation from others. Our discussion in this chapter deals with how work organizations (as outside sources) either help to frustrate or to satisfy people's need for esteem. It is critical that the reader keep these distinctions in mind.

Facets of Self-Esteem

A number of scholars have suggested recently that it may be important to distinguish between a person's global view of his or her self-esteem and self-esteem that is related more directly to specific tasks and activities (Rosenberg, Schooler, Schoenbach, and Rosenberg, 1995). The former idea has to do with a person's total view of himself or herself. As in the case of any attitude we hold, however, it is possible to have a positive overall attitude (such as "I like the city in which I live"), while having less general, more highly discordant attitudes toward facets of the object (such as "but I wish it wouldn't rain so much!"). Rosenberg et al. (1995) show that it is also possible to have specific attitudes about particular facets of one's self. In a massive study of more than 1,800 boys, they showed that global assessments of self were related to, but conceptually and empirically distinct from, the boys' "academic self-esteem." Moreover, they found that the former concept—global self-esteem—was positively related to a variety of measures of psychological well-being but not to the boys' actual academic achievement. On the other hand, the measure of academic self-esteem was strongly associated with the boys' actual performance in school.

Facets of Self-Esteem at Work

Similarly, Pierce, Gardner, Cummings, and Dunham (1989) have proposed a three-level construction of self-esteem. In their typology, they differentiate between three levels of self-esteem. The first is a global concept, similar to that of Rosenberg et al. (1995). They also have an organization-based concept, which they define "as the degree to which organizational members believe they can satisfy their needs by participating in roles within the context of an organization" (Pierce et al., 1989, p. 625). Finally, Pierce et al. (1989) delineate a concept of task- and job-based self-esteem, which is concerned with a person's views about her capacity to perform particular tasks. Of particular interest to our purposes is their second construct, organization-based self-esteem. They state: "Employees with high organization-based self esteem [OBSE] perceive themselves as important, meaningful, effectual and worthwhile within their employing organization. . . . [T]he determinants of OBSE may include managerial respect, organizational structure, and job complexity. Factors influenced by organization-based self esteem may include not only global self esteem but also job performance, intrinsic motivation, general satisfaction, citizenship behavior, organizational commitment, and general satisfaction" (pp. 643–644).

On the basis of many years of research on the topic of self-esteem in the workplace, Brockner (1988a, p. xi) observes that self-esteem influences employee behaviors and attitudes in two fundamental ways. First, employees bring to work with them their various levels of self-esteem, which, in turn, influence how they feel and behave on the job. Second, because of the powerful human need for esteem, much of what people do and feel on the job is at least partly related to their desire to satisfy that need, through seeking and mastering assignments, being promoted and advanced, and by developing their work skills. These two dynamics are in a sense circular and mutually reinforcing, and they lie behind a considerable amount of organizational behavior.

Korman (1970, 1976) has argued that a person's level of self-esteem even has a heavy influence on the nature of the careers and jobs that people seek to enter. Korman's theory holds that people are largely motivated to behave consistently with themselves; that is, people tend to prefer to engage in acts that are consistent with their beliefs and attitudes and—in particular—with their self-concepts. Therefore, a person who consciously espouses certain values and beliefs will be heavily affected by those values and beliefs as s/he seeks areas to study and careers to pursue. A person's self-esteem (which, we saw earlier, is a highly significant belief) plays a critical role. People with high self-esteem will shoot for the stars in tracking jobs and careers; people with lower self-esteem will tend to have much lower aspiration levels with regard to their working (and nonworking) lives. Movie fans will recall that the two down-and-outers played by Mickey Rourke and Faye Dunaway in the movie *Barfly* illustrate low self-esteem and low career aspiration levels.

Brockner (1988a) has consistently found support for the main tenets of Korman's theory, finding that people with high self-esteem tend to believe that their careers will be successful in satisfying their life goals and that they possess the right skills and abilities to be successful in their chosen careers (p. 17). The significance of employment for people's self-esteem was vividly demonstrated in a recent longitudinal study of more than 11,000 American high school graduates. The researchers found that periods of unemployment and job dissatisfaction were detrimental to people's self-esteem. Compared with graduates who had been employed over the seven-year period between 1980 and 1987, those who had been employed in dissatisfying jobs and those who had experienced great periods of unemployment showed less development of their self-esteem over that period than did grads who had been employed in satisfying jobs. Moreover, the greater the time of unemployment, the harsher were the effects on the students' self-esteem (Dooley and Prause, 1995).

Self-Esteem versus Self-Efficacy

Recent years in psychology have seen the emergence and study of a concept that is similar to, but different from, self-esteem. This newer concept, *self-efficacy,* plays a major role in a number of the formal theories of work motivation discussed later in the book. Its similarity to and tendency to become confused with self-esteem, especially self-esteem at the organizational level, requires that it be introduced at this point. Self-efficacy is a concept from *social cognitive theory,* a theory that posits that human behavior, human cognition, and the environment all interact in a mutually causal way to determine one another (Bandura, 1977, 1986). Specifically, it "refers to beliefs in one's capabilities to mobilize the motivation, cognitive resources, and courses of action needed to meet given situational demands" (Wood and Bandura, 1989, p. 408). Self-efficacy "is a judgement about task capability that is not inherently evaluative" (Gist and Mitchell, 1992, p. 185).

So, whereas a person may believe that she is not very competent at a specific task or job, such as painting, painting may not be important enough to the woman to affect her evaluation of herself in broader terms; that is, her low self-efficacy is unlikely to diminish her self-esteem. Again, self-esteem is a basic belief a person holds about his or her worth as a person, spanning a wide variety of situations (Brockner, 1988). Hence, self-esteem is not likely to be influenced by a person's feelings and perceptions of self-efficacy unless the person lacks skill and ability at most every task contemplated. Some confusion between these two concepts may have resulted from attempts by some researchers to invoke a concept of task-related self esteem. Brockner (1988a), among others, claims that the notion of task-specific self-esteem is synonymous with the concept of self-efficacy. Since the emergence and acceptance of self-efficacy, the idea of task-related self-esteem has received little attention.[6]

Later, in chapter 12, we will see that self-efficacy is similar to another construct in the popular expectancy-valence models of work motivation; we will deal with that apparent overlap at that point. In the meantime we return to our discussion of self-esteem and contrast its effect on work motivation with that of self-efficacy.

---

[6]There has been considerable confusion about the meanings of self-efficacy and self-esteem, in large part caused by lack of agreement among authors about the boundaries and definitions of the constructs. Some people refer to a trait called *trait expectancy, global, chronic self-esteem,* or *general self-efficacy* as a stable personality trait that accompanies a person from one context to another. Here we refer to this construct merely as self-esteem. Others have written about *state expectancy, specific self-esteem, particularized self-efficacy,* and *specific self-efficacy.* These all represent the beliefs a person holds about his or her capacity to perform a particular task in a particular setting and time (Eden and Kinnar, 1991). It is time the confusion stopped so that the field can enjoy the benefits of cumulative research and theoretical efforts via a single vocabulary (see Eden, 1988).

Self-Esteem, Self-Efficacy, Job Performance, and Satisfaction

Although it is true that self-esteem levels are positively correlated with job attitudes, there is little, if any, evidence that high self-esteem is causally related to high levels of job performance, at least when "performance" is measured as raw productivity. There are a number of reasons why this may be the case (see Brockner, 1988a, for a review of these arguments). For example, work motivation and performance are both determined by a variety of factors, personality variables (such as need for esteem) and cognitive variables (such as self-esteem) being only two of many. Moreover, people often engage in esteem-enhancing behaviors on the job, acts intended to bolster either their own self-esteem or their reputations in the eyes of significant others. Seeking feedback and/or paying attention to feedback about one's work can be two critical determinants of work performance (Ashford, 1993; Ashford and Cummings, 1983). Employees who are concerned with their status and self-esteem may elect neither to solicit help and feedback in relation to their work, nor pay attention to whatever feedback is available. One study found, for example, that people with low self-esteem avoided feedback about their personal task performance, although not necessarily about their performance in comparison to that of other people (Northcraft and Ashford, 1990). To the extent that performance feedback is avoided, nevertheless, the work performance of people may be impaired.

Whereas self-esteem has very little connection with task performance, self-efficacy has repeatedly been shown to predict task success (Bandura, 1986). Moreover, self-efficacy may have an interesting relationship with social facilitation and social loafing, two other concepts we examined earlier in the chapter. Experimental research reported by Sanna (1992), for example, suggests that people with high self-efficacy beliefs, working together but for individual goals (coacting), may work more effectively than high-efficacy people who work alone. This is what Sanna (1992) found, supporting the social facilitation hypothesis (described earlier in this chapter). In addition, when people had beliefs of low self-efficacy, they performed better when working toward group goals than when working toward individual goals. Sanna (1992) cites this as support for the social loafing hypothesis. In short, self-efficacy may help to explain and reconcile the fascinating effects of people on one another's work motivation through social facilitation and social loafing. More work is required on this possibility. Aside from its lack of clear effects on job performance, however, it seems that high self-esteem is positively related to other aspects of work performance, such as "prosocial" work behavior (good citizenship and work above and beyond the call of duty [Brockner, 1988a, and see chapter 10]).

Recent years have seen a number of efforts to refine our understanding of self-esteem and to differentiate among different levels of the construct. The interested reader is referred to Brockner's (1988) work for a complete theoretical exploration of the known and theoretically possible linkages among esteem motivation, self-esteem, and organizational outcomes such as work motivation, performance, and job attitudes.

In the remaining sections of this chapter, we turn our attention away from the individual worker and his or her esteem motivation to examine the contexts within which esteem-driven persons live and work: We examine status systems, particularly status systems within workplaces.

Status and Status Systems

What is social status? Sociologists offer a variety of definitions, and they tend to converge. For Faunce (1982), social status is a location in a hierarchy resulting from the unequal distribution of anything that is valued and that produces relations of deference, acceptance, or derogation (p. 172). Hence, status implies differences among people or social units in terms of honor, esteem, respect, and prestige (Zeldich, 1968). In some sense, status is a "gratification." To lose it is a deprivation. According to Zeldich (1968, p. 253), "opportunities to improve status are seized by almost everyone, even in societies that are not achievement-oriented. . . . When status is threatened, its loss is resisted. . . ."

The differences that exist among categories of working people are powerful indicators of their relative status, both at work and outside the work context. Hence, it is common practice upon meeting a newcomer in Western culture to inquire immediately about the person's occupation. The labels and categories that come as answers are critical, symbolic, and value-laden. Inherent in them are distinctions with status implications. We have work-related distinctions between manual and nonmanual employees, supervisors and nonsupervisors, "productive" versus "nonproductive" labor, professionals versus nonprofessionals, managers and routine workers, and credentialed versus uncredentialed workers (Burris, 1990). These days it may not even be polite or politically correct to refer to someone as a "worker," the preferred term being "employee," perhaps.

If people's occupational achievement is the primary determinant of their status in Western society, what is it that determines a person's occupational achievement? A complete answer is beyond the scope and purpose of this book, but one factor that may not come to mind readily but is worth mentioning is genetics. Elsewhere we have noted that some organization theorists have suggested that biology may play a factor in certain aspects of human work motivation and behavior (e.g., Arvey and Bouchard, 1994). Interestingly, there is preliminary evidence to suggest that biology, notably in the form of the male hormone testosterone, may play a role in the occupational achievement (and hence, in the social status) of North American men. In a large-scale study of Viet Nam war vets conducted by the Centers for Disease Control, Dabbs (1992) found that higher levels of testosterone were correlated with lower levels of occupational achievement. The sample studied comprised a representative cross-section of the U.S. population at large. The explanation offered was that higher levels of the hormone among young males led to higher levels of antisocial behavior, lower levels of intelligence, and lower levels of education, resulting, eventually, in fewer or lower levels of marketable job skills. Dabbs (1992) observes that the effects were small in statistical terms but important enough to be taken seriously, because testosterone levels are heritable and virtually fixed at the time of birth. The point here is that occupational status may be determined by a variety of factors, at least one of which is beyond the control of the individual.

For the concept of social status to have much psychological effect on people or to serve as an incentive for people to "get ahead" in life, it seems reasonable to expect that there be some degree of consensus among the people of a society regarding the comparative status of occupations. Such has not always been the case, however (e.g., Powell and Jacobs, 1983). In fact, a study by Guppy and Goyder (1984) found that although there was considerable consensus among people of high socioeconomic status (SES), there was much less agreement about occupational prestige among people of both mixed and lower SES levels. There was comparatively low consensus about occupational status among the black participants of the study as well. Gazenboom, De Graaf, De Trieman, and de Leeuw (1992) have developed and reported an approach to the scaling of occupational status, international in scope, that may help address many of the problems of previous attempts.

Notwithstanding the measurement problem, there has long been a powerful connection between work, working, and the status of people. The workplace is a potent *potential* forum for the satisfaction or the frustration of esteem needs and for the very definitions we apply to ourselves and to others. To denigrate the working category of a person is usually taken as insulting, and it becomes important for many people that they are seen as belonging to one of the more prestigious status groups (professionals, executives, entrepreneurs, etc.). More will be said on these matters shortly. In the following section, we will briefly review some of the knowledge related to esteem need satisfaction and the powerful role that work and work organizations can have in the satisfaction or frustration of esteem needs. The need for positive self-regard from others and for having a positive view of one's own worth motivates a lot of human behavior; it is certainly a powerful source of work motivation. Before we begin we take a brief look at the nature of status systems in general terms, to explore what they are and why they exist.

The Nature and Functions of Organizational Status Systems

One organizational scholar defined status with the workplace in mind as "the condition of the individual that is defined by a statement of his rights, privileges, immunities, duties, and obligations as well as the restrictions, limitations, and prohibitions concerning his behavior" (Barnard, 1946). Why do status systems exist? A first, simple answer is found throughout the current section of this chapter: Status systems provide for the possible satisfaction of human needs (such as the esteem needs). But what else do they do? What other functions are served by status systems?

First, they can serve as incentives. To achieve formally designated positions of high status can be rewarding, especially for those who value these rewards. High-status positions can be rewarding for their own sake, and they can also be instrumental for the attainment of other rewards and benefits (Barnard, 1946). Second, status systems can help develop and maintain a sense of responsibility and decorum among people. The threat of a loss in one's status can be a considerable impediment in work settings, causing people to adhere to company codes of conduct as well as the mores of society at large. The author knows of professional accounting firms that have strong informal rules about the conduct of their employees outside the workplace, during after-hours. Violation of these rules can be costly to the status and subsequent treatment of those who dare to violate. Reducing a person's status officially is one of the most dramatic and traumatic acts in organizational life. Having to discipline an employee is a dreaded part of most managers' jobs, and being the recipient of organizational discipline can be even more traumatic for the employee involved. Having to lay off people for economic reasons is bad; having to fire an employee for cause is the stuff of nightmares for most bosses and executives (see chapter 10). Status can be thought of as a cherished commodity, in life in general and particularly in the context of one's work. To be stripped of one's status is therefore a consequence of organizational behavior dreaded by most people. Hence, the maintenance of a strong status system makes control, reward, and punishment powerful managerial tools.

There is a mixed and complex relationship between status and interpersonal communication. On one hand, status systems can expedite communication (Barnard, 1946). A junior officer who receives an order from a commander has no legitimate reason to ask about "why's and wherefore's"—an order is an order. The uniform worn by the commander immediately lets the junior officer know that what the former has to say is to be taken seriously and acted upon. Communication is thereby expedited. Further, the recognition of rank by both parties determines the sort of language and decorum that is appropriate. People tend to speak and write to others in terms that are appropriate to the status of both the sender and the receiver of the message. Again, communication is enhanced by status. On the other hand, status differences between people can inhibit the open communication of ideas if the lower-status person is afraid to be frank, open, honest, and complete in what s/he communicates, or if the "superior" person resents being addressed by a status inferior.[7] Similarly, high-status persons may withhold information that is sensitive, classified, or beyond "the need to know."

The theory of status characteristics and expectation states that when members of a group are arranged in a certain rank order by their status, they will tend to have the same relative standing among group members in terms of the amount of interaction they have with other group members (J. Berger, Cohen, and Zeldich, 1972; J. Berger, Rosenholtz, and Zeldich, 1980). A massive field test of three key hypotheses from the theory recently supported it (B. P. Cohen and Zhou, 1991). The researchers investigated 2,077 respondents representing 224 research and development teams from 29 large corporations. They assessed all team members on a variety of "external" status indicators (education, gender, status within the company as a whole, seniority, and whether the person was a formally designated leader) as well as on two "internal" indicators (expert status and team status). The findings revealed that the external indicators all had a major impact on the scientists' status within their respective teams, and that this team status, in turn, was significantly predictive of the amount of formal interaction involving each person. The study suggests the pervasiveness and importance of society- and organization-level status systems and shows how they can affect the interaction of people inside formally designated work groups.

Differences between Occupations in Status and Prestige

An issue of long-standing interest to sociologists has been the comparative status of various occupations in the economy. Historians and political scientists can use the relative comings and goings of status differences as a means of tracking "the times," the importance of various current events, and the general values of the culture at large. For

---

[7]E. H. Porter (1962) tells the story of the invention of the spindle found in many restaurants. According to Porter, differences between highly skilled cooks and lesser skilled waiters and waitresses (called "servers" these days) was not culturally acceptable in many restaurants. Low-status people should not be in a position to initiate orders with persons of higher status. The introduction of the spindle on which a diner's order can be placed and then rotated into the view of the cook obviates the need for cross-status communication.

example, the author vividly recalls the tremendous negative impact that the Watergate hearings had on the social status of attorneys in the United States in the late 1970s and early 1980s. Nevertheless, the point is that societies typically stratify members of the workforce on the basis of the general occupations to which people belong. There is rarely a case where all occupations are viewed as equally prestigious.

The traditional bases for determining interoccupational status differences are the power, income, and/or necessary educational level associated with the occupations (Abbott, 1981). Accordingly, the professions are usually ranked in the higher echelons of a society's status hierarchy, and the issue becomes one of deciding and agreeing upon which occupations are professions and which are not. Another issue that emerges quickly has to do with the comparative status of the professions: Are nurses more prestigious, as a group, than school teachers? Are physicians of higher status than accountants? But that's not all: We also have a keen tendency to differentiate among ourselves within occupations.

Stratification within Occupations

The human desire to stratify usually causes stratification consciousness to occur within particular occupations. Among the members of any profession, for example, stratification occurs. All physicians are not seen as equal within the population of people accepted as physicians. In Canada, homeopaths are held in low regard and high suspicion by much of the rest of the medical "establishment." Similarly, not all lawyers are perceived as equally prestigious among members of that profession. Interestingly, it seems that the lawyers (or physicians, etc.) who are seen as the most prestigious by the outside community are held in much lower regard by members of the inside group of lawyers (or physicians). In other words, the eminent scientist who takes her work to the people by popularizing and making intelligible the current knowledge of her field via television or radio is likely to be held in relatively low regard by members of the same subdiscipline who prefer not to go public.

Abbott (1981) attempts to explain this paradox by arguing that professionals prefer to keep themselves "pure," unencumbered by what he calls nonprofessional issues or irrelevant professional issues arising from practice. Anything that entails human complexity, problems, or reality bespoils the state of purity, and accordingly, denigrates the status of the professional engaged in the activity. Hence the judge holds superior status to the district attorney because the former can maintain professional purity through the buffering rules of the courtroom. The theoretical engineer who works in a university lab is likely to enjoy much less status in the eyes of the general public than the famous engineer who is publicly acknowledged for constructing large public projects such as bridges or dams. Inside the profession, however, Abbott (1981) would predict that the comparative status of these two engineers would be quite the opposite. Biopsychologists enjoy higher status in the profession than that of social psychologists, who, in turn, look down on the industrial psychologist (whose work has the most to do with problems of real people in messy organizational settings). It seems that dealing with people and the real problems that people drag along with them, such as illness, laws, crimes, or troubles of any sort, create an opportunity for an erstwhile professional to lose her purity and, with it, some of the status she enjoys within the culture of her peers.

Status-Assignment Systems

The concept of *status-assignment systems* helps us understand the ubiquity of these inter- and intraoccupational status comparisons (Faunce, 1982, 1989). The basic elements of status-assignment systems, according to Faunce (1989), "are a set of persons or positions being evaluated, a set of people doing the evaluating, a set of values, and a resulting hierarchy of persons or positions. Any social encounter that includes relations of deference, equality, or derogation involves an explicit or implied status-assignment system" (p. 384). Moreover, these status-assignment systems occur within boundaries of varying size and degrees of inclusion. So, as we have seen above, an occupational status-assignment system may be circumscribed by the boundaries of a work group, office, firm, occupation, or set of corporations in a community or society (Faunce, 1989, p. 385). "Having a very rich brother-in-law may locate one differently in a family status hierarchy from having a highly-educated brother-in-law" (Faunce, 1982, p. 168). (The problem is moot, of course, when the same brother-in-law is both highly educated and rich.)

One study found that members of a common occupation will differ from each other in status on the basis of whether they match the dominant gender composition of the occupation in question (Powell and Jacobs, 1984). For example they found that women in female-dominated occupations (e.g., nursing) were regarded as having higher prestige than that of male nurses. Similarly, women truck drivers were regarded as having lower prestige than male truck drivers, the driving of trucks being a predominantly male preserve. Moreover, the gap in prestige between males and females within any given occupation was correlated with the degree to which the person was "misplaced" in comparison to the population at large.

In a related study the same researchers sought to determine whether there is an inherent gender-related status for occupations or whether the gender of typical occupants in the various occupations also played a role (Jacobs and Powell, 1985). They found that the general status of occupations seemed to reflect the prestige normally attributed to the gender-typical jobholders (men in male-dominated occupations, women in female-dominated occupations). The researchers concluded that "the seemingly sex-neutral concept of occupational prestige incorporates strong sex-linked assumptions. . . . [T]he prestige accorded to an occupation reflects the sex-typical incumbent—men in male-dominated occupations and women in female-dominated occupations" (pp. 1069–1070). Clearly, the relationships between gender, gender-role stereotypes, and the actual distribution of men and women across occupations are complex and subject to change as the nature of the workforce changes. Aside from how complex or tricky these relationships are, they do matter to people in the workplace.

The point here is simple: People, by nature, will stratify. Much of the desire to do so (not all of it) is driven by a universal need for esteem. The nature of work that people perform is a ready, handy, and common basis for forming horizontal layers between people, and as we have seen, there is almost no end to the fineness of the gradations people conjure or create to assure that some persons are superior to others while receiving less status and prestige than others.

Status Symbols in the Workplace

An integral part of virtually all status systems is any number of tangible and intangible symbols that serve to reflect the status of the people who use or possess them. Office size and decoration are an example. One study found that employees who were temporarily relocated to higher-status offices increased their work performance. Conversely, employees in the same study who were temporarily relocated to offices of lower status values than they were used to occupying demonstrated a reduction in work performance (Greenberg, 1988b). Many organizations invest considerable trouble, time, and expense to assure that there is a close relationship between the quality of the office space a person occupies and that person's status. Corner offices are coveted, for example, because they often tend to be larger and have more windows. Occupants of corner offices may claim that the extra space is appreciated because it permits easier access, more storage, or larger meetings; the real value, however, usually lies in the fact that there are a limited number of large corner offices and the recipients of these spaces are the higher-status members of the organization. People often go to great lengths to deny the sociological facts of status symbols ("The extra space is functional" really means "Look at me, I have arrived!"). The author knows of a professional engineering firm that prohibits the assignment of corner offices to individual employees because part of the managerial philosophy of the firm is to deny status differences ("We are all equals here"). Their corner offices are used for the firm's library, conference and meeting rooms, and for other purposes. Despite the firm's desire to deny status differences, other bases emerge, usually based on the subspecialty of the engineers themselves.

What is seen as a status symbol varies from culture to culture and from group to group. Status symbols are generally commodities that are rare and take on value in part because of the cultural belief that they are rare and valued. Possessing one's own price marker was a jealously sought-after and protected status symbol in the culture of a grocery store the author once worked in. To possess one's own price marker implied that the person was of high status. It was especially "cool" to possess one's own belt holster in which to carry the marker. Status symbols need not be tangible objects. Job titles are important: Never confuse an "assistant to the manager" with an "assistant manager." Privileges—to come and go at will, for example, or to set one's own work schedule—are nontangible indicators of status that people can grow to cherish, protect, maintain, and covet.

Military and paramilitary organizations place especially heavy importance on status symbols. Stars, stripes, chevrons, pins, badges, and other insignia are carefully assigned to officers and troops of various levels with the strictest of control and regimentation. That the symbols of military rank are taken seriously was vividly illustrated in two very recent cases. The first case involved Admiral Mike Boorda, who was the U.S. Chief of Naval Operations when he took his own life in the spring of 1996. A veteran of 40 years' service, Boorda was distressed when questions were raised about the appropriateness of his wearing two small bronze V pins among the considerable collection of decorations on his uniform. These insignia designate that the wearer saw combat in the war zones represented by the V's. Although Boorda had served in combat zones during the Viet Nam War and had earned two commendations for his service there, he had not actually earned the V's, the wearing of which implied that he had been exposed to personal hazard due to direct hostile action by the enemy. When he realized his mistake, Boorda stopped wearing the pins, but by this time, there were journalists and other people who were curious about his ever having worn them. Rather than permitting his error to cause a denigration of the symbolic value and meaning of the medals, Admiral Boorda killed himself immediately before a meeting with the curious journalists. For Boorda and other members of the U.S. miliary culture, it was a matter of honor (Zoglin, 1996).

In the second case, Otto ("Dutch") Bischoff, aged 97, was awarded the U.S. Military's Silver Star for his "great coolness and courage" during action against the German

Army at the Battle of the Argonne Forest in early 1918. For whatever bureaucratic reasons, the Army failed to award the Silver Star in due course, and it took the Fraternal Order of Trench Soldiers to research the case and to rectify the oversight. The medal was awarded to Mr. Bischoff in June 1996, 78 years after he had earned it. After all the intervening years, the Silver Star was still deemed of sufficient value to be awarded, and the military still believed in the symbolic importance of awarding it (*Vancouver Province,* June 27, 1996, p. A26).

There are countless other examples of status symbols, their importance, and the functions they serve. Anyone old enough to have held a job, seen a movie, or read a book about work will recognize the point here. Status systems require and are defined by status symbols. To possess these symbols implies high status. Not to possess them implies lower status, and to have them taken away is usually a source of great embarrassment and humiliation for the person involved.

A Theoretical Caveat

Most of the examples just provided to illustrate status symbols in work settings probably have a familiar ring. Yet for those who are concerned with theory development and the refinement of concepts of status, status symbols, and their potential for appealing to people's needs for self-esteem, a precaution is sounded by Faunce (1982). Using the specific substantive example of status and self-esteem, Faunce criticizes modern sociology for the slapdash way by which complex concepts (such as social status) are operationalized and interpreted without careful connections to theory. As examples, he notes that we might be tempted to equate status differences between occupations with the levels of pay they receive, or with the educational levels that they require, or with whether the work involved is manual or conceptual, and so on. In practice, these various "indicators" of status may be correlated among themselves (such that high-paying jobs tend to require greater training and education and tend to be conducted by people in white collars, using their minds rather than their hands, for example), but neither are these connections perfect and always predictable, and neither do the choices among the indicators find theoretical justification in a carefully articulated conceptualization of social status (Faunce, 1982):

> [M]any of the presumed consequences of occupational status differences rest on the assumption that people care about these differences. The assumption that occupational status influences self esteem without further specification of the mechanisms through which this may occur [is] an example of chain saw sociology. A theory explaining this relationship would have to identify various types of occupational status hierarchies, specify the conditions under which these hierarchies are more or less likely to become relevant to social experience, and detail the ways in which social evaluation involved in the experience of status differences influences self esteem. (p. 169)

In many ways, Faunce's observations and lament are related to those that we see in psychology and microorganizational behavior under the general heading of *construct validity* (see Schwab, 1980, and chapter 2 of this book). The point is that sometimes, our desire to make practical (managerial?) use of social scientific concepts induces us to grasp at handy, salient, or obvious indicators of those concepts, for the sake of getting on with practical matters, such as running a school or a business, raising a family, or providing assistance to those in need. The problem, according to Faunce (1982), is that such quick and loose interpretations of concepts by practitioners can obscure the essential meanings of the concepts themselves and inhibit the development of theoretical disciplines such as sociology. In addition to the meanings of the concepts is the problem of understanding why and how the various concepts are connected.

This author offered a similar lament two decades ago in relation to the "premature application" of theories of work motivation (Pinder, 1977). The reader with applied intentions may benefit from the wisdom regarding status symbols and self-esteem that was offered earlier in this section, but Faunce (1982) cautions that the connections between the "obvious" indicators of status and status differences and the true meaning of the concepts they purport to represent (in this case, social status) are only partial, imperfect, and without much in the way of conceptual wholeness. Point well taken, although we will see shortly that Faunce (1982, 1989) has offered a *constructive* example of how theoretically based connections can be made between concepts in social science, again using the specific substantive case of the relationship between status and self-esteem.

Status Assignment and Denigration

Status can be achieved either through ascription or by effort, merit, and accomplishment. When a person has earned the right to a higher level of status, there is often some form of ceremony involved to mark the event (see Trice, Belasco, and Alutto, 1969). The greater the transition in status, the greater and more extravagant the event tends to be (Ritti, 1994). Work organizations make frequent use of ceremonials in the more or less well-managed realities of status in the workplace. Promotions are advertised, demotions are kept hush-hush (unless the purpose is to damage the demoted person's pride and self-esteem), and retirements are frequently feted by lavish gifts and testimonials.

Interestingly, lateral career moves are seldom free of status implications (Pinder, 1989). It seems that as long as two jobs are somehow different from one another in terms of content, location, or mission, they are held not to be of equal status in most organizational status systems. Geographic moves within a company are similar. Moving from Toronto to Chicago in one company may be widely interpreted as a promotion ("She's really on the fast track"), whereas the same move in another company (other factors being equal) may widely be held as a demotion—that the person is being "put out to pasture" (see Pinder, 1983).

An issue of common concern in many companies these days is caused by the fact that most companies' formal structures are pyramidal and the demographics of the work population are uneven. This means that many people (especially in the baby-boom generation and in Generation X) are confronted with limited opportunities for upward movement within their organizations. Their bosses are still far from retirement. One solution that has been proposed is downward movement of people for the sake of keeping them interested and motivated in their work, and committed to the employer (see D.T. Hall and Isabella, 1985). Naturally, this solution meets with only limited success because of the traditional association in work organizations between career advancement, increased status levels, and *upward* movement in the hierarchy. Status and status consciousness are ubiquitous in work settings.

The Role of Occupational Status in Self-Esteem

Now that we have discussed the need for esteem and the potential of work and work organizations for either satisfying or denying these needs, we can directly ask the question: Does working in a putatively high status role necessarily result in the satisfaction of esteem needs? Faunce (1982, 1989) claims that the answer is no; the relationship is not so simple. According to Faunce (1989), the empirical research on the relationship between occupational achievement and self-esteem is confused, mixed, and ambiguous. He argues that "the effects of status on self esteem occur not simply as a result of *knowledge* of one's location in a status hierarchy but, more important, as a result of the frequency with which one is *reminded* of that location." In other words, Faunce is suggesting that merely possessing a superior position in a status hierarchy does not assure that a person will experience high self-esteem; rather, the system must frequently remind the person of his or her rank through any of variety of means. For example, frequent encounters with persons of apparently lower or higher status, frequent use of the perquisites of one's status, or frequent recognition by others of one's status are characteristics of status systems that can make one's status meaningful or central to one's definition of self. Faunce (1989) refers to this notion as *self-investment:* Different activities or attributes of a person's life take on different levels of significance for the way the person defines his or her value or success in life: "Self investment is defined as a commitment to achievement with regard to an activity or attribute based on the relevance of that activity or attribute for self esteem. High self investment in work, for example, means that occupational achievement in some form is necessary to maintain self esteem; those with low self investment can fail in this area with impunity" (pp. 381–382). Moreover, the more frequently a person is evaluated by others in terms of an activity or attribute, the higher will be the centrality of that activity (such as one's work) or attribute (such as one's skill or good looks). In short, if a person's work is not a central life interest (Dubin, 1956), or in Faunce's terms, if a person is not heavily self-invested in work, the attainment of status at any level will probably have no impact, good or bad, on the person's self-esteem.

Work is a major determinant of status for many of us, although not for all of us (Faunce, 1989). Among those of us for whom work is a central life interest, however, the status systems found related to work at all levels can be critical determinants of our self-esteem. If work is important to us and we fail to achieve sufficient status, we expect the person's self-esteem to suffer, to be frustrated. Work achievement for these people, on the other hand, will contribute greatly to their sense of self-worth. However, if a person does not have a high degree of self-investment in work, his success or failure in work-related pursuits may have no impact on his self-esteem. Other areas of his life (such as his family, religion, or leisure accomplishments) may be much more critical for the determination of self-esteem.

GENERAL SUMMARY AND A GLANCE AHEAD

In this chapter we continued our explicit examination of the human needs for social interaction and of the motivational consequences of these needs and interactions for organizational behavior. Whereas in chapter 5 we looked at power motivation and the human desires for love and sex as they appear in work settings, in this chapter we explored the human desire for affiliation and for the esteem of others and of themselves. We also explored the ways in which the needs for affiliation and esteem may be aroused and then either satisfied or frustrated by work settings and experiences. In the following chapter we turn our attention away from the relatedness needs altogether and focus on the human needs for psychological growth and self-determination.

CHAPTER

Growth Needs and Intrinsic Motivation to Work

It matters not how strait the gate
How charged with punishments the scroll
I am the master of my fate
I am the captain of my soul
—W. E. HENLEY

Imagine that you are walking with a friend through your neighborhood on a warm summer evening. As you walk, you notice a 9-year-old boy pushing a lawn mower in erratic circles and strips around the grass on his parents' front yard. The boy has his head lowered between his straight, extended arms, and he is bent over at the waist as he runs and pushes the mower. Upon getting closer, you hear him making sounds like an engine—an airplane engine. You stop and ask the young man what he is doing and learn that he is pretending to be a pilot flying an airplane. The sounds he was emitting, of course, were those made by the plane's motor. The young pilot seems friendly enough, so you stop to chat for awhile. The conversation reveals that the boy is having fun with his fantasy Beechcraft and that he did not consider his activity to be work. Further probing on your part informs you that the boy receives no pay or other form of direct compensation from his parents for cutting the grass (or flying his airplane). You part company, wishing him a safe flight.

Is the boy in this example working (cutting the lawn), or playing (flying his aircraft)? Or does it matter what you call it or how you classify his behavior? For the boy, the behavior clearly was playing. On the other hand, the boy's father would view it as work—a chore that he would now not have to perform himself. It may simply be a matter of one's perspective, as seemed to be the case when Tom Sawyer managed to lure his friends into whitewashing his Aunt Polly's fence. Using some of the concepts and tools of chapter 3 we can look a bit deeper behind the reasons for our young pilot's behavior, asking, for example, what motivated him to behave the way he did. We can probably rule out existence and relatedness needs as explanations for the boy's action, because he was not deriving monetary rewards for his play, nor did he seem to be seeking social interaction from it. If we assume that the boy's behavior was, in fact, motivated (as opposed to being simply random or compulsive), we are left with the conclusion that the boy must have been motivated largely by growth needs. What, you may ask, has growth got to do with the erratic flight of a low-altitude lawn mower?

Before proceeding, consider a second case, of a 55-year-old widow who attends noncredit courses at night school to study a variety of languages that are new to her. Although she enjoys traveling, she has absolutely no interest in visiting Russia or Japan, yet Russian and Japanese are the two languages she has studied and enjoyed most since the death of her husband. How do you explain this woman's behavior? There is no possible connection in her mind between mastering these languages—both of which begin with alphabets totally dissimilar from the Roman characters she is familiar with—and the satisfaction of any basic biological needs. At one level it appears that she is learning these difficult new languages, at least in part, because she enjoys the challenge.

The purpose of this chapter is to examine further a set of needs that we classified in chapter 3 as growth needs, and then study the role of growth needs in a phenomenon called *intrinsic motivation* or *intrinsically motivated behavior.* We then move to an analysis of alternative perspectives on intrinsic motivation and present some of the controversy that has surrounded this fascinating concept. The chapter concludes with a discussion of some currently popular managerial concepts, such as job enrichment and employee empowerment, that have both historical and conceptual links with the theory of intrinsic motivation.

WHAT IS INTRINSIC MOTIVATION?

Current thinking in work motivation would view both the boy's and the woman's behavior as being *intrinsically motivated.* Or we might say that each was intrinsically motivated to do what he or she was doing. Intrinsically motivated behavior can be defined, loosely, as behavior that is performed for its own sake rather than for the purpose of acquiring any material or social rewards. But there is much more to it than that. One scholar who has investigated intrinsically motivated behaviors extensively defines them as those "which a person engages in to feel competent and self determining" (Deci, 1975, p. 61). More recently:

> Intrinsic motivation is based in the innate, organismic needs for competence and self-determination. It energizes a wide variety of behaviors and psychological processes for which the primary rewards are the experiences of effectance and autonomy. Intrinsic needs differ from primary drives in that they are not based on tissue deficits and they do not operate cyclically, that is, breaking into awareness, pushing to be satisfied, and then when satisfied, receding into quiescence. Like drives, however, intrinsic needs are innate to the human organism and function as an important energizer of behavior. Furthermore, intrinsic motivation may interact with drives in the sense of either amplifying or attenuating drives and of affecting the way in which people satisfy their drives. (Deci and Ryan, 1985, p. 32)

Feelings of interest and enjoyment—even excitement—characterize intrinsic motivation, accompanied by what Deci and Ryan call a "sense of flow" of the sort that the young lawn mower pilot must have been sensing. Yet, even though feelings of competence and interest in the task are central to intrinsic motivation, a person must also feel free of pressures such as rewards or potential punishments. The person must feel that her "locus of causality" is internal, meaning that she is responsible for the choice of the activity, that she is in command of how she is spending her time. Hence, the notion of *choice* is central to the concept of self-determination—the person must be in control of the alternatives for action and be able to choose among them. Although choice is also a possibility in many extrinsically motivated activities, it is central to the concept of intrinsic motivation.[1]

In addition, the person must feel challenged: experiencing, finding, or creating situations that will provide opportunities for mastery, as in the cases of the boy with the lawn mower and the multilingual woman we described earlier.

> The intrinsic needs for competence and self-determination motivate an ongoing process of seeking and attempting to conquer optimal challenges. When people are free from the intrusion of drives and emotions, they seek situations that interest them and require the use of their creativity and resourcefulness. They seek challenges that are suited to their competencies, that are neither too easy nor too difficult. When they find optimal challenges, people work to conquer them, and they do so persistently. In short, the needs for competence and self-determination keep people involved in ongoing cycles of seeking and conquering optimal challenges. (Deci and Ryan, 1985, pp. 32–33)

Exploratory and inquisitive behavior is common among animals as well as human beings (see Harlow, Harlow, and Meyer, 1950). It is adaptive. If members of a species did not explore and take risks in seeking new places to live and new sources of food, they would surely perish. Psychologists have argued that such behavior is not only innately human, but that it is also characteristic of many cultures—such as those found in Canada and the United States—that emphasize individualism, self-fulfillment, and freedom (e.g., Eisenberger and Cameron, 1996).

The desire to be in control of one's circumstances manifests itself in work settings in many ways. In chapter 6 we saw how affiliation motivation plays a key role in how people attempt to "make sense" of uncertainties around them. Few places can be more threatening for adults than new work settings; at first most people feel that they have little control over what happens to them. In a recent study of newly graduated middle managers, Ashford and Black (1996) found that newcomers will try a wide variety of tactics to gather information for the sake of securing some semblance of self-control. In particular, people with comparatively stronger needs for control engaged more proactively than other employees in socialization tactics such as seeking job-related information, feedback about their behavior, networking, building relationships with their new bosses, and so on. It is one thing for newcomers to a work setting to accept passively the socialization procedures applied to them by management; it is another thing for people who have especially high needs for control to set about to secure control proactively.

In another study, a sample of shoe factory employees in New York state who reported having higher levels of autonomy, relatedness, and competence on the job expe-

---

[1]Consider the stanza from the poem "Invictus" that opened this chapter: It captures the notions of self-determination and internal control of one's activities and outcomes.

rienced greater overall levels of job satisfaction, higher self-esteem, and general well-being. These results were obtained when either the employees or their supervisors provided ratings about the presence of the intrinsic motivational features of the job. When the various effects of the three factors were examined separately, it was found that the autonomy factor contributed to general satisfaction, satisfaction with the work, and general mental health. Feelings of competence were associated with feelings of self-esteem (Ilardi, Leone, Kasser, and Ryan, 1993). In another study, 380 door-to-door sales personnel were shown to derive satisfaction from merely trying hard—from expending great effort in their attempts to sell products—even when their efforts failed to result in extrinsic satisfaction caused by the rewards for high performance (S. P. Brown and Peterson, 1994).

The reader will notice from the passages quoted above that Deci and Ryan (1985) sometimes write of the *needs* for competence and self-determination as if they are equivalent, or at least two elements of a single concept. E. A. Skinner and her colleagues take exception to the idea that competence and self-determination are one and the same thing. Building on de Charms (1968), she states that "the need for self-determination, or autonomy, is the desire to be the origin of one's own behavior, to be free, to choose one's course of action for one's self" (E. A. Skinner, 1995, p. 10). By comparison, *competence* refers to the "connection between behaviors and outcomes; it is the extent to which a person feels capable of producing desired and preventing undesired events; its opposite is helplessness. Autonomy refers to the connection between volition and action; it is the extent to which a person feels free to show the behaviors of his choice; nonautonomous behaviors include both compliance and defiance, which have in common that they are reactions to others' agendas and not freely chosen" (Patrick, Skinner, and Connell, 1993, cited by E. A. Skinner, 1995, p. 11).

We can link many of these concepts back to earlier notions advanced by writers such as Maslow (1954; recall chapter 3), who would relate intrinsic motivation to his "higher-order needs" or to what Alderfer (1972) would classify as growth needs—force directed toward behavior that is its own incentive. The distinction between internal and external work motivation originated with Herzberg, Mausner, and Snyderman's (1959) study of the determinants of job satisfaction (recall chapter 2). Although the concepts of intrinsic and extrinsic motives, rewards, and outcomes have not always been understood and used consistently (Dyer and Parker, 1975), the distinction is important; intrinsic motivation is a major factor in explaining much of the work behavior of many employees. In fact, intrinsic motivation (and hence the intrinsic rewards required to satisfy it) may well become increasingly important as the workforce becomes more highly educated and less threatened by challenging jobs (M. R. Cooper, Morgan, Foley, and Kaplan, 1979).

Intrinsic and Extrinsic Outcomes

In addition to distinguishing between intrinsic and extrinsic motivation, scholars have distinguished between intrinsic and extrinsic job outcomes (Lawler, 1969). Intrinsic outcomes relate to either the satisfaction or frustration of higher-level or growth needs. Examples of intrinsic outcomes include positive feelings of accomplishment or a sense of diminished self-esteem. Intrinsic outcomes occur immediately upon the performance of the acts that produce them. They are, in a sense, self-administered by the person rather than distributed by others. Extrinsic outcomes tend to relate more to the gratification and frustration of the existence and relatedness needs. They include such things as pay, promotions, and social interaction with one's colleagues. Moreover, they tend to be mediated by outsiders, such as one's supervisor or peers.

There have been disputes for many years about the precise dividing line between intrinsic and extrinsic outcomes (see Dyer and Parker, 1975), so some writers discourage continued use of the distinction (e.g., Billings and Cornelius, 1980; M. E. Ford, 1992; Guzzo, 1979; Thierry, 1990). One recent critique of the intrinsic motivation literature has found that different "extrinsic" outcomes (such as money and praise) have different effects on people receiving them (Cameron and Pierce, 1994), so lumping praise and pay in the same category may be more convenient than valid from a scientific perspective.

Alternative Explanations of Intrinsic Motivation

According to Deci and Ryan (1985, chap. 2), there have been at least 20 conceptualizations of intrinsic motivation and intrinsically motivated behavior. Three of these—those first discussed at length by Deci (1975)—have attracted the most attention and bear the most interest for those interested in work motivation. In the interest of space, we focus on the three viewpoints that Deci (1975) first identified, as well as a theoretical link with self-efficacy, a concept presented in chapter 6. In short, what are some useful ways of understanding intrinsic motivation when work is our primary interest?

The Optimum Arousal Approach

The first approach, represented by the work of Hebb (1955), posits that human beings seek preferred or optimum levels of arousal (where arousal is seen as the stimulation of the brain and central nervous system). Arousal levels result primarily from stimulation found in a person's environment. If the arousal level is too low in comparison with someone's desired level, the person will be motivated to behave so as to increase it. For example, an employee who is used to a fairly hectic work pace but who finds things slower than usual on a particular day will be motivated to seek out other people for conversation, set new tasks to be accomplished, or do something simply to "stir things up." On the other hand, if the person's level of arousal is greater than the level preferred, the person will attempt either to withdraw from the highly arousing circumstances or take steps to slow things down toward the level desired (e.g., by turning off a noisy radio or moving into a job that is less demanding). In this view, then, intrinsically motivated behavior is behavior intended to increase or decrease the physiological stimulation that a person experiences, to bring it into line with the levels desired. The implications of activation/arousal theory for the motivation of employees through the design of work have been reviewed by Gardner and Cummings (1988) and W. E. Scott (1966). We return to their work later in the book when we address job design issues explicitly.

The Optimum Incongruity Perspective

A second approach (which is similar to the first) posits that people desire and behave to achieve an optimum level of uncertainty or incongruity, where incongruities consist of psychological inconsistencies in a person's beliefs, thoughts, perceptions, values, or behaviors (Zajonc, 1960). Unlike Festinger (1957), who posited that people find cognitive dissonance aversive and that they are motivated to minimize the number of inconsistent cognitions they hold, this approach claims that people vary in the number and intensity of the disparate beliefs, acts, and perceptions they prefer in their lives. When a person is experiencing either too little consistency ("Things just don't add up") or too much consistency ("The world is in total harmony with itself"), behavior is instigated either to reduce or increase the level of congruity in the person's mind. Whereas the optimum arousal approach described above is physiological in orientation, the optimal congruity approach stresses the level of psychic comfort or discomfort that a person experiences as a consequence of his or her acts and perceptions. The work of Hunt (1965) and Berlyne (1973) represents this second approach to explaining the origins of intrinsically motivated behavior. More recently, Amabile (1988) has shown how high levels of intrinsic motivation can contribute to creativity and innovation in work organizations.

The Need for Competence and Self-Determination Approach

The third approach to intrinsic motivation identified by Deci (1975) is best represented by R. White's (1959) concept of competence (or effectance) motivation and de Charms' (1968) notion of personal causation. According to R. White (1959), competence refers to a person's capacity to master and deal effectively with the surroundings—to be in charge of them. The exploratory behavior of children characterizes a desire to be competent, as do adult behaviors that are intended to enquire, to manipulate, and to learn about things. Competence motivation represents a need that is always available to instigate and direct behavior, although this need is less urgent (or *prepotent,* to use Maslow's term) than are the types of existence needs we examined in chapter 3. Once aroused, however, competence motivation causes people to seek out challenging situations in their environments and then to conquer those situations, leading to feelings of competence and efficacy.

Similarly, according to de Charms (1968), Burger (1992), and E. A. Skinner (1995), people desire to be the origin of their own behavior rather than the pawns of circumstances beyond their control. People strive for personal causation, to be in charge of their own lives and for the outcomes that accrue to them. Similar to Deci's concept of self-determination is Burger's (1992) concept of *desire for control.* This is defined as "the extent to which people generally are motivated to see themselves in control of the events of their lives" (p. 6). Burger views the desire for control as a personality trait, one that generalizes through the various arenas of a person's life. Therefore, if a person has a strong desire for control in his marital relationship, he probably has a strong desire to be in control of his work situation, his social activities, and his friendships. Whereas Burger is concerned with a desire for control that he views as a stable personality trait, E. A. Skinner (1995) is concerned with *perceived control,* seen as a "flexible set of interrelated beliefs that are organized around interpretations of prior interactions in specific domains. . . . [T]hey are open to new experiences and can be altered" (p. 4).

Another, less well-known approach to intrinsic motivation was advanced by Weick (1969), although he did not use the term. For Weick, the very process of organizing consists of the activities associated with the removal of "equivocality" and the construction of procedures and systems to make this possible. *Equivocality* implies multiple meanings and mixed and confusing messages. It is represented by puzzles; in humor, by puns. For Weick, people tend to enjoy the process of organizing through removing uncertainty from their environments as well as the processes of planning to continue to deal with these uncertainties. Being somewhat enjoyable in themselves, these activities will motivate a person to be productive in one way or another: planning, sense-making, and resolving uncertainties. Therefore, as long as productivity is a path to the removal of uncertainty, we will see people being both highly motivated to engage in tasks and deriving pleasure from the process (Weick, 1969, p. 99). In many ways, Weick's concept of equivocality removal is similar to Deci's concepts of self-determination and control: In fact, they have common roots in the theoretical work of R. White (1959), discussed earlier.

Intrinsic Motivation and Self-Efficacy

In chapter 6 we encountered the concept of self-efficacy. This concept has to do with a person's perceptions of his or her capacity to perform a particular task in a given set of circumstances. This view of self-efficacy is largely cognitive; it has to do simply with people's perceptions and beliefs. But self-efficacy has also been interpreted in a different, albeit related way, one of interest to us here. Self-efficacy can also be seen as the *need* that underlies much of the thinking on intrinsic motivation presented here. That is, another way of thinking of R. White's (1959) need for self-determination is to think of that need as a need for self-efficacy (Gecas, 1989).

When the same commodity or concept has more than a single meaning, or when the same noun is used to refer to more than one concept, analysis of motivational processes is made more difficult. For example, the term *power* is seen as both a need and as a goal or set of goals that one seeks to satisfy that need (see chapter 5). When we examined theories of emotions in chapter 4 we saw that the term *love* is used to represent a wide array of *feelings*. So love is an emotion; but it is also a need, and a goal (see chapter 3). We have the same sort of difficulty here. The term *self-efficacy* is generally referred to in the context of this book as a belief (regarding one's capacity vis-à-vis a task), yet when we look closely at it, it becomes clear that self-efficacy is the stuff that theorists of intrinsic motivation are talking about when they use terms such as *self-determination* (Gecas, 1989), implying that it might also be considered a goal. The reader is cautioned about the difficulties and confusion that multiple meanings of the term may cause.

In short, then, intrinsically motivated behaviors are those behaviors that a person engages in to feel competent, self-determining, and in command of the situation at hand. These behaviors are of two general types: those intended to find or create challenge and those intended to conquer it. Hence, the adult who deliberately takes a clock apart merely to see how it works, or who learns a foreign language simply for the sake of learning it, are two examples of intrinsically motivated behavior from this third perspective.

To summarize, there have been at least three conceptual interpretations of intrinsic motivation, each predicated on a different fundamental assumption regarding human nature: The first is primarily biological/physiological; the second, cognitive/perceptual; and the third, based on a need-fulfillment model of human functioning. Does this mean that there is no similarity or overlap among the three approaches?

Similarities among the Four Approaches

Notice that the challenge associated with any of the exploratory behaviors mentioned in connection with the third approach above might serve to increase or decrease a person's level of arousal and/or the level of consistency experienced, suggesting that the various general approaches to understanding intrinsic motivation are somewhat compatible with one another. For example, a person who disassembles a machine that does not need repair opens up (literally) a great deal of new arousal as he perceives and manipulates the delicate internal mechanisms. This provides some degree of physiological arousal. Further, there is a strong chance that he may either confirm or disconfirm his prior beliefs about what he would find inside the machine, thereby either reducing or increasing the net level of congruity he holds in mind about the way things operate. Finally, if he were successful at reassembling the machine, he is likely to experience feelings of mastery, competence, and self-efficacy.

The point is that the three concepts of intrinsic motivation cited by Deci (1975) are compatible (or at least reconcilable) with one another, so one might conclude that in a sense, a process of increasing incongruity, arousal, and challenge followed by attempts to reduce this incongruity, arousal, and challenge constitute the psychological mechanisms behind behaviors we refer to as intrinsically motivated behavior. Thus, Deci (1975) states: "Only when a person is able to reduce incongruity . . . and only when a person is able to conquer the challenges which he encounters or creates will he feel competent and self-determining. He will feel satisfied when he is able to seek out pleasurable stimulation and deal effectively with over stimulation. In short, people seem to be engaged in the general process of seeking and conquering challenges which are optimal" (pp. 61–62). According to Deci, the need to be competent and self-determining is innate in humans, although the specific types of behaviors required to satisfy it vary from person to person. Deci considers self-actualization to be a common manifestation of the need for competence and self-determination; he sees achievement motivation as another manifestation. In fact, achievement motivation has been one of the most thoroughly researched needs in psychology and is one that has special relevance to work behavior. Let's take a close look at this particular human need.

Achievement Motivation

Henry Murray (who provided us with the general definition of need that we adopted in chapter 3) generated numerous lists of human needs. One of these needs is the need for achievement, which he defined as a need to "accomplish something difficult. To master, manipulate, or organize physical objects, human beings, or ideas. To do this as rapidly and as independently as possible. To overcome obstacles and attain a high standard. To excel oneself. To rival and surpass others. To increase self regard by the successful exercise of talent" (Murray, 1938, p. 164). The overlap between this need and Maslow's notion of self-actualization is apparent, although not complete. The essence of achievement motivation might be seen as a struggle *against one's own standards of excellence*, which clearly is consistent with the idea of becoming all that one is capable of becoming. But the element of achievement motivation having to do with mastering objects and overcoming obstacles and challenges is not necessarily part of self-actualization, although the two can, in practice, go hand in hand. Further, the aspects of the need for achievement pertaining to mastering and organizing the environment are clearly consistent with R. White's (1959) concept of competence motivation and de Charms' (1968) notion that people prefer to be responsible for their outcomes rather than merely being pawns.

In short, these various growth needs are not identical, in large measure because they have been identified and studied by scholars working more or less independently of one another, but they do converge considerably in terms of the types of behaviors they instigate. David McClelland, a student of Henry Murray, has devoted much of his career to developing our understanding of achievement motivation and the role it plays in entrepreneurial behavior and the economic prosperity of nations (Stewart, 1982). His work is far too extensive to be summarized completely here, so the reader is referred to some of the original sources (e.g., McClelland, 1961, 1962, 1965; McClelland and Winter, 1969). But a number of features of this work of particular relevance to our understanding of employee work motivation will be discussed here.

The Origins of Achievement Motivation

First, McClelland believes that all motives are learned from experiences in which certain cues in the environment are paired with positive or negative consequences. Accordingly, the need for achievement is learned when opportunities for competing with standards of excellence become associated with positive outcomes. Hence, child-rearing practices that encourage youngsters to tackle challenges independently and to do well are critical. In fact, McClelland (1961, pp. 340–350) holds that child-rearing practices are the most important determinants of the level of a person's achievement motivation. McClelland has also shown that deliberate programs of training that involve the development of an achievement-oriented mentality can induce entrepreneurial behavior among adults where it did not previously exist (McClelland, 1965; McClelland and Winter, 1969). In other words, adults can be trained to create and respond to opportunities to strive against challenges and to behave in the ways described in the definition above.

Gender and Achievement Motivation

It is important to recognize that most of McClelland's research evidence pertains to boys and men. Similarly, most of the early work on the matter failed to address gender differences (as was the case in most of behavioral science in the early years). Some research studies intended to generalize the theory to women and girls have been attempted, but many were flawed, as is often the case in research on human motivation (recall chapter 2). After a thorough review of studies that did investigate gender differences in how achievement motivation is aroused among women, what forms it takes, and what consequences it has among females, Stewart and Chester (1982) concluded: "It seems . . . that an intellectual and cultural climate of unconscious sexism has led researchers to adopt untested assumptions, ignore evidence, and make interpretations that depend on attending to only some of the data" (p. 184). Until a sufficient number of valid studies have been designed, executed, and reported on the matter of gender and achievement, there is no reason to conclude that either the need or its arousal, force, or goals is different among men and women. That leaves us with the question: What does achievement-oriented behavior look like?

Characteristics of Achievement-Motivated Behavior

It was stated in chapter 3 that we can sometimes detect the existence of many particular needs in a person by observing the person's behavior and drawing inferences from it. Accordingly, the behavior of achievement-motivated persons is commonly characterized by three features. First, achievement-motivated people prefer tasks of moderate levels of difficulty. Second, achievement-motivated people prefer tasks for which successful performance depends on their efforts rather than on luck. Finally, achievement-motivated people demand feedback and knowledge about their successes and failures to a far greater degree than do people who are low in achievement motivation.

The preference for tasks of moderate levels of difficulty deserves special attention. According to Atkinson (1964), the total achievement-oriented force affecting a person who confronts a task is determined by three variables. Further, the three combine multiplicatively, so that if one of them is inactive, or "zero," there is no psychological force to engage in the task. The first factor is the strength of the person's underlying need for achievement. This remains constant from one day to the next, although as suggested above, it can be developed among adults using focused training procedures. The second factor is the level of difficulty of the task, as the person perceives it. Whether a particular task will be viewed as easy or difficult depends on a host of variables, such as the person's perception of his or her ability to perform the task, for example. The third factor that determines the strength of achievement-oriented motivation is the degree of intrinsic reward (or feelings of accomplishment) that the person expects to experience by accomplishing the task. Naturally, meeting a difficult challenge will bring a person greater feelings of accomplishment than will achieving a task thought to be simple. Therefore, the value of this third factor is related inversely to the second factor, the perceived level of difficulty of the task. Symbolically,

$$\text{T.A.F.} = \text{Nach} \times \text{P.S.} \times \text{I.S.} \qquad \text{and} \qquad \text{I.S.} = 1 - \text{P.S.}$$

where

T.A.F. = total achievement-motivated force
Nach = strength of the person's underlying need for achievement
  P.S. = perceived probability of task success
  I.S. = intrinsic feeling of accomplishment

To illustrate how this works, consider the net force operating on an employee if (1) he has a very low level of the need for achievement, or (2) he perceives the task to be too difficult for him to succeed, or (3) he perceives the task as very easy. In all three cases, we would not expect much achievement motivation in the person contemplating the task. His level of effort toward performing the task would be determined by the strength of other needs and incentives he believed would result from task success (such as recognition by a woman he was trying to impress).

The Importance of Perceived Task Difficulty

Notice that insofar as a person's level of underlying need strength is constant in the short run, the net level of achievement-related force acting on the person to engage in a particular task will be determined by the perception of the level of difficulty of that task. The implication of this for the design of jobs and for the assignment of people to jobs is clear: To arouse motivational force associated with achievement needs, a supervisor must structure jobs and assign people to them so that employees see their chances of job performance as 50/50: not too low, but not too high. A moderate level of challenge must be perceived. In practice, application of this principle can be difficult, because it requires that a supervisor be capable of accurately perceiving the difficulty level of a task as the employee sees it. A supervisor who overestimates or underestimates an employee's ability vis-à-vis a task will probably fail to arouse and take advantage of a certain amount of the natural achievement motivation of that worker. In theory, the principle is relatively simple; applying it effectively can be another matter.

CONTROVERSY: DOES INTRINSIC MOTIVATION MIX WELL WITH EXTRINSIC REWARDS?

Return for a moment to the hypothetical case of the boy and the lawn mower that opened this chapter. Consider what would happen if the boy's father elected to compensate him for cutting the lawn using pay or some other form of extrinsic reward. Further, assume that the father agreed to pay the boy some amount of money for cutting the grass each time, thereby making the receipt of the money contingent upon his cutting the lawn. What would happen to the boy's net level of motivation to cut the lawn, and what would happen to the amount of fun the boy would have in cutting the grass/flying his imaginary airplane?

Common sense, widespread practice, and considerable theory and research evidence (Lawler, 1971) support the proposition that compensation systems that tie pay and other rewards to the performance of an activity can *increase* the level and rate of performance of a task. It would stand to reason, therefore, that paying the boy to "fly" the lawn mower would add considerable extrinsic motivation to the level of intrinsic motivation the boy already has for that task. In other words, the boy's net level of motivation to cut the lawn should now be greater than before, because the extrinsic motivation provided by the money will somehow combine with his prior level of intrinsic motivation, resulting in a greater overall level of motivation than the boy had before he started to receive the pay. Again, common sense would support this reasoning, as do some formal theories of work motivation (e.g., Galbraith and Cummings, 1967; Porter and Lawler, 1968). However, a series of experiments by Deci (e.g., 1971, 1972) and others (e.g., Condry, 1975; D. Greene and Lepper, 1974; Pritchard, Campbell, and Campbell, 1977) suggested that intrinsic and extrinsic motivation may not always "add up" (in a psychological sense) the way that common sense would have it. Instead, these experiments suggested that in some circumstances, the addition of an extrinsic, contingently paid incentive (such as money) to a work context in which the employee is intrinsically motivated to do the work may result in a loss of some (or all) of the employee's prior level of intrinsic motivation toward that task and perhaps also toward tasks perceived to be similar.

The possibility that intrinsic and extrinsic incentives may not be additive generated considerable research activity in the 1970s and 1980s. Scientists pursued the idea that rewards may diminish people's propensity to engage in an otherwise-attractive activity once the rewards are discontinued. Also investigated was the possibility that rewards might be detrimental to individual creativity and innovativeness. The results of these studies, most of which were experiments conducted in laboratory settings, were mixed. Sometimes extrinsic rewards appeared to reduce intrinsic motivation; other times the opposite effect seemed to occur—the contingent rewards enhanced intrinsic motivation (Wiersma, 1992). A number of attempts were made to build theories that would reconcile these contradictory results, some of which we review briefly here.

Staw (1976) reviewed the evidence regarding the *overjustification hypothesis* and suggested that whether extrinsic rewards enhance or reduce intrinsic motivation[2] depends on at least five factors: (1) the degree of saliency of the reward; (2) the prevailing norm regarding the appropriateness of payment for the activity in question; (3) the prior level of commitment of the person to the task; (4) the degree of choice the person has to perform, or not to perform, the task; and (5) the existence of potential adverse consequences. So, according to Staw, extrinsic rewards are more likely to reduce subsequent levels of intrinsic motivation if the reward is highly salient, meaning that it is obvious to those who are to receive it and that it is understood that the reward will be received upon the performance of the act. The more salient the reward, the more likely it is to have an adverse impact on a person's intrinsic motivation to perform the task in question (M. Ross, 1975).

Second, Staw suggested that rewards that are normally provided for a behavior in our culture are less likely to reduce a person's intrinsic motivation to engage in that behavior. He notes that in many of the studies in which rewards have been observed to reduce intrinsic motivation, the rewards were provided for the performance of acts that are not usually followed by reward (such as participating in games and puzzles in a laboratory setting). On the other hand, behaviors that are normally compensated in our culture (and that we might be inclined to classify as work) are less likely to be influenced by the provision of extrinsic outcomes. Hence, rewards may be more damaging to play and learning behaviors than they are to work behavior.

Third, if the person is initially very committed to the task being rewarded, according to Staw, extrinsic rewards are less likely to dampen intrinsic motivation. Those studies that have demonstrated an adverse impact of extrinsic rewards have tended to involve tasks of only moderate prior levels of intrinsic motivation (compare Arnold, 1976, with Pinder, 1976).

A fourth factor is the level of choice or compulsion a person feels with regard to performing a task. If the person feels a high level of external pressure to engage in a task, she is more likely to believe that she is extrinsically motivated to behave in that manner, so little intrinsic rationale is available, and little damage can be done by the provision of extrinsic rewards. The explanation for this effect can be found in traditional attribution theory (see S. T. Fiske and Taylor, 1991) and self-perception theory (Bem, 1967). It is similar to the idea of the saliency of the reward: If a person is acutely aware that there are "external" reasons or explanations available to explain why she is doing something (such as "There is a lot of money in it for me" or "Because I might lose my job if I don't do it"), she is more likely to conclude that these outside forces are in fact the reason for her behavior. No internal or intrinsic explanation seems as plausible under such circumstances.

Finally, the perception that failure to perform the task might result in adverse consequences also contributes to the chances that the person will not attribute her own behavior to internal causes.

The point here is this: It is believed that people observe and rationalize their own behavior in a manner similar to that by which they observe the behavior of others and make attributions about the causes of that behavior (Bem, 1967). When an act is conducted in the context of a highly salient, highly compelling set of extrinsic circumstances

---

[2]Notice that the focus here is on intrinsic motivation, not on performance.

(such as the fear of threats or the inducement of rewards), people are more likely to attribute their own behavior to these external causes. When there are few apparent external forces to which their behavior can be attributed, people are more likely to assume that they are behaving in a certain manner because they want to—they like doing so. It seems that the presence or absence of external factors largely determines whether people make intrinsic or extrinsic attributions about their own acts as well as the cultural appropriateness of those external factors.

Money is an interesting issue in this regard. The many psychological implications and meanings that pay has in work settings was acknowledged more than 30 years ago (Opsahl and Dunnette, 1966), and a major text of the 1970s explored the motivational qualities of pay in the workplace (Lawler, 1971). On the surface it makes sense to tie people's pay to either their work effort or their performance (recall chapter 1 of this book). Yet it may not be so simple, according to critics of the sort we look at later in the chapter (see Kohn, 1993).[3] The mixed impact of money on people's work motivation continues to be an ongoing topic; we will return to it later.[4]

Cognitive Evaluation Theory

Deci and his colleagues (e.g., Deci, 1975, 1980; Deci and Porac, 1978; Deci and Ryan, 1985) proposed the *cognitive evaluation theory* to reconcile the contradictory evidence pertaining to the relationship between intrinsic and extrinsic motivation. According to the theory, rewards can bear at least two fundamental features for the person receiving them. The first of these is referred to as *feedback,* meaning that rewards given for performance of a task can convey information to the individual concerning *how well* she is doing at the task. A second feature of rewards can be the messages, if any, they have for the individual about *why* she is performing the task. Deci refers to these as *control* perceptions (i.e., "Why am I doing this job? For the reward, of course!"). The theory states that which of these two features is more salient serves either to enhance or to reduce a person's intrinsic motivation toward it. If control perceptions are more salient, they may cause a shift in the person's perceived locus of causality, such that she attributes her reasons for engaging in the task to the external inducements surrounding it rather than to any internal satisfaction provided by the task itself.

This notion also draws on self-perception theory (Bem, 1967), which states that people examine their own behavior, much as they do the behavior of other people, and make attributions about their motives for behaving as they do. In Deci's theory, control perceptions arising from a reward are said to shift from self-perceptions of intrinsic motivation ("I am cutting the lawn because it is fun") to extrinsic self-attributions ("I am doing it for the money"). As the perceived locus of causality shifts, the person's intrinsic motivation to do the task diminishes. Highly contingent rewards (such as in a piece-rate or commission payment system) seem more likely to imply control perceptions, and thereby reduce intrinsic motivation, than do less contingent pay systems

---

[3]The author's butcher recently exclaimed loudly, "Money, money, money, of course!" when a recent shopping trip occasioned a discussion of the fact that the author was writing a book. "A book on work motivation: What other than money is there?" asked the butcher. "Do you think I'd come into this bleedin' place every day if I didn't have to do so for the money?"

[4]Recall the hypothetical case at the beginning of this chapter of the little boy who enjoyed mowing the lawn before he was paid for doing so.

(such as monthly salaries or hourly wages), largely because they are salient and undeniably connected with behavior.

According to Deci, feedback perceptions may either enhance or reduce intrinsic motivation. If the feedback indicates to the person that he is doing well at a task, his feelings of competence are enhanced, and his intrinsic motivation for the task is increased (because, for Deci, competence and self-determination are the essence of intrinsic motivation). But if the person perceives that he is doing poorly as a result of the feedback implied by the rewards (or lack of rewards), his feelings of competence will be diminished, as will his intrinsic motivation, and the person will be less likely to engage in the task in the future without some form of extrinsic incentive.

A major shortcoming of cognitive evaluation theory is that it fails to specify the conditions under which either of the two facets of reward (feedback or control) will be more salient for a particular person in a given situation (Guzzo, 1979; Wiersma, 1992). In one statement of the theory, Deci and Porac (1978) state only that " 'individual differences and situational factors' are related to the way people interpret the meaning of the rewards they receive" (pp. 163–164). Arnold's (1976) work suggests that when a person's prior level of intrinsic motivation for a task is very high, feedback perceptions may be more salient, although one experiment failed to confirm this hypothesis (Pinder, Nord, and Ramirez, 1984). Another problem with the theory is that it is imprecise about the exact *types* of rewards that may diminish intrinsic motivation (Eisenberger and Cameron, 1996). That is, rewards can be provided merely for engaging in a task, or they can be provided only for completing the task. Similarly, quality of performance may or may not be a basis for receiving rewards. Cognitive evaluation theory is not sufficiently developed to make sharp differential predictions about the effects of various rewards on intrinsic motivation (Eisenberger and Cameron, 1996).

Validity of the Theory

As we explained in chapter 2, most theories arise after behavioral scientists have made observations under more or less well-controlled research conditions. In the case of cognitive evaluation theory, it was the early experimental work of Deci (1971, 1972) that ultimately led to the development of the theory. In fact, as is often the case, the theory was advanced as an effort to reconcile mixed experimental results, most of them gathered in laboratory settings that simulated work or in educational settings in which children's play behavior was observed. Similar to the case of Herzberg's two-factor theory (recall chapter 2), Deci and others observed that the theory was supported in some circumstances but not in others. A quarter of a century has elapsed since Deci's (1972) early work, and fully two decades have passed since theories appeared to reconcile contradictory conclusions about the effects of rewards on intrinsic motivation, task interest, and creativity. As often occurs, researchers have conducted meta-analyses[5] of previous, independent studies, hoping that combining results across studies would provide greater statistical power and more definitive answers. Such is the case with the "Deci effect," the alleged effect of rewards (of various kinds) on intrinsic motivation (and other outcomes).

---

[5]A *meta-analysis* is a study in which the results of many earlier studies are combined, especially when the earlier studies have been yielding inconclusive or mixed results. The procedures used in meta-analysis are beyond the scope of this book; the interested reader is referred to a book by Hunter, Schmidt, and Jackson (1982).

One of the first meta-analyses found that when the concept of intrinsic motivation was operationalized by whether research participants continued to "work" or play at the experimental task in what they believed was "free time" following the termination of the study, extrinsic rewards did seem to reduce intrinsic motivation. In other words, when experimental subjects were rewarded with an extrinsic payment that varied with their performance levels, their propensity to engage in the task during a free interval was lower than the same propensity among the control participants, who received either no reward or a flat payment unrelated to their behavior or performance. The results suggested that we still cannot be sure whether extrinsic rewards actually have a deleterious effect on intrinsic motivation. Rather, all that could be concluded was that *withdrawing a previously administered extrinsic reward may have such an effect* (Wiersma, 1992, p. 110). On the other hand, when the researchers operationalized intrinsic motivation as performance levels during the experiment itself, the payment of contingent external rewards combined to *increase* overall levels of motivation (Wiersma, 1992). The overall findings again remind us of the importance of carefully defining motivational constructs. They also provide another example of how the experimental procedures used by researchers can influence the content of the theory that results from their research (recall chapter 2).

A more recent meta-analysis, this one based on a larger number of studies, was even less supportive of the proposition that rewards diminish intrinsic motivation (Cameron and Pierce, 1994; see also Eisenberger and Cameron, 1996).[6] These researchers made an interesting observation about the effects of differing paradigms and theoretical perspectives on the findings that had emerged *prior to their analysis:* "The overjustification effect, cognitive evaluation theory, and the recent behavioral explanations each attempt to account for the disparate effects of reward and reinforcement on intrinsic motivation. . . . [R]eviewers on all sides of the issue tend to be highly critical of research designed outside their own paradigm, and, more often than not, findings from studies in opposite camps are not considered relevant" (Cameron and Pierce, 1994, p. 372).

This meta-analysis addressed three fundamental questions: (1) What is the effect of reward on intrinsic motivation? (2) What are the effects of specific features of reward on intrinsic motivation? and (3) What is the effect of reinforcement[7] on intrinsic motivation? The study included the findings of 96 experiments that had focused on four different operationalizations of intrinsic motivation: free time spent on a task once reward is removed, self-reports of attitude, performance during the free time period, and willingness to volunteer for more of the same type of work. Cameron and Pierce's (1994) meta-analysis concluded that rewards do not have a negative effect on intrinsic motivation in terms of any of the four dependent variables studied. In fact, they concluded that "people who receive a verbal reward spend more time on a task once the reward is withdrawn; they also show more interest and enjoyment than non-rewarded persons" (p. 391).

The only decremental effect of rewards on intrinsic motivation, across studies, seems to have occurred when expected rewards (as opposed to unexpected rewards)

---

[6]The author is grateful to Edwin Locke for drawing his attention to this study.

[7]The concept of *reinforcement* comes from a body of theory presented in chapter 14. For the present purposes, the term has two major interpretations: (1) it is a consequence of an act that increases the rate or probability of the occurrence of the act, or (2) it is something deemed positive that is provided as a consequence of an act.

are administered simply for engaging in a task (as opposed to being based on perfor-mance at the task). In this case the decrement was on the "free time spent after reward withdrawal" measure of intrinsic motivation. Cameron and Pierce (1994) noted that this effect is consistent with cognitive evaluation theory:

> According to cognitive evaluation theory, competence and self-determination underlie intrinsic motivation. Rewards can facilitate or hinder competence and self-determina-tion depending on whether they are perceived as informational, controlling or ainfor-mational. From this perspective, results from the meta-analysis would suggest that ver-bal rewards increase a person's intrinsic motivation because of their informational value. Verbal praise would be seen to lead an individual to feel competent in perform-ing a task; hence, intrinsic motivation would increase. Because the cognitive evaluation is said to take place while the rewarded activity is occurring, unexpected rewards would not alter a person's intrinsic motivation. On the other hand, rewards offered to people for participating in a task, in spite of how well they perform, would be perceived as con-trolling and would decrease intrinsic motivation. (p. 395)

But that was about all the support the meta-analysis revealed for cognitive evaluation theory: It was based on a single indicator of intrinsic motivation. The theory was not supported when attitudinal measures of intrinsic motivation were used, although Cameron and Pierce (1994) acknowledged that many of the studies included in their analysis may not have used valid measures of task attitudes (p. 396).

This meta-analysis has serious consequences for our thinking about intrinsic mo-tivation as well as about the effects of rewards on intrinsic motivation. Although it is true that many laboratory experiments have individually suggested that rewards have a negative effect, the size of the effects in most of those studies now appears not to have been substantial enough to lead to major policy conclusions against the use of re-wards in either the workplace or the classroom. Rigby, Deci, Patrick, and Ryan (1992; cited by Cameron and Pierce, 1994, p. 396) have suggested that the simple dichotomy between intrinsic and extrinsic motivation may be too simple and that a shift of em-phasis is in order toward further development of the concepts of competence and self-determination. As in the case of most theories in social science (and most theories of work motivation), the theories related to the effects of rewards on intrinsic motivation are scrutinized and either supported, rejected, or altered (recall chapter 2). So it is and will be with cognitive evaluation theory and the *overjustification effect* hypothesis.

Is it time to abandon the notion of intrinsic motivation altogether? The author's position is that it is premature to do so. The statistically low effects of rewards on intrin-sic motivation suggested by Cameron and Pierce's work should be kept in perspective. Their meta-analytic results do not provide grounds for abandoning the notion of intrin-sic motivation: they justify only a careful reexamination in work and organizational set-tings of policies that restrict the use of rewards for achievement, creativity, and learning.

Rewards, Intrinsic Motivation, and Performance in Real Workplaces

We have noted that the majority of the research that led to the advancement and sub-sequent testing of cognitive evaluation theory was conducted in contrived (or artifi-cial) work settings or in educational settings where the focus was on children's intrinsic motivation to continue or engage in play behavior (see Cameron and Pierce, 1994). But what about the process of tying extrinsic rewards to employee behavior and performance in real work settings?[8] The major implication of the Deci effect for industrial work settings is that pay for performance may offset whatever intrinsic motivation workers experience as a consequence of initiatives such as job enrichment or employee empowerment programs. There is still only limited empirical evidence that this occurs in practice, despite our common, everyday encounters with surly employees who refuse to perform duties that are not strictly within the formal definitions of their jobs ("I'm not paid to do that"). In keeping with the conclusion of Rigby et al. (1992), field research into intrinsic motivation may better be focused on feelings of competence self-determination. In fact, one study investigated the issue.

Self-Determination in Real Work Settings

An 18-month field study of nearly 1,000 technicians and field managers working for a large office machine corporation examined the effects of supportive leadership styles on employee job attitudes (Deci, Connell, and Ryan, 1989). The experimental manipulations were designed to influence the degree of self-determination the employees would experience. The hypothesis was that higher levels of felt self-determination, brought about by supportive supervision, would yield higher levels of satisfaction with a variety of work-related outcomes, including levels of trust in the company. The results were largely supportive of the hypotheses, especially when the general economic condition of the company was favorable (when times were not good, the supervisory support had little impact on the satisfaction variables). As impressive as this experiment was, we must keep our attention on the fact that it was self-determination that was manipulated and it was a set of attitudinal variables (rather than performance or motivation) that served as the dependent variables of interest. Although self-determination is a critical element of intrinsic motivation according to cognitive evaluation theory, there is more to it than that, as described above.

Pay for Performance in Real Work Settings

Drawing heavily on the experimental literature that led to the meta-analyses described earlier, Kohn (1993) has published warnings in the popular literature about the harmful effects of rewards on *employee performance*. He states that "rewards typically undermine the very processes they are intended to enhance" (Kohn, 1993, p. 54). He claims that rewards used in work organizations, such as stock options, pension plans, sales commissions, bonuses, and vacations generally result only in "temporary compliance." Once such rewards are withdrawn, the desired behavior vanishes, and no fundamental change is made in the person's basic attitudes and belief structures. "They do not create an enduring *commitment* to any value or action" (p. 55). He also claims that performance at tasks requiring cognitive skills, such as problem solving and creativity, is especially vulnerable to the deleterious effects of extrinsic rewards. Executive bonuses are not related to corporate performance; in fact, according to Kohn, there are often slight negative correlations between executive pay and performance.

---

[8]In the discussion that follows, keep in mind the distinctions we made in chapter 1 between motivation and performance. It may be that extrinsic rewards have negative effects on performance whether or not decreased intrinsic motivation per se can explain such effects.

Kohn offers six reasons why rewards can backfire in real settings, none of which relate to the sort of explanations by Deci and his colleagues having to do with shifts in locus of causality, loss of control, or feelings of reduced self-determination. Rather, Kohn's concerns are with the negative effects on *performance,* per se. First, although pay is a valued outcome from work (for most people), it is not by any means always the most important consequence. Further, even though pay is valued, it does not follow that greater and greater levels of pay will result in greater and greater levels of motivation—it has diminishing returns.

Second, rewards are often seen by employees as manipulative, so they can have a punishing effect. " 'Do this and you'll get that' is not really different from 'Do this or here's what will happen to you' " (Kohn, 1993, p. 58). Not receiving a reward when one is expected is also punishing; the more desirable the reward, the more severe the feeling of punishment.

Third, rewards can "rupture" relationships. Competition among employees for rewards, particularly when they are in scarce supply, can undermine collaboration among colleagues and co-workers. This effect can be especially damaging in work settings that are otherwise designed to foster collaboration for joint creativity and innovation (see Amabile, 1988). Advertising who earned the most rewards is also difficult on relationships, causing envy and invidious comparisons among people.

A fourth explanation offered by Kohn is that reliance on rewards such as pay to overcome problems at work ignores the underlying causes of such problems. If employees are in need of training, or if insufficient resources are available to get the job done effectively, bribing higher performance with pay does nothing to find the systemic problems.

Fifth, rewards can discourage people from taking risks, from venturing to try things on the job other than precisely what they have been instructed to do to be rewarded. Again, there is some evidence (Amabile, 1988) that work climates that are low in individualized performance-contingent rewards are most conducive to creativity and innovation.

Finally, Kohn cites the work of Deci and Ryan (1985) having to do with how contingently paid extrinsic rewards can undermine intrinsic motivation. Clearly, Kohn (1993) did not have the benefit of the knowledge of meta-analyses such as that reported by Cameron and Pierce (1994).

To repeat, although some of Kohn's explanations require us to consider some types of internal states (such as commitment and attitudes, both discussed later in the book), it is not only through the mechanisms of cognitive evaluation theory as such that he indicts the use of extrinsic rewards. Further, he has no original evidence to offer in support of the hypothesis that rewards decrease intrinsic motivation or performance in the field; he merely extrapolates from the evidence of Deci and his colleagues that has been reviewed here. Nevertheless, because his focus is broader than intrinsic motivation, his points should be of interest to anyone—parents, teachers, or supervisors in the workplace—who must manage the performance of other people and who may or may not be interested in intrinsic motivation as such. In sum, the relationship between intrinsic and extrinsic motivation is not as simple as originally assumed (see Lepper and Greene, 1978), and further study, especially in real work settings with adult populations, is needed before final conclusions are warranted.

INTRINSIC MOTIVATION
THROUGH THE DESIGN OF JOBS

Earlier in the chapter we saw that intrinsic motivation consists of energy expended, first to increase and then to reduce a person's levels of arousal, challenge, and incongruity. People are viewed as seeking levels of stimulation in their environments that provide degrees of both physiological and psychological arousal that are neither too low nor too high for their personal preferences. An emphasis on the physiological basis for understanding job design is desirable from a scientific point of view because it permits an objective, quantifiable insight into the impacts of jobs on people, without the necessity of relying on subjective self-report explanations of employees. On the other hand, there are a variety of difficulties associated with a strictly physiological approach—difficulties that make such an approach difficult to put into managerial practice. Therefore, a greater understanding of how jobs might be sources of motivation can be gained if we consider both physiological and psychological perspectives on the matter rather than adopting only a single view. Further, we will see that the two approaches are generally quite consistent with one another, such that a practical manager who relies, of necessity, on cognitive and perceptual models of job design will in most cases enact policies that are consistent with those that would follow from a strict physiological perspective. Therefore, let's look first at the design of jobs from the point of view of the physiologically based activation theory as proposed by W. E. Scott (1966) and expanded by Gardner and Cummings (1988).

Activation-Arousal Theory

The principal thrust of the activation theory approach to job design is that jobs are themselves sources of activation for the people who perform them. *Activation* is ultimately conceptualized as "the degree of excitation of the brain stem reticular formation" (W.E. Scott, 1966, p.11). Certain properties of any stimulus object or setting (such as a job) generate greater levels of activation and arousal. In particular, the intensity, variation and variety, complexity, uncertainty, novelty, and meaningfulness of objects and situations are of special importance. Therefore, a job that has little variety, few component tasks, little novelty, and no uncertainty or unpredictability, will be less activating than a job that features the opposite characteristics. That is, jobs that feature elements of novelty and change, unpredictable requirements, and multiple tasks, other things being equal, should be comparatively quite capable of generating arousal.

Notice that the theory does not suggest that more activation is better. Instead, it suggests that these characteristics of work determine the overall levels of arousal experienced by the employee. But the level of arousal most comfortable for a particular employee is the critical issue. Again, too much stimulation is dissatisfying, as is too little. When an employee encounters a work situation in which the stimulation level is either slightly higher or slightly lower than her preferred level, she will enjoy it. For example, not having to attend a regularly scheduled meeting may make a manager's day a bit less hectic than normal and therefore somewhat more satisfying than usual. Similarly, a spontaneous gathering of colleagues in a person's office, followed by an unusually brisk flurry of telephone calls, may be viewed as exciting and pleasurable.

On the other hand, extreme deviations from a person's optimum arousal level are aversive and instigate efforts to restore normality by either generating or reducing stimulation. Daydreaming, clown play, and kibitzing on the job are common examples of the former; escape behaviors such as tardiness or malingering are examples of the latter. Employees can often increase or decrease the stimulation of a job situation by modifying the content or flow of the work itself. For example, ways of increasing stimulation would include informally trading jobs with other employees, reversing the sequence of certain tasks, or designing new techniques for performing tasks. Alternatively, breaking complex jobs down into constituent elements, or simply postponing or ignoring certain parts of a job, are examples of means of reducing job-related stimulation. The point is that workers can often adjust the level of activation provided by a job or create means of magnifying or reducing the degree of arousal a job provides. As a result of the efforts that a person expends to adjust stimulation levels closer to what is "normal," that person's performance at whatever other tasks he is doing usually suffers. In balance, therefore, the relationship between activation level and task performance is best summarized by an inverted U, such that performance of a job is compromised when the job is either too dull or too hectic for the person involved (Yerkes and Dodson, 1908).

Individual Differences in Arousal Preference

People differ at least three separate ways in the amount of stimulation and arousal they prefer (Korman, 1974). First, for a given time of day, some people desire greater stimulation and resultant activation than other people. Students who share housing accommodations with friends who seem perversely "night people" or "morning types" are aware of the fact that people vary considerably among themselves as to when they seek and enjoy stimulation and activity from their surroundings.

Second, a given person varies across the period of a day in the level of stimulation he or she finds desirable. A common pattern is for people to prefer relatively low levels of noise and commotion early in the morning, before a sufficient quantity of caffeine has been ingested. Later in the day, greater levels of excitement are desired until bedtime approaches, when, again, less excitement is preferred. But this pattern is not universal by any means.

A third form of individual difference that pertains to activation arousal theory is a tendency for people to adapt, within limits, to progressively higher or lower levels of stimulation at particular times in a day. Whereas a junior clerk comes to accept relatively little stimulation from his entry-level position, he manages to desire and seek increasing levels of stimulation as he is promoted upward through a series of jobs that involve increasingly higher levels of stimulation, and as a result, higher levels of overall arousal.

In short, people vary a great deal, both from others and within themselves in terms of their preferred levels of stimulation. These differences are of vital importance in understanding how to use arousal theory to design jobs, but as discussed in the next section, they make formal, precise application of the theory by managers virtually impossible.

The Value of the Optimum Arousal Approach

In a sense, W.E. Scott's (1966) activation-arousal theory provides a number of very simple suggestions for job design. Specifically, this approach suggests that job-related motivation is maximized when the job is neither too complex nor too simple for an employee; therefore, jobs should be designed to feature optimum, balanced levels of complexity, novelty, and stimulation. But applying this advice in practice is far from easy, for a number of reasons. First, it is not possible for job design specialists (let alone line supervisors) to gain precise measures of either the level of stimulation that a job generates or of the effect that particular objective stimulation levels (even if they could be determined) have on a particular employee. Moreover, the between- and within-person differences in arousal preferences add to the problem: How are managers to appreciate the differences among their employees in their preferred levels of arousal for particular times of the day? Further, how can a job be designed such that it arouses greater activation in the employee at precisely those times of day that match the person's preferences for more or less arousal? Finally, how can a manager accurately measure the changes that occur for particular people in their preferred levels of arousal as they change and adapt to sequences of job assignments, as described earlier? In brief, the precise adoption and application of this approach to job design seems impossible in practice. On the other hand, it would be a mistake to discard or ignore it altogether, for several reasons.

One reason is that the optimum arousal approach provides a relatively sound physiological basis for understanding why and how other approaches to job design function as they do. As we show in the following sections, a variety of other general strategies for job design have been advanced, most of which offer concrete detail concerning how jobs should be designed for the purpose of making them intrinsically motivating, but there have been few explanations of why their prescriptions can be motivating for employees. Although the optimum arousal approach is not fully consistent with all other formal theories of job design, it is consistent with enough aspects of them to provide us with some biological insights into how the design characteristics of jobs may influence people.

A second major value of the optimum arousal approach is that its principles can be kept in mind by managers for their use on an informal day-to-day basis, both as a guide to the assignment of people to jobs and a basis for understanding effective and ineffective job behaviors and attitudes. In other words, although it is impossible for managers to calibrate stimulation and arousal levels precisely (as argued above), it is possible for managers to pay attention, in a less formal fashion, to the differences among their people in the levels of challenge, excitement, and activity they seem to desire. Moreover, it is desirable for managers to fully appreciate the differences among the jobs that fall under their purview in terms of the types and amounts of challenge, excitement, and activity they entail, especially for an employee newly assigned to perform them.

A third point of value of this theory (one that is related to the second) is that the concepts it provides can be useful both for explaining certain personnel problems after they occur, and/or in preventing problems before they occur. For example, the so-called *Peter Principle* (Peter and Hull, 1969) suggests that promotion systems in organizations tend to advance people upward in hierarchies until they are ultimately assigned to jobs at which they are not competent. There is little scientific evidence in support of this proposition, but it does fit the observations of many of us and therefore holds some intuitive appeal. To the extent that the Peter principle has any validity, the mechanisms described in the optimum arousal approach help us understand it. Translated into the terms of the theory, the Peter Principle might be paraphrased as follows:

There is a tendency in many organizations, in which promotions and transfer are based on merit, for employees eventually to be moved into jobs in which the level of physiological and psychological stimulation featured in these jobs is high enough to arouse activation levels that are sufficiently too great in comparison to employees' preferred levels. When this happens, these employees are motivated to reduce activation through avoiding or reducing the net stimulation generated by the job, thereby limiting their effective performance of these jobs.

A related example concerns the use of job transfers as a means of fostering experiential learning for the sake of developing employees so as to prepare them to take over senior-level positions in geographically dispersed organizations. It may be that the stimulation and traumas associated specifically with undergoing a move (see Brett, 1981) can add to the increment in arousal that normally accompanies a job reassignment (such as a promotion) that does not entail geographic mobility, thereby resulting in net levels of activation that are dysfunctional for experiential learning to occur (Pinder and Schroeder, 1987; Pinder and Walter, 1984).

To summarize, the two preceding examples illustrate that a manager need not be a physiological psychologist to benefit from the key concepts provided by W. E. Scott's (1966) activation theory approach to job design. As we will see in the following sections, managers who attempt to follow the explicit guidelines of other, more subjective, formal theories of job design will inadvertently be adhering to much of the advice that activation theory would propose. These subjective theories of job design seem easier both to researchers who wish to construct theories without monitoring brain activity and to managers who simply wish to match people and jobs in an enlightened fashion. Accordingly, in the following sections we present the central ideas found in three of the most popular and well understood of these subjective approaches: Herzberg's two-factor theory, Hackman and Oldham's job characteristics approach, and Staw's expectancy theory approach. Less emphasis is placed here on Herzberg's model because it received so much attention in chapter 2.

The Two-Factor Theory

The motivator-hygiene (or two-factor) theory of work attitudes and motivation was presented and discussed in detail in chapter 2, where it was argued that the asymmetry posited to exist between the origins of job satisfaction and job dissatisfaction has made the theory very controversial, so much so that it has fallen into disrepute with many critics. But it was also argued that it is not always necessary to adopt or reject a theory of work motivation totally to be influenced by it; sometimes it is wise to accept certain elements of a theory while reserving judgment on or rejecting other, less defensible elements. This seems to be the case for Herzberg's motivator-hygiene theory. Specifically, it is not necessary to accept Herzberg's notions of the independence and asymmetry of positive and negative job attitudes to accept (and benefit from) the advice provided by the theory for job design.

Herzberg (1966) was among the first industrial psychologists to consider and write explicitly about the notion of human growth needs. Although his theory borrowed somewhat from Maslow (1943), it was not identical to Maslow's theory and made substantial additions to it. (For example, Herzberg rejected Maslow's notions of hierarchical differences in prepotency among human needs.) The point is that Herzberg's theory argues that jobs must feature a number of characteristics to permit them to arouse and then satisfy growth needs. To repeat in part the discussion of chapter 2, jobs should permit achievement as well as recognition of that achievement, they should be interesting to perform, they should permit feelings of growth through advancement, and they should provide feelings of responsibility on the part of the employee executing them. In short, jobs should feature those factors that Herzberg, Mausner, and Synderman (1959) came to call the *motivators.* It is not necessary to assume that the absence or removal of these job characteristics does not result in low job attitudes. But there is some evidence that when jobs are changed so as to build in higher levels of these factors, positive consequences can accrue for both the employee and the organization (R. N. Ford, 1973; Paul, Robertson, and Herzberg, 1969). Few of Herzberg's toughest critics deny this.

The Job Characteristics Approach

Perhaps the most popular current perspective on job design is one developed by Hackman, Oldham, and their associates. Their approach is similar to Herzberg's insofar as it proposes a set of features that should be built into jobs in order that they be satisfying and motivating, although the two approaches differ somewhat with regard to the specific characteristics of work that make it desirable. The interested reader is referred to the early work of Turner and Lawrence (1965), Hackman and Lawler (1971), and especially to chapter 3 of Hackman and Oldham's (1980) book.

Elements of the Theory

According to Hackman and Oldham (1980), an employee will experience *internal motivation* (which is taken to be the same as intrinsic motivation as discussed earlier in the chapter) from a job when the job generates three critical psychological states. First, the employee must feel personal responsibility for the outcomes of the job (such as its levels of quantity and quality). Second, the work must be experienced as meaningful; that is, the employee must feel that his efforts "count" or matter somehow, to someone. The third critical state is knowledge of the actual results of the person's work efforts. In other words, an employee should be aware of how effective he is in converting his effort into performance (see our discussion of VIE theory terms in Chapter 12): He should have a knowledge of the results of his efforts. In short, jobs should be designed to generate experiences for the employee of meaningfulness, responsibility, and a knowledge of the results of one's effort.

Notice that Herzberg's model of job design would agree completely with Hackman and Oldham's requirement for feelings of responsibility, and that Herzberg's achievement and advancement for achievement factors are consistent with Hackman and Oldham's suggestion concerning knowledge of results, insofar as knowledge of one's success is necessary for feelings of achievement to occur, and that, in addition, advancement often serves as a formal recognition of positive results. There is thus some degree of consistency between the two approaches with regard to the role of responsibility and knowledge of results in the design of motivating work. The question remains: How can jobs actually be designed to make it possible for employees to experience these three critical psychological states?

Generating Experienced Meaningfulness

For Hackman and Oldham, three specific core factors of jobs are particularly important for making work feel meaningful. The first factor, referred to as *skill variety,* is defined as "the degree to which a job requires a variety of different activities in carrying out the work, involving the use of a number of different skills and talents of the person" (Hackman and Oldham, 1980, p. 78). The need for competence (R. White, 1959) expresses itself, in part, by behaviors that involve exploring and investigating the environment, as explained earlier in the chapter. One aspect of this searching and exploring entails the use and development of the person's various skills and abilities. Accordingly, Hackman and Oldham propose that jobs which require the use of multiple talents are experienced as more meaningful, and therefore more intrinsically motivating, than jobs that require the use of only one or two types of skills. Also notice that the exercise of numerous skills would probably result in the stimulation of a greater number of the employee's senses, thereby resulting in higher overall levels of activation and arousal. (See Schwab and Cummings, 1976, for a discussion of the issue of the stimulation of multiple sensory modalities when designing jobs.)

Hence, the inclusion of task variety as an element of job design is consistent with the concept of growth need satisfaction as well as with the more physiological approach taken by activation theory. It is not consistent, however, with Herzberg's approach, which refers to the simple addition of tasks as horizontal job loading or job enlargement (as opposed to job enrichment). This difference between the Hackman–Oldham approach and that of Herzberg is crucial because, as will become evident in the following sections, the addition of varied tasks to a job can be one practical means of generating some of the other key features prescribed by both theories.

A second job characteristic that is seen as contributing to experienced meaningfulness, referred to as *task identity,* is defined as "the degree to which a job requires completion of a 'whole' and identifiable piece of work . . . doing a job from beginning to end with a visible outcome" (Hackman and Oldham, 1980, p. 78). Over the years the popular press has paid considerable attention to the worker *alienation* that results from repetitive jobs in which employees perform the same simple operations hundreds or thousands of times every day with only a minimal understanding of how the work they do relates to the "bigger picture." For example, auto assembly workers who install the same three or four parts in the hundreds of partially constructed cars that pass their workstations every month have little understanding of how those few parts fit in with the effective functioning of the completed vehicle. Work is experienced as more meaningful, according to Hackman and Oldham, when employees are capable of gaining a greater understanding of how their jobs fit in with those of other employees and with the completion of an integral unit of product or service. For example, the famous curvilinear assembly lines used in Scandinavian auto assembly plants are designed, in part, to permit employees to participate in much larger subsections of finished automobiles than is possible in conventional straight-line assembly plants in North America (Gyllenhammar, 1977).

How does the notion of task identity fit with the other viewpoints presented here? On the surface, simply providing task identity does not seem particularly relevant for the satisfaction of the major growth needs we have examined. On the other hand, insofar as stimulus complexity and meaningfulness determine the stimulating capacity of objects and events (D. W. Fiske and Maddi, 1961; W. E. Scott, 1966), a job with task identity should be more stimulating from the point of view of activation theory. Finally, Herzberg's approach would probably admit that task identity contributes to the motivator factor referred to as *interesting work*.

The third factor that makes work more meaningful, referred to as *task significance,* is defined as "the degree to which the job has a substantial impact on the lives of other people, whether those people are in the immediate organization or in the world at large" (Hackman and Oldham, 1980, p. 79). For example, munitions employees during World War II worked long, hard hours in miserable production plants, maintaining high levels of motivation and morale because of the important contribution they knew they were making to the war effort (Turner and Miclette, 1962). The *task significance* component of Hackman and Oldham's experienced meaningfulness concept is harder to relate to other job design approaches than are the skill variety and task identity components, with the possible exception that performing work perceived as significant might contribute to the satisfaction of esteem needs (both the need for the esteem of others and for a positive regard of one's self).

In summary, Hackman and Oldham's (1980) theory suggests that experienced meaningfulness is important for a job to arouse intrinsic motivation and that it, in turn, requires that the work be integrated, important, and demanding of the use of multiple skills and abilities.

Generating Experienced Responsibility

Whereas three core job factors are seen as contributing to feelings of meaningfulness, only one factor—autonomy—is required for an employee to experience the psychological feelings of responsibility. *Autonomy* is defined as "the degree to which the job provides substantial freedom, independence, and discretion to the individual in scheduling the work and in determining the procedures to be used in carrying it out" (Hackman and Oldham, 1980, p. 79). Autonomy and responsibility have long been recognized as important facets of employee motivation and satisfaction. They are explicitly recognized in Herzberg's two-factor theory (see chapter 2), McClelland's (1961) theory of achievement, and de Charms' (1968) thinking about pawns and origins (recall our earlier discussion). Moreover, autonomy was treated as a separate category of higher-order need by L. W. Porter (1962, 1963) in his early adaptation of Maslow's need hierarchy for studying managerial job attitudes. From the point of view of activation theory, it is reasonable to assume that people who are responsible for their own job outcomes will be more fully activated than people who share with others responsibility for success or failure on the job. Hackman and Oldham's suggestion that autonomy (and the responsibility feelings it fosters) is motivating is quite consistent with the other perspectives and approaches to job design that we have considered.

Generating Knowledge of Results

The third critical psychological factor in Hackman and Oldham's model is referred to as *knowledge of results.* They see two basic types of feedback as the essential determinants of the degree to which an employee understands how well he is doing on the job. The first type of feedback comes from the job itself, such as that which occurs when a worker assembles an alarm clock and tests it to see whether she has put it together properly. The second type comes from other people, such as one's superior, who informs the worker how well he is doing on the job. Hackman and Oldham recognize the role that both forms of feedback can have for providing knowledge of results, but stress the importance of designing jobs so that they regularly provide the former type, feedback from the job.

Why would we expect that feedback from the job itself would be more motivating than feedback mediated by other people, such as one's supervisor? One reason is that when the feedback comes from the person's own observation of how well she is doing, it often comes immediately after the employee has done the work. Second, this form of feedback is not as susceptible to the interference that can result from a variety of social-psychological processes, such as those that have to do with the perceived credibility of the source of the message or the relative power of the sender of the message. In short, feedback from the task itself is simple, direct, and impersonal, and seems to be a more powerful means of providing motivating information than is feedback from outside sources (Ilgen, Fisher, and Taylor, 1979; J. M. Ivancevich and McMahon, 1982).

The importance of feedback for intrinsic motivation is recognized explicitly in Deci's cognitive evaluation theory (recall our discussion earlier in the chapter), in which it was seen as critical for either enhancing or reducing a person's feelings of competence and subsequently the person's level of intrinsic motivation, or alternatively, affecting the person's locus of causality and subsequent intrinsic motivation. Similarly, a strong desire for task-related feedback is one of the most important traits displayed by males who are high in achievement motivation (McClelland, 1961). Feedback can clearly affect a person's level of self-esteem as well, depending on whether it is favorable or unfavorable. Finally, from the perspective of activation theory, feedback from a task may contribute to both the complexity and novelty of that task for the individual.[9] A full summary of the critical psychological states as well as the major core factors seen as producing them is provided in Figure 7-1.

Measuring the Dimensions

Hackman and Oldham have developed an instrument called the *job diagnostic survey* (JDS), which is used to assess what they refer to as the overall motivating potential score for a particular job. Perceptions of the job incumbent are used to calculate the amount of skill variety, task identity, task significance, autonomy, and feedback found in a job. When combined, scores on these dimensions enable a job analyst to assess the degree to which a job may be capable of arousing intrinsic motivation for particular individuals. Detail concerning the content and psychometric properties of the JDS is beyond the scope of this book. The interested reader is referred to Hackman and Oldham (1975, 1976, 1980), and Hackman, Oldham, Janson, and Purdy (1975) for more detail on the development of the theory and the instrument, and to Aldag, Barr, and Brief (1981) for a positive assessment of the JDS itself. Finally, it should be noted that there is some evidence that people's perceptions of these task characteristics of their jobs remain stable over time (see our discussion of the stability of beliefs in chapter 9), although their affective (emotional) reactions to them may be less stable (Griffin, 1982a).

---

[9]We will see in chapter 13 that feedback is also a critical ingredient in the effectiveness of goal-setting and control theories of work motivation.

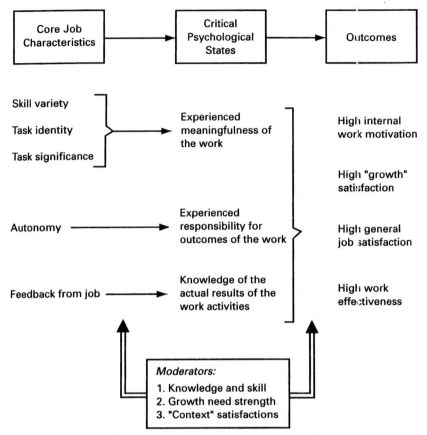

Source: From J.R. Hackman and G.R. Oldham, *Work redesign* (figure 4.6, p. 90). © 1980 by Addison-Wesley Publishing Co., Inc. Reprinted with permission of Addison-Wesley Longman, Inc.

FIGURE 7-1 Job Characteristics Model of Task Design

Expectancy Theory and the Job Characteristics Approach

More than two decades ago, Staw (1976) proposed a model for job redesign that applies a formulation of VIE theory[10] to the job characteristics approach described above, thereby providing an additional theoretical understanding of why certain features of jobs may arouse intrinsic motivation. The version of VIE theory that Staw adopted had been proposed by House (1971) and House et al. (1974). In essence this model explicitly recognizes the fact that overall work motivation can be determined by both intrinsic and extrinsic factors. More important, the model delineates the separate effects of two specific types of intrinsic motivation: (1) that which is associated with simply doing a job, and (2) that which is associated with effective achievement of the job. Specifically, the House et al. (1974) expectancy model can be represented as follows:

---

[10]The reader is referred to chapter 12 for a complete treatment of this theory of work motivation.

$$M = IV_a + (P_1)(IV_b) + \Sigma \, (P_{2i})(EV_i)$$

where

M = total task motivation
IV_a = intrinsic valence associated with task behavior
IV_b = intrinsic valence associated with task accomplishment
EV_j = extrinsic valences associated with outcomes for task accomplishment
P_1 = perceived probability that one's behavior will lead to task accomplishment
P_2 = perceived probability that one's task accomplishment will lead to extrinsically valent outcomes

A number of features of this model deserve highlighting. First, the reader is reminded of the crucial distinction between valence and importance: It is the *expectation* of the satisfaction associated with an outcome that attracts a person to engage in a task. Second, the strength of the valence associated with task behavior for a person (IV_a) rests largely with the strength of the person's need for competence. It consists of the enjoyment that people anticipate receiving from merely attempting a task, regardless of how successful they expect to be at it. The reader is reminded of Murray's (1938) belief (see chapter 3) that satisfaction consists of the pleasure of the process of reducing need-related tension, in addition to the pleasure of the feeling that one has once the need has been satisfied. The first component of the House et al. model is consistent with this element of satisfaction.

On the other hand, the strength of the intrinsic valence associated with task accomplishment (IV_b) is determined largely by the strength of the person's need for achievement. Therefore, the net force attributed to the achievement component of the model is seen as being determined by the mechanisms described in the discussion earlier in the chapter: Overall achievement-oriented motivation is determined largely by the person's *perception* of the probability of task success. Tasks that are anticipated to be either too easy or too difficult arouse little achievement motivation, because the intrinsic thrill of mastering an easy goal is small, whereas difficult goals are judged to be unattainable, thereby discouraging a person from attempting them. In short, the achievement-related component of the Staw–House et al. model requires consideration of both the anticipated probability of success and the anticipated thrill from succeeding. Moreover, because of the inverse relationship between perceived probability of task success and this form of valence, the net motivational force associated with achievement outcomes will be maximized when the person perceives the odds of success as moderate.

The final component in the equation consists of the person's *expected value* from various extrinsic outcomes that might be available. It is determined by the strength of her belief (or perceived probability, P) that performance, if it occurs, will result in outcomes such as pay, recognition, promotion opportunities, discredit with co-workers, and so on. Valence is the expected level of satisfaction or dissatisfaction with each of the extrinsic outcomes. As described by the formula, the perceived probabilities are multiplied in the person's mind by the expected levels of satisfaction or dissatisfaction and the mathematical products summed across the various outcomes that the person considers relevant. We explore the intricacies of these types of motivation models in greater depth in chapter 12.

Independence of the Intrinsic Components

As presented here, the model implicitly assumes that the two forms of intrinsic motivation are independent of one another. For example, it suggests that a person could continue to expect to derive pleasure from engaging in a task even if he constantly fails at the task. Hall's theory of career success experiences (D. T. Hall, 1976) and the impact they can have on feelings of competence and self-esteem suggests that this may not in fact be the case (see also Bandura, 1982). Instead, Hall suggests, repeated success experiences at a task may, up to a certain limit, serve to increase a person's attraction for a task, whereas continual failures eventually reduce the person's affinity for it. Nevertheless, Staw's adaptation of the House et al. (1974) expectancy theory to job design provides a theoretical rationale for a number of prescriptions for the design of work. These are summarized in Figure 7-2.

Design Implications from the Expectancy Model

Figure 7-2 suggests that overall task motivation can be influenced if a job is designed to affect the intrinsic valence of doing it, the intrinsic valence associated with succeeding at it, and the person's perceptions of her chances of succeeding. Specifically, the figure suggests that jobs which feature a variety of tasks, jobs that are not overly routine, and jobs that require the employee to interact a great deal with others will, *ceteris paribus,* have a greater likelihood of appealing to employee needs for competence: that is, they will foster relatively high levels of the intrinsic valence associated with doing the task. In other terms, such tasks will tend to be comparatively enjoyable, and satisfaction will result from the very act of doing them and reducing the tension associated with the need for competence.

FIGURE 7-2   Expectancy Theory Approach to Intrinsic Motivation

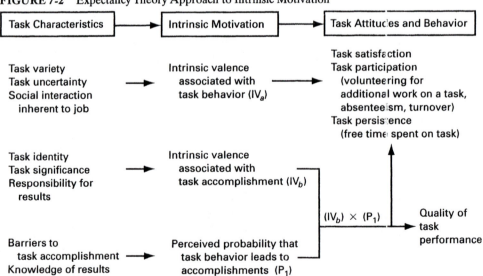

Source: B. M. Staw, *Intrinsic and extrinsic motivation.* © 1976 by General Learning Press, an imprint of Silver Burdett Ginn; Simon & Schuster Education Group. Reprinted with permission.

Figure 7-2 also suggests that the valence associated with success at a job will be comparatively high when the person sees it as comparatively high in Hackman and Oldham's (1980) task identity and task significance dimensions and when the person expects that he will be largely responsible for his success or failure at the job. In other words, a person will expect a greater thrill from accomplishing a job goal when he believes that his efforts (as opposed to luck or the efforts of other people) determine success or failure and when he is able to see how his accomplishments fit into the larger picture and are of value to the organization or to someone associated with it. Intuitively, this argument makes sense. But recall that net achievement-oriented motivation also depends heavily on the person's judgments about whether he will be able to perform the task. Figure 7-2 illustrates that a host of factors in the job itself, or in the context of the job, can serve to influence the employee's views about his ability to perform it. The interactive nature of the valence associated with achievement (IV_b) and the perceived probability of achievement (P_1) in determining the individual's overall achievement-oriented motivation is reflected in Figure 7-2.

Individual Differences and Job Enrichment

We know that people differ considerably in terms of the strength of their growth needs—the learned needs that, when aroused, account for what is called intrinsic motivation. In addition, in an earlier section we discussed the complexity of the difference, both between people and within a single person, in terms of the levels of stimulation desired from the environment (including jobs). To the extent, therefore, that individual differences exist in the strength of the needs and preferences that people have for the outcomes that job enrichment can provide, it should follow that enriched jobs will be more attractive to (and more highly motivating for) some people than to others. In other words, we would logically expect considerable individual difference between people in their attitudinal and behavioral reactions to enriched work. In fact, many theories of job design explicitly recognize the fact that many people view their jobs as secondary sources of need satisfaction and simply do not wish to work in jobs that feature high levels of challenge and responsibility. Let's take a brief look at the role attributed to individual differences in the theories discussed above.

Herzberg has often been criticized for ignoring the role of individual differences in the motivation styles that people display, although later statements of his theory readily acknowledge that certain people are abnormally preoccupied with the satisfaction of hygiene needs, for various reasons (see Herzberg, 1976, chapt. 2). Similarly, research of Turner and Lawrence (1965) on the motivational characteristics of jobs suggested that employees from rural backgrounds respond much more positively and favorably to job enrichment than do employees with urban backgrounds. The work of Hackman and Lawler (1971) followed directly from that of Turner and Lawrence, although Hackman and Lawler attempted to measure the strength of the growth needs of each person in their study, reasoning that a more precise prediction of the effects of job enrichment could be gained by considering individual need states rather than a person's general sociological–geographic background. Their reasoning made logical sense and their empirical results provided support. There were higher correlations between the existence of enriched job characteristics and outcomes such as intrinsic motivation, job satisfaction, and attendance among employees with high growth need strength than among employees who were low in growth needs. Later studies by Wanous (1974), Brief and Aldag (1975), and Giles (1977) supported Hackman and Lawler's conclusions, and the current theory of job design forwarded by Hackman and Oldham (described earlier) includes provisions for assessing the strength of employee needs for growth before implementing changes in their jobs (Hackman and Oldham, 1980, p. 118).

But as is often the case, the matter is not so simple. A review of the evidence by J.K. White (1978a) concluded that the majority of studies in which employee responses to job design were found to depend on employee traits of some form or another failed to hold up in replication studies. That is, sometimes a particular variable (such as the strength of employee growth needs) determined the effect of job characteristics on work outcomes, but sometimes those same variables failed to make any difference. J. K. White (1978a) concluded that individual difference factors that influence the impact of worker responses to job characteristics are situation specific. In other words, certain variables may be important in some situations, whereas other variables may be important in other situations, where jobs are designed to be enriched. A separate review of the evidence by Pierce and Dunham (1976) reached essentially the same conclusion. White added strength to his argument by showing in a vast study of his own (J. K. White, 1978b) that not one of 73 individual variables that he investigated consistently affected the impact of job characteristics on employee responses. A disappointing state of affairs, to say the least.

Other researchers, including Dunham (1977) and Sims and Szilagyi (1976), have attempted to show that organizational factors (as opposed to individual factors) may determine whether job enrichment has positive consequences for employees. Still, the results are very inconsistent and inconclusive. It may be that the most accurate and most practical way of predicting whether job enrichment will have a positive benefit for a particular person is simply to ask the person, as Cherrington and England (1980) once did, how much he desires enriched work, rather than relying on less direct predictors such as work values or need states. There is abundant evidence that not everybody desires to work at jobs that feature the enriching characteristics proposed by the theories described in this chapter. But it is still very difficult to predict which categories of people will or will not benefit from and enjoy job enrichment. Surrogate measures such as assessments of individual needs and personality traits are unreliable predictors, although simply asking the people involved directly about their desire for job enrichment may be useful.

Practical Issues in Job Design for Enrichment

Now that a number of theoretical approaches to job redesign have been discussed, there are a variety of practical issues that deserve attention, issues that are important for understanding how job enrichment can be applied to real settings, as well as in explaining some of the successes and failures that job enrichment has had in the field.

Where Might Enrichment Be Attempted?

Below are a number of clues, most of which can be gathered from documents such as union contracts, personnel manuals, organization charts, and organizational folklore, that can sometimes help to identify situations in which job enrichment may be of value (Drake, 1974).

1. *Repetition of functions.* If an operation is performed at one point in a work flow and repeated by someone else later in the same flow, it may be that the two jobs involved are not sufficiently different to justify their separation into two jobs. Perhaps the jobs can be combined into a single job that features more stimulation, variety, meaningfulness, and feedback than is possible in either of the separate jobs.

2. *Unusual reporting relationships.* People whose jobs require them to report to more than one supervisor will encounter role conflict and probably not enjoy as much autonomy as they might otherwise experience from their jobs. On the other hand, a high frequency of one-to-one reporting relationships may suggest that many employees are expected to perform the menial and unmotivating tasks that are neglected or discarded from the jobs of their superiors.

3. *Layering.* Some organizations feature multiple levels of authority among jobs in which the work performed is basically identical. For example, allowing low-level employees to provide refunds to customers up to a certain maximum amount, and requiring successively higher amounts to be passed upward in the organization's structure, limits the potential for employee feelings of responsibility, autonomy, and to a lesser extent, knowledge of results. Similar-sounding job titles, such as junior file clerk, intermediate file clerk, file clerk, and senior file clerk, may signal the existence of layered functions that might be rearranged for the sake of job enrichment.

4. *Supergurus and troubleshooters.* The smooth functioning of many work settings often relies heavily on the existence of a small number of gurus, who seem to know virtually everything about the company, its customers and suppliers, and all other aspects of the operation. Such people are, of course, very important and usually very powerful as a consequence of their wisdom. Moreover, they are often quite jealous about their roles and unwilling to share their knowledge. But their monopoly often robs other employees of responsibility, meaningfulness, and autonomy in the work they perform, while leaving the organization as a whole vulnerable to their departure.

5. *Special checking or inspection jobs.* Investigation may show that special inspections are unnecessary. Permitting employees to check the quality of their work adds potential task meaningfulness, autonomy, and knowledge of results to their jobs.

6. *Excessive number of job titles.* Drake (1974) suggested that if the ratio of people to job titles in a work setting is not at least 5:1, it may be the case that the work is too fractionated and that enrichment may be appropriate.

7. *Pools.* Drake (1974) also suggested that the existence of pools of people performing similar work, such as typing, keypunching,[11] or word processing, is a signal that certain people in the organization are casting off the routine (and boring) parts of their jobs onto other people. On the other hand, operators in such a pool may receive more variety and task identity than do operators who work for only one or a few persons.

8. *Liaison personnel.* Highly differentiated organizations often require special people to coordinate and integrate activities that involve more than one group (Lawrence and Lorsch, 1969). Whereas entrusting such special functions to particular people may

---

[11]Although keypunching is now obsolete, the general principle behind Drake's (1974) is worth considering.

facilitate integration, it may also impoverish the motivational potential of those jobs being integrated, depriving them of task significance, task identity, and skill variety.

9. *Existence of several jobs requiring the same equipment.* Duplications of equipment use suggest that the work being done on these jobs is too highly specialized and fractionated. Is it possible that a single job (with many incumbents) might be created that combines all the tasks that were previously assigned to many different jobs, thereby providing potential for higher levels of skill variety and task identity?

There are a variety of characteristics of organizational structure that may suggest places in which jobs might benefit from enrichment and/or restructuring. After noting such clues, the interested manager would have to proceed to investigate more thoroughly the potential for and feasibility of job redesign. Some aspects of this feasibility assessment are the topic of the next section.

Implementing Job Enrichment

Two of the leading proponents and developers of the theory and practice of job enrichment recognized from the outset that taking the theory and putting it into effective practice can be very difficult because of the constraints that are often encountered in real organizational settings (Hackman and Oldham, 1980). Changes in job design cannot usually be implemented without changes in (or at least accommodation to) other elements of the organization and its various programs and procedures. In fact, many early failures of job redesign programs can be blamed on failure to recognize these other organizational considerations.

Obstacles in Implementation

What, then, should be attended to in addition to the diagnosis of jobs and people for the sake of installing job enrichment successfully? Oldham and Hackman (1980) identified a number of constraints to the effective installation of such programs, including the following:

1. The technological system (i.e., the basic nature of the production or work process) can drastically curtail the degree to which jobs can feasibly be enriched. The assembly line is a classic example of such a technology. Any type of work process that depends heavily on the use of particular machinery will typically be very expensive to modify, perhaps prohibitively so (see Anderson, 1970a).

2. Personnel systems, such as job analysis and the development of more or less rigid job descriptions, which are often enshrined in labor–management collective agreements, can limit the feasibility of job enrichment. Enriching jobs means changing jobs, and seldom only one or two at a time. Tradition, bureaucratization, and formal agreements can make this sort of change very difficult.

3. Control systems (such as budgetary and accounting systems or production and quality control reporting systems) can also impede job redesign efforts because by nature they are often designed to limit individual discretion, autonomy, and flexibility. Groups that traditionally have been responsible for these control functions are often quite resistant to giving them up.

4. Training programs must be available that can permit whatever levels of effort are induced by the enriched work to result in useful performance. Otherwise, the motivated effort created by the work will be frustrated and result in employee frustration (see chapter 8).

5. Career development practices must also be appropriate. For example, we noted earlier that job enrichment may not be appropriate for all employees; some people neither want, nor are capable of handling, the challenge and responsibility that enrichment entails. Without career development strategies (such as transfers or reassignments) to accommodate or deal effectively with employees unsuited for job enrichment, frustration, job dissatisfaction, and resentment can be expected and one can anticipate limited benefit from job enrichment programs.

6. The levels of pay and the methods of payment are also important. Equity theory (see chapter 11) would predict that increased levels of pay would be expected by employees who perceive the increases in responsibility that result from enrichment to constitute additional inputs they must make to their jobs. Alternatively, employees who perceive enrichment as resulting in greater satisfaction (or in greater outcomes) may not make such pay demands. One practitioner with considerable experience in job enrichment has suggested that if the redesign of jobs is done properly, employees do not necessarily demand more money for the responsibility added to their positions. In fact, he notes that most job evaluation programs in organizations are designed to deal easily with the added levels of responsibility and skill levels that can result from enrichment, should the issues be raised (Caulkins, 1974). Nevertheless, very little research has been directed toward the issue of pay-level implications of job enrichment, although there is some theoretical basis to worry that the form of payment is important. Recall from our earlier discussion that Deci's (1975) cognitive evaluation theory suggests that contingently paid money (as in piece-rate pay plans) may undermine intrinsic motivation, the very goal sought by enrichment programs. Finally, whether the pay is distributed on an individual, group, or organization-wide basis must be compatible with the means by which the work is accomplished (i.e., by individuals, groups, or by overall organizational performance).

Similarly, Sirota, and Wolfson (1972) noted other obstacles to the installation and success of job enrichment. While these other factors are a bit more subtle than those noted by Oldham and Hackman, they are no less critical. For example, it is often very difficult to overcome the long-standing biases and beliefs held by many managers concerning the virtues of job design according to the classical principles of previous times (see Massie, 1965). But even when traditional beliefs are challenged successfully, it is still necessary to educate managers in the theory and techniques of job enrichment so that they can provide the types and amounts of support that are necessary for success.

Many managers who have considered job enrichment for their organizations have expected to see real returns on the financial investments involved in unrealistically short periods of time. Demanding evidence of return on investment is fine, but the payoffs that are possible (although not guaranteed) from enrichment interventions seldom appear immediately. Moreover, an honest "sales job" by someone proposing that an organization venture into job enrichment cannot *promise* meaningful return on investment, whether in the long or the short run. Such promises simply are not well founded, especially today, after so many attempts have been observed to fail. It is no wonder that many managers concerned with costs and profitability are skeptical about allowing enrichment changes in their organizations. To make matters worse, unless top management is at least somewhat enthusiastic, any new enrichment attempt is bound to fail—a sort of self-fulfilling prophecy of disaster. This has been the experience with the implementation of management-by-objectives programs as well as we will see in chapter 13.

Another barrier to effective installation of job enrichment can be generalized fear of the unknown among those who will be affected most heavily, especially middle managers, who often expect that such programs will undermine their authority and possible make them redundant. ("If I give away all my power to my subordinates, what need will there be for me in this organization?") There is also a natural tendency on the part of many managers to accept the idea of enrichment in abstract terms but to deny that it might be feasible, or even necessary, in their organizations. Sirota and Wolfson (1972) also note a tendency among many enrichment specialists to be dogmatic in the techniques they employ either to diagnose or to install enrichment strategies. There are many cases where the particular problems facing an organization require eclecticism on the part of the interventionist (Sandler, 1974), but successful applications brought about by a method often encourage continued use of that method alone.

Unions and Job Enrichment

There is at least one other set of factors that can influence the effective installation of job redesign: labor unions and the collective bargaining process. Although the majority of formal job enrichment programs have been conducted in nonunion settings or among only the nonunion personnel in organizations where unions are represented (Schlesinger and Walton, 1976), there have been a number of instances where formal enrichment has been attempted in the midst of unionized settings. It would be an oversimplification to say that labor unions have a typical or unitary attitude about such programs (Donahue, 1982), but there are a number of issues that normally must be dealt with when a union is involved. First, it is often the case that union leaders are wary about job enrichment (and other formal programs aimed at improving the quality of work life). This wariness comes from the concern that their own positions may be undermined. That is, to the extent that the enrichment design entails greater responsibility and autonomy for dealing with job-related problems, union stewards may fear that their traditional role as representatives of the rank and file may be diminished. A second common concern for labor officials is that the union membership may perceive any joint union–management cooperation over the planning and installation of enrichment with suspicion that they are "in bed" with management.

Unions are often suspicious that programs such as job enrichment are simply newfangled methods of "speed-up" designed primarily to extract higher levels of productivity per hour of labor. Often, this sort of suspicion has been well founded. Unions may accept managerial prerogatives to redesign work so as to make more efficient use of capital equipment and other resources, but they rarely agree to programs they perceive as designed primarily to increase productivity through exploitation of their membership (Schlesinger and Walton, 1976). But perhaps the biggest difficulty in installing programs such as job enrichment successfully in unionized settings is the fact that by its very nature (in North America, at least), the labor–management relationship is adversarial rather than cooperative—hardly the sort of relationship to foster collaboration and joint decision making (Ephlin, 1973).

It is commonplace to argue that organizations are systems and that change in certain of their parts necessitates change in other parts (e.g., D. Katz and Kahn, 1978). Oldham and Hackman (1980) and Sirota and Wolfson (1972) have provided specific illustrations of the meaning of this concept: Job enrichment cannot be implemented effectively without regard to various subsystems in the organization's structure, policies, and practices. Pursuant to the discussion presented in chapter 2, it is unfortunately the case that the precise nature of the interdependencies among new managerial techniques (such as job enrichment) and other organizational considerations are not appreciated until a significant number of costly and disappointing failures are experienced. This raises the question of the validity of the theory (or theories) of job enrichment and of their "track records" in applied organizational settings.

The Validity and Value of Job Enrichment

In chapter 2 the twin issues of validity and applied utility were introduced as they relate to theories and techniques from behavioral science. It is timely now to inquire into the scientific validity and applied utility of the predominant approaches to job enrichment. Just how good are they? Sadly, there is no simple answer to this question, although there are a variety of answers pertaining to the different approaches that are available. First, the author is not aware of any empirical tests or applied applications of the Staw–House et al. model presented above, although there are myriad tests of various expectancy theories, if not the precise one underlying Staw's model. The reader is referred to chapter 12 for a summary of the evidence concerning expectancy (or VIE) theory.

Similarly, there are no specific empirical tests of the activation/arousal theory approach to job design per se, with the possible exception of a study reported by Standing (1973), who found that steel mill inspectors who were particularly high or low on a measure of cognitive complexity (which may be a surrogate measure for preferred activation levels) were more satisfied with various aspects of their jobs than were inspectors (performing virtually the same job as the others) who attained moderate scores on the cognitive complexity scale. More direct tests of Scott's theory have not been conducted, in large measure because of the obvious difficulties involved in operationalizing it.

The bulk of the research and applied evidence is old, and it pertains mostly to Herzberg's approach and the job characteristics model of Hackman, Oldham, and their colleagues. A complete study-by-study review of the evidence is beyond the scope of this chapter, but a brief summary of the evidence is appropriate here. The interested reader is referred to the following sources for more detail: T. G. Cummings, Molloy, and Glen (1977); L. E. Davis and Taylor (1979); Fein (1974); Gyllenhammar (1977); Hackman (1977); Hackman and Oldham (1980); Luthans and Reif (1974); and Yorks (1979).[12]

Before the mid-1970s, the majority of job enrichment programs attempted in North America were based on Herzberg's motivator-hygiene theory or on some variant of the sociotechnical approach of Davis and his colleagues (see L. E. Davis and

---

[12]The reader should note that these empirical assessments of job enrichment are old, many being published approximately two decades ago. This is another indication that scientific interest in job enrichment has declined sharply since the publication of Hackman and Oldham's (1980) major text.

Taylor, 1979; J. E. Kelly, 1978). The early literature reported these projects as generally quite positive and encouraging (e.g., R.N. Ford, 1973; Paul, Robertson, and Herzberg, 1969), although it is probable that most of the failures and disappointments were less likely to be reported. Nevertheless, Herzberg-inspired job enrichment programs have enjoyed a reasonable track record, despite the limited and/or unknown validity of the theory behind them (recall chapter 2). As stressed earlier, the concept of asymmetry between what Herzberg calls motivators and hygiene factors is less important for the practical purposes of job redesign than the fact that jobs which feature the motivators seem to result in more favorable consequences than those that do not.

Since the mid-1970s, new theories, such as the job characteristics approach described above, have emerged and have influenced organizational development via job enrichment. How valid is the job characteristics approach? As has been the case so many times in this book, the best answer to this question is that the scientific validity of this theoretical model is unknown, despite the considerable amount of research that lies behind it. The reason for this conclusion is that much of the research that generated and sought to test the validity of the job characteristics approach has been flawed by problems in design and execution (Arnold and House, 1980; Roberts and Glick, 1981). For example, the theory holds that *changing* jobs so as to build in higher levels of the core factors (task identity, skill variety, etc.), will result in increases in intrinsic motivation and job satisfaction and reductions in employee withdrawal behaviors such as absenteeism. Yet the majority of the research pertaining to the theory has not, in fact, shown that changes in job design at one time result in changes of the sort predicted later. Instead, most studies have been synchronous, or cross-sectional, meaning that measures of job characteristics have been gathered and correlated with measures of employee reactions that were gathered at the same time. Thus, although the evidence based on data of this sort has revealed encouraging simultaneous associations between the strength of the core factors and favorable employee reactions, it cannot itself support the type of causal claims made by the theory. In addition, the research has featured a number of other shortcomings which collectively reduce the conclusiveness of the findings and leave uncertainty about the actual validity of the job characteristics approach. Nevertheless, theories often gain popularity, even hegemony, despite weakness in the research on which they are based (Bourgeois and Pinder, 1983), and it is important to remember that failure to support a theory of this sort unequivocally does not necessarily imply that it is wrong. Hackman, Oldham, and their colleagues have made a contribution, and time and further research will reveal how valuable that contribution is.

Putative Benefits of Job Enrichment

It was stated earlier that the most important goal of job enrichment is to increase and sustain intrinsic motivation among employees. Presumably, higher levels of intrinsic motivation will be accompanied by higher levels of performance and job satisfaction as well as reduced levels of withdrawal such as absenteeism and turnover. What is the evidence in this regard? Does job enrichment deliver the sorts of things that it was hoped it might deliver?

With some exceptions, the research that might have provided an answer to this question has not been as well conducted as one might have hoped. It is very difficult to establish sufficient experimental control in real organizational settings to permit either a researcher or a manager to rule out all possible explanations for observed changes in employee behavior when an experiment has been attempted. Moreover, as suggested earlier, there is more chance that we will see and hear about the supposed successes than about applications of job enrichment that have failed. These considerations aside, what evidence there is on the matter suggests that job enrichment is probably much more useful for influencing employee attitudes than it is for improving performance levels (e.g., Orpen, 1979). Thus, enriched work may contribute to organizational effectiveness indirectly through the impact it has on the consequences of healthy work attitudes much more than directly through increases in employee productivity per se (Dowling, 1973a).

Although research into the matter has tended to be of questionable quality (Griffin, Welsh, and Moorhead, 1981), positive changes in work attitudes do not usually seem to be accompanied by increases in productivity as a consequence of job enrichment. There may be a number of reasons for this, but two seem most plausible. First, the reader is reminded of the tenuous relationship that exists among beliefs, attitudes, intentions, and behaviors (see chapter 9). Changing jobs so as to change employee perceptions of task characteristics (as proposed by Herzberg, Staw, and Hackman and Oldham) can be expected to have only a very indirect impact on employee effort levels, because beliefs must be positively evaluated and then converted into specific intentions to act. As we will see in chapter 9, for a given person, some beliefs about particular stimulus objects will be positive, whereas others are negative. In the case of job redesign attempts, this means that employees may perceive many things about enriched jobs, some desirable, some averse. Presumably, it was hoped that individual differences in growth need strength would be important; people high in these needs were assumed to assess their beliefs about enriched jobs favorably. But models such as that of Hackman and Oldham (1980) fail to take into account the possibility that employees will hold beliefs about enriched jobs other than those pertaining only to their capacity to satisfy growth needs. As a result, it may be that not all beliefs that are generated by enriched work are evaluated positively. Consequently, there is a diminished likelihood that net perceptions of enriched work will lead to the types of intentions that are necessary to instigate the sort of behavior that is required for higher levels of performance. In short, any model that tries to build predictive bridges between employee beliefs and employee behaviors overlooks the important intermediary roles of attitudes and intentions (Fishbein and Ajzen, 1975) and will result in only limited predictive effectiveness.

A second reason why enrichment may not easily result in increases in job performance has to do with the fact that many factors can operate to dampen the conversion of employee effort (even if it is increased by enrichment) into performance. A number of the specific impediments that can interfere with enrichment programs have been identified above. In conclusion, one can argue that increased job satisfaction and possibly reduced levels of withdrawal may be the major benefits that are potentially attainable from enrichment efforts; and that these positive benefits seem attainable without accompanying cost in productivity to management (e.g., Dowling, 1973a). Accordingly, one might argue that job enrichment is a desirable strategy for management to adopt. But there remains too little solid evidence to claim that enrichment results in higher levels of effort or job performance per se.

Criticisms of Job Enrichment

We have argued that a healthy skepticism must accompany any assessment of the success of job enrichment, because of the difficulties that researchers and managers naturally encounter when trying to gain the sort of rigorous experimental control that is necessary to demonstrate that observed changes in employee attitudes and behavior can be attributed to enrichment attempts. In addition to this set of criticisms, however, a number of others have been aimed at job enrichment in general, based on a variety of considerations of a nonscientific nature. One of these has to do with the problem of individual differences as we discussed them earlier in the chapter. Briefly, the argument is that job enrichment is not for everyone: Some workers would much prefer increases in pay or job security, better working conditions (Fein, 1974), or more social interaction (Reif and Luthans, 1972) from their jobs rather than the more amorphous things attributed to job enrichment.

Further, R. Katz (1977, 1978, 1980) has argued that some people will benefit from enrichment much more at some stages in their careers than they will at others. For example, newcomers to a job setting will be oriented primarily toward establishing social ties that will assist them in becoming established and making sense of their new surroundings, whereas employees who have been at their jobs for long periods of time will be oriented toward pay, security, and other factors that Herzberg would refer to as satisfying hygiene needs. For Katz, only those employees who have been established in their jobs for moderate periods of time will be likely to benefit from the potential outcomes offered by enrichment.

Another criticism concerns the application of job enrichment, the argument being that this technique has been treated as only one of a series of programs distilled from behavioral science for application to management problems as a sort of panacea (Hackman, 1975; Pinder, 1977, 1978, 1982). When this occurs, management groups are prone and/or susceptible to adopting job enrichment without first establishing that the problems being addressed, if any, are the sorts of problems for which the technique might be appropriate.

Finally, some critics have suggested that job enrichment is doomed to failure as a means of really increasing the quality of working life because like most or all other management techniques, it takes as given the very socioeconomic conditions that give rise to organizational problems for human beings—the nature of the fundamental means of ownership and distribution of wealth. This radical attack (D. M. Jenkins, 1975; Nord, 1977; Nord and Durand, 1978) holds that no managerial technique will cure the ills caused by work designed according to the principles of classical management and scientific management, because they do not address the most basic cause of these ills, the fundamental assumptions made by the capitalist system itself.

CONCLUSIONS

Job enrichment was once one of the most popular and most written about of the applied motivational techniques based on behavioral science. However, much of the scientific and managerial experience with job enrichment has not been as impressive or as encouraging as its proponents anticipated. It is clear that any hope that job enrichment would help make work universally more humane, and help make the workforce more productive, simply has not been realized. But it is also clear that much of the research done to develop and test new approaches to job redesign has not been of sufficient quality to permit an accurate estimate of either the validity of the scientific theories involved or of the applied utility of the techniques that arise from those theories (Hackman, 1977).

The reader must not be too critical of either the theories or of the scientists who have attempted to develop them. As we saw in chapter 2, it is extremely difficult to conduct research in real organizational settings that permits us to generate unequivocal evidence in support of the validity or utility of behavioral science ideas. As has been the suggestion in many other parts of this book, it may be that the theory (or theories) of job enrichment is, in fact, more valid and of more potential applied utility than we are presently capable of demonstrating.

What's New in Job Enrichment?

Whatever the case, the dramatic drop in the level of attention paid to job enrichment theory and practice since the early 1980s is remarkable: Very little new theory has been advanced since that time, nor have there been many published reports of job enrichment attempts in real-world settings. It is hard to determine whether job enrichment is moribund as an applied motivational technique or whether the recent lack of new theory on the matter is responsible for the silence we observe in the literature. Lawler (1992) believes that job enrichment has tended to move away from production and manufacturing settings in recent years and is now more commonly found in white-collar and service jobs. Customers prefer to deal with as few service staff as possible to get their needs met, so expanding the authority and responsibility of first-line service personnel makes good sense. It seems that job enrichment has evolved since the 1980s and taken on new names and added new wrinkles for our consumption in the 1990s. To the degree that is so, the currently most popular "new" concept in the job enrichment tradition is employee empowerment.

Employee Empowerment in the Workplace

Recent years have seen the emergence of a concept referred to as *empowerment,* a phenomenon that implies making it possible for people to attain control and to employ suitable power to make their lives effective. We can speak of empowerment at many levels and in many contexts, such as empowering entire communities to make decisions about their own police protection, health-care services, and the like. Our focus here is on empowerment of employees in the workplace (see Conger and Kanungo, 1988; Frey, 1993; Shipper and Manz, 1992; Spreitzer, 1995, 1996).

One of the earliest treatments of empowerment in the workplace was provided by Conger and Kanungo (1988). They proposed that empowerment functions to enhance employee feelings of self-efficacy (see Schwartzer, 1992, and chapters 6, 12, and 13 of this book). Briefly, since we discuss it elsewhere, *self-efficacy* refers to a person's beliefs about whether he or she "can do" a particular task. Accordingly, self-efficacy is thought to have powerful motivational implications: If a person believes that she can, in fact, perform a task, she is more likely to do so (see K.W. Thomas and Velthouse, 1990). Most treatments of self-efficacy in the organizational literature consider it to be a state into which people can move or be moved, a consequence of certain managerial actions or policies rather than a stable personality trait (e.g., Spreitzer, 1995a, 1995b, 1996).

Following Conger and Kunungo (1988), K.W. Thomas and Velthouse (1990) advanced a model of empowerment that hinges on the concept of intrinsic motivation as we discussed the concept earlier in the chapter. According to Thomas and Velthouse, if a person becomes "empowered," she witnesses changes in what they call *task assessments,* which represent increases in a sense of impact, competence, meaningfulness, and choice. The overlap and similarity between these cognitive elements and the essence of intrinsic motivation as we described it earlier should be apparent, as should the overlap among the four factors and the psychological mechanisms thought to mediate the relationships between job design and employee outcomes in Hackman and Oldham's (1980) theory of job design. To empower someone means to give them power, and that power can be of *at least* two varieties. One form is legitimate authority; the other is represented by energy. It is this notion of energization through task assessments that lies at the core of the Thomas and Velthouse notion of empowerment.

It is critical to keep in mind that these internal cognitive states come about through perceptual interpretation of a person's context (such as a job or any other situation). The objective circumstances are contributing factors (such as the level of trust, information, and resources actually available to a person), but it is one's *perception* of the availability of these resources that will determine whether the person will assess the situation as providing possible impact, competence, and so on. If the circumstances do not yield a sense that the person has impact, choice, competence, or meaningfulness, then, by definition, she is not empowered—she has no heightened intrinsic motivation to engage in the task in question.

The design of jobs, organizational structures, and policies, rules, and procedures are key: They can collectively provide opportunities for empowerment or constraints against it (Spreitzer, 1996). Thus, one would expect higher levels of empowerment in organizational structures with wide spans of control, requiring employees to take on more initiative with less supervision from their superiors (Spreitzer, 1996). Similarly, people who work in jobs in which they are unclear about what is expected of them will feel less empowered, according to Spreitzer. Such people will not be confident of their level of authority and may be hesitant to act.

In a cross-sectional study of a sample of Fortune 500 executives, Spreitzer (1996) found that managers who experienced clear goals, a wide span of control, sociopolitical support from their peers, access to information, and a positive work climate reported higher levels of perceived empowerment than did those who did not experience these features in their jobs. Spreitzer cautions that because her design was cross-sectional rather than longitudinal or experimental, we are limited in our capacity to conclude that these contextual factors actually *caused* the first group's managers' feelings of empowerment. This constraint on causal conclusions characterized much of the early work on job enrichment as well, limiting its proponents' capacity to make strong causal arguments (see Roberts and Glick, 1981).

What is the financial impact of empowering employees by changing jobs the way that empowerment theorists suggest? This is a difficult question. Nevertheless, a recent study of 30 American steel minimills found support for the idea that organizational policies and procedures related to the management of employees can yield positive bottom-line economic benefits. Arthur (1994) categorized the mills in his sample as being of either of two types. Here is how Arthur (1994) characterizes the two categories: "Control and commitment represent two distinct approaches to shaping employee behaviors and attitudes at work. The goal of control human resources systems is to reduce direct labor costs, or to improve efficiency, by enforcing employee compliance with specified rules and procedures and basing employee rewards on some measurable output criteria. . . . In contrast, commitment human resource systems shape desired employee behaviors and attitudes by forging psychological links between organizational and employee goals. In other words, the focus is on developing committed employees who can be trusted to use their discretion to carry out job tasks in ways that are consistent with organizational goals" (p. 672). After sorting the mills into the control and commitment categories, Arthur compared the two sets in terms of their manufacturing performance and their rates of employee turnover. As expected (and consistent with what one might expect from an employee empowerment perspective), the mills in the commitment set performed better on both counts than those whose personnel policies were aimed more at employee control.

Employee Dysempowerment

One of the most current approaches to employee empowerment is based directly on Spreitzer's work, as described above. It is represented graphically in Figures 7-3 and 7-4 (see Kane and Montgomery, 1996; Spreitzer, 1995, 1996). As shown, Spreitzer's (1996) "organizational antecedents" are seen as responsible for creating psychological states of either empowerment or *dysempowerment*. These core psychological dimensions (which include *meaning, competence, self-determination,* and *impact*) are familiar to us after a reading of the theories of intrinsic motivation at the beginning of the chapter. The organizational antecedents that give rise to these psychological states are factors such as low role ambiguity, low supervision, sociopolitical support, access to information (see Eylon, 1994), and a participative climate (Spreitzer, 1996). Dysempowerment is defined as "an interruption with an individual's motivation to perform a work role, manifested in one or more affective reactions in an individual employee to the receipt of certain types of negative messages from another organizational actor" (Kane and Montgomery, 1996, p. 7). Hence, the origins of dysempowerment consist of negative information, originating from another employee, the work group, or the organization itself. The core of the phenomenon is the receiver's emotional reaction to such messages. The medium of the message can be either verbal or nonverbal. Dysempowering information may be transmitted either deliberately or inadvertently (Kane and Montgomery, 1996). Such messages are harmful to work motivation because they convey a lack of consideration of the person's dignity and well-being, either personally or professionally. They may have tones of distrust, insincerity, rudeness, disrespect, disinterest, and tactlessness. Their effect is to deflate the recipient's work-related energy, in part through the effect they have on his or her perceptions of fairness, justice, and trust (Kane and Montgomery, 1996).[13,14]

---

[13]The tones of contempt and exasperation with which some parents address their children are dysempowering; they imply a fundamental lack of respect, patience, and trust.

[14]Eylon (1994) attempted to test a model similar to that described by Kane and Montgomery (1996). Although there was some negative impact on participants' job satisfaction, Eylon failed to demonstrate the predicted negative effects on their work performance. Nevertheless, considerably more empirical work seems warranted to pursue both the dynamics of empowerment and dysempowerment and to continue to refine our understanding of intrinsic motivational processes.

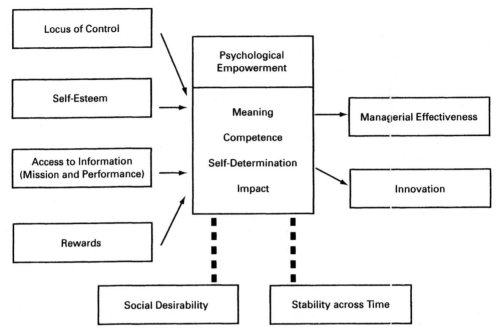

Source: G. M. Spreitzer, "Psychological empowerment in the workplace: Dimensions, measurement, and validation," *Academy of Management Journal,* 38, 1442–1465. Reprinted with permission.

FIGURE 7-3 Partial Nomological Network of Psychological Empowerment in the Workplace

Empowerment and Related Concepts

The fundamental assumption underlying employee empowerment is that people need and desire control, to be in charge of decisions that affect them, and to be equipped to make things happen. Theoretically, it is rooted in much of what we discussed earlier: people's needs for feelings of control and self-determination, to be origins rather than pawns, and so on (Burger, 1992; de Charms, 1968; Deci, 1975; Deci and Ryan, 1985; E. A. Skinner, 1995). In practice, the mechanics of the empowerment process are similar to those found in the job enrichment movement of the late 1960s, 1970s, and 1980s (see Hackman and Oldham, 1980). Nevertheless, whether empowerment is old wine in new bottles or really a new tool for understanding and managing organizational behavior, it has been applied with vigor in recent years and appears to be here to stay for a while (see R. C. Ford and Fottler, 1995; M. Hammer and Champy, 1993). Hanson, Porterfield, and Ames (1995) report, for example, that between 60 and 80 percent of Fortune 500 companies have either implemented empowerment programs or are experimenting with them (see also Lawler, Mohrman, and Ledford, 1995). The concept of empowerment is a standard prescription in current best-sellers addressed to management audiences, although it is often referred to by other terms (e.g., Kouzes and Posner [1995] suggest that managers *enable* others to perform effectively, and Covey [1989] suggests that successful people *synergize*).

A search of the literature produced since the mid-1980s reveals that academics have paid very little attention to job enrichment per se. There has been very little, if

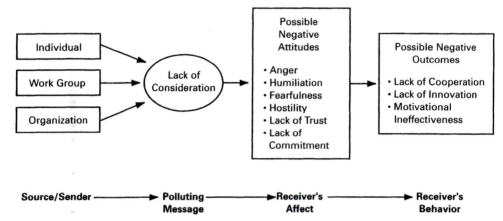

Source: K. Kane and K. Montgomery, "A theory of dysempowerment," paper presented at the Western Academy of Management, Banff, Alberta, Canada (1996). Reprinted with permission.

FIGURE 7-4   Model of Dysempowerment

any, new theory advanced on the topic and only a handful of reports from various industrial sectors reporting on the use and success (or failure) of job enrichment attempts. Yet while job enrichment may have gone underground over the past decade, the desire to build workplaces with intrinsic motivation, job satisfaction, and high performance has not disappeared. Our foregoing discussion of employee empowerment provides ample evidence that the sentiments in favor of intrinsic motivation are alive and well but that different applied techniques are being used to foster "high involvement" work. In vogue to varying degrees are programs such as employee ownership, self-directed work teams, quality circles, quality of life programs, and a number of others. (See Cotton, 1993, for a survey of the various forms.) Although the means used to attain them may move in and out of fashion every few years, the goals associated with intrinsic work motivation and intrinsic job satisfaction remain as sought after and as important as they were when Coch and French (1948), Deci (1972), Herzberg (1966), and others began the search for the means of providing people with a sense of worth, dignity, and self-control in their workplaces.

SUMMARY AND A GLANCE AHEAD

In this chapter we looked at such human growth needs as achievement, self-actualization, competence, and self-determination. We examined the nature of the intrinsic motivation that consists of the forces originating in these needs and attempted to show their relevance for employee work behavior. We reviewed the controversy related to the alleged negative effects of rewards on intrinsic motivation and found that the hypothesis stating that rewards diminish intrinsic motivation is either oversimplified or not valid. Nevertheless, we concluded that it is premature to abandon the concept of intrinsic motivation altogether. We then focused on job enrichment and employee empowerment, two latter-day concepts that have both philosophical and conceptual roots in the theory of intrinsic motivation. The essential goals that these managerial programs have in common are to make work interesting and a source of dignity and self-control for the people who perform it. Notwithstanding their wide coverage and popularity, programs of this sort have enjoyed only limited success to date.

We turn in the next chapter to the problem of need frustration—situations in which people are prevented from attaining the goals they pursue to satisfy the needs we have been examining throughout part two.

CHAPTER

Frustration at Work

*Perseverance is more prevailing than violence; and many things
which cannot be overcome when they are together,
yield themselves up when taken little by little.*

—PLUTARCH

On the afternoon of August 24, 1992, Professor Valery Fabrikant of Concordia University in Montreal entered the ninth floor of the engineering building where he worked, carrying a briefcase containing three handguns and many rounds of ammunition. He proceeded to shoot the president of the Concordia Faculty Association three times, killing him. He then shot two colleagues who had entered the scene, wounding one in her leg and fatally wounding the other. He then deliberately crossed through a maze of aisles and corridors, fatally shot the head of the electrical and computer engineering department, and fell into a scuffle with another colleague who was visiting the department at the time. Losing his first gun, Fabrikant shot to death another engineering professor while his previous two victims were tending to each other's traumas. Fabrikant finally grabbed another professor and a security guard and locked them away in an office with him while he called 911 and sought access to a television reporter. Eventually, the captive professor and the security guard overpowered Fabrikant and ended the crisis (Wolfe, 1994). Ultimately, four people died in the incident.

The Concordia University massacre shocked the Montreal community at large and the academic community all across Canada. How could such a terrible and unpredictable horror occur, especially in the otherwise safe and benign context of a university? After a period of time, investigations revealed that Dr. Fabrikant, a mechanical engineer with an international reputation, had been repeatedly frustrated by the university and by his colleagues and superiors, ultimately reaching the point where he felt he had to take control of his career by his own means. The means he used was violence. The event is still highly salient to academics and administrators in Canada and elsewhere.

Otherwise civilized and highly educated people are quite capable of resorting to violence in response to continued frustration in their lives and in their workplaces in particular. Fabrikant was known as a loner but as a highly prolific scholar (Wolfe,

1994). He placed heavy demands on department heads and other superiors for resources and research support and never seemed satisfied with what he received as a result of his demands. In the spring of 1991, for example, he was awarded a merit pay increase, the highest granted in his department. But he continued to demand more and was constantly in the "bad books" of most of the key players in his group. Eventually, an administrator examined his personnel file, found "minor discrepancies" (Wolfe, 1994, p. 18) in his résumé, and asked Fabrikant for proof of his academic qualifications. This led to an escalation of conflict between Fabrikant and the rest of his colleagues, who met to discuss disciplinary actions against him. One sanction applied was an increased teaching load, including courses Fabrikant claimed were outside his area of expertise. The case started to receive media coverage outside the university's boundaries and again, the conflict escalated. A former student alleged that she had been raped by Fabrikant. Meanwhile, Fabrikant was writing letters to at least two colleagues, demanding that they acknowledge that they had not made sufficient contributions to some of his papers to have earned the credit received, threatening them with lawsuits. Fabrikant was frustrated in the court battle and was charged with contempt. Eventually, he managed to obtain the three guns that allowed him to relieve his stress and frustration by murdering four colleagues.

In earlier chapters we discussed a number of human needs that may seek gratification through working. This chapter is about frustration: It deals with situations in which people's behaviors fail to result in the attainment of sought-after goals. In the sections that follow we examine some common causes and a number of predictable consequences of need frustration in work settings. The concepts discussed here come primarily from the work of Norman Maier (1956, 1961, 1973) and his associates, Leonard Berkowitz (1989, 1993b) and Paul Spector (1978, 1997).

NEEDS AND GOALS

Before we begin it is essential to sort out the meanings of two terms: needs and goals. Successful understanding and application of our knowledge about frustration depend largely on keeping the distinction between the two concepts in mind. As we have discussed at length, *needs* are hypothetical concepts that represent the basic internal forces posited to explain motivated behavior (recall chapter 3). They are characteristics of individuals and are relatively fixed, at least in the short run. On the other hand, *goals* are things that people seek and try to attain for the sake of fulfilling their needs. Goals such as food and sleep are necessary, respectively, for satisfying the human physiological needs called hunger and fatigue. In work settings, pay, promotions, recognition from one's superior, and a chance to show one's skill are examples of goals that people may seek to satisfy their existence, relatedness, and growth needs on the job and through their work. It bears repeating that the frustration model that follows is of value only if we keep the distinction between needs and goals in mind: Needs are internal to a person, part of the personality; goals are external agents or states.

As we noted in chapter 3, different people often pursue different goals to satisfy the same need. For example, relatedness needs may be expressed by a gregarious employee through constant chitchat during work hours, whereas another employee may attempt to satisfy that same need by seeking election to the organization's social committee. Further, a given goal, if achieved, may satisfy several needs simultaneously. A promotion, for instance, may be instrumental for the fulfillment of a person's existence, relatedness, and growth needs. In short, there is no one-to-one correspondence between needs and goals, and it is essential to keep the two concepts separate when we consider the causes and consequences of frustration. The relationships between needs and goals is represented in Figure 8-1.

Before we explore the nature and consequences of frustration in the workplace, we examine briefly the formal theory of frustration presented by Maier (1956, 1961), an American psychologist whose early work still figures prominently on this subject. The reader will see some basic similarities between the definition of motivation and motivated behavior offered by Maier and the definitions offered earlier in the book. The key point in what follows is to understand how motivated behavior differs from instinctive behavior and frustration.

MOTIVATION, FRUSTRATION, AND BEHAVIOR

For Maier (1956, 1973), motivated behavior is controlled by both an internal and an external condition. The internal condition is a need or desire. The external condition is a goal: "Either condition may be present without the other and produce a stimulus–response behavior, but both are essential for creating the state of motivation which selectively arouses behavior that may be goal oriented. Behavior called forth by the state of motivation tends to relieve the internal condition and this in turn leads to satisfaction. So-called 'adaptive behavior' is characterized by the fact that it leads to a reduction in need" (Maier, 1961, p. 96).

To be adaptive, of course, the behavior must be aligned appropriately with the nature of the need, and learning occurs over time—learning that associates the accomplishment of certain goals with particular need states. Maier defines instinctive or innate behavior as acts that occur in the presence of both need states and goals but

FIGURE 8-1   Needs, Goals, and the Frustration of Behavior

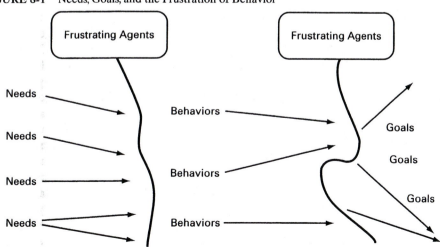

without the learning of associations between need states and goal acquisition. Jumping back in the presence of a sudden loud noise is an example. Whereas motivated behavior indicates a choice among alternative possible goals, there is no goal orientation in frustration behavior.

> When frustration is experienced behavior is a terminal response to frustration and not a means to an end. No need is satisfied because no goal is involved. Any satisfaction that occurs must be in the form of relief, not in the form of consummation. [We must distinguish] therefore . . . between two possible forms of satisfaction: relief from frustration, and the removal of a need through the attainment of a goal.
>
> Frustration, although it may be set up through need deprivation, initiates behavior which may be unrelated to the conditions that lead to the frustration. . . . Goals no longer serve as guides, so that frustration-instigated behavior is behavior that is forced by the condition of the organism. In this sense all frustrated behavior has the character of a compulsion. (Maier, 1961, p. 99)

Defining Frustration

Leonard Berkowitz (1989) has spent much of his career studying frustration and its consequences, especially aggression (to which we turn shortly). After surveying the set of possible definitions of frustration, he notes that this term is used frequently in everyday speech. People are always claiming to be "frustrated" for some reason or another. However, Berkowitz (1989) adopts a precise scientific definition of frustration for his work, a definition that was first advanced in 1939 by a group of Yale psychologists. For them, *frustration* is "an interference with the occurrence of an instigated goal-response at its proper time in the behavior sequence" (Dollard, Doob, Miller, Mowrer, and Sears, 1939, p. 7). Berkowitz (1989, pp. 60–61) points out that this definition implies a number of things, including (1) an impediment to a goal is not a frustration unless the person involved is striving, implicitly or explicitly, to reach the goal; and (2) the person involved anticipates satisfaction of a need through the attainment of the goal in question. Therefore, Berkowitz observes, poor people lacking the good things in life need not be defined as frustrated unless they are actually pursuing them and are prevented from attaining them. In concert with Berkowitz, we adopt the Yale University definition he adopts in his work (see Dollard et al., 1939) along with the nuances he identifies as following from it.[1]

Causes of Frustration

People tend to associate certain goals with satisfactions of their particular needs (although there is not always a one-to-one correspondence). Each of us tends to find certain things satisfying and other things less so. A simple example is the act of going to the refrigerator for a cold drink (the goal) for the sake of quenching one's thirst (the need). The more frequently a particular goal object proves successful in meeting a need, the more likely the person is to seek that same goal in the future when the need arises. To

---

[1]In everyday usage, people frequently claim that they are "frustrated." But statements of this sort are usually inaccurate from a technical point of view. Although people who make such statements are, in fact, frustrated, what they usually mean by their statements is that they are angry or depressed as a result of not being able to accomplish their goals. Frustration is formally a *situation,* not an emotional reaction. See chapter 4 for a complete discussion of emotions in the workplace.

some extent, we form habits (although Maier is careful to distinguish between habits and fixated behavior—one common response to frustration that we discuss shortly).

What happens when a traditionally successful behavior fails to reach the goal being sought? What happens when, for whatever reason, the behavior itself is not possible? Or what happens when a person's behavior tends to make goal accomplishment more difficult rather than easier? Situations of this sort are common in virtually all job settings. They are often difficult to identify and difficult to ameliorate. Nevertheless, the behavior that tends to occur in response to frustration is common in organizational settings and is usually (although not always) dysfunctional. Managing frustrated behavior is a major challenge for supervisors, and it is not always done effectively.

What types of things block a person's learned behavior from reaching work goals? In other words, what causes frustration in work settings? We can classify causes of frustration into two categories for the sake of discussion. The first includes factors that are, for the most part, external to the person, although they may or may not be beyond her control. Examples abound in organizations. The structure of the organization is a common cause of need frustration, because hierarchies, which tend to be pyramid shaped, prevent most of us from reaching the top. Other examples are policies that prevent people from interacting with one another on the job, that stipulate when a person may take a rest, or that prevent people from taking a vacation when they want. A job that is boring and repetitive is another example, one faced by many of us. A supervisor who will not cooperate and help an employee can frustrate that employee. Similarly, low-performing employees constitute barriers that prevent supervisors from achieving their job goals. Co-workers who exclude a newcomer and ignore his attempts to be friendly, and situations of ongoing conflict between co-workers, are other examples. People may attempt a myriad of behaviors to meet their needs, and there are countless potential barriers external to a person that can interfere with those behaviors, preventing her from meeting her basic needs at work (see Peters and O'Connor, 1980; Peters, O'Connor, and Eulberg, 1985).

A second category of potential frustrators consists of characteristics of the person being frustrated. A lack of ability to do the work (where work accomplishment is the goal) can block a person's attempts and leave his needs unfulfilled. Similarly, characteristics such as gender (Bartol, 1978; Larwood and Wood, 1977), age (Rosen and Jerdee, 1976), or departmental affiliation (M. Dalton, 1959) are other factors that can pose barriers and prevent people from getting jobs, promotions into new jobs, or even access to information that they need to be effective on their jobs. Disabled employees provide a powerful example of how a personal characteristic or set of personal characteristics can prevent a person from reaching work-related goals.

It tends to be easier to identify causes of frustration external to the person being frustrated than it is to identify internal causes, and people often blame factors other than themselves for their frustrations at work (Harvey and Albertson, 1971; Mitchell, Green, and Wood, 1981; Vroom, 1964). Diagnosing the real causes of an employee's frustration can be difficult, for many reasons. First, frustrated people are not always aware of the barriers to their goal achievement, especially when these barriers are internal to themselves or when they are rooted in organizational factors that are beyond their cognizance. An employee with unusual religious beliefs is an example of the former; a company's advertising campaign that projects an unfavorable image of the product he is attempting to sell illustrates the latter.

Second, the behavior that results from need frustration will vary from person to person. There is no universal one-to-one correspondence between the force of particular needs and the behavior that results (recall chapter 3). Also recall the human tendency to project our own need–behavior linkages to others, even when they are not appropriate. A supervisor who observes frustrated behavior by one of her subordinates may have difficulty both in diagnosing the need(s) seeking satisfaction and in detecting the nature of the barrier(s) responsible for the frustration of the behavior aimed at those needs—a complex problem indeed.

To summarize, frustration is defined as a situation in which habitual and learned behaviors are thwarted regarding the effective attainment of goals sought for meeting human needs. The barriers thwarting the behavior are often difficult to identify. Moreover, because of the complicated links between needs and the behaviors aimed at them, outsiders face a tough task when trying to help someone else who is frustrated. It is easier to talk about and understand the frustration of existence and relatedness needs than to understand and identify the frustration of growth needs. This is in large part because the goals typically sought for the satisfaction of existence and relatedness needs are usually relatively concrete and tangible. But as noted in chapter 7, growth needs are responsible for a considerable amount of the behavior we observe at work, and they may become even more important in the future. The goals that people seek to satisfy their growth needs are more often amorphous and idiosyncratic, making their attainment difficult at times. In fact, most of the jobs we perform in our economy do not readily satisfy human growth needs. As a result, the frustration of growth needs is a major problem in organizations, one that manifests itself in job-related boredom and dissatisfaction (as we will see in chapter 10). There are limits to the degree to which jobs can be structured to allow the ongoing satisfaction of human needs for competence, self-esteem, and self-actualization, although we will see that several formal managerial programs have been advanced to try to ease the situation and to make it more possible for people to satisfy their growth needs through their work.

Consequences of Frustration

Need frustration tends to result in any of a number of typical classes of behavior, although people manifest these classes of behavior in different ways. In fact, Maier notes (1961, p. 100) that motivated and frustrated behavior processes may appear simultaneously, in equal strength. In these cases, some of a person's behavior may be goal-oriented and some of it may simply be driven by the inner state, with no particular goal in mind. Sometimes the frustration may be relieved and the person's behavior becomes almost (or entirely) goal-oriented (a good scream or the utterance of an epithet are common means by which this occurs). Alternatively, goal-oriented behavior can vanish and most of the force driving the person is frustration—no goal is in mind or in sight.

The most constructive reaction to frustration is exploration and problem solving, by which the person sets about (with or without the help of others) to diagnose the cause, or barrier, and to remove it (Wong, 1979). This sort of behavior occurs regularly in our lives, so much so that we usually take it for granted. Problem solving in response to frustration can contribute to the satisfaction of most human needs. A second constructive adaptation to frustration is the adoption and pursuit of alternative goals. Rather than seeking to increase her income through a promotion or a raise in pay, a single working mother might take on a part-time job. Similarly, an employee who works in physical isolation from his co-workers may seek fulfillment of his social needs by pursuing friendships off the job. The need(s) remains the same, but the goal(s) changes.

Frustration and Aggression

In 1964, a burly produce manager poked a 18-year-old male part-time clerk in the deltoid muscle of the arm. It hurt. The manager stood passively in the 35° cooler and looked challengingly at the boy. The youngster dropped the knife on the floor. Another poke on the deltoid, harder this time. The produce manager looked with glee at the boy and poked him again. "Don't drop the goddammed knife, you jerk. Now, pick it up and get going."

This is a close re-creation of a real scene that occurred in Vancouver, Canada, about 25 years ago. The produce manager was reporting to a strict store manager who had to show a profit from each of his departments every day, every month, every quarter, every year. The right shoulder of the boy hurt, and in his fantasies he wanted to slug the produce manager in the face for the cruel indignities. Many people had hoped this sort of exploitation was long past. The idea was to terrorize young people, who earned union wages, into cost-reduction behaviors that would make each store more profitable. The young people ran to check prices on cans of peas when the marks were not clear on the cans. Dignity was not an issue; profit by the hour was at stake. The young people, most of whom were students, ran rather than walked because they were told to do so by the manager of the store. He thought that running by his young people to catch the price of a can of peas was the best way to manage. "If these kids want to earn union wages, they will earn it." Scientific management in the 1960s, alive and well in a Canadian grocery chain. There are probably still hundreds of thousands of unskilled or semiskilled workers in North America who work under such conditions of fear and frustration. There is no doubt that coercion plays a major motivating role among the populations of illegal immigrants who work in the farm fields and sweatshops of Canada and the United States. Conditions of this sort are charged with emotions of fear and anxiety and are kept alive by coercion based on superior power. These are situations rife for aggression.

Aggression is a common and highly predictable reaction to need frustration. The connection between frustration and aggression is so strong that 60 years ago the Yale psychologists mentioned earlier pronounced that "aggression is always a consequence of frustration" and "the occurrence of aggressive behavior always presupposes the existence of frustration" (Dollard et al., 1939, p. 1, quoted by Berkowitz, 1993, p. 59). Since then we have learned that there are more causes of aggression than only frustration, and that frustration can result in events other than aggression. Nevertheless, the connection between the two concepts is still regarded as powerful.

Usually defined as some form of attack accompanied by anger (Maier, 1973, p. 73), *aggression* can be open and aboveboard, or more covert and less obvious.[2] Berkowitz (1989) adopts the view that there are two varieties of aggression: hostile and instrumental. *Hostile aggression* is intended to hurt or to cause damage. *Instrumental*

---

[2]The Yale group (Dollard et al., 1939) whose definition of frustration we have adopted, defined aggression simply as any "sequence of behavior, the goal-response to which is the injury of the person toward whom it is directed" (p. 7).

aggression is intended to attain an objective, such as money, land, the affections of a mate, or another commodity (p. 62). Examples of hostile aggression might include bawling out a subordinate or hitting a co-worker. Less obvious examples include gossiping about someone behind his back or voting against a colleague's project proposal in an executive committee meeting. Overt or covert, hostile aggression is intended to somehow damage, hurt, or frustrate its target. The majority of our focus here is on hostile aggression and its causes and consequences for work motivation and the workplace.

When and under what circumstances does frustration lead to aggression? We adopt Berkowitz's (1989) recent position that "frustrations can give rise to aggressive inclinations because they are aversive [and] only to the extent that they are unpleasant to those affected" (p. 68). What makes a frustration aversive? One factor is the assumed intentions of the parties who cause the blockage. If we believe that there has been a capricious, unwarranted, or malicious intention driving the actions of other people to thwart us, the experience is aversive and aggressive impulses are more likely to result. Similarly, if the blockage represents the failure to attain something we wanted badly, the experience is likely to be more aversive than otherwise and therefore more likely to produce aggressive desires. Current thinking represented by Berkowitz (1989) adheres quite closely to the original frustration-aggression formulation advanced by Dollard et al. (1939) but is modified to allow for the *emotional reaction* of the frustrated person and the attributions he makes about the cause of his circumstances. If the blockage is aversive, aggression is likely to occur. If the blockage is not experienced as aversive, the connection between frustration and aggression is attenuated.

The targets of aggressive acts are often not the actual causes of the frustration. This phenomenon is referred to as *displaced aggression* or *scapegoating*. In organizational settings, a middle manager who is disciplined or frustrated by a superior may in turn vent his frustration on his own subordinates. Similarly, employees whose education levels are blocking them from receiving further promotions may turn their aggression against their supervisors or co-workers, none of whom are responsible for causing their frustration. Finally, assembly-line employees who deliberately sabotage the products they build (e.g., Dubois, 1979; Jermier, 1988) can be seen as taking out the aggression caused by the monotonous nature of their jobs on a handy, convenient scapegoat. It was clear to Maier (1961) that behavior of this sort is clearly not motivational because goal orientation is not involved, there is no apparent attempt to solve problems, to remove barriers, or to make things right again. Aggression of this sort is a product unto itself, not a means to another end (the accomplishment of a goal). Relief comes (or can come) merely through the expression of the act. It is, by definition, frustration-instigated behavior. The principle of availability is a potent predictor of the targets against which a person may select to aggress. People or objects nearby and unable to strike back are frequently the objects of a frustrated person's aggression. Wife beatings and child abuse by chronically unemployed workers are examples.

One reason that aggression so commonly results from frustration is that it often works to remove the frustrating barriers. A bully who usually wins through intimidating others soon learns that intimidation and the threat of force is quite effective in helping him achieve his goals. People do those things they find to be rewarding (see chapter 13). Moreover, aggressive styles may evolve as a person ages and advances from the simple use of brute force to the use of less physical, but equally forceful tactics such as sarcastic verbal attacks. Employee behavior ranging from theft and pilfering to the formation of a union may be seen as aggressive responses against organizational realities that perpetuate frustrate human needs (Hamner and Smith, 1978; Stagner, 1956). Employees who feel locked into their jobs have limited constructive means for dealing with their frustration and as a result are more likely to resort either to aggression or displaced aggression on their jobs.

It has recently been estimated that $5 billion to $6 billion are lost every year in the United States economy because of real or perceived abuse of employees by employers (Wilson, 1991). In addition, billions more are lost as the result of wrongful dismissal, sexual harassment, defamation suits, and workplace violence. Conditions of such workplace trauma cause the "actual disintegration of an employee's fundamental self, resulting from perceived or real continual and malicious treatment" (Wilson, 1991, p. 47).

In the past decade mass murders in the office place have risen by as much as 200 to 300 percent (Stuart, 1992); between 900 and 1,600 persons are murdered each year. In fact, these estimates may underrepresent the actual frequency (Elliott and Jarrett, 1994). According to the National Institute of Occupational Safety and Health in the United States, workplace homicide is the third-leading cause of death on the job, entailing more than 1,400 lives. Seven thousand work-related injuries due to violence occur every year (secondary data cited by P. R. Johnson and Indvik, 1994). Why all the mayhem at work?

A variety of factors contribute to this shocking rate of workplace violence (Elliott and Jarrett, 1994; P. R. Johnson and Indvik, 1994). Some of it is caused by violence based on frustration that originates outside work, such as in the home or family setting. Some of it is triggered when events at work dredge up suppressed violence that people witnessed as children. The workplace is a forum of hierarchy, frustration, and real and imagined threat for many people. Job insecurities based on organizational changes such as mergers, acquisitions, work redesign, and the introduction of new technology can pose threats and opportunities for aggression to be expressed. In fact, a combination of economic factors, including the tough economic times we have been having, combined with high rates of competition for fewer and fewer good jobs, immigration, and the multiculturalism and diversity brought about by immigration, can comprise real or imagined barriers for career advancement in the minds of many North Americans who are willing to take up arms against their co-workers or bosses (Elliott and Jarrett, 1994).

The "typical" workplace murderer is a middle-aged Caucasian male who is both homicidal and suicidal and who has, in many cases, suffered termination from his work, setbacks he equates with a loss of his basic existence (Elliott and Jarrett, 1994). The dynamics associated with layoffs from work are treated in chapter 11, where we discuss the critical importance of how they are handled. The current discussion will be of particular importance then. One factor that seems to underlie many of these sources of threat and frustration is violation of psychological contracts between workers and employers (Robinson and Rousseau, 1994; Rousseau, 1989; Rousseau and Parks, 1993). When agreements and promises appear to have been broken, career expectations are dashed. Persons seen as the cause of such events can quickly become the targets of aggression of the sort and scale described above.

A less dramatic form of aggression in the workplace is sabotage: a deliberate action or inaction intended to damage, destroy, or disrupt some aspect of the workplace environment, including the organization's property, product, processes, or reputation, with the net effect of undermining goals of capitalist elites (LaNuez and Jermier, 1994, p. 221, following L. Taylor and Watson, 1971). We normally think of sabotage as perpetrated by unskilled or semiskilled personnel. In fact, sabotage is frequently the tactic of choice among managers, professionals, and "technocrats" (Jermier, 1988; LaNuez and Jermier, 1994). Besides obvious acts of sabotage such as shutting down production lines, damaging equipment and supplies, or generally "throwing a wrench in the works," managerial and professional personnel can conduct sabotage by deeds such as divulging company secrets, circulating bogus rumors, erasing company computer files, and so on. Anything that hurts the company's best interests qualifies as sabotage, and anyone may participate.[3]

According to LaNuez and Jermier (1994), there are two common antecedents of acts of sabotage among managerial and professional employees: diminished control and negative affect. The reader will recall the treatment of intrinsic motivation provided in chapter 7. The essence of intrinsic motivation was reported as feelings of self-determination and personal control over one's environment. LaNuez and Jermier have described how such control has been stripped from managerial and professional employees in many workplaces by factors such as organizational restructuring, increased measurement and accountability for one's work output, advancing technology, and hegemony of electronic devices such as computers, pagers, and various surveillance techniques. Control has also been reduced for professional employees by determination by managers and quasi-professionals of how the work is to be done and how it is to be used. Finally, LaNuez and Jermier observe how rewards such as promotions and tenure have become harder for many professional employees to achieve, as many organizations prefer to hire and advance newer, younger, and more currently trained personnel. In fact, the trend away from permanent employment toward the use of part-time, temporary employees who serve as consultants on command exacerbates the problem. The point is that managerial, professional, and technical employees have been suffering reduced levels of control over their work lives. Like many lower-level employees, they are motivated to strike back at their employers through various forms of sabotage. Need frustration, especially the blockage of higher-level needs for growth, self-esteem, and self-actualization, is reasoned to lie at the bottom of much of the sabotage, especially when accompanied by strong negative emotions (see Berkowitz, 1989).

Related to sabotage is the simple act of theft—theft by employees of their employers' money, inventory, or other assets. Theft is a big-time concern in North America, costing employers approximately $20 billion a year by one estimate (Stoffman, 1991). A variety of techniques and tactics are used, including simply dipping into the till, gaining control of cash receipts and reporting bogus totals to senior management, withholding some of the cash actually taken in, finding small sums that senior mangers don't know about (such as small fines and refunds that are normally not accounted for), having work or services provided by suppliers to one's own home or property and charging it to the employer, stealing inventory, writing company checks to oneself, and so on. Filing false and padded expense accounts may be one of the most common tactics of theft. Wherever there are considerable stocks and flows of money and resources,

---

[3]Jermier's (1988) treatment of sabotage assumes that it is based on inherent conflictual forces in the workplace, where the interests of various groups such as owners, executives, managers, professionals, and production workers cannot be assumed to be in harmony merely because they are all associated with a common "organization." Jermier's chapter is rich with examples.

there will always be a chance that someone in a position of trust or knowledge will be tempted to steal. How many people? Stoffman (1991) quotes a forensic accountant who works for a large consulting/accounting firm: "Twenty percent are crooks who will steal all the time, 20 percent will never steal, and 60 percent will steal given motive and opportunity" (p. 56). Frustration and a sense of having been treated inequitably by the employer are definitely factors accounting for some of the theft.

In short, frustration often begets aggression, at work as in any other human forum. Aggression is usually aimed at the perceived source of the frustration. Therefore, the recipient of the aggression in work settings is often a supervisor or a co-worker. We have seen how violence, including even murder, has entered the North American workplace. On the other hand, the frustrated person may simply wish to strike back at the employing organization. Sabotage and theft are two very common examples of how this is accomplished. Similarly, aggression and perceived aggression frequently beget aggression in return, at work as anywhere else. The availability of weapons must exacerbate the frequency of shootings and murder, but physical violence can be executed without firearms in any or most work settings. This general concept often takes specific form when people are fired or laid off their jobs (Stuart, 1992). For example, in late 1991 and early 1992 there was a flurry of shootings of managers and supervisors associated with the terminations of former employees in U.S. industry (Stuart, 1992). Instances of violence, even those that fall short of shootings and murder, are serious disruptions to the social fabric of workplaces and comprise a major scar for the employing organization(s) involved. Frustration in the extreme can yield extreme consequences.

Other Nonaggressive Responses to Frustration

In our discussion of Alderfer's ERG theory, the concept of frustration-regression was introduced. *Regression* consists of the use of behaviors that are less sophisticated and less mature than those befitting a particular person (Maier, 1961, p. 107). They are childlike, or at least characteristic of behaviors learned during one's earlier developmental stages, or alternatively, simply less mature, even if they were not practiced and learned by the frustrated adult when he was younger (Maier, 1961). Common manifestations of regression include behaviors such as horseplay, swearing, humor (Duncan, Smeltzer, and Leap, 1990), crude and cruel joking (especially in male-dominated workplaces; see Collinson, 1992; Kahn, 1989), and among women, crying. Women are as capable as men at most forms of regression (see Collinson, 1992). For example, a female employee of Deere and Co. of Moline, Illinois, was caught several years ago photocopying her bare bottom on a company copier and was dismissed as a result. The concept of availability also pertains here. People may tend to engage in regressive acts that are easiest to accomplish or that more readily cause relief. Again, this is behavior without a goal other than the expression of the behavior itself. It may reduce tension, but it is not motivated by the attainment of an external goal.

Crying represents a particularly complex example, as does the use of foul language or physical violence. On the one hand, these styles of behavior represent adaptive responses that a youth or adolescent might employ in reaction to frustration. They may even have been useful during a person's younger years for removing frustrating barriers. When employed as a response to frustration by adults, however, regressive acts often function to increase the intensity of the frustration. For example, a woman who characteristically cries in response to frustration or attack in board meetings can inadvertently increase the tendency of her male colleagues to discount her managerial "cool" and ability. Similarly, a foul-mouthed male may add to his own exclusion from the inner circles of a management group simply by reconfirming that as an immature lout with a dirty mouth, he deserves to be excluded. Regression sometimes works to assist in the removal of the barriers that cause employee need frustration, but it can boomerang and make the frustration worse.

Fixation is another common behavioral response to need frustration. It involves repeated use of the same goal-seeking behaviors despite their ineffectiveness. For example, a student who continually approaches a mathematics problem using only one or two strategies, despite evidence that those strategies are not appropriate, is engaging in fixated behavior. Repeated failures breed even greater feelings of futility and make the adoption of more adaptive behaviors less likely. In work settings, fixated behavior can be pathetic because unlike aggression or regression, which sometimes result in goal accomplishment, it cannot, by definition, lead to success. Resorting to fixated behavior can be damaging to one's self-concept because of the image of helplessness it entails (see Korman, 1970, 1976, and D. T. Hall, 1976, for discussions of the importance of success experiences for one's self-esteem).

It is worth noting at this point that one reason behind the oft-noted resistance to change in organizations (Zaltman and Duncan, 1977) is that change can make learned and familiar behaviors by employees obsolete and frustrating. In other words, change (such as a redesigned organizational structure or a new work process) can generate very real barriers to the behaviors that employees have used in the past, barriers to the behaviors associated with goal accomplishment, and with it, need satisfaction. There are many examples of how the introduction of new computer technology (e.g., Mann and Williams, 1972) has been seen by workers as a threat and source of frustration, resulting in considerable unhappiness for them as well as reduced effectiveness of the new technology.

Another response to frustration that has particular relevance to work behavior is *resignation.* In simple terms this amounts to "giving up"—becoming docile, uninspired, and nonchalant. In many ways it is a nonresponse, insofar as the frustrated person merely continues to show up for work, performing to a minimum expected standard, obeying the rules, and getting by. This style of adaptation is in essence the style that reinforces belief in Theory X, according to McGregor (1960). Argyris (1957) claims it is the natural response that one can expect when employee needs for growth collide with organizational structures and procedures designed to achieve efficiency and control. It accounts for much of the half-hearted service we observe from workers in service industries and much of the apparent lack of intelligence and creativity exhibited by many people in various industrial settings. People adapt to the frustration caused by their job experiences by simply bringing their bodies to work and leaving their hearts, minds, and souls at home. We return to resignation and other forms of withdrawal from the job (such as absenteeism and turnover) in chapter 10 when we examine work-related beliefs and attitudes in detail.

The Choice of a Response

People will select from an array of responses to frustration according to how well they (or which ones) are believed likely to be most effective at restoring the person's apparent ability to cope effectively with the world (Gloria, 1984). Frustration scenarios can mostly be categorized as situations of failure (e.g., at a task), attack (against oneself from another person), or obstruction (such as when someone or something gets in our way, blocking goal attainment). Regardless, it seems that the particular type of response (or responses) we can expect to see exhibited in reaction to the frustration of a particular employee will depend on a host of factors, including the following: (1) the number and relative importance of the needs being blocked from satisfaction, (2) the degree of deprivation and/or its duration, (3) the extensiveness of the blocking and the completeness of the frustration that results (i.e., whether it is constant or intermittent), (4) the perceived motives (if any) of the source of the frustration, (5) the person's prior experiences of success and failure in using various reactions to frustration, and (6) the probable threats or costs perceived to be associated with the various response alternatives.

For example, we might expect to witness the use of aggression in cases where a person's existence needs are blocked (because they are so prepotent), where the frustration is intense and prolonged, and/or where the person attributes malevolent motives to the supervisor (for example), who is perceived as the source of the frustration.[4] More passive responses (such as fixation and/or resignation) are more likely when, for whatever reasons, aggression is impossible or is seen as too risky. According to R. Katz (1980), passive resignation and goal displacement are very common responses by many or most working adults who have mastered their jobs, so that no challenge remains.

Spector (1997) has recently formalized a similar model of workplace frustration that takes into account the cognitive interpretation of the frustrated person in predicting the type of response that is likely to result from frustration. Spector's model is presented in Figure 8-2. As shown, if the frustrated person sees the source of frustration as being arbitrary, an angry response is more likely than if the blockage is seen as innocent, unintentional, or accidental. The importance of the goal being blocked, the number of goals being blocked, the number of frustrators perceived to be involved, and the severity of the frustration will all affect the assessment made by the victim of frustration and, accordingly, influence her response to the frustration situation. For example, if a person is prevented from seeing her boss for a scheduled appointment because the boss's busy schedule of morning meetings is running late, the subordinate may be slightly disappointed but is more likely simply to seek an alternative meeting time than to threaten her boss or to withhold the ideas she was planning to share. In this case there is little urgency to the meeting: There are few goals at stake, they are not urgent, and it will be only a matter of time until the worker can see her boss on another occasion. By contrast, an employee who is trapped in a warehouse fire is more likely to become violent and aggressive in finding a way out of the warehouse. In this example the need for survival is paramount, and the heat and smoke of the fire make escape difficult as well as imperative.

Summary

There are a variety of responses to frustration, and the one chosen in a given circumstance will be affected by the frustrated person's interpretation of the frustration situation. The foregoing examples suggest that cool problem solving is not always the reaction of choice to frustration situations. There are a variety of other, less constructive

---

[4]One theorist denies a simple link between the choice of a response to frustration and the severity of the frustration itself (see Gloria, 1984).

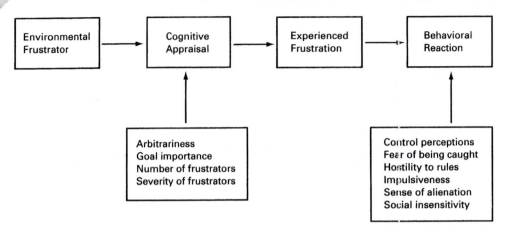

Source: From P. E. Spector, "The role of frustration in antisocial behavior at work," in R. A. Giacalone and J. Greenberg (Eds.), *Antisocial Behavior in Organizations* (Thousand Oaks, CA: Sage, 1997). Reprinted with permission of Sage Publications, Inc.

FIGURE 8-2   Spector's Model of Organizational Frustration

ways of responding to frustration—forms of behavior that are often found in organizational settings, such as that of Professor Fabrikant of Concordia University.

The reader is encouraged to use the frustration framework for viewing, understanding, and dealing with dysfunctional employee behaviors ranging from tardiness and absenteeism to poor quality and low levels of work effort. The insights into employee attitudes, emotions, behavior, and performance that this model can reveal are among the most useful available at present for understanding work motivation (or the lack of it) from the perspective of need-based models. The frustration model is especially useful for understanding deviant, aberrant, and antisocial behaviors such as theft, lying, tardiness, sabotage, whistle-blowing, and litigating against one's employer (Giacalone and Greenberg, 1997). When we think of it, most human behavior occurs in states of relative deprivation, so frustration, in varying degrees, is the normal condition for most of us most of the time.[5]

OVERVIEW OF NEED-BASED THEORIES AND A GLANCE AHEAD

This concludes our treatment of need-based approaches to work motivation. It is critical to note at this point that need-based theories of work motivation comprise only one approach to the issues discussed in this book, albeit one of the most popular approaches in the history of the organizational sciences. The popularity of these theories of work motivation has declined dramatically among social scientists since approximately the mid-1970s. The attack on need-based theories of job satisfaction (and of motivation and related concepts) by Salancik and Pfeffer (1977) seemed to precipitate

---

[5]The principles of frustration discussed here will be especially important as background when we explore problems of equity, justice, and fairness in the workplace in chapter 11.

a shift in emphasis in the field away from needs and toward models that are predicated on different root assumptions regarding human nature.

This author believes that a total abandonment of need-based models is inappropriate (see Snyder and Williams, 1982). It is true that need-based models have limitations and ambiguities. Many of them (such as Maslow's theory) are vague and hard to operationalize for scientific testing. Others, such as Herzberg's motivator-hygiene theory, simply seem to be wrong or severely limited in validity. There is the problem of complex connections between needs and behaviors (as illustrated in Figure 8-1), making it difficult to predict precise behaviors on the basis of knowledge of a person's predominant need states, or for that matter, to interpret the need states in the first place. Cognitive theories such as those we examine in part three have similar difficulties in subjectivity. We are left with the question: Are people need-driven, goal-seeking creatures? Notwithstanding the many difficulties of extant need-based models, the author's answer is: Yes, indeed, we are, at least in part. The difficulties scientists have had in testing the validity of need theories is as important as the disappointing results usually yielded in scientific tests. Meanwhile, human needs such as power, love, sex, achievement, and self-esteem continue to manifest themselves constantly in human affairs, especially in the workplace.

In part three we turn our attention toward theories of work motivation that are predicated on the root assumption that human beings are information processors, and that their work motivation and behavior can best be understood by reference to their beliefs, attitudes, intentions, and goals. These theories have been dominant for two decades among organizational behavior scholars. Their ascendancy can be explained in part, but not completely, by the problems featured in need-based models. Early forms of many of the cognitive theories to be discussed in part three were developed in the 1950s and 1960s, when need-based theories were dominant in the field as well as in practice among managers.

C H A P T E R

Beliefs, Attitudes, and Intentions

He that complies against his will
Is of his own opinion still
—SAMUEL BUTLER

The purpose of this chapter is to examine in general terms the meaning and importance of beliefs and attitudes and how they are related to human behavior, setting the stage for a discussion in subsequent chapters of many particular beliefs and attitudes that are of special interest in the context of work and work motivation (such as job satisfaction, organizational commitment, job involvement, equity, and fairness). Given that the body of research and theory on human attitudes is as voluminous as it is, however (see Pratkanis and Greenwald, 1989), we must restrict our focus somewhat. We refer the reader who wants a comprehensive treatment of the psychology of attitudes to scholarly reviews such as those of Eagly and Chaiken (1993) and J. M. Olson and Zanna (1993). Here, we focus on the work of Ajzen (1991), Ajzen and Fishbein (1977), and Fishbein and Ajzen (1975), along with a little help here and there from other sources and scholars as needed. The work of these scholars has proven the most useful to date in understanding work attitudes and behavior.

The current chapter also serves as a sort of transition point in the book as a whole: It will turn our attention away from models of human functioning that are primarily need-based and toward a set of theories that assume human beings to be information-processing creatures. As is the case when we adopt a need-based model of behavior, there is plenty of controversy about the relevance and usefulness of relying on hypothetical constructs such as attitudes, beliefs, and the like. Nowhere has the debate on this matter been more heated than in the organizational sciences, and it has been under way for years (see, e.g., Karmel, 1980). There are some camps in the discipline that, following schools of behaviorism in psychology, do not deny that people hold attitudes toward objects and phenomena, but they do dismiss as unnecessary the invocation of concepts such as attitudes for explaining or predicting work behavior. What are attitudes?

THE NATURE OF HUMAN ATTITUDES

People have attitudes. People hold attitudes toward many or most of the other people in their life spaces. They also tend to form attitudes in relation to tangible as well as intangible objects, causes, concepts, acts, and other phenomena with which they are familiar. The holding of attitudes is clearly one of the characteristics of human beings. Much of a person's identity is definable and understandable in terms of the attitudes s/he holds, how firmly the attitudes are held, and how easily changed his or her attitudes are. This is a book about work motivation and behavior. Of necessity, it is also about people's attitudes regarding their work, their careers, their occupations and professions, and toward the companies and other employers for whom they work. In other words, a comprehensive treatment of work motivation and behavior requires a thorough understanding of human attitudes because attitudes play a central role in much of the most important current thought about why and how people work.

THE NATURE OF ATTITUDES IN GENERAL

In a recent review of the literature on attitudes, J. M. Olson and Zanna (1993) claimed that there are a variety of definitions of attitudes and no single commonly accepted definition. (This is a familiar theme throughout this book: a failure of social scientists in general and motivation theorists in particular to agree on definitions of common terms.) Nevertheless, there appear to be three common themes or elements that run through the most common definitions, according to J. M. Olson and Zanna (1993):[1]

The first element is that attitudes generally involve an evaluative component. An attitude doesn't normally form until a person has made some evaluation of an attitude object (such as toward her car, her boss, or her job). A second common component of definitions of attitudes is that they are "represented in memory" (J. M. Olson and Zanna, 1993). That is, attitudes are often conceived of as links between belief structures and knowledge structures, such that the invocation of one attitude often triggers other mental events. When topics are somehow interrelated for a person (such as long working hours and the comparative willingness of supervisors to grant days off for sick leave), thinking about one of these matters can quickly lead to thoughts of the other.

The third common element of definitions and conceptualizations of attitudes is that they entail cognitive, affective, and behavior components and "correlates." As we detail below, the cognitive component might be a piece of information, a simple fact about some subject ("That house is painted blue"). Current thinking has it that not only can cognition of this sort be part of an attitude, but such a fact can trigger attitudes (J. M. Olson and Zanna, 1993, p. 120). Thus, the very blueness of a newly constructed house may cause a person to form an attitude about blue houses for the first time ("I've never considered whether I like blue houses until now. I sort of like them, I guess"). Similarly, all attitudes have long been seen as having an affective component, usually some degree of emotional reaction based on a person's values ("I hate the

---

[1]The "tripartite" definition of attitudes is popular and has dominated thinking in the literature on attitudes for centuries, but it is not the only view. A review of radical criticisms of the tripartite view is provided by Tesser and Shaffer (1990).

color blue"). Current thinking now has it that such an affective reaction may trigger an attitude, similar to the way the cognitive fact about the blue house may cause a newly formed attitude. Finally, attitudes have generally been seen as including a behavioral intention ("I plan to paint my house blue next summer"). Again, it is believed currently that being exposed to such a behavioral intention may initiate an attitude that wasn't there previously. ("If McPhillips is going to paint his house blue, maybe that's a good color for a house; in fact, I think I actually like blue houses.")

In short, current thinking about attitudes by social psychologists is that the traditional components of attitudes—the cognitive, the affective, and the intention—not only continue to comprise the three key elements of an attitude but can also be antecedents of attitudes, although "these domains will not necessarily all apply to a given attitude" (J. M. Olson and Zanna, 1993). For the sake of convergence, we offer a straightforward definition of *attitude* that is consistent with the thoughts of Olson and Zanna. This one comes from Eagly and Chaiken (1993): "Attitude is a psychological tendency that is expressed by evaluating a particular entity with some degree of favor or disfavor. . . . [P]sychological tendency refers to a state that is internal to the person, and evaluating refers to all classes of evaluative responding, whether overt or covert, cognitive, affective, or behavioral" (p. 1).

Functions of Attitudes

Attitudes serve many functions for human beings, one of which may be judged as positive, others as not so positive. Pratkanis and Greenwald (1989) have identified the following list of uses of attitude as a heuristic in conceptual processing:

1. Attitudes can help us interpret and explain social events.
2. Through their formation of halo effects, attitudes can bias the expectations and inferences we make about people simply on the basis of our knowledge that they belong to certain groups or categories.
3. Attitudes toward the conclusions of syllogisms can have an influence on whether we accept the conclusions as valid or not valid.
4. Whether a person's attitude toward a person or object is positive or negative can influence whether the person offers counterarguments against attempts by other people to persuade them into believing things about the object in question.
5. When people encounter others with attitudes similar to their own, there is a positive influence on the interpersonal attraction between them.
6. When people hold a certain attitude toward another person, they tend to believe that person holds attitudes similar to their own.
7. People sometimes believe that the attitudes they hold are more popular and more widely held than is actually the case.
8. Holding an attitude can lead to the selective reconstruction and recollection of past events.
9. A person's recollection of her past attitudes and behavior can be revised to be consistent with her current attitudes toward the same attitude objects.
10. Through a mechanism referred to as an information error technique, people will be biased in selecting among bits of false information to choose those that are most consistent with their own current attitudes.

11. Holding an attitude can influence the predictions we make about future events. Wanting something to occur because we have a positive attitude toward it causes us unduly to expect it to occur.

To summarize, one way we can think of attitudes is to examine them from a functionalist perspective, asking: What services (or disservices) do attitudes perform for us? What are the functions of attitudes? Pratkanis and Greenwald's (1989) compilation of the scientific evidence suggests that there are many answers to these questions: Attitudes serve a variety of functions in the way people perceive and behave toward the social world. Interestingly, many of these functions are driven by the human tendency toward consistency: To varying degrees, people prefer their attitudes, beliefs, and behaviors to be in concert (Cialdini, 1993). It will be important to keep both this list of functions of attitudes and the principle of attitudinal consistency in mind in subsequent chapters when we examine people's beliefs and attitudes about such things as their employers, their co-workers, and the treatment they receive at work.

THE THEORY OF REASONED ACTION

For the purposes of this book, in which the focus is on work motivation and employee attitudes, we rely most heavily on the theory of attitudes that is still the most commonly used when the issue is the connection between attitudes and behavior (J. M. Olson and Zanna, 1993), called the theory of reasoned action (Fishbein and Ajzen, 1975). If this book were devoted purely to social psychology, a variety of formulations would have to be presented. Because we are interested here primarily in employee attitudes and the relationships between employee attitudes and behaviors (e.g., performance, absenteeism, and prosocial acts), the theory of reasoned action, although 20 years old, is the most useful tool for our purposes (J. M. Olson and Zanna, 1993; Tesser and Shaffer, 1990).

The *theory of reasoned action* "is based on the assumption that human beings are usually quite rational and make systematic use of the information available to them. We do not subscribe to the view that human social behavior is controlled by unconscious motives or overpowering desires, nor do we believe that it can be characterized as capricious or thoughtless. Rather, we argue that people consider the implications of their actions before they decide to engage or not engage in a given behavior" (Ajzen and Fishbein, 1980, p. 5). Figure 9-1 is a schematic representing the theory of reasoned action. It is offered as a visual guide to our explanation of how beliefs and attitudes may or may not result in employee behavior.

The reader will note that this is an entirely different perspective on the origins of human behavior than we featured throughout the earlier chapters. No reference is made to forces such as needs or environmental pressures, although this theory makes use of hypothetical constructs of its own, such as beliefs, values, and expectancies. We adopt here the definition of attitude that Fishbein and Ajzen offered in 1975. An *attitude* is defined as the degree of positive or negative feeling (or affect) a person has toward a particular attitude object, such as a place, thing, or other person (Fishbein and Ajzen, 1975). Thus, when we speak of positive job attitudes, we mean that the people involved tend to have pleasant internal feelings when they think about their jobs, although different aspects of one's job are bound to cause different sorts of feelings. On one level, this concept of attitude makes intuitive sense and fits with our everyday un-

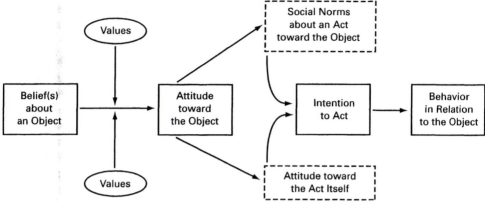

Source: Adapted from I. Ajzen and M. Fishbein, *Understanding attitudes and predicting social behavior* (Upper Saddle River, NJ: Prentice Hall, 1980).

FIGURE 9-1 Representation of the Theory of Reasoned Action

derstanding of the meaning of the concept. On the other hand, we must still address the question of the origins and causes of these affective reactions. In other words, what causes us to feel particularly good or bad about specific things or people?

The Nature of Beliefs

Part of the answer to the question regarding the origin of affective reaction lies in the beliefs we hold about the objects, persons, or things in question. A *belief* is a person's "subjective probability judgement concerning a relation between the object of the belief and some other object, value, concept, or attribute" (Fishbein and Ajzen, 1975, p. 131). It is a mental linkage tying an entity to a property in a probabilistic manner. For example, we might hold the belief that a certain occupation is challenging. The attitude object here is the occupation. The attribute is the property of being challenging. The strength of a person's belief about an attitude object consists of the magnitude of the probability in her mind that the object is associated with the attribute (Fishbein and Ajzen, 1975, p. 134).

How are beliefs formed? According to Fishbein and Ajzen (1975), we can think of three different types of beliefs, each formed by a different means. These are called descriptive beliefs, inferential beliefs, and beliefs formed on the basis of information from outside sources. Let's take a brief look at these. *Descriptive beliefs* are formed on the basis of a person's own observations. For example, an employee may notice that his supervisor keeps his office neat and form the belief that his supervisor is generally a tidy person. *Inferential beliefs* result from logical connections that people make in their minds between certain thoughts. For example, consider a person who holds antiunion attitudes and also believes that promotions should be based on merit rather than seniority. Assume further that this person has never considered the possible link between these two concepts (unions and the various bases for promotion). When asked to indicate whether he believes that unions normally favor seniority or merit as the primary basis for promotion, it is likely that the person would reply that unions probably favor seniority. The person would reach such a conclusion for either of two reasons. First, because it is inconsistent for a person to hold conflicting or unbalanced perceptions and beliefs about objects and issues (Heider, 1958), it is unlikely that he would associate something he positively evaluates (promotion on the basis of merit) with something else that he evaluates negatively (unions). Therefore, out of a desire to be internally consistent, he would probably conclude that unions favor promotions on the basis of seniority rather than merit. A second reason for his probable conclusion has to do with probabilistic reasoning on his part, such as the following: (1) antimanagement groups naturally tend not to favor promotions on the basis of merit; (2) unions are generally antimanagement; therefore, (3) unions probably favor promotions on the basis of seniority rather than merit. In short, inferential beliefs result from either the desire to be internally consistent and/or any of a number of logical processes.

A third source of beliefs consists of other people or outside information sources, such as newspapers. Once they are accepted, beliefs originating from external sources are similar in nature to beliefs formed through personal observation (Fishbein and Ajzen, 1975).

Several important points follow from Fishbein and Ajzen's concept of belief. Notice that beliefs may or may not be valid, depending on the accuracy of the information on which they are based. Descriptive beliefs are less prone to the influences of a person's prior beliefs and attitudes than are inferential beliefs (Fishbein and Ajzen, 1975). In other words, people are much less likely to formulate false beliefs based on their personal observation of events than they are when their beliefs are based on any of the types of inferential processes described above.

Second, notice that because of the potential role of personal bias in the formation of inferential beliefs, it is quite possible for any two people to hold differing beliefs about the same attitude object, even when they share common experiences. For example, two students may both spend a summer working as interns in the same accounting office. One of them may conclude that accounting is a dull occupation, but the other may have the opposite belief. Even descriptive beliefs vary between people when they pay attention to different aspects of their experiences with attitude objects.

A third point worth emphasizing has to do with the important influence that outside sources can have in the structuring of beliefs (see Salancik and Pfeffer, 1978). This phenomenon is particularly powerful for newcomers to work settings, who must learn new jobs, become acquainted with new colleagues, and assimilate a myriad of other details about aspects of that work setting (see Graen, 1976; Van Maanen, 1977; Wanous, 1980).

A fourth point concerns the number of beliefs that people hold about attitude objects. Because of the natural limits to human cognition, it is likely that most attitudes are formed on the basis of no more than five to nine beliefs concerning an attitude object. Of course, many people seem to desire fewer than five pieces of information about another person or object. Beliefs differ in the salience as well as in the importance they hold for people, such that individuals formulate their attitudes about objects because of those characteristics that stand out for them or seem most crucial. For example, an employee who is acutely aware of his low rate of pay is likely to mention it early in any conversation he has about his job.

A final important feature of beliefs is that they tend to be internally consistent with one another. For example, there is evidence that people tend to link personal attributes of other people in predictable clusters, such that a belief that a person is poised will lead to the assumption that the same person is also calm, composed, and nonhypochondriacal (Fishbein and Ajzen, 1975). Clusters about attitude objects other than people also tend to go hand in hand, largely because human beings tend to prefer consistency among their beliefs, actions, and attitudes (Festinger, 1957; Heider, 1958).

Beliefs and Attitudes

As suggested earlier: "An attitude represents a person's general feeling of favorableness or unfavorableness toward some stimulus object. . . . [A]s a person forms beliefs about an object, he automatically and simultaneously acquires an attitude toward that object. Each belief links the object to some attribute; the person's attitude toward the object is a function of his evaluations of these attributes" (Fishbein and Ajzen, 1975, p. 216). To return to our previous example, one summer intern may have a positive attitude about accountancy because he believes that it is interesting and because he evaluates positively the property of being interesting. Similarly, an employee may dislike his job because he believes that he is underpaid for the work he does, and he evaluates negatively the condition of underpayment he perceives. In this view attitudes are the affective (emotional) reactions people hold about attitude objects based on the way they evaluate the attributes they associate with those objects.[2]

The general attitude a person has toward an object is seen as an aggregation of all the beliefs that she holds about it, each weighted by the positive or negative evaluations she places on the various beliefs. Therefore, two employees may have the same set of beliefs about a job ("It's repetitive") but hold different attitudes toward it because one of them prefers routine work whereas the other desires more uncertainty. Alternatively, the same two employees may have differing beliefs about an object or person (such as their common supervisor) but have similar attitudes toward him. For example, one employee may be aware of the supervisor's prowess at the pub after work and admire him for it, whereas the second employee may positively evaluate the supervisor for what he believes to be his characteristic fairness.

To summarize, we can say that the connection between beliefs and attitudes is the following: If a person approves of or positively evaluates the attributes that he associates in his belief structure with an object, he will tend to hold a positive general attitude toward that object. On the other hand, if the attributes he connects in his beliefs with an object are characteristics he evaluates negatively, he will hold a negative overall attitude toward the object. So to influence a person's attitudes about an object (say a job), we might introduce new information about that job information that links the job with attributes that the employee evaluates positively (such as its variety and status). Alternatively, we might attempt to change the employee's assessment of the desirability or undesirability of the attributes the employee now associates with a job.[3]

---

[2]The reader is reminded, however, that people differ in the degree of incongruity and inconsistency they tolerate in their minds (recall chapter 7, where we discussed intrinsic motivation).

[3]Notice again the potential role of inaccurate beliefs for the formation of attitudes. Propaganda programs designed to change people's attitudes toward enemy groups focus heavily on introducing belief-structuring information to the populace about the enemy more than upon trying to make the populace evaluate differently the information they hold.

Stability and Change of Beliefs and Attitudes

How stable or susceptible to change are human beliefs about attitude objects? Traditional thought on this matter has held that attitudes (and the beliefs on which they rest) are relatively permanent predispositions of people toward attitude objects (other people, jobs, organizations, or whatever). More recent thinking (e.g., S. T. Fiske, 1993; S. T. Fiske and Taylor, 1991; Levine, Resnick, and Higgins, 1993) recognizes that attitudes—particularly attitudes that people form and hold about one another—are heavily influenced by the social contexts in which people exist; that is, how people feel about attitude objects is heavily influenced by the descriptive and evaluative information they acquire through their social interactions with other people. This alternative view, however, fails to recognize that there is some consistency and stability to attitudes over time—they do not swing wildly from one social setting to another. Therefore, a third view has been advanced that balances both the "attitudes as fixed dispositions" position and the "attitudes as socially constructed beliefs" position. For the sake of discussion, we refer to this third position as the information-processing approach (Calder and Schurr, 1981).

For Calder and Schurr (1981), an attitude is an integration of the evaluative meaning of sets of thoughts that a person holds in memory (p. 287; see also J. M. Olson and Zanna, 1993). Thoughts are similar to beliefs, as we discussed them above. Thus an attitude might be reflected in statements such as the following: "I think the company's transfer policy is quite liberal" or "I think the people I work with are dull and uninteresting." These thoughts need not be uttered in any way; they can be held privately by a person. (Notice the role of evaluation in this conception of attitudes. It corresponds with the evaluative nature of attitudes in the Fishbein and Ajzen model presented earlier.)

The concept of storage in memory is important (J. M. Olson and Zanna, 1993). This view considers both long- and short-term memory. The former serves two functions: the ongoing storage of information pertaining to an attitude object, and the interpretation of new information that is being processed in a particular setting by the person's short-term memory. As a person interacts with his surroundings, information is gathered about attitude objects. This information is processed with the assistance of information stored by the person in long-term memory, the contents of which help the person make sense out of new information, as it were. For example, if an employee hears a manager promise to redistribute workloads to make it possible for her staff to get away early on a long weekend, she will process this promise while remembering other promises made by the supervisor on past occasions. As new information is interpreted through the perceptual apparatus provided by memory, it, in turn, enters long-term memory and modifies or updates the contents of the memory bank. Thus, attitudes are influenced by the characteristics and nuances of the settings in which attitude objects are considered, but they are also heavily subject to the interpretive assistance provided by past experiences, thereby featuring some degree of stability over time. We might say that the information-processing approach sees attitudes as structured and developed according to a type of dynamic equilibrium process.

A study by Griffin (1982a) illustrated that one type of belief that is of particular interest to this book is in fact relatively slow changing—the nature of the perceptions people have about the capacity of their jobs to bring about intrinsic motivation and satisfaction. In chapter 7 we examine job redesign, the most popular of which relies heavily on employee beliefs that their jobs possess motivating qualities. Griffin's research suggests that these beliefs are relatively stable over time, although people's affective reactions to these beliefs (their attitudes) may be less stable.

Attitudes, Intentions, and Behavior

There has been considerable debate over the years concerning the nature of the relationship between attitudes and behavior. As mentioned earlier, it seems to make intuitive sense to many people that attitudes are major causes of our behavior: We behave in certain ways toward various people and objects because of the way we feel about them. An alternative view has it the other way around: that people's behavior toward objects and other people may help shape their attitudes toward them (Bem, 1967, 1972a). A few explanations are available for this possibility (J. M. Olson and Zanna, 1993; Tesser and Shaffer, 1990). The first is that sometimes an individual's internal states such as emotions and attitudes are weak and ambiguous, so they must infer these states by referring to knowledge about their overt behavior and the contexts in which the behavior occurred. Cialdini (1993, especially chap. 3) provides several powerful examples of how even the smallest of acts committed by people can lead to major shifts in espoused attitudes.

A second explanation is based on dissonance theory (Festinger, 1957), which claims that people experience an aversive psychological force when they say and do things that are logically inconsistent with one another, or when they find that their various beliefs, attitudes, and values are logically out of sync. The management of cognitive dissonance has been discounted somewhat as an explanation of attitude change toward consistency (Tesser and Shaffer, 1990). Therefore, a third explanation is possible: that people are concerned about the impressions they make on others, especially when they are accountable for their views. When a person is not expecting to be accountable to others but only to himself, he may readily change his attitudes to be consistent with his behaviors. If he expects to be accountable, however, he may be less quick to change his attitudes; rather, he may formulate "publicly defensible" opinions after carefully considering the issue at hand (Tesser and Shaffer, 1990).

On balance, and theoretical explanations aside, it seems that both causal arguments are valid: Attitudes can be both the antecedents and the consequences of behavior. According to the theory of reasoned action (see Ajzen and Fishbein, 1980), how do attitudes influence behavior? *Attitudes affect behavior only to the extent that they influence a person's intentions to act.* (Recall the earlier example: "Plan to paint my house blue next summer.") That is, attitudes can create a set of possible intentions to behave in certain ways toward the object in question, although a particular attitude usually does not relate to any single intention on a one-to-one basis. For example, an employee may have a generally positive attitude toward her new supervisor following a transfer. That generally positive attitude may predispose her to act in a variety of positive ways toward the supervisor, although it will not be useful as a predictor of any specific behavior (such as volunteering to help the supervisor on a special project without pay during off-hours). Nevertheless, it is possible that the generally favorable attitude will create an intention to do such free overtime work should the occasion arise. The point is that attitudes foster sets of intentions that are consistent with one another as well as consistent with the tone of the attitude itself. But single attitude–intention connections can seldom be predicted in advance.

On the other hand, every intention, once formed, is associated with specific behaviors. To the extent that behavior is volitional (as opposed to being strictly reflexive or coerced by the environment), people will attempt to do those things they intend to do (Ryan, 1970). Therefore, although the employee likes his new supervisor (because he positively evaluates the beliefs he holds about her), that general attitude may foster several positive intentions. When a specific behavioral opportunity presents itself, the positive attitude may (or may not) translate into an intention to act in a positive or helpful way toward the supervisor. The key is whether the person develops a positive or negative attitude toward the act in question (as we discuss shortly). Nevertheless, once an intention is formed to act in a way that is in keeping with the positive attitude, the employee will strive to behave in the way intended. To summarize: "[A]ttitude is viewed as a general predisposition that does not predispose the person to perform any specific behavior. Rather, it leads to a set of intentions that indicate a certain amount of affect toward the object in question. Each of these intentions is related to a specific behavior, and thus the overall affect expressed by the pattern of a person's action with respect to the object also corresponds to his attitude toward the object" (Fishbein and Ajzen, 1975, p. 15).

The Specificity of Intentions

To fully understand the connection between attitudes and intentions, it is necessary to understand more about intentions themselves, particularly about the importance of the specificity of the intentions involved. According to Fishbein and Ajzen (1975), intentions consist of four elements: the particular behavior being considered; the target object toward which the behavior might be directed; the situational context in which the behavior may be performed; and finally, the time at which the behavior is to occur. Each of these elements can vary in terms of how specifically it is considered. The most specific situation involves an intention to perform a clearly defined act toward a specific target in a highly specified place and time. For example, "I intend to walk off the job tomorrow morning after nine o'clock, as soon as I have convinced the rest of the gang to join me!"

Intentions are more closely connected to behavior when they are specific (Ajzen and Fishbein, 1977; Jaccard, King, and Pomazal, 1977). In other words, the more any of the four elements of an intention is left general (as opposed to specific), the weaker the connection is between the intention and subsequent behavior (Ajzen and Fishbein, 1977). For example, an employee might indicate that she intends to be more punctual in reporting to work. Left at this low level of specificity, we might expect this intention not to result in real punctuality as much as an intention of the form "I intend never to come to work later than nine o'clock again this year." In the second case, the particular behavior was more specifically articulated than it was in the first case (as was the time involved). Similarly, if the target object of an intention is left general rather than specific, behavior is less probable. Statements such as "I would never vote for a union" may prove to be poorer predictors of actual behavior than statements such as "I will never vote for the Sheepherders' Union, Local 123." The more specific the target of the intention, the more likely it will be associated with behavior that is consistent with the intention.

What about the specificity of the time element? Ajzen and Fishbein (1977) would suggest that statements such as "I plan to go on a diet" will not be as likely to lead to a loss of weight as a statement such as "I'll plan to start a diet in the New Year" (although we are all familiar with the fate of most New Year's resolutions). Finally, we can consider the specificity of the situation. If an employee says he intends to stop smoking on the job, we can expect to see less smoking on his part than if he were simply to say "I will stop smoking." The point is that increases in specificity with regard to the behavior, the target, the time, or the situation involved, will be associated with a higher likelihood that an intention will result in actual behavior that is consistent with it (Ajzen and Fishbein, 1977).

Intentions and Behavior

The final step in understanding why and how attitudes result in behavior requires that we examine how intentions, once formed (at whatever level of specificity), lead to behavior. According to Fishbein (1967), there are two important factors that determine intentions once attitudes have been formed toward objects. The first of these is itself an *attitudinal factor,* and the second is a *normative factor.* The attitudinal factor has to do with the person's feelings concerning the act being considered. In other words, it consists of the person's attitude toward performing the behavior in question under a particular set of circumstances. Moreover, this attitude (toward the behavior) is determined by the person's perceived consequences of the behavior and his evaluations of those consequences.

Caution! It is important not to confuse the attitude a person has toward an object (such as one's company) with the attitude he holds toward behaving a certain way toward that object (such as leaking the company's trade secrets to a competitor). The first of these attitudes, as we have said, consists of the individual's evaluations of the beliefs he holds about the object itself. Whether he develops an intention to act in a way consistent with that attitude depends on his attitude toward the action implied by the intention. This second attitude, in turn, is determined by the person's beliefs about the probable consequences of his action and his evaluation of those consequences.

To return to our earlier example, the new employee may hold a positive general attitude toward his supervisor and may therefore be generally predisposed to act positively toward her. Suppose the employee learns that the boss requires help at the office after hours on a particular night but that he would have to work without pay and therefore be violating the union contract if he were to volunteer. Will the employee's positive attitude translate into the specific act of offering assistance? Fishbein (1967) would suggest that the employee will form an attitude about the act of volunteering to help. That attitude will be determined by the consequences the person expects will follow from working after hours as well as from the person's evaluation of those consequences. On balance, whether our friend decides to volunteer for the job will depend, in this view, on whatever consequences he expects might result from volunteering and how favorably or unfavorably he evaluates these consequences. Again, we have an evaluation of a set of beliefs, although, to repeat, these beliefs pertain to the likely consequences of behavior, not to the supervisor per se. The theory predicts that if the employee believes that consequences he evaluates positively will outweigh consequences that he evaluates negatively, he will volunteer. If the employee believes that most of the consequences of volunteering will be negative (such as being reprimanded by the shop steward), he will not intend to volunteer and, accordingly, will not do so.

The second determinant of whether an attitude results in an intention, the normative component, concerns the influence of the social environment. That is, it has to do with the person's beliefs about what significant others around him expect him to do. Different people will be sensitive to the expectations placed on them by various people, such as one's spouse, one's co-workers, and so on. A person in a particular situation may consider the expectations of a variety of reference groups in the context of considering a particular behavior. So it may be that helping the supervisor at night without pay is something members of the work group expect of their youngest member, regardless of who it is and the fact that such work violates the union agreement. On the other hand, the employee's new spouse may have a different view of the situation, leaving the employee with some ambivalence and causing the generally positive attitude toward the boss not to result in an offer to work at night.

To summarize, whether an attitude toward an object results in a specific intention to behave in a certain way toward the object depends on the person's attitude about the behavior itself and on his beliefs about the expectations of relevant others regarding the behavior (see Figure 9-1). Notice two or three things about this theory. First, consider the important role played by the person's beliefs both about the attitude object and about the probable consequences of specific acts toward that object. Clearly, beliefs are not always accurate or valid, and they are certainly subject to change. Moreover, beliefs about either an attitude object or about the consequences of certain acts toward it can be heavily influenced by other people as well as by one's personal experiences. Notice too that a generally positive (or negative) attitude toward an object may not result in certain behaviors related to that object (such as helping one's supervisor at night) but may result in other behaviors that seem to outsiders to be quite similar (such as volunteering to help the supervisor with a special project during regular working hours).

Perhaps the most important thing to remember about using the theory of reasoned action is that it is highly unlikely that we will be able to predict a person's actions on the basis of our knowledge only of her attitudes toward an attitude object (Ajzen and Fishbein, 1980). Therefore, if we know that a small store owner does not generally like members of a particular ethnic group, it would be very risky to predict whether she would or would not hire a member of that group to work for her on the basis of that fact alone about the woman. There may be many reasons in her mind for hiring such a person: It is her attitude toward the act of hiring such a person, combined with the power of the subjective social norms that she perceives about hiring them, that will determine her intention, one way or another. As we have said, the more specific the intention in her mind, once it is formed, the more likely it is that she will (or will not) hire someone from the ethnic group.

Criticisms of the Theory

One of the main limitations of the theory of reasoned action is that it restricts itself to volitional or voluntary behavior, behavior(s) that people perform because they decide to perform them (Eagly and Chaiken, 1993). Therefore, the theory is limited in its capacity to predict behaviors that require skills, resources, or opportunities and conditions that are not available to people. Further, introducing intentions into the model between attitudes and behaviors, strictly speaking, precludes the possibility of understanding categories of behaviors that require little or no thought. Eagly and Chaiken (1993) cite examples such as spontaneous impulses that lead to violence against a hated minority group, behavior that results from a strong craving for a drug, and impulse buying that is driven by brand loyalty and plenty of practice. Similarly, some habitual behavior, such as smoking or fastening one's seat belt upon getting into a car, frequently requires no conscious thought. Merely possessing a well-ingrained attitude may be sufficient to provide a basis for predicting behavior (Eagly and Chaiken, 1993).

A recent study illustrates this. Bagozzi and Yi (1989) have shown that intentions may sometimes not need to play a role in connecting attitudes and behavior. They conducted an experiment with a sample of marketing students. The task they used was of a voluntary nature, to review and report on a marketing case. Half the students were given a warm-up exercise that was very similar to the case analysis they were asked to perform. The other half of the group was given a bogus exercise that had nothing to do with the marketing case. The researchers used these initial exercises to manipulate the strength of the intentions of the students vis-à-vis performing the voluntary case analysis. As they had hoped, the "relevant" preexercise caused the students' intentions to be much stronger than did the bogus preexercise. The researchers then observed the strength of the connections in the two groups between their attitudes about the case and their actual behavior. The results were interesting. The data from the students whose intentions had been manipulated to be the stronger of the two sets revealed that their intentions did come into play in explaining their actual behavior on the case. Among the students whose intentions had been weaker, however, the connection between their attitudes and actual behavior was not affected by those intentions by nearly the same degree. In short, the researchers concluded that when intentions are weak and the task is not something that takes much thought, attitudes and behaviors may be quite closely linked without a role being played by intentions. If results of this sort are replicated, we could see an interesting modification to the theory of reasoned action.

The formal theory deliberately restricts itself to reasoned actions. This restriction seems to be both a basis for the success of theory in predicting many behaviors (very well, as we shall see shortly) as well as its primary drawback. It cannot be used as a general theory of attitudes for the prediction of all human behavior (Eagly and Chaiken, 1993). Another criticism of the theory is based on the belief that there are many more determinants of people's intentions than one's attitude toward the behavior and subjective norms. For example, S. H. Schwartz and Tessler (1972) have suggested that people's personal beliefs about right and wrong, their sense of moral obligation, may also influence a person's intention to act in a certain way. This set of factors is internalized in a person's value system, independent, conceptually at least, from the subjective norm factor that Ajzen and Fishbein (1980) discuss. Similarly, some people will act in certain ways that are consistent with their self-identities. For example, if a person views herself as helpful by nature, she is more likely to form intentions to act in prosocial, helpful ways at work than if her self-identity did not include such a feature.

The upshot of these criticisms is not that they deny the critical, final role of intentions in inducing and directing behavior. Rather, they share the argument that the theory of reasoned action oversimplifies the matter of how intentions are formed in the first place. They claim that the theory overlooks many factors and forces by restricting the focus to attitude toward the act and the perception of social norms. Eagly and

Chaiken (1993, chap. 4) review these and other criticisms of the theory found in the literature.

Finally, some students and managers who wish to understand human behavior or work behavior and attitudes simply find the long, rocky road from beliefs, through attitudes, to intentions via attitudes toward behaviors (and social norms) counterintuitive and difficult to comprehend at first. Nevertheless, when we stand back and think carefully about life experiences in which we have seen people behave in ways that seem contrary to their attitudes toward other people or things (attitude objects), the theory of reasoned action takes on more credibility. This leads us to the question of the predictive validity of the theory.

Validity of the Theory of Reasoned Action

Notwithstanding the criticisms and shortcomings of the theory, how valid is it? Two different reviews of the scientific tests of the theory both conclude that the theory is very valid as a predictor of people's actions and, in addition, of the outcomes of people's actions (Eagly and Chaiken, 1993; Sheppard, Hartwick, and Warshaw, 1988). Sheppard et al. (1988) conducted a massive summary of the evidence related to the validity of the theory, beginning with this statement to remind us of what the formal theory does and does not purport to do for us: "[A] behavioral intention measure will predict the performance of any voluntary act, unless intent changes prior to performance or unless the intention measure does not correspond to the behavioral criterion in terms of action, target, context, time-frame and/or specificity" (p. 325). They then observe that the theory has frequently been applied to situations in which any or all of three conditions that violate the theory's assumptions are in place. One is that the target behavior is not completely under the person's control (see the discussion of the theory of planned behavior later in the chapter).

A second condition that is inappropriate to the formal assumptions of the theory has been where "the situation involves a choice problem not explicitly addressed by the theory itself." Finally, there have been cases where the theory has been used to predict people's acts in situations where they did or could not have sufficient information to make a completely confident intention. In short, there have been many studies that have attempted to test the theory "unfairly."[4]

Using the technique of meta-analysis (which has been used in many other studies reported in this book; see Hunter, Schmidt, and Jackson, 1982), Sheppard et al. (1988) surveyed 87 previous empirical studies and came up with an average correlation of 0.53 for the connection between intentions and behaviors. The corresponding correlation between attitudes and subjective norms, and intentions, was 0.66. Each of these results was based on work that included many thousands of participants in a variety of settings and in relation to a wide variety of intentions and behaviors. By any standard, these results are spectacular. Even more impressive is how the results remained strong when Sheppard et al. (1988) included in the analyses studies conducted more or less inappropriately, or unfairly, given the formal terms and conditions spelled out in the theory. The specific details of how they did this are too complex to be detailed here. The inter-

---

[4]Recall our discussion in chapter 3 of how Maslow's theory of needs has similarly been treated unfairly. We will run into this problem again and again.

ested reader is referred to the article by Sheppard and his colleagues (1988). The point is that the theory of reasoned action appears to be one of the best predictors of human behavior available in the social sciences. It is applicable to many behaviors and contexts and is remarkably robust to violations of some of the major tenets specified by the theory itself.

Recapitulation

Let's stop for a minute and review where we have been. So far we have seen that beliefs are the core of attitudes. They consist of perceived linkages between attitude objects and attributes. Strong beliefs consist of high subjective probabilities that particular objects are characterized by particular attributes. People tend to emphasize the most salient and most important beliefs they hold about objects as they form attitudes toward them. Attitudes are evaluative reactions that people have concerning the beliefs they hold about objects. The connection between attitudes and behavior, however, is unpredictable, for many reasons. For an attitude to result in behavior that is consistent with it, the attitude must result in an intention to act. For an intention to be developed, the person must hold a positive attitude toward the act itself and must believe that significant others would see the act as appropriate. Even then, the holding of a particular intention will result in a specific behavior only if the intention is somewhat specific regarding a variety of factors, including the exact nature of the behavior itself, the precise target toward which the behavior will be directed, the circumstances within which the act is contemplated, and finally, the time at which the act is to take place.

There is virtually never a simple connection between the holding of a particular attitude toward a person, a job, or some object, and specific behaviors toward that person, job, or object. Using attitudes to predict specific behaviors is a risky business. For example, an employee may like his job because he positively evaluates those things he believes about it (that it pays better than comparable jobs, that he can trust his co-workers, and that it may provide him with long-term security). On the basis of this attitude alone, we cannot predict whether he will work hard, seek promotions, take training courses, or help to organize a union. To make such behavioral predictions we would need a great deal more information about the employee's beliefs about the consequences of these particular acts as well as about his evaluative attitudes toward those beliefs and his understanding of what is expected of him by significant others. On the other hand, we can make predictions, in advance, that because an employee holds a generally positive attitude toward his job, positive job behaviors are more likely to result from him than are negative job behaviors, although the specific acts cannot be foreseen.

THE THEORY OF PLANNED ACTION

Before leaving our discussion of the theory of reasoned action, we note briefly that Ajzen (1991; Ajzen and Madden, 1986) has modified the theory slightly to take into account the possibility that although a person may be (1) positively disposed to perform an act, and (2) believe that the act is socially desired or expected, s/he may also have doubts about the feasibility of performing the act in question. (We alluded to this possibility earlier.) For example, a person may wish to drive to the store to buy groceries but find that his car doesn't work or be uncertain about whether the store will be open for business by the time he gets there. There may be forces beyond his control that limit the possibility of the act. Sometimes, according to the theory of planned behavior, a person may lack behavioral control. Ajzen refers to the additional construct "perceived behavioral control." The mitigating factors that cause perceptions of low behavioral control might be internal to the person, such as perceptions of low self-efficacy, or in the context in which the act would otherwise occur (e.g., a shortage of materials needed to make the task possible).

Ajzen and Fishbein (1980) have shown empirically how the addition of people's perceptions of behavioral control to the other two key factors in determining intentions—attitude toward the act and the social norms regarding the act—better explains the variability among people in the strength of their intentions to act. In other words, whereas the theory of reasoned action claims that two factors determine intentions, the theory of planned behavior claims that three variables determine intentions—it adds the person's perception of his or her control over the circumstances that will make an act possible. Research investigations of the predictive validity of the theory of planned behavior are summarized by Ajzen (1991) himself and by J. M. Olson and Zanna (1993), who observe that although the evidence is mixed, most comparative tests of the two theories conclude that the later, expanded theory enjoys more empirical support than the original theory, as impressive as that is (see above).

THEORY X AND THEORY Y REVISITED

Before leaving our discussion of the relationship between beliefs, attitudes, and behavior, it is worth recalling from chapter 3 two particular sets of beliefs commonly held by many managers concerning the nature of human beings. These beliefs, called Theory X and Theory Y, are seen as resulting in managerial behaviors that are consistent with either the view that people like to work, can be trusted with responsibility, and so on (Theory Y), or that they are lazy, dislike work, and cannot be trusted with responsibility (Theory X). According to McGregor (1960), Theory X beliefs are the cause as well as the result of apathetic and withdrawal behavior—a self-fulfilling prophecy. Although there is no claim that either Theory X or Theory Y beliefs are connected on a one-to-one basis with specific managerial behaviors, McGregor believed that these basic underlying beliefs are associated with managerial acts and policies that tend to be self-reinforcing. This association between a set of beliefs and a set of behaviors is entirely consistent with the model of beliefs, attitudes, and behaviors presented above (Ajzen and Fishbein, 1980; Fishbein and Ajzen, 1975).

Now that we have examined the general nature of human attitudes, at least from the perspective of one major and successful theory, we turn our attention to the more specific issue of people's beliefs, attitudes, and emotional reactions concerning their work, their jobs, and the organizations for which they work.

CHAPTER

Beliefs, Attitudes, and Emotions about Work

*If work was really good, the rich would have found a way
to keep it to themselves.*
—HAITIAN PROVERB

Anyone who has ever held a job can relate to the visceral and emotional underpinnings of this chapter; it is about people's beliefs, attitudes, and feelings toward their work. Positive attitudes about what we do for a living make a tremendous difference in the way we feel about life in general. To have a job that is annoying, frustrating, or full of fear and conflict can be a terrible experience. This chapter is about such job-related attitudes and emotions. Although the discussion is sometimes scientific and esoteric, the reader should keep in mind the human dimensions of the joy that comes from having a "good job" or "good career" and the worse, painful, private agonies that come from having to perform work that is dissatisfying, illegal, boring, or humiliating. This chapter, more than most others, appeals to the human, emotional side of work motivation. Job satisfaction, organizational commitment, and the identification that people have with their work are all at the very core of the issue of work motivation. It is here where the mind and the heart meet in this book more than in any other place: because work can be a major source of pleasure for people or the primary source of their own private hells.

A Precaution

A point of semantics is in order before we begin. Although much of the discussion in this chapter is about "job attitudes," it is important to recognize that, in fact, attitudes (as we have defined them in chapter 9) are only part of what this chapter is about. As we will find shortly, much of our experiencing of "job attitudes" in life and in common discourse deals, in fact, with job-related beliefs and emotions. So, as often happens in organizational science, terms from common parlance are often used to represent concepts that have different technical meaning in the discipline. We clarify the distinctions among job-related beliefs, attitudes, and emotions by the end of the chapter.

Why an Interest in Work Attitudes?

Since the early days of the organizational sciences, academics and other researchers have spent considerable time researching the nature, causes, and correlates of a variety of work-related attitudes, for a variety of reasons. Why is this so? P. C. Smith, Kendall, and Hulin (1969) provide four commonly accepted answers to the question. First, it has long been assumed by many managers, parents, teachers, and people in general that attitudes influence behavior. The importance of this assumption for our present purposes lies in the possibilities that it holds for managers and supervisors who wish to influence employee motivation and job performance. It has long been assumed that work-related attitudes must somehow be related to work behaviors (see Brayfield and Crockett, 1955; C. Fisher, 1980). Early forms of this belief held that higher levels of job satisfaction are associated with higher levels of job performance: "A more satisfied employee is a more productive employee." Although years of research have shown that the relationship is not so simple (Bassett, 1994), there is still some basis for believing that attitudes and behaviors can be related to one another in some circumstances (Ajzen and Fishbein, 1977; Cialdini, Petty, and Cacioppo, 1981). Accordingly, it remains important to develop a precise understanding of what attitudes are, the factors that influence them, and whatever connections they may have with behavior.

Second, P.C. Smith et al. (1969) point out that a great deal of management's activities with regard to personnel selection and placement, training, career counseling, and so on, are based in part on a concern for employee attitudes and, in turn, for employee behavior. Third, Smith and her colleagues note that improving employee job satisfaction is a desirable goal in its own right, for humanitarian reasons. In other words, one need not expect some form of managerial payoff to justify attempts to understand employee work attitudes. Finally, understanding the nature of job attitudes may be beneficial for the greater scientific concern of understanding attitudes in general: Work is only one arena in which human attitudes are formed and altered, albeit an important one. Social scientists are interested in the nature and change of attitudes for political reasons, for marketing research, and for a variety of other social purposes. Things that are learned about job attitudes contribute to this greater stock of knowledge about human attitudes in general.

In short, we are interested in the study of job attitudes because they are believed to be related to work behavior, because a great deal of managerial activity is concerned with positively influencing them, for humanitarian reasons, and for more general scientific reasons. The purpose of discussing them in this book is influenced by each of these reasons.

Job Attitudes of the Most Interest

Without doubt, the most commonly studied variety of job-related attitudes is job satisfaction, often defined as the degree to which a person's work is useful for satisfying her needs. (A more rigorous treatment of job satisfaction will be presented shortly.) Job satisfaction is widely viewed as a multidimensional concept, such that a person may be satisfied with certain aspects of her work ("I like my supervisor") while simultaneously being unhappy with other aspects of her work ("The pay and working conditions are terrible").

A second construct that has been investigated in recent years is variously referred to under the general rubric of *commitment* (or sometimes, *attachment*). This concept is also multidimensional and has to do with the attachment or adherence of persons to any or all of the following: to the work ethic in general, to one's occupation or profession, to one's actual day-by-day work experiences, and/or to one's employer (Morrow, 1993). As detailed by Morrow (1993), each of these four approaches to commitment has a number of variations that differ conceptually among themselves by minor degrees, and each is accompanied by one or more sets of scales and measures for their assessment. The interested reader is referred to Morrow's (1983, 1993) careful analyses and evaluations of the many nuances in meaning and measures of these concepts; we limit our discussion here to two of the major dimensions of commitment: those usually referred to as organizational commitment and job involvement.

The third concept treated in this chapter is referred to as *job involvement*. This construct has to do with people's devotion to their work per se, independent of the particular jobs they hold or the particular organization they work for. Job involvement concerns a person's views about the centrality of work to his life. For example, a person may enjoy being a machinist but may or may not be satisfied with his current job as a machinist and he may or may not have a sense of commitment to his employer.

In summary, then, the purpose of this chapter is to examine the theory and research related to job satisfaction, organizational commitment, and job involvement, considering their place in a broader study of work motivation.

JOB SATISFACTION

As mentioned earlier, job satisfaction is the job-related attitudinal construct that has attracted the most attention in modern times. Scientists, managers, and the "person on the street" are all familiar with the term and share a concern for understanding it. In fact, it is not unfair to state that most people believe themselves to be experts on the issue. The popular press as well as practitioners' management literature continually carry stories dealing with the matter of job satisfaction and employee attitudes or reporting sample surveys that study how people feel about their jobs.[1] One recent short piece that characterizes this genre was written by Ettorre (1994), who summarized a study by Martha Sanders, a professor at Wichita State University. In a sample of 250 male and female graduate students, all of whom had at least four years of organizational work experience, Sanders found that job satisfaction "continues" to be more important than any other work-related outcome, including financial remuneration, for both men and women. This author finds it significant that such short pieces continue to be researched and reported in newspapers and management journals: It is as if the possibility that job satisfaction is more important to people than money is still counterintuitive, despite recession, hard economic times, and high chronic unemployment. The purpose here is not to dwell on the substantive findings of Sanders' study (Ettorre, 1994); it is merely to refer to this half-page story from the *Management Review* to illustrate the continued public interest in the topic of job satisfaction and the relative importance it has in people's lives.

The popular importance of job attitudes is also reflected in the intermittent appearance in airport and other bookstores of straight-from-the-heart paperbacks that

---

[1]These days, a popular twist to many of these stories concerns gender differences: Do men and women differ in what they want from their jobs or in how they feel about their jobs?

represent in racy, living detail the thoughts and experiences of common folks about their work. An interesting example that is popular at the time of this writing is the irreverent and sometimes zany paperback entitled *The I Hate My Job Handbook* (Tien and Frankel, 1996), a series of interviews, stories, and snapshot insights into the miseries of office politics, bad bosses, organizational corruption, and everyday misery in office settings, particularly as they relate to women. What's the point here? The point is simply to demonstrate that as old as the concept is, job satisfaction (particularly job dissatisfaction) is a matter of timeless concern for anyone who works or for anyone who must interact with working people.

The proportion of people in North America who report being satisfied with their jobs has not changed a great deal over recent decades. A current chapter by Firebaugh and Harley (1995) reports, for example, that about 85 percent of U.S. workers are happy with their jobs and that men and women are approximately equal in this regard. Older workers tend to report higher levels of satisfaction than are reported by younger workers, in part because they tend to hold better jobs. In addition, the expectations of older workers may not be as high as those of younger employees because many older workers were raised during economic times when things were not as abundant as they have been more recently (Firebaugh and Harley, 1995). These figures are very similar to data reported 20 years ago. The authors did find, however, that there are some racial differences in job satisfaction levels: African-American women reported lower levels of job satisfaction than those reported by their white counterparts. On the other hand, at least one study has found that "morale" is very low these days among North American middle managers, in large part because of the severe cutbacks, layoffs, downsizings, and reengineering that has occurred over the past 10 years (A. B. Fisher, 1991).

The findings in Canada are similar to those in the United States. A recent study by WorkCANADA (Watson Wyatt Worldwide, 1995) has shown that the proportion of Canadians who report being satisfied with their jobs was 66 percent in 1995, down slightly from 71 percent reported in 1991, yet the percentage of people who reported being dissatisfied with their jobs fell during that four-year period from 21 percent to 9 percent. (This means that the group who claimed to be "partly satisfied or partly dissatisfied" grew dramatically, from 9 percent to 25 percent over the four years.) On balance, although people do complain a lot about their jobs, the vast majority of the North American workforce have been, and remain, reasonably satisfied with their jobs.

A literature review reported two decades ago (Locke, 1976) estimated that over 3,300 research projects had been conducted and reported up to that time on job satisfaction during the preceding 25 years. A more recent estimate is that there are probably now more than 5,000 articles and dissertations on the subject (Cranny, Smith, and Stone, 1992). Considering that only a fraction of the studies that are conducted by academics ever find their way into print, Locke's estimate is clearly conservative. In brief, job satisfaction is a popular issue. But what is it, exactly?

The Nature of Job Satisfaction

Many implicit and explicit definitions of job satisfaction have been offered over the years. The definition that has probably had the most influence in the field has been that of Locke (1969, 1976). For Locke, *job satisfaction* is an *emotional* reaction that "results from the perception that one's job fulfills or allows the fulfillment of one's important job values, providing and to the degree that those values are congruent with one's needs" (1976, p. 1307). Unless otherwise indicated, this definition will be the one intended whenever the term *job satisfaction* is used in the present volume, and its obverse will be intended whenever the term *job dissatisfaction* is used. It is interesting to note in relation to our discussion in chapter 4 that although job satisfaction is widely seen as an attitude, Locke's definition defines it in terms of an emotional reaction. Locke doesn't speculate about the particular emotions that are involved, and it is still largely a matter of speculation, insofar as virtually no empirical work has been done to isolate the emotions that comprise job satisfaction.

Nevertheless, a recent definition of job satisfaction offered by Weiss and Cropanzano (1996) gives emotion a greater emphasis than Locke (1976) did. They define it as "an evaluative judgement about one's job that partly, but not entirely, results from emotional experiences at work. It also partly results from more abstract beliefs about one's job. Together, affective experiences and belief structures result in the evaluation we call job satisfaction" (p. 2). These authors offer the *affective events theory* of employee attitudes, emotions, and behavior that provides a rich framework for guiding new empirical research into the study of emotions and job satisfaction. Until such work is conducted and reported, we can speculate on which emotions are most involved in the causes and experience of job satisfaction. In chapter 4 we speculated about the possible connections between job attitudes and a wide variety of human emotions, drawing on a typology offered recently by Lazarus and Lazarus (1994).

What about the emotions that accompany *job dissatisfaction?* Of those that we reviewed in chapter 4, a few likely candidates come to mind, including anger, fear, jealousy, and envy (see also Lazarus and Lazarus, 1994). So in keeping with the general tradition of the field, job satisfaction and dissatisfaction are discussed here primarily as if they are attitudes, although it is clear that emotions are also heavily involved in the experiences that people witness on the job.

Locke notes that job satisfaction is not the same thing as morale. Although satisfaction has to do with a retrospective assessment of one's job, morale is seen more as concerned with a positive desire to continue to work at one's job. Further, the term *morale* is often used to describe the overall attitudes of a work group rather than of a single individual. Locke's definition of job satisfaction is a conceptual one. In practice, researchers and managers often operationalize job satisfaction as having to do with the gratification of one's needs on the job or through the work setting. (Recall the discussion in chapters 3, 4, 5, and 6 of the multitude of needs that might be considered in such a context.) Moreover, interest is often directed at the satisfaction one has with a variety of specific aspects of one's job and the circumstances surrounding it. For example, the theory of work adjustment (Bretz and Judge, 1994; *Journal of Vocational Behavior,* 1993; Lofquist and Dawis, 1969) concerns itself with employee satisfaction and dissatisfaction with 21 aspects of work and organizations, ranging from creativity and recognition to social status and working conditions. Thus, as noted by Locke (1976) and confirmed by Ben Porat (1981), the list of potential causes of job satisfaction and dissatisfaction that have been investigated includes both *agents* (such as pay levels or one's supervisor) and *events* (such as the level of responsibility that one is usually permitted to assume on the job).

Moreover, different writers over the years have tended to contrive their own measures of satisfaction, making what is learned from one study difficult to compare with the results of other studies, although this situation has improved somewhat in recent years (Cranny et al., 1992, p. 2). Consequently, progress toward general agreement in the field on the nature of the construct has been impeded somewhat, and there have been intermittent attacks on the needs-based approach to job satisfaction that have detracted from the efforts expended in that tradition, although it still dominates the thinking and research of scholars and practitioners alike (see Stone, 1992). Still, we are left with a vast volume of research on job satisfaction and dissatisfaction that has yet to yield unanimous agreement on what it is, how it is influenced in work organizations, and what its consequences are for understanding and managing work organizations. Nevertheless, progress has been made, and our purpose here is to review that progress as well as some of the debate that still persists.

Job satisfaction has traditionally been assessed at either the global level or at the level of a number of facets. That is, employees are asked either for an overall assessment of their jobs ("How do you like your job?") or for more detailed assessments of facets such as the pay, job challenge, or supervision. A new approach has been suggested to assess the levels of satisfaction that people have with the various tasks that comprise their jobs. Allowing the 573 study participants (who represented a variety of different jobs) to define "tasks" according to their own definitions, Taber and Alliger (1995) concluded that global and facet measures of satisfaction were "consistent with, but only partially predictable from," the properties of the component tasks of jobs. The value added by this approach over the traditional approach remains to be seen, although this author expects that the greater precision it offers is likely to result in finer, although less generalizable predictions of work behaviors and attitudes. Time will tell.

The Causes of Job Satisfaction

What is known and agreed upon in relation to job satisfaction? As indicated above, most authors see job satisfaction as resulting from the fulfillment of needs through the activities one performs at one's job and from the context in which the work is performed. In other words, job satisfaction is a function of, indeed the same thing as, need satisfaction, or at least the degree of correspondence, congruence, or complementarity between a person's needs and the need-gratifying capacity of the work setting. Characteristic of this work is that of Betz (1969), Fredericksen, Jensen, Beaton, and Bloxom (1972), Lofquist and Dawis (1969), Mathieu, Hofmann, and Farr (1993), Ostroff (1993), Pervin (1968), L. W. Porter (1962, 1963), Seybolt (1976), and Tuckman (1968).

Other authors, including Ilgen (1971) and McFarlin and Rice (1992), conceive of job satisfaction as resulting from the size of the *discrepancy* that one perceives, if any, between what he expects to receive from his work and what he perceives he is receiving. Thus, large differences between the amount of pay an employee perceives he is receiving and the amount he expects to receive would result in dissatisfaction with pay, no reference being made to needs per se. Within this tradition is the issue of whether people are more or less concerned with various facets of their workplaces (e.g., the pay, the supervision, the working conditions) or whether overall, global satisfaction is more important.

A pair of recent studies, for example, found that discrepancies between what employees perceive to be receiving on the job and what they want from their jobs were critical when various facets were considered. Employees who placed high value on a specific facet were more satisfied with a small discrepancy and more dissatisfied with large discrepancies than those who placed lower importance on the same facets (McFarlin and Rice, 1992; see also Rice, Gentile, and McFarlin, 1991).

As we saw in chapter 3, recent experimental work has suggested that satisfaction results from at least three general types of perceptions. First, the person must see that there is a positive increment in the level of desired outcomes she receives. Second, the shorter the period over which the improvement occurs, the greater is the feeling of satisfaction (called the notion of velocity). Third, positive increases in the rate of positive change also add to the sensation of satisfaction: People want to see things get better for themselves over time, and the faster the improvement, the better (Salovey, Hsee, and Mayer, 1993). To the knowledge of this author, no empirical work has investigated this so-called *emodynamic theory* as it pertains to job satisfaction and dissatisfaction.

The importance of global measures, reflecting overall satisfaction with the work, is discussed by Cranny et al. (1992), who believe that global satisfaction may be both a contributing cause and a partial effect of facet satisfaction and that global satisfaction may make workers more receptive and cooperative in reaction to management-initiated changes to the workplace. In other words, it may be that as people become satisfied with one or a few aspects of their jobs, they tend to form positive global attitudes about those jobs. On the other hand, a person may have, for whatever reason, a generally positive view of her job and will therefore tend to report satisfaction with specific aspects of it (e.g., the promotion opportunities), if only because her general attitude is positive.

A third approach considers employee values, which are defined as those things that one sees as conducive to his or her welfare. It is important to distinguish between needs and values. As defined in chapter 3, needs are basic forces that initiate and guide behavior for the sake of the preservation and health of the individual. Values are those things that a person believes are conducive to his welfare. Thus, whereas the author might place a high value on a new sports car, he might have trouble convincing his wife that he really needs one. The point is that some approaches to satisfaction, such as that of Locke (1976), emphasize the role of values being met as the key determinant of job satisfaction, at least to the degree that these values are congruent with one's needs.

Still another view sees satisfaction or dissatisfaction resulting from comparisons that a person makes between herself and others around her. In this view (see chapter 11) a person is most likely to be dissatisfied when she perceives that the relationship between the contributions she makes to the organization and the benefits she derives in return is less satisfactory than the relationship she perceives between the inputs and outcomes derived by some other person or group of persons. Feelings of inequitable treatment have been shown to be predictive of intentions to quit organizations. A more thorough treatment of equity theory is presented in chapter 11.

Recent debate on the origins and nature of job satisfaction has hinged on the issue of whether it is determined by situations (i.e., the contextual factors of the workplace) or by disposition, as if some people are generally more disposed toward positive attitudes of all sorts, their jobs in particular. Brief mention was made of this issue earlier in the book (see chapter 1), and a full discussion of the matter is beyond the scope of this chapter as well. In a nutshell, there is a school of thought which believes that human beings vary in a general trait toward happiness or unhappiness, a disposition that accompanies them in many different aspects of their lives. When in a positive mood state, people may be more likely to engage in "prosocial" behaviors, offering help to one another or customers, for example (see Brief and Motowidlo, 1986; Isen and Baron, 1991), although the evidence is mixed on whether positive affectivity as a trait has such an effect (compare Organ and Konovsky, 1989, with George, 1991; and see George, 1992, and Judge, 1992).

The *dispositional approach* to job attitudes assumes that job satisfaction may be a function of a stable personality state. The individual differences that we often observe in job satisfaction, as well as the relative stability of job attitudes within people but across times and contexts, adds to the notion that attitudes may be at least partly dispositional (George, 1991, 1992). It is important to note, however, that this approach is not inconsistent with the idea that contexts can also affect attitudes in general and job satisfaction in particular. Rather, the dispositional hypothesis predicts that people of all sorts are subject to increases and decreases in their job attitudes, but that people who have the positively affective disposition will maintain a higher rank order across situations than those who do not possess this disposition (Watson and Slack, 1993). More will be said on this matter later in the chapter.

The work in this new tradition is different from efforts of previous times to explain organizational behavior by reference to personality variables; the newer tradition referred to as the dispositional approach considers such dispositions as affective (emotional) in nature (Judge, 1992). One group of researchers has argued that people can actually be born with a partial predisposition toward positive or negative job attitudes (see Arvey and Bouchard, 1994). Research in this area is still in its infancy and has been fraught with difficulty. A thorough review is provided by Judge (1992) for the interested reader.

The Nature and Causes of Job Dissatisfaction

Traditional thought on the matter has always held that job dissatisfaction is simply the opposite of job satisfaction, such that if an employee becomes more satisfied with her job, she necessarily becomes less dissatisfied, and vice versa. In chapter 2, Herzberg's challenge to this assumption was presented and discussed at length. To review it briefly, Herzberg and his colleagues argued that the concepts of job satisfaction and dissatisfaction are not the opposite of one another; rather, they are independent of one another. The reader will recall from that discussion that this asymmetrical aspect of the motivator-hygiene theory is the one responsible for much of the so-called Herzberg controversy.[2] Because of the lack of clear and consistent support for the two-factor approach that has *not* been based on questionable research, the perspective adopted here is the traditional one: Satisfaction and dissatisfaction represent opposite ends of the same continuum. Nevertheless, it is clear that jobs have multiple facets, so it is recognized that people can be satisfied and/or dissatisfied with different aspects of their jobs simultaneously (Rice, Gentile, and McFarlin, 1991). (See T. A. Mahoney, 1979, for an approach that reconciles the two-factor approach with the more traditional one.)

It is important to note as well the connection between what was presented in chapter 8 as need frustration and what is commonly viewed as job dissatisfaction:

---

[2]In fairness to Herzberg, and as noted in chapter 2, much of the research that purports to refute the motivator-hygiene theory was also flawed (Grigaliunas and Weiner, 1974).

When dissatisfaction is conceived of as an emotional reaction to the blockage of attempts on the job to satisfy one's needs, job dissatisfaction amounts to the same psychological state of frustration as we discussed in chapter 8; and we can expect any of the usual human responses to it (see Spector, 1978). What causes such blockages? Organizational policies that prevent people from being effective, despite their best efforts. Fellow employees who don't cooperate. Too much work to be done in the time permitted, such that none of it can be accomplished effectively. Shoddy machinery or supplies. A supervisor who doesn't listen or who fails to provide assistance when it is needed. An organizational structure that prohibits rapid advancement or promotion. One's gender (being the wrong one), or lack of abilities. Inconsistent expectations from one's bosses or members of one's job environment. Being assigned to undesirable working hours, such as the night shift. In short, frustration results from a blockage of one's efforts in pursuit of goals, and the blockage can emanate from any of a countless number of sources in an organization. The emotional reaction to frustration on the job is job dissatisfaction, although as we noted earlier, the specific emotions felt during job dissatisfaction have received little empirical attention and may, in fact, vary widely from person to person. Work is required on this issue.

To understand job dissatisfaction as a specific form of frustration, we must understand the nature of the needs that can be blocked on the job. Remember that there are a variety of human needs in addition to those for existence and relatedness. The various forms of growth needs have become more important to members of the modern workforce than they were in previous times, in large measure because of the relatively high levels of education and economic abundance enjoyed by Western society over the past generation. The point is that the modern workforce expects greater challenge and stimulation, greater opportunities to self-actualize on the job, more chances to feel competent and efficacious, and more frequent opportunities to achieve and develop than did previous generations (O'Toole, 1981). But there are not enough jobs in business and industry that provide sufficient challenge and stimulation to make this sort of universal need satisfaction possible from work. People seek alternative activities to meet their needs for challenge and stimulation.

Earlier, we focused on Locke's (1968) definition of job satisfaction as an emotional reaction to one's work. It follows that job dissatisfaction is also an emotional reaction, although the blend and intensity of the emotions involved have not received systematic study. Nevertheless, the concept of *emodynamic* satisfaction (and dissatisfaction) must be mentioned here again. From this view a person's emotional experience of job dissatisfaction will be greatest when she loses desired outcomes, when the loss occurs suddenly rather than gradually, and when the rate of loss increases over time (see Salovey et al., 1993). Empirical research into this dynamic, temporal perspective on job dissatisfaction remains to be conducted.

Social Information Processing and Job Dis(satisfaction)

The foregoing discussion of the nature and causes of job dissatisfaction was, as we said, rooted in traditional thoughts on the matter. A more recent approach that has attracted considerable attention and controversy is referred to as the *social information processing* approach (see Salancik and Pfeffer, 1978; Pfeffer, 1981b). The proponents of this view are among the harshest critics of needs-based models of job attitudes (see

Salancik and Pfeffer, 1977, and a reply by Alderfer, 1977). Their basic tenet is that a person's reactions to his or her job are heavily influenced by the interpretation of cues provided by other people and other sources. Employees make use of the nouns and verbs provided to them by the social contexts of the workplace to describe and to think about their jobs. They learn about the relative desirability of the work by watching and speaking with co-workers and other people.

Two proponents of the social information processing approach describe it this way: "Social information refers to comments, observations, and similar cues provided by people whose view of the job an employee considers relevant. It may be provided by people directly associated with the job, such as co-workers, supervisors, and customers, or it may be provided by people not employed by the company, such as family members and friends" (J. G. Thomas and Griffin, 1989, p. 65).

Social information from these sources provides the employee not only with ideas about what things are important in the workplace but also about the relative importance of these features (Pfeffer, 1981b). In addition, they can provide insight into formation of the employee's evaluation of these features—are they favorable or aversive? Hulin (1990), who is a harsh critic of this view, states:

> An extreme version of this approach argues that individuals experience little affect about their job satisfaction until they are *asked* (usually by social scientists). This view argues that social attitudes and affect are latent and unrecognized until some event triggers an evaluation. The nature of the triggering event (e.g., an attitude survey) may influence the resulting expressed and experienced attitudes much as the events that presumably formed the latent attitudes. If asked, the respondents will produce an answer *because they are expected to;* they will then search their environments for information to justify their response—they enact subjective environments that provide a justification for their response. (pp. 455–456)

As is usually the case in social science, the introduction of a radically new approach to a sacred tradition sparked a number of studies that attempted to pit the old theory against the new one. In this case the question was: Which is correct, the belief that objective features of the work environment are responsible for people's attitude, or are job attitudes merely the result of socially constructed realities? The reader is referred to Griffin (1987), Griffin, Bateman, Wayne, and Head (1987), and J. G. Thomas and Griffin (1989) for summaries of these studies. As often occurs in situations such as this—the debate between competing views on a matter—the conflicting data that result from research studies cause someone to proclaim that there is an element of truth in both viewpoints. Hence, Griffin et al. (1987) concluded: "The conclusions of researchers seeking to validate the social information processing model notwithstanding, it appears that perceptions of tasks are, in fact, partially determined by their objective properties and partially determined by social cues in workplaces" (p. 505). This author concurs with this conclusion.

Summary

There are a variety of theoretical perspectives on the nature and experience of job dissatisfaction. The reader is encouraged to consider the proposition that all the models we discussed here have elements of truth: None is more "right" or "wrong" than the others, and perhaps the most important thing to remember is that job dissatis-faction can be a terrible drain on the spirits and health of people, both when they are at work and when they are trying to be away from it. We turn now to a look at some of the consequences of disliking one's job.

Some Consequences of Job Dissatisfaction

Setting the theory of frustration aside for a moment, it is instructive to consider what job dissatisfaction feels like to those who are experiencing it. It often carries feelings of gloom and despair, sometimes anger and resentment, sometimes futility. Jobs that are frustrating tend to make people tired and more mentally fatigued than they would otherwise be. Dissatisfying jobs can fill up lives, such that people feel depressed off the job as much as they do while at work, making the pursuit of leisure activities more critical, yet often less rewarding at the same time. Moreover, job dissatisfaction can be a major contributor to poor mental health as well as to poor physical health (Herzberg, 1976; Jamal and Mitchell, 1980; Kavanaugh, Hurst, and Rose, 1981; Korn-hauser, 1965).

For example, consider a study reported by Stanley Bigos of the Department of Orthopedics of the University of Washington (see *Canadian Business,* 1991). After a four-year study, Bigos found that employees at Boeing Corp. who "hardly ever" en-joyed their work were 2.5 times more likely to report back injuries than were employ-ees who indicated that they "almost always" enjoyed their work. Ergonomics officials with the Canadian Centre for Occupational Health and Safety agree, claiming that job attitudes are related significantly to the incidence of muscular skeletal injuries such as back injuries (*Canadian Business,* 1991). Job dissatisfaction hurts.

When a blockage occurs and frustration follows, we can expect the same sorts of reactions as occur in response to frustration in off-the-job settings, such as aggression, regression, fixation, and withdrawal (see chapter 8). Which of these general classes of reaction will occur and the specific manifestation that it will take vary from one person to the next and from one job situation to the next, depending on a number of factors. But we can anticipate bickering, theft, deliberate tardiness, substance abuse, insubordi-nation, sabotage, espionage, and union activity, for example, to reflect impulses of ag-gression and anger directed at the job or the organization. We can also expect a certain amount of displaced aggression, such as child and spouse abuse, in cases where a per-son cannot (or dares not) focus the aggression toward the job. Regressive responses such as pettiness, gossiping, complaining, crying, or foul-mouthing can also probably be expected more frequently than aggressive behaviors, but sometimes in conjunction with aggressive acts. (Physical violence, for example, can be classed as both aggression and regression.)

The diversity of conceptual and operational definitions of job satisfaction (and dissatisfaction) used by investigators and managers (e.g., Wanous and Lawler, 1972) makes it somewhat difficult to generalize the findings of research into the organiza-tional consequences of holding favorable or unfavorable job attitudes. It has been as-sumed for many years that job attitudes may be more closely related to employee de-cisions to participate in organizations than they are to employee decisions concerning performance levels (see March and Simon, 1958). In other words, job satisfaction and dissatisfaction have been assumed to be much better predictors of attendance (or absenteeism), tardiness (as opposed to punctuality), and turnover than they are of performance levels. In the following section we focus on the evidence behind these conclusions and discuss the costs and benefits of the consequences associated with unfavorable job attitudes.

Job Dissatisfaction and Withdrawal Behaviors

Withdrawal in response to job dissatisfaction takes a number of characteristic forms, sometimes together. Tardiness, absenteeism, and turnover are the three most commonly acknowledged forms of withdrawal, but psychological withdrawal is also a problem. Psychological withdrawal consists of passive compliance and minimal attempts to perform on the job, demonstrating a general lack of desire to excel, to be creative, let alone to perform "above and beyond the call of duty" (see George, 1991; Organ, 1990). It sometimes manifests itself as laziness, sometimes as stupidity. While tardiness, absenteeism, turnover, and psychological withdrawal are separate phenomena, they do tend to be related to one another, to appear hand in hand (Beehr and Gupta, 1978; P. K. Edwards, 1979; Stumpf and Dawley, 1981).

Research evidence suggests that job satisfaction will be conducive to lower levels of absenteeism (Breaugh, 1981; Dittrich and Carrell, 1979; Ilgen and Hollenbeck, 1977; Mirvis and Lawler, 1977; Nicholson, Wall, and Lischeron, 1977), higher levels of motivation to attend work on a given day (F. J. Smith, 1977; Steers and Rhodes, 1978), lower levels of tardiness (Adler and Golan, 1981), and lower levels of voluntary turnover (Arnold and Feldman, 1982; Dunnette, Arvey, and Banas, 1973. Karp and Nickson, 1973; Nicholson et al., 1977), possibly including early retirement (Schmitt and McCune, 1981). For example, a simple two-year longitudinal study of 93 California-based supervisory personnel found that employees who left the organization were significantly lower in measured job attitudes, higher in a composite measure of job performance that had been provided by their supervisors, shorter in tenure with the company, and characteristically better able to cope to satisfy their growth needs (T. A. Wright and Bonett, 1993). In other words, job dissatisfaction was related to a propensity to leave the company, and understandably, it was the better performers who left, as well as those people who had developed styles for taking care of their needs for growth.

A number of other studies have shown that employees' expressed intentions to leave an organization are more closely correlated with actual subsequent turnover than are other indicators of job dissatisfaction (Kraut, 1975; Mitchel, 1981). Note that this finding is entirely consistent with the theory of reasoned action presented in chapter 9. Intentions, once formed, are more closely connected to behavior than are attitudes (Ajzen and Fishbein, 1980; Fishbein and Ajzen, 1975; and recall chapter 9).

The importance of these findings from a management perspective lies in the fact that the various forms of withdrawal can be disruptive to smooth organizational functioning, and very costly. For example, it was found in a study of a U.S. bank that the average cost (during the mid-1970s) of replacing a teller was over $2,500. The attendant cost savings potentially associated with an improvement in job satisfaction of 0.5 standard deviation among a group of 160 tellers would be approximately $17,600 (Mirvis and Lawler, 1977). When other factors, such as comparable increases in levels of intrinsic motivation (recall chapter 7) and job involvement (discussed later in this chapter), were added to the analysis, it was estimated that the employer might have saved as much as $125,000 over a one-year period. The point is that turnover can be very costly to an organization. In addition to the disruption that turnover can cause in the work process, there are costs associated with recruitment, training, and supporting new employees until they are creating enough value to offset the compensation they earn on the job (Pinder and Das, 1979).

Absenteeism from Work and Job Attitudes

It has long been an article of faith among researchers and managers that a primary cause of absenteeism behavior is low job satisfaction, low organizational commitment, or some other blend of unhappy attitudes toward one's work and the workplace. Although it may be true that on the margin, unhappy workers are less likely to report to work than happier ones, there is much more to the absenteeism syndrome than job attitudes and the research evidence shows that the connection between absenteeism and job satisfaction/dissatisfaction is not very strong. For example, more than a decade ago, Johns and Nicholson (1982) argued that there are many different reasons for people to be absent from work, and the psychological factors related to absence behavior should be treated case by case. In fact, two meta-analytic studies of the matter have reported that facets of job satisfaction count for less than 5 percent of absence behavior.

Later, in a meta-analysis of 31 studies that had investigated the linkage between job attitudes and absenteeism to that point in time, Hackett and Guion (1985) concluded that the relationship between the two concepts was very small and weak, notwithstanding the apparent appeal of the belief that people who dislike their jobs are more likely to stay away from those jobs. Like other researchers before them, Hackett and Guion blamed, in part, a sort of dogmatic tenacious belief in the human relations notion that poor job attitudes are naturally related to unfortunate work outcomes, such as low performance and various forms of withdrawal, including absenteeism.

Taking an entirely different approach that combined modern costing models (Cascio, 1987) with the theory of reasoned action (recall chapter 9 and see Ajzen and Fishbein, 1980), Martocchio (1992) estimated the cost to a U.S. employer of the absence behaviors of 440 white- and blue-collar workers over a three-month period in 1988–1989. Measures of job satisfaction and organizational commitment were taken, and the variable costs of their absences (their wages, paid at the rate of only $5.10 per hour, on average) were computed. The average variable cost per absence for the blue-collar workers was $58.34; for the white-collar workers in the sample, the average cost per absence was $62.18 over the three-month period. In aggregate, the costs of absence to the company for three months was greater than $25,000 (in 1988–1989 dollars).

The role of intentionality was clear in the results. Among those employees who at the beginning of the study intended to be absent, 423 days were lost; among those who originally claimed that they did not intend to be absent, there were only 15 days lost, a ratio of 28:1. Clearly, intentions, once formed, are powerful predictors of organizational behavior (as we saw in chapter 9), so any means of reducing intentions to stay away would be worth investigating from the company's perspective. In short, absenteeism behavior is frequently a matter of choice and a form of organizational behavior that costs money.[3]

---

[3]We will see in chapter 14 that absenteeism is a problem that *can* be managed, however.

For example, Martocchio and Judge (1994) recently formed clusters of employees who worked for a large university on the basis of the common origins of their absenteeism behavior. Factors such as personal illness, the illness of others in one's household, community activities and hobby or leisure activities, and having children were considered. The results suggested that following Johns and Nicholson (1982), there are many reasons, and combinations of reasons, for people to be absent from work. Of interest to our purposes here, job dissatisfaction was a statistically significant factor, but the effect was not large, particularly compared to some of the other factors included, such as personal illness.

Although absenteeism does not appear to have many redeeming qualities, it has been argued that *turnover* is not without its benefits to the organizations and individuals involved, as well as to society as a whole (Dalton, 1981; Dalton and Todor, 1979, 1982a). For example, it can be shown that an organization can reap real dollar cost savings through turnover, especially in cases where those who leave can easily be replaced by newcomers who are compensated at lower rates of pay and benefits (Dalton and Todor, 1982a). In addition, turnover can help introduce new ideas, new "blood," and the potential for change and adaptation of the organization involved, a necessity for organizations facing even moderate levels of change in their environments (Aldrich, 1980; Gross, 1965). People who leave tend to be the ones who withdraw in other ways, so turnover may help reduce absenteeism, tardiness, psychological withdrawal, and their associated costs (Mobley, 1982).

Turnover may also be the only solution in cases of extreme conflict between organizational members, as often occurs following mergers and other forms of reorganization (Mobley, 1982). For the individual, moving to a new organization can serve as an adaptive escape from a job that is stressful or conducive to marital discord, alcohol and drug abuse, or general life maladjustment (see Hulin's [1990] discussion of withdrawal behaviors of all sorts as adaptive responses to job dissatisfaction and frustration). From a societal point of view, turnover helps cross-organizational institution building, as ideas and techniques developed in some organizations are taken into others, often at the cost of individual organizations but often for the benefit of entire industries or networks of organizations. (See McKelvey, 1982, for a discussion of the transmission of "genes" among organizations.)

Voluntary versus Involuntary Withdrawal

It is important to distinguish between voluntary and involuntary absenteeism, tardiness, and turnover, and to realize that job attitudes can be predictive only of withdrawal behaviors that are voluntary in nature (Steers and Rhodes, 1978). Many times, employees are late for work, absent from work, or must quit their jobs for reasons that are somewhat or totally beyond their control. For example, many employees find they must quit their jobs to accompany their spouses to new job sites in other cities following transfers. It would be unreasonable to include turnover of this sort in any analysis of the connection between job attitudes and turnover. The point is that job dissatisfaction is not the only cause of the various types of withdrawal behaviors that we have discussed here, although it does contribute to many people's decisions to quit.

Second, although job dissatisfaction may generate a desire to leave one's organization in favor of employment elsewhere, we cannot assume that low levels of turnover are indicative of generally positive work attitudes in a workforce. A number of things can lock in disgruntled employees, preventing them from leaving dissatisfying work settings (Flowers and Hughes, 1973; Hershey, 1973). For example, while an employee may be very dissatisfied with some aspects of her job (such as the nature of the work itself), she might be quite unwilling to leave it and lose the high levels of pay it brings her. (Some critics claim that such has been the case in the auto industry, where the production work is terribly boring but where the United Auto Workers have managed to negotiate handsome hourly wages for its members, to somehow "buy them off" for suffering the tedium of assembly-line work.) Similarly, tight labor markets often prevent dissatisfied employees from turning over, as do a host of familial and economic factors. ("I like it here in Prince Rupert; why should I leave?") Sometimes a generalized fear of the unknown, often based on real or imagined self-perceptions of obsolescence, prevents dissatisfied employees from quitting.

Many organizations inadvertently prevent their employees from leaving them because of the "golden handcuffs" they manage to lock onto their workforce over the years through pension plans, health insurance plans, and other benefits. The importance of this point is that although there is no necessary connection between job attitudes and individual job performance, disgruntled employees are often those who perform their jobs at the minimum levels required and who seldom demonstrate any desire to be creative or to excel "above and beyond the call of duty" when the occasion to do so presents itself. Moreover, there is evidence, presented earlier, that dissatisfied personnel are more likely to be absent and tardy, disrupting the normal flow of events for their employers, customers, and co-workers (T. A. Wright and Bonett, 1993). Hence, an organization may benefit from ridding itself of those who are dissatisfied.

On the other hand, workers who leave are often the most competent and (therefore) the most marketable. These are people who, when they do leave, represent a loss of talent to the organization losing them and an equal increase in the stock of talent that works for other employers (such as the competition). Whether turnover occurs among an organization's high performers or low performers may depend on its reward system. Competent personnel seem less likely to leave when pay and other rewards are contingent on performance, whereas they are more likely to leave when rewards are not distributed in accordance with performance (Dreher, 1982).

In summary, while job dissatisfaction is a contributing factor to voluntary turnover, it is not responsible for most cases of involuntary quitting, and for the reasons just listed, we cannot assume that turnover will rid an organization of either its most dissatisfied or its lowest-performing employees. Hence, turnover may be beneficial for the employee who leaves and for the organization to which he goes. But turnover may be either beneficial or detrimental to the organization that suffers it, depending on the costs associated with the economic and noneconomic considerations discussed above. An exhaustive analysis of the causes, costs, and benefits of turnover is beyond the scope of this chapter.

Job Satisfaction and Individual Productivity

At least since the beginning of the human relations movement in the 1940s, it has commonly been assumed that employees who are more satisfied with their work tend to be more productive. Among many managers, politicians, and social critics, it makes intuitive sense to assume that "a more satisfied employee is a productive employee."

Notwithstanding the intuitive appeal of the idea, after countless studies into the relationship between these two variables, it can be concluded that there is no simple, bivariate relationship between job attitudes and individual performance, where "performance" is conceived as short-term productivity and task accomplishment.

Recall from our discussion in chapter 9 that it is seldom the case that attitudes lead to specific behaviors in a predictable fashion. Sometimes high levels of satisfaction are associated with high levels of productivity; other times, the opposite is the case. It may be, for example, that a dissatisfied employee will become quite productive if she perceives that high performance levels may help her earn a promotion, a raise in pay, or even a chance to attain a job elsewhere. Alternatively, highly satisfied employees can become complacent, resting on their reputations and assuming that contributions made in the past have earned them the right to "coast" on the job, perhaps until retirement or layoff.

Why do general attitudes about one's work not predict job performance? C. D. Fisher (1980) observed years ago that it is unreasonable to expect *general* attitudes (such as a generally positive attitude toward one's job) to be predictive of *specific* acts (such as performing at a high level of productivity). Fisher points out that we can reasonably expect only *specific attitudes* to predict *specific actions.* More to the point— using concepts from the theory of reasoned action (recall chapter 9)––rather than expecting to predict a specific behavior (such as expending high job effort) with a global attitude toward one's job, we should attempt to use people's *attitudes toward the act in question* (expending high levels of effort on the job) to predict that behavior. Unless and until attitudes and behaviors are conceptualized and measured at the same levels of specificity, C. D. Fisher (1980) observes, it is hopeless to expect job satisfaction to predict individual job performance.

One intriguing theoretical approach suggests that satisfaction may be responsible for high levels of individual productivity only when the person believes that productivity will be successful as a means of removing "equivocality" (Weick, 1969, p. 99). Equivocality is disorder, ambiguity, multiple meanings, and a touch of chaos. We noted in chapter 7 that people are frequently motivated to increase and then reduce the amounts of uncertainty in their lives. The energy expended in creating these cycles is called, in one view, intrinsic motivation. The actual behavior associated with increasing and removing uncertainty is called intrinsically motivated behavior. Weick (1969) suggests that there is pleasure in the removal of equivocality from one's environment, and so if an employee believes that equivocality can be mastered through high energy expenditure and that pleasure occurs in the removal process, performance and satisfaction will covary: As one increases, so does the other. Historically, it is interesting to note that Weick's hypothesis was apparently derived, at least in part, from some of the same intellectual roots that inspired Deci and his colleagues, although the latter two authors do not acknowledge one another. The common roots are found in R. White's (1959) writing about *effectance motivation* (see chapter 7). Direct comparison of Weick's thinking and that of Deci (1975; Deci and Ryan, 1985) would require us to equate the concept of equivocality (Weick) with that of uncertainty (Deci).

About a decade ago, a meta-analysis of previous empirical studies found that when rewards are contingent on productivity, the connection between satisfaction and performance is higher than in those situations where pay and productivity are not tied together (Podsakoff and Williams, 1986), but that is about as much success as there has been in the search for a satisfaction–performance link. More typical are the results of a study reported by Katzell, Thompson, and Guzzo (1992), who advanced a complex theoretical model summarizing a great deal of the existing evidence on the complex relationship between job satisfaction and job performance. In the research that followed, Katzell and his team assessed the job-related attitudes and performance of 1,200 employees from a wide variety of organizational units. They found, as have other researchers before them, that the connection between positive job attitudes and high levels of performance are low (or nonexistent, depending on whether employees or their supervisors provide the performance data) or simply nonexistent. They also concluded that both performance and satisfaction are probably best thought of as consequences of many other organizational and attitudinal factors, and that when they are connected with one another, it is usually very indirectly, through the effects of other such variables. For example, the work must yield intrinsic rewards. There must be highly valued extrinsic rewards tied to performance and administered equitably. Job involvement must be high, and clear, challenging, and acceptable goals must be set (Katzell et al., 1992). This summary is reminiscent of a much earlier formulation presented by Porter and Lawler (1968) and a more recent one by Locke and Latham (1990b).

The Katzell et al. (1992) study was remarkable, making use of many more measures and more current data analysis techniques than most other studies of the matter, but their findings have the same general conclusion as that reached by others before them: There is no simple, direct, reliable association between job attitudes and job performance, despite how much common sense lies behind the hypothesis. In short, despite the intuitive appeal of the commonsense axiom that job satisfaction leads to individual job performance, there is abundant evidence to show that this is simply not reliably true (see Bhagat, 1982; Brayfield and Crockett, 1955; Schwab and Cummings, 1970; and Vroom, 1964, for reviews of the evidence). Some authors have suggested that even in those cases where individual performance and satisfaction are related, it may be that performance levels cause satisfaction levels rather than the other way around (e.g., Lawler and Porter, 1967) or that a host of organizational factors influence satisfaction and performance simultaneously, causing them to appear to be causally interrelated (Katzell et al., 1992).

Job Satisfaction and Other Forms of Performance

So why are positive job attitudes important if they are not related to bottom-line indicators of performance? Farrell (1983), C. D. Fisher and Locke (1992), and P. C. Smith (1992), among others, provide some answers. Although it is true that positive job attitudes are not reliably predictive of the performance levels of individual employees (as detailed above), job satisfaction may be related to a variety of other outcome variables that have largely been ignored until recently. An alternative way of stating the same thing is that current thinking requires a broader definition of performance than has traditionally been used in the past by organizational scientists.

Building on the work of Farrell (1983), for example, C. D. Fisher and Locke (1992) have constructed a typology of outcomes that can result from negative job attitudes. These categories include avoidance acts such as quitting one's job outright, avoidance by minimizing effort or dodging difficult tasks, psychological adjustments (e.g., using drugs or other substances), constructive problem solving or forming a union, defying authority and resisting managerial directions, and outright aggression, such as acts involving sabotage, rumor mongering, and the like. Fisher and Locke's categories include many other specific examples, but their point is made: "Performance" consists of much more than simple efficiency and measures of individual productivity, as has usually been construed in the past (see Staw, 1984). On the positive side, an entire set of prosocial behaviors (or what Fisher and Locke call "helping behaviors") often result from positive employee attitudes. Originally conceived of as work that lies outside the individual's formal job description (D. Katz, 1964), four more specific forms of work above and beyond the call of duty have been studied in recent years, usually in relation to positive job attitudes. These positive behaviors have been referred to as extra-role, prosocial, altruistic, and citizenship behaviors (see Organ, 1990).

Clearly, most organizations would rather have their employees engage in such acts than not do so: We have all experienced the chill of the bureaucratic employee who prefers not to extend himself beyond minimal treatment, and a few of us have actually enjoyed the relief and satisfaction that can occur when an employee extends himself beyond normal expectations to be especially helpful. Good citizenship behavior by employees becomes particularly important in service industries, where courtesy, sympathy, and energetic creativity and positive attitude toward customers' problems can mean the difference between profit and loss (George, 1991). Consider the following sections of an internal memo written and circulated by General Telephone of the Southwest:

> As the issue of employee commitment in an organization is examined, there are two types of commitment perceived. First, the organization defines the minimum amount of effort (or commitment) which is required to avoid being fired or penalized. The feeling organizationally is that there is a benefit to be derived by establishing a corporate culture and climate which will initiate a second "above minimum" commitment. This commitment, known as discretionary effort, is the difference between the minimum expectation set by the organization, and the maximum amount of effort and care an individual *could* bring to the job. . . .
>
> We are looking for the key to the "hidden productivity" in [our] work force, both management and craft. We need to find a formula which, when applied, will result in a work force excited about, involved in, and committed to the strategies involved in our current corporate direction. We need a clue to the commitment phenomenon. . . . (cited by Heckscher, 1988, p. 89)

The executive(s) who wrote and circulated this memo used the term *commitment* where we would prefer the word *motivation*—*commitment* having a special meaning explained later in the chapter. Regardless of the specific terms that the executive used, it is clear that s/he is talking about the extra energy that was expected to give the telephone company an edge on the competition. Current thinking—returning to that begun long ago by D. Katz (1964)—considers positive job attitudes to be very important to job performance as long as *performance* is defined more broadly than to include simple output measures of productivity.

Job Satisfaction and Life Satisfaction

There may be other reasons to be concerned with generating and fostering positive job attitudes—having more to do with mental and physical health and personal well-being than they do with corporate profit and individual job performance. As suggested earlier, there is a renewal in the belief that positive attitudes in one forum of a person's life "spill over" into positive mental health and happiness in other arenas of life. This idea was first proposed decades ago but has enjoyed a recent resurrection by major job satisfaction theorists such as P. C. Smith (1992), who has written about general feelings of happiness and trust that people may generate and enjoy through their work. Their feelings of happiness and joy also contribute to similar emotions in nonwork settings, such as in their family lives, recreation activities, and so on (see Schmitt and Bedeian, 1982; Schmitt and Pulakos, 1985). A general sense of joy and a predilection toward being happy fosters positive job attitudes as well, so the causality between general happiness and context-specific happiness prevails. According to P. C. Smith (1992), people blessed with such feelings of happiness and trust are much more open to change in their lives, particularly changes in their work situations. Their generally positive disposition tends to transcend time and situations, although as we noted earlier, they too are subject to negative feelings. It is a matter of relative rank order among their peers who don't possess the predisposition. At work, they are less resistant to managerial initiates and approach new work procedures more constructively and with minimum suspicion.

A longitudinal study conducted in the mid-1980s and reported recently involved a sample of full-time employees of a private U.S. university. This study illustrates the concept of spillover and the statements that Cranny et al. (1992) have made about the benefits of positive general life satisfaction. The study also extended previous work to examine the effects of two (rather than just one) dimensions of emotionality: negative affectivity and positive affectivity (Levin and Stokes, 1989; Watson and Slack, 1993). Each of these moods can be experienced either as a passing state or as stable traits, although the focus in this project was on the trait forms of affectivity. People who have strong negative affectivity tend to view the world from a negative, pessimistic perspective. They witness higher levels of distress and dissatisfaction in most settings in which they find themselves. On the contrary, people high in positive trait affectivity have fun in life, viewing things positively and with a generalized optimism. They may even have heightened capacities to enjoy positive stimuli.

In their study, Watson and Slack (1993) gathered data on both positive and negative affectivity at two points in time, spanning two years. They controlled for a number of other variables relating to their participants' work and assessed job satisfaction at the end of the two-year period. A total of 82 of the original 151 employees stayed with the project to provide complete sets of data. The results confirmed that both positive and negative trait measures of emotionality were related to at least some dimensions of job satisfaction. Thus, negative trait affect was associated with lower satisfaction with one's work and one's co-workers; positive trait affect was predictive of positive assessments of employees' work, promotions, and overall job satisfaction. They also found that these traits/predispositions remained stable over the two years of the project. The authors concluded that job satisfaction can reasonably be understood "in the context of the broader emotional lives of employees." It is not just a result of organizational policies, procedures, and job design; it is a reflection of the greater, more general degree of individual happiness or unhappiness of the person. To the extent that this is true, there is plenty of reason to study job satisfaction, aside from the relentless quest for its link to productivity, performance, and other aspects of organizational effectiveness.

Another recent study examined the notion that job and life satisfaction are related to one another using a large survey data base from the early 1970s (Judge and

Watanabe, 1993). These researchers found a strong cross-sectional link between the two variables but a much smaller connection between job satisfaction and life satisfaction when the latter was measured five years later than the former.

In contrast to the argument that job satisfaction and life satisfaction are related to one another (Cranny et al., 1992) presumably in the sense that one is responsible for much of the other (i.e., that job satisfaction causes some or much of life satisfaction), there is another possibility. A study of 631 people in their homes, combined with data analysis techniques appropriate for the purpose, has recently suggested that any relationship that does exist between job and life satisfaction is due, at least in large measure, to the effects of one or more other variables (Frone, Russell, and Cooper, 1994). In other words, it may be that the oft-observed bivariate relationship between satisfaction at work and satisfaction with life in general (or, alternatively, dissatisfaction in both arenas) is spurious. This means that the correlation between them may be because some other variable(s) is driving both of them, although life and work satisfaction may not actually be causally related. By now, the reader will probably suspect the types of third variables these researchers offer as candidates to explain the spurious correlations: personality predispositions toward being either positive or negative, genetic factors, and/or even methodological artifacts. Once more in this book we see the debate between those who believe in the role of personality predispositions and those who would minimize the role of such forces (see George, 1992; Judge, 1992).

Criticisms of the Debate Itself

On balance, there are some recent, compelling, and intuitively appealing arguments both for and against the spillover hypothesis and, with it, arguments both advocating and minimizing the importance of job satisfaction in the workplace, notwithstanding the weak relationship between job attitudes and individual productivity. Two very recent arguments have been made on the "nay" side, however. One of these arguments (O'Reilly and Chatman, 1994) was addressed to the concept of dispositionalism in the context of motivation rather than of satisfaction, but it is certainly relevant to the current discussion. It is of a methodological nature, an argument that echoes a point made repeatedly throughout this book. The authors write:

> In the past several years, organizational researchers have engaged in a rather artificial debate about the extent to which individual differences or dispositions predict job outcomes such as attitudes and behaviors. . . . While the debate is provocative, a careful examination indicates that there may be less substance to this debate than it seems. By now, most organizational researchers acknowledge the fundamental importance of situational effects, the existence of stable individual differences, and their interaction as causes of behavior. . . . The controversy lies in questions about the usefulness of measuring dispositions that are sometimes poorly specified and lack reliability and validity, the absence of well-developed theoretical justifications for constructs for given situations, and the frequent use of cross-sectional research designs that do not permit adequate longitudinal testing of clearly specified hypotheses. (p. 603)

Is There a Case *against* Employee Satisfaction?

Another author has advanced what he calls "the case against job satisfaction" (Bassett, 1994). He reviews the literature summarized above in this chapter, literature that reports consistent failure to find simple connections between individual satisfaction and productivity (or performance). He then cites data that report correlations between job satisfaction and worker health but dismisses these findings on the grounds that it is far from clear whether employee dissatisfaction causes poor health or whether it is the other way around: Unhealthy people tend to be dissatisfied with their jobs (and perhaps with their lives in general). Finally, he notes that both job satisfaction and health may be determined by entire sets of other factors, so that any correlations that appear between the two variables are entirely spurious (Kenny, 1979).

Bassett discusses the virtual impossibility of achieving overall high levels of job satisfaction while managing human resources according to other basic principles of management. As long as organizational structures are pyramidal in shape, not everyone who wished to be promoted will be promoted; many or most will be disappointed. As long as managers reward merit for superior performance, there will be people who receive fewer rewards than others and feel slighted. Further, Bassett (1994) invokes the dispositional arguments explained elsewhere in this chapter to suggest that some people are prone by nature of their personalities to be either positive and happy or negative and unhappy, regardless of the circumstances surrounding them (see Judge, 1992). To the extent that this is true, it is futile for management to try anything and everything to develop strong positive work attitudes among everyone.

Bassett (1994) also points out that organizations can benefit from employing people who are more or less dissatisfied. Dissatisfaction can motivate people to find better ways to get things done, leading to innovations in products and services or improvements in the way the work is performed (see March and Simon, 1958). On balance, this author concurs with *some* of the conclusions offered by Bassett (1994), specifically and only those related to the human relations–driven hope to inspire greater individual performance through improving people's job satisfaction:

> Striving to bring satisfaction to the workforce goes on. Whether it may or may not be an element of future high-performance management systems is open to argument. Certainly the expectation that worker satisfaction must always be the foundation of high-performance output systems is naive and perhaps even dangerous. Worker satisfaction is a complex matter that deserves careful thought and consideration in any management systems design decision. But it cannot and should not be the touchstone of efforts to invent high performance systems. The *satisfied worker is a productive worker* paradigm doesn't work. It is much more complicated than that! (p. 67)

Conclusions on Job Satisfaction

But that is as far as this author's support goes for any argument against fostering job satisfaction in work organizations. Indeed, the position taken here is that job satisfaction is a valuable emotional experience whether or not it spills over into the rest of our lives. By contrast, job dissatisfaction is a painful experience, sometimes chronic in nature, that hurts employees and their mental health. It can also be a source of misery for people close to the dissatisfied employee, such as innocent and powerless family members and loved ones. The position taken here is that after all the conceptual and methodological arguments are considered and then set aside, it is abundantly obvious that people in a modern world need and deserve a minimum level of enjoyment from their work. Anyone who has suffered extended unhappiness at work with few or no options to exercise will understand and agree with this position, as will those people who are fortunate enough to look forward to their work on a daily basis and who derive joy and a sense of self-worth from their work. These things seem obvious.

Reminder of Purpose and a Glance Ahead

The key purpose of spending so much attention on job attitudes derives from the importance of attitudes in general in the determination of behavior in general. We are interested in this book in the motivation to work, which consists of people's desires to join and remain with work-related enterprises and to produce well once they have joined. Whereas part two of this book approached the motivation to participate and the motivation to perform from a needs perspective, part three looks at these two elements of work motivation from the perspective of people's attitudes and beliefs. In short, the purpose here is to understand how certain job-related attitudes may or may not be related to the desire of people to participate in organizations and to perform well for those organizations. Now that we have examined job satisfaction in detail, we turn our attention to organizational commitment, a set of attitudes, beliefs, and intentions that people form in reference to their employers, as opposed to their jobs per se.

ORGANIZATIONAL COMMITMENT

Whereas job satisfaction generally has to do with the degree to which one's needs or values are satisfied by one's job, work commitment is a multidimensional construct that is somewhat broader in scope. Specifically, *work commitment* is currently seen as comprising several dimensions, such as adherence to a work ethic (see chapter 1 of this book), commitment to a career or a profession, job involvement (degree of daily absorption in everyday work experiences), and organizational commitment—the degree of loyalty a person holds for a particular employer (see G. Blau and Paul, 1993; Morrow, 1993). Space limitations here require that we focus primarily on the third and fourth varieties of work commitment identified by Morrow (1993): job involvement and organizational commitment. The interested reader is referred to Morrow (1993, chapter 1) and to chapter 1 of this volume for a discussion of the issue of the Protestant work ethic, and to Morrow (1993, chaps. 2 and 3) for an examination of a relatively new concept, career commitment. We examine organizational commitment in the following sections and conclude the chapter with job involvement.

Varieties of Organizational Commitment: What Is It?

Organizational commitment has attracted more attention among organizational scientists than any other variety of work commitment, and it has been conceptualized in a variety of ways, although there is some convergence among the best developed perspectives (Morrow, 1993). For example, L. W. Porter, Steers, Mowday, and Boulian (1972) see organizational commitment as consisting of three interrelated (although not identical) attitudes and intentions: (1) a strong belief in, and acceptance of, the organization's goals and values; (2) a willingness to exert considerable effort on behalf of the organization; and (3) a definite desire to remain a member of the organization (L. W. Porter et al., 1974). The Porter approach, which has been the predominant one for two decades, has come to be referred to as an *affective* view of the concept (e.g., Meyer and Allen, 1997; Meyer, Paunonen, Gellatly, Goffin, and Jackson, 1989). "Employees with a strong affective commitment continue employment with the organization because they *want* to do so" (Meyer and Allen, 1991, p. 67).

A second component of organizational commitment is referred to as *normative commitment* (Meyer and Allen, 1991). It consists of "the totality of internalized normative pressures to act in a way that meets organizational goals and interests" (Weiner, 1982). In this approach, commitment causes individuals to behave in ways that they believe are morally right rather than in ways that are going to be instrumental for their own goals. It involves a belief that *a person simply ought to be loyal;* it is a matter of intrinsic responsibility. Beliefs and values of this sort are believed to originate in one's family and culture and through organizational socialization (Meyer and Allen, 1991). People who are normatively committed to their organizations are more likely to make sacrifices for them, to persist in their attempts to serve them, and to be preoccupied with them, devoting a considerable proportion of their time and energy to the pursuit of the objectives of their organizations. It is seen simply as the right thing to do.

A third approach to organizational commitment has been referred to as *calculative* (Morrow, 1993) or *continuance commitment* (Meyer and Allen, 1997; Meyer et al., 1989). Originating with H. S. Becker (1960), this form of organizational commitment is concerned with the individual's attachment to an employer by virtue of transactions that occur between the employee and the organization, resulting in various forms of side bets and investments over time (e.g., seniority rights, personal attachments to other workers, pension plans, company-specific work skills). In this view an employee is committed to an organization because the costs of leaving become too high. A person's attachment is not based on emotion or good feelings toward the company (as in the affective view), or upon any normative beliefs about the inherent goodness and value in being loyal (as in the second approach). Rather, this third understanding of commitment is based on sheer economics and pragmatic considerations: It simply becomes too expensive for the person not to adhere to the company or other employer.

In short, we can think of organizational commitment as a form of extreme loyalty to one's organization. The important aspect of this construct for our present purpose is that the attitude object here is the organization per se, not the person's particular job, department, work group, occupation, profession, or career. Meyer and Allen (1997), two of the leading scholars in this area, suggest that we think of the three dimensions of commitment discussed above as components (of an underlying construct) rather than as types of commitment (which would imply less underlying unity of the construct).

Is Organizational Commitment a Trait, a Value, or a Propensity?

Earlier in this chapter we touched briefly upon the notion that job satisfaction and job dissatisfaction may represent personal dispositions among people—that some people possess a propensity toward either positive or negative affective states that influence the way they evaluate their jobs and their general work lives. Similarly, some researchers think of organizational commitment, or at least certain aspects of it, as parts of a person's personality or personal value system (e.g., Angle and Lawson, 1993). In one study, a sample of 400 employees who were transferred en mass by their employer more than 1,000 miles for a corporate relocation were measured for organizational commitment twice, both at the time of the relocation and then again two years later (Angle and Lawson, 1993). The researchers found that affective and continuance commitment were only modestly related to one another, but more important, they tested and supported a model that treated normative commitment as a personal value that predisposes a person toward possessing high affective and continuance commitment (Angle and Lawson, 1993). By this view, then, normative commitment is a more or less stable trait—a value—that people bring with them to any and all workplaces. Although a person's values are subject to change over time (see chapter 3), normative commitment is seen by this perspective as being more or less constant: Either a person values commitment or does not, regardless of the circumstances.

Another study, this one with a sample of U.S. Air Force cadets, investigated Mowday, Porter, and Steers' (1982) concept of *commitment propensity* (Lee, Ashford, Walsh, and Mowday, 1992). This concept is seen as representing all the personality factors, experiences, expectations, and values that a person brings to bear when considering going to work for an employer (Mowday et al., 1982). Commitment propensity is a summary concept that reflects the likelihood, in advance of being employed by an organization, that the person will become committed to the organization after being hired. It also takes into account the degree of volition a person has in choosing to work for a particular organization. The Air Force study showed that the various experiences (situational factors) and the cadets' varying degrees of commitment propensity both had an effect on their survival in the Air Force. Specifically, preentry commitment propensity was related to initial commitment, which in turn was related to organizational commitment in the longer term, as measured by lower levels of voluntary withdrawal from the Academy.

The Lee et al. (1992) study is important for several reasons. First, it provides an example of the new variety of research that attempts to disentangle the various effects of personal variables from situational variables (recall the discussion in chapter 1 and see Judge, 1992; Organ, 1990; and Schneider, 1983). Second, it provides another illustration of the critical importance of early experiences for a person after he enters an organization or new job setting for the first time. Earlier in this chapter, for instance, we saw how important it is for newcomers to have challenging first assignments, participation in the decisions about their jobs, and a chance to be "heard" about the work itself for satisfaction and commitment to the organization. This same effect has been well documented among engineers (Badawy, 1982).

Psychological Bases for Organizational Commitment

O'Reilly and Chatman (1986) have built upon an earlier typology of attitude change proposed by Kelman (1958) to delineate three distinct psychological bases that can underlie organizational commitment. The issue is: What, psychologically, forms the basis for a person's commitment to an organization? The three bases are referred to as compliance, identification, and internalization. *Compliance* occurs when a person is attached for the sake of gaining rewards or advancement of some sort. It is an instrumental form of commitment that has little or nothing to do with adherence to the organization's mission or the values of its key members. *Identification* occurs when a person accepts influence to establish or maintain a satisfying relationship. This may entail pride in membership in a group, "respecting its values and accomplishments without adopting them as his own" (O'Reilly and Chatman, 1986, p. 493). Affiliation with another person or group, for the sake of affiliation, is the key. The third basis for commitment that O'Reilly and Chatman borrowed from Kelmans (1958) is referred to as *internalization*. In this case the person accepts a group's attitudes and behaviors as congruent with his or her own. There is commitment that goes beyond mere identification: Internalization means the closest association between one's own motives and the motives of whatever group or organization is at issue.

In two different studies, O'Reilly and Chatman (1986) found that identification and internalization forms of commitment were positively related to prosocial behaviors and negatively related to both intentions to quit and actual quitting behavior. Commitment based on compliance was not related to prosocial behaviors or actual quitting behavior, but it was correlated with people's expressions of an intention to leave. The distinctions among these three "bases" for commitment are important and have roots in organizational science from many years past. We will see shortly that keeping the psychological bases for organizational commitment disentangled from one another allows for even further refinement of the general concept of organizational commitment (see T. E. Becker, 1992).

Why Is Commitment Thought to Be Important?

Why has there been so much interest in organizational commitment among managers and academics? There are a number of reasons, some of which have legitimate scientific grounding, and some of which have been shown to have little or no basis in reality. On an intuitive level, it has been believed that high commitment is beneficial for both employers and employees. From the individual's perspective, high commitment provides a sense of identity and perhaps even status and prestige (Romzek, 1989). High commitment provides an opportunity for the person to receive both intrinsic and extrinsic satisfactions through their association with the employer, the other employees, and the business or industry in general. An employee who is committed to his employer may suffer less anxiety about the prospect of losing his job and may generally feel much more secure and content as a result. Commitment is accompanied by feelings of nurturance and mutual trust and fosters a generally positive outlook in life. For those who have it, commitment can be a source of comfort, identity, and security (Mowday et al., 1982).

Ashforth and Mael (1989) have described the value to people of *identifying* with an organization. While committing to an organization is related to identifying with it, the concepts are slightly different. "According to SIT [social identity theory], people tend to classify themselves and others into various social categories, such as organizational membership, religious affiliation, gender, and age cohort. . . . Social classification serves two functions. First, it cognitively segments and orders the social environment, providing the individual with a systematic means of defining others. . . . Second, social classification enables the individual to define *him- or herself* in the social environment" (pp. 20–21). It is possible for a person's social identity to adhere to a work group, a department, or a union (Ashforth and Mael, 1989), but our focus here is on the identification that comes with high organizational commitment. Once a focus for the identification has been selected ("I am an employee of the University of Nebraska's Alumni

Association"), the person will derive a sense of pride and self-concept, defined in part through that association. In short, identification that comes with commitment can be beneficial to a person.

Management's Stake in Commitment

What is important about commitment from an employer's perspective? Organizations value high levels of commitment on the parts of their employees for a number of reasons (Randall, 1987). It has been widely believed that highly committed employees perform better on the job and are less likely to be absent, late, or to leave altogether. Such people are assumed to be more likely to engage in good citizen behaviors or work above and beyond the call of duty (D. Katz and Kahn, 1978; Mowday et al., 1982; Organ, 1990; Organ and Konovsky, 1989). At a societal level, high commitment may be associated with lower rates of overall mobility, higher levels of stability, greater national productivity, and higher aggregate levels of quality of life (Mathieu and Zajac, 1990). On the face of it, then, intuitive reasoning suggests that high levels of organizational commitment will benefit both individuals and employers: Everyone wins.

In the following sections we examine the ways in which organizations attempt to build commitment for the sake of gaining the benefits it is thought to produce. We then look closely at the evidence on the matter: What are the actual costs and benefits of high commitment?

Organizational Socialization and Commitment

From the time they enter the employment of organizations, most people witness attempts to make them committed and devoted to those organizations. Again, the purpose of these attempts is based on the hope and belief that highly committed workers are likely to be more effective. Thus, organizational rules are designed to assure that employees behave according to the norms and expectations of the organization. Often, an attempt is made to impress the newcomer with the merit of the organization's mission and major goals as well as to provide a sense of the history and traditions of the organization (Pondy, Frost, Morgan, and Dandridge, 1983).

For example, induction programs and other socialization rituals attempt to inculcate the employee with an understanding of, and an appreciation for, "our way of doing things" (D. C. Feldman, 1977, 1981). Pensions and other benefit plans sometimes constitute so called "golden handcuffs," which make it increasingly difficult for employees to consider leaving (see Angle and Perry, 1982). Organizational logos and insignia, off-the-job social functions, and programs for employees' spouses are all designed, in part, to build loyalty. (See H. S. Becker, 1960, on the role of social involvement in commitment building.) Company newsletters are common in large organizations, serving more to build a sense of loyalty and commitment than to communicate real news.

It has been suggested that even certain formal personnel transactions conducted upon employees once they are "on board" facilitate commitment, binding them to the organization as a primary source of emotional and social support. For example, Edstrom and Galbraith (1977) suggested that the transferring of employees to positions at the various operating sites of geographically dispersed organizations functions, in part, to make them less likely to build connections outside the organization that may be distracting or that may serve to compromise their complete and undivided devotion. Finally, there is some evidence that reward systems (including promotions and merit pay) that link performance to rewards will tend to make employees more committed (Dreher, 1982). Many of these commitment builders are more deliberate than others, and some of them can be very subtle. The point is that organized activity requires commitment among organizational members (D. Katz, 1964), so organizational procedures are necessary to generate and sustain such loyalty.

Several researchers have shown that in addition to active and deliberate organizational procedures for building commitment, other factors can contribute to it: factors related to the employees themselves, to their jobs, as well as to other elements of the work environment (e.g., Angle and Perry, 1982; Morris and Sherman, 1981; Steers, 1977). For example, in a study of scientists, engineers, and hospital employees, Steers (1977) found that individual needs for achievement, education, and age were associated with commitment to their organizations. (Education was inversely correlated: Higher levels of education were related to lower levels of commitment. This is a common phenomenon among professional employees, whose loyalty is devoted to the profession first and to the employer second.) Pro-organizational attitudes of the person's work group were associated with greater commitment. Jobs that permitted the employee greater degrees of voluntary interaction with co-workers, and jobs that permitted employees to understand how their work related to the jobs done by others in the organization, also seemed to be conducive to commitment (probably through the satisfaction these job characteristics fostered). However, Steers' (1977) results showed that certain work-related experiences were more powerful as predictors of commitment than were either the personal, job, or other organizational factors considered. Specifically, Steers found that positive group attitudes among one's peers, feelings that the organization had met the person's prior expectations, feelings that the organization could be relied on to carry out its commitments to its personnel, and feelings that the individual was of some importance to the organization collectively seemed to be the most important influences on commitment levels. Similar results were found in separate studies by Angle and Perry (1982), Buchanan (1974), and Morris and Sherman (1981). For the sake of instilling and maintaining commitment, these results are encouraging to the manager because they suggest that commitment can, in fact, be built and that it is not going to be determined simply by the inherent characteristics of employees.

A number of work-related experiences have been shown to foster organizational commitment, such as confirmation of preemployment expectations (Arnold and Feldman, 1982), job satisfaction (O'Reilly and Caldwell, 1981), participation in decision making (Rhodes and Steers, 1981), role clarity and freedom from conflict (Jamal, 1984), and organizational dependency or concern for employees (Steers, 1977). As pointed out by Meyer and Allen (1988), however, most of these early studies were cross-sectional, so the direction of the causality is hard to determine. In other words, such research designs do not permit us to discern whether job satisfaction causes organizational commitment, or vice versa. (Another possibility is that both variables are the consequences of one or more other systemic variables, such as organizational policies, leadership style, or whatever.)

One work-related experience that seems to have definite positive impact on organizational commitment early in a person's career is the nature of the early assignments they are given on being hired. Two related studies of Canadian university graduates by Meyer and Allen (1987, 1988), for example, found that measures of self-expression (being allowed to be one's own person), participation in decision making, and confirmed preentry expectations during the first month after being hired were positively related to organizational commitment later (after 6 and 11 months). These two studies both employed longitudinal designs, allowing for more confidence in the causal conclusions reached than is the case with cross-sectional designs. Other, earlier studies that tried to link early experiences with commitment much later in employees' tenure with employers have failed to find such an effect, so the impact may erode after a year or so on the job (Meyer and Allen, 1987, 1988). The critical thing, then, seems to be that managers must be clear about what employees can expect on the job, before they are hired, and then assure that early job assignments both fulfill those expectations and permit the employee to express herself in the planning and execution of her work, especially during the critical first month or two of employment (Meyer and Allen, 1987, 1988; Wanous, 1980).

The Evidence on Organizational Commitment

Earlier we noted that employers attempt to generate and sustain high commitment because many of them believe that high commitment yields high business benefits. Is this actually the case? Since an earlier examination of the matter (Pinder, 1984), considerable effort has been invested to confirm or disconfirm the validity of people's beliefs about the benefits of high commitment. As might be expected, the evidence does not support most of the popular beliefs and expectations (Mathieu and Zajac, 1990).

Commitment and Performance

First, there is no evidence for a simple, strong, overall relationship between organizational commitment and job performance (Mathieu and Zajac, 1990; Mowday et al., 1982). However, when the general notion of commitment is dissembled, there is some support for the notion that certain varieties of commitment may have different relationships with employee performance (see the discussion above of varieties of commitment). Hence, Meyer et al. (1989) found, as they had hypothesized, that affective commitment (that which is characterized by positive beliefs and attitudes about the organization) was correlated with performance, whereas continuance commitment (which is based on economic necessity and side bets) was inversely correlated with performance. Affective commitment is also positively related to organizational citizenship behavior (see Organ, 1990).

Commitment and Withdrawal

A number of attempts have been made to link different types or elements of organizational commitment to different types of withdrawal behavior. A very recent example is provided by a study by Somers (1995), who found that affective commitment was the best predictor of the various forms of withdrawal considered (which included intentions to withdraw, turnover, and absenteeism). By comparison, normative commitment was associated only with intentions, and continuance commitment had no direct effects on any of the withdrawal variables studied. (The reader is referred to our earlier discussion of the three psychological bases of commitment.) However, most of the correlations found between commitment and leaving behavior have varied in size and strength and have depended in part on how one defines organizational commitment—as normative, affective, or continuance (Jaros, Jermier, Koehler, and Sincich, 1993), leading to at least two closer examinations using meta-analysis (A. Cohen, 1993; Mathieu and Zajac, 1990).

In one of these meta-analyses, as expected, A. Cohen (1993) found that the relationship between commitment and turnover was much stronger when the two variables were measured relatively close in time: When the time between the measurement of commitment and the observation of departure was longer, the relationships have been weaker. The reader will recall that we discussed this matter in chapter 9 in relation to the theory of reasoned action. In short, it seems clear that organizational commitment, in some of its various forms (as was discussed earlier), is predictive of employees' staying with or leaving their organizations. The effects of commitment, however, appear to be indirect (Jaros et al., 1993). That is, the effects of high or low commitment on turnover behavior seem to work through the person's *intentions* to withdraw (see Jaros et al., 1993, and recall the theory of reasoned action in chapter 9). If the intention to leave is not formed, the likelihood of leaving is low.

Mathieu and Zajac's (1990) meta-analysis confirmed the conclusions reached a decade earlier by Mowday et al. (1982), that there is very little relationship between organizational commitment and individual worker performance (see Mathieu and Zajac, 1990, p. 184). As in the case of A. Cohen's (1993) meta-analysis, there were significant inverse correlations between commitment and lateness, turnover and intention to turn over. High commitment was also associated with attendance. Although significant in statistical terms, none of the relationships in Cohen's study between commitment and withdrawal and attendance behaviors was large in magnitude.

In a recent summary of the link between commitment and withdrawal behaviors, Meyer and Allen (1997) state:

> On the basis of these findings, it might be tempting to conclude that if an organization's goal is to develop a stable workforce on whose continued membership it can count, any form of commitment will suffice. . . . [H]owever, we caution strongly against this conclusion unless employee retention is the organization's *only goal*. An emphasis on employee retention to the exclusion of performance is unlikely to characterize many organizations. Indeed, it is now widely recognized that some voluntary turnover is helpful, rather than harmful, to the organization in that it includes resignations from employees who perform poorly or are disruptive. . . . Most organizations—and most managers—want much more from committed employees than simply their continued membership in the organization. (p. 26)

A comparison of the general findings of studies that consider constructs at the most general, undifferentiated levels (e.g., Mathieu and Zajac, 1990) with more fine-grained analyses such as that of Meyer et al. (1989), which look at the more precise subconstructs, highlights the importance of defining constructs carefully and precisely before expecting to find relationships among variables, such as commitment and performance (Schwab, 1980). We saw the same issue arise earlier in this chapter in connection with the long-sought-after linkage between job satisfaction and job performance (see C. D. Fisher, 1980). Morrow (1983) is responsible for first pointing out the multidimensionality of commitment; the wisdom of her observation and argument set the stage for the deliberate examination of *elements* of the overall construct in relation to performance by Meyer et al. (1989). There is a lesson to be learned.

Costs to Employees of High Commitment

In the foregoing sections, we examined the value of high worker commitment from the organization's point of view. What about the individual's perspective? People who become highly committed often tend to anthropomorphize or reify their organizations. We noted earlier in this book that although organizations are made up of human beings, they are not themselves human beings. Organizations are complex social systems that structure themselves and behave so as to survive. They do not have memories, and they do not have hearts. Senior managers and executives may be capable of remembering who deserves support and loyal treatment for jobs done well in the past, but senior executives come and go. Loyalty earned during one era can lose all value as new managerial regimes evolve. The survival of the organization is tantamount; if it is expedient to continue to support the faithful servants of the past, they will be supported. But when economic or other exigencies arise to threaten the survival or effectiveness of an organization, the highly committed individual's loyalty is often unrequited, and the individual may be left with organization-specific skills that are limited and that restrict her mobility to find new employment (Randall, 1987).

The author was personally acquainted with the senior executive of a large foreign airline who devoted most of his adult life to the profitability and effectiveness of the firm. The executive's hard work led to a stroke at age 46, although he eventually recovered most of his physical abilities and all of his mental skills. The company kept him on, but organizational policies requiring that he have his health examined by corporate doctors (rather than local doctors) precipitated a second stroke 12 years later. Obeying the firm's orders rather than acting according to his own best interest, the executive undertook to travel halfway around the world for a medical check, despite his protestations that his health was poor at that time and that it would be further threatened by a trip of such demanding proportions. His local doctors were able to perform the necessary work, making the journey unnecessary. The trip killed the executive, and his wife was granted a small settlement. The high levels of commitment the executive had to the airline and the obedience that derived from that commitment compelled him to pursue corporate advice that was not in the best interest of his health.

Aside from the possibility that commitment may not be reciprocated by one's organization, leaving the person abandoned in hard times, there is the issue, of course, of the nature of the organizational goals to which individuals commit themselves. Clearly, if a person becomes enthralled by the goals of an organization, the legality and the morality of those goals have important implications for the committed employee (Y. Weiner, 1982). Many cases of corporate corruption and crime have been perpetrated by highly committed employees whose zealous pursuit of their employer's goals required them to engage in illegal and immoral activities in which they probably would not have otherwise engaged.

Two authors have recently advanced the idea that work organizations can be seen as addictive substances, and that adherence to the goals and work expectations of these organizations can result in a condition of process addiction for employees (Schaef and Fassel, 1988). According to these authors:

> Nothing in and of itself is addictive. *Anything* can be addictive when it becomes so central in one's life that one feels that life is not possible without the substance or process. Organizations function as the addictive substance in the lives of many people. We recog-

nized [in our work] that for many people, the workplace, the job, and the organization were the central foci of their lives. Because the organization was so primary in their lives, because they were totally preoccupied with it, they began to lose touch with other aspects of their lives and gradually gave up what they knew, felt, and believed. (p. 119)

The point is this: Organizations require the commitment of their members in order to survive, so they do what they can to develop and foster it. But economic necessities can force even the most benevolent of employers to lay off, or otherwise abandon, those who have helped to make them effective. Even in Japan, where loyalty to one's organization is an inherent part of the culture, managers and employees at all levels have been laid off, North American style, as the economic advantage previously enjoyed by Japanese industry has declined over the years (e.g., Rifkin, 1995, p. 105; Watanabe, 1996). In short, although commitment is necessary for the organization's survival, it may or may not be best for a person's long-term interests, notwithstanding all the things our parents told us.

Romzek (1989) has pursued the old hypothesis that beneficial experiences at one's work can "spill over" and have a positive influence on a person's nonwork life. She has reported a study in which she followed a panel of 485 public employees through two waves of data collection, in 1982 and then again in 1984. Of interest to Romzek in this longitudinal project was whether the consequences of employee commitment are positive or negative on nonwork and career satisfactions. Although the effects were not strong, she found consistent support for the proposition that organizational commitment has positive benefit for people's lives outside the employment relationship, in areas such as satisfaction with their families, the cities in which they lived, their friendships and hobbies, and so on. She also found that high levels of organizational commitment as measured in 1982 were predictive of high levels of job satisfaction and career satisfaction two years later. One of the interpretations Romzek placed on her findings is that people tend to possess a disposition toward either positive or negative attitudes in life in general, and that these predispositions cover most or all aspects of a person's life, including work and nonwork activities. This dispositional hypothesis was discussed earlier in this chapter; there is no need to review it again here (see George, 1992; Judge, 1992).

Multiple, Conflicting Commitments?

One interesting consequence of extreme levels of organizational commitment may be reduced levels of commitment to other sources of support (as mentioned earlier). Sometimes this can be dysfunctional for the organization involved. For example, Rotondi (1975) found that research and development engineers who were more committed to their organization tended to be less creative and innovative, probably because devotion to one's scientific discipline can often clash with devotion to one's employer (see H. Shepard, 1956).

On the other hand, some feel that work organizations represent arenas for multiple forms of commitment for the employees involved. Hence, according to Reichers (1985), many employees experience allegiance to the goals, products and services, values, or people associated with multiple constituencies associated with their workplaces, such as unions, suppliers, customers, managers, professional associations, and so on. Therefore, the nature of the "commitment" experienced by any one person is likely to be entirely different from that experienced by another, because the foci of the commitment(s) vary from person to person. "Thus one individual's 'organizational commitment' may be primarily a function of the perception that the organization is dedicated to high quality products at a reasonable price: another person's commitment may depend to a great extent on the individual's belief that the organization espouses humanistic values towards [its] employees" (Reichers, 1985, p. 473).

Taking the multiple constituencies concept a step further, T.E. Becker (1992) has argued that we should differentiate between the foci of commitment, meaning the various individuals and groups to whom an employee might be attached, and the bases of commitment, the motives that explain the attachment (recall the three bases mentioned above: compliance, identification, and internalization). The reason for the argument is that attachment to foci may be predictive of different organizational outcomes than is attachment, which is predicated on different psychological "bases."

In fact, Becker was able to demonstrate that this may be the case. He found negative correlations between people's commitment to their organizations, work groups, and supervisors, and their intentions to quit. In other words, attachment to the various groups tended to reduce a person's desire to leave an organization. At the same time, he found positive correlations between these interpersonally based bonds and job satisfaction and the occurrence of prosocial behaviors of the sort we discussed earlier in the chapter.

Different results were found when the focus turned to the psychological bases for organizational commitment. Becker assessed the employees' levels of compliance, identification, and internalization (see O'Reilly and Chatman, 1986). As predicted, when the basis for commitment was either identification or internalization, higher levels of job satisfaction and prosocial behavior resulted, while commitment based on compliance was associated with higher levels of intention to leave the organization. In short, it appears that the global concept of organizational commitment is, in fact, a blend of attachments to various groups and individuals, on the one hand, and an array of psychological dynamics, on the other—a sort of apples and oranges concept in totality. The work of Reichers (1985) and, particularly, of T. E. Becker (1992) points to the wisdom of disentangling the foci of commitment (the people to whom we are committed) from the bases of the commitment (the psychological motives for the attachments). For as O'Reilly and Chatman (1986) have shown, different psychological bases for one's attachment to an organization can result in entirely different outcome dynamics for people.

Dual Commitment to an Employer and a Union

The issue of multiple loyalties and commitments takes on a special meaning in the context of unionized work settings. Can a member of a union be organizationally committed to both the company and the union? The "dispositional" school of thought described earlier suggests that people who are positively disposed to life in general (or negatively so disposed, on the other hand) should be capable of being devoted both to the company or agency that employs them as well as to the union that represents them under a collective agreement. What does the evidence say?

For decades, researchers had a hard time determining whether dual (union *and* company) commitment was anything more than an aggregate of the two separate forms of commitment (see Bemmels, 1995). The ins and outs of the issue are beyond our purpose here. Nevertheless, Bemmels (1995) addressed the question head-on and demonstrated that dual commitment to one's union *and* to one's employer *is* a distinct construct, with explanatory power beyond that of separate commitments to one's company and to one's union. In other words, Bemmels states, dual commitment to union and company is not simply an epiphenomenon. In short, Bemmels' research provided a conceptual base that permits substantive research on dual commitment to proceed.

Accordingly, one interesting study of nearly 300 blue-collar workers found that employees who had once been members of the union but who had subsequently withdrawn their memberships were less committed to both the union and to the employer. In addition, the correlation between the two commitment measures used in the project (toward the union and toward the company) correlated more highly among this group (the leavers) than they did among either of the other two groups (people who were active members and people who had never been members). Even though all the employees in the study received the benefits of union membership, regardless of whether they were members, those who were members had the greatest commitment to the union. The authors concluded from these results that efforts by unions to enhance commitment among nonmembers must go further than the negotiation of agreements for all, members and nonmembers alike (Conlon and Gallagher, 1987). The group of workers who had never been members of the union reported the highest levels of intrinsic satisfaction, extrinsic satisfaction, and commitment to the employer. Finally, the overall correlation between the two measures of commitment in this sample of 300 employees was 0.22—statistically significant but not very large in absolute value. The corresponding correlations among the members, nonmembers, and former members were 0.14, 0.08, and 0.48, pointing out the key message of this study: The relationship between commitment to the union and commitment to the company must take into account the different membership statuses of the people involved. Only in closed shops where union membership is mandatory will the employees be homogeneous enough to make general statements about dual loyalty safe.

Another study also demonstrated that employees are capable of holding dual loyalties (to employers and to unions, simultaneously) *if* certain conditions are in place. In other words, whether dual loyalty is possible depends on certain considerations. In this project Angle and Perry (1986) measured both company commitment and union commitment among a sample of 1,057 rank-and-file employees of 28 separate municipal bus companies in the United States. Angle and Perry predicted—and found—that dual commitment would be most likely in those work settings in which the prevailing labor–management climate was positive. They also found, as expected, that the strength of the correlation between the two forms of commitment was higher among workers who were active participants in the union. In summary, people can be committed to more than one constituency at the workplace, so thinking about "commitment to work" or "organizational commitment" as a unitary concept is futile and overly simplistic.

Gender and Organizational Commitment

Some people have thought that there may be gender differences in the propensity of people to become committed to their work organizations. One theory has it that women may be less committed than men to employers because women's first forum for loyalty is the home; career is second (Loscocco, 1990). This theory is based primarily on affective commitment, as opposed to either normative or continuance commitment. An alternative view postulates that women are more committed to employers than men are, although their commitment is of the continuance variety: Women are bound by necessity and side bets to an employer once a job relationship has begun. The reasoning behind this idea is that women often must try harder than men to secure jobs in the first place and that they have fewer alternatives should they chose to leave.

Chusmir (1982) has suggested that many of the common stereotypes about women at work—particularly beliefs about their longevity on the job, their comparative rates of illness and absence, and the benefits that can be derived from training women—are myths, and that it is not a matter of gender per se but of a number of other variables. For example, men and women are likely to exhibit the same rates of absenteeism and turnover when they are in similar circumstances. Generally, women hold more low-level positions than men, and turnover and absenteeism are more frequent among low-level jobs. Hence, Chusmir argues, whether they are women or men, people in such jobs are more likely than people in higher-level jobs to be absent and to quit.

It should be noted that Chusmir (1982) was focusing on what we call in this book "job involvement," not on organizational commitment per se. Job commitment, for Chusmir, is "an attitude or an orientation toward the job that links or attaches the identity of the person to the job" (p. 596), as opposed to the organization per se. Nevertheless, we can learn from his analysis. Chusmir develops a comprehensive model of factors that are associated with commitment and shows that the model can be applicable to either men or women. The model included variables and considerations both within and outside the place of work. The similarity breaks down somewhat when one considers the gender-role conflicts that woman may suffer (and that few men encounter), and that men in our society are expected to be less in charge of the family and more highly committed to work outside the home. However, if a woman does not encounter these gender-role expectations and is able to hold the same jobs as a man does, for whatever reason, there is no reason to expect that the nature or levels of job commitment should vary by gender, according to Chusmir (1982). To balance these findings, however, a large-scale meta-analysis of 27 separate studies, encompassing more than 14,000 employees, failed to find any systematic differences between men and women in affective commitment (although continuance commitment was not studied) (Aven, Parker, and McEvoy, 1993).

The Past, Present, and Future of Organizational Commitment

It was an article of faith among many people of previous generations that being committed to one's employer was a wise and proper thing to do (Randall, 1987). The virtues of organizational commitment seemed self-evident—again, if not for the instrumental benefits that would accrue, but also because it was somehow inherently virtuous. This sentiment was summarized in an important book of the mid-1950s, *The Organization Man* (W.H. Whyte, 1956).

A few generations of experience in North America of intermittent recessions and the attendant layoffs, cutbacks, downsizing, and "right-sizing" that comes with recessions has seen a change in the common values as they pertain to organizational commitment. More than a decade ago, for example, three influential American scholars in the area of work motivation and commitment wrote that they anticipated a marked decrease in the commitment of North American employees to their companies. Among the reasons they cited to back their prediction were that more people would be wanting jobs, more people would be wanting *good* jobs, increasing demands for personal growth and personal freedom, greater expectations for immediate need gratification, greater concern for minority rights, greater numbers of dual-career families, people's demands for more than work in their lives, better awareness of job alternatives than in the past, and, interestingly, a sort of acceptance at societal levels that low commitment is legitimate: If it were to become a cultural norm to reject high organizational commitment, more people would feel free to do so (Mowday, Steers, and Porter, 1982).

Now, in the late-1990s, a trend away from organizational commitment is quite clear, and scholars are predicting that the trend will continue. Parks and Kidder (1995), for example, cite fierce competition among companies as well as among whole economies in days of free trade blocks and international competition as causes of continued layoffs and right-sizing (this decade's euphemism for layoffs). They also note high fixed costs and "bloated bureaucracies" as sources of letting people go. They observe that the amount of work that must be accomplished in many organizations does not diminish after people are laid off, so surviving workers are expected to work harder and longer hours to pick up the slack (see Schor, 1991). All of these factors militate against high organizational commitment.

Longitudinal studies conducted throughout North America by Hay Management Consultants confirm these impressions (Grey and Johnson, 1988; G. C. Johnson and Grey, 1988a, 1988b). Their work suggests that a major decline in organizational commitment has occurred, at least in large part, because of a sharp decline in promotional opportunities for North American employees, blue collar and white collar alike. The causes for the reduction in promotion opportunities are similar to those cited by Parks and Kidder (1995): high rates of competition both within companies for jobs and between companies for markets. Increases in computer and information technology and leaner, meaner organizational designs that reduce the numbers of people required to get the work done. The Hay people also note that there has been a disgruntlement factor as well, caused by people feeling not well informed about their chances and career possibilities (G. C. Johnson and Grey, 1988a). That is, employers are seen as not having responded to the anxieties caused by reduced promotion opportunities with commensurate levels of openness with employees—openness with regard to issues such as "reasons behind business decisions," "where the company is headed," and "how can I best improve my job performance?" (G. C. Johnson and Grey, 1988a). In the face of all these pressures it is little wonder that people turn away from a belief in the inherent virtue of organizational commitment and toward an ethic of "looking out for No. 1."

Meyer and Allen (1997), two scholars who have championed the commitment construct over the past 15 years, take a more positive view of the value of commitment in the future. They note that although many organizations are becoming smaller, they are not disappearing altogether. Therefore, they must rely on core groups of devoted people who will offer the energy and citizenship behavior that has been so important to organizations in the past. Second, even though many organizations are outsourcing much of their work to other organizations, they must be concerned about the commitment of the personnel in these other organizations. "Admittedly, the commitment may be different, perhaps being of a shorter duration and with a focus on a contract or project rather than on the organization itself" (Meyer and Allen, 1997, p. 5).

Finally, Meyer and Allen (1997) believe that commitment develops naturally in people. Not to be committed to *something* is to be alienated. So workers who do not commit to employers will naturally seek commitment with some other source of gratification, such as a hobby, a church, a friend, a job, or an occupation. Hence, even if *organizational commitment* itself declines, it will remain important for social scientists to pursue an understanding of commitment in its varied forms.

Consequences of Low Commitment

We have discussed how, in part by definition, organizational commitment is related to the propensity to stay in the employment of a company. On the flip side, low commitment, again in part by its very definition, is predictive of voluntary turnover. But what are the effects of low commitment among employees who stay and maintain the employment relationship? Two writers on the subject suggest that employees in such circumstances alter the quality of the work they contribute in exchange for the poor treatment they associate with their low commitment (Parks and Kidder, 1995). There is a wide range of service quality that an employee may contribute. At one end of the scale is altruism and civic virtue. In the middle of the scale are conscientiousness and simple compliance. At the other end are shirking, negligence, and even theft, harassment, and overt damage. Workers who feel violated by their employers will manifest more behaviors toward the latter end of this scale and fewer of the positive behaviors that characterize the former end of the scale (Parks and Kidder, 1995).

Elsewhere in this book we have noted that theft by employees of employers' supplies, materials, and money costs more than $40 billion annually in the United States; there is no doubt that low commitment, especially when it erodes into resentment, frustration, and a desire to "strike back," accounts not only for much of the theft we have cited, but also much of the overt damage, sabotage, negativism, and grudging compliance that we observe every day among turned-off employees. So it may still be a matter of opinion and of one's values whether there is anything inherently valuable or virtuous about high commitment, but it is much more than a matter of opinion when we objectively look at the consequences in our economies and our culture of low organizational commitment.

Conclusion: The Ebb and Flow of Organizational Commitment

The author has been teaching students in several North American business schools for 25 years, observing the changing attitudes of students regarding life's important issues. It is true that values swing like a pendulum on most issues, the issue of commitment being no exception. A few years ago, it was heretical to suggest to business school students that to become committed to an employer was foolish. In recent years, young people who are leaving college and joining the workforce for the first time seem to be fully aware of the issues of loyalty and commitment. Many or most of these students have known someone who was the victim of harsh or inconsiderate treatment at the hands of an organization. Most have known people who were laid off because of downsizings, mergers, and other corporate necessities for survival. Whether it is wise or noble for a person to expect commitment from an employer, and whether it is fair of an employer to expect loyalty from its workers are matters of opinion, rooted in the values each of us hold. The author hopes only that the foregoing discussion will bring the matter of commitment, its costs and its benefits, to a conscious level for consideration by readers of this book. We turn next to a study of a similar work-related attitude, job involvement.

JOB INVOLVEMENT

A third psychological construct related to work behavior that has received considerable attention in recent years is job involvement. There have been a number of attempts to define this term and to differentiate it from related constructs such as job satisfaction and intrinsic motivation (Lawler and Hall, 1970; Lodahl and Kejner, 1965; Saleh and Hosek, 1976). *Job involvement,* loosely defined, has to do with the strength of the relationship between a person's work and his or her self-concept. Specifically, a person is said to be involved in his job if he (1) participates in it actively, (2) holds it as a central life interest, (3) perceives performance at it as central to his self-esteem, and (4) sees performance on it as consistent with his self-concept.

People who are highly job involved tend to be obsessed with their work. When they perform poorly, they feel poorly. They like others to know them for their work and to know that they do it well. For a highly job-involved person, work is one of the most important aspects of life, if not the most important. There is some evidence that job-involved people tend to be more satisfied with their work (Gorn and Kanungo, 1980) and more intrinsically motivated (Lawler and Hall, 1970), but it is important to repeat that involvement, satisfaction, and intrinsic motivation are distinct constructs (Lawler and Hall, 1970). Moreover, this construct has to do with one's commitment to her job, not to her employer per se, and these two forms of commitment are only slightly related to one another (Stevens, Beyer, and Trice, 1978; Y. Weiner and Vardi, 1980).

Causes of Job Involvement

What determines the level of involvement a person has in his job? A number of studies suggest that as was the case in the determinants of commitment, characteristics of both the individual and of the organization must be taken into account. For example, Rabinowitz and Hall (1977) found that job involvement was correlated with the strength of the person's growth needs (see chapter 7) and with the strength of one's belief in the "Protestant work ethic." In addition, the length of time the person was on the job, as well as the scope provided by the job, were positively associated with involvement. Another study found that employees whose jobs served to satisfy their most salient needs (regardless of whether these were intrinsic or extrinsic) were higher in both involvement with the particular jobs they held at the time, as well as with work in general (Gorn and Kanungo, 1980). In a third study it was found that employees who participated more in the decision making related to their jobs were more involved in those jobs (A. Siegel and Ruh, 1973).

In short, the level of involvement people feel with regard to their jobs is probably determined by the interaction of their own needs and values with a variety of features of the job and the job setting. Consequently, we might assume that job involvement may be somewhat manipulable through the enactment of appropriate organizational policies and procedures.

Consequences of Moderate Job Involvement

As we did in our discussion of commitment, we can suitably ask whether job involvement is a good thing; and as before, we must conclude that the answer may depend on who provides it. There is some evidence that job-involved employees tend to be more satisfied with their jobs than are employees who are less job involved (Cheloha and Farr, 1980; Gannon and Hendrickson, 1973; Gorn and Kanungo, 1980; Lawler and Hall, 1970). Similarly, there is suggestive evidence that job-involved employees are likely to be somewhat happier with their organizations (Schwyhart and Smith, 1972), as well as more committed to them and less absent from them (Cheloha and Farr, 1980), although as mentioned earlier, the relationships are mixed and of only moderate strength (Gorn and Kanungo, 1980). This means that it is quite possible for employees to enjoy their jobs but not feel fully involved in them. Or it is possible for people to be attached to their jobs and to enjoy them but not be very committed to their employing organization. This is often the case with managerial, professional, technical, and other highly skilled employees. Physicians working under terribly constrained budgets and limited resources in equipment and supplies often are terribly unhappy with their jobs, totally uncommitted to the hospitals in which they function, yet remain unflaggingly committed to their chosen profession of medicine.

Is there any relationship between job involvement and employee effort and performance? Very little research has been reported on this issue, so caution is necessary. One study found moderately strong linkages between involvement and self-report measures of effort and performance (as measured by salary) among a group of insurance sales representatives who worked on commission (Gorn and Kanungo, 1980). It is critical to note that virtually all of the studies reported above were conducted in a cross-sectional manner, making it impossible when there were relationships observed to determine which variables were causal and which were the results of the workings of others. For example, are highly involved employees more likely to devote higher levels of effort to their jobs because of the fulfillment it provides them? Or is it the other way around: Could more highly involved employees become more satisfied with their jobs because their devotion to them results in mastery and feelings of achievement and competence? What seems most plausible is that certain characteristics of employees, their jobs, and their organizations are likely to be responsible for causing levels of commitment, satisfaction, and involvement; these in turn both influence, and are influenced by, the person's performance level. Therefore, managers may be able to affect this cluster of events and associations by thoughtful application of enlightened policies and practices, but it is probable that the characteristics of their employees will limit (or magnify) the impact that they can have on these various outcome variables.

In simple terms, the job involvement construct has to do with how seriously people take their work. Therefore, it would follow that people who are characteristically high in job involvement may be more prone to permit the stressors they encounter on their jobs to "get to them," to be more deleterious to their well-being, than would be the case for people who are lower in job involvement. In fact, a study by Frone, Russell, and Cooper (1995) suggests that this may be the case. After controlling for a set of sociological variables that is normally associated with poor health, the researchers found that job involvement exacerbated the relationship between job stressors and employee health. Although the results were mixed across the various dependent variables studied (such as depression, alcohol use, and physical symptoms), they are consistent with our understanding of the job involvement construct as well as with common sense. People who "eat, breathe, and sleep their work" seem more susceptible to health difficulties, particularly if they do not engage in practices that are designed to assuage tension and relieve the stress that their work entails for them. What about people who are exceptionally committed to their work? We turn next to an examination of people who become addicted to their work, commonly referred to as *workaholics.*

Work Addiction: Involvement and Commitment in the Extreme

Before we leave our discussion of the benefits of job involvement, we should ask whether extreme levels of job involvement, like extreme levels of commitment, might have any unfortunate consequences for the employee. The person on the street often uses the term *workaholism* to refer to the construct labeled job involvement by students of organizational science. What is workaholism? Killinger (1991) points out that not everyone who works hard is a workaholic. She notes that "work is essential for our well-being. Through work we define ourselves, develop our strengths, and take our places in society. Work gives us satisfaction, a sense of accomplishment, and mastery over problems. It provides us with a sense of direction, and gives us goals to reach and hurdles to overcome" (p. 5). For Killinger (1991), work *addiction* is a different matter. It usually happens to middle-class people who are necessarily driven by economic necessity. A workaholic is "a person who gradually becomes emotionally crippled and addicted to control and power in a compulsive drive to gain control and success" (p. 6). Such people are competitive and driven to acquire the "fix" of fame, recognition, and success that comes with hard work and long hours. Without this fix, the workaholic feels pain in the form of anger, hurt, guilt, and fear. Working becomes a state of mind more than simply a job. Working permits people an overly inflated sense of responsibility and an escape from intimacy with other people (Killinger, 1991).

Workaholics are people who live to work. They plan their work during periods when they are otherwise at play, such as during holidays and vacations (Killinger, 1991). Machlowitz (1980) estimates that about 5 percent of the adult population are workaholics, but that the proportion of the workforce who are workaholics is probably higher, since, almost by definition, these people tend not to be unemployed. Although not all hard workers are workaholics, all workaholics are hard workers. They plan their lives around their jobs, and love it. Both men and women can be workaholics, although the difficulties faced by female workaholics are different (and sometimes worse) than those faced by male workaholics. Many workaholics contribute to the effectiveness of their organizations at levels that are detrimental to their own health (Caplan and Jones, 1975) but don't mind doing so and are often not aware that they are doing so (Killinger, 1991).

The author is not aware of any research that has attempted to apportion workaholic tendencies between people's organizational commitment and their job involvement, as we have defined these phenomena here. Research on workaholics suggests that people who work too hard for their own good can be driven by either high commitment to their institutions, or to their occupations, or to some blends of both. The precise origins of the phenomenon are less important than the consequences of workaholism for the people who are afflicted as well as for those who love them or work with them.

Types of Work Addictions

According to Fassel (1990), there are at least four categories of workaholics. The reader will notice the similarities among the names of the categories, the characteristics of the people in the categories, and the nouns and verbs that are used in common reference to addictions and addicts related to other substances and processes. There is the *compulsive worker,* the person who is simply driven to work all the time. This is the category we usually associate with workaholism. They keep long and strange hours, they never plan vacations, and they seldom make plans in their outside lives because they are always concerned about what might come up for them at work. But these people are not the only category or type of workaholic, according to Fassel (1990).

There are also *binge workers,* people who work with high intensity when they work, even if it is only at intervals. When work has to be done, they are obsessed and driven to get it done. Fassel likens the patterns of these people to those of binge drinkers, who "save it up" and then go on working with nothing else in their lives for short, sharp spurts of it.

A third category are referred to by Fassel (1990) as *closet workers.* People in this category have "a niggling awareness that" something is dysfunctional about their work style (p. 20). They tend to make promises to reform themselves but seldom keep their promises. They hide work-related files and problems away similar to the ways that alcoholics hide bottles of liquor in closets, basements, and nooks and crannies. They often pretend not to be working, as when they are on "vacation," but they are thinking, dreaming, and making plans about their work. They are the types of people who take cellular telephones with them to museums, libraries, and gymnasiums, into places and into activities where, otherwise, they might be thought of as relaxing or not working. They are basically dishonest about their priorities and cheat in the way they relate to others about those priorities.

A fourth category of workaholic identified by Fassel (1990) are people whom she refers to as *work anorexics.* They are people who act as if the way to get out of their problems (analogous to overeaters) is by not doing it at all. Their theme, according to Fassel (1990, p. 23), is "I'm darned good at what I do, but I seldom do it." Work becomes such an addiction to these people that they do everything they can to avoid it, to pretend that it is not a problem for them. They procrastinate and then feel guilty about their procrastination. So they place themselves in positions of lateness, deadlines, and pressures where they must produce to survive and to save face. They force schedules upon themselves because pacing and spacing of assignments fail to provide the thrill of an emergency in which the work must get done at once. They like to "slip under the gate just as it is closing," according to Fassel (1990, p. 24).

Is There a Problem?

In an economy worried about the motivation of its workforce to sustain itself and be competitive, we can ask: Is workaholism a good thing? A quarter of a century of research and writing on the issue has brought mixed answers (see Fassel, 1990; Killinger,

1991; Machlowitz, 1980; Oates, 1971). Without workaholics, many organizations could not function as effectively as they do (Oates, 1971). Workaholics are always there to backstop the errors made by others. (Of course, they are also often the cause of many of these errors themselves.) They often make up for the low commitment of others. They can be counted on to perform the jobs others avoid, and generally, to attack them with passion. They work hard; they provide management more "bang for the buck." Every person reading this volume must be familiar with at least one workaholic, as well as with how others around that person have grown dependent on him, or her, in the job setting.

There has been disagreement over the years among people who have studied workaholics on the issue of whether they are healthy or normal. One early authority, for example, claims that workaholics are generally healthy and happy people (Machlowitz, 1980). On the other hand, it is common to pity workaholics, or even to look upon them with disdain, as if they are afflicted with some form of social or occupational disease. For example, H.S. Schwartz (1982) defines involvement as a manifestation of neurotic obsession/compulsion, while Schaef and Fassel (1988) and Fassel (1990) cast overly involved work as an addiction, a "process addiction that features all the common characteristics of other addictions." According to Schaef and Fassel (1988) and Fassel (1990), these symptoms include confusion, self-centeredness, dishonesty, perfectionism, a preoccupation with control, frozen feelings, ethical deterioration, stress, low self-esteem, an inability to relax, depression, negativism, and a variety of other forms of maladjustment. Workaholism is a major source of marital breakdown. It is a substitute for normal religious experiences for many who are afflicted by it (Killinger, 1991).

Most commonly, addicts of all types make great use of *denial:* They claim steadfastly that there is nothing wrong with them, that they have no problems (Fassel, 1990; Killinger, 1991). An interesting comment once made by a friend to this author about work addiction is that "people are workaholics who work harder than I do." In other words, for many hard-working persons, the pace they set and the goals they accomplish are, to them, defined as somehow "normal." Anyone else who significantly exceeds these standards is typically defined by anyone else as being abnormal, as being a workaholic.

Workaholics typically come from dysfunctional families, families in which behavior and interpersonal relations deviate from normal. Frequently, these families feature addiction to substances such as alcohol or drugs or to processes such as sex, perfectionism, or orderliness (Killinger, 1991). In fact, workaholism is often "the addiction of choice" of adult children of alcoholics (Schaef and Fassel, 1988). Typically, these people are better at work than they are at personal relationships, so they fill their lives with work—too much of it. Therefore, employees who are addicted to their work, in the extreme, are anything but healthy, according to Fassel (1990) and Schaef and Fassel (1988).

Machlowitz (1980) claims that while they spend long hours of intense effort at their jobs, workaholics are often very poor performers, for a variety of reasons. One reason is that they have an inherent aversion to delegating responsibilities to other people. They insist on maintaining control and would generally rather do everything themselves. As a result, they often spread themselves too thin and take on so many tasks that they simply cannot be effective at all of them, despite the long hours they spend at their work. Workaholics often try to create and foster the impression that they are indispensable (due to their reluctance to delegate, this is often the case). But much of the flurry surrounding them is artificial rather than truly warranted. Moreover, workaholics tend to intimidate and annoy others around them who are not so completely obsessed with work. As supervisors, they push their subordinates with impunity, often causing high levels of stress and low levels of job satisfaction among them, and sometimes driving away talented people. There is no cause to believe that the high levels of energy they expend necessarily result in greater levels of performance efficiency than would be attainable by working at more "normal" speeds. Workaholics often lose sight of work priorities; in their attempts to get everything done, they often get little actually accomplished. Their obsession with their own time and time schedules means they frequently fail to honor the time requirements of others; they are characteristically late for meetings and frequently leave in the middle of meetings. Cast in the terms we discussed in chapter 8, workaholics can be major sources of frustration for people around them, both on the job and off.

Fassel's work indicates that workaholics become hooked on both a physiological (or "substance") level but also on a process or activity level, making this form of addiction especially pernicious. The substance is adrenaline; the rush comes when the person is under pressure. The process aspect comes from the acts of applying effort, of spending the hours and of feeling the thrill of accomplishment when (and if) it arrives, just in time. Like others writing on this topic, Fassel (1990) use the terms *workaholism* and *work addiction* interchangeably because they categorize the condition as they do other forms of addiction, as sharing many of the characteristics and problems seen in other addictions. What are some of these symptoms of work addiction that are so similar to other addictions to substances and processes?

Fassel argues that like other addictions, workaholism can be a one-way slide toward personal destruction. Combinations of the symptoms listed above can ultimately result in hospitalization, physical illness, and death. Workaholics kill themselves via stomach ailments, alcoholism, accidents brought on by physical fatigue, excessive smoking and eating, insomnia, and even suicide. Fassel (1990) argues that in our society, the syndrome can be especially perilous for women, especially women who try to establish and maintain occupations outside of the home. "A woman's work is never done . . ." (p. 53). She acknowledges that work addiction is gender neutral, though, in the sense that many men also become victims, although the specific tasks and role expectations placed on them (or which they place on themselves) are different in type, although not in ultimate effect. For many men in our culture, the self-concept of innate superiority must be fulfilled and maintained, according to Fassel (1990), so the drive to produce, to provide, can be constant and unrelenting. Space limitations prevent a full treatment of the theory and research evidence here; the interested reader is referred to Fassel (1990), Schaef and Fassel (1988), and Schor (1991).

So the prevailing current answer to the question: Is workaholism a good thing? seems to be a resounding "no!" Nevertheless, this author expects that we will see more and more of it in the future as the number of jobs available in our economies declines, as more people are put out of work, and as those who are employed hold onto their jobs tenaciously (see Bridges, 1994; Rifkin, 1995).

CONCLUSION

Employees' work attitudes are important both to the people who hold them and to the organizations that employ people. Although the connections are unpredictable, attitudes can result in behaviors that can have either positive or negative consequences for both people and organizations. Managers often assume that the connection between employee attitudes and behaviors is stronger than in fact it is, and sometimes they overreact to what they see as extreme attitudes of either positive or negative tone. Up to a certain point, both organizational commitment and job involvement are necessary and potentially beneficial for both employees and employers. In the extreme, however, too much commitment may make employees emotionally and occupationally vulnerable, and too much job involvement may result in the sorts of human consequences associated with workaholism. To date, however, there has been nothing to indicate that too much job satisfaction has any harmful effects, but we seem to be a long way from reaching the stage where, on a macro level, this will ever be the case. In the foreseeable future, a vast number of undesirable jobs will continue to need to be done (see Faltermayer, 1974).

Finally, it is important to note that the three job-related attitudes discussed in this chapter are not the only ones that have been investigated by organizational scientists. Job satisfaction, organizational commitment, and job involvement were singled out for discussion here both because they have been the subjects of considerable research in recent years and because they are important. It is critical to note that these three constructs do not exhaust all the possible forms that employee attitudes may take. Identified and articulated in the ways they have been presented here, these constructs represent only three of an infinite number of mental and visceral reactions people may have toward their work. In many ways, these concepts are arbitrary: Who is to say that they represent the most common or even the most important attitudes that can be found in the minds and hearts of working people? In short, the careful reader will pay attention to these three constructs as important but will realize that in many ways they represent the mental events of the researchers and scholars who have identified (created?) and discussed them (see Schwab, 1980).

Relationships among the Concepts

The various components of work commitment are thought of as conceptually distinct from one another, yet as interrelated in that they share some common bases conceptually and because a person who tends to be high on one of these dimensions will tend to be relatively high on the others (G. Blau and Paul, 1993; Morrow, 1983, 1993). One study of more than 700 U.S. men and women found that job satisfaction had a significant effect on job involvement, but the obverse was not the case (Mortimer and Lorence, 1989). Although the researchers failed to show that satisfaction at one time may predict levels of involvement four years later, their cross-sectional analysis did support a weak but significant satisfaction-causes-involvement connection. This particular paper is cited because it is typical of the many that have been conducted on these matters, as are the findings reported.

In fact, the empirically observed relationships among job satisfaction, organizational commitment, and motivation are so consistent (although not overwhelmingly high) that two reviewers have suggested that the three variables "may be conceived of as rather specific aspects of a more generalized affective response to the work environment" (Mathieu and Zajac, 1990). In other words, the phenomenological experiences that people have at their work during their careers may result, for many, in an overall positive or negative feeling about work and things related to it. This dispositional view was presented and discussed at length earlier in this chapter as well as in chapter 1. Some working people may not be able or willing to disentangle their feelings about their jobs from their beliefs and attitudes regarding their employers. That explanation may have a lot of merit; not everyone we study is as cerebral or as contemplative about work-related matters as organizational researchers wish them to be.[4] Another explanation is that organizational researchers may simply not be able to measure these various dimensions with sufficient validity and precision using the particular time sequences in longitudinal designs that are appropriate to the phenomena involved, to find any relationships that actually exist among these variables. Difficulties of this sort were introduced and discussed at length in chapter 2.[5]

The author suspects that the truth lies in some combination of these two explanations. There are plenty of intuitive grounds to believe that people who are satisfied with parts of their jobs may become committed to their employers, out of gratitude or for no particular reason, such that we would expect satisfied employees to be more committed employees. The causal connection may work the other way: People who, for whatever reason, are committed to their employers may tend to see their work as satisfying (Mathieu and Zajac, 1990). As is the case on many points throughout this book, the author suspects that the intuitive truth about matters related to work motivation may not be totally discernible by the crude tools of behavioral researchers. Hence in this case there is still just cause to expect causal relationships between motivation, commitment, and other job attitude variables, although the relationships may be complex and circular.

Before we leave our extended discussion of job satisfaction, organizational commitment, and job involvement, it is worth briefly considering how these concepts might interact in practice. Consider what it may be like for someone who is high in job involvement (meaning they live to work) but who is exceptionally dissatisfied with her company or with conditions of her current job. Consider the case of the person who is high in job involvement but who has no job or who is capable of holding only part-time work. People of this sort are commonplace in current work settings and are, by definition, cases of frustration (recall chapter 8). Futurists would suggest that cases such as these may be much more than commonplace in the next few years; they may become the norm. There will then be major consequences for people to redefine the concept of careers as we have known them, and for many people, there may be a regression to an increased importance to simple survival needs, to do "whatever work needs to be done" (Bridges, 1994).

---

[4]Nevertheless, at least two studies, involving different categories of workers, have found that measures of job involvement, organizational commitment, and job satisfaction are distinct from one another; that is, that the people studied did differentiate among the three forms of work-related attitudes (Brooke, Russell, and Price, 1988; Mathieu and Farr, 1991).

[5]On the other hand, some progress has been made: A recent study examined four possible causal models linking commitment and satisfaction (satisfaction causes commitment; commitment causes satisfaction; the two are related reciprocally; and that there is no simple bivariate relationship between the two constructs). The evidence supported the "commitment causes satisfaction" alternative (Vandenberg and Lance, 1992).

LOOKING AHEAD

In chapters 9 and 10 we introduced the cognitive approach to understanding work motivation and behavior. In chapter 9 we studied the nature and functioning of human beliefs and attitudes. In the current chapter we surveyed the scientific literature dealing with three important types of work-related attitudes: satisfaction, commitment, and involvement. While attitudes are not motivation, per se, attitudes can instigate behavior: Job attitudes can instigate work-related behaviors such as joining an organization, leaving it, staying with it, forming a trade union, working hard, stealing from the organization, and so on. Attitudes are slippery and hard to discern or observe directly. But job attitudes are common, powerful precursors to organizational action. They provide the basis for work motivation. In the following three chapters we present three separate bodies of formal theory of work motivation, all of which rely on the cognitive model of human functioning introduced in chapter 9.

CHAPTER

Equity, Justice, and Fairness in the Workplace

You remember Thurow's answer . . . you never expected justice from a company, did you? They have neither a soul to lose, nor a body to kick.
—Rev. Sydney Smith

Systematic interdependencies among people and social units following a norm of reciprocity are critical in keeping a society together. That is, *exchange* is the essence of social interaction. At some level, sooner or later, people expect to receive from one another goods, services, and social benefits commensurate in value with those they contribute and provide (Gouldner, 1960; Parsons and Shils, 1951). People like to be treated fairly in their exchanges with one another and develop norms concerning what is fair and what is unfair treatment.

The workplace is an important forum in which people experience the joys and miseries of fairness and unfairness in the exchange of their talents, efforts, and ideas for economic and noneconomic benefits. The norms of reciprocity and fairness that function in the greater society are critically important in the functioning of economic organizations such as businesses, government agencies, and other employment settings. According to one leading theorist in this area (Greenberg, 1990), people have a strong urge to see themselves and to be seen by others as fair. They will go to great lengths of self-image management to attain and maintain these perceptions. In fact, Greenberg (1988b) found that mangers deemed it more important to be seen as fair by co-workers than actually to be fair.

Distributive and Procedural Justice

This chapter deals with a variety of issues related to fairness, equity, and justice in the workplace. We begin with a study of the traditional body of theory and research on *equity* and *distributive justice*. These concepts have to do with the distribution of benefits and sanctions among people and deal with questions such as who is to receive how much, and how fairly are these outcomes distributed? As part of this discussion, we provide an extended treatment of the doctrine of comparable worth. In the second part of the chapter we move to an examination of *procedural justice,* which is concerned with the fairness of the policies and procedures by which people interact. We will see that not only are the official practices used to distribute rewards and punishment in organizations important, but that the nature of the interpersonal relationships during the administration of justice are important as well. (This is the domain referred to as *interactional justice.*) We end the chapter with a survey of a number of organizational practices, such as downsizing and firing, from the perspective of procedural justice. To begin, what is meant by the terms *fairness, justice,* and *equity?*

Defining Fairness, Justice, and Equity

According to R. L. Cohen (1991), justice is thought to exist when people receive those things they (and others around them) deserve or are entitled to. These receipts can be either benefits (such as pay increases) or burdens (such as a transfer to an undesirable city or region). Injustice involves a violation of a moral contract for goods, services, opportunities, or treatment. An employee who is hired by a large bank with the clear expectation that she will be moved quickly through a series of new and challenging jobs will feel a sense of injustice if these reassignments are not forthcoming (see Robinson and Rousseau, 1994, for an empirical example of the violation of such contracts). Generally, we follow the practice of Sheppard, Lewicki, and Minton (1992), who use the terms *justice* and *fairness* interchangeably, although, as we will see, many of the nuances associated with justice and fairness concern the procedures by which people are treated rather than (or in addition to) the outcomes of their treatment. The notion of equity is the most researched justice-related topic in the organizational sciences. So we begin our discussion with it.

EQUITY THEORY: THE MAINSTAY
OF DISTRIBUTIVE JUSTICE CONCEPTS

Professional athletes often make the news by demanding that their contracts be torn up before their terms expire. The reason for this apparent lack of respect for contract law usually involves feelings by these athletes that the previously agreed upon rates of pay are, by some standard, no longer "fair." If Michael Jordan is worth $25 million for a single year, the challenge is to decide what is "fair" or "equitable" for Shaquille O'Neal in a seven-year contract. These considerations are not unique to professional athletes. People hold beliefs about the value of their contributions at work and how well these contributions are recognized and rewarded. These beliefs are formed in a social context in which people compare how well they are being treated with how well they believe others are being treated. When people believe that relative to others, they are being undercompensated or somehow underrecognized, they become unhappy and motivated to do something about it. R. H. Smith (1991) argues that the primary emotion experienced at times like these is envy (see chapter 4). Professional athletes have been known to sit out entire seasons over contract disputes of this sort, and labor unions in many nonsports industries go on strike every year for similar reasons. In this chapter we describe a collection of theories generally and collectively referred to as *equity theory.* There are a variety of theories that fit under this general heading. Due to limitations of space, the discussion here will be general and relevant to all of them rather than devoted to a precise analysis of the nuances of each and the differences between them.[1]

The Elements of Equity Theory

Equity theory rests on three main assumptions (Carrell and Dittrich, 1978). First, the theory holds that people develop beliefs about what constitutes a fair and equitable return for their contributions to their jobs. Second, people tend to compare what they perceive to be the exchange they have with their employers with what they perceive to be the nature of the exchange *other individuals* have with their employers (although the employers being considered need not be one and the same). Finally, the theory holds that when people believe that their own treatment is not equitable relative to the exchange they perceive others to be making, they will be motivated to do something about it, as in the examples of the millionaire athletes mentioned earlier.

The theory states that individuals hold perceptions about the number and value of the contributions they make to their work, usually referred to as *inputs.* For example, people may consider the education and training they bring to their jobs, the number of hours they work, and how hard they try to perform. Different people tend to pay attention to different inputs, and there is a tendency for people to place greater emphasis on the inputs they have to offer (e.g., L. L. Cummings, 1980). For example, highly educated people often place great importance on their schooling, even in work contexts where what they have learned in college is not related to the nature of the work they do. The college graduate with a major in German literature, for example, may become frustrated when she learns that her degree is discounted by prospective employers seeking to hire computer operators. Equity theory assumes that people aggregate their perceived inputs into a sort of psychological total, representing the net value they believe they contribute to their jobs.

People also hold beliefs about the nature and quantity of the consequences or *outcomes* they receive as a result of doing their work. Pay, fringe benefits, job satisfaction, status, and opportunities to learn, as well as physical outcomes such as company cars, represent the range of things people might consider as outcomes. Different people tend to recognize different outcomes, depending on what their own jobs provide. For 115 years, members of Canada's prestigious Royal Canadian Mounted Police have enjoyed tremendous status and respect from the citizenry, somewhat offsetting what many of them believed to be comparatively low pay levels. Similarly, junior professors at highly prestigious universities are often expected to work for lower starting salaries than they might receive elsewhere, in part because of the status they are expected to derive from being affiliated with these institutions, a phenomenon known as "eating ivy."

---

[1]The interested reader is referred to J. S. Adams (1963, 1965), Homans (1961), E. Jacques (1961), and Patchen (1961) for treatments of many of the specific versions of equity theory. It is acknowledged that the following discussion is influenced most heavily by the work of Adams (1963, 1965), because his version seems to have been the most influential in the research and theoretic work among organizational scientists interested in work motivation and behavior (R. D. Pritchard, 1969).

Equity Ratios

Equity theory holds that people evaluate their outcomes relative to their inputs and form opinions about how well they are being treated. Most (but not all)[2] versions of the theory stress that this evaluation often takes place in a comparative, social sense, such that people consider their inputs and outcomes relative to the inputs and outcomes they perceive other people contribute and take away from their work. The crucial aspect of this social comparison process is the belief that inputs and outcomes are considered in ratio terms rather than absolute terms. For example, the reader may believe that Karen makes twice as much money as he does. Whether or not that belief results in annoyance will depend on his beliefs about the value of the contributions Karen makes to her work compared to the value of the contributions he believes he makes to his own job. People can tolerate seeing others earn more money and other benefits than they do if they believe that the others also contribute more in the way of inputs. When we see other people making a lot more money (or other forms of outcome) than we do but not appearing to be contributing more in the way of relevant inputs, a tension results that the theory says will motivate behavior to equalize the ratios. The tension is particularly strong when the other person's outcomes are perceived as higher than ours but that person's inputs are simultaneously perceived to be lower (J. S. Adams, 1963).

Symbolically, we can represent these two ratios for a hypothetical person (named Richard) as follows:

$$\frac{\text{Richard's beliefs about his own outcomes}}{\text{Richard's beliefs about his own inputs}} \quad \overset{?}{=} \quad \frac{\text{Richard's beliefs about someone else's outcomes}}{\text{Richard's beliefs about that person's inputs}}$$

If Richard perceives that, psychologically, his ratio of outcomes to inputs compares favorably with that of some other person with whom he compares, the theory suggests that he will be content. Tension builds, however, when Richard perceives that the ratio of outcomes to inputs of his comparison person is more favorable than the ratio he attributes to his own situation. However, life is rarely so simple, as we discuss next.

The Eye of the Beholder

A number of points must be made clear. First, the ratios represented above reflect Richard's view of the world; they may not be shared by other people, such as Richard's supervisor, or the person with whom Richard compares himself. Therefore, the same two people could compare themselves with each other and each conclude

---

[2]For example, R. D. Pritchard (1969) states that "feelings of inequity arise first and foremost from the correspondence between the person's own inputs and outcomes. . . . If his inputs are greater than outcomes he will experience inequity, which will lead to feelings of dissatisfaction regardless of the input–outcome ratio of anyone else" (p. 206). However, Pritchard is a bit inconsistent, because elsewhere (1969, pp. 205–206; R. D. Pritchard, Dunnette, and Jorgenson, 1972) the role of external referents is included in his thinking and empirical research (Tornblom, 1977).

that the other has a better deal. It depends entirely on the degree to which their beliefs about each other's (and their own) inputs and outcomes matched. Often, supervisors get themselves into considerable trouble by distributing rewards and punishments in a way they perceive to be *equal* among employees—so that the norm of equity is immediately at risk if the recipients don't perceive their inputs to be equal. Alternatively, supervisors who attempt to recognize a norm of equity can err by distributing rewards (or punishment) in doses that the various parties don't perceive to be commensurate with the efforts, performance, seniority, or other inputs they have provided. Hence, distributing rewards and punishments among subordinates is widely acknowledged as an anguishing task among parents, teachers, and supervisors in many diverse settings. Sometimes it can be a matter of "damned if you do and damned if you don't!"

That justice and fairness can be a matter of "the eye of the beholder" was illustrated by a simple study. The employees of a company were asked how they thought *a lump sum* of money should be divided among members of their organization. Highest-level executives thought organization-wide equity should be used; departmental mangers suggested intradepartmental equity; lowest-level employees did not differentiate between equity and equality of distribution as a basis for distributing the money (Lansberg, 1984).

Bazerman (1993) has suggested three mechanisms, or standards, by which people may be seen as irrational in their judgments of fairness. The first is caused by any deviation from what would normally be considered rational by broad economic standards. The second criterion is based on any outcome or circumstance that can be judged to be Pareto-inefficient. "An agreement is defined as Pareto efficient when there is no other agreement [between two parties] that would make one party better off without decreasing the outcomes to any other party" (Bazerman, 1993, p. 190). This implies that either an equal or an unequal distribution of resources or outcomes may be best for the society at large, depending on prior circumstances. Deviations from such decisions are irrational by this criterion. The third basis for a person's fairness judgments to be seen as irrational is when they are inconsistent. The inconsistencies may result from intransitivity or be based on irrelevant concerns. Or if a person changes his decisions about outcomes on the basis of irrelevant data, he would be seen as irrational.

The Choice of a Referent

A second point concerns the choice of a referent for comparison. With whom does Richard compare ratios? Some equity theorists suggest that people often experience equity or inequity in terms of the degree of balance they perceive between their own inputs and outcomes compared to some internalized standard (e.g., Weick and Nesset, 1968). Alternatively, there is cause to believe that many people evaluate their current equity situations with situations they recall from other jobs in the past. ("Damn! I was better off at my last job!") Finally, some people compare their equity situation with their expectations when they first started their jobs. When a person begins a job, she develops a set of expectations about the types and amounts of inputs and outcomes that will be involved. When this psychological contract (Rousseau, 1989; Rousseau and Parks, 1993; E. H. Schein, 1970) is violated, inequity perceptions develop, and the person becomes less satisfied with her job and more likely to withdraw from it (Ilgen and Seely, 1974; Robinson and Rousseau, 1994).

Early social comparison theory predicted that people attempt to compare their beliefs and attitudes with other people whom they perceive as being similar to themselves, either in terms of the issues they wish to have confirmed or, failing that, in terms of perceived demographic characteristics (Festinger, 1954).[3] Hence, Richard may have someone in mind who performs the same job he performs, either at his own organization or elsewhere. Labor unions frequently construct their wage demands using this principle, comparing their own wages (usually unfavorably) to the wages earned by workers in the same industries in other places or to the wages earned by unions in similar industries at the same location (A. Ross, 1948).

Professionals seem to be more inclined than nonprofessionals to compare their equity situations with people outside their own organizations (Goodman, 1974), and people from different cultures may or may not consider equity issues as we do in North America (Weick, Bougon, and Maruyama, 1976). There is even some evidence that different racial groups in North America may consider and approach concepts of equity differently (e.g., L. S. Perry, 1993). For example, a graduate student from China related a story in class that sheds light on the foregoing discussion and, at the same time, may help us to understand what happened in 1991 at Tiannenman Square. The student reported that there were major differences between the perceptions held by the young students who protested in the square (and paid so heavily) and those held by the elder politicians and military personnel who suppressed the protests. On the one hand, the students were comparing their standards of living, their freedom, and their progress toward a better society with what they believed to be the standards of young people in other societies (such as in North America, for example). On the other hand, the basis for comparison used by the elders was the China of previous decades, when conditions had been much worse. The young protestors employed referents abroad who were presumably their own age and whom they saw as enjoying greater freedom and a better life at the current time. The elders employed a different set of referents and had a hard time accepting and tolerating the impatience of the new generation.

A major theme of this book is that most or all social and individual behavior is overdetermined, or caused by more than single factors. Historians and political scientists can no doubt furnish other explanations for the Tiannenman Square massacre. However, differences in the referent groups used by widely divergent generations of Chinese provided a feasible explanation of the causes of the event for the student.

Beliefs, Attitudes, Inequity, and Behavior

A third key point in equity theory is that it deals with people's beliefs and attitudes. The beliefs consist of thoughts such as "Richard has a key to the executive washroom, and I don't." Attitudes consist of evaluations of these beliefs ("Who cares about having a key to the executive washroom, anyway?"). Beliefs and attitudes about equity are formed and modified in the same manner as other beliefs and attitudes (see chapter 9).

---

[3]More recent thinking has suggested that in the context of opinion verification, at least, people may choose others "to the extent that the information they are expected to provide is compatible with the chooser's motivation" (Kruglanski and Mayesless, 1990, p. 197).

Moreover, the beliefs and attitudes of equity theory are related as unpredictably to employee behavior as are all beliefs and attitudes. To result in relevant behaviors, they must be converted into intentions.

Consequences of Inequity Perceptions

Nevertheless, the theory claims that people find conditions of perceived inequity uncomfortable or dissonant (Festinger, 1957), and when the tension becomes great enough, the person will do something to redress it. States of perceived inequity are seen as constituting a need of the sort examined in chapter 3, possessing all the characteristics of needs discussed there. Notice that it is possible for a person such as Richard to perceive that he is being overly well treated in relation to his comparison person. The theory states (and research supports) that people have a greater tolerance for this sort of inequity situation than for cases where they believe they are being poorly treated. However, the theory predicts that eventually they will be motivated to equalize the ratios as they perceive them (J. S. Adams, 1963; Andrews, 1967; Weick and Nesset, 1968).

Theoretically, how is equity restored? First, remember that equity is in the eye of the beholder. The theory states that people will be motivated to change elements of either (or both) of the ratios they perceive. For example, Richard might demand a raise from his boss if he feels he is being poorly treated compared to his co-worker. Or he might demand some other form of increased outcome, something he values enough to feel that justice has been done. Alternatively, Richard might attempt to change the nature of the denominator of his own equity ratio by, for example, reducing the quantity or quality of his work. ("Fine, if that's all you wish to pay me, you won't be seeing me around here on Sundays anymore.") The author has known colleagues who have proclaimed that their employers "seem able to afford less of my time every year!"

Changing Effort to Restore Equity

It is important to note that the theory makes different predictions about whether an employee (who believes she is being inequitably treated) will increase or decrease her effort level, depending on the nature of the payment system under which she is working. If the employee is working for a piece rate, for example, the theory predicts that feelings of underpayment inequity (as a result of a belief that the rate of payment per unit produced is too low) will lead to attempts to increase productivity levels, thereby maximizing the net level of pay earned overall. On the other hand, underpayment inequity is predicted to result in reduced performance levels in situations of hourly pay. Similarly, equity theory predicts perceptions of overpayment under a piece-rate pay plan to result in restricted output and increased quality, thereby limiting the net amount of overpayment the person earns while providing greater input to the exchange. Finally, overpayment perceptions under an hourly compensation plan would be expected to result in increased performance levels, because higher productivity is one means of increasing one's inputs and restoring balance. Reference to the equity ratios represented earlier helps explain why different behavioral reactions are predicted in the various underpayment and overpayment conditions.

Notice that Richard might be able to restore equity in the ratios he perceives by influencing either the numerator or the denominator (or both) of the ratio he attributes to his comparison person. If Richard were brash enough, for example, he might enquire about the inordinately high level of pay being earned by his co-worker. More likely, Richard might attack the numerator of his co-worker's ratio: He may behave in such a way as to assure that his comparison person actually earns his fancy salary and key to the executive washroom.

The point is that perceptions of inequitable treatment generate motivational forces (using the terminology of chapter 9, we would call them beliefs and attitudes with the potential to become intentions) that instigate behavior to reduce tension, and that often a variety of behaviors is available for correcting a situation of perceived inequity. But we know from chapter 8 that not all goal-directed behavior is successful—people do not always succeed at what they attempt to do. Moreover, it is not always feasible even to try certain acts. For example, it would be quite risky in most circumstances for Richard to attempt to have his co-worker's pay cut or to try to get the other person to contribute more to the organization. Consequently, people in Richard's position often find that they have more control over elements of their own perceived ratios, particularly over the level and quality of inputs they provide. In other words, the theory predicts that people like Richard may deliberately reduce the level of effort they put into their jobs. But even this can be difficult or risky at times. What if Richard's job is machine-paced, so that it is not possible for him to reduce the quantity of work he performs? What if Richard cuts back on the quality of his work? If he did so and was caught by his boss, his frustration would become even greater.

An interesting study by Greenberg and Ornstein (1983) is relevant here. These researchers employed undergraduate students in a proofreading task. Each of two groups of students received a "high-status job title," one group on the basis of what they thought was their superior performance on the job, the other for no apparent reason. Both groups were asked to contribute more work to the proofreading project for no additional pay. The people who believed they had actually earned their elevated titles sustained their performance at the task for no extra pay. In the group granted the higher status for no stated reason, the performance level increased for a short period, then fell off dramatically. (The employees who were given added responsibility but no title reduced their performance over time.)

Cognitive Reevaluation of Outcomes

If behavior to influence the value of any of the four main elements of the two equity ratios in Richard's mind is impossible, what can Richard do to reduce the motivational force? Remember that the elements of the two ratios are simply Richard's *perceptions* of the nature and quantity of his own and his partner's inputs and outcomes. The theory says that when reality cannot be changed, the perceptions that give rise to the motivational force will be changed. Hence Richard may reevaluate any (or all) of the beliefs he holds about either the numerators or the denominators he has in mind. For example, he may investigate and learn that his apparently overpaid co-worker has a better set of credentials than Richard initially thought he had. Richard may notice that the other person actually works harder than he had given him credit for previously. Or Richard may decide that his own Ph.D. in anthropology really is not a material input to his job as a dishwasher. Finally, Richard may reevaluate his beliefs about his outcomes, noticing that the people he works with are very congenial, and that low paying as it is, at least his job is clean.

Greenberg (1989) has reported one of the few studies demonstrating that people can and do alter their beliefs about the value of the outcomes they receive in their exchange ratios vis-à-vis their employers. In a study of 114 salaried clerical workers whose pay was cut by natural circumstances, Greenberg found support for equity theory in the form of an increase in the perceived importance of nonsalary rewards as a means of reducing feelings of inequitable treatment. He had the employees rate the value of a number of physical features of their working environment, such as the amount of floor space, desk space, privacy, the number of co-workers who shared their offices, the number of windows in their offices, and so on, both while their pay was below normal and after their salaries had been reinstated to normal levels. As hypothesized by equity theory, the clerical employees attributed higher value to these physical amenities during the period when their pay had been reduced than they did many months later, after their regular salary levels had been restored to normal levels. In summary, when behavior is not possible to restore a perception of equity, the theory predicts that the person will try to change his beliefs about his equity ratios and/or his evaluative reactions to those beliefs.

What if it is simply not possible to change one's beliefs about equity matters sufficiently? The theory predicts that when behavior is not possible, and when it is not possible to change perceptions sufficiently to restore feelings of equity, people will respond with denial, repression, or withdrawal, as they do when faced with other types of frustrating circumstances (recall chapter 8). Hence, perceptions of being inequitably treated contribute to job dissatisfaction (R. D. Pritchard, 1969), which, in turn, results in higher rates of absenteeism and turnover (Carrell and Dittrich, 1976; Telly, French, and Scott, 1971) and other forms of withdrawal, such as silence (R. L. Cohen, 1990; Harlos, 1995).

There is evidence that both distributive and procedural justice have an effect on employee attitudes toward work but that the two forms of justice may affect different types of attitudes. One study of 188 public utility engineers, for example, found that perceptions of distributive justice were more closely related to what the authors called personal-level outcomes such as pay satisfaction, whereas procedural justice was more closely linked to organizational-level outcomes such as organizational commitment (Sweeney and McFarlin, 1993). This particular model of the findings was the most effective of four alternative theoretical approaches studied by the authors. We return to the matter of procedural justice later in the chapter.

Dysfunctional Reactions to Perceived Inequity

Greenberg (1990, 1993) has demonstrated in both laboratory (1993) and field (1990) settings that one reaction that people may have to being treated inequitably is to steal from their employers. In the simple terms of the equity ratios discussed above, theft of property,[4] money, ideas, or information from one's employer constitutes an increase in the outcomes that a person takes away from the employment exchange, albeit not an outcome or benefit that the employer had in mind (Greenberg and Scott, 1996). In one of these studies, Greenberg (1990) observed the theft rates among employees

---

[4]One estimate, although more than 10 years old, placed the cost to employers of industrial theft by employees at more than $40 billion annually (Hartnett, 1991; U.S. Congress, 1990). Presumably the cost is considerably higher in current dollars.

who worked for a midwestern company at three different manufacturing plants. Because the company lost two major contracts, it cut the employees' wages by 15 percent in two of the three plants. In one of the two plants, management explained to the employees in advance that their pay was going to be cut for a temporary period, outlining the causes of the pay cut and expressing regret that such action had to be taken. Management took great care to make the employees believe that the pay cuts were unavoidable and that they were sorry. In the second plant, a brief meeting was held and minimal information was provided about the cuts. Management expressed little or no sorrow or regret. No pay cuts were required in the third plant. There were no significant differences in theft rates among the three groups before the pay cuts were instituted or after wages returned to normal. There was no significant change during the experiment among the control (no-wage-cut) employees. However, there was an increase in theft rates among both wage-cut plants during the period of the cuts. The increase was particularly dramatic among the employees who had received only a brief explanation of the necessity for the cuts. The results of this study are among the few available *from field settings* that demonstrate how employees can be motivated to restore equity in their exchange with their employers. They also illustrate the importance of interactional justice, a concept we focus on later in the chapter.

Silence

Many years ago, Hirschman (1970) offered one of the most useful models for understanding employee reactions to unfavorable treatment by employers. He advanced a typology of three reactions: exit, voice, and loyalty. Exit implies withdrawal from the company. Voice implies speaking up: complaining, protesting, or initiating action intended to make things right. Loyalty implies accepting the inequity and remaining more or less committed to the company, despite the circumstances. One consequence of perceived injustice that has received some recent attention might be seen as the flip side of voice mechanisms—employee silence. That is, one reaction that people can have to injustice is remaining silent, neither protesting nor attempting to make their views heard. They withdraw but stay on-board. This sort of silence might be interpreted by management as a sign of contentment: After all, if no one is complaining, things must be all right. Ironically, in many cases it is the most disadvantaged of groups who choose to remain silent about injustice, even when formal procedures for action are available (Crosby, 1984; Harlos, 1995).

By its very nature, silence in the context of justice and injustice is hard to discern and understand. Cohen (1990) has argued, for example, that silence may be seen as support for, and endorsement of, the status quo, or it might be a reflection of objection. Silence might also reflect a lack of information or means for expression. Employee silence might indicate that voice mechanisms are bogus or ineffectual. Finally, silence may reflect fear of speaking up. Therefore, both voice and silence may be signs of either justice or injustice (R. L. Cohen, 1990; Harlos, 1995). To date, not much work has been done on the nature and consequences of employee silence, so we can only speculate on what those consequences might be. Earlier we saw that theft can be a vehicle for employees who feel they are being treated unfairly. Presumably, theft is accompanied by silence—people are not likely to brag about or advertise their own acts of larceny. However, others who are adapting to injustice through silence and who are also aware of theft and other forms of subterfuge (e.g., espionage, sabotage, malignment of the company's image) are also less likely to speak up, to "blow the whistle" (see Near, Dworkin, and Miceli, 1993).

Silence also implies not making positive, innovative suggestions about how the work might be performed more effectively. Silence implies withholding of information on a day-to-day basis—simply not communicating. It is important to repeat that these thoughts are merely speculation and that empirical work needs to be done to explore the significance of silence as an employee response to inequity. Meanwhile, the key point here is to emphasize that silence among people in the workplace may reflect satisfaction and contentment, or it may also be a sign that people are feeling unjustly treated. Of the two possible errors one might make in interpreting employee silence, the author suspects that management is more likely to misattribute silence caused by dissatisfaction to a belief that things are fine than to dissatisfaction when things are in fact running well.

Individual Differences and Reactions to Inequity

Years ago, Tornow (1971) suggested that researchers and theorists should take individual differences into account when testing predictions from equity theory. He based his suggestion on the observation that some people tend to classify certain elements of their work experiences as inputs whereas others may classify the same elements as outcomes (responsibility on the job is an example). More recent work tried to improve the predictive accuracy of the theory by considering the possibility that different types of people may have characteristically different cognitive and emotional reactions to conditions of perceived inequity and, if they do, taking into account these characteristic reactions when making predictions in equity research. A relatively new individual differences variable, one designed especially for embellishing and sharpening equity theory, has been offered by Huseman, Hatfield, and Miles (1985, 1987), and E. W. Miles, Hatfield, and Huseman (1994). On the basis of this construct, known as *equity sensitivity,* people are classified into one of three categories. One group, called *benevolents,* are people who can tolerate having their own perceived equity ratios in a disadvantaged position relative to others. A second group, the *equity sensitives,* are posited to adhere to the traditional predictions of equity theory, responding with a degree of discomfort to positions of either felt overpayment or felt relative deprivation. The third category is comprised of *entitleds,* people who prefer to have things imbalanced in their favor.

One study has shown that members of the three groups may place greater emphasis or importance on different types of work-related outcomes in equity/inequity circumstances (E. W. Miles et al., 1994). Four different factors (or groupings of outcomes) were created statistically after 20 specific outcomes were rated for importance. Some examples of the specific outcomes included "sense of accomplishment," using one's abilities, "pay," "appreciation from others," and "job security." Factor analysis resulted in four clusters of outcomes. The entitleds placed greater importance than the other two groups of employees on extrinsic, tangible outcomes such as pay, fringe benefits, and job security. There were no systematic differences between the three groups in terms of the importance they placed on extrinsic intangible outcomes such as recognition for good work and friendships on the job. Finally, the results revealed that, of the three types, the benevolents placed the highest importance on strictly intrinsic outcomes from the work, items such as "a sense of accomplishment," "doing challenging work," and "a feeling of achievement."

One of the key criticisms of equity theory over the years has concerned its predictive validity—a general weakness in making accurate, better-than-chance predictions of individual behavior and attitude changes (Mowday, 1991). As we will see later in the chapter, there may be a number of reasons for this failure. The attempt made by Huseman, Miles, and Hatfield to introduce an individual differences variable into the model may be a useful step in the right direction. Moreover, there is something to be said in favor of tailoring such a new moderator variable to the theory itself rather than attempting to increase validity by subgrouping people on the basis of a common demographic variable such as age or race.[5] On the other hand, the use of such idiosyncratic constructs for the sake of improving the predictive validity of any theory—constructs that have little or no relevance or use in other scientific constructs—is a costly proposition. Taken too far, this approach could result in a proliferation of single-use, single-context variables, cluttering the landscape and militating against the development of useful middle-range theories. In the limit, approaches such as this can border on tautology. Nevertheless, at least one new independent test and application of the equity sensitivity construct has proven useful (W. C. King, Miles, and Day, 1993), so it is too early to be critical of the idea.

Racial Differences?

Another approach to finding variables that might help the predictive validity of a theory is to resort to group-level factors, such as age, gender, education level, or other demographic indicators. This was attempted in the context of equity theory in a recent study of nearly 800 African Americans. We mentioned on two earlier occasions that the theory posits discomfort for people who perceive themselves to be either overpaid or underpaid. The results of this study confirmed the researcher's hypothesis that the relationship between payment and satisfaction was linear—that there was no evidence among this sample of black Americans that overpayment inequity was uncomfortable for them (L. S. Perry, 1993). The reason? Perry argues that black American employees whose pay is somehow higher than what it would otherwise be would take into account discrimination and other barriers they typically have to cope with in the marketplace, viewing them as other varieties of "inputs" that whites or majority-group employees do not encounter. Therefore, any perceived overpayment would help to restore an overall sense of balance and equity. L. S. Perry's (1993) study constitutes an interesting variant in the research on equity theory by offering and supporting a hypothesis that at first glance might appear contrary to the tenets of the theory.

Inequity and Individual Reactions: The Research Evidence

As with the case of every other major theory of work motivation presented in this book, equity theory has come under a great deal of scrutiny and criticism from researchers and theorists. In fact, this particular theory seems to have received some of

---

[5]This is similar to the strategy used nearly 20 years ago by Cherrington and England (1980) in the context of making better predictions about people's reactions to job redesign after previous attempts using large-scale sociological variables proved to be relatively ineffective (e.g., Hulin and Blood, 1968).

the most voluminous and fine-grained inspection among most of the theories in this book. Perhaps one reason for this is that equity theory has been of interest not only to organizational psychologists interested in motivation and job attitudes, but also to social psychologists interested in social exchange dynamics in contexts other than the workplace (e.g., Walster, Berscheid, and Walster, 1976). Our review of the validity of the theory and of the quality of the research conducted to assess that validity will be limited here to work done on equity theory in the work motivation context.

There have been many summaries of the findings and apparent validity of equity theory in the workplace over the years (e.g., J. P. Campbell and Pritchard, 1976; Carrell and Dittrich, 1978; P. A. Goodman and Friedman, 1971; R. D. Pritchard, 1969, among others). The most recent assessment of these reviews and the paper that best provides a balanced assessment of the theory is provided by Mowday (1991), who concludes that it appears that there is

> general support for equity theory predictions. In the overpayment-hourly condition, a number of studies have provided some support for the prediction that overpaid subjects will produce higher quantity than equitably-paid subjects. . . . Several studies have either failed to support or provided mixed support for equity theory predictions in this condition, although they have differed from the supporting studies in the manner in which perceived inequity was experimentally manipulated. . . . In the overpayment-piece-rate condition, support for the theory has been found [by a number of studies]. Although fewer studies have examined the underpayment conditions, support for both the hourly and piece-rate predictions have been reported. . . . (pp. 115, 119)

At first blush, Mowday's assessment appears to provide good news for equity theory as applied to work motivation and attitudes. However, Mowday (1991) demonstrates a host of problems in research design, unanswered conceptual questions, concerns about the construct validity of many of the experimental manipulations, and other shortcomings in the studies that have purported to test the validity of the theory. Some of these issues and problems will be discussed shortly, together with other concerns brought to light by scholars other than Mowday. The interested reader is referred to Mowday's work for a careful discussion of the scientific problems that have plagued so much equity theory research and that, notwithstanding the appearance of high validity, leave a careful reader worried about the net validity of the theory as it applies to work motivation and employee attitudes.

Problems with Equity Theory Research

In chapter 2 we discussed the necessity for conducting research to evaluate the validity of theories of work motivation. We also discussed the difficulties associated with doing research that provides fair tests of these theories. Since then we have seen a number of instances where the research conducted to evaluate certain theories has been flawed or somehow inappropriately executed. Research into the validity of equity theory is no exception. Researchers pursuing this theory have made a number of mistakes that leave us with only an uncertain feel for its scientific validity. For example, many of the experiments conducted to test the theory's predictions of behavior under conditions of perceived overpayment have utilized a ploy that probably generated in the minds of experimental subjects feelings that they were unworthy of the pay they were receiving.

In other words, the experimental induction used may have influenced their feelings of self-esteem rather than simply manipulating their equity beliefs per se. As a result of this confounding, the results yielded by these experiments are equivocal. We cannot be sure whether they reflect the impact of inequity perceptions or the effects of esteem degradation (Mowday, 1991; Schwab, 1980).

Second, despite the obvious importance of comparison subjects to the dynamics posited by the theory, many studies to date have ignored the issue of which referents experimental subjects use to compare themselves. In those studies in which referents have been identified, researchers have failed to control or observe the types and amounts of information provided to their subjects about the inputs being provided by the referents (Middlemist and Peterson, 1976). On the one hand, the theory states that people will pay attention to a variety of inputs provided by themselves and by comparison others. On the other hand, researchers have been lax, on the whole, in manipulating or even monitoring the information available concerning the (real or imagined) levels of qualification or effort being contributed by comparison referents. Without such control, the results obtained in these studies are hard to interpret. Related to this issue is the conceptual (and experimental) matter of whether the referent being used is an unidentifiable group of other employees in the work organization or a friend or associate. It would seem that people would be better able to reconcile feelings of inequity in the former case than in the latter.

A third problem with much of the research is that *pay* has been the primary outcome provided to experimental subjects in exchange for their work. The reason for such a heavy reliance on money is understandable and may comprise both the greatest strength and the greatest weakness of this body of work (Mowday, 1991). Money is easy to measure and dispense, and it is generally valued by people. But the theory claims that people may recognize a variety of outcomes as they form mental images about how equitably they are being treated, and that many of these outcomes are nonpecuniary as well as nonphysical. The reliance on pay, Mowday (1991) notes, seems to have blinded most researchers from considering other alternatives, task satisfaction being the major exception (Weick, 1967), until recently (e.g., Greenberg, 1988a, 1990b; Greenberg and Ornstein, 1983).

Another problem with the almost exclusive reliance on pay as the experimental outcome is that money has been found to have a variety of influences on the perceived value of other outcomes, such as intrinsic satisfaction with the task (recall chapter 7). Related to this problem is the possibility that outcomes of various sorts simply do not aggregate in value psychologically the way the theory has implicitly assumed (see Porac and Salancik, 1981, for an example). Again, the point is that the ease of measurement and control gained through the use of money by researchers may have added to the other deficiencies of the research on equity theory, compromising our ability to assess the theory's merit.

A fourth problem with this research (albeit one that is not unique to equity theory) is that it has predominantly been conducted in contrived laboratory settings, using college students working on tasks of limited degrees of realism, generally over very short periods of time. People tend to use a much longer time frame to formulate their beliefs about how equitably treated they are than might have been implied either in the original theory or in many of the earliest studies, particularly laboratory experiments. Landy and Becker (1987) cite the work of earlier theorists to interpret the findings of

Greenberg and Ornstein (1983) and argue that beliefs about one's own treatment at the hands of an employer may not develop in real life as quickly as might be concluded on the basis of laboratory evidence with undergraduates. This author echoes that thought and suggests that this is especially the case among people in our economies who are older (40-plus?), who have limited job skills, or who are unable to relocate.

Further, most experimental manipulations of inequity, both in lab settings and in the field, have, of necessity, been relatively tame and inconsequential. Having people believe that they have been comparatively underpaid for short-term, often-contrived exercises may yield certain forms of attitudinal and behavioral reactions, but how realistic are they in comparison to deprivation in real work settings? Accordingly, J. Martin (1993) asks us to consider what might happen if it were possible to disadvantage or deprive people of such benefits as their incomes in large-scale, long-term conditions, so that serious economic and psychic impact would result. Naturally, researchers have rarely, if ever, done such a thing, both because of ethical considerations and because it would be impossible to gain access to people and organizational functioning in order to perform such "realistic" equity manipulations. Few organizations would permit such treatment of their personnel. Therefore, what we have is a body of knowledge about people's reactions to "tepid" forms of injustice. We may not be able to extrapolate this knowledge to realistic situations of egregious injustice and violations of people's desires for fairness (J. Martin, 1993).

The author believes that laboratory research is a valuable means for developing and refining hypotheses derived from theory, but that it must be combined with observations gathered in real-life settings. (The reader is referred to Runkel and McGrath, 1972, for a thorough discussion of the iterative use of different research methodologies and sites.) The reason for the heavy reliance on the lab is, of course, the convenience it offers to researchers and the experimental control that can be exercised over variables. There have been a few valiant attempts to increase the realism of the settings in which equity theory has been tested (e.g., Evan and Simmons, 1969; R. D Pritchard, Dunnette, and Jorgenson, 1972), but they have been rare (the most promising exception has been the work of Greenberg and his colleagues: Greenberg, 1988a, 1990b; Greenberg and Ornstein, 1983).

A fifth problem is the way that perceptions of equity and inequity have been created and assessed by researchers. For example, the tendency has been to manipulate either the numerator or the denominator (or both) of the research subject's equity ratio and/or those of some comparison person, assuming that the feelings of inequity created are similar in terms of the impact they have on people (see Tornow, 1971). In fact, there is a range of possible situations of inequity that can influence people's beliefs about the treatment they receive (Tornblom, 1977), so that the nature of the actual feelings of inequity created in research participants' minds has been poorly understood to date (Mowday, 1991). Greenberg (1990b) has pointed out that the heavy emphasis placed by equity theorists on intrapsychic processes has fallen into disfavor, largely because we now recognize that the outcomes of exchange at work are only part of the problem: Hence the importance and emergence of interest in procedural justice (described next).

J. Martin (1993) has pointed out that the bulk of the work on equity theory has implicitly adopted a managerial bias. He argues that the reliance on studying people's perceptions of the inputs they have provided has blinded distributive justice researchers from considering other bases for assessing justice, such as people's needs or desires for equality of treatment (see Sheppard et al., 1992). For example, most research participants have been college students or managers. Martin suggests that if disadvantaged populations were to participate, people for whom "middle class levels of prosperity were . . . unattainable" (p. 301), the results of equity studies might be considerably different. Such people might choose to compare themselves with those they judge as better off than they are and conclude that the treatment they have been receiving is unfair and unjust. Martin summarizes how a number of early equity studies found low-level employees who wanted to do just that, to compare themselves with managerial-class persons. The authors of these studies rationalized these reactions as reflecting people's chronic discontent and envy.

Is There Cause for Hope for the Theory?

A final observation about equity theory offered as a criticism by some theorists is that most of its hypotheses may be capable of being handled by expectancy-valence theories (see J. P. Campbell and Pritchard, 1976; Lawler, 1973; and chapter 12 of this book). The reader is referred to Mowday (1991) or to Lawler (1973) for an explanation of this claim. This author believes that any theory should be parsimonious, and that if one theory can legitimately subsume another, it should do so. But equity theory has more to offer the discipline than just the motivation-related hypotheses it may share with expectancy-valence theories, justifying a place of its own in the field. For example, it comprises a significant part of what has come to be called *distributive justice,* along with relative deprivation theory (see J. Martin, 1993), which, in turn, combines with theory on procedural justice to yield a more comprehensive middle-range theory of fairness in work and nonwork settings than is available elsewhere. Similarly, as part of the broader body of work in social exchange, equity theory may prove useful in understanding parts of the dynamics of leadership behavior through the insights it provides into the relationships between leaders and followers, or managers and subordinates (Mowday, 1991).

On balance, the evidence attesting to the validity of equity theory as a predictor of changes in work effort and performance is not as impressive as the elegance of the predictions made by the theory, despite first impressions. But again, who or what is at fault here: the theory or the research that purports to test it? The foregoing summary and review should make it clear that for a number of very understandable and practical reasons, the research on equity theory has generally not been conducted well enough to provide us with a fair sense of its validity. Although the theoretic propositions advanced by Adams and others seem to make considerable intuitive sense, many specific features of the theory remain unsubstantiated, and its nuances are far from understood. In other words, it may be, as with so many other theories discussed in this book, that the theory is more valid than researchers are able to demonstrate. The author believes this to be the case. Concepts of fairness, justice, and equity are still thriving in the organizational sciences, suggesting that other social scientists also believe in the likely validity of the basic notions of these theories, notwithstanding the paucity of empirical success.

Many of these criticisms and difficulties have been noted and taken into account. Garland's (1973) work, for example, illustrates a way around the use of self-esteem reduction as a by-product of attempts to create feelings of overpayment. Similarly, other researchers have tried to avoid the problems caused by the identification and addition of inputs and outcomes by making use of a person's net perceptions of the *fairness* of exchange relationships (see Carrell and Dittrich, 1978, for example). Finally, the urgency of understanding the nature and consequences of equity and inequity generated by the ongoing concern for human rights will continue to support the development of new theories of distributive justice and the means for testing them. The issues of comparable worth and procedural justice at both the organizational and societal levels are two current examples that will be discussed shortly. Notwithstanding these difficulties, we accept the theory at face value and discuss a variety of practical applied issues that arise from it.

Organizational Causes of Perceived (and Actual) Inequity

What creates feelings of inequity among employees? Most answers to this question involve the sensitivity and responsiveness of organizational reward systems. Feelings of inequitable treatment tend to occur when people believe they are not receiving fair returns for their efforts and other contributions. To prevent this sort of perception from developing, an organization must structure its reward system so that it distributes rewards in accordance with employee beliefs about their own value to the enterprise. In practice, this is very difficult. One reason is the difficulty of achieving agreement among people concerning what constitutes value ("Is your MBA degree really relevant to the work you perform here? I don't think so. . . ." or, "Who cares if you held several other farm laboring jobs before coming to this one? I can train someone much younger than you are to pick as many berries as you can; probably more. . . .").

Another problem is the difficulty of recognizing good performance when it occurs. Performance appraisal is a very complicated process that is fraught with potential for errors and the creation of inequities, either real or imagined. Union contracts often require that seniority be rewarded. For those who are senior, such provisions seem very equitable, because they tend to see their seniority as valuable experience (a type of input) that should be compensated. On the other hand, junior employees often do not agree, especially when they also believe that they contribute more or better job performance to the organization than that of their older colleagues. Favoritism, in all its manifestations, tends to generate feelings of inequitable treatment. Nepotism is a particularly interesting example. Members of the boss's family are often in the difficult position of making sure their co-workers see that they deserve any and all benefits they receive, sometimes to the point where the boss's family members feel they are maltreated in relation to other employees.

Alternative Distribution Rules

People also develop perceptions of inequity because their managers make no attempt to exercise reward and punishment systems according to the tenets of a norm of equity. Equity is only one of many "distribution rules" possible for allocating rewards and punishment in organizations (G. S. Leventhal, 1976; Sheppard et al., 1992). Depending on other goals and priorities, reward systems may be based on norms of *equality* rather than equity. The norm of equality deliberately avoids most of the intrapsychic subtleties and risks of managing by the norm of equity (see G. S. Leventhal, 1976). Equality may be chosen to maximize harmony and minimize conflict among employees.

Equal treatment is easier to manage than equitable treatment because, in part, no one is required to try to imagine the perceptions of relative inputs and outcomes held by other people. Further, a norm of equality may be highly justified when there is a considerable amount of interdependence and cooperation among members of a work group.

Sometimes a norm of *social responsibility* is the criterion or guiding principle used by management. Under these conditions, people are deliberately treated according to what they need rather than on the basis of what they deem to be fair. This principle for distributing rewards may be best when one is dealing with a friend or with someone for whom the manager feels responsible. This type of standard may be deemed more paternalistic than norms of equity or equality. It can certainly be open to problems of real or alleged favoritism. Nevertheless, it is an alternative basis for the distribution of work-related outcomes, both positive and negative, that can result in feelings of inequitable or unfair treatment by employees (see G. S. Leventhal, 1976; Sheppard et al., 1992). The point is that there are myriad practical factors in most work settings that contribute to feelings of inequity among employees. Many of these factors are difficult for managers to control. One particularly intractable problem is caused by the clash between internal norms of equity and the cost of labor in the external marketplace.

Internal and External Equity in Formal Compensation Systems

Most large organizations (as well as many smaller ones) employ some form of job evaluation system, designed to assure that there is a relationship between the amount of pay provided to incumbents of its various jobs and the value of those jobs to the organization. A complete treatment of these programs is beyond our purpose; the interested reader is referred to a comprehensive treatment of formal pay plans by Henderson (1989). Although plans of this sort are often capable of providing reasonable degrees of pay equity within an organization at a particular time, they generally do not account for fluctuating labor market conditions, which can heavily influence the compensation levels necessary to attract new employees from outside. Sometimes there is a trade-off between internal and external equity considerations. This can make it very difficult to maintain perceptions of equity inside an organization while permitting it effectively to recruit new employees from the labor market.

One solution often adopted, in part to deal with the internal versus external equity trade-off, is to keep pay levels secret throughout the organization—people are not told how much money others earn (M. G. Miner, 1974). Pay secrecy policies have a number of interesting features. First, people often talk informally about salaries and wages, sometimes about their own and sometimes about the compensation earned by others. Often the "rumor mill" on the issue of money is not accurate, as people knowingly or inadvertently distort figures they associate with themselves and with others. There is also evidence that managers may tend honestly to underestimate the compensation levels of their superiors and overestimate the compensation levels earned by their peers and subordinates. When this occurs people are likely to feel that there is underpayment inequity vis-à-vis their subordinates. Furthermore, the belief that higher organizational levels don't fetch that much more compensation may tend to reduce the incentive value of promotions (Lawler, 1965, 1967a; Milkovich and Anderson, 1972).

As a result, it has been suggested on theoretical grounds that compensation levels should not be kept secret (Lawler, 1972), but that they should be opened up to the scrutiny of all concerned, despite the initial difficulties the opening-up process may create. A great brouhaha erupted in the spring of 1996 when the Ontario government required publication of the names of all its employees who earned more than $100,000. The facts revealed a number of glaring apparent inequities. For example, the president of the University of Toronto, Canada's largest and arguably best university, earned considerably less salary than his counterpart at Wilfred Laurier University, a much smaller and less prestigious university in the Ontario system. Doctors, lawyers, university professors, senior bureaucrats, and cabinet ministers immediately began the nervous process of comparing their own salaries with those of others on the government payroll, often concluding, as one might expect, that they, personally, were not being compensated fairly (see Fennel, 1996). Monica Belcourt, a professor of human resources management at York University, opined that "people are going to start comparing their salaries and saying 'Am I making enough, and is he worth what he is getting?' " (Fennel, 1996). The public (taxpayers who pay government employees) got into the act as well, demanding to know *why* civil servants were earning such "high salaries" while many people in the province were unemployed or on welfare. One early study on the matter concluded that open pay schemes do not necessarily result in more accurate perceptions of other people's pay, despite the availability of the necessary information (Milkovich and Anderson, 1972). Moreover, it is not always the case that open pay schemes result in the higher levels of pay satisfaction that equity theory would predict (T. A. Mahoney and Weitzel, 1978). This is a thorny issue.

The author was once part of a two-person consulting team asked to intervene in a number of personnel management problems being tackled in a small federal government agency. Central to these problems was a pay structure that had grown willy-nilly without much rationalization. There was evidence of pay discrimination on the basis of gender and a host of other anomalies that had emerged slowly over time as people's jobs had changed and as the traditions and customs of the small office prevailed over the best principles of compensation management. The author and his partner suggested (among other recommendations) that the new pay structure being proposed be opened up and made public to all members of the office. The agency's board of directors flatly refused, largely because of the opinion of one retired career personnel administrator who was afraid the roof would come off immediately after employees became aware of the proposed new realignment of salaries. The management group agreed that changes had to be made, and they realized that gossip and rumors would quickly flourish among the staff about "who makes how much now." Despite being warned about the likelihood and risks of false rumors, the managers refused to implement an open salary system. Parenthetically, they quickly accepted and adopted the many suggestions made by the author's lawyer partner in relation to other matters in the office, presumably because so many of his recommendations were shrouded in Latin terminology.

In short, the fact that organizations must recruit and retain a labor force from external markets can make the maintenance of equitable internal compensation plans a tricky problem for which no easy solution seems available. Moreover, plans of this sort can deal only with the equitable distribution of pay. They have virtually nothing to do with the equitable distribution of other forms of compensation (such as fringe benefits) or informal rewards (e.g., recognition, praise). It is very difficult, in practice, to administer rewards in a manner that will be perceived as equitable by everyone concerned.

COMPARABLE WORTH: AN ISSUE, A MOVEMENT, AND A DOCTRINE

Matters of fairness and equity take on major significance when we cast them in the light of one of the major social and economic movements of the past two decades in North America (R. M. Kelly and Bayes, 1988; Killingsworth, 1990). This movement is referred to as *comparable worth* in the United States and as *pay equity* in Canada. The movement's focus is on the pay that employers provide to people who perform jobs of varying degrees of similarity, especially, as we shall see, when the workers involved are of mixed genders. The movement itself rests on a doctrine whose essential meaning has been described by T. A. Mahoney (1987) as "equal pay for jobs of comparable (equal) worth." The surface similarity of the jobs in question is of minor importance, nor do the jobs need to be from the same organization. Therefore, comparable worth ignores (or even counteracts) the effects of the marketplace on wage rates on the grounds that entire classes of apparently dissimilar jobs have been undervalued by the market forces of supply and demand because they have traditionally been held by women. For example, if the services that a public nurse provides are considered equal in value to those provided by a person who trims trees in the same community, the doctrine of comparable worth would have the two incumbents paid the same compensation by their common employer. Quite simple *in principle*, really.

What Is Comparable Worth?

There are at least four different levels, or categories, of policy and practice that deal with the comparability of remuneration between and among jobs (M. J. Moore and Abraham, 1992). The practical and policy implications vary significantly among them. To make our discussion of these matters as clear as possible, let's take a brief look at these four categories. The least debated category is referred to as *equal pay for equal work* (Moore and Abraham, 1992, p. 456). Under the terms of the Equal Pay Act of 1963, there are four basic factors on which jobs are to be compared to determine equality or inequality: skill, effort, responsibility, and working conditions. When these four criteria (or compensable factors) are applied to two or more jobs and the jobs are found not to differ very much on these factors, they are deemed to be substantially equal. When two jobs are believed equal in terms of the four factors but still not seen as substantially equal, we have the case of *equal pay for similar work* (M. J. Moore and Abraham, 1992, p. 456). Comparable worth advocates argue that differences in pay are not justified in such cases. A third category is referred to as *pay parity.* "This requires that the average salary for women must equal the average salary for men, aggregated on a national basis. This is the most extreme view" (M. J. Moore and Abraham, 1992, p. 456). Finally, comparable worth is the category in which we have *equal pay for equal worth.* "This means that jobs that are dissimilar, but equal in terms of value or worth to the employer, should be paid the same" (M. J. Moore and Abraham, 1992, p. 456). Any variety of job evaluation scheme or formula may be used to determine "value" and "worth," but when two or more jobs somehow are deemed to have a similar number of points of value as measured by these schemes, they should be paid the same. Of the four levels or standards for comparison just described, this one—comparable worth— is the most controversial (p. 456).

As noted above, simple notions of equality and equity are represented in varying forms and degrees within each of the four categories. We focus our discussion here on the fourth of these because it has resulted in legislation and a great deal of resistance and controversy in organizational practice. Before we begin, we note that most of the work conducted on comparable worth issues has been cast as a matter of distributive justice—a matter of the perceived fairness, or lack thereof, of the distribution of remuneration among people and across gender groups. We recognize there are several issues concerned with *how* pay is distributed that also have relevance for the concept of comparable worth. The interested reader is referred to a paper by Greenberg and Mc-Carty (1990) for a discussion of the relationship between procedural justice and comparable worth. The primary orientation here will be to view comparable worth as a matter of distributive justice.

Origins of the Doctrine and Movement

A number of interrelated origins provided the impetus for the comparable worth movement: the emergence of greater numbers of women in the workforce, the rise of the feminist movement, the observed disparity between the earnings made by men and women, and the powerful association of certain types of work with men and other types of work with women (Kovach and Millspaugh, 1990; T. A. Mahoney, 1987). The translation of the doctrine into legislation and practice is a major political struggle. By and large, the struggle consists of finding gender-unbiased methods for determining wages and salaries in occupations filled primarily by women, even though, in principle, the doctrine of comparable worth is a gender-neutral concept (T. A. Mahoney, 1987).

The Gender Pay Gap: The History of its Size and Importance

Earlier we alluded to the traditional gap existing between the earnings made by men and women. This gap, referred to here as the *gender pay gap* and *gender earnings gap* is an interesting and durable social phenomenon. Marini (1989) has traced the history of the size of this gap and has contributed to our understanding of its origins (see also Bayes, 1988; T. A. Mahoney, 1987; M. J. Moore and Abraham, 1992, 1994). The gap is usually referred to or calibrated as a ratio of the average earnings made by women compared to the average earned by men. The figure hovered around 60 percent during the 1970s and began to grow in the 1980s. By 1995, the ratio stood at approximately 72 percent (*The Economist,* June 8, 1996; Steele, 1995), depending on how certain factors were taken into account, such as the precision of the estimates of actual wages paid, whether wages from more than one job per person are considered, the inclusion of self-employment income, the age range over which the estimates are made, and the amount of reporting error that slips into the estimate (Marini, p. 344). Thus, one estimate of the ratio varied from 62 to 68 percent as a function of the types and numbers of adjustments made to the assumptions used (L. O'Neill, 1985).

The gender wage gap changed very little in the United States between 1920 and 1980, hovering around 60 percent, sometimes rising, sometimes falling. In fact, the gap widened between 1939 and 1981 (Bayes, 1988; Marini, 1989). By 1983 the ratio was estimated to be 64 percent, the same as it was in 1955. Marini (1989) reports that women's relative wages decline with age relative to men's wages until about age 40, when the earnings ratio levels off. Finally, although there is a wage gap in all racial groups, the gap is larger among whites than among blacks and Hispanics (Marini, 1989). *The Economist* (1996) claims that a woman's "typical" hourly wage was barely two-thirds that of a man in 1973 but that by 1995 women had increased the ratio to 77 percent. Moreover, *The Economist* study indicates that well-educated women have made the greatest strides over the past decades and that women have been especially active in starting their own small businesses during that period, so that the overall condition of women in the North American economy has improved in recent years. Nevertheless, the gap persists.

Causes of the Gender Pay Gap

Why does this gap exist? Several explanations have been offered. Early in the debate, L. McDonald (1977) suggested that approximately half the gap was attributable to the fact that women tend to occupy lower-paying jobs than men and that the other half can be attributed to discrimination against women, meaning that women are simply paid less than men even when they do the same jobs (see Konrad and Langton, 1994). On the other hand, P. England and McLaughlin (1979) argued against the simple discrimination explanation. They suggested that the gap exists because in addition to occupying lower-paying jobs, women tend to be at the lower pay brackets within the jobs they occupy because so many of them have entered the labor market only recently.

In this section we take a look at two sets of theory that have been offered to explain the earnings gap between men and women. The first set comes largely from economics and sociology; the second comes primarily from psychology.

Economic Perspectives on the Pay Gap

Marini (1989) has categorized the causes for the wage gap into two groups, labeled supply- and demand-side causes. *Supply-side explanations* focus on the "characteristics and decisions of individual workers" (p. 348), including such things as the qualifications, intentions, and attitudes that women and men bring to the workforce, factors lumped under the heading of human capital: "To the extent that men possess greater education, skill and experience than women, they would be expected to earn more than women," and, in fact, such has been the case in North America (T. A. Mahoney, 1987, p. 221). For example, some writers note that compared to men, women frequently have more discontinuous careers, dropping out of the job market more frequently and spending, overall, a smaller percentage of their lives working for remuneration. Similarly, women tend to take on a much larger share of the domestic duties than that of men. Even when women try to pursue upwardly mobile jobs where more pay might be earned, they are frequently limited in the amount of time and energy they can devote to pursuing their careers (see T.A. Mahoney, 1987; M. J. Moore and Abraham, 1992). The author has a close woman friend who earned a Master's of business administration as well as her C.A. designation and became the major authority on Canadian–U.S. tax laws in a large chartered accountancy firm in Vancouver. The woman also took care of the bulk of the responsibility for raising her child, allowing her husband more time to pursue his professional career. One day the senior partners at the firm gave the woman an ultimatum: Either spend more time at her job or face limited promotion opportunities. "Aren't you committed to the firm?" they asked.

The alternatives and the trade-offs among them were simple. The woman could either comply with the partners' demand for more work (i.e., more time away from home), she could renegotiate the distribution of domestic chores with her husband, or she could quit the firm. She was unwilling to work longer hours away from her child, and it was not possible for her husband to take on more of the responsibility at home. She quit the firm, sacrificing 10 years of postsecondary education, a high-status professional career, and a substantial income. This case is representative of countless similar cases throughout North America. Although econometric studies on these human capital matters have had mixed results, Marini's (1989) summary of the research concludes that these human capital factors can account for no more than half of the gender wage gap.[6] Thus, there is more at work here than systematic gender differences in human skills and abilities.

Demand-side explanations focus on the differential value that members of a society place on different goods and services, tradition, discrimination, and systemic features of the marketplace that perpetuate the effects of discrimination: factors such as prejudice, differential performance expectations, and unjust assessment procedures (see Marini, 1989). These forces are the sort that psychologists and students of organizational behavior typically offer as explanations. T. A. Mahoney (1987) observes that every society places differential degrees of value on different types of skills and services. He reports, for example, that the U.S. Census found that physicians were paid 6.5 times as much as nursing aides and orderlies. The reason? In this culture we place more value on what physicians can do than on what nurses' aides and orderlies can do. To the extent that men tend to occupy the more highly valued occupations, they will earn more money; and such is the case (see M. J. Moore and Abraham, 1992). Men and women tend to work in different types of jobs and occupations, notwithstanding the woman's movement and other social forces and norms of egalitarianism. The North American labor force has virtually always been segregated by gender, and, it would seem, a pernicious self-fulfilling prophesy prevails in which one of the reasons that women and men continue to hold certain types of jobs is because they have always held those jobs (see below, and see T. A. Mahoney, 1987, for more on this).

There are also industry factors that affect the demand for (and therefore the value of) different forms of labor. In brief: "Certain industries appear better able to pay than do others, and exploit this ability by offering higher wages. In a very real sense, a given occupation is worth more in one industry than in another" (T. A. Mahoney, 1987). There are also a number of institutional factors that can account for some of the observed earnings gap. One of these is trade unions. Women are proportionately underrepresented in industries in which trade unions organize workers and bargain for

---

[6]One observer of the debate has noted that the actual size of the gap seems to depend on many issues, such as how the gap itself is actually defined and measured. He also notes that there is considerable disagreement among other scholars about how much of the gap can be attributed to nondiscriminatory factors (Rhoads, 1993). His analysis, especially as presented in chapters 1 and 2 (Rhoads, 1994), is interesting and compelling.

collective agreements with management, and other things being equal, unionized employees tend to earn more money than do nonunionized employees (Freeman and Medoff, 1984). Certain organization-level factors may also contribute. Ironically, since there are typically fewer senior women managers and executives in most organizations, there are fewer people available to serve as role models and mentors for less senior women. Therefore, women are less able to build and use networks than men, and the cycle is reinforced (see M. J. Moore and Abraham, 1992, p. 457).

In summary, there are a number of powerful "big picture" factors that can be cited as contributing to the systematic differences that we observe between the earnings of men and women in North America. The sheer intractability of these forces helps explain why and how they have continued to perpetuate the gender wage gap—they are not easily turned around or overruled. Although they may not be as "big" by nature, there are also many other factors of a more micro nature that may be just as difficult to change when we consider pay inequality in the workplace. We look at some of these phenomena next.

Psychological Perspectives on the Gap

From what is primarily a psychological perspective, Bartol (1978) provided an early examination of a phenomenon she referred to as the "sex-structuring of organizations"—the tendency of men to occupy the higher-status, higher-paying jobs within most North American organizations.[7] Although similar to the arguments advanced by economists and sociologists, Bartol's reasoning adds a different perspective, based largely on the psychology of beliefs and attitudes, primarily the former (refer to chapter 9). First, many women simply do not enter labor pools in search of jobs that are traditionally male dominated, in part because of the cultural norm just mentioned and the socialization of females that fosters it (A. H. Stein and Bailey, 1973). In addition, the lower starting salaries offered women by many organizations discourage them from seeking employment in male-dominated occupations. At the time of Bartol's (1978) analysis, there was also evidence that when they compete for jobs, women are frequently offered lower-paying positions, often of the clerical variety or some type that is consistent with the gender-labeling norm (Cash, Gillen, and Burns, 1977; S. L. Cohen and Bunker, 1975; Rosen and Jerdee, 1974a, 1974b). Moreover, women who have been admitted to managerial jobs are often not provided with the early task assignments that give them the chance to demonstrate their competence and get off to as fast a start as their male counterparts (Rosen and Jerdee, 1974b; Terborg, 1977). In addition, work done by women is often not as highly evaluated as work done by men, even when women evaluate the jobs. Finally, there was evidence in the 1970s that when women did perform well at certain tasks, people were more likely to attribute their success to luck rather than to ability (Garland and Price, 1977) and both males and females were likely to attribute failures on the job to the contributions made by female group members (Heilman and Kram, 1978).

Personality traits generally associated with being "male" have traditionally been more closely related to those associated with being a manager than are "female" traits, by both males and females (V. Schein, 1973, 1975), reinforcing the tendency to exclude

---

[7]These days, the term *glass ceiling* is the metaphor of choice to refer to the forces that systematically inhibit the upward movement of women in work organizations.

women from managerial positions. Studies of women who have succeeded in climbing the corporate ladder suggest that females may have to demonstrate traits that are usually defined as male in our culture (A. H. Stein and Bailey, 1973; Van Der Merwe, 1978). Sometimes "token" women are hired into responsible positions for the sake of window dressing, often when they are not really qualified for these positions. The failures that result tend to further reinforce the prior beliefs about the competence of women for male-type (read *managerial*) positions.

We note that Bartol's (1978) theory of the gender structuring of organizations was solidly predicated on theory, research, and practice that was current when she published it. Caution is urged in deciding how much of her theory is still valid because nearly 20 years have elapsed and there is cause to believe that things may have changed in some of the phenomena she depicted (e.g., the size of the gap has been shrinking since 1991, as we will see shortly). Nevertheless, many of the factors that Bartol identified, such as child-rearing practices and difficulties in job evaluation and performance appraisal techniques, for example, are slow to change. The author believes that Bartol's reasoning deserves serious consideration in any 1990s examination of the gender gap in earnings, since the business world is still largely a male arena.

As just suggested, job evaluation is a key concept and set of techniques that figure largely in any discussion of the gender gap in wages (Wittig and Turner, 1988). This is the name for the pseudoscientific techniques used in organizations to determine the relative value of jobs. T. A. Mahoney (1987) has discussed how the processes of job evaluation probably also perpetuate the gender pay gap. Although research reviewed by Mahoney has failed to show that either the gender of job analysts or the gender of job incumbents systematically biases the relative values that raters place on jobs, some studies have shown that the gender stereotypes associated with jobs do affect the evaluation process. That is, the proportion of employees who, at the level of the economy, are female can help to explain the variance in the wages that raters would attribute to different jobs (see T. A. Mahoney and Blake, 1987). Moreover, Grams and Schwab (1985) have shown in an experiment using business school students how a person's knowledge of the current, prevailing wages paid to particular jobs can influence the value the person places on that job. They demonstrated that it is possible during the job evaluation process for current market pay rates to help perpetuate whatever gender-based inequities already exist. This form of "indirect bias" could "work backward through the job evaluation process to produce relatively deflated evaluations for jobs held predominantly by women without the need for any direct bias based on gender composition" (Grams and Schwab, 1985, p. 288).

Another ubiquitous practice in work organizations that can contribute to gender-based inequities is *performance appraisal,* the assessment of people's performance in their formal positions. One recent study has shown how inequities on the basis of race may be perpetrated in performance appraisal settings. In this study of several hundred U.S. managers and their supervisors, the researchers (Greenhaus and Parasuraman, 1993) asked hundreds of black and white supervisors of both genders to rate the job performance of managers who reported to them. They then asked the supervisors to make assessments of the probable causes of, or reasons for, the success of those managers rated at least minimally successful. As they expected, the researchers found that among the most highly successful male managers, the attributed causes for the success were "internal" factors, such as effort and skill, while among the parallel group of highly successful female managers, factors external to the ratees were suggested, such as "she was lucky," the job is easy, or "she had the help of others." Similarly, the black managers' successful job performance, at all levels, was judged to be attributable to ability much less often than was the case among the white managers.

This study is consistent with similar ones conducted in the early 1970s (e.g., Heilman and Guzzo, 1978), although it went beyond the study of gender and looked at the effects of race on performance evaluations. Further, the results of this study showed that the level of ability attributed to the managers was in turn predictive of ratings made about them in terms of their probable career prospects. Women and black managers were viewed as relying more than white male managers on factors other than ability for their success. These ratings of ability seemed to predict the supervisors' expectations for the future prospects of the managers reporting to them. In other words, the study demonstrates how self-fulfilling prophesies (see Jussim, 1986) may help to fuel the processes responsible for the glass ceiling effect (C. King, 1993; A. M. Morrison, White, and Van Velsor, 1987). People whose successes are written off to luck and the help of others rather than attributed to their own ability are less likely to develop high self-esteem, self-efficacy, and expectations that they can succeed. The way that rewards and punishments are distributed in our society is an important social issue. It is especially important in the workplace, where we spend so much of our lives. Managers who ignore or overlook the power of the sentiments associated with distributive justice and the perceptions of fairness and equity do so at their own peril as well as at the peril of those who work for them. Yet, as strong and as important as these forces are, they are very difficult to manage.

There are still a variety of psychological and sociological reasons why women tend not to occupy managerial and other high-paying jobs. Long-standing and internationally shared (Bayes, 1988; Leacock and Safa, 1986) cultural beliefs about the role of females and the nature of what constitute men's work and women's work[8] perpetuate the gap between male and female earnings more than two decades after the enactment of legislation to outlaw such practices. In the following section we take a brief look at the role of legislation in the battle against gender-based pay discrimination in Canada and the United States.

Legislation against Pay Discrimination

Although both Montana and Michigan had adopted equal pay legislation as early as 1919, followed by Illinois, New York, Massachusetts, and Washington in the 1940s, they were the only U.S. states with such provisions for a quarter of a century. As of 1994 (see M. J. Moore and Abraham, 1994), about half of the 50 U.S. states had implemented comparable worth legislation for public-sector employees. Many U.S. states have begun adjusting the salaries of female state employees as a result of comparable worth analyses conducted in accordance with their state laws (e.g., Idaho, Iowa, Minnesota, Massachusetts, New York, New Mexico, and Washington; M. J. Moore and Abraham, 1994).

---

[8]In 1995, 20-year-old Shannon Faulkner resigned after one week in boot camp at the Citadel, a venerated military academy in Charleston, S.C. Ms. Faulkner spent two years of legal and administrative struggle to be admitted to the academy, making her the first woman cadet in the 152-year history of the male bastion. She and her family suffered vandalism and even death threats during her campaign to be admitted. Eventually, the strain of the experience caused her to withdraw (Carlson, 1995; Lacayo, 1995).

Things at the United States federal level were much slower to develop. It took the civil rights movement in the United States in the 1960s to provide the necessary sociopolitical background for the more widespread emergence of federal legislation to make pay discrimination illegal. The Civil Rights Act of 1964 (particularly Title VII of the Act) and the Equal Pay Act of 1963 outlawed wage discrimination, the latter bill forbidding wage discrimination "between employees on the basis of sex when employees perform equal work on jobs in the same establishment requiring equal skill, effort, and responsibility and performed under similar working conditions." Exceptions to these terms were allowed where seniority was a bona fide basis for pay differences or where merit was to be rewarded on the basis of the quantity or quality of work performed. It became federal U.S. law that men and women must be paid equally when they are performing substantially identical jobs, other things equal.

Title VII of the Civil Rights Act was met with some resistance when introduced to the U.S. Senate and was amended such that gender differences in pay can occur if these differences are consistent with the provisions of the Equal Pay Act (as discussed above). Nevertheless, the Civil Rights Act led to the establishment of the Equal Employment Opportunity Commission (EEOC) to enforce the provisions of the act in the private sector. "The guidelines bar, among other discriminatory acts, hiring based on stereotyped characterizations of the sexes, classification or labelling of 'men's jobs' and 'women's jobs,' and advertising under male or female headings" (U.S. Department of Labor, Women's Bureau, 1977, p. 2). In practice, however, the Senate amendment has limited the activities of the EEOC to the scope of the Equal Pay Act of 1963, and this interpretation of the 1964 act has stood up in the courts (see M. J. Moore and Abraham, 1994, p. 266). Therefore, the EEOC guidelines do not provide for Title VII pay equity claims, as such, so many cases have been set aside without investigation, leading to considerable litigation. Just the same, the many requirements that must be met to bring these cases to court have resulted in only a few of them being brought, and the courts have managed to avoid dealing directly with the comparable-worth issue. The legal fine points pertaining to litigation of comparable worth cases are beyond the scope of this book. The interested reader is referred to a readable recent summary provided by M. J. Moore and Abraham (1994).

Pay Equity in Canada

In Canada, the flow of events has been very similar to that in the United States. A Royal Commission report by Federal Judge Abella (1984) provided the most important legitimate argument favoring the intervention of the government into matters related to gender differences in pay and conditions of employment. The phrase *pay equity* is used rather than *comparable worth,* but it is essentially the same concept. The Canadian Human Rights Act provides virtually the same protection to Canadian citizens as do the Equal Pay Act and the Civil Rights Act in the United States. The federal law states that wage differentials between men and women are illegal if both are performing "work of equal value." Similar laws have been passed in seven of the 10 provinces and in the federal domain. A key difference between the United States and Canada, however, is that in Canada, pay equity legislation applies to both employees in the public sector and employees working in organizations whose enterprises fall under federal (as opposed to provincial) jurisdiction (since the Canadian Human Rights Act of 1978). In fact, Canadian pay equity legislation applies to both the 512,000 employees in the public sector (*Government Finance Review,* 1994) and more than 600,000 employees working in crown corporations and private organizations whose enterprises fall under federal jurisdiction. The act requires employers to develop, display, and put into practice plans for every bargaining unit and for all groups of nonunionized employees. This plan must identify all the categories of jobs dominated by either male or female employees, and it must explain how the value of each job is determined. The law also requires that wage differences be justified where they are found to exist, providing exceptions for those circumstances that include recognition of merit and/or seniority. In short, the Canadian law, as written, entails a lot of detail and effort by government and nongovernment employers in federally regulated organizations.

In January 1991, the Canadian government released its annual report on the gender pay gap. The figures showed that the average earnings for women over 15 years of age who were working full time was $26, compared to $38 for men of the same category. This means that the gap was slightly more than 30 percent, although it had narrowed by 2 percent since 1990 and by 11 percent since 1967 (N. Miller, 1993). The size of the gender gap varied from province to province. The ratio of women's to men's earnings for the same period in Prince Edward Island was 80.8 percent; it was lowest in Alberta at 64.5 percent. By the end of 1992, the government had paid more than $500 million in both one-shot and recurring pay equity settlements to approximately 74,000 men and women, about one fourth of the public payroll (*Government Finance Review,* 1994). This is, to say the least, a lot of money, about $375 million in U.S. dollars.

In Ontario, the province that enacted the toughest pay equity legislation, firms with between 50 and 99 employees were to have made adjustments to pay inequities by January 1993. By January 1, 1994, the same deadline applied to companies that employed between 10 and 49 employees. These were the dates set by the law; they were certainly not the dates of actual compliance with the law by many employers, who struggled to implement it or avoid it altogether (N. Miller, 1993). As in the case of the federal jurisdiction, there was a lot of work and a lot of "catching-up" involved. No wonder there was a commensurate amount of complaining and resistance. For example, a major newspaper in Ontario found during its required pay equity review that inequities ranged from 16 cents an hour to as much as $8.06 an hour (among nonunion employees). Among its unionized personnel, adjustments ranged from 91 cents an hour to $3.57 an hour.

Enacting equal pay laws is one thing; seeing them have real impact on practice is another. Seven years after the law was passed in Canada, there were still wide male–female disparities in wages and salaries, largely because the law was being interpreted and there were few, if any, provisions for enforcement (Kovach and Millspaugh, 1990).[9] Another reason, of course, was the sheer scale of the task: Defining comparable worth is a very difficult operation (Milkovich, 1980) and depends largely on arbitrary standards and decisions and idiosyncratic views of what constitutes value (T. A. Mahoney, 1987; Waluchow, 1988).

---

[9]One perspective on pay equity in Canada from a women's point of view is provided in the March 1996 issue of *Chatelaine* magazine (H. Schacter, 1996).

Criticisms of the Comparable Worth Doctrine

Reference was made earlier to the resistance that comparable worth has encountered by people who have to implement it and manage it as policy. Let's take a brief look at the sources of this resistance with the help of Waluchow (1988) (see also M. J. Moore and Abraham, 1994). One of the key sources of difficulty, Waluchow claims, is that some people adopt the position that it is not clear that the reason for the gap is discrimination; rather, the main causes are legitimate human capital factors of the sort reviewed above (e.g., women are less educated than men, or have less seniority in many cases).

A second source of resistance is fear of the very high cost that businesses and government would incur if the pay gap was closed. Grams and Schwab (1985) have estimated that the aggregate cost of doing so in the United States would have been between $250 billion and $300 billion per year (note that their estimate is at least a decade old; the cost in current dollars would be hard to estimate, because although the dollar is worth less now, some of the gap has been closed; see J. O'Neill and Polachek, 1993).

A third source of resistance identified by Waluchow (1988) is related to the second. Some critics fear that closing the pay gap would decrease the demand for labor, especially in those sectors of the economy dominated by women employees. According to this view, well-intentioned policies designed to bring about social equity and fairness would backfire, hurting the very people the policies are designed to help.[10] Empirical studies on this matter have yielded contradictory results (see Killingsworth, 1990; Sorenson, 1994).

What Is Equal Value?

Finally, there is the problem of deciding how to determine when work of equal value is, in fact, of equal value. In other words, how can we decide which jobs are of equal value? Whose criteria are to be used? Who is to decide? This puzzle has been cited by a number of authors over the years, but few have addressed it other than to state that "the market" will determine relative value (we will see that argument developed shortly). Waluchow (1988) lists eight possible answers to the question: How does one determine the worth or value of someone's work so as to compare it with the work of others? He generates the following list:

1. By whatever value the existing market (i.e., an employer) will pay for it
2. By whatever a fair market would pay for it
3. By what she deserves for doing it
4. By how much her work contributes to the success of the firm
5. By how much her work contributes to the community
6. By whatever the going rate is in "the industry" for people who perform the same work
7. By whatever value her work is assigned by her employer's explicit wage policy
8. By whatever value her work is assigned by her employer's implicit wage policy

---

[10]A somewhat similar concern was identified by R. M. Kelly and Bayes (1988): that equalizing pay for women's jobs may discourage women from seeking employment in occupations that are normally male dominated.

R. M. Kelly and Bayes (1988) identify another fundamental source of disagreement that is somewhat hidden in those listed above. There is a simple lack of agreement among interested parties concerning who should *implement* comparable worth policies even if they are accepted in principle: legislatures, unions, courts, or executives.

In summary, there are many ideological and practical sources of resistance to the doctrine of comparable worth, notwithstanding how acceptable it might seem at face value. The resistance is often quite passionate and even hostile. Consider, for example, the following excerpts from a column by Barbara Amiel (1985), a right-leaning critic who appears in a number of magazines around the world, including *Maclean's* in Canada. The title of her column was "The Dangerous Cost of Equal Pay." In accordance with the market value concept (A. Smith, 1937, cited by T. A. Mahoney, 1987), Amiel wrote:

> Of all the concepts that the totalitarian instinct of our times has bequeathed to society—including racial and gender job quotas and laws against free speech—the seemingly-harmless slogan "equal pay for work of equal value" is potentially the most destructive to a free society. . . .
>
> Of course, all work has equal value in a purely moral and abstract sense. The most complicated brain surgery could not be performed without the steady contribution of electricians who install equipment or the orderlies who prepare the patient. But to view things so abstractly and demand that everyone be paid the same would be ludicrous.
>
> The value of a job is determined by nothing but supply and demand. Value depends upon how many people require a service and how many others are willing to provide it. Nobody in his right mind would decide that a performer of pop tunes is a more skilled musician than the concertmaster of a symphony orchestra, but the demand for one outstrips the other and often so does the pay. My own classical preference may be for a classical violinist, but that is a minority view; most people want to hear Madonna. . . .
>
> To stop this steamroller policy will require fighting shortsighted and narrow-minded feminists as well as cowardly politicians. But if our society wishes to retain equality of opportunity and liberty, the fight must be won. (p. 9)

For Amiel and many other critics, the entire process of equating jobs that are inherently different amounts to replacing the natural forces of supply and demand in a democratic, capitalist society with a contrived, arbitrary set of wages and salaries of the sort found in controlled economies.

Recent Trends in the Gender Pay Gap and Their Causes

Earlier we noted that the gender earnings gap has narrowed by about 1 percentage point per year between 1976 and 1989 (J. O'Neill and Polachek, 1993). In 1976, the ratio of female to male income was 0.602; by 1990, it was estimated to be 0.716. The primary causes of the closure, it appears, have been changes in the human capital factors that have been proposed as the most potent explanations for the existence of the gap in the first place (see T. A. Mahoney, 1988; Sorenson, 1991). J. O'Neill and Polachek (1993) demonstrated that during the 13-year period just mentioned, there were corresponding increases in the marketable skills of women as well as in the years of experience they bring to the marketplace. J. O'Neill and Polachek (1993) estimate that these factors accounted for between one-third and one-half of the narrowing of the gap. They speculate that during the period there may might also have been a decrease in discrimination, resulting from both legislative pressure and a change in employer attitudes and practices, but their data fall short of providing support for such a contention. Sorenson (1991) believes that there has been a reduction in simple discrimination and a convergence in the distribution of men and women by occupation. Hence, Sorenson's (1991) analysis is similar to that of J. O'Neill and Polachek. On the whole, it appears that things are changing in a positive direction for women in the North American workplace. However, there is still a long way to go until parity with men is achieved. While 70 percent is better than 60 percent, women are still paid less than men in North America.

The Current Social/Historical Context of the Comparable Worth Doctrine

Since the doctrine of comparable worth was first proposed, there have been many court decisions, many billions of hours of day-to-day experience, and still, the force and the social acceptability of that concept are in flux. Libertarians would propose that people who perform different jobs that are somehow deemed equal by any civilized social accounting scheme should be paid comparable wages. The student of these matters learns to recognize that the feasibility and acceptability of abstract concepts with social implications such as comparable worth are limited by the prevailing sociopolitical values at the time.

Affirmative action is another example. During the days when liberal philosophy was in vogue (or accepted, tolerated, or forgiven), the idea of making explicit, bald attempts to right the wrongs of discrimination of past generations against disadvantaged groups such as women, racial minorities, and the physically handicapped were accepted. As time goes by, we have seen a shift to the right in North America, especially in the United States, where social assistance programs such as President Clinton's health bill went down to defeat. In the United States, the Reagan administration oversaw and fostered a decline in interest in comparable worth (M. J. Moore and Abraham, 1994), and the recent election of a majority Republican membership in Congress reinforces this ideological shift. In Canada, the people of Ontario, the province with the most "advanced" practices in the pay equity domain, elected a majority government of Progressive Conservatives in 1995. The new government promised to repeal much or all of the employment equity legislation enacted by the previous New Democratic Party (NDP) government (see Janigan, 1995).

As social historians as far back as Karl Marx would tell us, the pendulum will swing back and forth. Implications for the enactment of legislation to assist the disadvantaged will be a result of these ideological swings. It was much more popular and acceptable to speak and write about employment equity, affirmative action, and minority rights 15 years ago (Pinder, 1984) than it is in the mid-1990s. Accordingly, the author expects the gender pay gap to continue for at least another quarter century. Women will continue to be paid less than men for performing work of equal value. The only question will be whether the gap widens, stays fixed, or somehow manages to continue to close.[11]

---

[11]The International Labor Organization (ILO) released a study in August 1995 that concluded, among other things, that it will take at least 500 years to "get women into managerial and administrative positions at the top equally with men" (Morris, 1995).

An Editorial Note on Comparable Worth and Pay Equity

The author acknowledges the scholarship of Michael Evan Gold (1983) for drawing his attention to the following passage from the Old Testament to help frame and motivate the following section of this chapter: "And the Lord spoke to Moses, saying, Speak unto the children of Israel, and say unto them: When a man shall clearly utter a vow of persons unto the Lord, according to thy valuation, then thy valuation for the male from twenty years old even unto sixty years old, even thy valuation shall be fifty shekels of silver, after the shekel of the sanctuary. And, if it be female, then thy valuation shall be thirty shekels" (Lev. 27:1–4). Although the author is neither a Biblical scholar, a Jew, nor an adherent of the dictates of the Old Testament, the power of this passage reflects the importance of the comparable worth doctrine when we take into account the point made by T. A. Mahoney (1987) on the phenomenological significance of pay equity and, with it by extension, employment equity. Mahoney wrote: "In other words, there is more to comparable worth than fairness in economic treatment of people by their employers. There are issues of human dignity and self-esteem deeply associated with the simple pay aspects of the work relationship" (p. xx). In chapter 6 we saw how important human dignity and self-esteem are in a person's life in general and as factors in the motivation to work in particular. The rest should be self-evident.

A Glance Ahead

To this point we have taken a careful look at the key principles of distributive justice and equity theory, focusing attention on the issue of comparable worth. The key point underlying the discussion is the fact that the concern is with the ways that valued outcomes such as pay are *distributed* among people. In the following sections we direct our attention away from the outcomes of distribution decisions and toward the fairness dimensions *in the means* by which rewards and punishments are distributed in a society (or a workplace). We will see that attention can be paid to both the formal procedures that an organization prescribes for the administration of justice and to the informal, interpersonal dynamics that actually characterize the management of rewards and sanctions. The first of these topics is referred to as procedural justice. We investigate it next, then turn to the second issue (interactional justice) at the end of the chapter.

PROCEDURAL JUSTICE IN THE WORKPLACE

The procedures by which managers distribute work-related outcomes have justice implications that are different from the actual decisions themselves. Accordingly, the last two decades have witnessed considerable theory and research under the rubric of *procedural justice*. This new school of thought has not supplanted the earlier focus on distributive and equity matters, but it has provided fresh insights into matters of fairness and justice at work (Greenberg, 1987, 1990a). Folger and Greenberg (1985) "conceive of procedural justice as the perceived fairness of the procedures used in making decisions" (p. 143). They note that regardless of "whether the outcomes are pay raises to be distributed to employees, labor disputes to be settled, or performance evaluations to be recorded, a key determinant of these decisions involves *how* they are made" (p. 143).

The earliest focus of procedural justice in organizational behavior and human resources management was on the procedures used to resolve disputes in the workplace (see Thibault and Walker, 1975, 1978). Since then, scholars have broadened their attention to the procedural justice issues related to a variety of workplace matters, such as personnel selection (Arvey, 1979), reward allocation (see G. S. Leventhal, 1976, 1980), performance evaluation procedures, discipline, compensation systems, and participatory decision-making systems (see Folger and Greenberg, 1985, for a review). There are even elements of the comparable worth issue related to procedural justice, as pointed out by Greenberg and McCarty (1990). During times of organizational downsizing and employee layoffs, distributive justice has become especially important as a standard for managerial decision making. Before we begin, it is worth repeating that procedural justice is similar to interactional justice, as we discussed in the preceding section. The difference lies in whether we are dealing with the quality of the person-to-person interactions that characterize outcome distribution, or whether we are concerned with the *official procedures* that lie behind the processes for making decisions about people and the allocation of rewards and punishments. As we saw, interactional justice deals with the former set of issues. Procedural justice deals with the latter set of concerns. Parts of this research may have more relevance than others for a general treatment of work motivation. We will rely most heavily on the concepts presented by Sheppard et al. (1992), although no attempt is made to summarize their entire theory of procedural justice. Readers who desire much more comprehensive treatments are referred to excellent works by Cropanzano (1992), Feuille and Delany (1992), Greenberg (1987), and Lind and Tyler (1988).

Dimensions of Procedural Justice

One of the earliest attempts to define distributive justice in social psychology identified six dimensions in the construct (Leventhal, 1980). By this view, procedures are fair if they are made (1) with consistent procedures, (2) without self-interest, (3) on the basis of accurate information, (4) with opportunities to make corrections, (5) with the interests of all legitimate parties taken into account, and (6) while observing moral and ethical standards. For the sake of emphasizing the distinction between procedural and distributive justice, notice that none of these six criteria (or dimensions) mention the nature of the *outcomes* of decisions. Rather, they all deal with the nature of the formal procedures used.

Fairness

About a decade after the work of Leventhal and his colleagues, Sashkin and Williams (1990) identified nine facets of *fairness*[12] and showed how differences in employee perceptions on these nine dimensions were related to the differences in employee sickness rates and accident compensation costs among 20 outlets of a large retail organization, 10 in each of two regions of the country. The nine dimensions were as follows:

---

[12]The reader will note that some of these dimensions of fairness might be classified as perceived outcomes from the employment process, as much as they reflect procedural processes. Nevertheless, the entire list is presented here for the sake of coherence in relating the work of Sashkin and Williams (1990).

1. *Trust:* confidence that employees have in management and the degree to which employees believe what management tells them

2. *Consistency:* regularity, steady continuity, or predictability of management action such that employees are not surprised . . . by management actions

3. *Truthfulness:* management's fidelity and sincerity in action

4. *Integrity:* management's adherence in action to values, ethics, or a moral code

5. *Expectations:* provision of clear statements by management as to what task activities are desired of employees and what consequences will result

6. *Equity:* demonstration through action that all employees are treated alike in terms of rewards and punishments for similar behaviors and results

7. *Influence:* provision of authority to employees equal to their responsibility, so that employees have a sense of "ownership" of their actions and achievements

8. *Justice:* adherence to a code of standards that is perceived as appropriate and administered impartially

9. *Respect:* management's expression of concern, consideration, and regard for employees

Sashkin and Williams (1990) developed scales to measure perceived fairness in terms of their nine dimensions (as well as a final scale to assess overall fairness). They asked the store managers to rate their own fairness on these scales. Similarly, they had the department managers rate themselves in terms of the 10 fairness dimensions. Finally, they had the employees use the rating scales not to assess themselves, but to assess their bosses in terms of fairness. The reader may anticipate the findings. The store managers in both the high-illness/accident-cost stores saw their own behavior as fair, as did the managers from the stores with the lower illness rates and accidents costs. By their own admission, then, all of the store managers were equally fair. Similarly, when the researchers compared the department managers' ratings of their own behaviors, there were no systematic differences related to whether they were from high- or low-accident/ illness stores. Finally, when the researchers compared the ratings provided by department managers of their store managers, a different picture emerged. Fairness ratings on two dimensions were related to the health statistics: expectations and influence. Even more interesting were the differences between the high- and low-health-statistics stores when the researchers compared the ratings of fairness provided by the nonsupervisory employees (who had assessed their bosses). There were differences across all 10 dimensions of fairness, five of them statistically significant. In a nutshell, the results showed that employees who worked in the stores with the lowest accident rates and health costs systematically and consistently rated their supervisors as lower in fairness.

The factors that were especially critical in differentiating among the two groups of stores were what the authors referred to as "warm and fuzzy" factors: factors of fairness such as trust, truthfulness, integrity, and justice. On the basis of these findings, Sashkin and Williams concluded that fairness does make a difference—even on hard bottom-line-outcome variables such as employee sickness (and, therefore absenteeism) and accident compensation costs. The point of this simple, relevant study is that treating employees is important. It can make a difference to do so, not only in terms of soft, attitudinal measures but also in terms that managers frequently care about the most: the bottom line.

Balance, Correctness, and the Eye of the Beholder

For Sheppard et al. (1992; see also Minton, Lewicki, and Sheppard, 1994) a decision is perceived as fair if the outcomes are seen as *balanced* and *correct*. Their concept of balance is central to distributive justice, which we dealt with earlier. By *balance,* they mean that an act by (for example) a manager "is compared to similar actions in similar situations. If the act is seen as roughly equivalent to actions in these situations, it is seen as fair; if it is seen as not equivalent, it is judged as unfair. . . . [T]he same punishment should be applied to all who commit the same crime" (Minton et al., 1994, p. 139).

Their concept of *correctness* also gets at the nub of the matter of procedural justice. Minton and colleagues argue that perceptions about the correctness of the procedures followed in decisions are as important as perceptions about the outcomes of those decisions. "By 'correctness,' we mean that quality which makes the decision seem right—a determination that the decision seems to be compatible with qualities of consistency, accuracy, clarity, procedural thoroughness, and compatibility with the morals and values of the times" (Minton et al., 1994, p. 140). For example, an employee may be unhappy about the absolute amount of pay increase he receives, but he may ultimately feel that he was treated fairly if the procedures used to determine that amount are explained to him and are seen as appropriate. In other words, "perceived procedural fairness may help mitigate the effects of perceived unjust outcomes (i.e., low raises, missed promotions, or small budgets)" (Sheppard et al., 1992, p. 17).

In sum, to be seen by others as fair, a decision must feature both balance and correctness. If either facet is missing, a decision is not perceived as fair. The key point here is that it is an observer's perception of balance and correctness that matters. We return to this point later.

The interactive effects of outcome and procedural fairness were illustrated recently in a study of the fallout effects from company layoffs (Brockner et al., 1994). Following from Folger's (1986) referent cognitions theory, Brockner and his colleagues reasoned that "the joint presence of negative outcomes and low procedural fairness will elicit particularly negative reactions. To state the predicted interaction differently, when procedural justice is low, outcome negativity should have an adverse effect on individuals' reactions . . ." (p. 398).

Studying three different groups of employees who had been affected one way or another by layoffs by their employers, they supported their hypothesis. One group consisted of 218 layoff victims who were applying for the first time for unemployment benefits. Most of them had worked in the service sector. The second group (of 150 people) were referred to as layoff survivors: They had kept their jobs in a financial services organization that had undergone layoffs about half a year earlier than the study. The third group studied were 147 employees who were about to be laid off from a large unionized manufacturing plant in the southern United States. Because the people in each of the three groups were in entirely different circumstances, the researchers used different measures of what they called *outcome negativity* as their dependent variable. The researchers were especially interested in the role played by advance notice among those who had been laid off (group 1) and who were about to be laid off (group 3).

Without getting into the nuances of the different measures for the different groups, we can summarize the findings by reporting that, as predicted, the employees reported lower levels of outcome negativity (such as low levels of organizational trust and commitment) when they perceived that appropriate steps had been taken to treat them fairly in the context of the various layoff experiences they had had. It seems that perceived fairness in process helped to assuage some of the bitterness and dissatisfaction that employees experienced, whether they had been laid off, survived a layoff, or were about to be laid off.

A later study in this tradition has suggested a possible explanation for the interaction of distributive and procedural justice on employee attitudes (P. A. Siegel, Brockner, and Tyler, 1995). Employees who have experiences that they perceive to be fair in terms of process and procedures will be more likely to develop feelings of *trust* toward their employers. These positive feelings may then serve to make the effects of harsh or undesirable outcomes (e.g., disappointing pay increases) less damaging to their feelings toward the employer. In other words, procedural justice may help to build trust, which in turn, may help to offset or assuage the negative impact of distributive decisions. Siegel and her colleagues also suggest that the procedural justice–trust development connection is probably not as strong during times of scarcity of resources (P. A. Siegel et al., 1995; see Brockner and Siegel, 1996, for a summary of the interactive effects of trust and distributive and procedural justice). We return to the issue of procedural justice and fairness in employee layoffs later in this chapter.

Levels of Justice

In addition to the issues of balance and correctness, fairness perceptions are seen as operating on at least three different *levels,* referred to as outcome, procedure, and system: "At the outcome level, judgements are made about the balance and correctness of particular results, for example, a pay raise, a layoff, or a dismissal. At the procedural level, judgements are made about the balance and correctness of the procedures and processes by which decisions are made: how a raise is determined or how a layoff decision is implemented. Finally, at the systemic level, judgments are made about the broader organizational systems in which procedures are generated and embedded" (Minton et al., 1994, p. 141). This three-way distinction implies that judgments about the fairness of the system must usually be based on the observation of a number of treatments and decisions by some people about others. For example, an employee may feel that a co-worker has been treated harshly and unfairly by a supervisor upon coming to work late for the first time. The observer may have feelings about the balance and correctness of the outcome (a verbal reprimand) and even about the procedure used (the supervisor decides that the employee was late even though there was a misunderstanding about the starting time). But a decision about the fairness of the system as a whole must be based on the observation of *many* instances of lateness and disciplinary acts for lateness, as well as upon occurrences of other forms of crime and punishment.

In short, the concepts of balance are seen as independent (Folger and Greenberg, 1985) of the levels of the judgment. Perceptions of either or both balance and correctness may be made by an employee about specific outcomes ("I didn't get a raise"), about procedures ("The boss didn't refer to my performance review before she denied me a raise"), or about the broader system that governs decisions ("I think the company should refer to our formal performance reviews before making decisions about our raises!").

The Goals of Decision Making

For Sheppard and his colleagues (Minton et al., 1994; Sheppard et al., 1992), perceptions of balance and correctness can also be affected by the *goals* of a person or an organization in decision making. One goal is *performance effectiveness.* A second goal is a concern for a *sense of community.* Here the goal and the basis for assessment of fairness is whether people manage to coalesce, to form groups, and to work in harmony. A third goal involves a concern for *individual dignity and humaneness.* If the purpose of decision making has implications for these goods, the assessment of fairness (via balance and correctness) takes on yet another frame of reference.

Sheppard and his colleagues (1992) point out that the goals associated with decision making can often be in conflict. For example, if rewards and punishments are distributed with performance as the primary goal, individual or group achievement will be rewarded, possibly undermining the sense of esprit de corps of those who did not do so well (thereby compromising the community goal). Yet if rewards are distributed *equally* among employees for the sake of maintaining harmony, the incentive value of the rewards is diminished and the goal of performance effectiveness is compromised. These clashes among goals are especially common in work settings where different parties may favor different goals, such that any set of decisions about reward distribution may alienate all but a few people (whose own goals have been served at the expense of the goals of those who are not rewarded).

To make matters even more complex, perception plays as big a role in the determination of procedural justice as it does in assessments of distributive justice, as discussed earlier in the chapter. For example, a manager may distribute rewards and sanctions according to a strict norm of equality because she wishes to serve a goal of community and harmony. Her employees may or may not understand that the benefits are being distributed equally, even if they all accept the wisdom of her choice of goal. As a result, many of the employees may be disgruntled and lose faith in the manager. As in the case of distributive justice, fairness is in the eye of the beholder when we consider the procedures by which decisions are made.

Looking Ahead

Later in the chapter we explore several common types of organizational transactions and issues that have procedural justice dimensions. Many or most of the decisions that a manager or supervisor makes on a day-to-day basis about the treatment of his subordinates are subject to perceptions by others (including the subordinates themselves) about the procedural fairness of these decisions. When we address the various substantive decisions (e.g., discipline, layoffs, and firings) the trick will be to keep in mind how the three dimensions in the theory of justice interact to determine perceptions of fairness (balance and correctness, level—as it relates to outcomes, procedures, and systems—and the goals in force at the time).

Procedural Justice, Discipline, and Punishment

One of the areas of management and work motivation that has strong associations with the concepts of justice discussed in this chapter is employee discipline and punishment (see chapter 14). Our purpose here is to look at discipline and punishment from the perspective of *perceived* justice, particularly as assessed in the eyes of third parties, such as co-workers of the individual(s) punished. To begin, let us define our terms. Although they ultimately decided to use the two terms interchangeably in their analysis of the matter, Arvey and Jones (1985) drew a distinction between punishment and discipline as they are found in work settings. For them, following Kazdin (1975, pp. 33–34), *punishment* is defined as "the presentation of an aversive event or the removal of a positive event following a response which decreases the probability of that response" (p. 369). This definition has its roots in the school of operant conditioning (which we examine in chapter 14).

Although the roots of their adopted definition may lie in behaviorism,[13] Arvey and Jones acknowledge that there are social cues associated with punishment and that the concept of *discipline* differs from it in a number of ways. First, punishment implies negative motives on the part of the person using it. The punishment itself has the connotation of retribution, or payback. Discipline, on the other hand, is more future oriented. The goal of discipline is to point the way to new, anticipated behavior. There is also a distinction based on the formality or informality of the act: "Typically, employees use the term discipline to refer to the *formal* sanctions delivered by the organization (e.g., write-ups, formal warnings, etc.) whereas punishment implies aversive stimuli delivered in a less formal fashion. It is not necessary that punishment occur within the actual structural confines of the organization; it could occur in outside social settings which include organizational members" (Arvey and Jones, 1985, p. 370).

A Brief Aside on the Basic Issue

In the context of an extended discussion of equity, fairness, and justice in supposedly voluntary work situations in a free society, one might ask a number of fundamental questions about the right of any employer to "discipline" or "punish" an employee. The existence of discipline procedures in the workplace in Western societies implies something about the unstated rights of employers and the unstated appropriateness of the use of discipline by one party over another. What about human freedom and dignity? What about people's rights under the eyes of their gods or under the legal constitutions of the countries in which they live? How often does an employee challenge the right of a boss, supervisor, or enterprise owner to apply sanctions of any kind? Clearly, company policies, social standards of judgment, and even the decisions of arbitrators place limits on the types and degrees of sanctions that are tolerated in work settings. The fundamental fact of their existence, however, goes unstated in Western business practice. Seldom do students of management think such thoughts about the fundamental nature of the work relationship; not until, perhaps, they themselves have been on the receiving end of retribution for violating some organization's formal or informal rules. We seem to take it for granted.

---

[13]A nonbehaviorist definition is offered by Trevino (1992, p. 649): "Punishment is defined as the manager's application of a negative consequence or the withdrawal of a positive consequence from someone under his or her supervision." No mention is made of the punishment's effects on the future probability of the occurrence of the punished act. In the behaviorist model, discipline amounts to punishment, by definition, only when it alters the probabilities of future behaviors.

The Social Effects of Discipline and Punishment at Work

Let's return to the basic point. People frequently witness the administration of discipline and punishment in work settings, notwithstanding the sentiments raised in the preceding paragraph. Through the dynamics of social learning, modelling, and vicarious reinforcement and punishment (see chapter 14), employees other than those upon whom the sanctions are delivered learn something about the rules and about the consequences of running afoul of those rules (see Trevino, 1992). In earlier times, punishment by the state or by the church was deliberately administered in public for all to see, presumably to allow the powerful effects of social learning to obviate the need to administer punishment to any and all who might otherwise sin, left to their own devices and personal tendencies.

Previous reviews of the work on punishment in the workplace have tended to focus on the consequences of the punishment for the behaviors and attitudes of the victims. The results of these studies have been mixed and inconclusive (see Arvey and Jones, 1985). Nevertheless, interest in the topic remains and may in fact be growing, in part because the field is increasingly turning away from behaviorism toward social cognitive theories such as that of Bandura (Bandura, 1986; Krietner and Luthans, 1991; and see chapter 14). A question for today's workplace is: What are the effects *on other people* of the administration of organizational discipline and punishment?

Current thinking that abandons the behaviorist perspective (e.g., Ball, Trevino, and Sims, 1994) throws organizational punishment in a somewhat different light, suggesting a number of potential *positive* consequences of its use (Trevino, 1992): "For example, punishment may serve to uphold social norms within a group, signal appropriate and inappropriate behaviors to observers. . . , deter misconduct in . . . group members, and create perceptions of the supervisor and the organization as just or unjust" (Trevino, 1992, p. 674). Observers of punishment form opinions about its fairness when it is administered, and they base these judgments on several factors (Arvey and Jones, 1985). These factors include many considerations, such as their own knowledge about the alleged offense, whether the punishment seems to fit the crime, and whether other people had committed similar offenses and gone unpunished. These factors sound quite similar to many of the factors contained in the theory of procedural justice of Sheppard et al. (1992), described earlier.

Trevino (1992) points out that another key factor determining the reactions of observers is whether they view the "misconduct" as being, in fact, misconduct. An act may violate company rules but still be seen as acceptable by employee-observers. Other issues that may enter a person's assessment of the fairness of discipline include employee characteristics (such as gender, age, and race), the consequences of the rule infraction or crime, the person's disciplinary history, and even the person's skill or ability to do the job properly in the first place (T. R. Mitchell, Green, and Wood, 1981; Shingledecker, 1983, cited by Arvey and Jones, 1985, p. 393). Individual assessments of the severity of the punishment, taking into account the severity of the crime, are also important (from an equity perspective).

Lest it be thought that employee reactions to the application of discipline to their peers is always negative, we must observe that there is a norm in Western society for rule violation to be dealt with by retributive justice in some form or other, and the workplace is no exception. Thus, workers who all live under a set of rules and procedures that are more or less well accepted grow to expect the authorities to apply some form of punishment to those who seriously violate the rules (Trevino, 1992). Violation of the rules with the strongest general support tends to motivate the strongest desire among group members for severe retribution. By these norms, when an important rule is violated and the perpetrator is not punished, others in the group will feel a sense of injustice. When punishment is not meted out in such circumstances, the "group's belief systems, norms, and values are open to question and may be viewed as degrading" (p. 654) to those people who suffered the effects of the rule transgression.

Another key factor is the degree to which the accused person is seen as actually having been *responsible* for the crime, or whether there were external or extenuating factors beyond her control. Similarly, if the offensive behavior is viewed by observers as intentional, and if the consequences of the offending act are seen as severe, there tends to be a greater desire among observers for retribution (Trevino, 1992). There is some evidence that the severity of a witnessed punishment affects the probability that an observer's own misconduct behavior will be affected. The more severe the outcome, the more likely it is that observers will pay attention to the occurrence of the punishment and then be discouraged from committing the punished deed themselves. However, this seems to be the case only when the perceived costs of the punishment are believed to outweigh the perceived benefits of the misconduct in question (Trevino, 1992). It also seems that one of the most influential forms of punishment in the workplace is sanctioning and disapproval by one's peers—rejection by one's co-workers.

Summary

Because discipline and punishment are social events, witnessed by observers other than the direct recipients, a considerable amount of learning about such a culture occurs—people learn either vicariously or personally just what *is* valued, believed, and felt by the organization's key players. This learning can have major effects on the willingness and tendency (i.e., motivation) of employees to engage in particular forms of behavior in the context of their work (see Cropanzano, 1993, for another recent review).

Procedural Justice and Downsizing

Earlier we reported a study that demonstrated how procedural fairness helped to offset some of the negative impact of layoffs on employees (Brockner et al., 1994). In this section we examine this more closely, drawing on several authors who offered advice to human resource managers on the process of "downsizing" during the mid- and late 1980s, when organizations found they had to lay off countless thousands of people in order to survive. Although many of the "lessons" were derived from our experiences of the 1980s, it is clear that downsizing and mass layoffs are not a phenomenon of that decade alone. One observer has estimated that U.S. manufacturing companies cut more than 2 million workers from their payrolls between 1980 and the early 1990s, referring to corporate restructuring and the carnage that goes with it as the "[business] epidemic of the 1990's" (Cascio, 1993, p. 95).

Defining Downsizing

For the sake of this discussion, we rely on Cascio's (1993) and Brockner's (1988b) definitions of *downsizing:* planned elimination of positions or jobs. Downsizing can refer to the elimination of whole groups, departments, or levels of an organization, usually necessitated by economic exigencies or organizational redesign. People are laid off permanently and involuntarily (although in some cases, people are called back to work if and when economic conditions improve). Downsizing is different from firing people for cause, although principles and considerations of procedural justice are definitely relevant in the case of firing for cause as well, as we will see later. The authors whose work was cited here all have based their suggestions on real experiences with downsizing in major North American enterprises. Before we begin, we must note that there are at least two major groups affected by downsizing and layoffs: the victims and the survivors. We concern ourselves here with the motivational effects of downsizing on both groups, beginning with the victims.

The Motivational Effects of Layoffs on Victims

The involuntary loss of a job can be one of the most stressful events in a person's life. Even if the person is placed out of work because of economic necessity as seen by the company (as opposed to being fired for "cause"), the impact on the person's sense of worth and self-esteem can be devastating. Many people witness depression, decreased life satisfaction, increased social isolation, and feelings of powerlessness. Some people also experience a loss of their sense of time and the development of feelings of apathy, passivity, and resignation. Many studies have reported that people experience a degeneration of their physical health and well-being. Suicide is not unusual (see Ahlberg, 1986). Although it is true that some people experience more positive reactions, such as a sense of relief and hope that they can restore more hope into their lives (Leana and Feldman, 1994), the vast bulk of the work in social science has been devoted to the negative effects on people and the means they use to cope with the emotional and physical damage caused by job loss (e.g., see Latack, Kiniki, and Prussia, 1995, for a recent model of coping strategies for job loss victims).

The first reaction is usually to assess the seriousness of the job loss for the person's own life and circumstances. The more intensely the loss is experienced, the more the person attributes the cause to herself, the less reversible the loss is seen to be, the higher is the short-term stress experienced by the person (Leana and Feldman, 1994). In the longer term, people who lose their jobs can suffer difficulties of financial hardship, strains on marital and familial relationships, increasingly greater isolation from friends and acquaintances, and new or renewed careerist attitudes (i.e., less willingness to commit to an employer while adopting a mercenary attitude about working). Frequently, when unemployed people manage to find new jobs, they accept positions of lower quality and value than the ones they originally lost, and the diminished sense of pride and self-esteem may not rebound to levels that existed before the layoff. Simply finding a new job may not end the emotional and physical damage that result from job loss; these problems may become chronic conditions (Leana and Feldman, 1994).

Earlier, we said that being the victim of downsizing can have deleterious effects on victims' attitudes toward work and working. A recent study has suggested that these negative effects do tend to dissipate over time, and that people who are earlier in their careers may be affected more negatively than employees who are at more advanced career stages when they are outplaced (T. D. Allen, Freeman, Reizenstein, and Rentz, 1995). The types and amounts of social support offered by the company during layoffs is critical to the severity of the initial impact on the victim as well as upon his or her success in dealing with the longer-term considerations of adjustment and finding reemployment. Accordingly, let's look at what experience has taught us about the policies and procedures that have been used to assuage some of the negative effects of layoffs. As we do, let us keep in mind the three dimensions of outcomes, procedures, and systems and how they all may have elements of both balance and correctness in how we view them. (We will also keep in mind that different goals are served by managerial decisions on downsizing, although the continued survival of the enterprise is usually paramount in these cases.)

Employer Policies and Practices in Layoffs: Implications for Victims

First and foremost, advance notice of layoffs is clearly an important managerial tactic when downsizing is required (see A. M. Baker, 1988; D. C. Feldman and Leana, 1989; Settles, 1988). There is virtual agreement on this policy among all authors and practitioners. Notice that we are talking here about multiple or mass layoffs caused by economic exigency facing the organization, not dismissal for cause. Some authors have stressed the importance of adequate severance pay and extended health benefits (D. C. Feldman and Leana, 1989; Settles, 1988). Outplacement assistance in the form of office space, secretarial help, personal counseling, and job search training has been offered by many organizations that have laid people off (see D. C. Feldman and Leana, 1989; Settles, 1988).

It is important to make the *reasons* for the layoffs clear to people and to make the criteria used to select among victims and survivors explicit and honest (D. C. Feldman and Leana, 1989; A. B. Fisher, 1988). This is a matter of interactional justice: If sound reasons are offered for the bad news, the bad news is easier for recipients to take. If management wishes to use performance as its criterion, it becomes especially critical that performance appraisal procedures be valid, regular, and perceived as fair. One study of the criteria favored by unions and management for selecting among employees found that seniority, not job performance, was preferred by both management and union respondents, presumably out of a shared norm of fairness and respect for employees who have given more of their time to their companies (McCune, Beatty, and Montagno, 1988).

Treating layoff victims with dignity and respect, both at the time of the layoffs and afterward, is important (Brockner, 1988b; D. C. Feldman and Leana, 1989; A. B. Fisher, 1988). This means that disparaging comments about the departed after they have left must be discouraged (see Bies and Moag, 1986). Settles (1988) suggests the use of exit interviews with departing employees and a system of employee tracking that can be used in case of call-backs. It is usually recommended that layoffs be conducted all at once rather than a few at a time (D. C. Feldman and Leana, 1989). D. C. Feldman and Leana (1989) stress the importance of working with whatever unions are involved in a work site to determine the procedures to be used, although the evidence related to this suggestion is sparse (see Baker, 1988, for a discussion of some of the issues involved).

On the basis of his experience with downsizing at AC Transit, the two-county public transit located in Oakland, California, Settles (1988) has suggested that fairness in downsizing requires that management must be certain that it is necessary in the first place, by considering or attempting a number of alternatives. His list of possible alternatives include reducing the length of the workweek, offering attractive early retirement packages, offering part-time or contract work to erstwhile full-time employees, trimming waste in expenditures and procedures, across-the-board salary cuts, offering job retraining, lateral transfers, task forces charged with finding alternatives to layoffs, and negotiating wage rollbacks with unions. Clearly, not all or many of these measures may be plausible or relevant in the case of many organizations. Settles' (1988) point is that a norm of procedural justice requires management at least to consider them before resorting to layoffs. Work by McCune et al. (1988) yields similar recommendations.

Some authors discuss how companies can develop reputations from the unfair methods they use during layoffs (D. C. Feldman and Leana, 1989; Greco and Wood-lock, 1989; L. Newman, 1988) and how these reputations can affect the capacity of the company to attract new employees in better times. Presumably, reputations for being unfair can result from perceptions that layoff decisions are not balanced or correct, that they rely on capricious decisions by biased managers, and/or that there are either no policies or misguided policies in place to guide layoff decisions (see Minto et al., 1994; Sheppard et al., 1992). Again: Procedural justice is a matter of perception, and large, public organizations are under the scrutiny of many observers, both inside their boundaries and beyond those boundaries.

Earlier in the chapter we referred to a study by Brockner et al. (1994), which demonstrated in three different samples how perceptions of procedural fairness among layoff victims helped offset the negative impact of the experience on victims. Translating the general principles of procedural justice into active organizational policies is the trick. Principles of fairness such as those identified by Sashkin and Williams (1990), mentioned earlier, must be made to come alive and have real meaning for layoff victims if the motivational and other consequences of the trauma of job loss are to be minimized.

A Progressive Example

The Nova Corporation is a publicly held Canadian company with several divisions in gas services, gas marketing, gas pipelines, and petrochemicals. With their head office in Calgary, Nova employs more than 6,000 people and conducts operations in Canada, Australia, and throughout South America. A few years ago, the company began a series of corporate restructurings and undertook reengineering projects in many of its facilities. Anticipating that there would be considerable impact on their employees from these changes, Nova designed a multifaceted plan—a set of programs—to assist both employees who would be staying with the company as well as those who would probably be leaving. The company's official policy statement for these programs recognizes the need for the company to undergo changes, the fact that such changes will be ongoing, and the fact that these changes will have major effects on the careers of their employees. The policy states that Nova will "share in the responsibility" for the continued employment of its people, either within or outside its own employ. As we describe it below, the program clearly appeals to considerations of both distributive and procedural justice.

The program offers a generous menu of options for employees to consider. Work alternatives such as job sharing, reduced workweeks, sabbaticals, or seasonal leaves are offered for both individuals and teams. Severance packages are offered for those people who elect to leave the company to develop new skill areas, to start new businesses, or to return to school. These "selective voluntary separations" are not granted to everyone who applies, but if an employee does apply and is accepted for one of them, the company provides a variety of support services, such as priority for summer jobs, reimbursement schedules for school fees and tuition, partial salary continuance, and an option at the end of one year either to accept severance or to continue with the leave support.

Some of Nova's employees have become involved with their "Community Support" program for up to one year on half-pay from Nova. Under this option, the person works for another organization to assist with whatever growth or project assistance is required. As in many of these options, however, there is no guarantee of reemployment by Nova at the end of the year away. Finally (although the list is not exhaustive), Nova employees may apply for an opportunity to start up their own businesses with a sum of venture capital provided by Nova. These small businesses may, in some cases, actually deliver outsourced services to Nova or work on contact for them.

There are other features of Nova Corporation's program of employee assistance; the ones described here are among the most interesting. Stimulated by much less human downsizing practices that she witnessed in other companies during the 1980s, the corporate vice president of Nova's human resources section says that programs such as the ones described here help to maintain more company loyalty as well as more "organizational memory" than occurs when layoffs are made bureaucratically on the basis of simple seniority criteria.

Motivational Effects of Layoffs on Survivors

For a variety of reasons, downsizing often fails to yield the types and amounts of economic benefits that are intended (Cascio, 1993). Downsizing can have drastic effects on employees who are not cut, the "survivors." Survivors often find themselves in new, strange, and frequently anxiety-laden work environments, hardly the optimal type of environment for healthy work motivation to flourish (see Cascio, 1993, for evidence on this point). Survivors often change their expectations about future promotions and career advancements and may lose much or all of the trust they previously placed in their superiors. The performance and organizational commitment of those who remain can be diminished, especially depending on their perceptions of the fairness received by the victims (e.g., Brockner, Grover, Reed, DeWitt, and O'Malley, 1987). Dashed morale can be harmful to organizational attempts to increase or maintain high-quality service and a positive image in the eyes of customers (recall our discussion in chapter 17 of the consequences of low satisfaction). Frequently, the amount of work to be accomplished is not reduced, so more work is placed on the shoulders of those who remain.

About the effects of layoffs on survivors, Cascio (1993) writes: "From the perspective of the individual, the implications of all of this can be summarized succinctly: our views of organizational life, managing as a career, hard work, rewards, and loyalty will never be the same. Unfortunately, far too many senior managers . . . seem to regard employees as 'units of production,' costs to be cut rather than as assets to be developed. This is a 'plug-in' mentality—that is, like a machine, plug it in when you need it, unplug it when it is no longer needed. Unlike machines, however, employees have values, aspirations, beliefs—and memories" (p. 101). Cascio (1993) predicts that downsizing will continue in North American business as long as overhead costs remain uncompetitive with those of domestic and foreign competitors.

But are all the motivational effects negative? Brockner (1988b), who has done a considerable amount of work on the effects of downsizing, reports anecdotal accounts of how downsizing has sometimes resulted in positive effects on employee motivation, morale, and productivity. For example, *relief* (that one has managed to survive the cuts) is one of many psychological states that can result from downsizing. Similarly, the anxiety that downsizing produces may serve to heighten the activation and motivation of survivors (see Brockner, 1988b; Gardner and Cummings, 1988; Yerkes and Dodson, 1908) and may even result in increased effort through the forces of perceived overreward inequity that were described much earlier in the chapter (see J. S. Adams, 1963).

The point is that layoffs have the *potential* to generate either (or both) positive and negative psychological states among survivors. Accordingly, Brockner has developed and tested a theoretical model that enables us to make both predictions and prescriptions in regard to the downsizing process, especially as it affects survivors. A full treatment of Brockner's model is beyond the scope of this chapter. Suffice it to say that a number of variables are involved, such as the person's self-esteem (see chapter 5), the degree of interdependencies in the work flow between those laid off and those who remain, the types and amounts of social support offered by both the formal organization (i.e., management policies) and the informal organization, the friendship networks among the employees themselves.

Recapitulation: Downsizing and Procedural Justice

To summarize, there is considerable although not perfect convergence in the advice offered by authors addressing the layoffs of people from work organizations. Of primary concern to us here are the implications of these procedures for the perception, by all parties involved, of the procedural and interactional justice involved. The reason for the concern, again, is that people want to be treated fairly and with dignity, especially at times when their very self-identities are at risk, as is often the case when terminations are being experienced, be they general layoffs or firings for cause (which we examine next). Procedural and interactional justice matter to the job attitudes of survivors, to the self-concepts of the victims, and to the motivation and goals of the victims to continue with their working lives.

Dismissal: Firing for Cause[14]

Before we leave our discussion of the effects of job loss on people, we take a brief look at another traumatic event that occurs in many careers—one that also has serious implications for procedural justice. We are referring to situations in which people are released from their jobs when *the reason for the termination is not broad, general economic circumstances facing the organization but rather, the particular behavior of the individual.* This is organizational discipline in the extreme, and may be one area of human resource management in which the acuity of perceptions of balance and correctness are especially critical.

According to Morin and Yorks (1990), the reasons for firing people often vary with the level of employee involved. Lower-level employees are most frequently let go

---

[14]Discussion of firing and layoff can often be cast against the doctrine referred to as *employment at will.* This doctrine is defined as "the right of an employer to fire an employee without giving a reason and the right of an employee to quit when he or she chooses (Fulmer and Casey, 1990, p. 102), or "the absolute right to discharge an employee for whatever cause he might choose, without incurring liability" (Coulson, 1981, p. 111). Space limitations prohibit a detailed discussion of this doctrine; the interested reader is referred to Coulson (1981), Fulmer and Casey (1990), and Youngblood and Bierman (1994) for thorough treatments of the matter.

because of poor job performance, failure to comply with company rules and regulations, and/or insubordination. Senior managers and executives are more likely to be fired for reasons of personality or a judged lack of fit between them and the organization's goals (p. 33). Other reasons for firing people include "up-or-out" policies, in which a number of junior people are hired and developed with the explicit understanding that many of them won't make it. Professional accounting and law firms have made great use of this form of survival of the fittest strategy over the years when there was an abundance of eager young talent in tough labor market situations. Significant deviations from one's prescribed job duties is another reason often used to justify firing, as are instances of flagrant ethical misconduct (Morin and Yorks, 1990).

Morin and Yorks (1990) report that, in practice, terminations for cause tend to have a number of common features. For example, they are often executed on Friday afternoons, providing the fired person with little or no guidance about what to do next. Many people are treated so vaguely and "with so many euphemisms that they don't know they are being let go" (p. 7). For example, some people are told that they have been working too hard and that they need to take a break. Other people are treated with "excessive cruelty" (p. 7): Their personalities are attacked, they are yelled at, and they are roughly escorted out of the building, violating every tenet of interactional justice we considered earlier. Sometimes people are fired over the telephone. (In an age of E-mail and fax, the possibilities here are endless.) The author knows of executives who were fired from a Minneapolis-based corporation long distance, while they were on vacation in Florida ("Reach out and touch someone!"). Perhaps the worst cases are those in which the victim hears about the firing secondhand, via public media or by rumor. Professional athletes often complain of such treatment.

The psychological effects of being fired are similar to those that occur when a person is laid off for economic, noncause reasons. On the widely noted Holmes and Rahe (1967) Scale, being fired ranks eighth out of the 43 events considered by the scale. Grieff and Munter (1980; quoted by Morin and Yorks, 1990) write: "It doesn't matter what you call it, fired, axed, socked, canned, kicked upstairs, or allowed to resign. They are all the same. The only certainty about losing a job is that it hurts. It threatens everybody—the family, peers, even the executive who has to do the firing" (Grieff and Munter, 1980, p. 117). Although the author is not aware of any research into the matter, one would expect that being fired for cause would have even more psychological impact on a person than being laid off for reasons of corporate restructuring or economic exigency. In the former case, the message is that the person herself is to blame; in the latter case, the putative causes and responsibility are beyond the control of the individual. One would expect that the level of threat to self-esteem and the potential for shame and embarrassment are much greater when a person is fired for cause.

Employers have had to increase the care and attention they devote to their firing practices for a number of reasons. First, there is often a fear of discrimination charges if the victim is a woman or member of a visible or "protected" minority group. Even if the victim is not a member of one of these groups, litigation over unfair dismissal can be costly if it is undertaken. In response to this concern, many employers pay huge severance packages, hoping to obviate suit. Morin and Yorks (1990) report that common practice is to provide a middle or senior manager with as much as a year's salary in a lump sum. There are other reasons for paying close attention to the procedures an organization uses to terminate people (Morin and Yorks, 1990). One of these has to do with the organization's reputation and the effect it can have on the capacity of the organization to recruit new employees. The problem is especially acute in the context of recruiting senior executives, among whom there is often a small community of friendships and acquaintanceships. People talk, compare notes, and share experiences. In most cities and, indeed, in most industries, the population of senior people is a relatively small community, so word gets out about how companies treat their executives. At any level of the organization, if the firing victim's peers and colleagues view the treatment of the victim as having been unfair, morale can suffer among the survivors, who may develop fears that they too could be treated capriciously and fired. Finally, there are cases of vengeance in which fired people extract retribution by violence, even murder (R. E. Allen and Lucero, 1996, and see chapter 8 of this book).

Procedures for Dismissal with Justice in Mind

So with all of these psychological, economic, and organizational considerations in mind, how should employers deal with the termination of employees for cause? Morin and Yorks (1990, p. 69) observe that "consistency in the handling of firings requires a well-defined policy, *consistency of treatment* being one of the standards of fairness in procedural justice" (see Sashkin and Williams, 1990). Clearly, Sheppard and his colleagues (1992) would endorse this suggestion. The organization's dismissal policy should make it clear that terminations will not be used for vague or unsubstantiated reasons. This means that managers must keep records, documenting instances of poor performance, insubordination, and rule violations. This also means that valid performance appraisal procedures must be in place and used appropriately. It is the author's experience and the insight of countless authors in the human resources management literature that this is easier said than done. Performance appraisals take time and can be a source of hassle and embarrassment for everyone involved. Hence, in practice, this may be one of the least-well-performed activities in the management and supervision of workers by bosses. The point is that when it comes time to fire someone, both the law and human decency require that there be substantiated evidence that a firing is just and called for. (Consider how the principles of balance and correctness fit in here, as they apply to the assessment of the fairness of the organization's procedures and systems; see Sheppard et al., 1992).

There is some disagreement among the experts about the style and speed of execution of the firing once it has been decided that a dismissal is to take place. Coulson (1981) suggests that before firing takes place, the problematic employee should be told clearly that problems are perceived regarding his work. There should be counseling by the supervisor or other official to seek ways to sort things out. If this fails, there should be a written reprimand, followed, if necessary, by a "final warning." The final warning should contain copies of previous warnings, identification of specific areas in which the employee must improve, a period of time within which the employee has a chance to show improvement, and a statement that this is the person's final opportunity to bring performance up to standard. It should be made clear that this will be the final warning. A copy of the warning should be given to the employee and another placed in his file. If all of these procedures fail, the person's immediate supervisor should perform the firing.

All of these procedures are consistent with the advice of Sheppard and his colleagues (1992; Minton et al., 1994). But here is where they depart from Coulson's (1981) advice. Coulson claims that the message should be direct, fully explained, unequivocal, and leave no cause for the employee to believe that further chances are possible: There is no turning back (Coulson, 1981). On the other hand, Minton et al., (1994) favor the person's right to a hearing, including adequate time for the employee to prepare for it. The person may also have the right to representation at such a hearing and, ultimately, the right to appeal. At first blush, the two sets of prescriptions seem equally fair. At a second glance, they seem irreconcilable.

An organization's formal dismissal policy should also clearly spell out the nature of the support package that will be provided to terminated employees, if any. For example, it should be clear how much money will be awarded, and the terms and criteria for the amount should be spelled out in writing and provided to the person when he is fired. The person should be told whether he may use any of the company's employees as referees for future employment and, if so, who these people are. Provisions for counseling and outplacement support, such as the use of an office, a shared office, secretarial support, and the assistance of professional recruiters, should also be specified if they are to be provided at all (Morin and Yorks, 1991).

The rationale underlying these guidelines for the firing of employees is partly legal, motivated by the goal of protecting the organization from lawsuit. Aside from legal considerations, these types of procedures and policies should be grounded in principles of procedural justice as detailed by Lewicki and his colleagues (Sheppard et al., 1992). Life goes on after a firing,[15] for both the victim and the other employees of the organization, so it seems imperative that life be made as civilized and as pleasant as possible for everyone concerned. Keeping an eye on the basic principles of fairness as well as the legal issues concerned seems to be the most humane and businesswise way to proceed.

A final note: Those who have had to do it report that dismissing another employee can be among the most stressful assignments they have to perform as managers or supervisors. It would seem that some degree of comfort would be more available to those who bear the message when policies are structured with the principles of procedural justice in place than in situations where there are no policies or where the policies are ill planned, inconsistent, and inhumane. Translating the principles of procedural fairness and interactional justice into explicit policies of discipline may not be easy, because to some degree, every case requiring dismissal may have its own idiosyncracies and nuances. Moreover, investing the time to adhere to carefully designed policies can also be demanding on supervisors and managers who have other duties to perform. Nevertheless, a certain portion of every manager's pay is (under normal circumstances) provided for executing policies of discipline, including the intermittent need to dismiss other employees. The norms of *distributive justice* we examined at the beginning of this chapter require that those who are paid more because they bear these responsibilities must be willing and able to perform them, unpleasant as they may be.

INTERACTIONAL JUSTICE

The vast majority of research on theorizing about fairness in organizations has been devoted to distributive and procedural justice, as described in the foregoing sections of this chapter. Over the past decade, theorists have offered a distinction between procedural

---

[15]Actually, job loss and/or extended periods of unemployment can lead to death, either indirectly through the natural physiological impact of the experience or through suicide (see Ahlberg, 1986).

justice, which refers to the bureaucratic systems that make decisions about people, and another form of justice, *interactional justice,* which has to do with the quality and content of person-to-person interactions as people relate to one another: "Concerns about the fairness of interpersonal communication are representative of a set of issues dealing with what we refer to as interactional justice. By interactional justice we mean that people are sensitive to the quality of interpersonal treatment they receive during the enactment of organizational procedures" (Bies and Moag, 1986, p. 44). It is one thing to have formal rules and procedures that are more or less fair. The interpretation and enactment of these procedures is what interactional justice is about. How a boss relays bad news based on a new organizational policy may have as much impact on an employee's perceptions of justice as the nature of the news itself and the perceived fairness of the policies being enacted.

Bies and Moag (1986, p. 46) suggest that procedural justice and interactional justice are related to perceptions of the fairness of outcomes in a causal, sequential manner in the following way:

$$procedure \rightarrow interaction \rightarrow outcome$$

They state: "Each part of the sequence is subject to fairness considerations and thus, every aspect of an organizational decision (procedure, interaction, outcome) may create a potential justice episode" (p. 46). This means that it is possible for an employee to believe that the rules and procedures that result in a layoff, a cut in pay, or a disciplinary action are fair, but that somehow, the entire experience is taken as unfair. It is not the decision that is unfair. It is not the outcome that is unfair. As we saw earlier in the context of downsizing and dismissal for cause, *it is the way the bad news is delivered that matters.* The message must be delivered in a way that is seen as candid and truthful. It must be respectful to the receiver rather than rude or condescending. And it must be seen as appropriate and justified (Bies and Moag, 1986). In fact, the justification factor is especially critical.

The Role of Accounts and Justifications

One of the key factors influencing whether people view relationships to be fair in interactional justice terms is whether apparent violations of justice norms are accompanied by justifications, or causal accounts. If there is a causal account—an excuse—provided for instances of apparent mistreatment, a person who is treated unfairly is less likely to be unhappy with the treatment. But the existence of a causal account by itself seems not to be enough. The explanation offering details about extenuating circumstances must be seen as adequate; merely offering an excuse is not as effective as offering an explanation that is viewed as adequate or reasonable (Bies, 1987; Bies and Shapiro, 1987).

Let's look at an example that is relevant to the lives of students. Suppose that a professor is late or absent from his office hours and many students are kept waiting for her to arrive to help them with ideas for their term papers. If the professor eventually shows up and tells the waiting students that she was late because she "was delayed," she will not satisfy the annoyed students nearly as much as if she honestly explains that the reason she was late was because her daughter was ill and had to be taken to the doctor for medical attention. If no explanation given, the students will perceive low interactional justice. If they are told that the professor "had a delay," they may feel less interactional injustice. If they learn that there was a valid reason for the lateness—the illness of the professor's child—the students will perceive much more interactional justice and be more likely to excuse the professor for her tardiness.

When people in organizations feel unfairly treated, there is a tendency for them to experience feelings of anger, resentment, and moral outrage (Bies, 1987). People who feel they have been treated badly may be motivated to "get even," to seek revenge in some form or another. But provision of a social account—an excuse, an explanation, or a rationale—may mitigate feelings of resentment on the part of the maltreated party. Specifically, a social account is "an explanation containing a reason to mitigate the harmdoer's responsibility for some action, or as it is more commonly referred to, an excuse" (M. B. Scott and Lyman, 1968, cited by Bies, 1987, p. 298). Providing a social account can mitigate the sting associated with the delivery of bad news, even when that news is fair by strict procedural standards. So a manager who lays off employees and cites a downturn in profits and revenues will generate much less ill-will and moral outrage than a boss who provides no such explanation. In fact, a manager who fails to provide explanations for the delivery or the enactment of bad news is likely to lose authority and respect in the eyes of subordinates (Baron, 1993; Bies, 1987).

A key element of violations of interactional injustice is the perception of violations of *trust*. When one person feels that another has betrayed him, changed the rules on him, broken a promise, breached a contract, committed a lie, stolen an idea or a material object, disclosed a confidence, or publicly slandered him, the sense of injustice can be acute. Notice that many or most of these misdeeds involve interactions rather than outcomes or the execution of legitimate procedures. In other words, interactional justice (or injustice) lies at the heart of violations of interpersonal trust and the violation of trust. Trust is an interpersonal value that is earned slowly and over time, yet it can be lost or broken quickly, by only seemingly minor violations or transgressions (see Kramer and Tyler, 1996). People whose trust has been violated typically react in any of a number of ways, including withdrawing from the offender, denying the claims made, or striking back, seeking revenge (see R. E. Allen and Lucero, 1996; Bies and Tripp, 1996).

SUMMARY AND CONCLUSION

This chapter has reviewed what is known about the human need for fairness and justice and its importance in work settings. It is critical to keep in mind that the major theories dealing with the issue posit that equity is considered to be a *need,* possessing all the capacity to arouse and direct human behavior that other needs possess (recall chapter 3). By itself, however, equity theory does not discuss how this need state, once aroused, results in intentions to act. It is also important to keep in mind that people's feelings about whether they (or others) are being equitably treated are based on their own perceptions and beliefs, subject to the same influences as are other types of perceptions and beliefs. Also important is the notion that both the distribution of outcomes and the procedures used to determine the distribution are important in determining people's perceptions of fairness, equity, and justice. Finally, distributive and procedural justice interact with one another in determining employee reactions, and trust is the key ingredient. Fair procedures may engender positive feelings of trust, which, in turn, may help to soften the impact of outcome decisions that would otherwise be seen as unfair and harmful. In chapter 12 we examine another popular body of theory that has its roots in the cognitive tradition of organizational science, valence-instrumentality-expectancy (VIE) theory.

CHAPTER

Expectancy-Valence Theories of Work Motivation[1]

Never is there either work without reward,
nor reward without work being expended.

—LIVY (TITUS LIVIUS)

One of the most popular theories of work motivation among organizational scientists over the past three decades is referred to as Valence-Instrumentality-Expectancy theory or expectancy theory (Locke, 1975). Actually, a number of theories are included under this general title, although the similarities among them are more important than the differences. Each of these theories has its modern roots in Victor Vroom's (1964) book on work motivation, although earlier theory in psychology relating to general human motivation quite clearly predates Vroom's interpretation for organizational science (e.g., Atkinson, 1958; Davidson, Suppes, and Siegel, 1957; Lewin, 1938; Peak, 1955; Rotter, 1955; Tolman, 1959), and an early study by Georgopoulos, Mahoney, and Jones (1957) demonstrated the relevance of the theory for work behavior.[2]

We want to accomplish two things in this chapter. First, we discuss at length the most important versions of the valence-instrumentality-expectancy theories of work motivation. As in the case of most other approaches to work motivation in this book, we address the theories' weaknesses, methodological and scientific limitations, as well as present the theories in their pure form. We also discuss some of the most important implications they have for leadership in real work settings.

---

[1]The author thanks Professor Wilfred Zerbe of the University of Calgary for his contributions to this chapter.

[2]One notable expectancy-value theory is Fishbein and Ajzen's *Theory of Reasoned Action,* which we examined in chapter 9 (Ajzen and Fishbein, 1980; Fishbein, 1980; Fishbein and Ajzen, 1975). This theory proposes that a person's attitude toward performing a behavior (an act) can be estimated by the summed products of beliefs (b_i) about the outcomes of performing that behavior and the evaluations (e_j) of those outcomes $A_{act} = \Sigma_{ij} b_i e_j$. Although its similarity to VIE theory is evident, the theory of reasoned action has spawned a large body of work in areas outside of work motivation (e.g., Ajzen and Madden, 1986; Bagozzi, 1986; Budd, 1986; Crawford and Boyer, 1985; Craychee, 1987; Critchlow, 1987; W. A. Fisher, 1984; Hewstone and Young, 1988; Hughey, Sundstrom, and Lounsbury, 1985; Miniard and Cohen, 1983; Oliver and Bearden, 1985; Shimp and Kavas, 1984; Toneatto and Binik, 1987).

VROOM'S ORIGINAL THEORY

Vroom's theory assumes that "the choices made by a person among alternative courses of action are lawfully related to psychological events occurring contemporaneously with the behavior" (1964, pp. 14–15). In other words, people's behavior results from conscious choices among alternatives, and these choices (behaviors) are systematically related to psychological processes, particularly perception and the formation of beliefs and attitudes. The purpose of the choices, generally, is to maximize pleasure and minimize pain. Like equity theory, then, VIE theory assumes that people base their acts on perceptions and beliefs, although as we saw in chapter 9, we need not anticipate any one-to-one relationships between particular beliefs and specific behaviors (such as job behaviors). More specifically, VIE theory proposes that behavior is instigated and directed to the extent that (1) people believe that the behavior will lead to outcomes such as job performance, (2) people believe that such outcomes will be rewarded, and (3) people value those rewards. Referred to as VIE theory, we must examine the three key mental components that are seen as instigating and directing behavior. Referred to as *expectancy, instrumentality,* and *valence,* respectively, each of these components is, in fact, a belief (using the terminology developed in chapter 9).

The Concept of Valence

VIE theory assumes that people hold preferences among various outcomes or states of nature. For example, the reader probably prefers, other things being equal, a higher rate of pay for a particular job over a lower rate of pay. Here pay level is the outcome in question, and the preference for high pay over low pay reflects the strength of the reader's basic underlying need and value structure. Likewise, some people hold preferences among various types of outcomes (as opposed to greater or lesser amounts of a particular outcome). For example, many employees would seem to prefer an opportunity to work with other people, even if the only jobs featuring high levels of social interaction entail less comfortable surroundings, lower pay, or some other trade-off. The point is that people have more or less well-defined preferences for the outcomes they derive from their actions. (Notice that these outcomes correspond roughly with what we referred to in chapter 8 as goals in the discussion of employee frustration as well as to the outcomes we examined in chapter 11 in the context of equity theory.) Preferences, in short, relate to a person's relative desires for, or attraction to, outcomes.

Vroom uses the term *valence* to refer to these affective orientations that people hold with regard to outcomes. An outcome is said to be positively valent for a person if she would prefer having it to not having it. For example, we would say that a promotion is positively valent for an employee who would rather be promoted than not be promoted. Similarly, we say that an outcome which a person would prefer to avoid has negative valence for her, or simply that it is negatively valent. For example, fatigue, stress, and layoffs are three outcomes that are usually negatively valent among employees. Finally, sometimes an employee is indifferent toward certain outcomes; in such cases the outcome is said to hold zero valence for that person.

Expected Satisfaction, Not Real Value

The most important feature of people's valences concerning work-related outcomes is that they refer to the level of satisfaction the person *expects* to receive from them, not to the real value the person actually derives from them. For example, the reader may be enrolled in a program of business management because she expects that the outcomes to follow (an education and a diploma, among others) will be of value to her when she is finished. It may be the case that when the student graduates there will be little or no market demand for the services she has to offer the world of business and administration, so the degree may have little real value. The point is that people attribute either positive or negative preferences (or indifference) to outcomes according to the satisfaction or dissatisfaction they expect to receive from them. It is often the case that the true value of an outcome (such as a diploma) is either greater or less than the valence (expected value) it once held for the person who was motivated to pursue it. As a final example, consider the person who fears being fired but learns after actually being dismissed from a job that she is healthier, happier, and better off financially in the new job she acquired after having been terminated by her former employer. In this case, being fired was a negatively valent outcome before it occurred, but turned out to be of positive value after it occurred. One more time: Valence is the value that a person expects to achieve from an outcome; it is what contributes to the motivation to act. The actual value of an outcome is usually not known until after the fact, so it has little motivational power.

Performance as an Outcome

The expected levels of satisfaction and/or dissatisfaction brought by work-related outcomes indicated by valence include performance. In most organizational settings, besides being an outcome in itself, performance is likely to result in additional outcomes, such as pay, promotions, satisfaction, keeping or losing one's job, and so on. Performance can be thought of as a *first-level outcome;* outcomes that result from performance are second-level outcomes. *Second-level outcomes* are directly associated with valences; performance has valence through its connection with second-level outcomes. As we shall see shortly, the strength of the connection in the mind of the employee between effort and the performance level achieved is central to Vroom's theory. Performance is the most direct outcome of effort and usually the most important for understanding work motivation from a VIE theory perspective.

The Concept of Instrumentality

Instrumentality is the term used by Vroom to describe the connection between performance on the job and outcomes that result from it, that is, between first- and second-level outcomes. This connection is what determines the valence associated with performance. A given level of performance is positively valent if the employee believes that it will lead to second-level outcomes and that those outcomes are positively valent. In other words, if an employee believes (through all the belief construction processes we discussed in chapter 9) that a high level of performance is instrumental for the acquisition of other outcomes that he expects will be gratifying (e.g., a promotion), and/or if he believes that a high performance level will be instrumental for avoiding other outcomes that he wishes to avoid (e.g., being fired), the employee will place a high valence on performing the job well.

Consider the meaning of the adjective *instrumental*. The author's word processor at the present time is instrumental in the preparation of this book. It contributes to the job; it helps. Something is said to be instrumental if it is believed to lead to something else, if it helps achieve or attain something else. Studying is commonly seen by students as instrumental for passing exams. In turn, passing exams is often believed instrumental for the acquisition of diplomas, which, in turn, are believed to be instrumental for landing jobs in tight labor market conditions.

Vroom (1964) suggests that we consider instrumentality as a probability belief linking one outcome (performance level) to other outcomes, ranging from 1.0 (meaning that the attainment of the second outcome is certain if the first outcome is achieved), through zero (meaning that there is no probable relationship between the attainment of the first outcome and the attainment of the second), to −1.0 (meaning that the attainment of the second outcome is certain without the first and that it is impossible with it). For example, bonus pay that is distributed at random would lead to employees' having perceptions of the instrumentality between bonus pay and performance equal to zero ("Performance and pay have no connection around here"). On the other hand, commission pay schemes that tie pay directly to performance, and only to performance, are designed to make employees perceive that performance is positively instrumental for the acquisition of money. Finally, an employee who has been threatened with dismissal for being drunk on the job may be told by his supervisor, in effect, that lack of sobriety at work is negatively instrumental for continued employment, or alternatively, that further imbibing will be positively instrumental for termination. (The notion of negative instrumentalities makes Vroom's original formulation of VIE theory somewhat more difficult and cumbersome than it might otherwise be, so subsequent versions of the theory have avoided using it, choosing instead to speak only of positive instrumentalities.)

Consider the case of an employee who perceives that high performance will not lead to things he desires but that it will be more instrumental for attaining outcomes to which he attributes negative valences. High performance will not be positively valent for such a person, so we would not expect to see him striving to perform well. As a further example, an employee might perceive that taking a job as a traveling salesman will be instrumental for attaining a number of outcomes, some of which he expects will be positive, some of which he believes will be negative. On the positively valent side, meeting new people and seeing the countryside may be appealing to him, because he expects that these outcomes will be instrumental for satisfying his relatedness and growth needs, while the possible threat to his family life may be aversive to him.

In short, the I in VIE theory stands for instrumentality: the belief about the way in which performance and other first-level outcomes are related to second-level job outcomes. It serves as the connection between performance and valence. A first-level outcome is positively valent if the person believes that it holds high instrumentality for the acquisition of positively valent consequences (goals or other outcomes) and the avoidance of negatively valent outcomes. That is, for a first-level outcome to be positively valent, the outcomes to which the person believes it is connected must themselves be seen as positively valent. If an employee anticipates that high levels of performance will lead primarily to things that he dislikes, high performance will not be positively valent to him. Similarly, if the person perceives that high performance is generally rewarded with things that he desires, he will place high valence on high performance and, other things being equal, will strive for high performance. Of course, the valence of such second-level outcomes is determined by the nature of the person's most salient needs and values.

At this point the reader will be seeing implications for the design of reward systems in organizations. If management wants high performance levels, it must tie positively valent outcomes to high performance and be sure that employees understand the connection. Similarly, low performance must be seen as connected to consequences that are of either zero or negative valence.

Expectancy and Related Concepts

The third major component of VIE theory is referred to as *expectancy*. Expectancy is the strength of a person's belief about the degree to which a particular first-level outcome is the result of his or her actions. The author, for example, would place very little expectancy on the prospect of becoming an astronaut. He is pretty certain that no amount of trying on his part will see him aboard the space shuttle. If a person believes that he can achieve an outcome, he will be more motivated to try for it, assuming other things equal (the other things being the person's beliefs about the valence of the outcome, which, in turn, is determined by the person's beliefs about the odds that the outcome will be instrumental for acquiring and avoiding those things he wishes to acquire or avoid).

Vroom (1964) spoke of expectancy beliefs as action-outcome associations held in people's minds and suggested that we think of them in probability terms ranging from zero (in the case where the person's subjective probability of attaining an outcome is psychologically zero—"I can't do it") through to 1.0, indicating that the person has no doubt about his capacity to attain the outcome. In practice, of course, people's estimates tend to range between these two extremes. (The reader will recall from chapter 7 that achievement-oriented people tend to prefer tasks that are neither too difficult nor too easy, such that, for example, we might say they prefer tasks with perceived expectancy values near 0.5, meaning that there is a 50:50 perceived chance of success in performing the task.)

A variety of factors contribute to an employee's expectancy perceptions about various levels of job performance. For example, his level of confidence in his skills for the task at hand, the degree of help he expects to receive from his supervisor and subordinates, the quality of the materials and equipment available, and the availability of pertinent information and control over sufficient budget, are common examples of factors that can influence a person's expectancy beliefs about being able to achieve a particular level of performance. Previous success experiences at a task and a generally high level of self-esteem also strengthen expectancy beliefs (Lawler, 1973, and see chapter 6 of this book). Previous success is the essence of *enactive mastery,* which Bandura (1982) argues is the predominant influence on *self-efficacy,* or "one's belief in one's capability to perform a specific task" (Gist, 1987, p. 472).

Expectancy Beliefs versus Self-Efficacy Beliefs

During our discussion of self-esteem in chapter 6 we introduced the concept of self-efficacy, in part because it is frequently confused with self-esteem, although as we noted then, the two concepts are only remotely related. In similar fashion, it is appropriate to reintroduce the concept of self-efficacy at this point because it is also frequently confused with the notion of expectancy, or expectation. Clearly, the concept of self-efficacy expectations is closely related to the concept of effort-performance expectancy. Self-efficacy is, however, a somewhat broader construct. According to Daniels and Mitchell (1995), self-efficacy has to do with a person's judgment about whether s/he *can* do something; it is an estimate of ability relative to a task. If someone asks you if you can make a perfect martini and you answer with honest confidence, "Of course!" you are reflecting high self-efficacy for this exquisite task. Inasmuch as self-efficacy beliefs have to do with a person's confidence about her capability to perform a particular task in a particular context, deliberate training for the task-in-context ought to increase the strength of self-efficacy beliefs. Indeed, one study conducted at the U.S. Naval Recruit Training Command demonstrated that this is the case. More than 1,000 Navy recruits were assessed on the basis of their commitment, self-efficacy, and motivation levels both before and after rigorous socialization training. Comparison of pre- and posttraining self-ratings of self-efficacy showed significant increases as a result of the training (Tannenbaum, Mathieu, Salas, and Cannon-Bowers, 1991). Other, similar examples of this sort will be presented, both later in this chapter and in chapter 14.

But merely having such high self-efficacy for this task can actually stimulate you to engage in it; thus self-efficacy is said to have *generative* properties—it can actually stimulate the behavior in question.[3] It *is* possible to have high self-efficacy with regard to a task but not be motivated to perform it, however, so although high self-efficacy can be a major contributing factor to task motivation, it is not necessarily generative nor predictive of work motivation. The point is that self-efficacy concerns the question: Can I do it? By contrast, expectancy perceptions concern the issue of how a person believes that s/he will actually do at a task (Daniels and Mitchell, 1995). R. Kanfer and Ackerman (1989) refer to this judgment as "predicted performance"; Henry (1994) calls it a *performance prediction*. So if "self-efficacy can be thought of as a 'can do' construct . . . then an expectation can be viewed as a 'will do' construct" (Daniels and Mitchell, 1995). Thus, expectancies do not have the generative power that self-efficacy beliefs are thought of as possessing.

Gist (1987) suggests that self-efficacy may predict nonperformance of a task as a result of a person's belief that he is unmotivated. Gist and Mitchell (1992, p. 185) suggest that

> self-efficacy may represent a more comprehensive formulation of the rationale underlying the expectancy theory construct [expectancy]. For example, the most frequent conceptualization and empirical assessment of [expectancy] is in terms of the relation-

---

[3]Recent years have seen a number of attempts to postulate and define a concept of *group efficacy*, which has been defined by one team of authors as a "group's (or organization's) collective belief that it can successfully perform a specific task" (Lindsley, Brass, and Thomas, 1995). Noting that self-efficacy beliefs can link up with high performance such that these beliefs become both a contributor to high performance and a consequence of such performance, the notion is that groups can generate and enjoy such spiraling effects. Moreover, spirals linking efficacy and performance also work in a downward direction: Once things start going badly, self-efficacy beliefs decline and further poor performance becomes more likely. The author understands and appreciates the concept but would prefer that a concept other than self-efficacy be used in such analyses. Self-efficacy is an individual-level concept; linking it to group-level phenomena constitutes anthropomorphism (see chapter 4).

ship between effort and performance. . . . By contrast, Bandura asserted not only that self-efficacy subsumes variables typically not included in [expectancy] (such as mood), but also that "[s]elf percepts of efficacy are not simply inert predictors of future behavior" (1984: 242). Though both constructs involve forethought, self-efficacy is viewed as having *generative* capability: it influences thought patterns, emotional reactions, and the orchestration of performance through the adroit use of subskills, ingenuity, resourcefulness, and so forth. (Bandura, 1984, 1986)

Notwithstanding the distinction between expectancy and self-efficacy, the other influences on self-efficacy that Bandura proposed probably apply to expectancy as well. To the extent that this is so, expectancy will be influenced by vicarious experience (observing a successful model, preferably one similar to the observer), verbal persuasion aimed at convincing a person of her capability, and physiological arousal (such as when anxiety is interpreted as debilitating fear) (Gist, 1987). The point is that an employee's subjective estimate of the odds that he can achieve a given level of performance is determined by a variety of factors, both within his own control and beyond it.

Efficacy Spirals

There is a particularly interesting feature about self-efficacy beliefs that can have major importance for both people who work and for those who oversee the work of others. People often become engaged in efficacy spirals—periods in which successful performance of a task fuels higher beliefs of self-efficacy that, in turn, raise a person's confidence and facilitate further successful performance: The better one becomes at a job, the more confidence she feels and the better she does at the job. Within human and technological limits, things just keep getting better and better.

These spirals can also work in the opposite direction. If a person experiences one or two significant failures at a job, and if those failures are taken seriously, she may witness feelings of self-doubt, performance anxiety, and lowered beliefs of self-efficacy. The author has a young friend (a former student) who works in a human resources department in a large Canadian food retail company. Over the period of only a few days, this woman made two or three simple, yet innocent *adding mistakes* in the process of completing and submitting a report for her boss. The boss detected the errors and made mention of them. The woman took these errors to heart and the concern expressed by her boss crushed her. She reported to the author that she felt her supervisor would no longer trust her and that she was beginning to doubt whether she was capable of performing her job satisfactorily. She was convinced, in fact, that she had been performing below standard since the event and that it was only a matter of time until she would be detected as an incompetent and fired. The spiral in this case worked in the opposite direction: The worse things became, the worse still they became. This is a true story about a woman who was president of her graduating class at college, had a first-class average in her courses, managed to find a professional job (during a time when it appeared that there were no jobs), and had performed at least to standard during the first 18 months following her graduation: A woman who is a leader, a "winner." The popular *The I Hate My Job Handbook* (Tien and Frankel, 1996) is full of case stories of this variety. Few people who begin to slip into one of these spirals of poor performance → self-doubt → further poor performance may think of these situations as involving problems of self-efficacy, but that is what they are called in the organizational behavior literature.

The Pygmalion and Galatea Effects

Readers who are fans of Greek and Roman mythology may be amused to learn that two heroes from the classics lend their names to psychological effects related to the notions of expectancy and self-efficacy. The Israeli professor Dev Eden is largely credited for bringing these effects some personality by advancing and describing the Pygmalion and Galatea effects.

For the Romans, Pygmalion was the sculptor of Cyprus. He hated women and was determined that he would never be married. Despite his resolve, working on the beautiful statue enthralled him and he feel in love with it. He was distraught that his love object was merely a stone idol and prayed to Venus (who was in charge of love) to provide him with a real-life version of the statue. The maiden who materialized from the statue was Galatea (Encarta, 1993b). For the Greeks, Galatea was a sea nymph who was loved by the Cyclops Polyphemus, an ugly fellow with a single eye in the middle of his forehead. Galatea rejected his advances and mocked him, then teased him into believing that perhaps she could love him. But he never truly won her affection. Meanwhile, Galatea fell in love with Acis, a young prince, whom poor Polyphemus killed in a jealous rage (Encarta, 1993a).

In the realm of modern work motivation theory, the *Pygmalion effect* is a general increase in an employee's performance that results from raising a manager's expectations about the possible performance levels of employees (Eden, 1984). Managers who truly believe that people working for them are capable of high performance act in ways that instill confidence and that result in high performance. This sort of effect has been demonstrated time and time again in classroom settings. Teachers in controlled experiments who believe that their students are superior eventually end up with superior-performing students, when in fact, the students are randomly chosen and assigned. Believing that someone can excel seems to make us cause them to do so, even when we are not aware of doing so.

By contrast, the *Galatea effect* is a performance gain that results from an employee's expectations about her own performance (Eden, 1988; Eden and Kinnar, 1991). One interesting field experiment dealt with Israeli military inductees. In the usual approach, prescreened recruits who are eligible for special forces on the basis of aptitude and motivation are provided with information about the special forces and then solicited to volunteer. The purpose of the experiment was to entice a number of these young soldiers into serving in special forces units by manipulating their self-efficacy beliefs. First, the inductees were split into two groups, each of which was exposed to a veteran member of one of the special forces, who told the candidates about life in the forces. In the experimental group, the veterans making the presentations stressed that they had once been raw recruits and had wondered whether they would have had the ability to succeed in the special forces. In other words, the presenters attempted to manipulate the self-efficacy beliefs of the experimental soldiers, influencing them to believe that they were capable of doing well in these elite groups. The control soldiers received the same stories from the veterans, but the veterans made no mention of similarities between themselves when younger and the new recruits in the audience. In short, this simple experimental manipulation, aimed at creating an association in the minds of the new recruits between themselves and the successful soldiers, was used to boost the self-efficacy beliefs of half of the recruits. Self-efficacy was measured among all the recruits after their exposure to the veterans.

As expected, the self-reported self-efficacy scores of the experimental inductees were significantly higher than that among the control inductees. More important, 84 percent of the recruits exposed to the experimental induction volunteered for service in the special forces, compared to only 16 percent of the controls, a ratio of about 5:1. They volunteered because they believed they could perform well in the special units because they believed they were similar in ability to the successful special forces soldiers who talked to them. The experimenters concluded that this special induction was successful in increasing the young soldiers' beliefs that they had "the right stuff" to make it in the especially demanding roles of the special forces (Eden and Kinnar, 1991). In chapter 14 we revisit the development of self-efficacy beliefs and see that there are a variety of general approaches available. Eden and Kinnar's (1991) powerful demonstration of the influence of heightened self-efficacy on real behavior is compelling evidence of the importance of these psychological effects.

Empowerment

In chapter 7 we examined the concept referred to as *empowerment,* a buzzword of the 1980s that has survived until today. Although the concept has applications and relevance for a variety of settings and disciplines (Eylon, 1994; Spreitzer, 1996), it has particular relevance for the management of people in work settings. Conger and Kanungo (1988) were first to define empowerment for the organizational literature; for them, it is merely the motivational concept of self-efficacy. K. W. Thomas and Velthouse (1990) argued that empowerment is a multidimensional construct that includes elements of four cognitions related to a person's beliefs about her work: its meaning or purpose; the person's competence to perform the task; her degree of self-determination in how to approach the task; and *impact,* the degree to which she can influence the strategic, administrative, or operating outcomes at the workplace (Spreitzer, 1995a). "Together, these four cognitions reflect an active, rather than a passive, orientation to a work role and context. The four dimensions are argued to combine additively to create an overall construct of psychological empowerment.... [T]he lack of any dimension will deflate, though not completely eliminate, the overall degree of felt empowerment" (p. 1444). In this view, empowerment is not a trait that transcends settings; rather, it is a set of beliefs held by a person in a particular work setting (K. W. Thomas and Velthouse, 1990; recall the discussion in chapter 1 of this book). Spreitzer (1995a, 1995b) has reported the development and validation of scales to assess this conceptualization of empowerment and some encouraging empirical results connecting empowerment to effectiveness and innovativeness among two samples of employees.

Recapitulation

The purpose of the foregoing sections has been to explain the major elements of Vroom's (1964) original VIE theory, by explicating the meaning of valence, instrumentality, expectancy, and force. The last few paragraphs have taken us somewhat off course because our discussion of expectancy naturally lead us into a discussion of other concepts similar to expectancy, such as self-efficacy and empowerment. We now return to our treatment of Vroom's (1964) major concepts by examining what he meant by *force.*

The Concept of Force

Vroom (1964) argued that expectancies, instrumentalities, and valences interact psychologically to create a motivational force to act in ways that seem most likely to bring pleasure or to avoid pain. "Behavior on the part of a person is assumed to be the result of a field of forces each of which has a direction and magnitude" (p. 18). Vroom likened his concept of force to a variety of other metaphorical concepts, including things such as performance vectors and behavior potential.

Force as Intention

In keeping with the terminology developed in chapter 9, we can think of force as representing the strength of a person's intention to act in a certain way. For example, if a person elects to strive for a particular level of job performance, we might say that the person's beliefs cause the greatest amount of force to be directed toward that level, or that he intends to strive for that level rather than for other levels. Symbolically, Vroom (1964, p. 18) summarizes his theory as follows:

$$F_i = f\left(\sum_{i=1}^{n} E_{ij} V_j\right) \quad \text{and} \quad V_j = f\left(\sum_{j=1}^{n} I_{jk} V_k\right)$$

where

F_i = psychological force to perform an act (i) (such as striving for a particular level of performance)
E_{ij} = strength of the expectancy that the act will be followed by the outcome j
V_j = valence for the person of outcome j
I_{jk} = instrumentality of outcome j for attaining second-level outcome k
V_k = valence of second-level outcome k

or, in his words, "the force on a person to perform an act is a monotonically increasing function of the algebraic sum of the products of the valences of all outcomes and the strength of his expectancies that the act will be followed by the attainment of these outcomes."

So people choose from among the alternative acts those corresponding to the strongest positive (or weakest negative) force. People attempt to maximize their overall best interest using the information available to them and their evaluations of this information. In the context of work motivation, this means that people select to pursue that level of performance that they believe will maximize their overall best interest (or subjective expected utility). Notice from the formula that *there will be little or no motivational force operating on a person to act in a certain manner if any of three conditions hold:* (1) if the person does not believe that acting in that manner will have any result (i.e., if her expectancy is effectively zero); (2) if she believes that there is no association between the result of her behavior and any second-level outcomes (if her instrumentality is effectively zero); or (3) if she does not value the second-level outcomes (if her valence is zero).

The Choice of Performance Level

When we think of the levels of job performance that an employee might strive for as the outcome of interest, Vroom's theory suggests that the person will consider the valences, instrumentalities, and expectancies associated with each level of the entire spectrum of performance levels and will elect to pursue the level that generates the great-est positive force (or lowest negative force) for him. If the person sees more good out-comes than bad ones associated with performing at a high level, he will strive to per-form highly. On the other hand, if a lower level of performance results in the greatest degree of psychological force, we can anticipate that he will settle for such a level. The implication is that low motivation levels result from employee choices to perform at low levels, and that these choices, in turn, are the result of beliefs concerning the va-lences, instrumentalities, and expectancies held in the mind of the employee. These be-liefs are formed and modified in the ways described in chapter 9 and suggest, accord-ingly, a number of implications for the management of work motivation. We address these implications later in the chapter.

REFINEMENTS TO THE THEORY

Since the publication of Vroom's book in 1964, a considerable amount of both theoret-ical and empirical attention has been paid to expectancy models of work motivation. Aside from attempting to test the validity of the theory in its simple form, most of these efforts have sought to study the characteristics of people and organizations that influence valence, instrumentality, and expectancy beliefs, or to examine the types of conditions within which VIE predictions of work motivation can be expected to apply. A complete discussion of these refinements could easily constitute an entire book, so it is well beyond our present purposes. The reader who is interested in pursuing major theoretical advances in VIE theory is referred to the following sources: J. P. Campbell, Dunnette, Lawler, and Weick (1970); Dachler and Mobley, 1973; J. M. Feldman, Reitz, and Hiterman, (1976); Graen (1969); House, Shapiro, and Wahba (1974); Kanfer (1992); Kopelman (1977); Kopelman and Thompson (1976); Lawler (1971, 1973); Nay-lor, Pritchard, and Ilgen (1980); L. W. Porter and Lawler (1968); Reinharth and Wahba (1976); Staw (1977); and Zedeck (1977). Thorough reviews of the research evidence pertaining to VIE theory are provided by Heneman and Schwab (1972), T. R. Mitchell and Biglan (1971), and J. P. Campbell and Pritchard (1976).

For the purpose of the present discussion, only one of the many theoretical ad-vances in VIE theory is presented, followed by a brief summary of the validity of the theory and a number of difficulties that have been encountered in determining its va-lidity. We conclude with a discussion of the major implications of VIE theory for the practice of management. To begin, let's take a look at one of the most important mod-ifications and extensions of Vroom's work: the model offered by L. W. Porter and Lawler (1968).

The Porter–Lawler Model

Vroom's (1964) statement of VIE theory left a number of questions unanswered. Per-haps the most important of these concerned the origins of valence, instrumentality, and expectancy beliefs and the nature of the relationship, if any, between employee attitudes toward work and job performance. L. W. Porter and Lawler (1968) developed a theoretic model and then tested it using a sample of managers and revised it to explore these is-sues. The revised statement of their model is provided in schematic form in Figure 12-1.

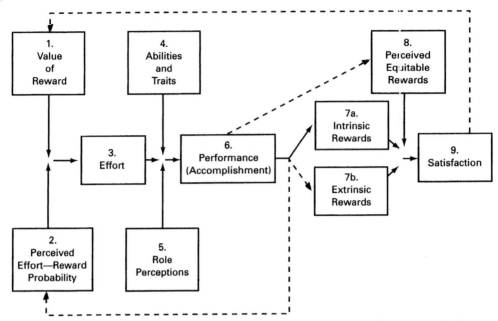

Source: From L. W. Porter and E. E. Lawler, *Managerial attitudes and performance* (Homewood, IL: Dorsey Press, division of Richard D. Irwin, 1968). Reprinted with permission.

FIGURE 12-1   Revised Porter–Lawler Model

In a nutshell, their theory suggests the following. Employee effort is determined by two key factors: the value a person places on certain outcomes and the degree to which the person believes that his effort will lead to the attainment of these rewards. As predicted by Vroom, Porter and Lawler found that these two factors interact to determine effort level; in other words, they found that for people to put forth further effort, they must both positively value outcomes and believe that these outcomes result from their efforts. However, effort may or may not result in job performance, which they defined as the accomplishment of those tasks that comprise a person's job. Why? For two reasons: the level of ability the person has to do his job and his role clarity, the degree of clarity of the understanding the person has concerning just what his job consists of. Thus, a person may be highly motivated (putting out a lot of effort), but that effort will not necessarily result in what can be considered performance unless he has both the ability to perform the job and a clear understanding of the ways in which it is appropriate to direct his effort. The reader is probably familiar with at least one classmate who has high motivation to learn and succeed in college but who lacks either the ability or the savoir faire needed to direct his energy into what can be considered performance in an academic context: learning and self-development. In short, all three ingredients are needed to some degree, and if any one is absent, performance cannot result.

Next, what is the relationship between performance (at whatever level) and job satisfaction? As reflected in Figure 12-1, Porter and Lawler argue that performance and satisfaction may or may not be related, depending on a number of factors. First, they note that it is not always the case that performance results in rewards in organizations. Further, they recognize that there are at least two types of rewards potentially available from performance: intrinsic and extrinsic. (We dealt with the distinction between intrinsic and extrinsic outcomes in chapter 7) Porter and Lawler recognize that intrinsic rewards can be much more closely connected with good performance than extrinsic rewards, because the former result (almost automatically) from performance itself, whereas the latter depend on outside sources (both to recognize that performance has been attained and to administer rewards accordingly).

Porter and Lawler suggested that the level of performance that a person believes she has attained will influence the level of rewards that she believes will be equitable (see the discussion of internalized standards of equity in chapter 11). So if an employee believes that her efforts have resulted in a high degree of performance, she will expect a greater level of reward than would be the case if she believes that her performance is not as high. As a result, a particular reward, if any is forthcoming, will be assessed in terms of its level of equity in the mind of the employee rather than in terms of its absolute level. We sometimes hear statements such as "That pay increase was an insult considering all I do for this company," reflecting Porter and Lawler's belief that it is not the absolute amount of reward that follows performance which determines whether it is satisfying; rather, for it to be satisfying, the amount, however large or small, must be seen by the employee as being equitable. Satisfaction was defined in Porter and Lawler's research as "the extent to which rewards actually received meet or exceed the perceived equitable level of rewards" (p. 31). As suggested by the feedback loop at the top of Figure 12-1, the level of satisfaction or dissatisfaction experienced by the person as a result of his treatment by the organization helps determine the value he will place on the rewards in question in the future. Moreover, notice the feedback loop at the bottom of Figure 12-1. It suggests that the strength of the person's belief that effort will result in rewards is also determined through experience.

Comments and Criticisms of Porter and Lawler

A number of points must be made about this model. First, the primary focus of the research that accompanied its development was on pay and the role of pay in employee motivation. Although the authors limited their consideration of outcomes other than pay, they argued that the general model should be relevant for consequences other than pay. In addition, since pay was the focus, the emphasis was on positive consequences only rather than on both positive and negative consequences (such as fatigue, demotions, or various forms of punishment). Second, Porter and Lawler tested the propositions they derived from their model cross-sectionally (rather than over time), using only managers from the extreme ends of the distributions on the important variables in that model, excluding those who fell near the middle in each case. This is a common practice in research but one that causes overestimates of the validity of the model being tested (E. K. Taylor and Griess, 1976). Additionally, they measured job satisfaction using a technique that is also commonly used, but one subsequently shown to be inappropriate, probably reducing the apparent validity of the model (J. R. Edwards, 1994; Johns, 1981).

A third point is that although their model posits the importance of ability as an interactive factor with motivation as a determinant of job performance, Porter and Lawler's own research did not pay much attention to the specific role of ability. As noted in chapter 1 of the present volume, however, other researchers have addressed this issue, and the results seem to suggest that whereas ability has an important influence on performance, it may not interact with motivation in the manner believed by Vroom (1964) and L. W. Porter and Lawler (see Terborg, 1977). Fourth, although Porter and Lawler use the term *value* rather than *valence,* it seems clear that they had the same concept in mind as Vroom. The reader is reminded again of the importance of distinguishing between valence and value when considering motivation from a VIE theory perspective: It is the anticipated value (valence) of an outcome that is crucial in determining effort, not actual value.

Another point has to do with the way the connection between effort and rewards was conceptualized and measured. Current theories recognize that employee beliefs about the strength of the connection between effort and reward distribution can usefully be broken down into two components: (1) the strength of the belief that a person's effort will result in job performance, and (2) the strength of the person's belief that performance, if achieved, will eventuate into rewards. Porter and Lawler acknowledge the prospect for breaking this overall cognition down into its component parts, and subsequent work by Lawler (1973) and others maintains this distinction.

Performance and Satisfaction (Again)

A major contribution of the Porter–Lawler model consists of the implications it holds for the issue concerning the relationship between performance and satisfaction. According to the theory, will satisfaction and performance be related? If so, when? Figure 12-1 suggests that these two factors may or may not be related, but that when they are, the order of causality is far from simple. How might satisfaction be a contributing determinant of performance levels? A number of conditions must hold:

1. Satisfaction must leave the person desirous of attaining more of the same outcome(s). Recall from chapter 3 that satisfied needs tend to lose their capacity to motivate behavior, although growth need satisfaction seems to increase the strength of these needs.

2. Even if the reward maintains its valence, effort will result only if the person believes that effort results in attainment of the reward (which, as we have discussed, is not always the case).

3. For someone's effort to result in performance, the person must have the ability to perform as well as a clear idea concerning how to try to perform—where to direct his effort.

4. The performance must result in rewards, and these rewards must be perceived as equitable, for the reasons discussed earlier.

In short, for satisfaction to be a contributing cause of performance, as was believed during the days of the human relations movement (and as is still commonly believed by managers and people on the street), all of the foregoing individual and organizational conditions must apply. Rather complicated, to say the least.

Can performance be a cause of satisfaction? The model implies that it can. As noted earlier, high performance can be an immediate cause of intrinsic satisfaction, assuming that the job provides sufficient challenge to appeal to growth needs (recall chapter 7). In addition, performance can contribute to extrinsic satisfaction if at least three conditions hold: (1) Desired rewards must be tied to performance (as opposed to being tied to chance or other factors), (2) the person must perceive the connection between his performance and the rewards he receives, and (3) the person must believe that the rewards he receives for his performance are equitable. Again, not a very simple relationship, but Porter and Lawler's model helps explain why the relationships observed between performance and satisfaction have traditionally been so low, although in their research, the two factors were found to be more strongly connected than is usually the case.

In conclusion, Porter and Lawler provided a useful elaboration of the fundamental concepts of VIE theory as presented by Vroom. The dynamic features of their model (as reflected in the feedback loops) indicate the ongoing nature of the motivation process and shed light on why some employees are more productive than others, why some employees are more satisfied with their work than others, and when we can expect to find a relationship between employee attitudes and performance. The reader may wonder about the age of the Porter and Lawler revision: It was published nearly 30 years ago. More recent models have been proposed, but they offer few major innovations over those of L. W. Porter and Lawler (1968)—demonstrating again that the simple age of an idea is not sufficient grounds to reject it.

THE VALIDITY OF VIE THEORY

Despite the fact that there have been innumerable tests of the scientific validity of VIE theory, it is unclear whether or not researchers have conducted fair tests of the theory given the claims made by the theory itself and problems with the way that studies have been conducted. In their 1976 review, J. P. Campbell and Pritchard identified 12 common problems in the many studies conducted to that time. In the two decades since then, some of these have been seemingly resolved, others have not.

The Between/Within Issue

Probably the most widely cited of these problems has to do with what has come to be called the *between/within issue*. This concerns the argument that VIE theory is intended solely to make behavioral and attitudinal predictions within, not across, persons (Arnold, 1981; Klein, 1991a; Kopelman, 1977; T. R. Mitchell, 1974; Nickerson and McLelland, 1989; Wolf and Connolly, 1981). *In other words, is Vroom's theory intended to make predictions about which behavioral alternatives a single person will choose from among those that confront him, or to make predictions about the relative likelihood of different people choosing from among the alternatives confronting them?*

Vroom states that the alternative which is perceived to maximize a person's overall expected utility and satisfaction will be the one selected. This implies that the theory is concerned with choices across alternatives but within persons. On the other hand, in many investigations purporting to test VIE theory, expected levels of motivational force (or effort) for a number of people were computed using those people's scores on VIE factors, and then the scores predicted were correlated across persons, with ratings representing actual behavior or attitudes.

To illustrate more completely, suppose that we were to compute expected effort scores for a sample of 20 people, using the information these people provide us through interviews or questionnaires. We would calculate these scores using some form of $E(\Sigma \text{ VI})$ formula. Then suppose that we rank-ordered these people on the basis of the magnitude of this overall predicted effort level. Next, we gather supervisory ratings of the actual typical effort levels of the same people and rank-order them again, this time on the basis of their supervisory ratings. Finally, assume that we correlate the rated effort scores with our predicted effort scores, attempting to determine whether the people with the highest predicted scores tended to have the highest supervisory ratings and whether those with the lowest predicted scores also had the lowest ratings.

Proponents of the within-persons approach have argued that the between-persons approach is invalid for two reasons. First, on theoretical grounds they argue that it does not test VIE theory per se. Then, on empirical grounds they argue that the tendency of findings of between-persons studies to be weaker shows that the between approach is not valid. Here, we discuss these arguments in terms of three interrelated issues. The first is statistical, concerning the relative ability of the two approaches to show empirical support for the theory. Between-persons versus within-persons experimental designs have differential power to detect existing empirical relationships. The second issue is methodological. It concerns the vulnerability of the two approaches to alternative explanations (recall chapter 2). The third issue is theoretical, concerning whether or not VIE theory makes between- as well as within-persons predictions.

Using the terms defined by Cook and Campbell (1979) in their definitive work on the validity of propositions, these three issues correspond to concerns about *statistical conclusion validity, internal validity,* and *construct validity.* Our position is that conclusions about the validity of the within- as opposed to between-persons approaches cannot be made on the basis of empirical results (Nickerson and McLelland, 1989) but must be made on theoretical grounds. Further, we hold that advancements in conceptualization and operationalization of VIE theory concepts make between-persons studies valid extensions of Vroom's theory.

Statistical Conclusion Validity

Tests employing the within-persons approach have often been more supportive of VIE theory predictions than those adopting a between-persons approach. That is, they have been more likely to find statistically significant relationships between predictor and criterion measures of VIE concepts. For example, D. F. Parker and Dyer (1976) were able to make better-than-chance predictions about the decisions reached by naval officers as to whether or not to retire voluntarily. Similarly, Arnold (1981), D. D. Baker, Ravichandran, and Randall (1989), and Fusilier, Ganster, and Middlemist (1984) made predictions supportive of the theory concerning the choices of jobs made by students (see also Wanous, Keon, and Latack, 1983, for a review of within-persons studies of occupational choice); Butler and Cantrell (1989) predicted the research productivity of business faculty; Matsui, Kagawa, Nagamatsu, and Ohtsuka (1977) predicted which of six insurance policies agents would prefer to sell; Nebeker and Mitchell (1974) and Matsui and Ohtsuka (1978) predicted the leadership styles of supervisors in different settings and in different cultures.

At the same time, although generally finding weaker relationships, the between-persons approach has also supported VIE theory (see Schwab, Olian, and Heneman, 1979, for a review of early between-persons research). The results of studies that purport to contrast the within- and between-persons approaches are mixed. Snyder, Howard, and Hammer (1978), for example, found that the between-persons approach outperformed the within-persons approach in predicting job choice. By contrast, Muchinsky (1977) and C. W. Kennedy, Fossum, and White (1983) found that within-persons predictions of effort were stronger than between-persons predictions.[4]

In chapter 2 we introduced the concept of statistical conclusion validity. This issue concerns whether a researcher makes correct inferences about the true relationships among constructs of interest to him (e.g., between predicted effort scores and actual effort ratings provided by supervisors in a VIE theory study) on the basis of the statistical measures and statistical relationships that he found in his research. Of the numerous threats to this kind of validity listed by Cook and Campbell, three are particularly relevant here: (1) the greater statistical power of within-persons designs, (2) the low reliability of measures, and (3) the random heterogeneity of respondents.

First, VIE studies employing the within-persons approach generally have significantly greater power to find relationships than do between-persons designs. By asking the same people to provide repeated measures, the number of observations given the same number of participants is much higher. Baker, Ravichandran, and Randall (1989), for example, conducted a within-persons study of VIE theory in which they obtained 25,800 observations from 101 participants.

Second, the low reliability of VIE measures (de Leo and Pritchard, 1974) is a problem for both within- and between-persons studies. However, given the lower ability of between-persons approaches to find effects for the other reasons given here and the small proportion of total variance in behavior often explained by VIE measures, the effect of low reliability may be to attenuate relationships found in between-persons studies to below traditional significance criteria.

Third, and probably most important, one of the reasons that within-individual tests of VIE theory often outperform between-persons tests is that they control for differences for random heterogeneity across individuals. Between-persons tests require strong assumptions about the comparability of people, assumptions that are often not met (Dawes and Smith, 1985; Hammond, McLelland, and Mumpower, 1980; Jaccard, 1981; Nickerson and McLelland, 1989; Wolf and Connolly, 1981). In within-persons experimental designs each person acts as his or her own control; thus differences between people in ability, experience, personality, preferences for different rewards, instrument response tendencies, and various other things are held constant for each person (C. W. Kennedy, Fossum, and White, 1983). To the extent that such things are relevant to what the experimenter is trying to predict, as is very much the case for VIE theory, experimental designs in which they are held constant are likely to show stronger relationships between predictor and criterion measures than those in which they are left to vary. In between-persons designs the effect of such differences is left to vary randomly, thus reducing the proportion of the variance in the criterion measure that is predicted by VIE theory constructs.[5]

As Nickerson and McLelland (1989) state: "[P]ossible distortions in the across-persons correlations render meaningless any comparisons between across-persons and within-persons predictions" (p. 266). In effect, VIE theory is an incomplete specification

---

[4]Later we argue that such comparisons are meaningless.

[5]Nickerson and McLelland (1989) show that, in fact, factors such as response bias can yield higher across-persons than within-persons predictions, depending on how such biases are manifested and how differences between individuals being studied interact with VIE theory measures.

of employee behavior. For example, ability is an obvious determinant of performance, yet it is not included in VIE theory; if performance is used as the criterion in tests of the theory, it will be predicted imperfectly. Similarly, we pointed out earlier that employee self-esteem is likely to have an effect on expectancy beliefs. Indeed, incorporating individual differences improves the predictions of VIE theory (L. E. Miller and Grush, 1988). To the extent that these or other relevant variables are not held constant, their effect on effort will be counted as error variance, reducing the apparent validity of the theory. The effect of this fact is to make fair comparisons of the between- and within-persons approaches to VIE theory very difficult.

To state the problem another way, every theoretical proposition contains an implicit *ceteris paribus* clause. Vroom, for example, hypothesized that people will choose outcomes that maximize their overall best interest, *all other things being equal*. Yet most research designs do not hold all other things equal. Within-persons designs come closest by comparing a person's behavior in one instance with his or her behavior in another instance (such as when facing two job choices), thus holding individual differences constant. Between-persons designs allow individual differences to vary but intentionally randomize this variance. In both approaches the validity coefficient is the effect size divided by the random error. But in between-persons designs this random error includes the effect of individual differences, whereas in within-persons designs it does not. Using the magnitude of predictor–criterion relationships to judge the differential validity of the two approaches biases the comparison in favor of within-persons studies.

Finally, lest we be misunderstood, it is important to note that every theory of human behavior is incomplete. None predicts behavior perfectly for every person in every situation. Theorists attempt to build theories that are as descriptive as possible, using as small a number of concepts as can get the job done. It is a truism that theories cannot be general *and* parsimonious simultaneously. Our point is that different research designs account for this incompleteness in different ways. Each has advantages and disadvantages, in terms of such things as the power to detect differences, vulnerability to alternative explanations, realism, and practicality (Runkel and McGrath, 1972). Choosing effectively among them is a matter of managing the trade-offs among these factors. Evaluating the validity of the within- and between-persons designs, therefore, requires considerably more than merely comparing the magnitude of empirical results.

Internal Validity

Having concluded that a relationship between a predictor and a criterion measure exists, internal validity concerns the question of whether the effect on the criterion can be correctly attributed to the predictor. That is, having made the decision that repeated measures of VIE concepts are statistically significantly related to repeated measures of choices among alternatives, can we conclude that the latter is a consequence of the former? For a complete review of threats to internal validity, the reader is referred to Cook and Campbell (1979), Runkel and McGrath (1972), and chapter 2 of this book. For our purposes here, the threats that are particularly relevant to the between- versus within-persons debate include the effects of repeated testing in within-persons studies and the interaction of this with the awareness of participants that they are being studied.

When people are asked to respond to similar questions repeatedly, they are vulnerable to testing effects such as learning and familiarity. Familiarity can "enhance performance because items and error responses are more likely to be remembered at later testing sessions" (T. D. Cook and Campbell, 1979, p. 52). As Keren and Raaijmakers (1988) point out for studies of utility theory: "A likely effect . . . of such repeated stimuli is to evoke the subjects' awareness to provide consistent responses (even if they do not reflect the true preferences)" (p. 237).

Further, when people are aware that they are participants in a study, they may behave in ways that introduce bias into experimental results. Their responses may tend to confirm implicit hypotheses rather than reflect their unbiased motivations. They may try to be "good" participants by providing responses that are consistent with what they think the researcher wants. This is true for both between- and within-persons designs. However, in within-persons studies, participants may be more likely to guess the experimenter's intent and be more able to act on that. For example, in within-persons experimental designs, participants may be cued by the multiple choices placed in front of them (Greenwald, 1976; Nickerson and McLelland, 1989). In between-persons designs, participants are usually aware of only one condition. For example, they might be asked to report only one set of measures of expectancy, instrumentality, valence, and choice. In contrast, in within-persons designs, participants are asked to report multiple sets of measures corresponding to a number of alternative choices. These repeated measures may cue participants to the experimental hypothesis. That is, participants may be more able to guess the experimenter's hypothesis and to fulfill their desires to be good experimental subjects (Rosenthal, 1976).

Artifacts of this sort can lead experimenters to avoid within-persons designs; they also contribute to the ability of such designs to appear to support theoretical predictions. Our point here is that the within-persons approach has advantages (and disadvantages) that affect its ability to claim support for VIE theory quite independent of whether or not VIE theory makes within- or between-persons predictions.

Construct Validity

Construct validity concerns the correspondence between empirical operations and the theoretical constructs they are intended to represent (recall chapter 2). It concerns the very question of whether the comparisons made in VIE studies are appropriate tests of the theoretical propositions of VIE theory as well as the question of whether operational measures of VIE constructs are valid. In other words, do the statistical comparisons made in VIE studies test the form of the relationships specified in the propositions of VIE theory, and do the measures employed validly represent VIE constructs? As we shall see, these two issues are connected.

Most proponents of the within-persons approach to VIE theory studies argue that this is the approach that Vroom (1964) intended and that therefore between-persons studies are inappropriate. Yet it must be said that Vroom did not write the last (or the first) word on VIE theory.[6] This is to say that if we wish to believe that the development of motivation theory is an ongoing, progressive enterprise, we cannot allow

---

[6]Interestingly, studies of the theory of reasoned action (see chapter 9), which some researchers do not distinguish from VIE theory (e.g., Nickerson and McLelland, 1989), tend to employ a between-persons approach without any attendant controversy about its appropriateness.

ourselves to be ideologically fixed to a single conception of the relationships among expectancies, valences, and behavior. The developments of the past 30 years in VIE theory have been just that, developments. Surely Vroom intended to describe the behavior of employees rather than prescribe one best, unchanging way of making choices about occupations or effort. Advancements and refinements to the theory, such as the addition of constructs and propositions and the development of improved measures, are part of the cycle of theory building and testing that leads to better description and prediction of employee behavior. To adhere to one conception does not assist this enterprise.

Leaving this issue aside, what did Vroom intend? His formulation says that people will choose from among the alternatives available to them the one that has the highest valence. On the face of it this is a within-persons prediction. Yet it is also the case that if two people are faced with two identical alternatives and we know that for the first person the first choice has higher valence than the second and that for the second person the reverse is true, VIE theory will predict greater motivational force toward the first choice for the first person and the second choice for the second person. This is clearly a between-persons prediction. It is, in fact, an example given by Vroom himself (our "first" and "second" persons correspond to persons 1 and 4, respectively, on page 192 of Vroom, 1964). He also gave the following example of three people: The first has high expected payoffs for both high and low effort, the second has high expected payoffs for high effort but not for low effort, and the third has high expected payoffs for neither high nor low effort. Vroom argues that only the second person is highly motivated to perform effectively and says that these cases "illustrate the kind of predictions that can be derived from the model."

So it seems that Vroom's intent may have included between-persons VIE theory predictions. The example he gives shows that between-persons predictions are possible if we have information about the relative preference *within persons* for choices about alternatives. In other words, if we know the relative preferences of a sample of employees for choosing to expend high as opposed to low effort, it makes sense to correlate those preferences with ratings of their performance (keeping in mind the other factors affecting the relationship between motivation and performance). Critical readers may wish to argue that Vroom's definition of expectancy speaks of preferences for only a single level of effort. Recall, however, that every theoretical proposition contains an implicit "all other things being equal" clause. Thus every theoretical statement about one effort level (or choice) refers implicitly to other choices.

Ironically, the argument that a person's motivational force toward one choice can be compared meaningfully only to the same person's scores for other choices (Dachler and Mobley, 1973; C. W. Kennedy, Fossum, and White, 1983; Kopelman, 1977; Mobley and Meglino, 1977) has been used against the between-persons approach. Yet if this requirement is incorporated into measurement of expectancy concepts, the argument is negated. This brings us to the second component of construct validity: the validity of measurement of VIE theory concepts.

As we said earlier, Vroom suggested that expectancy beliefs be measured in terms of a person's subjective probability that a particular first-level outcome (e.g., task performance) would result from his or her actions (e.g., effort). As a result, expectancy has been most often operationalized by asking people to provide a rating of the likelihood that given a high level of effort, they would be able to achieve a given level of performance. There has been a steady trend, however, toward incorporating multiple effort levels into the measurement of expectancy. Kopelman (1977) and Staw (1977) proposed that expectancy scores be calculated by subtracting the likelihood of an outcome given low effort from the likelihood of the same outcome given high effort. The resulting measure would reflect the incremental value of increased effort rather than just the value of high effort. This has been labeled the *return on effort method*. A number of studies have claimed that it is superior to the conventional method (Biberman, Baril, and Kopelman, 1986; C. W. Kennedy, Fossum, and White, 1983; Kopelman, 1977).

Continuing this line of thinking, Hollenbeck (1979) proposed a *matrix method* for expectancy research that asks respondents to provide assessments of the likelihood that each of a range of effort levels will result in a range of levels of performance. Instrumentality is measured similarly for combinations of performance levels and various outcomes. Matrix multiplication is applied to calculate the motivational force associated with each level of effort. Hollenbeck proposes, finally, that a probabilistic approach be taken to relate effort to these multiple force scores in which a person exerts effort in proportion to the relative attractiveness of each level of effort.

Building on Hollenbeck's work, Sussman and Vecchio (1985) proposed a fourfold model which includes the measurement of subjective probabilities associated with combinations of levels of effort and outcomes. They point out that their approach resolves the problems associated with traditional approaches to expectancy theory, in which variables measured on interval-level scales are subjected to impermissible transformations such as multiplication (Schmidt, 1973).

Ilgen, Nebeker, and Pritchard (1981) have come closest to empirical validation of such measures of VIE theory concepts. They proposed multiple effort, performance, and outcome measures of expectancy and instrumentality and compared these to traditional measures. For example, they constructed both an expected value index and covariation measures of expectancy, the latter corresponding most closely to the approaches advocated by Hollenbeck and Sussman and Vecchio. They then sought to validate these measures by comparing the scores of respondents who completed work in high and low objective expectancy conditions. Contrary to their own hypothesis that expectancy is best conceptualized as the covariation between effort and performance, they found that this measure "showed little responsiveness to the expectancy manipulation" (p. 215). The reason for this, we propose, is that their manipulation of objective expectancy did not in fact manipulate the covariation between effort and performance. They sought to create a high-expectancy condition by using a relatively easy task and a low-expectancy condition by using a relatively difficult task. It is possible, however, for tasks with very different degrees of difficulty to have the same relationship between working hard and achieving outcomes. That is, a person can increase his effort by 10 units, say, and see 10 units of increase in performance in both a relatively easy and a relatively difficult task. Similarly, tasks can create very different relationships between effort and performance, yet have the same overall probability of success (Eden, 1988). In sum, task difficulty and expectancy are not necessarily inversely related (Garland, 1984).

The importance of these developments in measurement is that they explicitly incorporate the comparison of multiple levels of effort and performance; they make explicit the within-person nature of the theory in the operationalization of VIE theory concepts. In so doing, they make possible between-persons predictions. This resolves part of the debate between advocates of the within- and between-persons approaches. On the one hand, by incorporating comparison of multiple effort and performance levels into measurement, it is possible to test hypotheses that people with higher motivational force toward particular choices will be more likely to make those choices than will people who have lower motivation toward those choices. On the other hand, this is different from saying that motivational force scores are determined by the particular multiplicative function specified by Vroom. In other words, *the between- and within-persons approaches test different hypotheses of VIE theory.* In their criticism of between-persons studies, Wolf and Connolly (1981) put it bluntly. They say that between-persons studies have "without doubt, established that individuals commonly shape their work-related behaviors in a manner somewhat responsive to their anticipation of the likely outcomes of those behaviors—a finding we see as less than surprising. They certainly have *not* cast light on the cognitive processes of individuals in regard to their work choices" (p. 44).

Other Research Difficulties

In addition to the between/within and measurement problems just described, a variety of other problems have been tackled by researchers interested in VIE theory (J. P. Campbell and Pritchard, 1976). Most of these have to do with the complex nature of the theory, making very difficult the operationalization of measures and research designs so as to be isomorphic with the theory. For example, as we noted earlier, VIE theory studies often use supervisory ratings of *performance* as the criterion against which predictions of employee force is compared, whereas the theory purports to predict *effort*.[7] Because effort is only one determinant of performance, the results of these studies have been negatively biased against the theory.

VIE theory also speaks of *changes,* at one point in time, of V, I, and E perceptions being predictive of *changes* of effort at a subsequent time. Yet cross-sectional designs (whether within or between persons) cannot assess such changes (see Kuhl and Atkinson, 1984, and Mayes, 1978a, for a discussion of this problem and Kopelman, 1979, and Lawler and Suttle, 1973 for attempts to get around it). VIE theory proposes that valence, expectancy, and instrumentality beliefs combine multiplicatively. This imposes the assumption that the beliefs that people hold are independent of one another, but that may not be true. People may place higher valence on outcomes that are believed more difficult to attain. Indeed, many researchers have sought to evaluate the tenability of the multiplication hypothesis (e.g., Baker, Ravichandran, and Randall, 1989). Finally, VIE theory assumes a high degree of rationality among employees. Yet we know that people have limited cognitive capacities and that much of human behavior is habitual and subconscious (Locke, 1975; Mayes, 1978b; Simon, 1957; Staw, 1977).

Summary

The self-correcting cycle of research activity we examined in chapter 2 has raised questions about these and other common problems in the research on VIE theory, and some studies have taken many of them into account. Nevertheless, significant lack of

---

[7]Recall from chapter 1 that employee effort (or motivational force) and job performance are not the same thing. Using performance to measure motivation is an error in construct validity (recall chapter 2).

consensus remains with respect to research operations. In 1979, Schwab, Olian, and Heneman found that 42 percent of the variance in the results in between-persons VIE studies was attributable to methodological factors. A similar study today, particularly one that included both within- and between-persons studies, would probably conclude that the problem remains at least as large. It appears, then, that VIE theory may be a more valid representation of work-related attitudes and behaviors than has been concluded by many who have surveyed studies that were fraught with the problems identified above. We conclude that the situation for VIE theory may be similar to that for Maslow's need hierarchy theory (recall chapter 3), equity theory (chapter 11), and perhaps even Herzberg's two-factor theory (recall chapter 2): Although many studies have been conducted with the intention of testing its validity, only a few studies have been free of the methodological and conceptual errors we have detailed in this section. On balance, we are left with the optimistic belief that VIE theory is probably a valid model of the causes of work behavior. At the very least it is probably an accurate representation of how people form work-related intentions (see chapter 13).

THE PATH-GOAL THEORY OF LEADERSHIP

VIE theory inspired a formal theory of leadership called *path-goal theory*. This theory suggests ways that leaders can make work groups more effective through the impact they can have on employee beliefs about valences, instrumentalities, and expectancies. More specifically, the theory discusses the ways in which leaders may use any of at least four types of behavioral styles to influence employee satisfaction, the acceptance of the leader by employees, and employee beliefs that effort can result in performance and that performance will result in desired rewards (House and Mitchell, 1974). The four leadership styles considered are the following:

1. *Directive:* The leader structures the work, assigns tasks, clarifies his or her role with subordinates, and creates and enforces standards of performance.
2. *Supportive:* The leader shows genuine respect for employee needs and status, attempting to make the work more pleasant Such a leader treats subordinates as equals and is friendly and approachable.
3. *Participative:* The leader consults with subordinates about problems and decisions that must be made and takes subordinates' suggestions into account when possible.
4. *Achievement-oriented:* The leader sets challenging goals and shows confidence that subordinates can reach the goals.

Path-goal theory assumes that individual managers are capable of exhibiting more than one of these styles depending on the circumstances. In other words, it is a mistake to assume that a particular manager is simply a participative or a supportive leader. In fact, the theory specifies the types of conditions under which it is more appropriate for a leader to employ each of these behavioral styles. Based on VIE theory, it is assumed that the effective leader will behave in ways that recognize and arouse employee needs for the types of outcomes that the leader has at his disposal and then attempt to increase the payoff to employees for successful performance when it occurs. Moreover, the successful leader will try to influence subordinate expectancy beliefs by assisting with the accomplishment of difficult tasks and by clarifying ambiguous task assignments. Finally, the effective leader will attempt, where possible, to make the distribution of rewards contingent on the successful accomplishment of work. "To summarize, the motivational functions of the leader consist of increasing the number and kinds of personal payoffs to subordinates for work-goal attainment and making paths to these payoffs easier to travel by clarifying the paths, reducing road blocks and pitfalls and increasing the opportunities for personal satisfaction en route" (House and Mitchell, 1974, quoted from Downey, Hellriegel, and Slocum, 1977, p. 226).

Limitations of space prevent more elaborate treatment of the path-goal theory here. The interested reader can trace the development of the theory by reading Evans (1970, 1974), Fiedler and House (1988), House (1971), House and Dessler (1974), and House and Mitchell (1974). Research testing the theory has been reported by Al-Gattain (1985); Childers, Dubinsky, and Skinner (1990); Dessler and Valenzi (1977); Dobbins and Zaccaro (1986); Downey, Sheridan, and Slocum (1976); C. N. Greene (1979); Keller (1989); Mossholder, Neibuhr, and Morris (1990); Sagie and Koslowsky (1994); C. A. Schriesheim and De Nisi (1981); J. F. Schriesheim and Schriesheim (1980); C. A. Schriesheim and Von Glinow (1977); Thomas and Tartell (1991); and Wofford and Liska (1993), among others.

Unfortunately, as in the case of research testing VIE theory, research on path-goal theory has been hampered by the complexity of the theory and by the use of many different operationalizations of its components. In a definitive meta-analysis, Wofford and Liska (1993) found limited support for the theory, citing three principal deficiencies. First, the degree to which research findings tended to support the predictions of path-goal theory depended on which measures of leader behavior were used. It seems that measures of leader behavior lack convergent validity. Moreover, although House and Mitchell's (1974) description of path-goal theory described four styles of leadership, most tests of the theory have only tested the effects of directive and supportive leadership. Second, whereas path-goal theory makes predictions about the effect of leader behaviors on employee beliefs about expectancies and instrumentalities, research testing the theory has used surrogate measures of these constructs, such as satisfaction, performance, role clarity, and organizational commitment. Because other factors also influence these, tests of path-goal theory predictions are weakened. Finally, in most of the studies included in Wofford and Liska's meta-analysis, measures of both the predictor and criterion variables were subjective reports obtained from the same participants, making them subject to common method variance. In sum, they conclude that while the predictions of path-goal theory probably have not received a fair test, it may also be the case that the theory is not a valid description of the determinants of effective leadership.

IMPLICATIONS OF VIE THEORY FOR MANAGEMENT

We noted in chapter 9 that beliefs about work (or about life in general) are based on a person's perceptions of the surrounding environment and that these perceptions are influenced by information stored in the person's memory. It is assumed here that valence, instrumentality, and expectancy beliefs are established and influenced in the same manner as are other beliefs. Therefore, it follows that because beliefs may not be valid or accurate, the person's behavior may not seem appropriate to observers. It also follows that because these three beliefs are merely beliefs (as opposed to intentions), they may not result in behavior at all, or at least, they may not result in specifically predictable behaviors. They should, however, influence a person's intentions to act certain ways. Accordingly, a number of implications follow from VIE theory for any supervisor who wishes to try to "motivate" a staff. Many of these suggestions were implicit in our discussion of the path-goal theory.

Expectancy-Related Factors

To generate positive expectancy forces, a supervisor must assign her personnel to jobs for which they are trained and which they are capable of performing. This requires that the supervisor understand the skills, strengths, and weaknesses of each subordinate as well as the nature of the skill requirements of the jobs to which she is assigning them. If people are assigned to tasks they are not capable of performing, according to VIE theory, their expectancy perceptions will be low and we would not expect to see them trying to perform.

Consider how difficult it is, in practice, for supervisors to appreciate completely the skill requirements of the jobs their employees must perform and to recognize that it is the level of skills of the employees vis-à-vis the jobs, not their own skill levels, that matter. Jobs often change with time and as incumbents come and go, making it difficult to keep track of what they require. In addition, supervisors who have performed some or all of the jobs under their purview may forget how difficult these jobs are to newcomers, so they may either over- or underestimate the difficulty level of jobs for any of these reasons. Finally, it is important to recognize that employees' skills and abilities change over time, both as a result of formal training and education and from the natural consequences of maturation and simple work experiences.

But adequate skill levels are not sufficient to assure positive expectancy perceptions. In addition, the employee must believe that the other circumstances surrounding his effort are favorable and conducive to success. For example, the supervisor must be sure that machinery and equipment are in good repair and that the employee's own staff, if any, are trained and capable of being of assistance. Similarly, there must be sufficient budget to make success possible. In short, the job must be capable of being performed by an employee if we are to expect the employee to try to perform it; and more important, the person must perceive that it is so. But countless practical factors can combine to make it very difficult for any supervisor to estimate accurately the expectancy beliefs held by particular employees about specific jobs; accordingly, they make it difficult for supervisors to fully implement the implications that follow from the expectancy component of VIE theory.

Of particular importance for supervisors is the structuring of the expectancy beliefs of newcomers to a work setting (D. T. Hall, 1976). Managers often take a "sink or swim" approach with new employees, assigning them work duties that are too difficult given their relative lack of familiarity with the rules, procedures, and the myriad other circumstances that must be understood to make work efforts successful. An alternative approach is to underchallenge newcomers, requiring them to work through a tedious series of trivial jobs before being given a real challenge. Recent college graduates often complain of this treatment upon landing their first jobs after graduating, and as a result, turnover among recent graduates is usually very high (Mobley, 1982).

A third approach, the desired one, is to strike a balance using a combination of achievement-oriented, supportive, and directive leadership styles (as defined in the preceding section), attempting to make the newcomer's initial experiences challenging and successful. Success experiences are necessary for developing strong expectancy beliefs and for maintaining a positive self-concept about one's work: a feeling of competence, self-determination, and high self-esteem (see Bandura, 1982; Deci, 1975; D. T. Hall, 1976; Korman, 1970, 1976).

Instrumentality-Related Factors

To operationalize the concepts of instrumentality and valence, supervisors must make sure that positively valent rewards are associated with good job performance and that their employees perceive this connection. In practice, this also is difficult for a number of reasons. Most supervisors have a limited stock of rewards available to them for distribution to their subordinates. Company policies with regard to pay and benefits are usually restrictive, for the good reasons of control and the maintenance of equity. Further, union contracts are generally quite clear about the bases of reward distribution and often require that pay and other rewards be based on seniority rather than merit, further restricting the capacity of individual supervisors always to know who their meritorious employees are. This problem is especially common among managerial, professional, and technical personnel, in whose jobs good performance is normally very hard to measure, even when someone tries diligently to do so. As a result of these and other practical difficulties, implementing the instrumentality implications of VIE is often (perhaps usually) very difficult.

Valence-Related Factors

Where does the notion of valence fit into practice? VIE theory would prescribe that rewards distributed for good performance should be the types of things that employees desire. All that we know from common sense and that which we have learned from research into human needs (see chapters 3 through 8) tells us that different people have different need profiles at different times, so it follows that different outcomes will be rewarding for different people at different times. Hence, even the same outcome (such as a job transfer to another city) may be positively valent for some people while being negatively valent for others. To the extent that satisfied needs tend to lose their capacity to motivate behavior (as is suggested by the need theories discussed in chapters 3 through 8), we can expect certain organizationally distributed rewards to be satisfying and perhaps motivating for a particular person in some circumstances but not in other circumstances. Hence, older employees often have no desire to meet and befriend new employees on the job: Their relatedness needs are already well met and secured by interactions with old friends and acquaintances. In short, implementing VIE and path-goal concepts with regard to providing valent outcomes for work can be very difficult in practice.

Individualized Organizations

One leading authority proposed decades ago that people be rewarded for their work with outcomes that are best suited to their individual needs (Lawler, 1973, 1976). His suggestions entail comprehensive analyses of both the employees and the jobs in organizations, followed by the careful assignment of people to those jobs in which they will find outcomes they desire, especially as a consequence of good performance. A notable attempt to structure rewards on a more-or-less individualized basis can be found in the concept of cafeteria-style compensation plans (Lawler, 1966; Nealey, 1963; J. R. Schuster, 1969). The general design of these plans is for the individual employee to be allotted a fixed dollar sum of compensation that she can distribute according to her own preferences across a variety of forms of compensation, including salary and any of a number of fringe benefits: deferred earnings, stock options, and the like.

A problem usually encountered by managerial attempts to individualize employee rewards in a fashion consistent with VIE theory concerns the difficulty of accurately determining the actual needs of individual employees. The reader is asked to recall the discussion in chapter 3 in which we examined the risks of inferring need states from observations of another person's behavior. Managers simply may not be able accurately to determine the needs of their employees, so they must rely on techniques such as attitude surveys and one-on-one discussions to learn about employee values.

The distinction between needs and values may appear academic, but it is more than that (recall chapter 2). According to Locke (1976), rewards may be satisfying as long as they correspond with employee values and are not inconsistent with employee needs. But when employee values deviate from needs (meaning that people desire things that are not actually conducive to their best interests), organizational reward systems aimed at fulfilling employee values may not be at all beneficial for either the individuals involved or for the organization as a whole.

The Content of Employee Surveys

Although a complete discussion of the design and use of employee attitude surveys is beyond our present purpose, VIE theory clearly has a number of implications for this process. Specifically, rather than including only questions dealing with employee attitudes (as is commonly the case), greater benefit can be gained from seeking insight into the nature of employee beliefs, particularly beliefs about whether people feel that it is typically possible to convert effort into performance and whether rewards are seen as being tied to performance and as being equitable (Lawler, 1967b). In addition, more can be learned from enquiring why employees hold high or low expectancy and instrumentality beliefs, as well as why they believe the distribution of rewards is seen as inequitable, should that be the case.

SUMMARY

The point here is that even those managers and supervisors who understand VIE theory and who are capable of distilling practical implications from it for application on their jobs are usually severely handicapped by countless practical features surrounding work groups, union contracts, standard practices and policies, history, and precedents. More important, however, we must remember that even if managers are able to structure work settings and reward distribution systems so as to comply with the implications of VIE theory and the path-goal model, they will not be successful unless their policies and practices result in employee beliefs and perceptions that are consistent with high performance levels. For example, employees might not realize that rewards are, in fact, distributed in accordance with merit, even if that is actually the case. Similarly, employees may underestimate their chances of succeeding at a task because they are not aware of the help that is available to them at the time. According to VIE theory, it is beliefs that ultimately determine employee behavior, so unless managerial practices translate into beliefs that are favorable toward high job performance, beliefs will not result in employee intentions to perform well. VIE theory offers a number of elegant implications for managerial practices aimed at generating and sustaining high levels of employee motivation. But putting these implications into practice can be difficult, because managers are often quite limited in the degree of control they have over the practical factors that must be manipulated to totally determine their employees' expectancy, valence, and instrumentality beliefs, thereby influencing their intentions to perform well.

One way of conceptualizing VIE theory is to think of it as a model designed to predict a person's behavioral intentions. When we assess a person's beliefs about expectancies, valences, and instrumentalities and combine them in the configurations described by the theory itself, we have a basis for predicting a person's choices or decisions. These decisions may be to select one job rather than another, to retire or not to retire, or to work hard rather than not so hard. In short, VIE theory helps us to understand what lies behind a person's intentions and goals. In chapter 14 we examine goal-setting theory, a body of work that explicitly starts with intentions—the place where VIE theory leaves off. As we will see, when we are capable of specifying and understanding a person's goals, we are a step closer to being able to predict his or her behavior. Goal setting is therefore a powerful motivational tool and a body of theory that enjoys considerable scientific validity.

CHAPTER

Goal Theory
in Work Organizations

Ah, but a man's reach should exceed his grasp,
Or what's a heaven for?
—ROBERT BROWNING

After a very short stint with an accounting firm, Ken Thuerback started a consulting firm and went into the business of helping to turn around more than three dozen international companies whose foreign development loans had gone sour. During this time, he and his colleagues had visited 83 countries and helped bring to fruition enterprises representing $729 million. These successes whetted his appetite for further challenges. He began a business in Montana that built an upscale variety of old-fashioned log cabins and sold them widely to CEOs, entertainment celebrities, and others. Along the way he generated considerable economic activity in western Montana, a region previously depressed. Eventually, his energies contributed to the establishment of the University of Montana's Entrepreneurial Center, which in turn has helped more than 700 businesses. Thuerback's self-stated formula for success is to set and to stay committed to goals. Being prepared to accept failure is also critical, he says. The trick is not giving up when failure occurs. Thuerback epitomizes the North American entrepreneur with a "can-do" attitude of vigorous goal setting. For him, it is a way of life.

In several earlier chapters we have presented formal theories of work motivation that assume a cognitive/perceptual model of human nature (Walter and Marks, 1981). Thus, both equity theory and VIE theory assume that people's perceptions of their work environment cause them to form beliefs and attitudes (about inputs and outcomes, or valences, expectancies, and instrumentalities, respectively), and that these cognitions, in turn, instigate and direct various work-related behaviors. The reader will recall from chapters 9 and 10, however, that the general connection between cognitive factors and behavior is quite tenuous, and that behavior is linked more directly to intentions than to either beliefs or attitudes. In other words, intentions, once formed, are more likely than either beliefs or attitudes to be useful for predicting and explaining behavior (Fishbein and Ajzen, 1975). It is suggested that the limited predictive validity of both equity theory and VIE theory can be explained, in part, in terms of their failure to address intentions. It would follow that if any cognitive theory is to be predictive of behavior, it will probably be one that bases its predictions on intentions. The theory of goal setting and task performance is such an approach. We examine it here in detail.

This chapter consists of five major sections. In the first section we examine briefly the formal theory of intentional behavior proposed by Ryan (1970). In the second part of the chapter we review related work on goal setting as developed by Locke, Latham, and their colleagues (see Locke and Latham, 1990a). The major tenets of the original formulation of goal setting are presented as well as more recent attempts to broaden its scope and increase its predictive power. As one might anticipate from the reasoning in the preceding paragraph, we will see that there is more scientific support for goal setting as a predictor of work effort and performance than for either equity theory or VIE theory.

In the third section we consider control theory, another cognitively based, goal-oriented theory of human behavior and work motivation that has come onto the scene in the organizational literature over the past decade (see Klein, 1989). We will see that control theory has a number of major elements in common with goal-setting theory and discuss some of the controversy that the ascendance of control theory has instigated. We then look at two applied areas of modern psychology and management that rely heavily for their theoretical legitimacy on the principles found in goal setting and control theory. The first of these, self-regulation, consists of a set of principles by which people can consciously and deliberately influence their own behaviors. Finally, we review very briefly the managerial technique known as management by objectives (MBO), which draws heavily (but not exclusively) on the principles of goal setting. We address the disparity between the relative success of goal-setting programs per se and management by objectives, and speculate on the future of MBO in work organizations.

To begin, then: What are intentions, and how are they formed?

THE THEORY OF INTENTIONAL BEHAVIOR

The fundamental theory of motivation underlying current work on goal setting assumes that people's intentions are an important factor in explaining their behavior, although not the only factor, as illustrated in Figure 13-1 (Ryan, 1970). For example, the theory does not reject needs as a force in initiating action, although it assumes that needs influence behavior primarily through the effect they can have on a person's intentions. According to the theory, behavior can be broken down into four interrelated stages or levels (Ryan, 1970). Each level helps explain the one that follows. As mentioned, the most immediate level of explanation consists of the intentions that people hold. Individuals strive to act intentionally, pursuing whatever goals they have in mind. Whenever circumstances permit, behavior that is consistent with those intentions can be expected.

The second level of explanation consists of three sets of factors that influence the person's intentions. These are (1) the person's perceptions concerning means–ends relationships (whether the person believes that certain acts will result in certain outcomes, as in VIE theory), (2) the level of intrinsic interest or attractiveness of the act

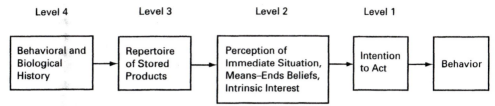

Level 4	Level 3	Level 2	Level 1	
Behavioral and Biological History	Repertoire of Stored Products	Perception of Immediate Situation, Means–Ends Beliefs, Intrinsic Interest	Intention to Act	Behavior

Source: Adapted From T. A. Ryan, *Intentional behavior* (New York: Ronald Press, 1970).

FIGURE 13-1 Simplified Representation of the Four Levels of Causality of Behavior

being contemplated, and (3) the appropriateness of the act in the particular social and physical setting in question (Ryan, 1970, pp. 26–27). A person's perceptions with regard to these three factors are the most important determinants of the person's intentions to act. The reader may notice the similarities between these three factors and the elements of VIE theory discussed in chapter 12, Fishbein and Ajzen's theory of reasoned behavior (recall chapter 9), and even the theory of intrinsic motivation presented in chapter 7. The point is that it is possible to invoke other bodies of cognitive motivation theory to help understand the origins of human intentions to behave in Ryan's theory.

The third level of explanation consists of those factors that influence the three factors comprising the second level. Third-level factors consist of explanations of why people perceive things the way they do, why they find particular acts intrinsically interesting, and so on. The theory assumes that people become "equipped with many prepared ways of perceiving, anticipating, and conceiving the world and their own activity" (Ryan, 1970, p. 28). People have ready-made reactions *to stimuli in their environment* that result from past history and learning. Ryan conceives these as repertoires, as stored products invoked in particular settings to make sense of the environment. These products consist of factors such as needs, values, preferences, plans, rules for behaving, and so on. At this third level, understanding behavior consists of understanding both the contents of the person's repertoire and the principles concerning which of its elements will be used in particular situations. It consists of seeking patterns in the person's reactions to situations, in the way the person perceives means–ends relationships, in the types of activities she finds intrinsically interesting, and in the way she deems particular types of acts as more or less appropriate, both practically and socially.

The fourth level of Ryan's theory consists of the historical and developmental background of the person, which explains why the person's repertoire is formed as it is. For Ryan (1970) this level is the most remotely connected with actual behavior and therefore of least interest in his theory. In short, for Ryan, a person's intentions are the most immediate determinants of her behavior. In view of the critical importance of intentions in his theory, let's take a closer look at the nature of human intentions.

The Nature of Intentions

Fishbein and Ajzen (1975) define an intention as a special form of belief. For them, an *intention* is a belief linking a person (the object of the belief) with a behavior (the attribute of the belief). As we saw in chapter 9, beliefs can vary in strength. Thus, we can speak of an intention's strength as the strength of the person's beliefs (in probabilistic terms) that he will actually behave in a particular manner. In more common terms, an intention is a conviction to act, a predilection to behave a certain way. This conception of intentions has prevailed in most of the social and organizational sciences for many years, often used interchangeably with the concept of *goal*. Intentions and goals have often been considered synonymous. We return to the issue of the relationship between these two concepts later in the chapter.

According to Ryan (1970), it is possible to consider a number of different dimensions of intentions—aspects that can be used to characterize them. For example, we might consider the degree of freedom of choice (the degree to which people are forced to behave by factors beyond their control, as opposed to the degree to which they feel they will behave in a particular manner, when and where they want) involved in the intention. Similarly, it is possible to consider the content (or direction) of an intention. For example, an intention may pertain to locomotion (going somewhere) or to modifying something (e.g., baking a pie, firing an employee, organizing a union). An intention may also pertain to communicating something to someone, seeking a skill, or acquiring new knowledge. The point is that people can hold many different types of intentions, dealing with convictions to act in an infinite number of ways toward any of an infinite number of objects. The reader is reminded of the importance of the specificity of an intention, however, in making predictions of particular acts (recall chapter 9; see Ajzen and Fishbein, 1977).

In summary, the basic concept underlying Ryan's theory is that intentions are the most immediate and most important causes of behavior. To understand the origins and nature of people's intentions requires that we understand the way people view the world around them. In turn, to understand why people perceive things the way they do, we must understand the nature of stored products, such as their needs, values, and norms. Finally, to understand why individuals hold particular repertoires of such products, we must examine their backgrounds. It bears repeating that other theories discussed in this book can be used to help understand the factors at each of these various levels of explanation, and that consistent with the model linking beliefs, attitudes, and intentions to behavior (Fishbein and Ajzen, 1975), intentions, once they are formed, are the most immediate causes and predictors of actual behavior.

The foregoing discussion of the basic theory of intentions is brief and considerably oversimplified. The interested reader is referred to Ryan's (1970) book for more detail. Now that the elements of the theory of intentional behavior have been introduced, we can examine the tenets of the theory of goal setting.

GOAL-SETTING THEORY AND RESEARCH

The fundamental tenet of goal-setting theory[1] is that goals and intentions are responsible for human behavior. In this context, goals mean the same thing as they did in chapter 8, where the frustration model was presented. A goal is something that a person tries to attain, achieve, or accomplish.

---

[1]Its major proponents often refer to goal setting as a set of techniques rather than a formal theory (Locke, 1975). Notwithstanding their view, we refer to the concepts and propositions related to goal setting as a theory for two reasons. The first is that the goal-setting framework is as coherent and well grounded as most other approaches presented in this book under the rubric of theory. The second reason is consistency with the terminology used with reference to theories presented in other chapters.

In work settings, goals may take the form of a level of job performance, a quota, a work norm, a deadline, or even a budgetary spending limit (Locke, Shaw, Saari, and Latham, 1981). We noted earlier that the terms *goal* and *intention* have frequently been used interchangeably. Locke and Latham (1990a) have argued that these two concepts should *not* be considered synonymous. They claim that an intention is a person's representation of a planned action, whereas a goal is the object or aim of such an act. Tubbs and Ekeberg (1991), meanwhile, advance an elaborate argument to the effect that people think and plan in such a way that intentions include both the planned action and the objective of the action, making intention a broader concept than goals. Each of these perspectives has merit, but it would be very difficult to pit them against one another in an empirical test to determine which is more meritorious. We adopt the Locke and Latham (1990a) here, if only to keep our treatment consistent with the dominant theoretical model extant in the goal-setting literature. For our purposes, a *goal* is the target of one's intentional acts, whereas an *intention* is a person's relationship with, or personal representation of, an act she will undertake to achieve the goal in question. There have been many attempts to develop categories or types of goals, which we will encounter as the chapter develops.

The second major tenet derives from the first. If goals determine human effort, it follows that higher or more difficult goals will result in higher levels of performance[2] than those resulting from easy goals. The third tenet of the theory holds that specific goals (such as "reducing employee turnover by 20 percent within six months") result in higher levels of effort than vague goals such as "let's cut back turnover as much as possible." A fourth tenet of the theory is that incentives such as money, feedback, competition, and the like will have no effect on behavior unless they lead to the setting and/or acceptance of specific, hard goals.

Notice again that this approach to work motivation relies heavily on the same cognitive/perceptual model of human functioning that underlies both VIE theory and equity theory, For a person to have a goal, he must be aware of his surroundings and be fully cognizant of the meaning of what constitutes his goal. Behavior is intentional (Ryan, 1970). It results from the deliberate adoption of one or more conscious choices of action. People engage in acts that are consistent with their intentions and goals.

Goal Difficulty and Task Difficulty

At first blush, these basic elements of goal-setting theory may seem trivial and self-evident. In fact, their simplicity is profound and leads logically to a number of important corollaries for application in work settings. The most important implication of the basic tenets of the theory concerns the most appropriate level of goal difficulty for maximum performance. A critical distinction must be made between *task difficulty* and *goal difficulty,* however, before we can proceed. According to Locke et al. (1981): "Since a goal is the object or aim of an action, it is possible for the completion of a task

---

[2]In chapter 1 we drew a distinction between work effort and performance, an important distinction maintained throughout the book. Although the concept of central interest in this book is *work motivation,* most of the research on goal setting focuses on *task performance.* That is, the successful accomplishment or the failure to accomplish tasks is the dependent variable in most of the work in this tradition. Both motivation and performance are discussed by the theory (see Locke and Latham, 1990a). The reader is exhorted to keep the distinction between the two concepts in mind: They are not equivalent and are not necessarily related to one another in real life.

to be a goal. However . . . the term goal refers to attaining a specific standard of proficiency on a task, usually within a specified time limit" (p. 126). Therefore, two people could be given the same task (such as to recruit 20 new sales representatives to the firm), but one person could have a much more difficult goal, such as being given half as much time as the other to complete the task, for example. Same task, different goals. The theory predicts that to the extent he is committed to it, the person with the harder goal will perform to a higher standard. As Latham and Locke (1991) note: "Knowing task difficulty . . . does not reveal the person's goals and thus makes it difficult to predict how well a person will perform the task."

The very difficulty of a task may also contribute to performance. For example, one early experiment of chess matches among undergraduate students found that goal difficulty was positively related to performance, as stated in the theory, but that the difficulty of the task itself contributed positively as well, in large part because it instigated exploration and learning, which paid off later (D. J. Campbell and Ilgen, 1976). The early empirical evidence in support of the goal-difficulty hypothesis was impressive. Locke, Latham, and their colleagues have conducted dozens of experiments in both laboratory (Locke, Cartledge, and Knerr, 1970) and field settings (Latham and Yukl, 1975) to show that difficult goals result in higher levels of performance than do easy goals (Locke et al., 1981; Locke and Latham, 1990a). The tasks included in the laboratory experiments have ranged from chess problems to arithmetic problems, card sorting, brainstorming, prose learning, and data coding, among others.

The early field studies were similarly diverse in nature and equally compelling. In one early experiment, for example, Latham and Baldes (1975) had forestry truck drivers set goals for the amount of wood they hauled to their woodyard on each load. Goals were set and measured in terms of the weight of each load as a percentage of each particular truck's gross vehicle weight. The additional wood hauled over a nine-month period as a result of the goal-setting program would have cost the company $250,000 to achieve (for the purchase of trucks) without the program.

In another early field experiment, Latham and Kinne (1974) showed how a one-day goal-setting training program resulted in both higher productivity and lower absenteeism among a sample of independent loggers over a 12-week period. In short, there is abundant evidence from advocates of this school of thought that difficult goals result in higher performance than do easy goals (see Tubbs, 1986). As we will see shortly, the simple hypothesis connecting task difficulty and task performance has been modified over time and as the result of considerable research and thinking since the theory's original promulgation. This prescription regarding the optimum level of goal difficulty appears at first glance to differ from that derived from VIE theory (which, as we saw in chapter 12, would suggest that motivation is maximized when expectancy beliefs are at a maximum) and McClelland and Atkinson's view (recall chapter 7) that achievement motivation is maximized when the person perceives the task to be of a moderate level of difficulty. Again, *the key is whether we are considering the task or the goal.* McClelland and Atkinson's work on achievement motivation concerned itself with task difficulty, whereas the goal-setting literature deals with goal difficulty. As mentioned, this is a critical distinction that is useful for theory development and understanding. In practice, however, the distinction may not be so easy to implement or manipulate. A person with low goals confronting a task that she finds difficult may encounter many of the same frustrations as a person who has high goals at an easy task.

Commitment to Goals

The goal-specificity and goal-difficulty tenets of the theory have assumed (first implicitly, then explicitly) that the person of interest is committed to the goals, that s/he possesses adequate ability and self-efficacy in relation to the task, and that feedback is provided in regard to progress toward the goal (Wood and Locke, 1990). Commitment "refers to the degree to which the individual is attached to the goal, considers it significant or important, is determined to reach it, and keeps it in the face of setbacks and obstacles" (Latham and Locke, 1991, p. 217). In one of their books, Locke and Latham proclaimed that commitment is the *sine qua non* of goal setting: Without commitment, the phenomenon does not exist (Locke and Latham, 1984). People seem most likely to choose and/or commit to them when they believe the goals are attainable and important (Klein, 1991a), so managers may have to use their powers of persuasion, their legitimate authority, and their technical expertise to facilitate subordinates' commitment to goals (Latham and Locke, 1991).

Commitment to a goal appears to have a direct as well as an indirect effect on performance. That is, when a person's goals are high, high commitment leads to higher performance than when commitment is low. But when goals are low, "high commitment may restrict performance because committed people will be loathe to raise their goals, whereas uncommitted people may set higher goals (perhaps because they want additional challenge)" (Latham and Locke, 1991, p. 217). We return to what has been learned about the commitment process later in the chapter when we summarize the recent developments in and refinements of the theory.

Commitment to What?

Tubbs (1993) noted that the motivational process in goal setting consists of three stages: (1) judgments and choices about whether to engage in goal-seeking activities, (2) the expenditure of effort, and (3) persistence toward the chosen goal. Therefore, he reasoned, we might consider the dynamics and consequences of commitment at any and all of these three stages. Most previous work had been unclear about where and when commitment was of the most value in the three stages of the goal-setting process. Tubbs undertook a series of studies to determine at which stage commitment is the most important in moderating the goal-performance relationship. As is often the case, there was critical controversy over Tubbs' (1993) attempt (see Tubbs, 1994; P.M. Wright, O'Leary-Kelly, Cortina, Klein, and Hollenbeck, 1994) and the issue does not seem to have been resolved at this time. The matter is raised here because of its theoretical importance and the significance of whatever resolution ultimately occurs.

Goal Specificity

In chapter 9 we noted that higher degrees of specificity in an intention are associated with more accurate levels of prediction of actual behavior (Ajzen and Fishbein, 1977). Similarly, an important tenet of goal-setting theory is that higher levels of performance result when goals are made specific. According to Ajzen and Fishbein (1977), intentions can be made more or less specific with regard to the nature of the act involved, the target of the act, and in terms of the time and circumstances in which the intended act might occur. As we will see, managerial techniques based on the goal-setting literature instruct practitioners to be as specific as possible with regard to each of these four dimensions. In short, the theory says that in addition to being difficult, goals should be specific. Again, the evidence is persuasive. Employee performance is consistently higher when goals are formulated in terms such as "Increase market share 8 percent per annum," "Sell 30 pounds of peaches by noon," or "Increase my grade-point average by one full grade by final exams," than when the target, the time, or the circumstances are not specified (Locke et al., 1981; Tubbs, 1986).

The Role of Incentives in Goal Setting

If, as the theory states, goals or intentions determine behavior, what about all we know from research and common experience about the influence of incentives (or even threats) on performance? According to Locke (1968), incentives are effective for influencing behavior only to the extent that they influence the goals that people strive to achieve. In other words, incentives work only if they change a person's goals and intentions or build commitment to those they already hold. For example, consider the effects of competition as a form of motivational device used by many managers, coaches, teachers, and even parents. Why is competition effective for changing behavior or increasing performance?

According to the theory, there are at least two reasons why competition may result in higher levels of performance. One is that competition may serve to build commitment to the task and to the goal of winning at the task on the part of the individual: Remember that the person must be committed to a goal to strive toward attaining it. However, a second feature of competition, particularly when it is "stiff," is that it serves to make the goal (winning) more difficult than it might be otherwise.

What about deadlines? Both common experience and research evidence show that people tend to accomplish a lot more when facing deadlines. In fact, some people seem to thrive under the pressure of meeting deadlines for work. Why might this be so? For the theory of goal setting, the answer is relatively simple: A deadline serves the same function as making a goal harder than it would be without it, and the theory states that more difficult goals result in higher performance levels. To illustrate, the classic field experiment by Latham and Locke (1975) showed that the performance levels of wood-harvesting crews increased dramatically when restrictions were placed on the number of days during which pulp and paper mills would buy the wood they hauled. In the same way that Parkinson's law (Parkinson, 1957) states that work expands to fill the time that is made available for it, this research, and the goal-setting principle on which it is based, suggest that people's work pace will increase according to the level of difficulty they attribute to the task to be accomplished.

Other incentives seem to influence motivation levels in a similar fashion. Money is probably the most widely used incentive. Goal-setting theory suggests that it will motivate higher levels of performance only to the extent that it results in higher levels of commitment by the person to the task involved. In chapter 12 we noted the importance, for example, of tying pay to good job performance and of having employees recognize the connection between merit and payment. In chapter 11 we noted that to result in positive attitudes toward work, rewards must be viewed as equitable. The relationship between these two principles and the use of incentives, from a goal-setting perspective, should be clear. If a monetary incentive is not seen as contingent on performance and/or if it is not seen as equitable, it is less likely to commit the person to a goal of high performance. In short, principles of equity theory and VIE theory help us understand the role of incentives, of all sorts, from the goal-setting point of view.

One interesting issue related to incentives and goals concerns the intrinsic reward value of attaining goals of differing levels of difficulty. There is mixed evidence on the matter, but it may be that people who set and attain low goals may be nearly as happy as people who set high goals and attain them (Latham and Locke, 1991). Similarly, a person who sets low goals and achieves higher-than-planned levels of performance will be even more self-satisfied than a person who achieves the same high performance standard but started with high goals. More work is required on these relationships before solid conclusions can be drawn.

The Role of Participation in Goal Setting

Should employees participate in the goal-setting process? There are a number of conceptual reasons why higher levels of motivation and performance may result when the employee involved has participated with her supervisor in the setting of work goals (T. R. Mitchell, 1973). The traditional reasoning is as follows. First, participatively set goals may sometimes be harder than goals set unilaterally by one's superior. In addition, an employee who has participated in goal setting is more likely to be ego involved in the successful attainment of those goals: Because they are somewhat responsible for the type and levels of the goals they are pursuing, employees will be more desirous of seeing them fulfilled. Thus, most of the early thinking about why and how participation may be beneficial was related to the effects of participation on employee motivation and commitment (Latham, Winters, and Locke, 1994). In other words, participation stimulates motivation and commitment to succeed at one's goals.

Despite the intuitive appeal of these arguments, the evidence that addresses them is decidedly mixed (Locke, Alavi, and Wagner, in press; Locke and Latham, 1990a; Shetzer, 1993). For example, Latham, Mitchell, and Dossett (1978) found that although a group of scientists and engineers who participated in setting goals tended to set more difficult goals than were set for a comparable group by a supervisor, the two groups did not differ significantly in actual performance levels. Moreover, other studies have shown that when the difficulty level of a goal is held constant among groups, people whose goals are assigned to them seem to perform as well, on average, as people who have participated in the setting of their work goals (Latham and Saari, 1979a; Latham and Steele, 1983; Latham, Steele, and Saari, 1982). It may be that the general level of supervisory supportiveness is more important than participation per se (Latham and Saari, 1979b), although the exact nature of the role of supportiveness in the goal-setting process is less well understood than other facets of the theory (Locke et al., 1981).

A series of studies conducted primarily by Latham (and summarized in Locke and Latham, 1990a, pp. 154–166) generated a considerable base for suggesting that participation may not have much of an impact on goal-related outcomes. Meanwhile, Erez and her colleagues reported a series of their own studies suggesting that participation may have significant salutary benefits (e.g., Erez and Arad, 1986), presumably for the theoretical reasons outlined above. In what must be one of the most unusual events in the organizational sciences when two researchers/theorists disagree with each other, Latham and Erez decided to place their differing views head to head by collaborating on the design of four experiments, using a mutually respected third party, Edwin Locke, as mediator (Latham, Erez, and Locke, 1988; Locke and Latham, 1990a, p. 163). The primary conclusion reached after this dramatic series of experiments was that assigned goals can have as much motivational effect as participatively set goals, as long as other factors are kept constant (such variables as goal difficulty and perceptions of self-efficacy).

One of the early hypotheses offered in favor of the participation effect in the success of goal setting was that participation may result in higher performance because *the employee is able to gain a better understanding of task requirements* through participation: She appreciates the reasons behind her goals as well as what to do to attain them (Latham and Saari, 1979b; T. R. Mitchell, 1973). This effect is better categorized as a cognitive rather than a motivational influence, as such. A recent experimental study by Latham et al. (1994) has suggested that participation in task strategy formulation can affect performance through two cognitive mechanisms: task strategies and the development of beliefs of self-efficacy. That is, participation may foster the development of effective strategies, which, in turn, influences the individual's beliefs of his or her self-efficacy. (The reader is referred to chapter 12 for our first discussion of self-efficacy; more will be said about it later in this chapter as well.)

In summary, it appears that participation may have weak and indirect effects on task performance. There are both motivational and cognitive explanations for this effect, and these mediating variables may be interrelated in complex ways. Research in this area may be yielding diminishing returns because of the difficulty scientists have in measuring these subtle mediating effects precisely and teasing out the causal linkages among them. The one consistent finding in all this is that the participation effect does exist but is not very powerful.

Other Forms of Employee Participation

While we are on the topic of the possible effects of employee participation on job performance and employee attitudes, it is worth examining the evidence related to the possible value of employee participation in management involving forms other than direct goal setting. Cotton, Vollrath, Froggatt, Lengnick-Hall, and Jennings (1988) instigated a debate by delineating a variety of forms of "participation," including techniques such as employee ownership and, of more interest here, direct participation in work decisions and a variety of forms of partial and indirect participation.

On the basis of their study, Cotton et al. (1988) concluded that different forms of participation are likely to yield different organizational and employee outcomes. Without going into the details of the debate, Wagner (1994) conducted some meta-analyses and pulled together the results of other scholars on the matter. He concluded that for the most part, participatory managerial practices have small statistically significant effects on outcome variables, but that the absolute size of these effects is not of practical importance. Wagner's conclusion is persuasive in large measure because he has not been part of any of the "camps" of researchers who may have developed vested interests in the participation phenomenon. He appears to be quite independent and dispassionate in his conclusions: Notwithstanding all the traditional and ideological rationale justifying it, participation—in any or most of its various forms—is generally not worth the resources required to make it work. In the final section of this chapter we address management by objectives, one of the most widely used and recognized formal programs of employee participation of the past four decades.

The Role of Feedback in Goal Setting

Feedback is information. When it is provided to a person in a goal-setting and performance situation, or when a person acquires such information by her own means, feedback interacts with goals to determine performance levels. In an early review of the research on goal setting, Locke and his colleagues concluded that both goals and feedback to people about their performance vis-à-vis their goals are necessary to sustain high levels of performance. In other words, neither the provision of feedback nor the setting of goals, taken alone, are as effective in motivating high performance as is the use of both goals and feedback (Locke et al., 1981; see also Bandura and Cervone, 1983, and Latham and Locke, 1991). So, how do they work together?

Latham and Locke (1991) describe the joint operation of goals and feedback as follows:

> The goal is the object or outcome one is aiming for as well as the standard by which one evaluates one's performance. Feedback provides information to the individual as to the degree to which the standard is being met. If performance meets or exceeds the standard, performance is typically maintained (although eventually the goal may be raised). If performance falls below the standard, subsequent improvement will occur to the extent that: (a) the individual is dissatisfied with that level of performance and, more importantly, expects to be dissatisfied with it in the future; (b) the individual has high self-efficacy, that is, confidence in her ability to improve; and (c) the individual sets a goal to improve over past performance. (p. 226)

For positive feedback to have its maximum impact on a person's motivation to carry on, it is important that the person believe that it is her own abilities and efforts that result in success (see K. M. Thomas and Mathieu, 1994). Greater satisfaction is derived when the person believes that she was responsible for the outcomes of goal-oriented behavior, and the impact on the person's self-efficacy is stronger than in cases where the person believes that external factors such as luck or the influence of other people were involved in the success. Hence, the nuances contained in the feedback that a person receives are especially critical. K. M. Thomas and Mathieu (1994) present a model that illustrates this principle.

Why Does Goal Setting Work?

Why is goal setting so effective as a motivational strategy? The authors of one major review (Locke et al., 1981) offered four reasons, reminding us that the concept of motivation is used to explain the direction, amplitude (level of effort), and duration (or persistence) of behavior (recall chapter 1 of this book). Notice in the following paragraphs how the fundamental tenets of goal setting relate to these facets of motivation.

First, goals direct attention and action. They identify the target of intended behavior (Ajzen and Fishbein, 1977), and if they are stated specifically (as is recommended), the focus of the person's effort becomes well defined. Similarly, the requirement that goals be made difficult relates directly to the effort level and persistence aspects of the motivation concept. If a goal is difficult, it will normally require more effort, over a longer period of time, to be attained. One element of persistence is tenacity—the refusal to quit trying, despite obstacles, until one's goal is achieved. Latham and Locke (1991) believe that commitment is one factor that contributes to tenacity, as does the sheer difficulty of the goal itself.

Locke and Latham (1984) offer a fourth explanation. They note that goal setting usually requires the development of task-related *strategy*. In other words, when people contemplate a goal, they must also consider means for its attainment, especially when that goal is seen as difficult. For example, in the aforementioned study in which truck drivers set higher goals for the capacity at which they loaded their trucks (Latham and Baldes, 1975), many of the drivers involved made recommendations concerning how their trucks might be modified to facilitate their attempts to carry more lumber. It may be that harder tasks are more likely to stimulate more strategy development than are easy tasks. Similarly, it makes sense that the more specific the task goal, the more likely it is that people will devise specific techniques to achieve it.

We return to the issue of strategy formulation and its role in goal-setting processes later in the chapter when we review the recent responses that goal researchers have made to refine and develop the original theory. In the meantime, another explanation is offered for the robustness of goal setting.

Goal Setting and the Theory of Reasoned Action

An addition to the four reasons offered by Locke and his colleagues (1981) for the success of goal-setting theory is the one suggested at the beginning of this chapter. If one adopts the approach of Fishbein and Ajzen (1975, and chapter 9), it makes considerable sense that goal setting is a comparatively successful theory of work motivation. Recall that according to Fishbein and Ajzen (1975), perceptions influence beliefs, which, in turn, typically result in evaluative attitudes. These attitudes may or may not result in intentions to act, depending on a number of factors. Nevertheless, in the causal chain linking perceptions, beliefs, attitudes, and intentions with behavior, intentions, once developed, are clearly the cognitive elements most closely connected with behavior. In fact, we can view the others (perception, beliefs, and attitudes) merely as factors that contribute to the development of intentions, but only imperfectly (see Mento, Cartledge, and Locke, 1980).

In other words, beliefs and attitudes contribute to the development of intentions, but they do not totally shape or determine them. Therefore, to the extent that beliefs and attitudes are only partially related to a person's intentions (for the reasons discussed in chapter 5), they will not be as effective as that person's intentions in predicting behavior. To repeat a point made earlier in this chapter, it follows that theories such as equity theory and VIE theory, which rely on beliefs and attitudes (which are merely predictors of intentions to act), cannot be as valid as goal setting, which takes intentions per se as its point of departure for predicting behavior.

The links between perceptions, beliefs, attitudes, intentions, and work behavior from the three cognitive theories (equity theory, VIE theory, and goal-setting theory) are presented graphically in Figure 13-2. (The reader is urged to refer to chapter 9 for a more complete discussion of these relationships.) In short, examination of the rela-

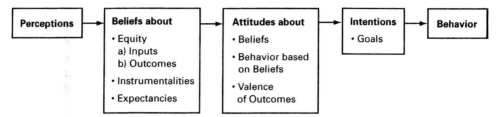

FIGURE 13-2   Summary of the Relationships among Beliefs, Attitudes, and Intentions in Three Cognitive Theories of Work Motivation

tionships represented in the figure helps explain the limited potential predictive and explanatory capacity of the theories presented in the preceding two chapters and suggests why goal-setting theory fares better by comparison.

An Assessment of Goal-Setting Research

The research conducted on goal setting has generally been far more rigorous and free of methodological error than that conducted on any of the other theories and approaches presented in this book. There are a number of reasons that may explain this, but two seem especially important. First, the theory itself is relatively simple by comparison with other theories of work motivation. For example, there are no requirements to develop psychometric measures of cognitive factors such as expectancies, valences, or instrumentalities. Similarly, the theory does not require the measurement of needs as is the case in Maslow's and Alderfer's hierarchical models (recall chapter 3). Time lags do not seem to play the important (but indefinite) role in goal setting that they entail in VIE theory. In short, the theory is comparatively simple and requires testing procedures that are accordingly simple and less subject to many of the types of methodological difficulties that have hindered the refinement of other theories presented in this book.

A second probable reason for the relatively high quality of goal-setting research is that a limited number of researchers have been involved. Whereas countless people have conducted research into equity theory and VIE theory, for example, only a limited number of people have been involved in the majority of the studies of goal setting. The goal-setting review by Locke et al. (1981) showed that Locke and Latham and their colleagues had carried the ball almost exclusively in developing this theory over the years. Now, 15 years later, the same point is still largely true, although some scientists unrelated to Locke and Latham have entered the field in recent years.

One result of this focused and ongoing attention by a limited number of researchers (and their academic progeny) has been the development of a set of research techniques and testing procedures (or experimental paradigms) that have proven to be effective and relatively sound from a scientific point of view. This author is not aware of any radical attacks on the research methods used by this relatively small school of scholars, attacks of the sort that have regularly been leveled at research into need hierarchy theory (e.g., Bandura, 1977; M. E. Ford, 1992; B. F. Mitchell and Moudgill, 1976; Salancik and Pfeffer, 1977), equity theory (see Carrell and Dittrich, 1978, and R. D. Pritchard, 1969), and VIE theory (see J. P. Campbell and Pritchard, 1976), for example. The cumulative experience in both laboratory and field settings by a limited number of people must account for part of this.

Evidence about the applied value of the theory continues to amass. For example, a recent survey of large U.S. businesses found small but statistically significant correlations between organizational profitability and the use of goal setting (Terpstra and Rozell, 1994). The researchers sampled 1,000 companies from *Dun's Business Rankings* and received usable responses from 201 of them. They compared the firms' profit margins and average annual growth in profit with replies from senior executives regarding their use or nonuse of "Locke's goal-setting theory." Sixty-one percent of the companies responding reported that they used the theory, and the correlations with the two financial indicators ranged from 0.10 to 0.54, varying from industry to industry.

Recent Criticisms and Refinements of Goal-Setting Theory

Nevertheless, it is to be expected that popular and robust theories in any social science will be subjected to close scrutiny and frequent attack from critics and scholars who desire to find flaws, weaknesses, and limitations in such theories. Such is the way that a discipline progresses (recall chapter 2). As the most successful theory of work motivation over the past two decades, goal-setting theory is no exception.

Scope and Philosophical Underpinnings of the Theory

One of the most thorough critiques of goal-setting theory and research was provided by Austin and Bobko (1985). Among other things, these authors noted that goal-setting work was developed in, and relied exclusively upon, logical positivism, and has avoided other approaches to the development and accumulation of knowledge. They conclude that goal setting comes from a "narrow, unidimensional" view of the world (p. 290) and that it could be informed by broader approaches, particularly those that permit constructionist understandings. Specifically, they cite Royce (1975), who would advocate a different philosophy of science, one that would assume that among other things, simple theories are not adequate to represent the complexities of human behavior, complex "pluralism" is necessary for a more complete view, and apparent paradoxes and contradictions must be expected and tolerated. Austin and Bobko (1985) pointed out that "goal setting literature consists mostly of published studies reporting short-term, laboratory experiments that neglect the spectrum of possible dependent measures. They serve more as demonstrations than as attempts to expand the parameters of a theory of goal setting" (p. 290). So, they concluded, goal-setting researchers have failed to explore limitations to the theory. This is pretty tough condemnation of any theory, particularly one that enjoys such relatively high status in the areas with which it deals.

As specific examples, Austin and Bobko (1985) pointed out that as of the early 1980s at least, the focus had been on unidimensional quantity (of performance) goals. Quality goals and multidimensional goals had been neglected, as had the prospect that quantity and quality goals can often be in conflict. (For example, the faster a person paints a living room, the poorer is the quality of the work one can expect.) In addition, the focus has been largely on individual-level as opposed to group-level goals. Finally, they complained that goal-setting work had been conducted too frequently in tightly controlled laboratory conditions and not sufficiently often in real-world organizational settings.

Task Complexity and Novelty

Other researchers and critics found that the simple original goal-setting formulation was ineffective in situations in which the person found the task novel or complex (e.g., D. J. Campbell, 1984, 1988; D. J. Campbell and Gingrich, 1986; Early, Connelly, and Ekegren, 1989; Wood, Mento, and Locke, 1987). One series of experiments reported by Early et al. (1989), for example, showed that assigning people the task of specific, difficult goals may be the worst thing to do; rather, asking people merely to "do their best" is most appropriate if the task is one that is novel and complex and for which there may be more than a single best way to approach it.

Responses to the Criticisms

One of the most impressive features of the goal-setting tradition is that its adherents have been conscientious in filling in areas where the theory has had gaps and in expanding the boundaries of the theory where new horizons have logically led them. For example, Locke and Latham and their colleagues have responded to at least two of the criticisms leveled by Austin and Bobko (1985). On the matter of conflict between a person's multiple goals, Locke, Smith, Erez, Chah, and Schaffer (1994) conducted and reported two studies. One was a laboratory experiment with undergraduate students and the other was a field study of the research productivity of professors. On the basis of these two projects, Locke and his colleagues (1994) concluded that conflicting goals (such as a dilemma between quantity and quality of production or one between research or teaching goals) can put pressure on people and lead to negative impacts on one of the performance goals under consideration. Similarly, in response to the allegation of an overreliance on laboratory experiments, Locke and Latham (1990a) counted and reported the comparative rates of use of field versus laboratory settings. (In fact, the comparative count of lab to field at that time was 239 versus 156, although a greater variety of tasks had been used in the field over the years than in the lab—53 versus 35.)

To reply to the issue of the relevance of goal setting for complex, unfamiliar tasks, Wood and Locke (1990) pursued the matter of task complexity. They propose that as tasks become more complex, the simple focusing mechanisms mentioned earlier (i.e., focus of attention, the devotion of specific energy, and persistence) become less adequate to explain goal-seeking behavior. As tasks become more complex or novel, the person is unable to rely on what Wood and Locke call stored universal plans and stored task-specific plans—strategies that have been learned in the past for approaching tasks and challenges. Task complexity requires the person to develop *new* task-specific plans, new ways of going about getting the job done. Stored universal plans are exemplified by routine, even mundane activities such as driving to work in the morning, whereas stored task-specific plans entail skill development such as operating a particular software program. The point is that task complexity and novelty can make both of these types of learned routines useless or even dysfunctional; the person has to discover news ways to act, which Wood and Locke (1990) refer to as *new task-specific plans.*

The joint effects of strategy and goals on a complex task were investigated explicitly to follow up on this line of reasoning (Chesney and Locke, 1991). Using a computer-based business game with a sample of senior undergraduate students, these researchers found that strategy development and goals both had positive effects on performance at the game, but that strategy had the stronger effect. In addition, more difficult goals resulted in a greater use of strategy, so that goal difficulty had both a direct and an indirect effect on performance through the strategy process (Chesney and Locke, 1991).

When strategy development is required, learning is taking place. The person tries to determine, either by trial and error or through other means, how to approach the task. When we speak of learning, we can consider the consequences under which the learning takes place. One critical variable in any teaching/learning context is whether the practice takes place in a massed, single period, or whether there are many practice periods, separated by breaks (Dempster, 1988, 1989). To pursue this matter, Kanfer, Ackerman, Murtha, Dudgale, and Nelson (1994) had psychology students perform a simulated air traffic control task under the guidance "do your best" as opposed to being assigned specific, difficult goals. The researchers also manipulated whether students worked with intermittent breaks to learn the task or on single massed trials. As expected, the students who had specific, difficult goals were superior in performance only when they were provided with rest periods during the learning and performance exercise; those who were required to learn and perform without the benefits of breaks did far less well.

This raises the question of the nature of the goals a person attempts to accomplish. *Outcome goals* focus "attention on a specific quantity or quality of something to be achieved (e.g., cut and delimb three trees per hour)" (Winters and Latham, 1996). In the research on goal setting to date, goals of this sort have been used predominantly. But the issue of novel tasks raises the importance of an alternative type of goal, a *learning goal* through "which individuals seek to increase their competence, to understand or master something new" (Dwek, 1986, p. 1040). Striving for learning goals, at least initially, "should increase performance when the person lacks the requisite knowledge to master a task. This is because it shifts the focus to task processes in terms of strategy development, and away from task outcome achievement" (Winters and Latham, 1996). When the person is unfamiliar with a task, a focus on outcome goals can be quite dysfunctional. The more appropriate goal on such occasions is a learning goal which, once accomplished, will facilitate performance in subsequent situations.

The point here is that this nearly 30-year program of research continues to expand its focus, refine its techniques, and respond to its critics in ways unmatched, in this author's opinion, in the history of the organizational sciences. Very impressive indeed.

Personality Differences and Goal-Setting Processes

For many years after goal-setting theory was introduced by Locke and Latham, little or no attention was paid to possible individual differences in the model. The effects of specific and difficult goals were assumed to apply universally across people of all personality types and predispositions. One recent study introduced a currently popular personality construct—*conscientiousness*—into the goal-setting literature. The researchers demonstrated that sales representatives who are high on this variable are more likely to become committed to their goals and, as a result, achieve them (Barrick, Mount, and Strauss, 1993). Known as one of the so-called "Big Five" factors of personality[3] to

---

[3]The so-called "Big Five" personality factors are extraversion, agreeableness, emotional stability, openness to experience, and conscientiousness (Digman, 1990). A recent paper by Mount and Barrick (1995) summarizes the relevance of this taxonomy of personality variables for the theory and practice of human resource management.

emerge in recent psychological research and theory (Digman, 1990), conscientiousness implies being responsible, dependable, planful, organized, persistent, and—of most importance to us here—achievement oriented (recall our discussion of achievement orientation in chapter 7). Barrick and his colleagues (1993) built on the "can do" and "will do" model proposed by Borman, White, Pulakos, and Oppler (1991) to help explain the origins of goal commitment. Recall that the early formulation of goal setting assumed, among other things, that specific and difficult goals are effective only when people are committed to them. The conscientiousness factor of human personality, which may be partially determined by heredity (Digman, 1990), may explain why some people commit to goals more readily.

A precaution is in order here. It is possible for a sort of tautology to occur over time as researchers and theorists pursue a theory of work motivation such as goal setting by adding more and more variables into the equation. For example, we must be careful not to fall into a loop such as the following: Conscientious people are more likely to commit to goals. Conscientiousness entails a cluster of traits that include being organized, dependable, and planful. The question arises: Is conscientiousness an independent causal factor that explains one's tendency to commit to goals, or is the tendency to commit to goals merely a defining characteristic of conscientiousness itself? Some thinkers may see goal-committing tendencies as a result of the personality trait, whereas others may see them as aspects of the same constellation of a person's personality. If we are not careful, we may confuse the two possibilities and lull ourselves into a false belief that we have explained a phenomenon such as goal commitment, when in fact all we have done is to define it as an element of the variables that are its putative causes. If the *definition* of conscientiousness did not sound so much like the tendency to commit to goals (and it does), we would have more reason to believe that we have learned something about the *causes* of goal commitment.[4]

Aside from this possible logical problem, there is evidence other than that presented by Barrick et al. (1993) that need for achievement may predispose people to be more likely to commit to goals. An interesting experiment conducted by Hollenbeck, Williams, and Klein (1989) using college students as participants found that people who are higher in achievement motivation (and those whose locus of control is internal) are more likely to commit to goals. In addition, Hollenbeck et al. (1989) found that people are more likely to become committed to goals when they make their goals public, a finding with plenty of previous support (see Salancik, 1977).

The Linkage with Self-Efficacy

The concept of self-efficacy has appeared many times in this volume (see chapters 7 and 12, in particular). The growing body of theory on goal setting has become integrally related to the work on self-efficacy. According to Latham and Locke (1991, pp. 220–221), self-efficacy is "broader in meaning than effort-performance expectancy"

---

[4]A similar problem in the work motivation literature was alleged by Roberts and Glick (1981), who attacked the popular job characteristics model of job design (Oldham and Hackman, 1980) by pointing out that some of the items in the instruments that were used to assess the "causal" elements in the model were the same as some of the items used by researchers to measure elements of other variables in that model. Hence, Roberts and Glick argued, it is no wonder that "perceived job characteristics" were found to be correlated with job attitudes: To a certain extent the concepts and the measures of job characteristics and job attitudes were the same concepts.

(recall our treatment of the two concepts in chapter 12) in expectancy theory, in that self-efficacy includes all factors that could lead one to perform well at a task (e.g., adaptability, creativity, resourcefulness, perceived capacity to orchestrate complex action sequences). It is believed that self-efficacy not only has a direct effect on performance by raising motivation levels, but it also has indirect effects, most notably by affecting people's choice of goals and their commitment to those goals (Latham and Locke, 1991). In other words, the theory holds that people with high self-efficacy beliefs are high performers because they are more likely to undertake difficult goals, to become committed to those goals, and—presumably—work with more intensity to achieve their goals (see Latham and Locke, 1991, p. 221).

Possible New Directions for Goal-Setting Theory

Goal-setting theory has at least a 30-year history and has become the most dominant, valid, and useful modern theory of work motivation. It is clear that its adherents will continue to pursue its theoretical and applied boundaries. Where else might their efforts be extended? One interesting issue concerns the emotional experiences associated with goal setting. As we saw in chapter 4 and elsewhere in this book, emotions and emotionality are areas of renewed interest in psychology and organizational behavior. To the knowledge of this author, little is known about how emotions are related to the various phenomena associated with goal setting, although a few hunches and hypotheses come to mind.

What types of emotional experiences are associated with the goal-setting process? Fear? Anxiety? Joy? What types of emotional states affect the difficulty of goals selected or the degree of commitment that a person attaches to a goal? What are the emotional experiences related to participation in goal setting? How does it feel when responsibility for setting goals is delegated to someone or removed from her? What emotions usually accompany the feedback process: seeking feedback, receiving positive feedback, or negative feedback? Do positive emotions or what has come to be called a trait of positive affectivity influence any of the stages and processes of goal setting, including goal determination, participation, feedback seeking, feedback acceptance, commitment dynamics, and/or the experience of goal attainment? Some work on the effects of goal-related progress has been reported by theorists and researchers working in the control theory tradition (e.g., Carver and Scheier, 1982; 1990b) and in the resurgent literature on the nature of human satisfaction (e.g., Brendl and Higgins, 1996; Hsee and Abelson, 1991), but a systematic expansion of goal-setting theory requires that more research be done that fully integrates emotionality into the various stages of the overall goal experience. The theoretical framework offered by Carver and Scheier (1982; 1990b) offers a fruitful place for research of this sort to begin.

A second area for possible goal-setting work deals with frustration. How does it feel to fail to achieve goals? Some early work by L. L. Martin, Tesser, and McIntosh (1993) provides a few clues (e.g., what they refer to as "passive" and "motivated" activation, depression, and rumination). Here again some interesting theoretical groundwork has been laid. It is time now for empirical research to complete and extend the work.

Summary, Conclusions, and a Glance Ahead

A recent paper by Locke et al. (1994) provides a succinct statement of the documented knowledge base related to goal setting: "Goal setting theory has established that specific, challenging goals lead to higher task performance than specific, unchallenging goals, vague goals or no goals, providing that: (1) there is feedback showing progress in relation to the goal; (2) appropriate task strategies are used when the task is complex; (3) individuals have adequate ability and situational constraints do not prohibit task-relevant performance; and (4) there is a commitment to the goals. . . . Goal-directed performance is also facilitated by high self-efficacy . . ." (p. 67). Locke (1996) has provided a brief, yet more complete delineation of the state of goal-setting theory summarized by 14 central "findings" over 30 years of work by himself and his colleagues. The interested reader will find this paper readable, current, and comprehensive. Considerably more detail about the philosophical background and development of the theory was written by Locke and Latham (1990b); and Kleinbeck, Quast, Thierry, and Hacker (1990) present the perspectives of other researchers and theorists who have investigated various aspects of goal setting.

This author stated years ago (Pinder, 1984) that it is appropriate to agree with Locke and his colleagues that "the beneficial effect of goal setting on task performance is one of the most robust and replicable findings in the psychological literature" (1981, p. 145). The same conclusion is warranted in the mid-1990s. But it is still important to reiterate the difference between a lack of scientific support on the one hand and negative evidence on the other. This point is of more than mere academic interest. Its relevance here is that it may be that other need-oriented and cognitively based theories are more valid than we are capable of demonstrating by normal scientific means (this argument has been raised in the discussion of several of the theories presented to this point). As mentioned above, it would appear that the propositions derived from Ryan's theory of intentional behavior are more easily operationalized, measured, and tested than are propositions derived from many of the other theories we have examined to this point, thereby making it easier to demonstrate the validity of this approach.

Two other points of balance are also in order. First, it must be noted that the scope of goal-setting theory is more focused than those of the need-based and the other two cognitive/perceptual theories presented in this book. Whereas these other theories might be applied to understanding people's career choices, their attitudes with regard to voting for a union, or their decisions to work for one organization rather than another, goal-setting theory only addresses the problem of employees' performance levels. One might expect, other things being equal, that a more limited-range theory should do a better job scientifically than one with a broader range of focus (Merton, 1968; Pinder and Moore, 1980).

Second, while we note that goal-setting theory has been exposed to more research in field settings than have most other theories of work motivation, there is still very little in the way of long-term field research that addresses the validity of goal-setting theory in its pure form, without the contaminating influences of other managerial programs (such as those that accompany management by objectives, for example). The field-based research that does exist is derived from comparatively short-term field studies (most of which support the theory) or from formalized MBO programs that entail encumbrances not related to goal setting per se but that frequently have caused such programs to fail (as we will see shortly). Notwithstanding these remarks, goal-setting theory continues to enjoy more scientific validity than any other theory or approach to work motivation. It holds more value and promise as an applied motivational tool for managers, especially when combined with principles found in behavior modification and social cognitive theory (see Wood and Bandura, 1989).

Before leaving our discussion of goal setting, it is worth noting again the potential that this theory has for integrating many of the other theories presented in this book (including some approaches and techniques still to be presented). Ryan's (1970) theory suggests the important role that needs may play in determining the repertoires that people develop for interpreting stimulus situations (see Locke, 1991a). Similarly, the work of Fishbein and Ajzen (1975) and Ajzen and Fishbein (1977) suggests how cognitive theories that rely on beliefs and attitudes (such as equity theory and VIE theory) contribute to the explanation of behavior. Their primary function is to provide a basis for predicting a person's intentions, not the direct prediction of behavior.

It stands to reason that managerial programs that attempt explicitly to influence employee intentions should be more effective for influencing employee behavior than programs designed to influence beliefs and attitudes. Later in this chapter we examine management by objectives, a popular managerial technique that attempts to do just that. First, however, we study a body of theory that has become a rival for goal setting, referred to as *control theory*.

CONTROL THEORY

Although control theory was first proposed a half-century ago (N. Weiner, 1948), it made its first appearances in the organizational sciences in the early 1980s (e.g., Campion and Lord, 1982). On first reading, the theory sounds and looks a lot like goal-setting theory, although some of the relevant nouns and verbs differ. In fact, we will see that considerable overlap exists between the two theories and that these similarities have generated controversy and criticism as well as positive attempts at integration between them. Although it appears to have had its origins in G. A. Miller, Galanter, and Pribrum's (1960) TOTE model[5] (Locke and Latham, 1990a, p. 19), this theory has been offered as a model of human behavior with applications in a variety of human contexts and problem areas, such as motivation, self-management, affective and behavioral reactions to work, stress, goal setting and goal changing, self-appraisal, and feedback seeking (Carver, 1979; Carver and Scheier, 1982, 1990b; Fellenz, 1996). We discuss self-management later in the chapter, and the relevance of control theory (and goal-setting theory) will be evident.

According to two leading proponents of control theory:

> [I]ntentional behavior [reflects] a process of feedback control.... When people move (physically or psychologically) toward goals, they manifest the functions of a negative

---

[5]TOTE is an acronym for "test–operate–test–exit," a sequence of operations by which early cognitive psychologists described how an organism (such as a person) behaves in an environment in pursuit of an end state, by sensing its progress toward the end state with the use of feedback, altering behavior on the basis of that feedback, and ultimately, ceasing the sequence (see G. A. Miller et al., 1960, chap. 1).

(discrepancy reducing) feedback loop. . . . That is, people periodically note the qualities they are expressing in their behavior (an input function). They compare these perceptions with salient reference values—whatever goals are being used temporarily to guide behavior (a comparison process inherent in all feedback systems). If the comparisons indicate discrepancies between reference value and the present state (i.e., between intended and actual quantities of behavior), people adjust (the output function) so that it more closely approximates the reference value. (Carver and Scheier, 1990b, p. 19)

The Genealogy of Control Theory

Control theory has its principal roots in cybernetics, the science of control and communication (Fellenz, 1996). In its most basic form, control theory is concerned with the self-regulation of systems, relying heavily on negative feedback loops that provide information to the system concerning how close it is coming to a desired goal state (Klein, 1989). Like a thermostat that operates a house's heating system, this model implies that a person (or any system) is in a constant state of seeking feedback, adjusting his functioning to accommodate any discrepancies detected between his achieved and desired state, and carrying on. The end point of the behavior is a still state of retirement, achieved once there is no discrepancy detected between one's goals and one's accomplishments. In simple terms, "when people pay attention to what they are doing, they usually do what they intend to do, relatively accurately and thoroughly" (Carver and Scheier, 1990b, p. 19).

Elements of Basic Control Theory

Lord and Hanges (1987) and Klein (1989) have offered comprehensive theories of control theory that have implications for work motivation. In the interest of space, we focus here on the model proposed by Klein (1989), because it is more recent and includes principal concepts from a variety of theories in addition to the fundamental notions found in cybernetics.[6] Klein's (1989) adaptation of the generic theory yields at least 33 testable propositions, although not much empirical work has been reported to this time. The generic model of control theory is presented in Figure 13-3, and the following explanation is presented in the generic terms used by control theorists.

The elements of this theory are as follows. The most important component of the theory is the feedback loop. As we saw earlier in the chapter, feedback is merely information provided to a person (or any system) about its circumstances. The feedback loop has four parts: (1) a referent standard (or goal), (2) a sensor, or input function, (3) a comparator, and (4) an effector, or output function. These four components are illustrated in Figure 13-3. For the present purpose, we assume that the terms *input, output, goal,* and *feedback* are familiar to the reader: They are used regularly in common parlance and elsewhere in this chapter. As Klein (1989) and most other control theorists do, we will return to the example of the typical thermostat controlling the heat of a room: "the referent standard is the temperature the thermostat is set at, the sensor is the element monitoring the current room temperature, the comparator is the mechanism that

---

[6]Hyland (1988) also offers a control theory model that integrates other theories of work motivation. In fact, Hyland offers his approach not as a theory of work motivation, as such, but rather "as a meta-theoretic framework for examining the relation between the core ideas of the different motivational programs" (p. 642).

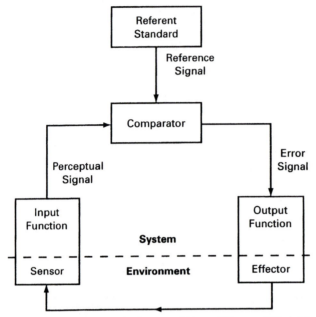

Source: From H. J. Klein, "An Integrated Control Theory of Work Motivation," *Academy of Management Review, 14,* pp. 150–172 (1989). Reprinted with permission.

FIGURE 13-3 Elements of a Control Theory System

compares the current and desired temperatures, and the effector is the furnace or air conditioner" (p. 151). In its most simple, mechanistic form, the system operates as follows. Some type of input is received by the sensor in the system, which, in turn, sends a signal to its comparator. The comparator tests the signal against the system's current standard or goal. If a discrepancy is found, an error signal is triggered and the system initiates action in its effector to reduce the discrepancy. If there is no discrepancy, no action may be taken by the effector (Klein, 1989). This is a description of how control theory works in its most basic, mechanical form.

Human systems are much more complex, of course, although Klein and others claim that the fundamental components and processes are similar. For humans, goals can be flexible and multiple. There are often many courses of action that can be selected to close any perceived discrepancies. The information contained in the feedback can be simple or complex, loaded with meaning or ambiguity. It can be subject to interpretation and either accepted as valid or rejected as suspicious or misleading. It may be judged as genuine or fallacious and devious. Klein (1989) continues: "Consider . . . a salesperson who has accepted a quarterly sales quota as a personal goal (the standard). The input function would be the information the salesperson perceives about his or her current sales performance. When this information is compared to the standard, the salesperson forms a perception of how well he or she is meeting the quota. If this comparison reveals a discrepancy, the salesperson will take some corrective action, possibly increasing the number of new contacts [he or she initiates with prospective customers]" (p. 151).

Control theory includes both cognitive and affective elements. The cognitive features hinge around the transmission and interpretation of information. The effective features arise from the perception of discrepancies and consist, at least in part, of the impulses to initiate or terminate action. If the salesperson is satisfied that he has surpassed his sales quota, he will feel a sense of joy and perhaps pride and relief (see chapter 4 for a discussion of these emotions). If he perceives that he has fallen short of his quota, he may experience anxiety, fear, anger, and possibly embarrassment or shame. It is easy and tempting to oversimplify control theory by ignoring or forgetting that it includes affective as well as cognitive processes (see Carver and Scheier, 1990a, 1990b).

Unlike most simple mechanical systems, human systems as depicted in control theory consist of hierarchies of feedback loops: "In such hierarchies, the *means* to reduce discrepancies in higher-order feedback loops become the *standards* of lower-order loops. . . . That is, the output function of one feedback loop [as illustrated in Figure 13-3] might consist of a string of other loops, and each of those, in turn, might contain other strings of loops, and so on . . ." (Klein, 1989). The salesperson will continue to serve to illustrate. The output function where we left off was the goal of increasing new contacts. It consists of several actions, such as telephoning current customers to inquire about competitors' needs, checking the Yellow Pages for other companies that might require his products and services, making initial contacts with everyone found by these search tactics, and so on. One output function consists of at least two feedback loops: finding and contacting. Each of these feedback loops will have the basic elements described above: an input function, a sensor, a comparator, and an output function. These hierarchies exists like wheels within wheels until, at the most basic level, there are loops that "[involve] neural signals and changes in muscle tension associated with turning the pages in a phone book. The result is a hierarchical plan for increasing sales through increasing new contacts. Powers (1973) proposed that the human nervous system embodies a detailed hierarchy of such feedback loops" (Klein, 1989, p. 152).

A Control Theory for Work Motivation

Now that the generic model has been presented, we can look briefly at how Klein interprets its basic elements for application to our study of work motivation. Klein (1989) substitutes *goals* for referent standards, and the person's behavior replaces the notion of effector. *Feedback* represents the sensor, and Klein maintains the notion of comparator. Klein's adaptation of the generic model is reproduced in Figure 13-4. The label on top in the boxes that contain two labels is Klein's term for the corresponding generic term below it. For example, box (1) represents the common notion from work motivation of a goal; translated into the generic terms of control theory, the concept represented in that box is a standard. Klein refers to his model as an "integrated control theory model of work motivation" because it incorporates concepts from goal-setting theory (such as goals and feedback), script theory (recall our earlier mention of scripts in this chapter, and see Lord and Kernan, 1987), and attribution theory (Kelley and Michela, 1980). The reader is directed to Klein's important paper for a complete representation of his integrated model. It is one of the most creative and constructive attempts to integrate what are generally thought of as competing or incompatible theories of work motivation. (See also Klein, 1991a, for an empirical test of part of this model.)

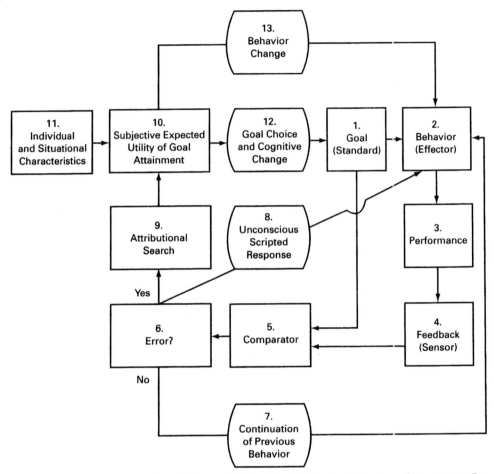

Source: From H. J. Klein, "An integrated control theory Model of Work Motivation," *Academy of Management Review, 14,* pp. 150–172 (1989). Reprinted with permission.

FIGURE 13-4 Klein's Integrated Model of Work Motivation

Goal Setting versus Control Theory

In chapter 2 we saw how it is part of the development of a discipline for researchers and theorists from one camp in a field to attack and criticize the theories and research methods used by scientists in competing camps. We have surveyed many examples of this sort of controversy throughout this volume. In this section we examine some of the heated controversy that has been directed at control theory, particularly the controversy that has emanated from partisans of the goal-setting camp, notably Locke, Latham, and Bandura. Their attacks have many dimensions and raise a series of issues. We do not deal with them exhaustively here; the interested reader is referred to the original sources as well as to a rejoinder offered by Klein (1991b).

Control Theory as Too Mechanistic

Locke and Latham (1990b) claim that control theory is a modern stepchild of behaviorism and that it is deficient because it deals only with discrepancy reduction by feedback monitoring, completely ignoring initial, natural goal-setting processes which they claim are inherently and definitively human. Locke and Latham object to the motionless end state that is the logical conclusion of human behavior under the control theory perspective (Locke and Latham, 1990b, p. 19). "The natural state of the organism is seen to be one of motionlessness, or rest. This is true of machines, but not of living organisms which are naturally active. It is, in effect, a mechanistic version of long discredited drive-reduction theory (Cofer and Appley, 1964)." (See chapter 1 of this book.) They continue with some vitriol: "At a fundamental level, discrepancy reduction theories such as control theory are inadequate because if people consistently acted in accordance with them by trying to eliminate all disturbances [discrepancies], they would all commit suicide—because it would be the only way to eliminate tension. If people chose instead to stay alive but set no goals, they would soon die anyway. By the time they were forced into action by desperate, unremitting hunger pangs, it would be too late to grow and process the food they would need to survive" (Locke and Latham, 1990b, p. 20).

On the same issue in another place, Locke wrote (1991b) "Discrepancy reduction is a consequence of goal-directed behavior, not a cause" (p. 13). "If tension-reduction or removal of discrepancies were people's major motive, then the simplest action for them to take (short of suicide) would be to adjust the goal or standard to their prior performance, thus obviating the need for any action to reduce the discrepancy. Or better yet, they would choose no standards at all so that any output would be as good as any other. But these alternatives are clearly at variance with how people usually act" (pp. 12–13). Fairly heavy criticism, indeed.

Similarly, Bandura (1989) has argued that *goal setting is first and foremost a discrepancy-creating process.* (Certainly, Deci and his colleagues in the intrinsic motivation theory tradition would agree; see chapter 7 of this volume and Harackiewicz and Stone, 1991.)

> It [human self-motivation] requires *feedforward control* as well as *feedback control.* People initially motivate themselves through feedforward control by adopting valued performance standards that create a state of disequilibrium and then mobilizing their effort on the basis of anticipatory estimation. Feedback control comes into play in subsequent adjustments of behavior to achieve desired results. After people attain the standard they have been pursuing, they generally set a higher standard for themselves. The adoption of further challenges creates new motivational discrepancies to be mastered. . . . Self-motivation thus involves a dual cyclic process of disequilibrating discrepancy production followed by equilibrating discrepancy reduction. (Bandura, 1989, p. 38)

Adherents and defenders of control theory take exception to the allegation that it is too mechanistic a model to represent human processes (e.g., Klein, 1989). "In human control systems, feedback involves much more than the mechanical sensing of environment, goals are not predetermined inflexible standards, and there are several alternatives for reducing discrepancies" (Klein, 1989, p. 151). Carver and Scheier

(1981) point out that control theory conceives of goals as existing in hierarchies, such that "the standard of comparison for the behavior of a subordinate loop is specified as the output of the loop at the next higher level of analysis" (p. 117). Moreover, human beings usually harbor multiple goal hierarchies (Eckblad, 1981; Fellenz, 1996), and their various goals may be mutually reinforcing, contradictory, or merely compatible and independent. *Human goals* can differ on a number of dimensions, such as their degree of generality, their time frames, whether they are related to activity and process or outcome states, the degree to which they are intended to influence a person's behavior, and the degree to which the person is even conscious of them (Winell, 1987, cited by Fellenz, 1996). The traditional body of goal-setting theory makes it clear that human goals can be manipulated in terms of their specificity, difficulty, and the level of commitment of the person holding the goals (Locke and Latham, 1990b).

This particular criticism of control theory seems unfair to this author. In a chapter published at about the same time as the Locke and Latham (1990b) critique, Carver and Scheier (1990b) reveal that they too believe that "human action [is] fundamentally goal-directed" (p. 5). They acknowledge that "the idea that human behavior—indeed, human personality—is best analyzed in terms of the goals that people adopt is one that has been prominent in the writing for many years. . . . [T]he central theme is that human action is defined in terms of the individual's goals" (p. 6). For Carver and Scheier (1990b), the origin of people's goals is their memories: behavioral knowledge about how people acted and responded in past situations similar to those they face at any given time in the present. People form *schemas*[7] and *scripts*[8] about the nature and

---

[7]More than 60 years ago, Bartlett (1932) introduced the idea of cognitive schemas as follows: "*Schema* refers to an active organization of past reactions, or of past experiences, which must always be supposed to be operating in any well-adapted organic response. That is, whenever there is any order or regularity of behavior, a particular response is possible only because it is related to other similar responses which have been serially organized, yet which operate, not simply as individual members coming after one another, but as a unitary mass. . . . All incoming pulses of a certain kind, or mode, go together to build up an active, organized setting: visual, auditory, various types of cutaneous impulses and the like, at a relatively low level; all the experiences connected by a common interest: in sport, in literature, history, art, science, philosophy, and so on, on a higher level" (p. 201, quoted by G. A. Miller et al., 1960, p. 7). For example, Shetzer (1993) has applied the notion of schemas to the processes associated with employee participation in decision making, providing not only a useful lens through which to consider the participation process but also a valuable example of how people form and utilize schemas to make sense of their work environments.

[8]A *script* is a particular type of knowledge schema, which Lord and Kernan (1987) define as follows: "Scripts are cognitive knowledge structures held in memory that describe the appropriate sequencing of events in conventional or familiar situations. . . . Scripts are a unique type of knowledge structure because they serve a dual purpose: They not only help one interpret the behavior of others, but they also aid in generating behavior. . . . Thus, they guide the planning and execution of familiar or repetitive activities" (p. 266). People develop and make use of scripts for most of the behavioral settings they have encountered more than a few times. For example, a student develops a script for taking a midterm examination in a university course—it consists of a series of mental images, concepts, expectations, and ideas associated with taking examinations in the past. The script contains knowledge and ideas about what forms of behavior are appropriate, what the student can expect from the behavior of other students taking the exam, and so on. Scripts are subject to change with the occurrence of new events and experiences. Thus, the occurrence of a fire drill in the middle of a particular examination period teaches the student (and alters her examination-taking script) that fire alarms are a possibility and that certain types of frantic and worrisome behavior can be expected from other students and the professor in charge. In the work setting, people are likely to form scripts that consist of expected and appropriate behaviors and events for a wide variety of occasions, such as meetings with colleagues, performance review interviews with one's boss, a Christmas party, or a labor walkout. Scripts help us organize our thoughts, expectations, beliefs, and behaviors so they can be invoked when appropriate to make our functioning in life efficient.

sequence of social events—scenarios about the way things work and about how events unfold. These scripts become part of memory, if not a part of a person's repertoire of action in future social situations similar to those in which the scripts were learned. Carver and Scheier (1990b) argue that "Saying that someone has taken up a behavioral goal is in some sense equivalent to saying that the person wants to manifest in his or her actions a particular quality that is represented in a knowledge structure in his or her memory. Accordingly . . . the behavioral goals underlying human action are specified in memory as elements of behavioral knowledge" (p. 5).

For this author, the origins and nature of goals, as noted in these published statements, are no less vague nor more scientifically helpful than those from Ryan (1970), whose explanation of the origins and nature of goals was presented earlier in the chapter. The primary difference appears to be that Ryan's (1970) thoughts rely on a theory of human needs as their bedrock, while those of Carver and Scheier (1990b) rely more on a cognitive, memory-based foundation. It seems ironic that Locke and Latham's (1990b) disapproval of control theory should be so hostile given the primarily cognitive basis of their own theory of goal setting. Whatever the truth, this author contends that the smoke and fury is more spectacular than the value of the underlying truth: Goals are critical to human behavior and, it follows, to motivation and behavior at work. The origins of these goals must be found in needs, cognition, memories, and more-or-less specific intentions—all of the above. Carving up the variance accounted for by each source hardly seems worth the time or trouble.

In short, there are many ways that are too simplistic to attack control theory as a mechanical or mechanistic representation of human functioning. There are definite parallels between the operations of human and lower-level systems (see Boulding, 1968; L. M. Miller, 1978), but to reject control theory on the basis of those similarities is unreasonable (see Fellenz, 1996, for a far more comprehensive review of the issues).

Originality and Induction versus Deduction

Another Lockean attack on control theory alleges that it does not have any original core content of its own. Locke (1991b) claims that the central notion—the negative feedback loop—is borrowed from cybernetics, and that all later embellishments of the theory have been ideas borrowed from other motivation theories. Goal-setting theory, by comparison, has a few core, original ideas (such as those pertaining to the setting of difficult, specific goals). The theory started and developed from the "ground up" in an inductive manner, adding variables and amendments as research has progressed over the years. Locke claims that the inductive approach is the preferred one, citing sociologists Glaser and Strauss (1967), who have extolled the virtues of "grounded theory."

Locke (1991b) also attacks the notion inherent in control theory of *goal hierarchies*. Control theory states that the goals a person has that serve as standards when discrepancies are detected are determined by higher-level goals or standards, which, in turn, are determined by still higher-level goals. Locke (1991) notes that "while it is true that people have goal hierarchies, this only pushes the tension-reduction problem back a step further. If tension reduction is the ultimate ideal, why have goal hierarchies at all?" (pp. 13–14). In other words, what is the ultimate source of these goals? Locke dismisses both the notion of instincts (an old, discredited theory) and the environment as the principal source of goals and standards, using the same bases that he and other cognitive theorists use to dismiss behaviorist explanations (see chapter 14). Hence Locke,

Latham, and Bandura discredit control theory as incomplete and lacking in one of the essential features of human behavior.

It is true that induction is a legitimate and appropriate method for theory development. This author believes the organizational sciences have not granted sufficient status and recognition to this approach over the past 25 years. Induction begins with the observation of real behavior by real people in situ and attempts to make sense out of that behavior, offering explanations and predictions, testing those predictions against further experience, and modifying the emergent theory to take into account any reliable differences between the predicted and the observed phenomena.

Locke (1991b) criticizes control theory for starting with the theoretical notions of cybernetics and mechanical systems and "working downward," filling in the holes and finding explanations for errors of prediction and understanding in other theoretical ideas. Justifiably, Klein (1991b) defends his approach: There is nothing inherently superior to induction over deduction in the development of new theory. Locke's attack on these grounds seems particularly duplicitous, inasmuch as so many of the current tenets of goal setting were advanced decades ago by Mace (1935) and others. In fact, Locke and Latham (1990b) acknowledge their debt to Mace as follows:

> Another academic influence on our work was the series of experiments conducted in England by Mace (1935). It is not clear what had influenced Mace to do this research, but so far as we know, his were the earliest experimental studies ever done of goal setting as an independent variable. He was the first to compare the effects of specific, challenging goals with goals such as "do your best," and to compare the effects of goals differing in level of difficulty. The results of one of his most successful experiments were reported in Ryan and Smith's (1954) early industrial psychology textbook, which the present first author [Locke] was assigned to read as a graduate student. (p. 13)

A Historical Note on the Controversy

It is somewhat ironic that goal-setting adherents are so critical of control theory, inasmuch as control theory was offered by some of its early advocates as a means of explaining why goal setting works. Campion and Lord (1982), for example, made three suggestions to explain why goal-setting theory, to that time at least, offered little insight into why goal processes work and why the goal literature had not yet been integrated with other theories of work motivation. This limited conceptual progress, they argued, was due partly to the inattention of goal-setting advocates to feedback processes, while people studying feedback had not paid any attention to goal setting.

In addition, Campion and Lord (1982) suggested there had been too much focus on static rather than dynamic processes in the goal-setting research tradition. Finally, they claimed that the very nature of the goals studied were limited, static, and isolated. They pointed out that, in reality, "goals may be imbedded in complex cognitive or motivational systems, goals may change frequently, and goals may be poorly defined. A comprehensive model of the goal setting process should be able to handle these types of goals" (p. 266). It is strange how, in retrospect, a theory offered in assistance of another has been so harshly criticized by its would-be benefactors.

The point for our purposes is that goal theorists have leveled highly critical attacks on the efforts of control theorists, and although some of their criticisms are apt, others are less so. Moreover, the similarities between the two theories are more important in practice than the differences between them. Both assume a cognitive human being who pays attention to goals and feedback from his environment and his own consciousness. Both theories provide tremendous insight into processes of self-regulation, as we will see later in this chapter (Bandura, 1989). In fact, one might claim that the two theories are sufficiently similar that the mere existence of both speaks to the truth value they both imply. If it is true that control theory can be faulted for ignoring the original goal-setting stage of human action (and the criticism is fair), it is true that goal-setting theory is limited in its scope and areas of application (see Austin and Bobko, 1985, and other sections of this chapter). The allegation of lack of originality is unfair. Theories evolve, compete, merge, and often become reconciled. The roots of control theory in cybernetics are no less legitimate than those of modern goal theory in the work of Mace (1935) and Ryan (1970). To this author, therefore, much of the criticism from the goal-setting camp seems petty and dysfunctional. Fellenz (1996) has reviewed a number of other criticisms directed at control theory by the Locke and Latham goal-setting school and offers reasonable rebuttals for many of them. The interested reader is referred to his paper for complete details.

In the final sections of this chapter, we turn our attention to management by objectives, a once-popular managerial technique that relied on goal setting as one of its principal theoretical foundations. In chapter 14 we study self-regulation, another set of applied techniques with tremendous potential implications for work motivation.

MANAGEMENT BY OBJECTIVES

The applied success of goal setting, even before it was developed and advanced as a formal theory of human behavior, contributed to the birth of a managerial technique that has been in wide use for nearly 40 years. *Management by objectives* (MBO) has been one of the most widely adopted managerial techniques for motivating and rewarding employees in Western economies since the late 1950s. Nearly 30 years ago, one of its first leading proponents claimed that MBO was the predominant form of management in modern business and government organizations and that this approach to management had been subjected to as much scientific investigation as any other (Odiorne, 1979). A cursory examination of the managerial literature confirms the widespread popularity of MBO, at least in terms of the number of organizations that have adopted it in some form or another. Similarly, as we saw in the first part of this chapter, the scientific literature on goal setting (the major body of research and theory related to a central aspect of MBO) suggests that many of the basic elements of MBO do rest on considerable scientific support. In the following sections we briefly examine MBO and discuss a number of related issues.

Origins of Management by Objectives

Although thinkers dating back to the classical philosophers have held that human effort is (or should be) goal directed (Odiorne, 1979), the modern origins of MBO are found in the work of Peter Drucker with General Motors and General Electric (Greenwood, 1981). Whereas earlier management theorists had assumed that objectives are an important part of managing, they placed little emphasis on the origins and consequences of objectives in organizational settings. Drucker recognized the problematic nature of objectives and built an approach to management centered primarily on them (Greenwood, 1981).

What Is MBO?

There is no *theory* of MBO, a feature that has brought it some harsh, recent criticism (see Halpern and Osofsky, 1990). In practice, there have been almost as many varieties of MBO as organizations that claim to have adopted it. In other words, the specific elements of MBO and MBO-like programs vary from one organization to another, sometimes causing confusion over just what is and what is not MBO. Nevertheless, one authority defined MBO as "a managerial process whereby organizational purposes are diagnosed and met by joining superiors and subordinates in the pursuit of mutually agreed goals and objectives, which are specific, measurable, time bounded, and joined to an action plan; progress and goal attainment are measured and monitored in appraisal sessions which center on mutually determined objective standards of performance" (McConkie, 1979, p 37). This definition is adopted in this chapter and elsewhere in this book.

Some Specific Features of MBO Programs

As noted above, the specific characteristics of MBO and MBO-like programs have varied in practice from one setting to another. However, the two most essential features of such programs are usually (1) a system for establishing work-related goals, and (2) some type of procedure for assessing a person's performance vis-à-vis those goals after a specified period of time. Beyond these two very basic characteristics, however, there is less unanimity in practice about what constitutes MBO. Nevertheless, McConkie (1979) reported varying degrees of agreement among a sample of experts concerning the following general statements about the goal-setting aspect of MBO:

1. Objectives should be reviewed periodically.
2. The time period for goal accomplishment should be specified.
3. The indicators of results should be quantifiable, if possible; otherwise, they should at least be verifiable.
4. Objectives should be flexible, changing as circumstances change.
5. Objectives should include a statement of an "action plan" for how they will be accomplished.
6. Objectives should be prioritized, some being agreed to be more important than others.

MBO usually consists of some combination of procedures for the setting of individual goals on the basis of broader organizational goals and the subsequent evaluation of individual performance in terms of the degree of accomplishment of these goals. The specific nuances with regard to the participation of subordinates in the goal-setting and performance evaluation processes vary across organizations as well as between units within particular organizations. The most important psychological processes that make MBO potentially successful are those that underlie goal setting, as explained earlier in the chapter.

Functions (Potentially) Served by MBO

Odiorne (1979) identified a variety of functions that MBO might be expected to serve, including the following:

1. Reduction of aimless activity and wasting of time and other resources
2. Reduction of conflict between superiors and subordinates as a result of greater clarity of each other's responsibilities
3. Improvement of individual performance and overall organizational effectiveness
4. Improvements in employee morale, employee development, quality of work, and delegation
5. Improvement in the capacity of the organization to change and adapt

It is claimed that MBO can help deal with a number of common problems faced by managers, such as deciding on who receives pay increases, how many people should report to a particular manager, the types of people who should report to a given manager, the types and amount of information communicated to subordinates, and the amount of delegation and decentralization most desirable in a particular situation. In short, advocates of MBO, such as Odiorne (1979), believe it is more than merely a set of techniques and procedures; rather, it is viewed as a total system of management, even as "a way of thinking about management" (p. 52).

Stages of the MBO Process

The use and administration of MBO can be broken down into four basic steps. First, managers at each organizational level confer and negotiate with each of their subordinates to determine organizational and personal objectives for some upcoming period of time (such as six months or a year). In practice, the degree to which the subordinate actually participates in this goal-setting process varies (as mentioned above), depending on the personal styles of both the superior and subordinate, as well as upon the degree to which they try to adhere to strictly prescribed MBO principles (which normally advocate participation). Second, the subordinate prepares an action plan describing how he will attempt to achieve the agreed-upon goals. These action plans may or may not be reviewed by the superior. Once agreed upon, however, the objectives and action plans guide the employee's work behavior during the following (and agreed-upon) period of time. The third stage consists of a performance review by the superior and the subordinate of the latter's progress toward the objectives set at the beginning of the period. This performance review, in effect, replaces more traditional methods of performance appraisal practiced in many organizations. In fact, problems with traditional methods were largely responsible for the rapid growth in popularity of MBO and MBO-like programs.

One classic paper, for example, pointed out how traditional performance appraisal systems place supervisors in the untenable position of "playing God" with subordinates. Invariably, the supervisor finds himself passing judgment on the personal worth of the subordinate (McGregor, 1957). As a result of the unpleasantness that naturally results from such a process, performance appraisal seldom accomplishes its purposes of constructively evaluating an employee's job performance. Instead, it generates defensive reactions on the part of the subordinate and/or attempts by the supervisor to avoid the process entirely. MBO was proposed as an alternative because it requires the superior and subordinate to focus attention on the behaviors and accomplishments of the employee in terms of objectives that the employee helps establish. The result, according to McGregor (1957), is a more analytic process, which is impersonal and objective, that makes constructive assessment more possible. McGregor's observations were made four decades ago. It is amazing how relevant they remain to this day.

The fourth and final stage of most MBO programs is the setting of new objectives by the superior and the subordinate for the next period of time.

Cascading

One general feature prescribed by advocates of MBO is that the goals set at each organizational level should be consistent with the goals set at other hierarchical levels. More specifically, the goals set at the highest level of the organization should be stated in relatively general terms, which can subsequently be translated into increasingly more specific terms at each lower level. The process of distilling increasingly more specific objectives as one moves down the hierarchy is referred to as *cascading* (see Raia, 1974). For example, an organization might have the objective of increasing profits by 10 percent over the next two-year period. This somewhat general objective is then interpreted into more specific goals for managers at lower levels of the firm. The vice president of administration of the company might generate objectives with his boss (the president) concerning cutting costs, whereas the vice president in charge of sales may translate the general organizational profit goal into more specific objectives about sales levels and market penetration. Each of these VPs would derive in turn even more specific objectives with each subordinate manager. To continue the example, the VP of administration might collaborate with his employment manager to set goals to reduce cost associated with turnover and the recruitment of new staff. The employment manager would then generate goals with each recruiter and personnel interviewer concerning specific techniques for reducing turnover and recruitment costs. The specific objectives derived at each level will vary from each department, depending on the type of work performed (e.g., sales, marketing, production).

Assumptions Underlying MBO

MBO programs rely on a number of assumptions (Barton, 1981). First, it is assumed that an organization may have more than a single objective. In fact, most organizations have multiple objectives (Gross, 1965). The hypothetical firm in the example above may have objectives dealing with new product development, the improvement of its corporate image, and diversification into different markets. Similarly, it is assumed that particular employees at each organizational level may have more than one objective and that objectives at any given level may result in more than one subobjective at subsequent lower levels. Second, it is assumed that when they are achieved, the various subgoals at each level cumulatively contribute to the achievement of the goals at each successive higher level, ultimately to the attainment of the organization's goals at their broadest levels (such as increasing profits by 7 percent over a two-year period). Third, the use of an MBO program implies that an organization's strategy and tactics are to be found in (and consist of) its goals and the action plans deriving from those goals. The means–ends links generated by an MBO program constitute organizational strategy and are the primary basis for organizational policy. It is in this sense that MBO has the potential to be much more than merely a goal-setting and performance appraisal system.

Finally, it might be assumed that ideally, the goals resulting from an MBO program should be mutually compatible and not counterproductive and mutually antithetical. In practice, of course, this is not normally the case. The opposite is more common: Organizational goals are commonly incompatible (Daft, 1983). For example, the hypothetical organization mentioned above may find that its goals of increasing profit and expanding markets interfere with its goal of improving its reputation in the community. Similarly, university students often feel that university goals dealing with research and publication activities are inconsistent with objectives pertaining to quality instruction in the classroom. This is sometimes the case, but not necessarily. Barton (1981) has recently discussed the problem of incompatible goals in MBO settings and has presented an approach for dealing with it.

How Effective Is MBO in Practice?

Now that we have looked at some of the claims made in support of MBO and a number of its principal characteristics, it is appropriate to examine the scientific evidence concerning the actual value and effectiveness of these programs. Just how effective has MBO been in practice? One early review of 185 case studies, surveys, quasi-experiments, and true experiments provided a somewhat discouraging conclusion, albeit one that will sound familiar to those who have read earlier chapters of this book. This review found an inverse relationship between the level of scientific rigor used in evaluative studies of MBO and the degree of support claimed for the program studied (Kondrasuk, 1981). When researchers employed carefully constructed experiments designed to rule out alternative explanations for their findings, the results tended to be less than favorable for MBO. On the other hand, in one-shot case studies in which no control groups were used and the basic fundamentals of experimental design were violated by the researchers in question, MBO appeared to have been effective. More recent surveys have found that the form taken by MBO programs varies widely, using different degrees and combinations of the basic elements described above (e.g., Kopelman, 1986). A meta-analysis reported by Rodgers and Hunter (1991) yielded the most positive and encouraging conclusions. In this study of studies, Rodgers and Hunter (1991) conducted a thorough search for research reports of other investigators who had examined MBO program effectiveness, reports that had not been included in previous meta-analyses. Their focus was on employee productivity, specifically on productivity gains apparently brought about by MBO programs. They found productivity gains in 68 of the 70 evaluation studies reviewed. The mean percentage increase in productivity across those studies that had used ratio-level (hard) indicators of productivity was 45 percent. When managerial ratings were used as the basis for assessment of MBO impact, the mean increase was found to be 42 percent of one standard deviation. No matter how productivity increases were measured, there was solid support for the positive effects of MBO programs (Rodgers and Hunter, 1991).

The Importance of Executive Commitment

Of special interest in this meta-analysis is the significance of the support provided to the MBO programs by the various senior executives in the organizations in which the programs had been installed. The results were strikingly clear: MBO had the greatest impact in those settings where senior executives not only gave positive endorsement but also practiced the technique at their own level. By contrast, productivity gains were weakest in organizations in which senior executives neither endorsed nor practiced their MBO programs, and the group in the middle of the support issue—those cases in which there was verbal endorsement but no actual practice of MBO among the executives—fell in the middle of the productivity improvement distribution. The productivity gains were five times higher among organizations with high executive commitment than among those with low executive commitment (Rodgers and Hunter, 1991). In a similar study of 18 previously reported studies, with their attention on job satisfaction (rather than productivity), similar results were found. The greatest increase in job attitudes was found in studies of organizations in which there were high levels of top management involvement. As before, there was positive improvement in the moderate-commitment cases and, finally, a slight *decrease* in job attitudes in MBO installations in which there was very low executive commitment (Rodgers, Hunter, and Rogers, 1993). Only 18 organizations were included in this meta-analysis of job satisfaction effects, so there were not many organizations in any of the three executive commitment-level groups, suggesting some caution in the interpretation of the results. Nevertheless, the two meta-analyses combined (Rodgers and Hunter, 1991; Rodgers et al., 1993) provide impressive empirical evidence to support the almost trite prescription from the managerial and organizational development literature that top management support is necessary for interventions such as MBO to have a chance of reaping positive results.

The Relationship between MBO Programs and Goal Setting

It was argued earlier in this chapter that goal setting has demonstrated more validity than any other theory of work motivation, and that goal-setting techniques constitute one of the two most common (perhaps universal) features of MBO programs in practice. In view of the success of goal setting per se, one might find the somewhat lower and mixed rates of success among formal MBO programs paradoxical or even contradictory. It is important to repeat that while goal-setting techniques constitute an integral element of virtually all MBO programs, there is much more to MBO than simple goal setting. As noted earlier, the performance review process is also an important element of MBO, as are the participation of employees in the goal-setting process, the technique of cascading, and the formalization of strategy, tactics, and policy. It may be that the transformation of the relatively simple principles of goal setting (as developed by Ryan, Locke, and Latham, for example) into formal MBO programs has introduced difficulties that may attenuate or dampen the positive effects possible from simple goal setting (see C. H. Ford, 1979; Muczyk, 1978; Reddin, 1971).[9] In fact, there is an abun-

---

[9] There is reason to believe that the translation of basic mentoring relationships into formalized, organizationally sponsored mentoring programs may have a similar corrupting effect on the value of mentor–protégé relationships (Schroeder, 1988).

dant literature dealing with the reasons most commonly responsible for MBO failures that supports such a conjecture. Let us now take a brief look at some of these reasons, to see what can be learned from them.

Some Common Causes of Failure of MBO Programs

There seem to be two general sets of causes of failure of MBO programs. The first set is concerned primarily with political issues at the implementation stage, while the second set entails behavioral reactions of organizational members after MBO has been installed.

Politics at the Implementation Stage

Organizations are typically very political social systems, featuring struggles among persons and coalitions of people for power, influence, and resources (Bacharach and Lawler, 1980). According to Jamieson (1973) and Odiorne (1979), failure to recognize and take the political reality of an organization into account at the time of the implementation of an MBO program is bound to result in its failure. What are some of these factors?

First, there is the organization's power structure. Moving from a nonrationalized form of management to one explicitly designed to be as rational as MBO is bound to threaten people inside the organization who already hold influence, often unofficially, over the way things are done. To formalize the setting of goals and the planning of policy in a broad-based fashion naturally challenges the power of those who have previously "had the boss's ear" and is bound to result in resistance from those people. Similarly, when power is diffused among more than one camp, the potential for political manoeuvering, "horse trading," and coalition formation (either in support of or against innovations such as MBO) is high. The result can often be difficult for any program that is introduced into such a climate.

On a related point, it must be remembered that MBO, properly practiced, entails the sharing of power between superiors and their subordinates at all levels. Often, managers at one level may be willing to encourage the involvement of their subordinates (in the setting of goals and action plans, for example) only as long as they receive a similar degree of downward power-sharing from their own superiors. Therefore, unless managers see more influence being passed downward to their levels from above, they will naturally fear that heavy participation by their own subordinates may make them redundant in the organizational hierarchy. As a result, the actual sharing of power is often an on-again, off-again sort of affair that can make a sham out of serious attempts to operate an MBO program. The results of the meta-analyses reported earlier (Rodgers and Hunter, 1991; Rodgers et al., 1993) suggest that active commitment by top executives to MBO programs may help prevent or at least reduce the negative effects of political resistance to the installation and effective performance of MBO programs.

A third factor (related to the first two) might be seen as a general resistance to change that can be anticipated whenever massive organizational change of any sort is attempted. For example, changes in cost accounting procedures, salary systems, and even the design of jobs that often accompany MBO naturally threaten people who believe (correctly or without justification) that they stand to lose something from the changes. Foot dragging and active resistance can be expected from such persons. Related to this problem is the one that normally occurs when tasks are reassigned: People who have tasks removed from them to be incorporated into other people's jobs naturally fear a loss of power, particularly when those tasks are central to the work flow, require particular expertise, and/or are concerned with dealing with any of the major problems facing the organization (Hickson, Hinings, Lee, Schneck, and Pennings, 1971).

A fourth factor noted by Odiorne (1979) is that people in organizations are often more loyal and committed to their immediate work unit than they are to the larger organization per se (see chapter 10 of this book). Thus, employees who start to set formal objectives for the first time may comply only to the extent that they believe the objectives being set are going to benefit their work unit per se. Otherwise, the loftier goals of the organization, as a whole, may not receive active support and participation during attempts to cascade them into specific objectives for particular groups.

Another political consideration has to do with possible individualists (often managerial, professional, and technical people, according to Odiorne) who are trained to be single-minded and independent. When people of this sort are confronted with a program they view as being overly routine, bureaucratized, and limiting of their professional freedom, they can be expected to resist it.

In short, failure to recognize and accommodate the political realities within an organization may be sufficient grounds for the failure of the system before it ever really has a chance to get started. However, although managing these political factors at the implementation stage may be necessary for the effectiveness of MBO, it does not appear to be sufficient to assure success. The point is that once installed, a number of other factors can function to limit the effectiveness of an MBO program. Let's take a brief look at some of the more common of these.

Postimplementation Problems for MBO

To survive once it is installed, an MBO program requires a number of other conditions. One of these is the quality of the organization's management information system: Without the capacity to set goals and monitor the performance of individuals and groups against those goals reliably, an MBO program cannot be effective. A second key factor is the leadership style of the organization's managers. If an organization has had a history of autocratic decision making throughout its structure for some time, the participatory style normally required to make MBO effective is less likely to be adopted, particularly if the organization in question has been relatively effective as a consequence of (or despite) its characteristic style. Especially critical is the skill of managers at conducting participatory interviews with their subordinates at the goal setting and performance review stage (Jamieson, 1973). Unless managers are trained and able to be creative, supportive, and nonthreatening when they jointly set goals and (especially) when they evaluate the performance of their subordinates against those goals, the organization will not derive the potential benefits that MBO offers. The ongoing, active support of MBO by senior executives is universally acknowledged as necessary for its success.

Similarly, key management personnel must not be averse to the idea of *planning*. Many organizations are quite effective despite an emphasis on future-oriented planning, particularly long-range planning. MBO requires a mentality that fosters planning at various intervals into the future, so unless managers are willing and able to engage in such an approach to managing, MBO will have limited success.

Traditionally, job descriptions and the operationalization of those descriptions have constituted an area of potential risk to MBO (Jamieson, 1973; Schoderbek and Plambeck, 1978). In stable or slowly evolving jobs, job descriptions must be kept as current as possible; otherwise, managers and their subordinates will not have a sound base for determining the types and levels of goals that should be set. On the other hand, it is seldom possible to translate all the elements of a job into specific goals. Care must be taken that those aspects of a person's job that cannot be set into goals are not ignored (Levinson, 1970). Moreover, many forms of modern work almost defy description and codification, so objectives may be difficult to set in precise terms in advance. Instead, it is often preferable to set plans that are less specific than in the past and are couched in terms of areas of activity rather than in terms of hard, quantifiable objectives. We saw earlier in this chapter that setting difficult, specific goals can actually be detrimental in task settings that are complex and/or novel for the person involved. As real jobs become less structured and codified, less reliance on specific difficult goals will be more appropriate and it will become more suitable for people merely to become committed to goals in which they will "do their best."

Much of the work performed in many organizations is accomplished through the efforts of groups rather than the work of single individuals. Therefore, the interdependencies between an employee and other people around him in the workplace must be recognized, both when goals are established and when performance is being reviewed. In some instances it may be desirable to set goals for groups of employees rather than for single individuals.

It is often found that as the initial enthusiasm for an MBO program starts to wane (for any of the reasons mentioned above), the daily practice of the program becomes less and less well maintained: Managers and subordinates delay goal setting and performance review interviews and/or conduct them in a half-hearted manner simply for the sake of appeasing the personnel department. Often, there is an increase in the level of authoritarianism in the setting of goals: Newly converted democratic managers gradually revert to their true underlying autocratic styles. Sometimes the emphasis at the appraisal stage reverts to assessing the personal traits of the subordinates rather than their objective accomplishments vis-à-vis their goals. The tying of rewards to goal attainment in MBO sometimes discourages innovation and risk taking and instead encourages conservative goal setting, interpersonal rivalries, and factionalism (C. H. Ford, 1979; Kohn, 1993; recall chapter 7 of this book). Sometimes the goal-setting and appraisal practices are extended too far down the hierarchy to levels where the nature of the work does not justify their use. The result is a proliferation of paperwork and a rejection of the program altogether. Sometimes the pursuit of established objectives causes an inflexibility of activities that prevents the organization from exploiting opportunities that arise during the middle of an MBO time period.

MBO requires a degree of monitoring and control to assure that it is not eroded over time in favor of managing by fiat, managing on a crisis-to-crisis basis, and/or managing with an evaluative style that discourages employees and managers alike from taking a positive, forward-looking approach. Recent evidence makes it clear that MBO has its best chance of survival and of being of value when there is active commitment by top executives.

Ethical Issues and MBO

One final reason that some MBO programs gradually break down may be because of what some employees see as unethical and unfair aspects of such programs. Questions of ethics are relevant in both the goal-setting and performance evaluation stages of MBO (Pringle and Longenecker, 1982). For example, the overly zealous implementation of an MBO program may coerce some employees into participating in the setting of goals when they have no desire to do so (Halpern and Osofsky, 1990). Not everyone wants to participate in the planning and control functions of their own work (Cherrington and England, 1980). On the other hand, ethical problems arise when employees are led to believe that they will be invited to participate in the setting of their own goals and the evaluation of their own performance, but after seeing the program in actual operation, they see that their inputs are either discredited, ignored, or unsolicited (Halpern and Osofsky, 1990). Two decades ago, the author noted: "MBO programs are often simply legitimized systems of phony participation, in which the fiction is maintained that the subordinate is making a real input into planning work objectives and procedures. Such situations smack of Machiavellianism and are quickly self-defeating" (Pinder, 1977, p. 388).

But other ethical issues may also be involved. The strong prescription to quantify objectives (as mentioned earlier) may force employees to focus on only parts of their jobs, ignoring other elements, such as concern for other people, adherence to moral standards of conduct, and commitment to principles of fair play. In fact, one study found that the requirement to quantify goals was the most commonly mentioned problem attributed to MBO programs among a sample of employees who worked under such systems (C. Stein, 1975).

Earlier, the problem of assessing individual performance in jobs in which the individual is interdependent with other employees was mentioned. Apart from its practical dimension, this problem has moral implications as well: Failure to take into account the effect of factors beyond a person's control while deciding the level of reward or punishment that person is to receive is blatantly unethical (see our discussion of procedural justice in chapter 11). There are also ethical considerations related to the performance assessment aspect of MBO programs (Pringle and Longenecker, 1982). To the extent that employees are evaluated exclusively on the *ends* of their efforts (i.e., the degree of attainment of their goals) and not on the means they use to achieve those goals, they may be compelled to engage in behaviors that are less than ethical. Longenecker and Pringle (1981) note that "setting very difficult goals and then applying pressure to reach these goals creates conditions favorable to producing unethical behavior. Is it always clear to personnel that they are expected to attain goals only within the confines of ethical performance? Or, is the emphasis upon goals so intense that attention is directed to the goals and not to means of achieving those goals?" (p. 89).

The sort of pressure that Longnecker and Pringle mention can become more intense, of course, to the degree that the employee influences the goals to which he is committed. Failure to accomplish one's own goals and living with the consequences of such failure is akin to being hoisted on one's own petard (Levinson, 1970).

Summary

If the basic principles of goal setting are to have a chance of being successful in work organizations, they must be accompanied by a host of organizational conditions, preparations, and (often) adjustments. The widespread application of MBO during the 1960s and 1970s in ignorance of these necessary organizational preconditions led to failures in the majority of organizations that tried it (Reddin, 1971; F. E. Schuster and Kindall, 1974). It would appear that organizational scientists have a better understanding of individual differences and the nature of human intentions to behave than they do of the critical features of organizations in which work behavior takes place. Accordingly, even the more successful theories of work motivation (such as goal setting) will provide limited scientific validity and practical value for managers until more is learned about how organizational variables interact with individual, psychological variables (see Mowday and Sutton, 1993).

What's New in MBO?

Not much. The reader will notice that the bulk of the documents cited in this section are fairly dated, many originating in the late 1960s and 1970s. Only a few refinements have been made to the practice of MBO since then. Most of what needed to be learned had been learned by the time summary reviews of the causes of success and failure in MBO programs, such as that by Kondrasuk (1981), were published. Other than a few details about the significance of top-level executive support (something most people knew intuitively anyway), there have been few lessons of significance to emerge about MBO over the past 15 or 20 years.

Moreover, E. A. Locke (personal communication, 1997) has suggested that the term *MBO* is not used in many organizations these days but that the principles of goal setting are applied, in varying degrees, in most organizations in the world. He is probably correct. There is no doubt that formalized MBO programs are less popular today than they were two decades ago (see Pinder, 1984), and there is also little doubt that goal-setting principles are ubiquitous, whether the people practicing them are aware of it or not. Nevertheless, there are still sufficient numbers of formal MBO programs in practice today that the reader who is interested in the application of work motivation theory ought to be appraised of what the technique is and is not, as well as of the many practices, conditions, and circumstances that can cause MBO programs to fail.

In fact, the managerial literature still carries "reports from the field" of successful attempts and bromides for action in the application of MBO principles. Of interest is the variety of industries in which MBO has been applied in recent years. A computer search in the spring of 1996 yielded papers from industries as diverse as banking, engineering, customer service, telemarketing, total quality management (TQM), distribution and transportation, public administration, voluntary associations, and even re-engineering projects. So although MBO is not as popular today as it once was, it is not yet dead. Still not clear is the efficacy of MBO in governmental settings. There are mixed reports on whether, how well, and under what types of circumstances MBO has a chance of succeeding in government bureaus and agencies (compare Rodgers, 1992, with Halpern and Osofsky, 1990).

The Prognosis for MBO

What is the future of MBO programs? Perspectives on this question vary, of course, depending on who holds them. Nevertheless, it is useful to recall the conclusions reached by Kondrasuk (1981), who has summarized the early research on MBO effectiveness. His analysis suggests that MBO seems to be more effective in the private sector than in the public sector, in the short run (as opposed to the long run), and in work settings that are buffered from customers. When we consider these conclusions in light of observations made by two organizational theorists, Hofstede (1978) and McCaskey (1974), we are able to understand them more clearly, as well as gain some basis for speculating about the future facing MBO and MBO-like programs.

Hofstede (1978) noted that to be effective, MBO and other managerial control programs like it require three necessary conditions. First, it must be possible to identify standards that represent the organization's objectives, presumably at all of its levels. Second, it must be possible to actually measure performance against these standards. Finally, it must be possible for the organization to implement any changes needed, to close whatever gaps are observed, when actual performance is compared with objectives.

In addition to Hofstede's (1978) observations, consider an argument raised two decades ago by McCaskey (1974). According to McCaskey, organizational planning does not necessarily require the setting and pursuit of goals. Instead, he claims, there are some situations in which it is more appropriate to plan by identifying domains and directions the organization wishes to pursue. A domain is a general area in which the organization wishes to operate (such as the production and sale of heavy equipment or the provision of medical care to low-income families). A direction consists of a person's (or an organization's) tendencies and favored styles of perceiving and acting (McCaskey, 1974, p. 283). In other words, planning without goals consists of deciding the general arena of activities in which the organization will operate and the general style of operations that will be undertaken. But it avoids setting targets and goals. The means are more important than the ends, and it is recognized that the organization may wish to change course at any time on the basis of its interactions with its environment.

According to McCaskey (1974), this type of planning is most appropriate in the following types of circumstances:

1. When it is too early in the organization's existence to set agreed-upon goals
2. When the organization's environment is unstable and highly uncertain
3. When members of the organization cannot build enough trust or agreement among themselves to make it possible to agree upon goals
4. When the people involved, because of a high tolerance for ambiguity or a preference for risk and excitement, prefer the uncertainty and flexibility that is most likely in the absence of goals

It is always difficult to forecast the future, and organizational theorists have been no more successful at it than any other futurists, but the creative application of the points raised by Hofstede and McCaskey helps explain some of the reasons for the comparative success of MBO in the types of settings noted by Kondrasuk (1981). First, it stands to reason that MBO has been more successful in short-run intervals than over longer periods. There are increasing odds that the appropriateness of goals and action plans in pursuit of those goals will diminish as more time transpires after they are established. The total amount of change in the environment facing any organization will grow as a function of time, and as noted by McCaskey (1974), change and uncertainty make goal setting risky and inappropriate.

What about Kondrasuk's (1981) observation that MBO has been more effective in contexts that are removed from customers? The activities of the organization and people in any organization's environment are the major sources of uncertainty facing that organization. It is easier to program activities within one's own organization than it is to predict (let alone control) events beyond its boundaries (Thompson, 1967). Therefore, there is little wonder that MBO, which requires a degree of stability in the environment, fares better in contexts that are buffered from customers (whose tastes, expectations, and demands are constantly subject to change).

Now consider the superior performance of MBO in the private sector to that in the public sector (Halpern and Osofsky, 1990) and the three necessary conditions identified by Hofstede (1978): the setting of standards, the measurement of performance, and the capacity to change so as to bring performance into line with standards. It is generally much more feasible to set standards and measure performance against those standards in private enterprise than in government and public organizations (Bower, 1977). Consider, for example, the comparative ease of setting objectives for production, sales, inventory levels, and market penetration, as opposed to setting goals for the provision of social services. Although surrogate measures are often used in public (and service) organizations as a means of monitoring activity, these measures are often crude and relate primarily to inputs rather than outputs. As a result, the behavior of bureaucrats often becomes directed more toward "looking good" on input measures than toward actually pursuing the overall goals of the bureau or agency (e.g., P. M. Blau, 1963; Merton, 1968). In other words, goal attainment becomes more important than performance.

Similarly, even in those cases in government organizations where standards can be set and performance can be assessed, the political realities facing public organizations often prevent ameliorative action from being taken. In addition, many of the problems that governments tackle (such as reducing inflation or increasing trade with other countries) are almost intractable. Even within private-sector organizations, it has been noted that the setting and quantification of goals is one of the most commonly mentioned complaints about MBO programs (C. Stein, 1975). The point is that the very nature of government organizations and the work they seek to accomplish violate the three necessary conditions identified by Hofstede (1978) for the effectiveness of MBO and programs like it. A similar argument can be made for many service organizations in the private sector.

So—is there a future for MBO? The author agrees with E. A. Locke's position (personal communication, 1997) that although formal MBO programs are far less popular today than they were two decades ago, formal MBO programs are likely to become even less numerous in the years ahead, because the nature of work and of work organizations is moving further away from the conditions that Hofstede and others have identified as critical for it to flourish. Nevertheless, the setting of goals and many of the practices associated with goal-setting theory (as described in this chapter) are highly popular and are likely to grow in popularity. Practitioners are well advised to learn from goal-setting principles: They are a key element of the achievements of successful people and they are ingrained to varying degrees in the policies and practices of most work organizations (Covey, 1989).

LOOKING AHEAD: A SLIGHT CHANGE OF PERSPECTIVE

In the next chapter we turn from theories of work motivation that rely heavily on cognitive processes toward a different perspective—one that in its earliest and purest forms ignored and even denied the role of mental factors in the causes of behavior in general and work motivation in particular. We will see that this perspective has enjoyed less success in the past two decades than in the 1960s and 1970s, but that it has evolved to incorporate some of the insights found in cognitive models, particularly goal setting. In fact, the hybrized new theory and the techniques that derive from it comprise the most feasible approach to understanding and managing work motivation available today.

CHAPTER

Learning Theories of Work Behavior

14

*Men are the sport of circumstances,
when the circumstances seem the sport of men.*
—Lord Byron

*I don't believe in circumstances. The people who go on in this world
are the people who get up and look for the circumstances they want.*
—G. B. Shaw

Different general views about the fundamental nature of human beings come and go in the behavioral sciences. We saw, for example, that the idea of instincts was acceptable to psychologists in the early part of this century and that the concept of needs displaced instincts sometime during the 1930s. During the 1940s, a school of thought that came with a number of headings, but with *behaviorism* as its most common title, gained ascendancy. The single most basic tenet of behaviorism is that behavior is determined by its consequences: There is no need to refer to mysterious, unobservable inner states such as instincts, needs, emotions, or thoughts. The focus of this school of thought was upon *learning* rather than motivation per se, and internal processes such as motivation were not considered relevant.

Behaviorism grew in popularity and influence in psychology in the 1950s. By the 1960s it had nearly eclipsed other approaches to modern psychology. By the 1970s, behaviorism had gained a position of hegemony in many applied areas of psychology, such as clinical psychology, organizational behavior, and management. But by the 1980s, behaviorism seemed to have achieved its zenith and psychology was witnessing the ascendancy of cognitive theories and models of human functioning. A battle was under way in Western science about the relative merits of the behaviorist camp, the cognitive camp, and others. By then (e.g., Pinder, 1984), behaviorism had, in fact, made a number of important contributions to organizational behavior but it seemed that this school of thought in its purest, noncognitive manifestations had experienced its zenith and, perhaps, was on the way out of thinking about organizational behavior in general and about work motivation in particular. What remains of this school of thought today is a hybrid version of the original, one that adopts and incorporates many essential elements from cognitive psychology, such as those we discussed in chapter 13. In retrospect, the marriage of the two schools was not as difficult as one might have predicted 20 years ago given the entrenched ideological differences between the two basic schools of thought (see Karmel, 1980).[1]

Blending Learning and Motivation

In what follows it is important to remember that the focus is on human learning as much as it is on human motivation. In fact, the blend of attention between learning and motivation changes gradually as the chapter develops and we tell the story of how the "radical behaviorism" of the 1950s and 1960s gradually gave way to the hybrid models of social learning theory and social cognitive theory that dominate the field today.

Overview of the Current Chapter

The first part of the chapter deals with the basic tenets of radical behaviorism (or operant psychology). The second part adopts a historical dimension and deals first with behavior modification in general terms and then with *organizational behavior modification* (or *applied behavior analysis*), telling the story of how the behaviorist camp gradually incorporated elements of cognitive psychology into its thinking (see Komaki, 1986; Kreitner and Luthans, 1984). Then we examine *social cognitive theory,* the next body of thought to emerge from this tradition, a school that openly incorporates concepts from goal setting and control theory. The chapter finishes with a discussion of self-regulation, a set of applied techniques that people can learn to apply to encourage or discourage aspects of their own behavior.

Why Include Behaviorism at All?

If it is true that behaviorism has had its day—for the time being, at least—in the study of organizational behavior, why is it included in this book at all? There are a number of answers to this question. First, although it may no longer dominate thinking about work-related matters, behaviorism has left its legacy in the thinking and writing of much current theory and research in organizational behavior. Second (and related to the first point), there are still a number of people in the field who prefer the root assumptions made by behaviorism: They find it intellectually more reasonable to think about the antecedents and consequences of human action than of black box concepts such as needs, beliefs, expectations, values, and other hypothetical constructs. Third, there are still a number of precepts of the behaviorist model that have value in understanding and managing human behavior: Although the entire theory has been dis-

---

[1]There are cognitive theorists such as Locke (1979) who claim that there was little in the way of blending but that, instead, the operant approach merely gave way to cognitive theory out of necessity. At least one adherent of the behaviorist camp (e.g., Komaki, 1986) sees matters differently. She claims that her approach has enjoyed an ongoing, mutually beneficial relationship with the rest of the field, at least through the mid-1980s. This author believes that the truth is found in a blend of their two positions.

placed from its position of hegemony, it is not altogether "wrong" in what it has to say about the human condition. In fact, *functional analysis* (Komaki, Coombs, and Schepman, 1991) can be a useful perspective for helping us understand many organizational phenomena, after they occur, by breaking events down into their antecedents, the behaviors that occur, and the consequences of those behaviors (into A–B–C sequences). The current survey and analysis of theories of work motivation would be incomplete without a summary of what the behaviorist camp taught us over the past half-century.

Finally, who knows when the pendulum may swing back in the direction of a model of human functioning that revitalizes some or all of the tenets of behaviorism? As we will see, elements of it are to be found in the body of work referred to as *social cognitive theory*. With all of these historical issues and rationales in mind, we turn now to a study of the operant-conditioning camp in the study of human behavior. We begin by looking at the radical behaviorism of decades ago to provide a basis for understanding the tempered influence that it still has in our thinking about work motivation.

BASIC TENETS OF RADICAL BEHAVIORISM

In contrast to the need-based and cognitive/perceptual models of human functioning (Walter and Marks, 1981) that underlie the theories of work motivation presented in the rest of this volume, the major school of thought, variously referred to as *behaviorism, behavioral learning theory,* and/or *operant conditioning,* avoids reliance on concepts such as perceptions, beliefs, attitudes, intentions, and motivation for understanding and predicting human behavior. The emphasis is on human learning, not on motivation. The major tenet of the radical behaviorist approach is simply that behavior is a joint function of human genetic endowment and environmental contingencies. Although proponents of this school do not deny that people have needs, beliefs, attitudes, values, intentions, and the like, they do not invoke such concepts, either to study or to influence human behavior. To quote B. F. Skinner (1953),[2] the eminent psychologist whose work provides the foundation of this school: "When we say that a man eats because he is hungry, smokes a great deal because he has a tobacco habit . . . or plays the piano well because of his musical ability, we seem to be referring to causes. But on analysis these phrases prove to be merely redundant descriptions. A single set of facts is described by the two statements 'He eats' and 'He is hungry.' The practice of explaining one statement in terms of another is dangerous because it suggests that we have found the cause and therefore need search no further" (p. 31).

So to state that an employee works hard because she is loyal to her company does not really explain anything; it merely repeats the same information. The important thing

---

[2]It must be noted at the outset that there is no single, unified school of modern behaviorism, notwithstanding the common tendency to assume that there is (M. J. Mahoney, 1974, p. 9). Rather, a continuum of schools of behaviorism exists, representing a number of perspectives differing among themselves in a variety of ways, the most important of which have to do with the role and importance of cognitive processes in human learning and behavior (Kazdin, 1978; M. J. Mahoney, 1974, chap. 2). Accordingly, although we draw most heavily from Skinner's behaviorism in this chapter, the reader is cautioned that even by his own admission, Skinner (1974) did not represent the voice of all behaviorism. Our reliance here on his work is based on three things: (1) the fact that it is at least as well known as any other school of behaviorism; (2) its obvious importance in modern psychology during the 1960s and 1970s; and (3) the fact that it, more than any other brand of behaviorism, is most often cited by organizational scientists in particular.

is the behavior: The person either works hard or she doesn't. B. F. Skinner (1971) writes: "We may . . . be disturbed by the fact that many young people work as little as possible, or that workers are not very productive and often absent [from their jobs], or that products are often of poor quality, but we shall not get far by inspiring a 'sense of craftsmanship or pride in one's work,' or a 'sense of the dignity of labor.'. . . Something is wrong with the contingencies which induce men to work industriously and carefully" (p. 157).

Again, adherents to this school do not deny that people experience emotions, or that they perceive things in their environments and formulate beliefs. But they consider these hypothetical factors as merely accompanying behavior, not causing it. In one of his early books, B. F. Skinner (1953) wrote: "The objection to inner states is not that they do not exist, but that they are not relevant in a functional [causal] analysis. We cannot account for the behavior of any system while staying wholly inside it; eventually we must turn to forces operating upon the organism from without" (p. 35). Hence, an employee may experience what he calls pride in his work or "satisfaction with his employer," but these feelings simply accompany the behavior of the person on his job: They do not cause it or account for it.

Even the very concept of motivation is questioned by many behaviorists when the term is used to imply an internal causal force that cannot be observed directly (Luthans and Ottemann, 1977). To attribute behavior to motivation, as in the statement "Barry works hard at his job because he is a highly motivated fellow," is as redundant as the examples of eating, smoking, and piano playing cited by Skinner. Motivation does not cause behavior—the contingencies of the environment do. On the other hand, behaviorists often use mentalistic terminology out of necessity and convenience, and for descriptive purposes (B. F. Skinner, 1974). For example, a behaviorist who says "Barry is motivated" does not mean to imply that any real or physical entity called motivation exists within Barry, causing him to work hard; instead, the behaviorist would be utilizing the term *motivated* to summarize Barry's behavior descriptively. It is the process of reifying concepts (such as motivation) from descriptive terms into terms that imply the existence of inferred behavior-causing entities that is rejected by behaviorists (Craighead, Kazdin, and Mahoney, 1976).

Operant Behavior

According to B. F. Skinner and most of those who have followed in his tradition, it is useful to categorize behavior into two general types. One type is referred to as *respondent behavior,* which consists of acts that are reflexive, or unlearned. Sneezing or jerking one's knee when it is tapped with a doctor's hammer are examples. Respondent behavior occurs in response to something in the environment. The second general category of behavior consists of most of the important acts human beings display. These are learned behaviors that operate on the environment to generate consequences, hence they are called *operant behaviors.* Whereas respondent behavior is elicited by a prior stimulus, operant behavior is emitted to produce a consequence. The environment acts on the person to produce respondent behavior, while operant behavior consists of the person's acting on the environment. For example, an employee who is confronted by a hostile supervisor may witness an increase in heartbeat, a pair of sweaty palms, and a flight response. The stimulus that caused these behaviors is the boss, and the "nervous" reactions are respondent behaviors. Alternatively, the employee may approach his boss with a view to making peace and mollifying him. This action would be classified as operant behavior. It is initiated by the person to operate on a part of his environment, in this case, his boss.

What Is Operant Conditioning?

Operant conditioning is the process of changing the frequency or probability of occurence of operant behaviors as a result of the consequences that follow them. For example, the employee who applies diplomacy to the problem with his superior successfully will be more likely to try this sort of (operant) behavior again in similar circumstances in the future. Alternatively, the negative consequences of his attempt at diplomacy may teach him not to try it again. The mechanisms through which the future probabilities of operant behaviors are influenced are referred to as *reinforcement* and *punishment.* (We will return to them shortly.)

Functional Analysis and Contingencies

Most of the important behavior we observe in organizations is learned, either before or after people enter them. This learning occurs in the context of stimuli, or cues made up of such things as the organization's structure, the work group, the supervisor, the job description, telephone calls, and so on. Operant learning occurs when people behave in response to these cues in certain ways, and in turn, when consequences follow from their behaviors. The process of breaking behavioral events down into their antecedents, the behavior itself, and the consequences that follow it is called *functional analysis* (see Komaki et al., 1991). All three elements must be examined to understand behavior (B. F. Skinner, 1969). Important organizational consequences include the approval or disapproval of co-workers, money, fatigue, promotions, and the many other things that we have referred to as *outcomes* in earlier chapters. When consequences such as these are directly tied to certain behaviors, they are said to be *contingent* on those behaviors. For example, commission is a form of pay that is directly contingent on the volume of product sold by a salesperson. Similarly, fatigue is usually contingent on hard work. Finally, when consequences bear no relationship to behavior, they are said to be noncontingent upon that behavior, as is the case in pay schemes such as salaries under which people are paid simply with the passage of intervals of time. We will return to functional analysis later in the chapter, after we examine in more detail the concepts of contingency and the consequences of behavior.

The Consequences of Behavior

According to the operant-conditioning approach, behavior occurring in a particular context can be followed by any of three types of consequences. These are referred to as reinforcement, punishment, and neutral stimuli. *Reinforcement* is defined as a consequence of behavior that increases the probability that an act will occur again in the future. *Punishment* is a consequence of behavior that reduces the probability of further occurrences of the act. Finally, sometimes neither reinforcement nor punishment is contingent on an act. In other words, there is no change in the person's environment as a consequence of his behavior. When this occurs, the act tends to cease. For example, a person who repeatedly puts a coin into a candy machine and receives nothing in return tends to stop investing in the recalcitrant machine. As a second example, a whining child who is ignored tends (eventually) to stop whining. Finally, an employee who wisecracks to his superior will tend to stop if no one (including his workmates) provides him with any reinforcement. The process of disconnecting a behavior and the consequences that formerly reinforced it is referred to as *extinction* (Craighead et al., 1976).

The Law of Effect

The relationship between contingent consequences and operant behavior is summarized in the *law of effect*. Although the general gist of this law appeared as early as a century ago in the writings of Herbert Spencer (1870), its first formal articulation was made by Thorndike (1911): "Of several responses made to the same situation, those which are accompanied or closely followed by satisfaction to the animal will, other things being equal, be more firmly connected with the situation, so that, when it recurs, they will be more likely to recur; those which are accompanied or closely followed by discomfort to the animal will, other things being equal, have their connections with that situation weakened, so that, when it recurs, they will be less likely to occur. The greater the satisfaction or discomfort, the greater the strengthening or weakening of the bond" (p. 244). Thorndike was aware that many of his critics would object to his reliance on subjective terms, such as satisfaction and comfort (they sound very cognitive), so he explained further: "By a satisfying state of affairs is meant one which the animal does nothing to avoid, often doing such things as attain and preserve it. By a discomforting or annoying state of affairs is meant one which the animal commonly avoids and abandons" (Thorndike, 1911, p. 245).

The law of effect has been subjected to a variety of attacks over the years on numerous logical, philosophical, and empirical grounds. A review of these issues is beyond our present purpose. Suffice it to say that its modern form, the *empirical law of effect* (of which there is more than one version), remains one of the most important tenets of behaviorism today. The empirical law of effect states that "the consequence of a response is an important determinant of whether the response will be learned" (Wilcoxon, 1969, p. 28). In other words, people tend to do those things that they find positive and they tend not to do those things that they learn to be aversive. Hence, if an employee associates high rates of pay with high levels of job performance, she will tend to behave in ways that she has learned are conducive to high performance.

When a behavior occurs and is followed by a desirable consequence, that behavior is said to be reinforced (meaning strengthened). The odds will increase that the person will behave in a similar fashion on future occasions that are similar. On the other hand, if the behavior results in aversive consequences, that behavior will be less probable in future similar circumstances, and it is said to have been punished. But desirable and undesirable consequences in organizations are only partially contingent on the behavior or the performance of employees. Accordingly, we can consider a range of relationships that may exist between behavior and its consequences. These behavior–consequence relationships are referred to as *schedules of reinforcement,* and the control of these schedules constitutes the application of operant conditioning in work organizations, educational institutions, clinical settings, and the like. Figure 14-1 illustrates the most common forms of reinforcement schedules.

		Basis of Distribution of Reinforcement	
		Occurrence of Behavior	Passage of Time
Constancy of Schedule	Fixed	1. Fixed Ratio	3. Fixed Interval
	Variable	2. Variable Ratio	4. Variable Interval

FIGURE 14-1   Intermittent Reinforcement Schedules

Schedules of Reinforcement

The simplest type of reinforcement schedule is referred to as *continuous*. When every instance of a particular behavior is reinforced, the schedule is defined as continuous. However, if reinforcement is provided after only some occurrences of an act, the schedule is defined as *intermittent,* or *partial.* Continuous and intermittent schedules each have some important characteristics and some important differences. First, new learning occurs fastest when the behavior being acquired is reinforced continuously. For example, a new employee who is learning how to set up a jig on a lathe will learn more quickly if he is reinforced every time he does it correctly. On the other hand, behavior that is reinforced by a continuous schedule for an ongoing period of time is more susceptible to extinction when, for whatever reason, the reinforcement stops or fails to occur following any particular occurrence of the act. Moreover, once a behavior has been learned, it will occur at higher frequency levels (and perhaps more intensely) when it is reinforced intermittently. For example, employees who have been taught to be polite to customers through the use of continuous reinforcement will be more likely to continue being polite if their supervisors decrease the frequency of reinforcement for courteous behaviors to an intermittent schedule.

Types of Intermittent Schedules

It is possible to administer intermittent reinforcement in a variety of ways. Sometimes reinforcement occurs only after the emission of a certain number of the desired behaviors; in other words, it is possible to assure that the reinforcement is contingent only upon behavior. Such schedules are called *ratio schedules,* because reinforcers are dispensed according to some proportion of the instances when the behavior occurs (e.g., every fourth time). Alternatively, it is possible to administer reinforcement following the passage of certain periods of time, such that, for example, the first desired response following the designated period (say, one hour) produces a reinforcer. Schedules of this sort are called *interval schedules.*

Aside from whether they are granted on the basis of some ratio with the occurrence of behavior or whether certain periods of time must elapse as well, we can also consider intermittent reinforcement on the basis of whether the ratio or the time interval used is constant, or changing and variable. Hence, we can consider the four different types of reinforcement schedules illustrated in Figure 14-1. Let's consider some examples of these various types of intermittent reinforcement. A fixed-ratio schedule is one in which the reinforcement follows every *n*th occurrence of an act. For instance, an employee who is paid a fee after every fourth delivery of materials to a warehouse is being reinforced under a fixed-ratio arrangement (see cell [1] of Figure 14-1). Notice that continuous reinforcement is a special case of a fixed-ratio schedule in which the ratio is 1:1. However, if the employee is paid *on average every fourth time, but not every fourth time per se,* we would say that he is being compensated according to a variable-ratio schedule (cell [2] of Figure 14-1).

As an illustration of how interval schedules might work, consider a sales representative who is being encouraged by her sales manager to make follow-up visits with her customers. If the sales manager acknowledges only those visits that occur at the beginning of every month, for example, and ignores those visits made by the sales rep during the middle of the month, the manager is using a fixed-interval schedule (cell [3]), in which the interval is one month. However, if the manager reinforces only those customer visits undertaken by the rep after one week, then three days, then four weeks, then eight days (and so on), he would be employing a variable interval schedule (cell [4]). In short, the passage of a particular period of time is necessary for the administration of a reinforcer or punisher under an interval schedule, but it is not sufficient: In addition, once the designated interval has passed, the person must perform the act that is being encouraged or discouraged.

Once a behavior has been learned, it can be encouraged through the careful use of intermittent schedules. Ratio schedules are superior to interval schedules for this purpose (because they are directly contingent on the occurrence of the desired acts without the necessity of the passage of time), and variable-ratio schedules are more effective than fixed-ratio schedules. Notice that under a variable-ratio schedule (e.g., that in slot machines), the person knows that he will be "paid off" every *n*th time, on average. But he is never sure whether any specific occurrence of his behavior will be rewarded. Moreover, once the desired act has been acquired and developed, a variable-ratio schedule can be made more lean or "stretched," meaning that the ratio of reinforcements to occurrences of the behavior can be reduced. For example, after we train a sales representative to be courteous to customers by using a continuous (or nearly continuous) schedule, we can reduce the ratio of reinforcements to occurrences of polite behaviors by reinforcing, say, every fifth or sixth occurrence on average, and then eventually cutting back on the frequency of reinforcements so that, on average, the ratio of reinforcements to behaviors becomes smaller and smaller. In practice, it becomes increasingly less necessary to reinforce behavior after it is learned.[3]

In summary, we can state the following about reinforcement schedules: (1) New learning is acquired most rapidly when it is conducted under a continuous schedule of reinforcement; (2) however, once a behavior has been acquired, it is best to begin reducing the frequency of reinforcements to some form of intermittent schedule, because they are more resistant to extinction; (3) ratio schedules result in higher levels of per-

---

[3]Once again, the reader is reminded that the phenomenon of interest in operant psychology is learning, not motivation.

formance of an act than do interval schedules, because the former are entirely behavior-based, whereas the latter are based on both time and behavior; and (4) the highest rates of behavior occur under variable- (as opposed to fixed-) ratio schedules.

Although the foregoing discussion has focused on schedules of reinforcement, we must note that punishment also occurs according to either continuous or intermittent schedules as well, although the effects of punishment under these alternative schedules are different from the effects of reinforcement. More will be said about punishment shortly.

Negative Reinforcement

Organizational scientists and managers often misuse behavior modification terminology and concepts (Heiman, 1975; Mawhinney, 1975). Perhaps the best example of this concerns the misuse of the concept of negative reinforcement. *Negative reinforcement is not punishment.* Like positive reinforcement, negative reinforcement strengthens the probability that a person will perform an act. By definition, punishment reduces such a probability. In fact, punishment refers to the presentation of an aversive agent or event, or the removal of a positive agent or event following a response, reducing the probability of that response in similar future circumstances. To be considered punishment, however, the act of either adding or removing an agent must result in a reduction in the frequency of occurrence of the act.

Notice that what some people find punishing may be reinforcing for others. For example, some people enjoy an evening at a Broadway musical, whereas others hate it. But whereas positive reinforcement involves the application of some circumstance (such as a pat on the back or a Friday afternoon off work), negative reinforcement entails the removal of some circumstance that was previously part of the environmental context. For instance, being permitted to return to day shift as a consequence of good performance on night shift is a negatively reinforcing consequence of effective job behavior for those employees who find night work aversive. Being transferred from a remote outpost as a consequence of good work is another example of negative reinforcement (for many people at least). Notice that the things that are negatively reinforcing for some people may not be negatively reinforcing for others, just as what some people find positively reinforcing may have no impact on the behavior probabilities of others. (For example, many people are not bothered at all by the winter weather in Winnipeg and Minneapolis.) We can classify the concepts of positive reinforcement, negative reinforcement, and punishment quite simply by considering whether the consequence that follows an act increases or decreases the frequency of the act, and whether it is applied or taken away. See Figure 14-2.

Reinforcers: The Agents and Events of Reinforcement

Now that we have discussed the nature of reinforcement and punishment and have differentiated between positive and negative reinforcement, let's take a closer look at those consequences that are reinforcing to people—the reinforcers. As will be shown shortly, there are a variety of things that can be reinforcing, although it must be reiterated that different people will have their behaviors made more frequent (reinforced) by the administration of different types of positive and negative things (see Dickson, Saunders, and Stringer, 1993).

Effect on Frequency of Behavior	Consequence	
	Applied	Removed
Increases	Positive Reinforcement	Negative Reinforcement
Decreases	Punishment by Application	Punishment by Removal

FIGURE 14-2   Summary of Reinforcement and Punishment Terminology

Primary and Secondary Reinforcers

An agent or event that increases the probability of an act is referred to as a reinforcer. Many reinforcers (such as food and water) are called *primary reinforcers* because they are reinforcing unto themselves; a person does not need to learn of their reinforcing value. People who are hungry and thirsty can derive reinforcement from food and water without having them linked to any other reinforcers. On the other hand, certain reinforcing agents and events acquire their capacity to increase the probability of particular behaviors through their learned association with other (primary) reinforcers. These are called *secondary reinforcers.* Money is the most important example in organizational settings. By itself, pay has no primary reinforcement capacity, but people quickly learn that pay can be used to acquire those things that do possess primary reinforcing value (e.g., food, shelter, status). It is important to recognize that not all primary reinforcers will always have the capacity to reinforce behavior. For example, food may lose its capacity to change a person's behavior if the person is not hungry. Similarly, potential secondary reinforcers such as praise may not have the same reinforcing power for some people as they do for others.

Generalized Conditioned Reinforcers

Some reinforcers are particularly potent for influencing the probability of the occurrence of behavior because they are themselves reinforcing. Again, money is a good example: Because it becomes associated, through learning, with a wide variety of other consequences that have either primary or secondary reinforcement value, it is particularly reinforcing. Attention and the approval of other people are other examples of such generalized reinforcers (B. F. Skinner, 1953), because they are usually accompanied by physical contact, praise, kindly remarks, and support of various other forms, including the possibility of the provision of primary reinforcers (such as physical warmth or food).

Behaviors as Reinforcers: The Premack Principle

The reinforcers discussed to this point have all been stimuli of some sort or another, stimuli that are either provided or removed contingent on behavior. However, it is possible for behaviors to have reinforcing qualities of their own. That is, permitting a person to work at a favored task contingent on the completion of a less preferred task can actually increase the probability that the person will engage in the former task. This phenomenon is called the *Premack principle* (Mawhinney, 1979; Premack, 1971).[4] For example, an employee who dislikes the paperwork associated with inventory control but does enjoy using new inventory to build retail sales displays might be reinforced to keep better inventory records (and to keep them more up to date) if opportunities to participate in the design and construction of displays was permitted only upon the completion of inventory work. Like all of the other reinforcers that have been discussed, this activity reinforcer can be administered according to either a continuous reinforcement schedule or any of the intermittent schedules that were discussed above.

The Multiplicity of Reinforcers

It is important to recognize that social situations can include many sources of both reinforcement and punishment for people. Work settings are no exception (Komaki et al., 1991). In fact, the application of behavior modification principles, for either understanding or influencing employee behavior, must recognize that the organization's official reward system (or reinforcement system, in operant-conditioning terms) is only one of several systems that can dispense reinforcements and punishments for individuals. For example, employees who work in groups quickly learn that co-workers can control both reinforcers (in the form of social acceptance and social status) and punishers (through the removal of approval and status). The point is that managers must remember that they are only one source of reinforcement and punishment for their employees; attempts to shape or influence their subordinates' behavior through the use of formally sanctioned rewards and punishments will be limited to the extent that they are consistent with the reinforcement and punishment contingencies people receive from other sources in the work setting (Jablonsky and DeVries, 1972; W. F. Whyte, 1972).

Behavior Shaping

Sometimes the behavior we want to encourage in others is so complex that it does not occur spontaneously, in pure form. Complex behaviors that consist of a number of elements (such as swinging a golf club properly) may be developed, however, if successive approximations to them are reinforced. In other words, we begin by reinforcing behaviors that bear even the slightest resemblance to the behavior we ultimately wish to develop. Continuous and variable-ratio schedules are used initially, but the standard required for reinforcement increases as the person proceeds, meaning that behaviors increasingly closer to the final one become required for a reinforcement to be earned—a sort of successive approximations approach.

For example, an employee who has had difficulty interacting with customers would initially be reinforced for even the slightest attempts to be friendly, such as smiling at them or at least not leaving the room when customers enter. After a while,

---

[4]We anticipated a variant of this principle in chapter 4 and again in chapter 13, where we discussed the issue of self-regulation. Although the treatment in those earlier chapters did not espouse a behaviorist view of the world, the applied implications were virtually the same as those here: People can reward themselves by sequencing the events that impinge upon them, such that their preferred experiences are self-administered as rewards (or, as a behaviorist would call them, as reinforcers).

however, positive reinforcement would be received only for more friendly behaviors, such as asking customers whether they need service. Desirable behaviors are reinforced while irrelevant or inappropriate behaviors are extinguished. Eventually, the employee can be placed on a variable-ratio schedule of reinforcement for performing the ultimately desired acts, and the ratio gradually reduced. This process is referred to as *behavior shaping*. Many of the acts we perform every day, such as driving a car, writing a letter, and being a parent, are learned through behavior shaping. They are far too complex to learn all at once.

Functional Analysis

It was noted earlier in this chapter that functional analysis explains behavior by looking at both the conditions that precede it and the consequences that follow it. To this point, we have focused largely on the consequences of behavior. What about the antecedents?

Prompts

A reinforcement not only increases the probability of the behavior it follows but also contributes to bringing that behavior under the control of whatever stimuli are present when the behavior occurs (Reynolds, 1975). In other words, when a particular act occurs and is reinforced in the presence of a certain type of stimulus, the presence of that stimulus itself can increase the frequency of the act (or *prompt* it). For example, a manager's instructions to a group of employees can set the group in motion. A parent's gesture to her child can often control the child's behavior (but not always, of course). When a particular prompt (or cue) initiates behavior that is subsequently reinforced, it is called a *discriminative stimulus*. A discriminative stimulus sets the occasion for behavior to unfold; it increases the probability that a behavior will follow. It signals the fact that a reinforcement may be following, although by itself, it does not actually elicit behavior. Nevertheless, after such a stimulus has been associated with enough reinforcement experiences, it can take on reinforcing qualities of its own, permitting the person to learn elaborate sequences of behaviors called chains.

Chaining

A *chain* is a series of behaviors that are linked together by stimuli that act both as reinforcers and as discriminative stimuli. A chain starts with the presentation of a discriminative stimulus. When the person responds in the appropriate manner in the presence of that stimulus, a reinforcer follows. This reinforcer often serves as a second discriminative stimulus, which makes the next appropriate response more probable (but not definite). Similarly, if the response that results is appropriate, it, in turn, is followed by reinforcement, which then prompts a third behavior. The sequence can go on and on until, ultimately, a primary or secondary reinforcer results that is sufficient to put an end to the sequence and to reinforce all of it.

Consider the writing of a business letter to order a shipment of new raw materials for a production shop. The original discriminative stimulus might simply be the time of year (such as the end of September, when orders are normally placed), or a frantic telephone call from a foreman who is worried that the present inventory of materials is close to exhaustion. The chain that follows might be composed of a number of responses, such as uncovering a typewriter, putting a fresh sheet of paper in the roller of the typewriter, creating and typing the letter, preparing an envelope and sealing it (with the letter enclosed, of course), putting postage on the envelope, and depositing the letter in the mail slot early enough to make the morning's mail pickup. The stimulus that follows each behavior (such as a bare typewriter, a finished letter, an addressed envelope, and so on) prompts the next behavior in the chain, each of which, in turn, is reinforced by the stimulus which follows that. Ultimately, of course, the entire chain may be reinforced a week later by the arrival of new materials and by an end to the incessant reminders of the worried foreman. Notice that each of the behaviors in the chain can itself be composed of a chain of smaller behaviors. For instance, the very act of putting a fresh sheet of paper in the roller mechanism of a typewriter consists of a sequence of smaller microbehaviors, tied together in a sequence that has proven more or less successful in the past. Notice also the similarity between these chains and the concepts of feedback loops we encountered in connection with control theory in chapter 13.

Discrimination Learning

Not every discriminative stimulus, or prompt, results in reinforced behavior. In the context of some stimuli, a particular behavior may be reinforced, while in the context of other stimuli the same behavior may not be reinforced. For example, uttering a curse may result in the chuckles of one's workmates but pays off less well when one's spouse is present. People learn to discriminate among stimulus conditions in which particular acts are reinforcing and others are punishing. Accordingly, we can make use of this sort of learning by increasing or decreasing the probability of behaviors, by applying or removing the antecedent cues with which they are associated.

Let's look at an example. When a telephone rings (a discriminative stimulus), we are prompted to answer it, because previous experiences of a similar sort have generally been reinforcing. Each subact in the chain that constitutes answering the phone sets the stage for the one that follows. For instance, picking up the receiver is reinforced by hearing an open line, which, in turn, prompts the act of saying "Hello," which, in turn, is reinforced by the knowledge of who has called. Notice that the same behavior (lifting the receiver and saying hello) is not likely to occur without the presence of the initial discriminative stimulus (the ringing of the telephone's bell).

In summary, many behaviors consist of chains of less complex behaviors. Each of the elements of each chain sets the stage for, and simultaneously reinforces, other behaviors that follow from them. Functional analysis is the process of breaking a person's behavior patterns down into a series of antecedent–behavior–consequence (A–B–C) linkages for analysis. Only through a study of the specific cues that prompt a behavior, as well as of the particular reinforcers that follow it, can we understand behavior, let alone influence it.

Stimulus Generalization and Response Generalization

In the foregoing section, it was stated that people discriminate among stimulus conditions before behaving in certain ways. But human learning includes the opposite process as well. This is called *stimulus generalization*. University students are aware of the virtues of the various pedagogical techniques their professors use to teach them material. It is often said that cases are useful teaching (and learning) devices because they are more realistic or hands-on than are lectures or discussions of concepts and ideas. However, the best solution to one case may not be the best solution for any other case, either in reality or in the classroom setting.

Notice that if the process of discrimination went too far, the behavior of students would be idiosyncratic for every different problem they encounter. As a result, many professors try to have their students generalize their learning from one situation to another. In other words, students strive to recognize similarities among stimulus situations (such as case problems) so that they can invoke behavioral solutions that were learned in the context of one problem to deal with problems that are different to varying degrees (e.g., House, 1975). The skills of eating spaghetti are quite similar to those of eating linguini, so a gourmand who learns how to eat the former should also be proficient at eating the latter, through the process of stimulus generalization. Similarly, the behaviors necessary for negotiating with a union steward over an incipient grievance are similar to (but not identical with) those needed to negotiate a raise in pay from one's own boss. Similarity between antecedent contexts is a matter of degree, but effective functioning in our culture requires that we generalize our antecedent–behavior–consequences linkages from one setting to others that are sufficiently similar in important ways.

People also learn how to generalize the responses they make to stimuli. In other words, while stimulus generalization entails learning how to invoke the same behavior in response to a variety of similar antecedent conditions, response generalization entails learning to employ behaviors that are similar to one another in a given situation. To the extent that one behavior is similar to another (such as smiling and laughing), when one of the acts is reinforced, the other is also more likely to be reinforced.

An example from the work setting might be as follows: A supervisor instructs an employee to act safely when using dangerous equipment. The behaviors associated with "acting safely" are then reinforced. Other behaviors, such as speaking more quietly on the shop floor, keeping the work area clean, or even helping other employees improve the safety of their behaviors may also result. The employee's safety-related skills have generalized in this example to other behaviors that, for some reason, hold some similarity for the person involved. Research in behavior modification shows that it is not always possible to predict the exact form that response generalization may take for a given person. Two people may be reinforced for performing the same act but then generalize that act to entirely different subsequent behaviors. The analysis of operant behavior reveals that learning does not occur in a unique cue–unique behavior–unique reinforcement fashion. Rather, people respond to general similarities among stimulus situations using behaviors that have been learned in other circumstances. Similarly, the reinforcement of particular behaviors in situations may result in the reinforcement of similar behaviors in the same context.

To this point, the emphasis has been on influencing the probability of behavior through positive means. But we know that punishment can also be used to change the occurrence of behavior. Let's take a look at punishment and the nature of formal discipline procedures typically found in work settings.

Punishment

Of the three types of consequences that can result from behavior, none is more ubiquitous in nature and more controversial in practice than punishment. (Recall from our earlier discussion that reinforcement and extinction are the other two.) We learn a great deal from being punished. B. F. Skinner (1971) notes, for example: "A child runs awkwardly, falls, and is hurt; he touches a bee and is stung; he takes a bone from a dog and is bitten; and as a result he learns not to do these things again" (p. 60). Similarly, punishment and the fear of it are very common in day-to-day experience in organizations (Arvey and Ivancevich, 1980) largely because it is reinforcing to those who use it (e.g., G. L. Mayhew, 1979). In fact, the heavy reliance on punishment in the usual practice of management provided much of the impetus for the introduction of operant-conditioning techniques (with their emphasis on positive reinforcement) into the management literature (see Aldis, 1961; Nord, 1969). Yet, despite its ubiquity in work settings, very little work has been done to formally study the nature and consequences of punishment at work (Arvey and Ivancevich, 1980).

Defining Punishment

Recall that punishment is defined in terms of the impact it has on behavior. More specifically, punishment is "the presentation of an aversive event or the removal of a positive event following a response which decreases the frequency of that response" (Kazdin, 1975, pp. 33–34). It is important to remember that different people find different events punishing, just as differences exist among the things people find reinforcing. "Different strokes for different folks!" As a result, the conscious administration of punishment in organizational settings can be difficult: For example, whereas some employees find being assigned to night duty punishing, others favor night work (Frost and Jamal, 1979). Notice that the simple administration of aversive stimuli does not constitute punishment, according to this definition. Many negative things can occur in the workplace, but unless they are related to behavior and have the effect of reducing the future occurrences of that behavior, they cannot be classified as punishment per se.

The Effects of Punishment

It was stated above that the use of punishment has been controversial. Most of this controversy results from the actual and imagined effects it has on people. Skinner was responsible in some of his early work for giving punishment "a bad name," and many people accepted his position without question for many years, advocating the use of positive reinforcement instead, whenever possible. More recent evidence, however, suggests that although complex in its effects on behavior, punishment can be effective. In fact, it has been particularly useful in clinical settings as a therapeutic mechanism for dealing with a variety of deviant behaviors (Kazdin, 1975).

One review of the literature suggested that many of the adverse consequences traditionally attributed to it have not actually been demonstrated in research conducted in work organizations per se and that it is premature to discard punishment as a managerial technique (Arvey and Ivancevich, 1980). For example, conventional wisdom has held that punishment results in attempts to get back at the punishing agent or at least to avoid it. In organizational settings this would imply that punishment will result in deliberate attempts to seek revenge on a punishing supervisor, through acts such as physical aggression toward the supervisor or the work (displaced aggression). Alternatively, the conventional wisdom suggests that a punished employee will withdraw from the work setting either physically or psychologically.

Another belief about punishment is that its effects generalize to discourage behaviors similar to those being punished but that are not intended to be discouraged.

For example, it would be assumed that punishing an employee for aggressively questioning a client might generalize to reduce the likelihood that the employee will act in such a manner toward suppliers and competitors. A third criticism has been that punishment never totally eliminates a behavior. Rather, it has been assumed that punished behavior tends to disappear only when the punishing agent is present and that it often reappears when surveillance is discontinued. The implication is that managerial systems based on punishment require close supervision and all the costs associated with it. (One wonders, for example, whether reformed criminals are ever sorry for their crimes or whether their sorrow results only from having been caught and punished.)

In short, there have been a variety of dysfunctional side effects attributed to the use of punishment for changing human behavior, but the research evidence underlying these beliefs is sparse, particularly as it relates to work settings.

The Morality of Punishment

One interesting criticism raised about the use of punishment concerns its morality: Is it moral to punish another person? It is worthwhile to note that punishment can be either of two varieties: *retributional* and backward looking or *corrective* and forward looking. It may be that punishment that is intended to attain revenge is less ethical and less civilized than is punishment intended to prevent a person from behaving in undesired ways in the future. It is also useful to distinguish between punishment and the use of coercion (Walter and Marks, 1981). Whereas punishment involves the application of aversive consequences or the removal of positive consequences for behavior, coercion goes further. *Coercion* entails the extralegal use of threats, fear, terror, violence, and often the application of naked force. Coercion involves the misuse of power between two people or between a power figure and his followers (S. D. Cook, 1972). For example, the college professor who extorts sexual favors in exchange for grades is employing coercion, as is the supervisor who threatens to assign an employee systematically to unpleasant tasks if that employee participates in union organizing activities. It seems that coercion and retributional punishment are generally viewed in our culture as less ethical than corrective punishment—which is administered equitably, within the bounds of legitimate authority, and with a view to preventing further occurrences of dysfunctional or harmful behavior.

Making Punishment Effective

McGregor (quoted by Sayles and Strauss, 1977) noted years ago that to be effective, punishment should occur in practice, as similarly as possible, as it occurs in nature. In fact, he coined the *hot stove rule* to summarize his belief. According to this rule, the most effective punishment is that which is immediate, contingent upon behavior, intense (meaning not too severe but not without some pain), consistent, impersonal, and informational. In addition, an alternative to the punished act should be available. Hence, when a person touches a hot stove, what happens? The burn that results is punishing and it is felt immediately. It results from an unfortunate behavior (rather than from the passage of time or random events). If the stove is at all hot, the pain is intense. In addition, hot stoves play no favorites: They are impersonal and consistent, punishing anyone who touches them, every time they are touched. The experience also tends to be informational; that is, people normally infer quickly the cause of their suffering. Finally, there are usually alternatives to touching hot stoves, such as moving away and avoiding them in the future.

In short, according to McGregor, to be effective, punishment in organizations should have all these features. The review of the literature mentioned above (Arvey and Ivancevich, 1980) reconfirms most of McGregor's wisdom about punishment and adds that it is most effective when the punishing agent (e.g., a supervisor) has relatively close and friendly relations with the punished person, when the agent explains the reason for the punishment to the person, and when the person understands what the contingencies for punishment will be in the future. Finally, when alternatives to the punished behavior are positively reinforced, it is less likely to occur in the future (Arvey and Ivancevich, 1980).

Alternatives to Punishment

Although punishment occurs frequently on a day-to-day basis in organizations and may be more effective at eliminating behavior than has traditionally been believed, many supervisors would prefer to avoid using it when it is not necessary. Accordingly, a number of alternatives may be effective in some circumstances. One is to ignore the undesirable behavior and/or remove those aspects of the person's environment that reinforce it, thus bringing about extinction. Another alternative is to positively reinforce behaviors that are incompatible with the undesired behavior. For instance, many effective teachers have learned that reinforcing quiet, constructive study and play behavior can reduce the problems created by boisterous students.

Finally, it is often possible to combine these tactics into a careful form of environmental engineering. For example, many organizations in which smoking in particular rooms or offices is unwanted have found it beneficial to provide specially designated areas where smoking is permitted. Rather than displaying signs that say "No Smoking Allowed," they post signs saying "Smoking Allowed in This Area" in places where it is deemed appropriate. Many restaurants make active use of this approach. Similarly, it may be possible to reduce the amount of graffiti that is written on the walls of a washroom or work area if paper and pencils are provided in those areas as an alternative. The objective of environmental engineering is to anticipate the types of dysfunctional behaviors that might occur in particular settings and to take steps to make them impossible, or at least, nonreinforcing.

Organizational Discipline and Punishment

How do formal discipline policies and practices in work organizations compare to the principles of the hot stove? In many cases, not very well. For example, it is difficult in practice to make punishment immediate. This is particularly the case when policies require a series of appeals and quasi-legal investigations after a charge is laid. For example, more than a year and a half passed at a major Canadian university between the time when it was first alleged that a senior professor was misusing government research funds and the beginning of the period of suspension meted out as punishment for the offense. Compounding the problem, of course, is the difficulty of distributing punishments so that they are consistent and perceived as equitable (see chapter 11). Consistency can be difficult to achieve for a number of reasons. One of these is that different people are often responsible for distributing punishment. For example, the same employee may be susceptible to the approval and discipline of more than one supervisor, even though such reporting relationships violate the principle of unity of command. Sometimes an employee is punishable by his own superior as well as by his superior's boss.

A number of other factors can influence the consistency of the punishment administered by the same person, including, for example, the mood of the supervisor (Goodstadt and Kipnis, 1970) and the value of the employee to the organization (Rosen and Jerdee, 1974c). Also, a variety of factors in the work context can influence the degree to which accidents or mistakes are attributed to the individual employee (as opposed to factors beyond the employee's control). Hence, if supervisors are aware of the consequences of inappropriate employee behaviors, they are more likely to assume that the behavior will occur again and more likely to assume that the employee is responsible both for the behavior and for the outcome that follows from it (Mitchell and Kalb, 1981). Further, supervisors who have had experience working on a job are more likely to attribute mistakes made on that job to external factors beyond the employee's control.[5] As a result of these and other factors, the same supervisors can make differing interpretations of the culpability of their employees and, as a result, administer different types and amounts of punishment for the same misbehavior (Mitchell, Green, and Wood, 1981). Although hot stoves may be consistent in the way they punish, supervisors in complex work settings often are not.

Are discipline procedures intense? Generally, formal discipline policies are more progressive than immediately intense. This is commonly the case in unionized work settings, in which collective agreements may restrict the intensity of the punishment that can be meted out by supervisors. One writer, in fact, proposed a method of "progressive discipline" that he believed can obviate many of the negative side effects that have traditionally been attributed to punishment (Huberman, 1964). This approach entails a series of disciplinary measures that are applied following each transgression by a particular employee. For example, the first offense results in a casual reminder of the rules and a "note of correction." The second occurrence results in a private discussion in the boss's office. The third offense also results in a talk with the supervisor and includes a discussion of possible reassignment. Continued infractions result in suspensions, first with pay, then without. Ultimately, the employee is dismissed.

Although programs of this sort are common in organizations, they do violate the purely psychological prescriptions concerning the intensity of punishment. On the other hand, they favor the goals of consistency and impersonality and as a result are more defensible on legal grounds (see Fox, 1980–1981). Finally, they tend to be more readily accepted because of their apparent humanity and reasonableness.

Discipline in Arbitration Decisions

Arbitration decisions in unionized work settings have been studied to determine whether they are progressive and corrective or retributional, intense, and authoritarian (using the terms employed by the author of the study). The results suggest that correc-

---

[5]For a behaviorist, of course, the mood of the supervisor does not cause his use of discipline. Rather, the evasive behavior of the subordinate is the discriminative stimulus that occasions the use of discipline; the boss's mood is merely an accompanying (or collateral) emotional reaction.

tive and retributional decisions are almost equally common, although there are a number of offenses that tend to result more frequently in punitive decisions. These offenses are insubordination, illegal striking, and dishonesty (Wheeler, 1976).

Summary

Punishment is a major facet of the managerial styles employed in work organizations. It can be a very effective means of quickly eliminating undesired behaviors, so it is reinforcing to managers who employ it. A number of unintended side effects have been attributed to the use of punishment, although there is very little evidence that these occur in work settings among adults. In practice, disciplinary procedures tend to have features that make them only partially similar to the most effective forms of punishment found in nature, and formal organizational policies, as well as arbitrator decisions, seem to support this divergence, probably because nature's style of punishing people is deemed too harsh by civilized people. It must be remembered that, in practice, the use of punishment and discipline occurs within a social context in which norms of fairness are more or less in place and expected by everyone involved. As we saw in chapter 11, this means that organizational discipline must be administered in a manner that is fair and seen to be fair. It is not a simple issue.

Operant Conditioning and VIE Theory

At this point it may be instructive to compare and contrast the operant-conditioning approach to that of VIE theory.[6] First, we have mentioned many times that the two approaches make entirely different fundamental assumptions about human nature and the causes of behavior. VIE theory attributes behavior to internal beliefs and attitudes, while behavior modification rejects internal constructs in favor of the antecedent stimuli and external consequences of behavior (see Komaki, 1986, p. 301). Second, both theories include the notion of probabilities, but in different ways (Petrock and Gamboa, 1976). VIE theory speaks of the subjective probabilities in the minds of people in the form of expectancies and instrumentalities. Operant conditioning speaks of the probabilities and frequencies of behaviors occurring as a consequence of the reinforcements and punishments that result from behavior.

Both theories advocate that rewards (or reinforcers) be administered contingently upon behavior, as soon as possible after the desired behavior occurs. Notice, however, that operant conditioning holds variable-ratio schedules to be the most motivating in the long run, once a behavior has been learned, whereas VIE theory would suggest that instrumentality beliefs should be strongest when rewards are always tied to performance (as under a continuous reinforcement schedule). Research on this issue involving workers has been largely mixed and inconclusive, if only because of the difficulty of controlling reinforcement/reward schedules carefully in real work settings (see Latham and Dossett, 1978; Saari and Latham, 1982; Yukl and Latham, 1975; Yukl, Latham, and Pursell, 1976; Yukl, Wexley, and Seymore, 1972).

To this point we have used the terms *reward* and *reinforcement* somewhat interchangeably. In fact, however, it is important to differentiate between the two concepts. The term *reward* implies a set of subjective reactions experienced internally; it is

---

[6]See chapter 12 of this volume.

rooted in the cognitive/perceptual model of human functioning. On the other hand, *reinforcement* implies that a behavior is made more probable, or more frequent, by its consequences; no mention of internal states or perceptions is involved. In short, choice of either term implicitly indicates whether a person assumes the importance of internal or external factors as the primary causes of behavior. On the other hand, both theories assume that human beings are basically hedonists who seek to maximize pleasure (or at least survival potential) and minimize pain.

Until recently, there has been a tendency for operant conditioning to focus on extrinsic outcomes rather than intrinsic ones, if only because the former are objective, measurable, and do not require the invocation of need concepts. On the other hand, VIE theory has devoted considerable attention to the role of both intrinsic and extrinsic rewards, especially since these two types of motivation were both formally recognized in L. W. Porter and Lawler's (1968) revised expectancy model. Since then, some behaviorists have attempted to provide operant-conditioning interpretations of the impact of extrinsic reinforcement on intrinsic motivation (e.g., Mawhinney, 1979).

In balance, we can conclude that the differences between the two approaches are of more theoretical importance than they are of practical significance (Petrock and Gamboa, 1976). Both theories would propose that rewards (or reinforcers) be linked with performance (or desired behaviors). Both schools would suggest that reward and reinforcement contingencies feature outcomes that people desire or value. Finally, both acknowledge the importance of the context of behavior: the behaviorists, because they hold the antecedents and consequences of acts to be their cause, and the VIE theorists (e.g., Lawler, 1973) because they recognize that features of the work environment are important for structuring expectancy and instrumentality beliefs, which, in turn, result in intentions to act.

A Glance Ahead

Our purpose to this point in the chapter has been to introduce some of the most important traditional principles of operant psychology, laying the foundation for a treatment of the application of these principles to the issues of work motivation and behavior. The purpose in the following sections is to (1) examine the general principles of *behavior modification,* and (2) present the specific application of the principles to organizational motivation and behavior, usually referred to as *organizational behavior modification* or *applied behavior analysis.*

GENERAL PRINCIPLES
OF BEHAVIOR MODIFICATION

On the basis of the diversity of views discussed in the foregoing section, it is not surprising that there is no universally agreed-upon definition of *behavior modification.* Nevertheless, for the sake of discussion, the following definition is borrowed from Kazdin (1978) and adopted for use in this book: "the application of basic research and theory from experimental psychology to influence behavior for purposes of resolving personal and social problems and enhancing human functioning" (p. ix). Notice that this definition would imply that knowledge from all branches of experimental psychology constitutes the knowledge base of behavior modification, without regard to the particular schools involved. The definition also implies that behavior modification is not a fixed or final set of techniques. Rather, as new research and theory are developed in the various schools of psychology, the knowledge base and techniques of behavior modification will continue to change accordingly (Craighead et al., 1976). It should be clear that as discussed earlier in this chapter, the principles of operant psychology constitute the most important elements of behavior modification.

In addition to traditional operant principles, however, modern behavior modification includes a variety of other principles and processes, many of which are of a cognitive nature. Aside from goal setting (which we discussed at length in chapter 13) and self-management (treated at length later in this chapter), the most significant cognitive processes that have been adopted by modern behaviorists are attention, mediation, anticipation, problem solving, attribution, feedback, and modeling. We examine each of these processes briefly in the following sections.

Attention

Even if we adopt the assumption that behavior has its antecedents and consequences in the environment, we must recognize that people are usually faced with a vast array of environmental events and contingencies and that we are simply not capable of monitoring them all. Instead, we tend to restrict our focus to subsets of the environment, including subsets of all the possible antecedents to behavior and subsets of all of its possible consequences. Two people in the same situation may concentrate their attention on different aspects of the environment and behave differently as a result. Therefore, whereas one employee may be particularly inclined to stay abreast of his supervisor's moods, another may not recognize the fact that the same supervisor tends to have shifts in mood from one day to the next. Similarly, some employees are more susceptible to the reinforcements and punishments they receive via the informal system of the organization; others concentrate on the rewards and punishments administered by management. In short, it is the environmental events to which people attend that determine their behavior (Craighead et al., 1976, p. 135).

Mediation

As people experience the cues that prompt behavior and the consequences that are contingent upon it, they learn. However, the material that is learned can be organized into symbolic mental structures in an orderly fashion that facilitates recall and recognition, or it may not be so organized. Different people employ different mental techniques for organizing the things they have learned, such as mnemonics, poems, and various other types of associations ("The way I remember the name of my boss's wife is that it is the same as my mother's"). Current behavior modification recognizes the role played by such mental processes in human behavior.

Anticipation

Why do some people take an umbrella to work with them in the morning even when it is not raining when they leave home? Why do people abandon sinking ships? The answer is that human beings often anticipate events, including those they have already experienced in the past (such as being caught in the rain without an umbrella), as well as those they may not have experienced before (such as going down with a ship). The point is that learning from the past—be it personal learning or vicarious learning—causes people to anticipate reinforcement and punishment from their future behavior.

Problem Solving

When a person behaves in a certain way in response to a challenge or task, the reinforcement or punishment that follows will influence the probability that the person will behave the same way in the future when confronted with the same situation, and we say that a behavior has been learned. On the other hand, we noted in chapter 13 that it is not necessary for people to experience antecedent–behavior–consequence contingencies for all possible, specific circumstances they may encounter. People develop the capacity to generalize somewhat from one situation to another. In other terms, we tend to develop problem-solving skills that make it possible to consider an array of potential behaviors for dealing with problem situations, as well as to select the one(s) that is most likely to be effective.

Attribution

People observe events around themselves and make inferences about the causes of those events. The events may be the antecedents that provide the operant conditioner's prompts or cues for behaving, or they may be the consequences of the operant behaviors that follow the cue. Alternatively, the event may be something that has little to do directly with the person in question. The point is that people tend to be naive psychologists, trying to determine why things happen the way they do (recall chapter 3, and see Heider, 1958). In the work setting, managers frequently make attributions about the reasons for the quality of the work of their subordinates, attributing it either to hard work and effort (or a lack thereof), or to factors that are beyond the control of the employees involved (see Mitchell et al., 1981, for a formal theory pertaining to this process).

Feedback

As we have seen on a number of occasions, feedback is the provision of information to a system about its output (recall chapter 13, in particular). In human terms, feedback consists of telling people something about their behavior in either quantitative or qualitative terms. The provision of feedback is one of the most potent and most common elements of behavior modification, particularly when applied to work settings (Prue and Fairbank, 1980). Often, feedback is combined with the setting of goals, and in fact, the feedback usually consists of information concerning the employee's progress toward those goals (see Ashford and Tsui, 1991; Tsui and Ashford, 1994).

Advantages of Feedback

Of all the performance-improvement mechanisms used in behavior modification, feedback is usually the most inexpensive and generally the easiest to employ. It costs little, in most circumstances, to tell employees how well they are doing. Further, feedback is usually a more positive means of gaining behavior control than are punishment and discipline, consistent with the positive orientation of the philosophy of behavior modification. Finally, feedback is usually more feasible than other behavior modification practices in organizations with internal constraints concerning the distribution of rewards and punishments. Union agreements, for example, may limit the use of money as a reinforcer but seldom prohibit management from telling rank-and-file employees when they are performing well on their jobs.

In short, feedback has a number of advantages in behavior modification efforts, accounting in large part for its popularity in such programs (Prue and Fairbank, 1980). It is important to note that although feedback may be reinforcing (i.e., increasing the frequency of behavior), it is conceptually distinct from reinforcement per se. The reason, of course, is that information fed back can also reduce the frequency of behavior, thereby qualifying for the formal definition of punishment in some situations.

Dimensions of Feedback

A number of aspects of feedback must be taken into account when considering its use in behavior modification. Of particular interest is whether the feedback is provided to the person in public or in private. One summary of the evidence on this matter has concluded that private feedback is desirable when (1) the performance of the person receiving it is low; (2) supervisors have the necessary interpersonal skills to deal with subordinates on a one-to-one basis; (3) there are enough resources (such as supervisory time) to provide it; (4) workers are in close proximity to their supervisors; and (5) the person receiving it is being compared to his own baseline performance or some designated standard (Prue and Fairbank, 1980).

Another consideration is the means used to deliver feedback. It can be provided verbally, in written form, by mechanical means, or by the person himself as he records his own behavior and performance. There are costs and benefits associated with each of these approaches. For example, self-monitoring implies trust of the person and includes the employee in the intervention program. Verbal feedback can be quick and inexpensive to administer. Written feedback can help with the keeping of records for ongoing assessments of performance improvements.

Also of concern is the content of the feedback, or the standard that is implied in the message (see our discussion of control theory and goal-setting theory on this point in Chapter 13). For example, is the person's performance to be compared with that of other people (such as her work group), with her own previous performance, or with an external standard or goal? The reader is reminded of the value of specifying hard and specific goals, as we discussed in chapter 13, and is referred to Prue and Fairbank (1980) and Dickson et al. (1993), who have reviewed a variety of specific issues that should be taken into account to plan the content of the feedback that is to be provided to employees.

The *timing* of feedback is often important. Ideally, feedback should be provided as soon as possible after the behavior about which information is being fed back, although people vary in their capacity to effectively wait to learn how well they are doing at a task. Immediate feedback is particularly valuable when it pertains to a task that the person is learning for the first time and/or when the task involved is complex. It would seem that feedback should be made contingent upon behavior rather than the passage of time per se as is the case with reinforcement, but there is little research evidence on this point at present.

Who should give the feedback? It stands to reason that the greater the prestige of the person who provides it, the more attention will be paid to feedback, although there are circumstances where this may not necessarily be the case. For example, the trustworthiness of the person, her capacity to deliver reinforcers and punishments, her expertise, sincerity, and the nature of the relationship between the person delivering the message and the person receiving it also should be taken into account. Further detail about considerations relevant to the nature and use of feedback is provided for the interested reader by A. B. Anderson (1970), Ashford (1993), Dickson et al. (1993), Greller (1978), Prue and Fairbank (1980), and Walter and Marks (1981).

Modeling

Earlier in this chapter we discussed the development of complex behaviors from simpler ones through the process referred to as behavior shaping. It was noted there that a great deal of human behavior is the result of behavior shaping; in fact, shaping continues throughout our lives, as we become increasingly more sophisticated in dealing with our environments. On the other hand, Bandura (1969, 1977, 1986) and others have noted that many complex behaviors seem not to require the time and ongoing personal experiencing of reinforcement and punishment entailed in shaping processes. Instead, they note that some complex behaviors can often appear all at once for the first time. The primary means by which this occurs, according to Bandura, is through identification processes—we watch others and learn from them. For example, a new employee in a grocery store may stand beside an experienced clerk to observe how vegetables are trimmed and prepared for display. After watching the several microsteps involved in efficiently trimming and wrapping a head of lettuce, for example, the experienced clerk may say to the newcomer, "Here, you try." Of course, the rookie may not be as proficient as the veteran on the first attempt, but a little shaping (of both the lettuce and the rookie's behavior) can normally overcome the problem, and before too long, the entire behavioral sequence has been learned.

Primary Modeling Mechanisms

There are three basic means through which people model their behavior after others. The first, *imitation,* was illustrated by the example of the lettuce trimmer in the preceding paragraph. Notice that the person whose behavior is being modeled need not actually be alive or present for learning to take place. In fact, training films are commonly used in organizations to demonstrate how relatively complex acts are performed.

A second form of modeling involves the use of behavior that already exists in the person's repertoire but that is *cued* (or prompted) by the behaviors of others around him. For example, employees in a work setting may be much more likely to engage in clown play when one of their informal leaders does so than would normally be the case. Although this aspect of modeling is similar to imitation, the difference has to do with whether the behavior being displayed by the person is new (which is the case in imitation) or whether it is already known by the person but prompted by the behaviors of other people in the environment.

A third modeling mechanism is vicarious identification with the consequences of the behaviors of other persons. Public punishment in the days of old capitalized on this process: Several people could "learn" about the consequences of illegal acts without having to perform those acts and incur the costs personally. Thus, if we see others being reinforced for behaving in certain ways, we may be more likely to behave in similar fashion ourselves, almost as if we had experienced the reinforcement firsthand. Notice that it is possible for modeling to result in the learning of behavior (either new behavior or old behavior in new circumstances) without that behavior actually being put into practice. Whether people actually employ the behaviors they observe depends on a number of things, including who the model is and the consequences that the model incurs as a result of the behavior. Research indicates that people are more likely to imitate the behavior of or model those high in prestige or expertise (Craighead et al., 1976, p. 107).

Goal Setting and Self-Management

Two final cognitive processes included in many behavior modification settings are goal setting (recall chapter 13) and self-management, a process (or set of processes) by which a person selects from among those response alternatives that are available at a particular time those that otherwise would not normally be chosen (see Erez and Kanfer, 1983; Mills, 1983; Thoresen and Mahoney, 1974). Self-management consists of overriding one's natural predilections in favor of pursuing goals that are less naturally favored.

We return to address self-management (or self-regulation) in greater detail later in this chapter, but for the sake of the current discussion we can describe it as a three-stage sequence in which the person monitors his own behavior, evaluates that behavior against some goal or standard, and then administers reinforcers or punishment to himself on the basis of the evaluation (Kanfer, 1980). For example, an employee who has been instructed by his supervisor to reduce the amount of material he wastes on a construction site might be taught methods for actually measuring the amount of scrap he throws away or the number of times he actively makes use of materials that have been discarded by himself or someone else. The evaluation stage follows closely, of course, as the employee will normally be immediately aware of how well his performance measures up to the standards he or his employer have set for him.

The third stage, the self-administration of either reinforcement or punishment, is somewhat more complex. For example, the person may voluntarily deny himself certain normal pleasures (such as a routine coffee break) if he notices that he is not making progress toward his goal. Alternatively, if he manages to make considerable use of discarded materials on a given morning, he may administer any of a number of desirable consequences to himself, such as making a phone call to a friend, taking an extralong lunch hour, or merely uttering statements to himself such as "That's better!"

Summary and Preview

The foregoing discussion has listed a number of processes and techniques that are commonly employed by psychologists in behavior modification settings. When combined with the basic methods of operant conditioning and those of other schools of psychology, these techniques have proven highly effective in influencing a wide array of human behavior in educational, clinical, and rehabilitation settings. When these techniques are applied to organizational and management problems, they are frequently referred to as *organizational behavior modification*. In the following sections, we examine the key elements of this approach to work motivation and behavior and attempt to leave the reader with an understanding of the current status of this now-hybridized school among the other theories of work motivation discussed in this book.

ORGANIZATIONAL BEHAVIOR MODIFICATION

Aldis (1961) and Nord (1969) were among the first to suggest application of the principles of operant conditioning to work organizations. As mentioned earlier, the idea caught on and was very popular during the 1970s (Goodall, 1972) and into the 1980s (Komaki et al., 1991; O'Hara, Johnson, and Beehr, 1985). The approach was called organizational behavior modification (sometimes referred to as O.B. mod, organizational behavior management, or applied behavior analysis). Two journals in particular, the *Journal of Applied Behavior Analysis* and the *Journal of Organizational Behavior Management,* are devoted to disseminating knowledge about the application of these principles to managerial problems and reporting research conducted within the O.B. mod framework. For historical reasons it is important to repeat that whereas operant psychology was originally the most important parent discipline underlying O.B. mod, the actual techniques applied by its practitioners typically include combinations of cognitive concepts such as those discussed in the foregoing sections of this chapter (Fredericksen and Lovett, 1980; Luthans and Kreitner, 1975; L. M. Miller, 1978).

Managing Behavioral Contingencies at Work

Managers who wish to apply O.B. mod must, in simple terms, learn how to diagnose and influence the antecedents and consequences of the behavior of their employees. Luthans and Kreitner (1974, 1975) have proposed a general sequence for accomplishing this, called behavioral contingency management. It consists of five basic steps. First, the manager must identify those employee behaviors that are detrimental to job performance. It is important that the manager be precise about exactly which behaviors are undesirable and need to be dealt with, and, if possible, that they be countable.

The second step is to count the frequency of the problematic behaviors, establishing a baseline that can be used to determine the effectiveness of the manager's subsequent intervention. The count may be made by the manager or by the employee himself (recall our earlier discussion of self-monitoring). Often, tally sheets are designed for this purpose, or managers sometimes merely sample the behavior of their personnel, checking how frequently they engage in the behavior in question during randomly selected periods of time. Wrist counters or the judicious application of memory are recommended in cases when it is probable that the employee will change his behavior if he knows that his supervisor is observing and recording it (see W. F. Whyte, 1972).

The third step is to identify both the conditions that are antecedent to the behavior as well as the consequences that reinforce it. For example, the author once observed a number of work groups in a plant in which steel containers were manufactured. Foremen in each of the groups often complained that employees of the other groups stole parts and materials for use on their own projects. (The word they used, of course, was "borrowed.") Upon investigation, it was learned that most of the borrowing occurred toward the end of every month. Moreover, the foremen whose workers conducted the informal requisitions managed to keep their cost figures low while assuring that their project deadlines were met. (The consequences for victimized foremen were exactly the opposite, of course.) Here the antecedent of the dysfunctional behavior (borrowing) was the time of the month in which it occurred. The consequences? A formal reward system that reinforced the foreman for in turn reinforcing his staff for raiding the supplies and materials of the other work groups.

The next step in behavioral contingency management is the selection of an intervention strategy (Luthans and Kreitner, 1975). This can include the application of any of the following, alone or in combination: positive reinforcement, negative reinforcement, punishment, or extinction. The manager tries to make the chosen consequence contingent upon the behavior she is trying either to reinforce or eliminate. There are a variety of factors that can (and should) influence the precise strategy selected, such as the nature of the job, the organization's structure, history and precedents, union contracts, and other, more informal agreements. The manager or the employee continues to record the frequency of occurrence of the behavior in question. If the intervention is effective, the undesirable behavior will decrease in frequency (or cease altogether), and more favorable behaviors will take its place.

The final step is to evaluate the intervention by observing whether the desired behavior actually becomes more frequent, while undesired behavior becomes less frequent. Without evaluation, a manager cannot tell whether her attempt to change her employee's behavior has been successful. If it has not been successful, further remedial steps might then be possible (such as reexamining the antecedents or changing the consequences or the schedules by which they are administered). Luthans and Kreitner's (1974, 1975) five-step approach follows consistently from the operant conditioners' suggestions for functional analysis, focusing on the antecedents and consequences of behavior, as well as on the nature of the behavior itself.

Komaki and her colleagues (1991) reviewed more than 50 applications of O.B. mod that they felt were well enough controlled to permit valid conclusions. On the basis of their review, Komaki et al. (1991) distilled four steps or ingredients that the various researchers and interventionists employed. Their list is similar to that of Luthans and Kreitner (1974, 1975) but has a more positive tone. These four ingredients were the following: (1) Specify the desired behavior (as opposed to identifying behaviors that are not desirable); (2) measure the frequency of the desired performance [or behavior]; (3) provide frequent, contingent, positive consequences; and (4) evaluate the effectiveness of the ultimate job performance (Komaki et al., 1991, p. 92). It is worth comparing the advice given two decades ago by Luthans and Kreitner (1975) with the techniques actually applied and the results attained by interventionists since then (as summarized by Komaki et al., 1991). They are quite similar, indeed.

Varieties of Consequences

Petrock (1978) suggested a useful means for analyzing the consequences of employee behavior for contingency management. He noted that most on-the-job behavior is of either of two varieties: job-related or non-job-related. Moreover, each of these types of behavior can result in either positive or aversive consequences. Finally, regardless of whether they are positive or aversive, the consequences of employee behavior can be classified according to three important dimensions: (1) whether the impact is on the employee or the organization (or both); (2) whether the consequences are immediate or delayed; and (3) whether they are certain and highly contingent on the behavior or somewhat random and only partially contingent on behavior. Therefore, the management of employee behavior requires that the supervisor identify both the reinforcing and punishing consequences that accrue to the employee for both those behaviors that are deemed desirable as well as those that are undesirable (from a managerial point of view). Clearly, people will engage in desirable behavior on the job when it results in a positive net balance of reinforcing consequences rather than a balance of punishing consequences. On the other hand, when employees find that work demands result in more unpleasant outcomes than positive ones, we can expect that rules will be broken or ignored or that employees will actively engage in practices that are more reinforcing than is compliance with management's desires.

Komaki and her colleagues (1991) report that five different classes of consequences were in fact used by interventionists in the studies they reviewed through the late 1980s. There were (1) organizational, such as pay raises and special training opportunities; (2) generalized rewards such as cash, frequent flyer coupons, and trading stamps; (3) activities, such as rearranging the order of their tasks, applying the Premack principle; (4) social rewards, such as compliments, criticism, and commendations; and (5) informational, such as feedback, public announcements about progress toward goals, and so on.

According to Petrock (1978), the punishing consequences of desired work behavior are usually personal (rather than organizational), immediate, and directly contingent on those behaviors. For example, wearing safety equipment is often uncomfortable, obeying formal rules can be inconvenient, and doing things by the book is often a "hassle." On the other hand, the reinforcing consequences of desired behavior are frequently personal, delayed (rather than immediate), and contingent on behavior, making desirable behavior less attractive than undesirable behavior in many cases. In short, Petrock suggests that supervisors who wish to influence the behavior of their employees must carefully identify and attempt to balance the positive and aversive consequences of both positive and negative behaviors and then take steps to assure that desired behaviors result in more positive, and fewer aversive consequences than undesired behavior.

It is important to reiterate that many work behaviors are often reinforced informally by the social system of the workplace, despite the fact (or often because of the fact) that management officially discourages them.

The Positive Approach in O.B. Mod

While O.B. mod makes use of reinforcement as well as punishment, *the emphasis is on the application of positive control measures wherever possible.* Luthans and Kreitner (1975, p. 84) summarized this principle: "Reinforcement is the key to operant learning theory and the most important principle of behavior modification. The simple fact is that positive reinforcement, contingently applied, can effectively control human behavior.... With the possible exception of the contingency concept itself, the understanding and appropriate use of positive reinforcement is most important to success in O.B. Mod." The trick, of course, is to identify those things that people find positively reinforcing, for as has been noted repeatedly, different people find different consequences reinforcing.

Identifying Reinforcers

How can we identify the consequences that particular people find positively reinforcing? Strictly speaking from an operant-conditioning perspective, the only appropriate way is to conduct functional analyses of people's behavior: that is, to observe the antecedent conditions in which behaviors occur, the specific behaviors themselves, and the consequences of those behaviors, with a particular view to noticing increases or decreases in the frequencies of the behaviors of interest. For example, if a manager notices that a particular employee engages in clown play when he has too little work to do (the antecedent condition) and that he seems to attract the attention and support of his co-workers when he does so, thereby increasing his propensity to act in such a manner (the reinforcement effect), the manager might infer that the person's behavior can be influenced by the contingent application (or withdrawal) of interaction with his peers. That is, if social interaction is reinforcing to the employee, chances for social interaction might be adopted by the supervisor as a contingent consequence for encouraging the person to perform tasks on the job. Just as we can observe the brand of beer people prefer at the pub when they are thirsty, so we can make inferences about the specific nature of other reinforcers of a particular person's behavior.

In practice, however, it is not possible to observe all the consequences of every employee's acts and to observe whether these consequences function to increase or decrease the occurrence of specific behaviors. Therefore, other means are more feasible and more frequently used to identify reinforcers. One method is simply to ask people what they desire from their work (recall our discussion of attitude surveys near the end of chapter 7). There are a variety of standardized instruments for inquiring about the types of things people desire from their work. One of these is the Minnesota Importance Questionnaire (Gay, Weiss, Hendel, Dawis, and Lofquist, 1971). Another is the Job Orientation Inventory (Blood, 1973). In common practice, however, employee attitude surveys normally feature a number of tailormade questions pertaining to the types of potential reinforcers that may be more or less idiosyncratic to the organization involved. A third approach to identifying reinforcers is through the use of trial and error: The manager simply tries a variety of outcomes contingent on desired employee behavior and observes whether they actually function to reinforce (make more frequent) the behaviors in question.

There are a wide variety of potential reinforcers in some organizations; in others, managers are limited by organizational policies, precedents, or formal agreements (such as union contracts) in the types of things they can offer employees in return for behavior. Nevertheless, Luthans and Kreitner (1975) suggested several categories of potential reinforcers that might be available in practice. Their categories, with examples, are: (1) *consumables:* beer parties, Easter hams; (2) *manipulatables:* wall plaques, watches; (3) *visual and auditory:* piped-in music, redecoration of work environment; (4) *tokens:* money, stocks, vacation trips; (5) *social:* solicitations for suggestions, smiles; and (6) *activity based:* job with more responsibility, time off work on a personal project with pay (recall the Premack principle).

A recently popular management-oriented paperback lists "1001 ways to reward employees" (Nelson, 1994). There are a variety of outcomes that creative supervisors might attempt to employ as reinforcers with their staffs, although in virtually all organizations there are constraints of one sort or another. But the desire is to find something positive rather than to rely on negative influences such as punishment or threat of punishment.

O.B. Mod and Work Motivation[7]

One of its leading proponents stated a decade ago that the effect of O.B. mod on the organizational sciences has been "most apparent in the area of work motivation" (Komaki, 1986, p. 299). The most significant contribution, she claims, is in the way her school of thought emphasizes the antecedents and consequences of work performance. As we discussed earlier in this chapter, "antecedents are thought to function in an educational or cuing role. Instructions, rules, and goals, for example, are viewed as clarifying expectations for performance, specifying the relationship between behavior and its consequences, and/or signalling occasions in which consequences are likely to be provided contingent on behavior. Consequences, on the other hand, are thought to have the potential of increasing or decreasing the probability of behavior reoccurring" (Komaki, 1986, p. 300). In fact, Komaki claims that the unique feature of the O.B. mod approach to work motivation is that it places its emphasis on the events that occur *after* a person's "target behavior." (By contrast, need theories rely on internal states that are operative before, during, and after behavior; expectancy-valence models are concerned with prior expectations of a person's likely satisfaction after an act; and goal-setting theory hinges completely on forward-looking intentions.) As we saw earlier, the "consequences" available and useful in this school of thought are varied, although the ones most frequently used and mentioned are recognition, feedback, and incentives.

Earlier we mentioned the notion of antecedents and their role in cuing behavior. Komaki (1986) is careful to emphasize that although they do educate and cue people to act, adherents of O.B. mod "do not think they [antecedents] are primarily responsible for increasing or decreasing the probability of the behavior occurring again" (p. 301). She cites a number of studies from the 1970s to bolster her point. The common thread among these studies was that antecedents alone were not sufficient either to induce desired employee behaviors (such as attendance or job performance) or to sustain improvements. In most or all cases, there had to be desirable consequences used either alone or in conjunction with antecedent conditions. In part because Komaki (1986) cites cases from the 1970s to bolster her point about the contributions of applied behavior analysis, the following few sections will feature a historical dimension. The author believes that a historical treatment is instructive because of the conflict that occurred between the O.B. mod camp and other, more cognitively oriented camps since the 1970s, leaving us today with a hybrid view of the world that can legitimately claim to have at least two intellectual sources.

Early Application of O.B. Mod
to Employee Performance Problems

In the late 1960s, management at Emery Air Freight (Dowling, 1973b) investigated a large number of the firm's operations and concluded that there were widespread differences between actual employee practices and the practices that were prescribed and

---

[7]The reader is reminded that the terms *functional analysis, applied behavior analysis,* and *O.B. mod* are being used interchangeably throughout this discussion.

intended by company policy. For example, it was found that customer service representatives were much slower than desired in responding to customer inquiries about freight rates, flight schedules, and other issues. Management had employees monitor their own performance and record how well they were doing on measurable standards. Goals were set to increase performance levels, and constant feedback and positive reinforcers were provided for improvements.

Emery saved an estimated $3 million over a three-year period as a result of their program (Dowling, 1973b). They expanded it into 224 various other parts of their operation, including areas such as operations, sales and sales training, and shipping. Initially, the most commonly used reinforcer was praise, but eventually it began to lose its capacity to reinforce desired behavior. In fact, it understandably became a source of irritation. Therefore, supervisors began using alternative reinforcers, such as assigning employees to pleasurable tasks upon the completion of less desirable ones (again, recall the Premack principle), time off, freedom to attend business luncheons, letters sent home praising the employee, and so on.

The need at Emery to expand the range of reinforcers used raises an important point. Reinforcers are reinforcing, by definition, only when they actually increase the frequency of a behavior or set of behaviors. Therefore, a supervisor, parent, teacher, or other person who is attempting to modify someone else's behavior must remember that different outcomes reinforce different people. (We discussed this issue near the end of Chapter 12, in the context of individualized reward systems from the point of view of VIE theory.) Certain outcomes, particularly praise, may become transparent, appear phony and manipulative, and thereby lose their capacity to influence behavior (Staw, 1977, and see chapter 5). In fact, such consequences may become punishers. Supervisors and other behavior modifiers must be careful to monitor the actual reinforcing power of those things they distribute contingent on behavior; otherwise, rather than reinforcing behavior, they may find they are punishing those behaviors they are attempting to encourage.

As suggested above, the Emery Air Freight experiment became a focus of controversy soon after it was reported. The controversy concerned whether the design and execution of their program actually constituted an example of operant conditioning per se. Although not disputing the success of the program, some critics argued that operant psychology, by itself, could not account for what happened. Rather, because the employees involved were required to set goals, monitor their own performance improvements, and accept feedback about those improvements, it was alleged that a strict operant psychology explanation was insufficient to explain the results. Instead, a more cognitively based explanation, particularly that associated with goal-setting theory, was offered (e.g., Locke, 1977, 1978, 1979).

Whatever they did at Emery, it worked. Moreover, other studies since that time have successfully applied various blends of goal setting, feedback, and positive reinforcement to improve employee performance (e.g., J. M. Ivancevich and McMahon, 1982; Kim and Hamner, 1976; Komaki, Waddell, and Pearce, 1977; Latham and Baldes, 1975; Latham and Dossett, 1978; Latham and Kinne, 1974; L. M. Miller, 1977; Runnion, Johnson, and McWhorter, 1978; Runnion, Watson, and McWhorter, 1978; Saari and Latham, 1982; and others). See Andrasik (1979) and Hamner and Hamner (1976) for two reviews of these and other studies that followed the Emery controversy. In short, it became clear by 1980 that these techniques can be useful for the improvement of job performance among many occupational groups. But this particular blend had other successful applications to work settings in addition to the management of performance problems.

More Recent Applications

The Emery Air Freight case is reported here because of its historical importance, both as the first high-profile "example" of O.B. mod as well as the source of much of the controversy that ensued. Since Emery, there have been countless other applications of the O.B. mod approach to a variety of business and organizational outcome variables. O'Hara et al. (1985) summarize many of these studies, categorizing them according to the outcome variables of interest to the interventionists involved. Most of the cases reviewed were applied to performance quantity and/or quality, absenteeism, employee safety, customer service, theft reduction, and the conservation of raw materials by employees. A more recent review by Komaki and her colleagues (1991) found the same range of applications. A few studies that serve to illustrate are summarized below.

Improving Safety and Reducing Accidents

Organization behavior modification (or whatever it was) also demonstrated considerable promise for reducing accidents in a variety of work settings. For example, Komaki, Barwick, and Scott (1978) identified a set of "desired safety practices" in two departments of a wholesale bakery in which accidents had become an increasingly serious problem. Employees were shown slides of both safe and unsafe behaviors associated with getting their work done (thereby providing a basis for behavior modeling) and were asked to discuss the safe and unsafe aspects of the acts depicted in the slides. Feedback was provided by the use of a chart that reported the frequency of occurrence of safe behaviors, showing graphically how the employees' safety performance improved over the prestudy baseline period. In addition, supervisors provided verbal reinforcement to those employees whom they saw engaging in the desired behaviors on the job. As a result of these three intervention components (behavior modeling and instruction, feedback, and reinforcement), the proportion of safely conducted behaviors increased from 70 percent to 96 percent in one department, and from 78 percent to 99 percent in the other. Moreover, the company's employees seemed positive about the program.

Similar O.B. mod interventions were effective for improving safety and reducing accidents in other settings. For example, Komaki, Heinzmann, and Lawson (1980) enhanced the safety record of a sample of civic vehicle maintenance workers using a combination of behavior modeling, instruction, and feedback, finding that the feedback was necessary to keep the program effective after the 226 early modeling and instruction phases were completed. Finally (although this does not exhaust the list of possible early examples), Haynes, Pine, and Fitch (1982) reduced the accident rate of a sample of urban bus drivers, using a combination of feedback, competition, and monetary and nonmonetary incentives.

Reducing Absenteeism

The control of employee absenteeism was another area in which O.B. mod showed early promise (see chapter 10 for a discussion of the costs of absenteeism to work organizations). Although many of these studies were criticized for being of relatively short duration and for not reporting cost-benefit data (Schmitz and Heneman, 1980), many impressive interventions were reported (e.g., Kopelman and Schneller, 1981; Nord, 1970; Orpen, 1978; Pedalino and Gamboa, 1974). Two studies suggested that the combined application of positive reinforcement and punishment is particularly effective for controlling employee absences (Kempen and Hall, 1977; Kopelman and Schneller, 1981).

By the early 1980s it appeared that a number of work-related behaviors were more or less amenable to modification by the principles of O.B. mod. Yet most of the successes reported were of interventions featuring goal setting in conjunction with feedback and/or positive reinforcement (O'Hara et al., 1985). In fact, blends of goal setting and other behavior modification principles and techniques (such as those mentioned at the beginning of this chapter) seemed, at the time, to be more effective in applied work motivation settings than any other theory or set of techniques (Pinder, 1984, p. 227). Despite its apparent applied effectiveness, there was a period of heated controversy surrounding O.B. mod. In the mid-1990s, we are in the aftermath of that controversy and O.B. mod (functional analysis, applied behavior analysis, operant conditioning, and behaviorism) has been relegated to a position of minor importance, mostly because the theory itself could not explain the successes of the techniques it purported to justify. Let's take a look at some of the key points in the criticisms.

Controversy and O.B. Mod

Of the theories of work motivation discussed in this book, Herzberg's two-factor model has been the most controversial (recall chapter 2). Second in controversy, however, must be the theory and applications that have come from operant psychology for application to organizations. Since the relevance of operant conditioning for understanding and managing organizations was first mentioned by Aldis (1961), Nord (1969), Luthans and Kreitner (1975), and others, there have been a number of controversies, ranging from the theoretical and the philosophical through to the operational and ethical (see Schneier, 1974). We will briefly examine several of the most contentious issues and problems here.

The Morality of Control

One of the most common concerns directed at operant conditioning and behavior modification pertained to the ethics of controlling human behavior and the allegation that to do so with the help of applied psychology is denigrating to human beings. Is it moral to apply techniques for the explicit purpose of influencing the behavior of other people? What about the sanctity of human nature and the freedom we have all fought to attain and protect? Who has the right to control another person's behavior, to determine what they can and cannot do? There are many answers offered in response to questions of this sort.

Answers from the behaviorist camp generally took the following form. Because human behavior naturally can result in only one or more of three possible consequences—reinforcement, punishment, or extinction—all people are both conditioned and conditioners. In B. F. Skinner's own words, "We all control, and we are all controlled" (1953, p. 438). From the time we are born and begin to behave, we all find that our acts result in either positive or aversive consequences. The world is a giant Skinner box in which people formally and informally administer rewards and punishments to one another. Children who are reprimanded by their parents for speaking out of turn are affected with the same degree of external control as children who accidentally cut themselves when they fall on sharp rocks. Control is natural; it is unavoidable. It is constant and ubiquitous. To deny that control is everywhere in nature is to ignore reality, so to refuse to exercise control is to defer it to others. So how can there be organized work effort without some degree of formal control? How can our economy and our society, as a whole, function and be competitive without some system of control? When people go to work for an employer, they implicitly (sometimes explicitly) resign themselves to the authority of the formal control system implemented by that employer. Finally, employees in a democratic society are free to come and go from one work setting to another, seeking levels of managerial control that are most comfortable. In short, the formal application of procedures to reinforce or punish behavior was claimed to be little different from what occurs in the absence of such procedures. Hence we are collectively better off by consciously learning about and utilizing the laws of behavior to make life as safe and comfortable as possible (see Rogers and Skinner, 1956, for a classic debate on these issues).

The Ethics of Observation

A related ethical question concerns the observation of work behavior (Luthans and Kreitner, 1975). Is it ethical to monitor, sometimes surreptitiously, the work behavior of others, with a view either to measure it (for establishing a baseline before intervention) or to watch whether it changes in response to intervention? Still another question concerns whether it is possible to gain reliable measures of the work behavior of employees when they are aware that they are being measured (W. F. Whyte, 1972). Let's take these one at a time.

First, it is usually quite difficult in practice to gain realistic assessments of the work rate of employees when those employees realize they are being observed. This is especially so when the purpose of the observation is to set standards for performance and payment under piece-rate pay systems. Therefore, managers who desire to gain reliable information about the rates and levels of employee behavior and performance might benefit, in some settings, from the use of spylike techniques.

Moreover, defendants of O.B. mod have argued that if the benefit to be gained by the appropriate setting of standards and the fair monitoring of performance is to be conducive to employee welfare, such observation is justified. In other words, these particular ends justify the means used, within reason, of course (see Luthans and Kreitner, 1975, p. 185). Besides, managers have always observed the work performance of their employees; O.B. mod merely formalizes the process, and employees should be made fully aware that their behavior will be monitored with a view to managing it.

Dehumanization

Another contentious issue arose from the fact that much of the research that led to our knowledge of operant and respondent behavior had been conducted on animals. Critics reacted negatively to the application of animal-based knowledge to human behavior—are we no better than, or different from, animals? Defendants of operant psychology recognized that human behavior is more complex than animal behavior, but argued that much of it is ultimately determined by similar underlying principles. Animals were used merely for the obvious reasons of humanity, cost, and convenience.

Nonrationality

A fourth fundamental attack on operant psychology pertained to the issue of human rationality. To claim that human behavior is merely a function of its consequences ignores the rational side of human nature, and with it, the free will that humans exercise. In other words, critics argued that people have consciousness and the capacity to think, reason, and choose among alternatives. Although not denying the importance of the consequences of human acts, these critics proposed that Skinnerian psychology denied any role to human cognition, and thereby treated humans merely as automatons, or mindless creatures, without the capacity to behave with volition.

As we noted above, modern schools of behavior modification openly admit the importance of rational processes (e.g., Craighead et al., 1976; M. J. Mahoney, 1974), so some peace has been made on this point. Nevertheless, there are still some behaviorists who retain the position that internal processes, such as cognition, are useless for understanding behavior: They cannot be observed or measured, so they certainly cannot be influenced (see M. E. Ford, 1992, for a review). They claim that to attribute human behavior to internal processes is both redundant (for the reasons discussed at the beginning of this chapter) and unscientific. On the other hand, critics of strict behaviorism claimed that it is no more scientific to attribute behavior to environmental factors with a philosophy that "If it works, we should use it," than it is to posit the importance of unobservable internal events. They argued that it is as scientific to rely on internal (albeit hypothetical) causes of human behavior as it is to rely on unobservables to explain the nature of physical entities and phenomena. Who has observed an electron, for example?

The point here is this: The radical behaviorist and cognitive/perceptual approaches constitute two incommensurate sets of fundamental beliefs regarding human nature. In their pure forms, they cannot be reconciled. On the other hand, a few peacemakers have proposed eclectic approaches, claiming that each of these perspectives has something to offer an understanding of human nature—neither is totally correct or incorrect (e.g., Fedor and Ferris, 1981; Hitt, 1969; Kreitner and Luthans, 1984; Walter and Marks, 1981). Further, it makes little difference to many people with purely applied intentions (such as parents, teachers, therapists, or managers) which theoretical model is being utilized. In fact, the early success of behavior modification techniques that utilized both behaviorist and cognitive concepts illustrates that the difference between the two points of view holds more importance for philosophy, religion, and barroom debate than it does for applied problem solving (see Bandura, 1977). When we discuss Bandura's social-cognitive theory later in this chapter and see how it can be used in self-regulation of individuals' behavior, this point should be more than clear.

Other, Practical Criticisms

Several other criticisms have been of a practical nature, dealing with the application of behavioral principles in real work settings. One concerned the problems of gaining reliable measurement, as we discussed. Another concerned the difficulty of determining what is reinforcing and punishing for particular employees, and then making it feasible to dispense these reinforcers in a way that is economically feasible and equitable. Another had to do with the heavy administrative procedures and red tape that often accompanies any form of organizational action.

Then there was the language that is used by both the interventionist and the employees involved. On the one hand, precision of communication is necessary for professionals to communicate effectively with one another. In fact, operant terminology has been particularly subject to misuse and misinterpretation (Mawhinney, 1975). On the other hand, excessive jargon and the use of buzzwords can alienate employees and managers, whose cooperation is essential for the success of programs (Murphy and Remnyi, 1979). Behavior modification had a lingo all of its own, causing it to be rejected by many practitioners.

Still another practical issue concerned the time that is granted by management for change to occur and manifest itself. Management groups are reinforced to participate in enlightened managerial techniques when they show a payoff (especially in dollar terms). Yet because of the many complexities of the dynamics in organizations, positive results sometimes take a while to become evident. Although this problem is not unique to applications of O.B. mod, it certainly does apply to them.

Some early critics claimed that behavior modification proved to be much more effective in settings where the interventionist held a position of high authority and control over those whose behavior was to be modified, as is the case, for example, in prisons, mental institutions, and even school settings (Argyris, 1971). The control over outside influences that can interfere with strict application of the measurement, reinforcement, and punishment of behavior in these types of settings is most similar to that which is possible in the laboratory settings in which the principles of operant psychology were first developed. But when these techniques were taken to actual work settings in organizations that featured constraints such as traditions, suspicions, unions, budgets, and impatient management groups, they were much less easy to install and make effective (see Murphy and Remnyi, 1979; O'Hara et al., 1985; Repucci and Saunders, 1974).

The Decline of the Behaviorist Camp

It is not hard to find published statements declaring that behaviorism is on the decline in the organizational sciences, but the following observation will suffice to illustrate the trend and the status of behaviorism (or reinforcement theory): "[R]einforcement theory, with its emphasis on external incentives and behavioral learning, has been overtaken by goal-setting approaches in which salient outcomes serve as mental targets for behavior" (Staw and Boettger, 1990, p. 534).

At the time of the current writing, radical behaviorism is almost gone from the organizational sciences. The fundamental rejection of behaviorism is reflected in the following quotation from Albert Bandura (1991), one of the most influential scholars in the cognitive camp:

> If human behavior were regulated solely by external outcomes, people would behave like weather vanes, constantly shifting direction to conform to whatever momentary social influence happened to impinge upon them. In actuality, people possess self-reflective and self-reactive capabilities that enable them to exercize some control over their thoughts, feelings, motivation, and actions. In the exercise of self-directedness, people adopt certain standards of behavior that serve as guides and motivators and regulate their actions anticipatorily through self-reactive influence. Human function-

ing is, therefore, regulated by an interplay of self-generated and external sources of influence. (p. 249)

Even passionate advocates of O.B. mod such as Kreitner and Luthans (1984) acknowledged more than a decade ago that the "pendulum" had swung back and forth in the discipline, starting with a preponderance of attention on internal forces such as needs and beliefs, then moving sharply away from internal states to a focus on the consequences of behavior, then settling back in a sort of compromise position, which they referred to as social learning theory (which we will study shortly). Kreitner and Luthans' (1984) pendulum metaphor is presented in Figure 14-3. Although it was first offered in 1984, this author believes that the state of affairs it currently symbolizes remains reasonably accurate, excluding one major ingredient: human emotion (see M.E. Ford, 1992), which is making a resurgence in psychology and work motivation (see George and Brief, 1996; Weiss and Cropanzano, 1996).

In the following sections we study social cognitive theory, located at the "bottom" of the arc in Figure 14-3. This is essentially a learning-oriented approach to human behavior that has some of its roots in behaviorism but that has evolved dramatically over the years to incorporate significant elements of what the cognitive schools (such as goal-setting theory and control theory) have to offer.

FIGURE 14-3   Conceptual Pendulum of Organizational Behavior

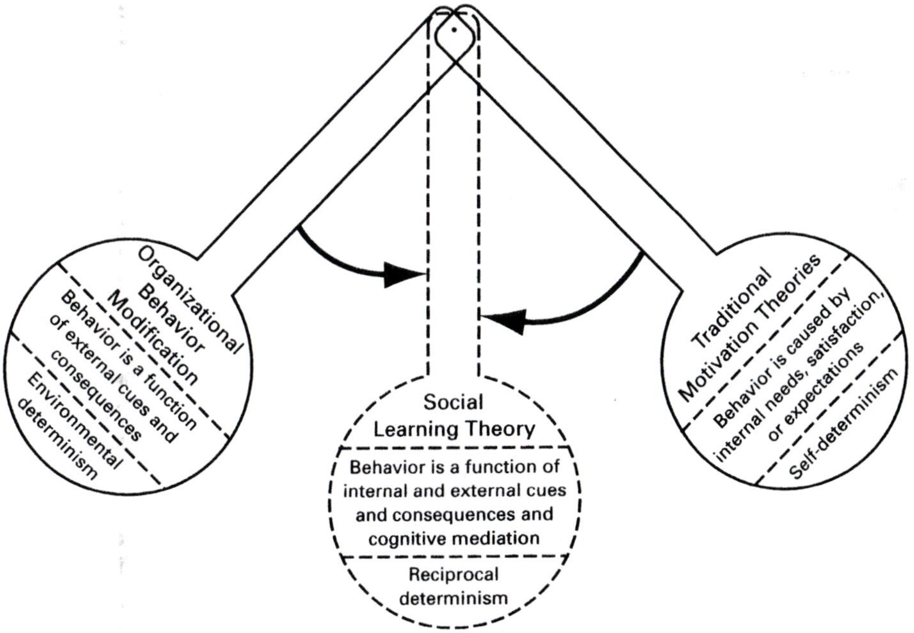

Source: From R. Kreitner and F. Luthans, "A social-leaning approach to behavioral management: Radical behaviorists 'mellowing out,' " *Organizational Dynamics Autumn 13 (2)* pp. 47–65 (1984). Reprinted with permission.

SOCIAL COGNITIVE THEORY

Kreitner and Luthans (1984) describe the emergence of social learning theory (now called *social cognitive theory*)[8] as follows: "When Albert Bandura, Stanford's noted behavioral psychologist, was conducting his pioneering experiments on vicarious learning, he became convinced that cognitive functioning must not be overlooked in explaining complex human behavior. He observed that mental cues and memory aids help people learn and retain behavior more effectively than trial-and-error shaping. This challenged operant conditioning as well as radical behaviorism." A practical example of Bandura's position is the salesperson who relies on a mental image of an apple to remember Applegate, the name of a prospective client. In Bandura's view, this way of learning is more efficient than rote memorization of clients' names in a structured training session. But "*unlike the radical cognitive theorists, Bandura gives a great deal of weight to the impact of environmental cues and consequences on actual behavior* [emphasis added]" (Kreitner and Luthans, 1984, p. 54).

The Flow of Causality

Whereas most previous theories of human behavior have placed their primary emphases on either internal personal states (such as needs, values, beliefs, or perceptions) or on external environmental conditions (such as antecedents and/or consequences), social cognitive theory "explains psychosocial functioning in terms of triadic reciprocal causation . . . In this model of reciprocal determinism, behavior, cognitive, and other personal factors and environmental events operate as interacting determinants that influence each other bidirectionally . . ."(Wood and Bandura, 1989, p. 362). This triangular relationship is shown in Figure 14-4. What is crucial about this three-way model is that it recognizes that people can have some control over their destinies while the environment sets limits on what is possible (Bandura, 1986, p. xi). The model places heavy emphasis on human thought processes, as is the case with goal-setting theory. Hence, it differs markedly from the behaviorist perspectives discussed earlier in the chapter. Yet this is a theory of learning and one that has been influenced by the powerful roles played by environmental factors, two reasons why it is being presented at this point in the current volume.

Bandura states that because the person, the behavior, and the environment all interact in a series of two-way (or dyadic) interactions, it does not follow that all three sets of factors are of equal importance.

Reciprocity does not mean symmetry in the strength of bidirectional influences. Nor is the patterning and strength of mutual influences fixed in reciprocal causation. The relative influence exerted by the three sets of interacting factors will vary for different activities, different individuals, and different circumstances. When environmental conditions exercise powerful constraints on behavior, they emerge as the overriding deter-

---

[8]Bandura (1986, p. xii) explains that social learning theory is the name usually given to his work (until a decade ago), but that subtle similarities and differences with other bodies of thought required him to relabel his work *social cognitive theory:* "The social portion of the terminology acknowledges the social origins of much human thought and action; the cognitive portion recognizes the influential causal contribution of thought processes to human motivation, affect, and action."

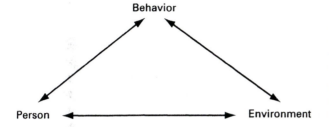

Source: Adapted from A. Bandura, *Social foundations of thought and action: A social cognitive theory* (Upper Saddle River, NJ: Prentice Hall, 1986).

FIGURE 14-4 Three-Way Casual Relationships in Social Cognitive Theory

minants. . . . There are times when behavior and its intrinsic feedback are the central factors in the interacting system. One example of this would be persons who play the piano for their own enjoyment. . . .

When situational constraints are weak, personal factors serve as the predominant influence in the regulatory system. In deciding what novel to check out from vast library holdings, people's preferences hold sway. . . . (p. 24)

Simple or Complex Solutions?

In this view, then, it is overly simplistic to accept simple answers to organizational behavior (or human behavior in any context) that rely exclusively on internal human causes. Consider the following, apparently simple question and the answer it might generate.

Q: "Why did Alice join the Navy?"
A: "She wanted to see the world."

Inherent in this answer is reference to a set of needs and possibly a set of expectancies. Left out of the analysis is any mention of how the environment might have influenced Alice's decision. For example, has recent Navy policy opened new opportunities for women? Or: What might be the effect of Alice's (and other women's) joining the Navy? The "Tailhook" incident of 1994 reminds us that women and men may still expect substantially different experiences in the Navy. Can we seriously answer our question about Alice joining the Navy with reference to the environment, such as the policies and procedures for the treatment of women sailors in the Navy? No, not according to social cognitive theory: The environment might have helped to induce Alice's behavior, which, in turn, may affect that environment (suppose that Alice became a ranking naval officer and was able to enact new naval policy about hazing activities).

The one-way causality offered by behaviorism was much easier than all of this: People respond to environmental cues and are either reinforced, punished, or ignored for their responses. But it is the environment that matters—the people involved are incidental. On the other hand, consider a simple, single-cause answer that makes reference only to internal personal factors (e.g., "Alice had strong needs for competence and perceived that joining the Navy would help her satisfy those needs"). They are a lot more manageable than gross sets of three factors, interacting in dyadic relationships, two at a time. But are simple one-way causal models realistic?

Bandura (1986) offers another example of how three-way relationships between a person (and his internal dynamics), his behavior, and the environment all interact; it is an example that most readers of this book will recognize—watching television:

> Personal preferences influence when and which programs, from among the available alternatives, individuals choose to watch on television. . . . Although the potential televised environment is identical for all viewers, their actual televised environment depends upon what they choose to watch. Through their viewing behavior, they partly shape the nature of the future televised environment. Because production costs and commercial requirements also determine what people are shown . . . the options provided in the televised environment partly shape the viewer's preferences. Here, all three factors—viewer preferences, viewing behavior, and televised offerings—reciprocally affect each other. What people watch exerts some influence on their preferences, thoughts, and actions. (p. 24)

The Social Factor

This approach also places heavy emphasis on the social origins of thought. People are believed to be influenced by the thoughts, beliefs, values, and actions of others around them. We also learn much of what we know vicariously, by observation of the events affecting other people and by identifying with their outcomes in life. Self-regulation is also important. People set goals and behave in ways intended to achieve their goals, monitoring their progress as they go along, adapting and changing their behaviors as the feedback they receive suggests. The reader should see commonalities here with goal-setting theory and control theory, as presented in chapter 13.

The Environment in Social Cognitive Theory

What is the role of the environment? Whereas behaviorism holds that environmental contingencies are all-important causes of behavior, Bandura's school of thought tempers that view: "External events may create the occasion for doing something, but, except in simple reflexive acts, they are not the originators of affect and action. External stimuli give rise to courses of action through personal agency" (Bandura, 1986, p. 12). In other words, people may elect to apply their own skills and abilities when their surroundings present them with opportunities to do so. The notion of triadic causality enters here. People are not assumed to be autonomous agents or mechanical conveyors of environmental forces. "Rather, they serve as a reciprocally contributing influence to their own motivation and behavior within a system of reciprocal causation involving personal determinants, action, and environmental factors" (Bandura, 1986, p. 12). Moreover, the environment does not influence people's behavior in some sort of mechanical, direct manner; rather, the person's perceptual and thought processes mediate the impact of the environment: A person may not notice information from her environment, and even if she does, she may or may not elect to act on the basis of that information. "During transactions with their environment, people are not merely emitting responses and experiencing outcomes. They form beliefs from observed regularities about the outcomes likely to result from actions in given situations and regulate their behavior accordingly" (p. 13). Later, Bandura (1986) writes:

A theory that denies that thoughts can regulate actions does not lend itself readily to the explanation of complex human behavior. Although cognitive determinants are disavowed by radical behaviorism, their causal contributions cannot be excised all that easily. Therefore, adherents of radical behaviorism translate cognitive determinants into stimulus operations, move them outside the organism, and then ascribe their effects to the direct action of the externally relocated events. . . . In fact, it is people's knowledge of their environment, not the stimuli, that is changed by correlated experience. Thus, for example, if a given word foreshadows physically-painful stimulation, the word assumes predictive significance for the individual, not the painful properties of the physical stimuli. (p. 15)

It seems almost strange that such an obvious point must be asserted, but its necessity at the time, a decade ago, speaks to the strength of the grip that behaviorism once had on modern psychology.

Distinctively Human Capabilities

In his most expansive statement of his approach, Bandura (1986) lists and documents the arguments in favor of a variety of human *capabilities*—inherent features of our humanity that were either ignored or denied by radical behaviorism. These capabilities are self-evident once they are identified, but again, it seems that someone had to describe these human dimensions explicitly to foster a shift away from a simplistic, mechanistic psychology of environmental determinism to one that recognized the self-starting, intellective nature of *Homo sapiens*. The most important of these capabilities permitting Bandura (1986) to advance his theoretical model are the following: anticipation and the capacity to form expectations; the capacity to symbolize—to form, manipulate, interpret, and communicate symbols and through symbols; the capacity to learn vicariously rather than only through personal experience; the capacity to self-regulate; and the capacity to reflectively think about one's self. We look briefly at each of these human capabilities.

Anticipation and Forethought Capability

People form expectancies about the *likely* consequences of their acts, not simply or primarily from the real consequences of those acts. "The notion that consequences influence behavior fares better for anticipated than for actual consequences . . ." (p. 13). The idea of anticipated consequences plays a key role in the cognitively based VIE theory presented in chapter 12 of this volume. So, to know how and whether outcomes will influence a person's behavior, we need to know how the person's cognitive apparatus processes these outcomes. Hence, Bandura rejects the simple, mechanical notion from behaviorism that "reinforcers" are the primary determinants of individual behavior. He also rejects the role of antecedent stimuli by citing work that shows that people are quite able to generate their own minds and emotions, not requiring features of their immediate environments to do so.

Symbolizing Capability

It bears repeating that this is a thinking person's theory of human behavior, although it does not imply that all behavior results from rational thought, clear thinking, or objective rationality. Biases abound, mistakes are made, and human mental aptitudes are not always well developed. Nevertheless, one major implication of this assumption is the observation that people formulate and make use of symbols in their everyday lives, and that symbolic action and the interpretation of symbols are critical in understanding behavior. "Through symbols people process and transform transient experiences into internal models that serve as guides for future action. Through symbols they similarly give meaning, form, and continuance to the experiences they have lived through" (Bandura, 1986, p. 18). People can use these symbols (including scripts and schemas, for example) to devise innovative ways of acting. People are capable of "playing out" scenarios in their minds, imagining the probable consequences of various forms of action. "Through the medium of symbols, [people] can communicate with others at almost any distance in time and space" (pp. 18–19).

Vicarious Learning Capability

People are capable of learning a great deal via the experiences of other people. In fact, "virtually all learning phenomena, resulting from direct experience, can occur vicariously by observing other people's behavior and the consequences for them" (Bandura, 1986, p. 19). This human capacity is one of the most important recognized by social cognitive theory, one of the tenets that makes it so much more realistic than radical behaviorism as a theory of human learning. Individuals and entire species might vanish if it were necessary for every one of us to learn how to deal with the world by trial and error.

Self-Regulatory Capability

Several times in this book, we have touched on the human desire for free will, self-determination, and individual freedom. Aside from a desire to be in command of our own acts, human history shows that we have considerable ability to be self-determining, for good or for bad. Nevertheless, one of the key capabilities that Bandura attributes to human nature is the capacity and the desire for what he calls self-regulation. "People do not behave just to suit the preferences of others. Much of their behavior is motivated and regulated by internal standards and self-evaluative reactions to their own actions" (Bandura, 1986, p. 20). Considerably more will be stated about self-regulation later in this chapter, particularly in the context of work motivation.

Self-Reflective Capability

Bandura (1986) states that "if there is any characteristic that is distinctively human, it is the capability for reflective self-consciousness. This enables people to analyze their experiences and to think about their own thought processes. By reflecting on their varied experiences and on what they know, they can derive generic knowledge about themselves and the world around them" (p. 21). Among the types of self-reflection that Bandura considers most important are the thoughts people have about their own abilities to engage in tasks. We have touched on his notion of self-efficacy at several points in this book (the reader is referred to chapters 6, 7, 12, and 13 for treatments of the topic). For our purposes here, the following should suffice: People will be more or less likely to take on tasks, set goals, alter goals, and attempt to master their environments if they assess positively their own capabilities vis-à-vis the world. Lacking self-efficacy beliefs would be terminal because people would be afraid to undertake any action. Overestimating their beliefs about self-efficacy can also have its problems in cases where people place themselves in situations in which they are doomed to fail. Whether our self-reflective beliefs are accurate or inaccurate, the point is that we all spend time thinking about ourselves, our thoughts, emotions, experiences, and desires. This trait makes us particularly human. It is not that behaviorists denied that we had the capacity to think, self-reflect, and emote; they merely denied the importance of these characteristics and processes as causes of human behavior.

Summary

For Bandura (1986), a defining characteristic of human beings is our almost limitless plasticity—our capacity to change ourselves and to be changed, within biological limits. The most important elements of human nature that form a pattern in his model of human functioning are our mental ones—our capacity to think, to plan, to make and use symbols, and our capacity to learn vicariously. It is not that Bandura believes that these mental skills give *Homo sapiens* total hegemony over the world; he does not. He simply gives us, as individuals, much more credit for our capacity to initiate action, to plan our own destinies, and to locate ourselves in environments of our open choice and our own making than did the behaviorists who immediately preceded him in the history of modern psychology.

Social Cognitive Theory and Work Motivation

Wood and Bandura (1989) state that three aspects of social cognitive theory have particular relevance for understanding work behavior. The first relates to the development of people's cognitive, social, and behavioral competencies at work through *master modeling*. This has to do with the way people can learn from one another in work settings by observing what other people do (and do not do) and then observing the consequences of those acts. It is not necessary for a newcomer to an organization, for example, to park his car mistakenly in the president's spot in order to learn that this is a "no-no." This lesson can be learned quite well by witnessing what happens to co-workers who do the same thing. The second area of relevance of social cognitive theory for organizational behavior is "the cultivation of people's beliefs in their capabilities so that they will use their talents effectively" (Wood and Bandura, 1989, p. 362). This has to do with the *development* of self-efficacy beliefs. The third area of direct relevance to us here is the enhancement of people's motivation through personal goal systems (Wood and Bandura, 1989, p. 362). We focus our attention here on the second and third areas, of particular value for social cognitive theory on work motivation: self-efficacy and goal systems. We have encountered both of these concepts before, so our treatment here will be brief.

Building Self-Efficacy

We have encountered this concept many times throughout this book, beginning in chapter 6. The reader is reminded here that *self-efficacy*

> concerns people's beliefs in their capacities to mobilize the motivation, cognitive resources, and courses of action needed to exercise control over events in their lives. There is a difference between possessing skills and being able to use them well and consistently under difficult circumstances. To be successful, one must not only possess the required skills, but also a resilient self-belief in one's capabilities to exercise control over events to

accomplish desired goals. People with the same skills may, therefore, perform poorly, adequately, or extraordinarily, depending on whether their self-beliefs of efficacy enhance or impair their motivation and problem-solving efforts. (Wood and Bandura, 1989, p. 364)

In short, people's self-efficacy beliefs will determine their levels of motivation, which, as we have defined it throughout this book, entails which tasks they undertake, how difficult a goal they will pursue, how much effort they will spend on the task, and how long they will persist in the face of failure or incompletion. Now the question becomes: What determines the strength of self-efficacy beliefs, given that they are so critical for determining the likelihood that a person will undertake tasks? There are four principal ways that efficacy beliefs can be instilled. The first is through *mastery experiences:* Performing a task well reinforces a person's belief that she can, in fact, do certain tasks as well as others like it. A second mechanism for building self-efficacy beliefs is *modeling,* which we have mentioned earlier: People learn a great deal by watching others, imitating them, and deriving vicarious rewards and punishments from the consequences of other people's actions.

A third mechanism for building self-efficacy is through *social persuasion.* This means having people encourage one another to do well and having other people assign us to tasks that will be challenging, yet manageable. People do not want to be induced into failure situations that will damage self-efficacy. Encouragements they receive should be realistic. The successes that follow should be against one's own goals rather than through triumphs over other people (Wood and Bandura, 1989). Finally, people pay attention to their own physical and mental health and fitness. "They read their emotional arousal and tension as signs of vulnerability to poor performance. In activities involving strength and stamina, people judge their fatigue, aches, and pains as signs of physical incapacity" (p. 365). So the fourth way that people can enhance their self-efficacy beliefs is by building their strength levels, reducing stress, and making the most of whatever bad news they receive about their limitations.

Group-Level Applications of the Theory

Recently, attempts have been made to apply variants of social cognitive theory to group-level performance. In one study, for example, Prussia and Kiniki (1996) examined the role of groups' affective reactions to their own performance accomplishments, group-level goals, and group-level feelings of "efficacy" on task performance. They found that two of the three factors (group-level affect and efficacy) mediated the relationships between feedback and exposure of the groups to films from which they could model effective behavior. Individual motivation also played a role. Interestingly, group-level goals did not have the sort of effects that individual-level goal-setting theory would have predicted. These preliminary results are interesting, although researchers must exercise caution in the ways by which they "translate" individual phenomena into group-level constructs.

Summary

In the foregoing sections, we have summarized social cognitive theory, showing how it emerged from the behaviorism of the 1950s and 1960s, evolving from the application of behavior modification and O.B. mod in the 1970s, acquiring and admitting cognitive elements as the decades passed. In its current form, social cognitive theory is an eclectic theory of human behavior that has subsumed most of the wisdom and contributions offered by these earlier approaches and has, in addition, picked up other useful concepts from cybernetics and goal-setting theory. We adopted a historical approach in this chapter to permit the reader to appreciate the origins of social cognitive theory, revealing how it contains and has adapted so many concepts that we have encountered under the umbrellas of other schools of thought. It is critical to see how behaviorism contributed to the blend: Although behaviorism may be moribund these days in its pure form, there is no doubt that it contributed, both directly and affirmatively but also through the backlash that it generated among its critics.

We close the chapter with a study of self-regulation, a body of applied techniques that is based upon social cognitive theory (and therefore upon elements of goal-setting theory), O.B. mod, and even control theory (recall chapter 13).

SELF-REGULATION

One of the most fruitful applications of psychology to everyday life over the past quarter-century has been in the area known as *self-regulation,* a set of principles and practices by which people monitor their own behaviors and *consciously* adjust those behaviors in pursuit of personal goals.[9] It is a process in which a person consciously elects to behave in ways that, otherwise, he would be less likely to behave (Mills, 1983; Thoresen and Mahoney, 1974). The person learns to recognize situations in which her habits may not serve her best interest, and to select nonhabitual options that may even be unpleasant or unfamiliar for her. For example, the author may routinely tune in the television program *Law and Order* after dinner on weeknights, curling up on his favorite sofa. Self-management in this case would occasion his recognizing that this comfortable habit is probably less desirable than other ways of spending the evening, such as reading the newspaper, going for a swim, or visiting a friend. Usually, self-management is accompanied by small rewards and punishments that the person applies or removes after he successfully engages in a consciously selected act that is an alternative to the most probable, habitual one.

Self-management can also entail considerable planning that removes or makes more difficult habitual options: Moving the television set to a drafty basement would continue our example. Most of us have witnessed the attempts that smokers make to kick their habit: They stop purchasing cigarettes, they attempt to eschew others who smoke (except when they want to "borrow" cigarettes), they avoid drinking beverages that have been associated in the past with smoking, and so on. If they succeed and are practicing self-regulation, they may reward themselves by consuming something special (other than tobacco smoke) or by engaging in a favorite activity (such as going bowling now that most public indoor facilities prohibit smoking).

---

[9]Consciousness is a defining element of self-regulation. Hence, any model of human nature or epistemology that denies or does not rely on human consciousness is alien to these principles.

Origins and Sources of Self-Regulation Concepts

As might be surmised from the foregoing examples, self-regulation owes much of its history and current status to clinical psychology.[10] In fact, Latham and Locke (1991) and others, such as Tsui and Ashford (1994), credit clinical psychologist Frederick Kanfer for his seminal contributions, although Kanfer (1970) himself observed that 4,000 years ago, Homer "reported some good advice for exercise of self-control through the admonitions of Circe to the sea faring Odysseus. To prevent the disastrous exposure to the bewitching songs of the Sirens, Odysseus was warned to plug his oarsmens' ears with soft beeswax. For his own control, he let himself be tied to the mast after cautioning the crew not to release him, 'shout as he may, begging to be untied' " (pp. 412–413). (This author wonders whether the same precautions might be effective against rap music.) Ironically, Kanfer also credits B. F. Skinner (1953) for his contributions to "self-control"; the irony lies in the fundamental differences that exist in the world views embraced by Locke and Latham on the one hand and Skinner on the other.

Nevertheless, self-regulation has been applied in a variety of other human settings and to a number of other human problems, such as personality and social psychology, abnormal psychology and psychotherapy, and education and learning, to mention a few (Karoly, 1993). In the clinical literature, self-regulation has been referred to as self-management, while in the organizational sciences it has also been labeled self-leadership, self-influence, self-management, self-control, and even "substitutes for leadership" (Mills, 1983).[11] Regardless of what it is called, the common feature of these techniques is that "the same person is both object and subject, both the doer and the target of the action" (Kanfer, 1970, p. 412). Our discussions of goal-setting theory and control theory in chapter 13 and of social cognitive theory earlier in this chapter will make the following description of self-regulation both familiar and possibly obvious to the reader. The essence of self-regulation is found in the concepts of goals, feedback, and control.

A Formal Definition of Self-Regulation

In a review of the theory, Karoly (1993) defined *self-regulation* as "those processes, internal and/or transactional, that enable an individual to guide his/her goal-directed activities over time and across changing circumstances (contexts). Regulation implies modulation of thought, affect, behavior, or attention via deliberate or automated use of specific mechanisms and supportive metaskills. The processes of self-regulation are initiated when routinized activity is impeded or when goal-directedness is otherwise made salient (e.g., the appearance of a challenge, the failure of habitual action patterns, etc.)" (p. 25). Self-regulation may be said to encompass up to five interrelated and iterative component phases: "(1) goal selection, (2) goal cognition, (3) directional maintenance, (4) directional change or reprioritization, and (5) goal termination" (p. 25).[12]

---

[10]See Pervin (1991) for some examples of self-regulation in the context of compulsions and addictions.

[11]Manz (1986) provided one of the earliest explications of self-regulation for understanding organizational behavior.

[12]Here is another example in the literature where different terms have been used to represent the same concept or process, or in which a given term may refer to two or more concepts or techniques. This point has been made in several places throughout this book. The term *self-management* in the context of organizational behavior and management has been used by authors such as M. de Waele, Morval, and Sheitoyan

Self-Regulation, Intrinsic Motivation, and Free Will

In many ways, the goal and gist of self-regulation is similar—perhaps identical—to the notion of self-determination that we examined in chapter 7: The core idea is that people have an innate *need* to be self-determining, to control their own behaviors, to affect their environments, and to be efficacious in those environments. People are driven to be captains of their own ships, masters of their own souls. Binswanger (1991) puts it this way: "Since regulation requires the expenditure of energy, self-regulation implies that the entity has its own energy source, one built into its structure. Its self-regulation is accomplished by using this energy source to initiate and steer its own behavior. An entity that is simply pushed and pulled about by external forces is clearly not regulating its motion. When a planet orbits a star, there is no self-regulation because the motion is the direct result of the sum of the external forces operating" (p. 154). Thus, self-regulation is really no more than a set of techniques that is based on scientifically validated concepts of goal setting and feedback that enable a person to achieve hegemony over her own behaviors, circumstances, and fate. Self-regulation is a technology designed to utilize what Deci and others (Deci, 1975; Deci and Ryan, 1985) refer to as *intrinsic motivation* (also see Hyland, 1988). Even more so, self-regulation can be seen as a modern behavioral technology intended for humans to pursue the age-old values of *free will* (Karoly, 1993).

The reader should recognize the link between the major concepts of goal-setting theory and control theory on the one hand, and the notion of self-regulation on the other. In fact, Latham and Locke (1991) state that "self-regulation is implicit in goal setting theory because . . . the setting of goals and their translation into action is a volitional process" (p. 233). Similarly, proponents of control theory easily apply their perspective to individual self-regulation (e.g., Carver, 1979; Carver and Scheier, 1990b). The terminology used by the two schools is similar but not identical. (For example, control theorists refer to "comparators," "output functions," and such [e.g., Carver and Scheier, 1990b], nouns that are not used by goal-setting theorists and proponents.) Let's take a look at the elements of the self-regulation process.

Elements of the Self-Regulation Process

First is the business of goal selection. A defining characteristic of self-regulation, in fact, is that a person sets his own goals (unlike much of the work done in the goal-setting tradition, in which people have their goals set for them or in which they determine their goals jointly with others). So a person adopts some goal for himself to accomplish over a set period of time. These goals may be *performance goals* (such as accomplishing so much work in a given period of time) or they may be *learning and mastery goals* (such as acquiring a new set of skills). For example, a new employee may set mastery goals such as becoming acquainted with the major customers of his new employer within his first six weeks on the job (which would represent a mastery goal) and then set other specific goals in terms of dollars of product he will sell each

---

(1992) to refer to a broad set of strategies and tactics that a person might employ to assure that she takes advantage of opportunities to advance her career on an ongoing basis and in a proactive manner rather than allow external events to determine her fate. This is a different use of the phrase *self-management* from the one we are dealing with here.

of those customers over the following two-year period (which would be a performance goal).[13]

Locke and Latham (1990b) report that self-set goals are as effective as goals that are assigned by other people or participatively set goals, but not *more* effective. Goals may be *distal* or *proximal;* their purpose is to plan the reduction of some discrepancy (as we described in chapter 13). The goal specifies the nature of the activity as well as the standard that the person desires to accomplish. Once set,[14] a person's goal instigates the three mechanisms underlying human motivation: effort, persistence, and direction (recall chapter 1). That is, a person consciously elects to follow one path or another (watch television or visit a friend; eat dessert or have a salad; skip class or attend class), and once chosen, the goal sustains the person's effort and tenacity until "the right thing" has been accomplished, even though it may not have been the preferred or the most pleasurable of the alternatives available. As we saw in chapter 13, if action results in a failure to reach the goal, some sort of negative self-appraisal occurs and the person engages in problem solving and further action to reduce the discrepancy. If the initial behavior is successful, the person may set higher or different goals. Generally, the person provides herself with small rewards or punishments for goal success or failure, just as she would if managing the behavior of some other person.

Self-Regulation of Organizational Behavior

Although self-regulation has an effective track record in dealing with a variety of clinical/behavioral problems such as stopping smoking, reducing weight, and overcoming drug addiction, demonstrations and applications of self-regulation in organized work settings are still not numerous in the literature, but they are becoming more common (Latham and Locke, 1991). One of the earliest studies of work behavior using social learning theory (now called social cognitive theory) was a controlled experiment reported a decade ago by Frayne and Latham (1987) and Latham and Frayne (1989). In this project, the researchers applied a training program in self-management techniques to 20 unionized state government employees with the purpose of reducing their absenteeism from work. The program consisted of eight weekly one-hour group sessions, followed by eight more weekly 30-minute sessions in which the employees were taught the essentials of self-management. A control group of 20 other employees received no training.

The workers in the treatment group listed their reasons for having been absent from their jobs as well as problem behaviors that they had been experiencing at work (such as difficulties with their supervisors). They went on to identify conditions in the

---

[13]Two authors have recently suggested a distinction between *target goals* and *purpose goals* (Harackiewicz and Stone, 1991). For them, target goals are specific goals that a person shoots for when undertaking a particular activity (e.g., memorizing a Shakespearian sonnet within one hour). A purpose goal, however, is a longer-term goal that is represented by the target goal but that is more general and of greater and longer-lasting significance. In our sonnet example, a purpose goal might be the development of mental imagery skills, of cognitive focusing skills, or the acquisition of mental command of all of the Bard's work. "Target goals guide an individual's behavior, and purpose goals suggest the reasons for the behavior" (Harackiewicz and Stone, 1991, p. 21).

[14]We are reminded that once identified, a goal must be accepted by the person involved—he must become committed to the goal to have any hope of attaining it (Erez and Kanfer, 1983). (We discussed the thinking on this earlier in this chapter.)

workplace that may have been related to these problem behaviors: factors that may have elicited or maintained them. Frayne and Latham considered these sessions to comprise the self-assessment component of self-management. The employees then engaged in goal setting—that is, establishing specific attendance goals for themselves over specific periods of time. The fourth phase of the program was to teach the employees how to monitor their own behavior, recording their own attendance behavior, making notes about failures to attend, and recording the particular steps that were ultimately used to return to work. As the authors put it: "Emphasis was placed on the importance of daily feedback for motivational purposes as well as accuracy in recording" (Frayne and Latham, 1987, p. 388).

The next stage entailed the identification of individualized rewards and punishers, such as purchasing gifts for one's self (as a reward) or performing certain disliked tasks (such as cleaning the garage). Each employee developed specific behavior–reward/punishment contingencies to administer to himself, contingent on his own behavior. The final stages emphasized what the authors called "maintenance." This involved discussions with the participants on topics such as the possibility and potential causes of relapse behavior, planning for these problems and for dealing with them, were they to recur.

Frayne and Latham (1987) cited Azrin (1977) to emphasize the importance of applying as many of these self-management tactics as possible to any behavior problem: "The assumption underlying self-management is that the treatment package should 'include as many of the component procedures as seem necessary to obtain, ideally, a total treatment success' (Azrin, 1977, p. 144). Empirical support for combining goal setting, feedback, and self-monitoring into a treatment package can be found in both the organizational behavior and clinical psychology literature" (Frayne and Latham, p. 389). The results of this study were impressive. Employees expressed positive reactions to the training, both immediately after the eight weeks as well as three months later. But more important, there was a marked increase in employee presence, the dependent variable of most interest, and it appears that increases in their self-efficacy was the principal reason. In other words, the trained employees experienced an increase in their beliefs about their ability to overcome the obstacles that had been keeping them away from work, and as a result, their attendance records improved.

Most impressive, however, was the fact that the effects of the self-management intervention stood up over time. Specifically, Latham and Frayne returned to the same job site studied by Frayne and Latham and monitored the effectiveness of their program on the same 40 employees (20 in the training group and 20 control participants). They found that the program remained effective both six and nine months after the original intervention. Moreover, the employees who had originally served as the control group underwent the same program, yielding similar positive results on their attendance records. Longitudinal research of this sort is rare in the organizational sciences.

How natural is the self-management process? There is some evidence that most people do not spontaneously engage in all of these processes (see Brief and Hollenbeck, 1985), although the project reported by Frayne and Lathan summarized above makes it clear that problem identification, personal goal setting, the monitoring of feedback, and the self-administration of minor rewards and punishments on the basis of choices made can be taught to people (e.g., Frayne and Lathan, 1987; Latham and

Frayne, 1989). Although people may not widely engage in these techniques, some people do, as illustrated recently in a project reported by Frayne and Geringer (1994). In this study of a sample of joint business venture managers, Frayne and Geringer (1994) found that executives who made use of self-management techniques enjoyed more success in their ventures. Specifically, the researchers assessed the success of joint ventures with a set of qualitative and financial measures. They found consistently strong and significant correlations between the use of self-management techniques (as described here) and satisfaction with the ventures (in the minds of parent companies' executives) as well as profitability measures.

More recently, Frayne and Geringer (1997) applied self-management techniques to a sample of 30 insurance salespeople and found, as expected, that job performance improved dramatically as a result of the self-management training. The effects lasted over a 12-month period and were then applied successfully to the group of sales representatives who had served in the role of control participants for the first, experimental group.

Self-Regulation and Career Management

Two advocates of self-regulation argue that use of these techniques may be especially critical during current times of organizational downsizing, mergers, acquisitions, and other forms of heightened workplace uncertainty. Tsui and Ashford (1994) suggest that

> under such conditions, it may be impossible and, indeed undesirable for organizations to control managers' behaviors using traditional control mechanisms such as job descriptions, standard operating procedures and static performance appraisal systems. . . . Instead, the processes most needed in the ambiguous and complex situations just described would seem to be those of self-regulation and self-control on the part of managers themselves. Managers skilled in self-regulation can respond to the complexity and dynamic pace of their intermediate environment in a timely fashion. In these situations, self-regulation by managers is not only a substitute for other sources of structure . . . it is a necessity if the organization is to survive and to prosper. (pp. 93–94)

Tsui and Ashford (1994; see also Ashford and Tsui, 1991) emphasize the importance for mangers under such circumstances to actively seek out information regarding the expectations that key stakeholders place on them (Ashford and Tsui, 1991). This may be a trickly business, according to Ashford (1993), who believes that managers must establish specific standards on which to assess their performance, they must learn how to distinguish among the many cues that are available to them from feedback they receive about their performance, and they must also accurately interpret those cues—all very subtle processes, indeed. Additionally, Tsui and Ashford (1994) believe that managers must develop the skill to assess which of the various roles and expectations being placed on them are more important at any point in time (rather than adhering to some predetermined programs or order of priority). They suggest that managers with strong self-efficacy beliefs are more likely to engage in active feedback seeking (as it relates to their behavior and performance), whereas managers who have low self-esteem (see chapter 6) will tend to avoid negative feedback and seek positive feedback about their performance.

Their proposed model yields a number of interesting hypotheses. In fact, an experiment reported by Northcraft and Ashford (1990) found that people with low performance expectations or low self-esteem may engage in low levels of feedback seeking: "Individuals forego inquiry if they believe the feedback will be negative, and especially if others will hear it" (p. 58). The point is that although some early theorists (e.g., Kanfer, 1971) indicated that self-management is a simple three-stage process, involving self-monitoring of one's own behavior, evaluation of that behavior, and the self-administration of rewards and sanctions, Ashford, Tsui, Northcraft, and others have delineated just how subtle and difficult these various stages may be, particularly the monitoring and evaluation of feedback.

Self-Regulation of Emotions

In chapter 4 we initially examined the notion of people's capacity to regulate or control their emotions, and in chapter 8 we paid particular attention to the connection between certain emotions, such as anger, and whether and how controlling anger in the face of frustration is possible or beneficial to human welfare. In these discussions we encountered the idea of emotional intelligence (Goleman, 1995; Salovey and Mayer, 1990; Salovey et al., 1993) and the purported value to people of maintaining control of their emotions and of their ability to read and respond appropriately to the emotions of other people. We return briefly here to the concept of the control of emotion in the present, broader context of self-regulation.

Emotional Intelligence

As we saw in chapter 4, the concept of *emotional intelligence* appears to have first been presented by Salovey and Mayer (1990) and made popular a few years later by Goleman (1995). The phrase refers to "a set of skills expected to contribute to the accurate appraisal and expression of emotion in oneself and others, and the use of feelings to motivate, plan, and achieve in one's life. The emotional intelligence framework suggests that there may be individual differences in people's abilities to exert effective control over their emotional lives" (Salovey et al., 1993, p. 258). A person's ability to regulate his own emotions depends on his capacity to interpret the information that emotional expression—both his own as well as that of other people—makes available. The making of "faces" is an example that was cited earlier: Some people are more capable than others of understanding the meaning of rude or provocative, deliberately projected faces (Salovey et al., 1993, p. 260). Similarly, some adults are limited in their ability to express their feelings in words, even though children have been shown to be capable of generating hundreds of words that reflect people's common emotions and of thinking of ways that they could moderate their own emotional expressions.[15]

In addition, people vary from one another in their abilities to harness their own emotions for problem solving. For example, changes in a person's mood may open up or suggest new solutions to problems. Creative and inductive reasoning may be served by happy emotional states, which may also cause people to "hang in there" longer

---

[15]Salovey et al. (1993) remind us that emotional intelligence includes the capacity to recognize, influence, or regulate the emotions of other people; our focus here will be limited to the interpretation and control of one's own emotions.

when the going gets tough. By contrast, sad states may be most effective in dealing with deductive reasoning tasks (see Salovey et al., 1993). Thus, it appears that possessing the skill to manipulate one's own emotional state may have benefit for the performance of many modern tasks. So, how is this accomplished? As we saw in chapter 3, recent evidence from the psychology of satisfaction and affect provides some clues (Salovey et al., 1993).

Simple hedonism implies that people are happier when they possess more of things they like. This simple hypothesis has been elaborated by a series of studies which show that in addition to the possession of desired outcomes, the rates at which we receive such outcomes and the changes that these outcomes imply over our baseline experiences are also critical in determining our satisfaction and pleasure (Salovey et al., 1993). In other words, we compare the level of outcomes we have at a given moment with the levels we have had in the past. Positive additions of good things bring pleasure, but after we have grown used to our new circumstances, the pleasure level drops. Thus, an employee who receives a sudden 10 percent pay increase may be ecstatic at first, but a month later the joy will probably subside as she grows used to the new level of pay.

In addition, when we lose valued commodities, such as occurs with a cut in pay, the anger initially felt is more acute than that which is likely after time has passed. So far, so good: People adapt to their new circumstances more or less readily. In addition, the *faster* things improve, the greater is our satisfaction, the happier is our mood. If pay increases come quickly, they bring more satisfaction than if they take longer. A person whose house increases in value by $10,000 over a year will be happier than a person whose house increases in value by $10,000 over two years (Salovey et al., 1993). So, in addition to positive changes from a baseline position, the rate at which the positive changes come also makes a difference in our satisfaction (Salovey et al., 1993). Researchers refer to this phenomenon as the *velocity* of change.

Finally, in addition to high velocity of change, people appear to gain even greater satisfaction *when the velocity itself changes from negative to positive*. That is, people are happiest when the desired value first decreases and then increases and the most unhappy when the velocity changes from positive to negative: "that is, when the desired value first increases and then decreases" (Salovey et al., 1993). We gain most pleasure from watching our favorite sports team win a game after falling behind in the early going and then making a valiant comeback to score the tying and winning goals late in the match. By contrast, the pain we feel for the same team is especially acute when they blow a lead and lose late in the game.[16] Salovey and his colleagues (1993) conclude: "This dynamic—indeed *emodynamic* view suggests that we are acutely sensitive to the pattern over which outcomes accrue in time, especially to their rate and shifts in that rate" (p. 269).

In summary, satisfaction derives not only from the level of one's outcomes but also from positive changes in that level and from increases in the rate of positive

---

[16]It is tempting to think of the notions of velocity and increases in velocity in mathematical terms such as first and second derivatives. In these terms, this neohedonism hypothesizes that satisfaction is greatest when both the first and second derivatives of the curve relating a person's level of desired outcome acquisition are both positive, and that dissatisfaction is at its worst when both mathematical terms are negative. The first derivative concept was tested successfully with Yale undergraduate students by Hsee and Abelson (1991).

change. The implications of these principles for the self-management of emotions are clear. It becomes a matter of arranging the order of events we encounter in life (and for our purposes, in our work experiences).

Arranging the Sequence of Events

Specifically, it follows that a person might regulate his emotional state to some degree if he can sequence events and activities so that they bring increasing levels of pleasure and/or in sequences that will minimize feelings of unhappiness and displeasure. Simple examples come to mind: Eat your (dreaded) Brussels sprouts before you turn your attention to your favorite ribeye steak. Organize your tasks at work on a given day so that the boring and distasteful ones are tackled first and the more pleasurable ones are attempted later. Open your birthday presents in the order that you expect them to bring you pleasure, the one with the most expected value last.[17] We discussed the Premack principle earlier in the chapter. It suggests that people engage in the tasks at work that are "most reinforcing" last, performing the tedious and least reinforcing tasks first—saving the "good stuff" until the end. The final piece of advice is to interact with and, where possible, help other people. There is evidence that helping others is generally a source of pleasure (Salovey et al., 1993).

With some effort given to thinking about the sequence of events we expose ourselves to, we can be capable of managing or at least moderating our own emotions and the expression of those emotions. To summarize, self-management works. In fact, research demonstrating connections between individual-level behaviors and organizational-level outcomes is more common in the literature on goal setting and its various derivatives, such as management by objectives and self-management, than it is in the literatures related to other bodies of work motivation theory (see Terpstra and Rozell, 1994).

GENERAL CONCLUSION

The theories and techniques of work motivation in this chapter are predicated on a model of human functioning that is different from those presented earlier in the book. This basic assumption is not based on human needs; that perspective was presented in part two. It is not based on perceptions and cognition; that assumption is featured in part three. Rather, the approaches presented in this chapter share a view of human nature that casts us as learning creatures. In this view the boundary between motivation and learning becomes somewhat blurred. This school of thought makes different ontological assumptions about people, different, at least, from the ontological assumptions made by theories elsewhere in our study of work motivation.

We adopted a historical approach in this chapter because it seems to be instructive of the ways in which theories and paradigms come and go in science. Behaviorism was the dominant school of thought in the tradition portrayed here until not long ago. Behaviorism does not deny the existence of human thinking or emotion; it merely

---

[17]In fact a series of experiments found that people prefer to open gifts in such an ascending order of expected pleasure, rather than in the opposite order, which would reflect a sense of impatience to get the fun over with as quickly as possible (see Salovey et al., 1993, for a summary of these studies).

discounts these internal constructs as useful explanations of human behavior. In the present context, behaviorism denies the relevance of thinking and feeling for explaining organizational behavior, and the very concept of "motivation" is alien or nonsensical. Behavior is determined by its consequences and limited by biological constraints. The antecedents of behavior contribute to our understanding, but only because these antecedent conditions have been learned to be the consequences of behavior. No need for difficult-to-measure, black-box concepts such as self-actualization, expectancy, self-efficacy beliefs, or pride in career progress.

But a lesson offered in chapter 2 is that theories come and go after researchers put hypotheses up against data and thinkers reason about *why* events occur as they do. So behaviorism faded in popularity in the late 1970s and is in disrepute now in the mid-1990s. It would be foolish to conclude that the behaviorist perspective is gone for good; it may be moribund but it may not be dead. The history of science (see Kuhn, 1970) teaches us (those of us who are willing to listen) that world views change and old ones come back, like Duncan's ghost. In the meantime, applications of behavioral psychology have been effective in clinical and educational settings. They have also been touted as effective in organizational settings, but it is not clear whether the root assumptions underlying these successes is as the behaviorists would have it. Instead, it seems that several cognitively based assumptions about human beings have to be included in the analysis to make sense of the results in work settings attributed to operant psychology. In the great picture of things, that is okay. Like the cycles of hemlines and the widths of neckties, behaviorism may come back. Duncan did.

CHAPTER

Work Motivation Theory: Assessment and Suggestions for the Future

All universal judgements are weak, loose, and dangerous.
—MONTAIGNE

For at least as long as the author has been a student of organizations and a participant in them, futurists have been making dramatic claims about the future of work and work organizations and, by implication, about the importance of the motivation to work. To varying degrees, the predictions of some of these organizational prophets (not many) have become reality, although not always within the time frames they imagined. At the time of this writing, Jeremy Rifkin's (1995) predictions about the future of work and jobs are catching the attention of many academics, business executives, and public policymakers. As we discussed in chapter 1, Rifkin offers a compelling argument that the world's societies and economies are evolving to the point wherein jobs, as we have known them, will eventually vanish. The concept of career will take on entirely new meaning, and rather than having jobs as such, people will be merely required, if not content, to perform whatever work needs to be done. Most of us will be replaced by technology and computers. Most organizations as we have known them will also disappear. A few people will continue to prosper, and a greater proportion of the population will live in poverty. Wealth will polarize as never before. If Rifkin is correct, if jobs continue to vanish and the economic benefits of automation are captured by an increasingly richer and smaller elite, those jobs that do remain in the interim will be especially valuable to those who can attain them and hold on to them. The motivation to work will become more acute that it has been in decades.

Even if Rifkin's predictions about the elimination of jobs are not correct, a variety of other large-scale forces and phenomena will cause the motivation to work to remain an important problem in the future (see Betcherman, McMullen, Leckie, and Caron, 1994). The ascendancy of many Asian national economies, the emergence of the North American Free Trade Agreement, the European Union, and the opening of trade between North America and many parts of the world are increasing the urgency for us to remain productive. Large-scale immigration from Latin America and Asia is changing the mix of North American languages, customs, work values, social security, and intercultural relations. Women are continuing to grow as a major force in our economies and are responsible for a disproportionate share of new small businesses. North American producers are competing more than ever to sell products and services in markets replete with goods and services produced by people who earn much less compensation per hour or per month than we earn. In fact, child labor is epidemic in many parts of Asia, Europe, and Latin America. Even on a less global scale, North American phenomena such as corporate downsizing, outplacing, right-sizing, and lay-offs are likely to continue well into the new millennium. Entrepreneurship, small business, network arrangements, and temporary organizational forms are likely to become much more the norm and much less the exception. Most of these forces and changes have serious potential consequences for the well-being of all of us.

Two questions arise. First, how much do we really know at present about work motivation? Second, how adequate will our current theories be for understanding and dealing with problems of work motivation in the future? In this chapter we assess the adequacy of current theory and suggest how research and theory building might be modified in the future to deal with the many changes we can expect in the world of work.

HOW MUCH DO WE KNOW AT PRESENT?

How much do we currently know about work motivation? This author's view is more positive now than it was in an earlier treatment of this topic (Pinder, 1984). At that time it seemed that both the quantity and quality of our knowledge about work motivation were less than commensurate with the obvious importance of the issue and the volumes of research and formal writing that had been devoted to it. But some progress has been made since then. The cycle of research and theory development depicted in chapter 2 has modified some work motivation theories (such as models of employee commitment, for example), reduced the importance of others (e.g., cognitive evaluation theory), and caused the reconciliation of still others (see chapter 14, for example). In addition, there have been some encouraging attempts to reconcile and integrate hitherto disparate bodies of theory, as we will see shortly.

In the following sections we summarize the most important propositions about work motivation that seem justified on the basis of theory and research from each of the four major perspectives on human nature examined in this book: human beings as need-satisfying creatures, as information-processing creatures, as emotional creatures, and as learning creatures.[1]

Human Beings as Need-Satisfying Creatures

The most important principles that follow from the theory and research predicated on this model of human nature are presented here. Most of these principles score well by our accounting on the practicality criterion (recall chapter 2 and see Brief and Dukerich,

---

[1]A similar list of propositions—all of which are based on empirical observation—has been advanced by Locke (1997).

1991) because they can be helpful in understanding why people behave the ways they do, and they have broad generalizability. But they rate less well on the "relevance" criterion (Thomas and Tymon, 1982) of being immediately applicable in a timely manner to nonobvious problems. They also fall short on their demonstrated scientific validity, in large part because of the difficulty researchers have had in operationalizing the concepts for rigorous scientific validity.[2]

1. Internal needs, some of which are innate and some of which are learned, are ultimately responsible for instigating and directing human behavior.

2. There are a variety of human needs; they operate in differing degrees of strength for different people as well as in varying levels of strength for particular people at different times.

3. It is difficult to assess the strength of needs directly; they are hypothetical constructs, the existence of which can be inferred only from observing behavior.

4. Certain human needs are more powerful in instigating and directing behavior than others, although there is less than total agreement about the comparative strength of the various nonphysiological needs (which are widely viewed as the least prepotent of all).

5. Since there is no one-to-one correspondence between particular needs and particular behaviors, it is difficult to make inferences about the influence of specific needs in other people simply from watching their behavior or listening to what they say.

6. Needs that have been more or less satisfied tend to lose their capacity to arouse and direct behavior.

7. Most behavior is determined by the force of more than one need.

8. Intrinsic motivation is energy directed at satisfying a set of learned needs, including needs for achievement, self-esteem, competence, and self-actualization.

9. The need for achievement is most likely to motivate behavior when the person perceives a moderate (or 50:50) degree of chance of success at the task.

10. To varying degrees, people have a need to be treated equitably and to treat others equitably.

11. People can be expected to vary in the degree of equity they find in the same reward/punishment circumstances; equity is "in the eye of the beholder."

12. Equality of treatment, therefore, does not assure equitable treatment.

13. Frustration occurs when behavior that is intended to achieve certain goals for the sake of meeting a need (or needs) is blocked.

14. Some blockages are external to the person being frustrated; others result from characteristics of the people themselves.

15. There are a variety of common human reactions to frustration, including aggression, regression, denial, and goal displacement (to mention a few).

16. These generic reactions to frustration manifest themselves in different ways in different people, often making it difficult to diagnose or recognize frustration-related behavior.

17. Values are similar to needs and are determined in large part by needs, but the two concepts are not identical. Values are objects, qualities, or standards that a person seeks to satisfy needs. Values are guides to human action.

---

[2]It bears repeating that many of the ideas presented in this book may be more valid than social scientists are capable of demonstrating; that point has been suggested several times.

18. People place value on end states (such as peace or wealth) as well as on means such as being honest, logical, or rational.

19. People's values change over time, in part because the composition of their most important needs changes.

20. There is a misleading tendency to attribute individual-level concepts such as needs and values to aggregates such as groups and organizations.

21. People often attribute their own motives to other people when attempting to understand or explain the behaviors of others. This also is a mistake.

Human Beings as Perceiving, Rational Information Processors

A similar set of the most important principles from theory and research predicated on the assumption that people are perceptual, rational creatures follows. The scientific validity of most of these points is superior to that of the points raised in the preceding set, in large part because scientists have been more effective at manipulating and measuring key variables in experimental work or merely measuring them in nonexperimental research. They are also more widely generalizable and practical.

1. Human beings are conscious animals. They perceive their environment and process information gathered from that environment. Beliefs and attitudes formed on the basis of this information provide the ultimate causes of behavior, but intentions are the most immediate causes.

2. The most effective means for changing volitional behavior is to alter people's perceptions, and accordingly, their beliefs, attitudes, and—of most importance—their intentions.

3. Perceptions of equity (or inequity) are based on a person's perceptions of the exchange relationships they have with other people or organizations (such as their employers).

4. Sufficiently high levels of perceived inequity will motivate attempts to restore perceptions of equity.

5. Strong feelings of inequity result in withdrawal behaviors if efforts to alter the exchange relationship fail.

6. People can be expected to alter their perceptions of exchange relationships if behavior aimed at actually changing them fails and if withdrawal is not possible.

7. As a result, absenteeism, turnover, and psychological withdrawal are commonly observed among people who feel inequitably treated.

8. People's level of confidence in their capacity to succeed at a task positively influences their motivation to engage in the task.

9. The degree of satisfaction expected from work-related outcomes influences the motivation to engage in a task; expected satisfaction—not actual satisfaction—is what matters.

10. The strength of the connection perceived between positively evaluated outcomes and work performance is a major determinant of work motivation.

11. The strength of the connection perceived by the person between work performance and the receipt of negatively evaluated outcomes also determines work motivation and decisions.

12. Specific task goals result in higher levels of performance than do vague goals or instructions to "do your best."

13. Incentives influence work motivation only to the extent that they influence people's intentions to act.

Human Beings as Emotional Creatures

We can consider a few principles of work motivation that arise from our analysis of the emotional nature of human beings, although there has been considerably less work performed from this perspective than from the other major perspectives studied in this book. The primary strengths of these following principles, in terms of the criteria we discussed in chapter 2, seem to be that they are universal in applicability (although the experience of emotion itself can be virtually idiosyncratic) and that they are quite practical, inasmuch as they should give rise to considerable thinking about people's motivation to work and their reactions to their jobs and careers. So what principles might be offered?

1. Emotions can be thought of as "readouts" of a person's inner need states, values, thoughts, and intentions. They can be very communicative.

2. People frequently use different terms to reflect different types of emotions, so flexibility is required when we attempt to communicate with other people about what they are "feeling."

3. Some people are characteristically happier and more positive about life in general than others. Similarly, some people are typically more negative than others about their life experiences.

4. Some emotions are like internal commodities or forces that require being "let out" or expressed.

5. People vary in the degree to which they can manage or regulate their emotions.

6. Some emotions can be denied expression until strategically appropriate times.

7. There is mixed evidence on the matter of the primacy of emotions and cognitions. Sometimes one of these facets of human nature seems to rule the other, but the dominant role can vary from time to time.

8. Being "highly emotional" does not imply being of substandard cognitive ability.

9. Women in our culture are, on average, better than men at understanding and addressing emotional issues.

10. People with a strong capacity to understand and manage their own emotions as well as those of other people can have an advantage in the workplace.

11. Emotion can serve as a motivational force that instigates behavior. It can also accompany behavior and be affected by one's own behavior.

12. Jobs requiring high levels of self-control over one's emotions may be damaging to the natural expression of a person's genuine behavioral impulses.

Human Beings as Learning Creatures

The fourth model of human functioning underpinning current approaches to work motivation is that provided by the learning approaches to work motivation presented in chapter 14. Many of the principles, although useful, may be so for reasons that early behaviorists and O.B. mod theorists rejected. The central controversy has to do with *why* the prescriptions and principles work as they do. We have addressed these controversies at length; here we summarize only the applied propositions offered by current learning models of work motivation.

1. Behavior is determined by its antecedents and its consequences.

2. Behavior that is reinforced in the context of a particular set of antecedent circumstances is more likely to be emitted on future occasions in those (and similar) circumstances.

3. Behavior that is punished in the context of a particular set of antecedent circumstances is less likely to be emitted on future occasions in those (and similar) circumstances.

4. Most behaviors occur in chains, in which the consequences of an act reinforce that act and serve as cues that make it more likely that the person will subsequently emit certain other acts, which themselves have been reinforced in the past.

5. A complete understanding of behavior requires, therefore, a knowledge of its antecedents and its consequences, as well as of the form of the behavior itself.

6. Consequences can be distributed on the basis of either interval or ratio schedules; the latter are more powerful than the former for influencing behavior.

7. Continuous reinforcement is most effective for the acquisition of new behaviors.

8. Extinction occurs most rapidly among behaviors that have been reinforced by continuous schedules.

9. Higher rates of behavior result from variable-ratio schedules than from any other schedule once a behavior has been learned.

10. People acquire many or most key skills from observing the experiences of other people and witnessing the consequences of the actions of others.

11. People are capable of manipulating their environments and those of other people so as to increase the likelihood of positive outcomes and minimize the likelihood of negative consequences for their acts.

12. People pay particular attention to the feedback that is available from their environments as it relates to their successes and failures in goal-related activity.

Summary and Caveat

Summary lists such those presented above are somewhat arbitrary. It is difficult to state the principles that derive from each perspective at equal levels of specificity. Moreover, it is hard to reach agreement about the amount of support that *should* be required for a body of theory before it or any of its tenets are proclaimed ready, or appropriate for application to real-world problems (compare Bobko, 1978, with Pinder, 1977, 1978). Nevertheless, the 58 points listed above (in addition to whatever corollaries derive from them) provide a set of principles that may be useful to those whose job it is to arouse or sustain the motivated effort of themselves or of others.

INTEGRATING THEORIES OF WORK MOTIVATION

One indicator of the progress that has been made since the mid-1980s is found in the attempts some scholars have made to integrate middle-range theories of work motivation into more general, holistic models. The importance of integrating theories was discussed 10 years ago by Ilgen and Klein (1988b). While discussing the role of *cognitive approaches to work motivation* in individual productivity, they wrote:

> The lack of integration is unfortunate. The diversity of perspectives gives the impression that there are few general principles across [organizational] positions. Yet this con-

clusion is unjustified. . . . Pritchard's expectancy theory interventions worked best when paired with goal setting, and transfer from behavior modeling training back to the job was better when performance goals were set (Wexley and Latham, 1981). For goals to be effective, it was assumed that the performer saw some connection between goal accomplishment and the receipt of some positive reinforcers; in other words, goals worked when nonzero instrumentalities existed between goal accomplishment and valued outcomes. Thus all three approaches explicitly included constructs from other theoretical positions.

A less explicit condition facilitating integration among the theories is the fact that the constructs developed within positions share a great deal in common across positions. This overlap has both negative and positive effects. . . .

Integration is, in our opinion, necessary. It is necessary because the theoretical perspectives rarely contradict and often complement each other. In fact, in one case, data gathered and interpreted from within one theoretical position could not be distinguished from those of another, in spite of very different interpretations offered for the same pattern of results. (See Locke's [1980] comparison of the goal setting of Latham with the behavior modification research of Komaki.) These conditions suggest that a summary of integrating concepts should be possible. (pp. 161–162)

On the basis of these observations, Ilgen and Klein (1988b) pulled together several points of overlap among various theories we have presented in this book. For example, they note that the idea of sense making is relevant or central to attribution theory, schema theory, expectancy theory, goal-setting theory, and equity theory. They point out that hedonism is an assumption underlying both VIE theory and goal-setting theory (they could have added equity theory). Concepts of value or valence (which is expected value) underlie VIE theory, equity theory, cognitive evaluation theory, and social cognitive theory. Experience and feedback are featured in control theory, goal-setting theory, social cognitive theory, and VIE theory.

The point? Ilgen and Klein (1988b) attempted to show that it is virtually impossible for differing theories of work motivation to be independent from one another because, after all, they all purport to reflect the nature of the same phenomenon. Holistic models of human nature have made such claims for years (see Walter and Marks, 1981). There have been other attempts to integrate work motivation theories. Klein (1989) followed up on his coauthored observations with Ilgen (cited above) with an integrative model of work motivation that builds around control theory and that includes parameters taken directly from various cognitive theories, portrayed in a single causal map (see chapter 13).

In similar fashion, Locke and Latham (1990a) have offered an integrated theory of "high performance" that combines elements of goal setting, expectancy, social cognitive theory, attribution, job design, equity, and commitment. A more fully developed version of this approach is Locke's (1991a, 1997) attempt to link motivation concepts into a sequential model that begins with needs and ends with satisfaction. Summarized in Figure 15-1, Locke's model proposes that human needs are the most fundamental set of factors for understanding work motivation and that they provide the basis for individual values. Values interact with expectancy and self-efficacy beliefs to determine key goal attributes such as difficulty and specificity, which, in turn, instigate the mediating goal mechanisms of direction, effort, persistence, and goal strategies. These mechanisms may or may not result in performance and outcomes, depending on a variety of

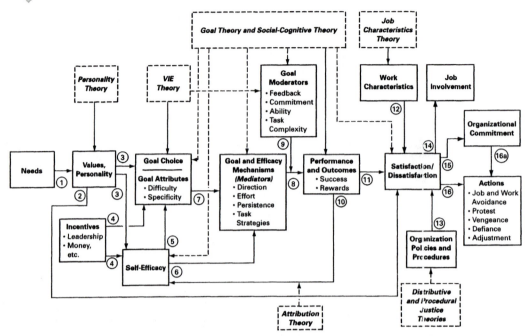

Source: From E. A. Locke, "The motivation to work: What we know," in P. Pintrich and M. Maehr (Eds.), *Advances in motivation and achievement,* vol. 10 (Greenwich CT: JAI Press, in press). Reprinted with permission.

FIGURE 15-1 Locke's Integrated Empirical Model of Work Motivation

factors, such as the nature of feedback, the employee's ability and commitment to the goal, and the complexity of the task being undertaken. Performance outcomes may or may not, in turn, result in employee satisfaction, depending in part on contextual factors such as the nature of the job itself and organizational policies and procedures. The level of satisfaction that does accrue may then affect the employee's levels of job involvement and organizational commitment. Finally, the satisfaction/dissatisfaction level and the degree of commitment the person has to the organization may cause any of a set of job actions, such as avoidance, protest, defiance, or adjustment.

To the knowledge of this author, Locke's (1997) integrative model is the most comprehensive currently available. It is especially significant because most of the causal connections it postulates are rooted in empirical evidence. The model implies that considerations of fairness and equity have only indirect influences on employee motivation and performance, and it excludes notions of intrinsic motivation altogether. The reader is referred to Locke's (1997) chapter for a complete explication of his integrative model. It is clearly the most defensible and comprehensive single summary of the evidence and theory available at this time.

Another approach to the integration of theories was offered by Mayes (1978b). His idea is to relegate different theories to the explanation of different work-related phenomena (e.g., habitual behavior versus deliberate decision making). In this tradition, Landy and Becker (1987) have suggested that need and equity models are best suited to exploring the emotional aspects of work motivation, while operant and goal approaches are best at *understanding* specific work behaviors. Finally, they suggest that

VIE theory be given the job of predicting people's behaviors from among the alternatives available to them (Landy and Becker, 1987).

Some theorists have attempted to gain "integration" simply by asserting (usually with the help of logic and appeals to metaphysical belief structures) that their preferred approaches are superior to those of others. Locke's attacks on O.B. mod (Locke, 1977, 1979; and see chapter 14 of this book) and his and Bandura's attacks on control theory (Bandura, 1989; Locke, 1991a; and see chapter 13) provide two examples of this approach to integration. A similar, related approach is to summarize extant theories and discard some while saving others on the basis of their scientific tractability (e.g., M. E. Ford, 1992).[3]

Taxonomies and Middle-Range Theories

This author has proposed in an earlier work (Pinder, 1984) that research and theory development on work motivation might be served by the development of middle-range theories that apply only to limited combinations of people and situations. Taxonomic procedures would be applied to develop categories of people and categories of organizational contexts, and different theories would then be pursued for relevance within the confines of different *people* × *situation* combinations. This approach is illustrated in Figure 15-2. To our knowledge, no one has yet undertaken a systematic pursuit of this research and theory-building strategy.

The Potential of Self-Concept Theory

Recently, however, Barbuto (1996) has suggested that work in the area known as *self theory,* particularly social identity theory (see Ashforth and Mael, 1989; Tajfel and Turner, 1985), self-presentation theory (Beach and Mitchell, 1990), and self-efficacy theory (Bandura, 1986) may provide the basis for forming motivational *types of people.* This body of work hinges on the fundamental notion of a "dynamic self-concept," which implies that a person's notion of his or her self can be "active, forceful, and capable of change. It interprets and organizes self-relevant actions and experiences; it has motivational consequences, providing the incentives, standards, plans, rules, and scripts for behavior; and it adjusts in response to challenges from the social environment" (Markus and Wurf, 1987, pp. 299–300).

FIGURE 15-2 Construction of Middle-Range Theories of Work Motivation

Type of Individual	Type of Work Setting			
	1	2	3	4
1	Theory 1,1	Theory 1, 2	Theory 1, 3	—
2	Theory 2,1	—	—	—
3		—	—	—
4		—	—	—

---

[3]Ford is harshly critical of need-based theories and behaviorist approaches and concludes that three sets of factors are necessary for workable theories of human motivation: goals, emotions, and "agency beliefs"—particularly self-efficacy beliefs.

The use of self theory as a tool for integrating work motivation theories is not new. Snyder and Williams (1982), for example, suggested this possibility years ago: "[It] is based on the premise that human beings have a fundamental *need* [emphasis added] to maintain or enhance the phenomenal self" (p. 257). The self is the entire personality of the person—the composite of things and attributes that a person uses to describe himself. All behavior is a function of what goes on inside the person and of how the person interprets objective situations as opportunities for maintaining and enhancing the self-concept. Snyder and Williams (1982) provided the following example:

> In the case of a low-performing individual, for example, self theorists would not view this person in the traditional sense of being "unmotivated" or "not influenced by the supervisor." Instead they would argue that individuals are always motivated to maintain or enhance their concept of self. The difference between a high performing individual and a low performing one, therefore, is not in terms of level of motivation. Both workers are motivated, but the high performer perceives high performance as a means of maintaining or enhancing the self, or, as is more likely, as a means of maintaining or enhancing the specific attributes of the self that are relevant to the particular performance involved. (p. 261)

Thus, self theorists would have us focus more on what goes on *inside* a person for an understanding of behavior. What goes on outside is relevant only as it is interpreted by the person in question, and as s/he sees external events and conditions as relevant to maintenance or enhancement of the self-concept.

An issue among self theorists concerns the nature of the self-concept itself. Sometimes it is viewed as a more or less stable *agent* that enables the person to operate on task environments that are stable, familiar, and nonthreatening. In these situations, theories that rely on needs, balance, equity, and expectancies are most useful for understanding work motivation. However, when the task environment is unstable, unfamiliar, or hostile, the self is more like an "evolving software program with subprograms to direct the person to be goal-oriented . . . to view acts as personally caused . . . to find a source of motives in internal cognitive structures . . . or to see themselves as in control of their lives . . ." (Sullivan, 1989, p. 355). Thus, theories such as goal setting and self-determination would be more relevant for understanding organizational behavior when the context is alien or unpredictable.

These unusual ideas had not attracted much attention among work motivation scholars until Leonard, Beauvais, and Scholl (1995) picked up the theme. They have argued that a self-concept-based theory of work motivation is needed for a variety of reasons. Specifically, such a theory would "(1) help to explain non-calculative work behavior; (2) better account for internal sources of motivation; (3) integrate dispositional and situational explanations of work behavior and (4) integrate existing self-theories" (p. 322). Accordingly, they have offered a five-way typology of *motivational sources* that includes *intrinsic process, instrumental motivation, external self-concept, internal self-concept,* and *goal identification.* Leonard et al. (1995) suggest that intrinsic process motivation occurs when a person engages in an activity for the sheer fun of it. The work is its own incentive (see chapter 7). Examples abound; people engage in an infinite variety of tasks and chores because they enjoy the activity for its own sake.

Instrumental motivation is aroused when a person perceives that action may result in extrinsic rewards such as money or recognition. It is based on calculative involvement (March and Simon, 1958) and is featured in the equity and VIE theories of work motivation (Leonard et al., 1995; and see chapters 11 and 12, respectively). External self-concept-based motivation entails behavior that is intended to meet the expectations of other people and significant reference groups, gaining their recognition, acceptance, and status. For example, a person might enroll in a weight-reduction program because his obesity is frowned upon by his colleagues and girlfriend. Alternatively, an employee might organize an office party because it is his turn to do so and he fears being rejected by his peers for not contributing his fair share to the social atmosphere of the workplace (see Leonard et al., 1995).

Internal self-concept-based motivation has the person setting personal, internal standards and then behaving in pursuit of those standards. This form of motivation is similar to achievement motivation and the aspects of intrinsic motivation involving competency and self-determination (see chapter 7). As an example, a person might set increasingly high sales or performance goals for herself, month after month. Finally, goal internalization occurs when people adopt attitudes and engage in behavior that is congruent with their personal value systems. This entails moral involvement (Etzioni, 1975) and the identification by the person with a cause or causes. An example would be fund-raising on a volunteer basis for a cancer society because one has lost a friend to that disease.

According to Barbuto (1996), a person's work behavior (and presumably her work-related attitudes and emotions) can be influenced by any and all of these five sources of motivation. For example, a different facet of the self-concept may explain why a person chose a particular program of study to prepare himself for a career and even the specific blend of courses he takes within his program of study. A different form of his self-concept may then explain the strategy he follows (if any) to seek and secure a job, or to start a business, or to travel abroad rather than seeking a job. Once in a work setting, different acts may be instigated, directed, and sustained by different facets of his self-concept, sometimes being influenced by his peers or his friends, other times by his own expectations of himself. The key thing is that membership in any given "category" is only temporary, as different elements of a person's self-concept predominate from one context to the next. Given that most deliberate human behavior is overdetermined, it will be important to think of blends of the different varieties of self-concept as contributing to work-related behavior, attitudes, and emotions.

The renewed interest in self-concept theory is still rudimentary, but it may offer one way to operationalize this author's notion of forming typologies or taxonomies of motivational types for the sake of developing middle-range theories of work motivation. A probable limitation of this approach would be operationalizing the constructs, so tests of the validity of the theory may be difficult, but perhaps not impossible.

Summary

Our purpose in the foregoing sections has been to address the question of how much is presently known about work motivation. Fifty-eight principles were offered to summarize our knowledge from four major perspectives on human nature, and we have reviewed a number of attempts that scholars have made to integrate bodies of theory that have hitherto seemed irreconcilable. On the basis of these principles and our examination of several conceptual suggestions for the integration of theories, we conclude that organizational science does offer a solid base of knowledge about work motivation—some aspects of it, at least.

OPPORTUNITIES AVAILABLE THROUGH NEW ROOT ASSUMPTIONS OF HUMAN FUNCTIONING

But the presentation of these lists of principles and integrative models highlights the necessity of multiple perspectives in order for us to make much sense of human work phenomena. Indeed, the celebrated complexity of human nature *requires* that we take into account multiple perspectives on work-related motivation, attitudes, emotions, and cognitions. The insights revealed by each of the major perspectives we have studied in this book are valuable but inadequate when considered one at a time. People *are* need-driven creatures, but there is more to understanding our behavior than considering only our needs and our goal-seeking activities. We are also motivated by our emotions and moods, and we are affected by the emotions and moods of others in our work lives. Likewise, we are information processors—much of our action can be understood when we take into account human perceptions, beliefs, attitudes, intentions, and other cognitive elements. Humans are also creatures who are capable of learning, both through personal means as well as vicariously through our communications with others. To attempt to reveal insight into any human behavior through the lens of only one of the major perspectives discussed in this book would be deficient, disappointing, and misleading. Which of the perspectives discussed in the foregoing chapters is correct? They all are, to varying degrees and in particular circumstances. Each provides some illumination, and each has its limitations. In fact, the strict adoption of any one of these perspectives can blind us to insights that may be available from the others. In summary, multiple perspectives on human nature are required to understand human work motivation. Collectively, the major perspectives presented here have revealed a great deal about the phenomenon, but more could still be learned through the development of perspectives not yet considered by work motivation researchers and theorists.

For example, there is a spiritual side of human functioning that has received virtually no attention in Western thinking on work motivation. A universal characteristic of human beings is our tendency to believe in some form of god or higher authority. Indeed, the history of the world is in large measure a story of the pursuit of human spirituality. But little or no theory has been developed to this point to explain the role of spirituality in our work motivation and behavior. Likewise, it is obvious that people are biological entities and that the biological capacities and limitations of our being affect our work habits. Yet little research and virtually no theory has been advanced on work motivation from a biological perspective on human nature.

In short, research and theory into work motivation may have been unavoidably attenuated in the past by the natural limitations each popular root assumption regarding human nature has placed on our thinking and observation. It follows that there may be room for advancement through the development of additional, alternative root assumptions of human nature that have hitherto been ignored by organizational scientists. In fact, our limited choice of lenses to date for the study of work phenomena may be understood when we take a close look at the precise types of people we have tended to study (and ignore) in the past, and when we step back and consider the comparatively limited range of problems we have studied so far. Three questions to consider are the following: Who have we focused our attention on, and which problems have we studied? How well will continued reliance on the same root assumptions we have used in the past enable us to understand work motivation in the future?

Whose Work Motivation Do We Understand?

Frost (1980) argued many years ago that the organizational sciences are too narrowly devoted to the study of a small, elite population of managers and professionals. He proposed that we have not spent sufficient time attempting to understand the realities of organizational life for lower participants in organizations. His point seems even more justified today than when he first made it. In fact, it deserves to be repeated and expanded.

For example, consider the organizational realities of immigrant laborers (both legal and illegal). They have received virtually no attention during the previous decades of research on work motivation. Likewise, we know very little about the work motivation of chronically unemployed or chronically underemployed people. What has been learned about the motivation and attitudes regarding the work of seasonal employees (such as farmers and fishers, for example)? Presumably, these primarily blue- and pink-collar workers hold beliefs, attitudes, values, and emotions relative to work, careers, and jobs, yet we have spent very little effort trying to understand their perspectives.

What about people who start their own businesses? What about outplaced people who return to school to improve their marketability and competitiveness? What about widows who have no marketable skills? What about single parents who have terrible difficulty taking care of their children while working to make their rent payments? What about underaged children who are compelled to sell their bodies into lives of sex and violence in order to survive from day to day? What about Native people who have low expectations of ever gaining and enjoying affluent status in a white person's world? How well do our current theories of work motivation guide us to understand the working lives and the significance of work among people in these groups? Not very well. The emotions, impulses, drives, attitudes, and spiritual states experienced by many people living and working in North America are poorly mirrored and understood by the theories of work motivation surveyed and summarized in this book. Heretofore many of these groups were considered "marginal" to the primary workforce, but they have become much more common and important in numbers as Rifkin's (1995) world of work unfolds. We must pay much more attention to them, so an expanded range of root assumptions regarding human nature may be useful.

Further, the motivation of people in many mainstream occupations is also hard to explain using our current models of motivation. For example, how can we explain the motivation of a person to be a nurse (see Driedger, 1997)? Consider their working conditions: shift work, exposure to foul and toxic substances (such as germ-infested blankets and bathrobes), abuse from patients and families of patients, doctors, and cleaning staff. There is constant risk of back injury. Why would a man or a woman become a nurse? The pay is usually poor and contentious. Nurses' shifts can create significant family difficulties and states of chronic sleep deprivation. Yet they are somehow motivated, in large numbers, to administer care and comfort in terrible circumstances to suffering people whom they *don't* know. How well can extant theories of work motivation explain nurses, or, for that matter, police officers or schoolteachers? Not very well, in the opinion of this author. Would a spiritual perspective help us to understand nurses?

The point here is that organizational scientists have tended to ignore work motivation issues for many significant segments of the working world. As Frost (1980) suggested, we have a subdiscipline devoted to the working executive, managerial, and middle classes of Western society. We know very little about the other classes and segments of society mentioned above. Portents of the world of work require that we shift our focus to study these other populations, and it may be that the adoption of new fundamental assumptions concerning human nature would open new ways of understanding these important but largely ignored populations of workers.

What Work Motivation Phenomena Do We Understand?

Paralleling Frost's (1980) plea for an expansion of study to broader and different populations of organizational participants was Staw's (1984) suggestion that the field of organizational behavior expand its attention to dependent variables other than the traditional ones: employee attitudes and performance. How well have research and theory on work motivation responded to Staw's (1984) plea? Listed below are brief overviews of the predominant foci of the major theories of work motivation discussed in this volume. Both the traditional dependent variables of interest in each theory as well as relatively new outcomes are cited. Naturally, the generalizations presented will overlook and miss a number of exceptions. The reader is referred to the appropriate chapters of this book to follow up on the generalizations offered. What have been the dependent variables of most interest to the dominant theories of work motivation to date, and how much is new since Staw's (1984) suggestion of a broader focus?

Goal-setting theory (chapter 13) purports to be a theory of motivation that uses individual task performance as its outcome variable of primary interest. (Recall from chapter 1 that motivation and performance are not the same concept.) Some recent attention has been devoted to learning goals in addition to performance goals, and goal-setting tactics are central to the new techniques of self-regulation in work settings. In short, goal-setting theory seems to be expanding the scope of its dependent variables, although comparatively little attention has been given to individual differences (see chapter 13).

VIE theory (chapter 12) has generally been used to build predictions of people's intentions and has been validated against ratings of their effort or performance, most frequently in a between-persons framework. Sometimes VIE theory has been used to predict individual choice behaviors such as retirement or job choice.

Equity theory (chapter 11) has traditionally been used to predict employee attitudes and motivation. Performance has been the criterion used in most of the studies of motivation. Lately, equity theory has demonstrated its value in the context of other behaviors as well, such as employee theft, and the overall scope has broadened from equity to wider concerns, such as fairness and varieties of justice. Procedural justice models have been applied to outcomes such as postlayoff adjustment of victims and survivors.

The theory of reasoned action (chapter 9) has not often been used in work motivation contexts. When it appears in the organizational literature, it is generally involved in studies of employee attitudes and intentions.

Social cognitive theory (formerly *social learning theory*) was rarely mentioned in the context of work motivation 15 years ago. Its emergence from the marriage of operant psychology and cognitive psychology makes it one of the most promising vehicles for progress in work motivation in coming years.

Operant models, O.B. mod, and especially *functional analysis* have been most useful in the form of functional analysis, in which the focus is on the connections between antecedent conditions, employee behavior (not attitudes), and the consequences of behavior. This theory has been subsumed for all intents and purposes by social cognitive theory.

Need-based theory and research have focused primarily on employee attitudes, motivation, and performance. Little innovation has occurred in this school of thought for decades.

In closing, although our review reveals that current theories of work motivation tell us a great deal about the initiation, direction, persistence, and cessation of work-related energy, they may be deficient for understanding the world of work that is coming. Current theories also fail to reflect the organizational and general life realities of many segments of today's population who are either working or eligible to be working. Moreover, current theories have focused too narrowly on a limited number of phenomena (employee job attitudes, individual performance, and emotions). Greater emphasis is now required on alternative root assumptions about people, on broader populations of workers and on the work motivation problems they face, and will be facing, in the new world of work. If organizational science broadens its focus to include a wider range of people and a wider range of work-related phenomena, our understanding of work motivation may be equal to the task: Individuals will have guidelines for making their own work-related decisions, and managers will have enlightened bases for the development and implementation of effective organizational policies and procedures.

A few years ago, Locke (1991a) concluded a survey of work motivation theory by writing: "[W]e do not know everything, but we do know something!" (p. 298). Indeed we do, but challenges remain.

References

Abbott, A. (1981). Status strain in the professions. *American Journal of Sociology, 46,* 819–835.

Abdel-Halim, A. A. (1980). Effects of person–job compatibility on managerial reactions to role ambiguity. *Organizational Behavior and Human Performance, 26,* 193–211.

Abella, R. S. (1984). *Report of the commission on equality in employment.* Ottawa: Minister of Supply and Services.

Adams, A. (1992). *Bullying at work.* London: Virago Press.

Adams, J. S. (1963). Toward an understanding of inequity. *Journal of Abnormal Psychology, 67,* 422–436.

Adams, J. S. (1965). Inequity in social exchange. In L. Berkowitz (Ed.), *Advances in experimental social psychology* (pp. 267–299). New York: Academic Press.

Adkins, C. L., Ravlin, E. C., and Meglino, B. M. (1992). *Value congruence between coworkers and its relationship to work-related outcomes.* Paper presented at the Academy of Management, Las Vegas, Nevada.

Adler, S., and Golan, J. (1981). Lateness as a withdrawal behavior. *Journal of Applied Psychology, 66,* 544–554.

Ahlberg, D. A. (1986). The social costs of unemployment. In R. Castle and D. E. Lewis (Eds.), *Work, leisure, and technology* (pp. 19–29). Melbourne, Victoria, Australia: Longman Cheshire.

Ahlberg, D. A., and Shapiro, M. O. (1983–1984). The social cost of economic decline: Some earlier evidence. *Journal of Keyensian Economics, VI(2),* 303–304.

Ajzen, I. (1991). The theory of planned behavior. *Organizational Behavior and Human Decision Processes, 50,* 1–33.

Ajzen, I., and Fishbein, M. (1977). Attitude–behavior relations: A theoretical analysis and review of empirical research. *Psychological Bulletin, 84,* 888–918.

Ajzen, I., and Fishbein, M. (1980). *Understanding attitudes and predicting social behavior.* Englewood Cliffs, NJ: Prentice Hall.

Ajzen, I., and Madden, T. J. (1986). Prediction of goal-directed behavior: The role of intention, perceived control, and prior behavior. *Journal of Experimental Social Psychology, 22,* 453–474.

Aldag, R. J., Barr, S. H., and Brief, A. P. (1981). Measurement of perceived task characteristics. *Psychological Bulletin, 90,* 415–431.

Alderfer, C. P. (1969). An empirical test of a new theory of human needs. *Organizational Behavior and Human Performance, 4,* 143–175.

Alderfer, C. P. (1972). *Existence, relatedness and growth.* New York: Free Press.

Alderfer, C. P. (1977). A critique of Salancik and Pfeffer's examination of need-satisfaction theories. *Administrative Science Quarterly, 22,* 658–669.

Aldis, O. (1961). Of pigeons and men. *Harvard Business Review, 39(4),* 59–63.

Aldrich, H. E. (1980). *Organizations and environments.* Englewood Cliffs, NJ: Prentice Hall.

Al-Gattain, A. A. (1985). Test of the path-goal theory of leadership in the multi-national domain. *Group and Organization Studies, 10,* 429–445.

Allen, N. J., and Meyer, J. P. (1990). The measurement and antecedents of affective, continuance and normative commitment to the organization. *Journal of Occupational Psychology, 63,* 1–18.

Allen, R. E., and Lucero, M. A. (1996). Beyond resentment: Exploring organizationally targeted insider murder. *Journal of Management Inquiry, 5,* 86–103.

Allen, T. D., Freeman, D. M., Reizenstein, R. C., and Rentz, J. O. (1995). Just another transition? Examining survivors' attitudes over time. *Academy of Management Best Papers Proceedings, 55th Annual General Meeting*. Vancouver, British Columbia, Canada: Academy of Management.

Amabile, T. M. (1988). A model of creativity and innovation in organizations. In B. M. Staw and L. L. Cummings (Eds.), *Research in organizational behavior* (Vol. 10, pp. 123–168). Greenwich, CT: JAI Press.

Amiel, B. (1985, August 5). The dangerous cost of equal pay. *Maclean's 98*(31), 9.

Anastasi, A. (1986). Evolving concepts of test validation. *Annual Review of Psychology, 37*, 1–15.

Anderson, J. (1970a). Giving and receiving feedback. In G. W. Dalton, P. R. Lawrence, and L. E. Greiner (Eds.), *Organizational change and development*. Homewood, IL: Irwin.

Anderson, J. W. (1970b). The impact of technology on job enrichment. *Personnel, 47*(5), 29–37.

Andrasik, F. (1979). Organizational behavior modification in business settings: A methodological and content review. *Journal of Organizational Behavior Management, 2*, 85–102.

Andrews, I. R. (1967). Wage inequity and job performance. *Journal of Applied Psychology, 51*, 39–45.

Angle, H. L., and Lawson, M. B. (1993). Changes in affective and continuance commitment in times of relocation. *Journal of Business Research, 26*(1), 3–15.

Angle, H. L., and Perry, J. L. (1981). An empirical assessment of organizational commitment and organizational effectiveness. *Administrative Science Quarterly, 26*, 1–14.

Angle, H. L., and Perry, J. L. (1983). Individual and organizational influences on organizational commitment. *Work and Occupations: An International Sociological Journal, 10*, 123–146.

Angle, H. L., and Perry, J. L. (1986). Dual commitment and labour–management relationship climates. *Academy of Management Journal, 29*, 31–50.

Argyris, C. (1957). *Personality and organization*. New York: Harper.

Argyris, C. (1971). Beyond freedom and dignity by B. F. Skinner: A review essay. *Harvard Educational Review, 41*, 550–567.

Armon, C. (1993). Developmental conceptions of good work: A longitudinal study. In J. Demick and P. M. Miller (Eds.), *Development in the workplace* (pp. 21–37). Hillsdale, NJ: Lawrence Erlbaum.

Armon-Jones, C. (1986). The thesis of constructionism. In R. Harre (Ed.), *The social construction of emotions* (pp. 32–56). New York: Basil Blackwell.

Arnold, H. J. (1976). Effects of performance feedback and extrinsic reward upon high intrinsic motivation. *Organizational Behavior and Human Performance, 17*, 275–288.

Arnold, H. J. (1981). A test of the validity of the multiplicative hypothesis of expectancy-valence theories of work motivation. *Academy of Management Journal, 24*, 128–141.

Arnold, H. J., and Feldman, D. C. (1982). A multivariate analysis of the determinants of job turnover. *Journal of Applied Psychology, 67*, 350–360.

Arnold, H. J., and House, R. J. (1980). Methodological and substantive extensions to the job characteristics model of motivation. *Organizational Behavior and Human Performance, 25*, 161–183.

Arthur, J. B. (1994). Effects of human resource systems on manufacturing performance and turnover. *Academy of Management Journal, 37*, pp. 670–687.

Arvey, R. D. (1979). *Fairness in selecting employees*. Reading, MA: Addison-Wesley.

Arvey, R. D., and Bouchard, T. J. (1994). Genetics, twins, and organizational behavior. In B. M. Staw and L. L. Cummings (Eds.), *Research in organizational behavior* (Vol. 16, pp. 47–82). Greenwich, CT: JAI Press.

Arvey, R. D., and Ivancevich, J. M. (1980). Punishment in organizations: A review, propositions and research suggestions. *Academy of Management Review, 5*, 123–132.

Arvey, R. D., and Jones, A. P. (1985). The use of discipline in organizational settings. In L. L. Cummings and B. M. Staw (Eds.), *Research in organizational behavior* (Vol. 7, pp. 367–408). Greenwich, CT: JAI Press.

Ashford, S. J. (1989). Self-assessments in organizations: A literature review and integrative model. In L. L. Cummings and B. M. Staw (Eds.), *Research in organizational behavior* (Vol. 11, pp. 133–174). Greenwich, CT: JAI Press.

Ashford, S. J. (1986). Feedback seeking in individual adaptation: A resource perspective. *Academy of Management Journal, 29*, pp. 465–487.

Ashford, S. J. (1993). The feedback environment: An exploratory study of cue use. *Journal of Organizational Behavior, 14*, 201–224.

Ashford, S. J., and Black, J. S. (1996). Proactivity during organizational entry: The role of desire for control. *Journal of Applied Psychology, 81*, 199–214.

Ashford, S. J., and Cummings, L. L. (1983). Feedback as an individual resource: Personal strategies of creating information. *Organizational Behavior and Human Performance, 32*, pp. 370–398.

Ashford, S. J., and Cummings, L. L. (1985). Proactive feedback seeking: the instrumental use of the information environment. *Journal of Occupational Psychology, 58*, pp. 67–79.

Ashford, S. J., and Northcraft, G. B. (1992). Conveying more (or less) than we realize: The role of impression-management in feedback seeking. *Organizational Behavior and Human Decision Processes, 53*, 310–334.

Ashford, S. J., and Tsui, A. S. (1991). Self-regulation for managerial effectiveness: The role of active feedback seeking. *Academy of Management Journal, 34,* 251–280.

Ashforth, B. (1994). Petty tyranny in organizations. *Human Relations, 47,* 755–778.

Ashforth, B. E., and Humphrey, R. H. (1995). Emotion in the workplace: A reappraisal. *Human Relations, 48,* 97–125.

Ashforth, B. E., and Mael, F. (1989). Social identity theory and the organization. *Academy of Management Review, 14,* 20–39.

Ashforth, B. E., and Saks, A. M. (1994, August). *Socialization tactics: Dimensionality and longitudinal effects on newcomer adjustment.* Paper presented at the Annual Meeting of the Academy of Management, Dallas, TX.

Atkinson, J. W. (1958). Towards experimental analysis of human motivation in terms of motives, expectancies, and incentives. In J. W. Atkinson (Ed.), *Motives in fantasy, action, and society* (pp. 288–305). Princeton, NJ: D. Van Nostrand.

Atkinson, J. W. (1964). *An introduction to motivation.* Princeton, NJ: D. Van Nostrand.

Austere, E. R. (1989). Task characteristics as a bridge between macro- and microlevel research on salary inequity between men and women. *Academy of Management Review, 14,* 173–193.

Austin, J. T., and Bobko, P. (1985). Goal-setting theory: Unexplored areas and future research directions. *Journal of Occupational and Organizational Psychology, 58,* 289–308.

Aven, F. F., Parker, B., and McEvoy, G. M. (1993). Gender and attitudinal commitment to organizations: A meta-analysis. *Journal of Business Research, 26,* 63–73.

Averill, J. (1982). *Anger and aggression: An essay on emotion.* New York: Springer-Verlag.

Azrin, N. H. (1977). A strategy for applied research: Learning based but outcome oriented. *American Psychologist, 32,* 140–149.

Babb, H. W., and Kopp, D. G. (1978). Applications of behavior modification in organizations: A review and critique. *Academy of Management Review, 3,* 281–292.

Bacharach, S. B. (1989). Organizational theories: Some criteria for evaluation. *Academy of Management Review, 14,* 496–515.

Bacharach, S. B., and Lawler, E. J. (1980). *Power and politics in organizations.* San Francisco: Jossey-Bass.

Badawy, M. K. (1982). *Developing managerial skills in engineers and scientists.* New York: Van Nostrand Reinhold.

Bagozzi, R. P. (1986). Attitude formation under the theory of reasoned action and a purposeful behaviour reformulation. *British Journal of Social Psychology, 25,* 95–107.

Bagozzi, R. P., and Yi, Y. (1989). The degree of intention formation as a moderator of the attitude–behavior relationship. *Social Psychology Quarterly, 52,* 266–279.

Baker, A. M. (1988, Fall). Plant closings: Lessons from the Maine experience. *Human Resource Management, 3,* 315–328.

Baker, D. D., Ravichandran, R., and Randall, D. M. (1989). Exploring contrasting formulations of expectancy theory. *Decision Sciences, 20,* 1–13.

Ball, G. A., Trevino, L. K., and Sims, H. P. (1994). Just and unjust punishment: Influences on subordinate performance and citizenship. *Academy of Management Journal, 37,* 299–322.

Bandura, A. (1969). *Principles of behavior modification.* New York: Holt, Rinehart and Winston.

Bandura, A. (1977). *Social learning theory,* Englewood Cliffs, NJ: Prentice Hall.

Bandura, A. (1982). Self-efficacy mechanism in human agency. *American Psychologist, 37,* 122–147.

Bandura, A. (1984). Recycling misconceptions of perceived self-efficacy. *Cognitive Therapy and Research, 8,* 213–229.

Bandura, A. (1986). *Social foundations of thought and action: A social cognitive theory.* Englewood Cliffs, NJ: Prentice Hall.

Bandura, A. (1989). Self-regulation of motivation and action through internal standards and external goal systems. In L. A. Pervin (Ed.), *Goal concepts in personality and social psychology.* Hillsdale, NJ.: Lawrence Erlbaum.

Bandura, A. (1991). Social cognitive theory of self-regulation. *Organizational Behavior and Human Decision Processes, 50,* 248–287.

Bandura, A., and Cervone, D. (1983). Self-evaluative and self-efficacy mechanisms governing the motivational effects of goal systems. *Journal of Personality and Social Psychology, 45,* 1017–1028.

Barbuto, J. (1996). *Motivation in the 1990's.* Unpublished manuscript.

Barnard, C. I. (1946). Functions and pathology of status systems in formal organizations. In W. F. Whyte (Ed.), *Industry and society* (pp. 207–243). New York: McGraw-Hill.

Barnowe, J. T., and Frost, P. J. (1982). *Career decisions upstream from QWL: Personality and situational influences upon choice of business specialty.* Unpublished manuscript, Faculty of Commerce and Business Administration, University of British Columbia, Vancouver, British Columbia, Canada.

Baron, R. A. (1993). Criticism (informal negative feedback) as a source of perceived unfairness in organizations: Effects, mechanisms, and countermeasures. In R. Cropanzano (Ed.), *Justice in the workplace* (pp. 155–170). Hillsdale, NJ: Lawrence Erlbaum.

Baron, R. A. (1994). The physical environment of work settings. In B. M. Staw and L. L. Cummings (Eds.), *Research in organizational behavior* (Vol. 16, pp. 1–46). Greenwich, CT: JAI Press.

Barrick, M. R., Mount, M. K., and Strauss, J. P. (1993). Conscientiousness and performance of sales representatives: Test of the mediating effects of goal setting. *Journal of Applied Psychology, 78*, 715–722.

Bartlett, F. C. (1932). *Remembering: A study in experimental and social psychology.* Cambridge: Cambridge University Press.

Bartol, K. M. (1978). The sex structuring of organizations, a search for possible causes. *Academy of Management Review, 3*, 805–815.

Barton, R. F. (1981). An MCDM approach for resolving goal conflict in MBO. *Academy of Management Review, 6*, 231–242.

Bass, B. M. (1981). *Stogdill's handbook of leadership: A survey of theory and research.* New York: Free Press.

Bass, B. M., and Vaughan, J. A. (1966). *Training in industry: The management of learning,* Belmont, CA: Wadsworth.

Bassett, G. (1994). The case against job satisfaction. *Business Horizons, 37*(3), 61–68.

Battle, J. (1990). *Self esteem: The new revolution.* Edmonton, Alberta, Canada: James Battle and Associates.

Bayes, J. (1988). Occupational sex segregation and comparable worth. In R. M. Kelly and J. Bayes (Eds.), *Comparable worth, pay equity, and public policy* (pp. 15–48). New York: Greenwood Press.

Bazerman, M. H. (1993). Fairness, social comparison, and irrationality. In J. K. Murnighan (Ed.), *Social psychology in organizations* (pp. 184–203). Englewood Cliffs, NJ: Prentice Hall.

Beach, L. R., and Mitchell, T. R. (1990). Image theory: A behavioral theory of decision making in organizations. In B. M. Staw and L. L. Cummings (Eds.), *Research in organizational behavior* (Vol. 12, pp. 1–42). Greenwich, CT: JAI Press.

Becker, H. S. (1960). Notes on the concept of commitment. *American Journal of Sociology, 66*, 32–40.

Becker, T. E. (1992). Foci and bases of commitment: Are they distinctions worth making? *Academy of Management Journal, 35*, 232–244.

Beehr, T. A., and Gupta, N. A. (1978). Note on the structure of employee withdrawal. *Organizational Behavior and Human Performance, 21*, 73–79.

Behling, O., Labovitz, G., and Kosmo, R. (1968). The Herzberg controversy: A critical appraisal. *Academy of Management Journal, 11*, 99–108.

Belcher, D. (1974). *Compensation administration.* Englewood Cliffs, NJ: Prentice Hall.

Bem, D. J. (1967). Self-perception: The dependent variable of human performance. *Organizational Behavior and Human Performance, 2*, 105–121.

Bem, D. J. (1972a). Constructing cross-situational consistencies in behavior: Some thoughts on Alker's critique of Mischel. *Journal of Personality, 40*, 17–26.

Bem, D. J. (1972b). Self-perception theory. In L. Berkowitz (Ed.), *Advances in experimental social psychology* (Vol. 6, pp. 2–62). New York: Academic Press.

Bem, D. J., and Allen, A. (1974). On predicting some of the people some of the time. *Psychological Review, 81*, 506–520.

Bemmels, B. (1995). Dual commitment: Unique construct or epiphenomenon? *Journal of Labor Research, 16*, 401–422.

Ben-Porat, A. (1981). Event and agent: Toward a structural theory of job satisfaction. *Personnel Psychology, 34*, 523–534.

Berger, C. J. and Cummings, L. L. (1979). Organizational structure, attitudes, and behaviors. In B. M. Staw (Ed.), *Research in organizational behavior* (Vol. 1, pp. 169–208). Greenwich CT: JAI Press.

Berger, J., Cohen, B. P., and Zeldich, M. (1972). Status characteristics and social interaction. *American Sociological Review, 37*, 241–255.

Berger, J., Rosenholtz, S. J., and Zeldich, M. (1980). Status organizing processes. *Annual Review of Sociology, 6*, 479–508.

Berger, P. L., and Luckman, T. (1966). *The social construction of reality: A treatise in the sociology of knowledge.* Garden City, NJ: Doubleday.

Berkowitz, L. (1989). Frustration–aggression hypothesis: Examination and reformulation. *Psychological Bulletin, 106*(1), 59–73.

Berkowitz, L. (1993b). *Aggression: Its causes, consequences, and control.* Philadelphia: Temple University Press.

Berkowitz, L. (1993a). Towards a general theory of anger and emotional aggression: Implications of the cognitive-neoassociationistic perspective for the analysis of anger and other emotions. In R. S. Wyer, Jr., and T. K. Skrull (Eds.), *Perspectives on anger and emotion: Advances in social cognition* (Vol. VI, pp. 1–46). Hillsdale, NJ: Lawrence Erlbaum.

Berlyne, D. E. (1973). The vicissitudes of aplopathematic and thebematoscopic pneumatology (or the hydrography of hedonism). In D. E. Berlyne and K. B. Madsen (Eds.), *Pleasure, reward, and preferences* (pp. 1–33). New York: Academic Press.

Betcherman, G., McMullen, K., Leckie, N., and Caron, C. (1994). *The Canadian workplace in transition.* Kingston, Ontario, Canada: Industrial Relations Centre, Queen's University.

Betz, E. L. (1969). Need-reinforcer correspondence as a predictor of job satisfaction. *Personnel and Guidance Journal, 47*, 878–883.

Bhagat, R. S. (1982). Conditions under which stronger job performance–job satisfaction relationships may be observed: A closer look at two situational contingencies. *Academy of Management Journal, 25,* 772–789.

Biberman, G., Baril, G. L., and Kopleman, R. E. (1986). Comparison of return-on-effort and conventional expectancy theory predictions of work effort and job performance: Results from three field studies. *Journal of Psychology, 120,* 229–237.

Bies, R. B. (1987). The predicament of injustice. In L. L. Cummings and B. M. Staw (Eds.), *Research in organizational behavior* (Vol. 9, pp. 289–320). Greenwich, CT: JAI Press.

Bies, R. B., and Moag, J. S. (1986). Interactional justice: Communication criteria of fairness. In R. J. Lewicki, B. H. Sheppard, and M. H. Bazerman (Eds.), *Research on negotiation in organizations* (Vol. 1, pp. 43–55). Greenwich, CT: JAI Press.

Bies, R. B., and Shapiro, D. L. (1987). Interactional fairness judgements: The influence of social accounts. *Social Justice Research, 2,* 199–218.

Bies, R. B., and Tripp, T. M. (1996). Beyond trust: "Getting even" and the need for revenge. In R. M. Kramer and T. R. Tyler (Eds.), *Trust in organizations* (pp. 246–260). Thousand Oaks, CA: Sage.

Billings, R. S., and Cornelius, E. T. (1980). Dimensions of work outcomes: A multidimensional scaling approach. *Personnel Psychology, 33,* 151–162.

Binswanger, H. (1991). Volition as cognitive self-regulation. *Organizational Behavior and Human Decision Processes, 50,* 154–178.

Bird, R. M., Bucovetsky, M. W., and Foot, D. K. (1979). *The growth of public employment in Canada.* Montreal, Quebec, Canada: Montreal Institute for Research on Public Policy.

Blair, J. M. (1975). Inflation in the United States. In G. C. Means et al. (Eds.), *The roots of inflation.* New York: Burt Franklin.

Blanchard, K., and Johnson, S. (1981). *The one-minute manager.* New York: Berkley Books.

Blankenstein, K. R., Flett, G. L., Koledin, S., and Bortolotto, R. (1989). Affect intensity and dimensions of affiliation motivation. *Personality and Individual Differences, 10*(11), 1201–1203.

Blau, G. (1993). Operationalizing direction and level of effort and testing their relationships to individual job performance. *Organizational Behavior and Human Performance, 55,* 152–170.

Blau, G., and Paul, A. (1993). On developing a general index of work commitment. *Journal of Vocational Behavior, 42,* 298–314.

Blau, P. M. (1963). *The dynamics of bureaucracy* (Rev. ed.). Chicago: University of Chicago Press.

Blood, M. R. (1969). Work values and job satisfaction. *Journal of Applied Psychology, 53,* 456–459.

Blood, M. R. (1973). Intergroup comparisons of intraperson differences: Rewards from the job. *Personnel Psychology, 26,* 1–9.

Boal, K. B., and Cummings, L. L. (1981). Cognitive evaluation theory: An experimental test of processes and outcomes. *Organizational Behavior and Human Performance, 28,* 289–310.

Bobko, P. (1978). Concerning the non-application of human motivation theories in organizational settings. *Academy of Management Review, 3,* 906–910.

Bobko, P. (1985). Removing assumptions of bipolarity: Towards variation and circularity. *Academy of Management Review, 10,* 99–108.

Bockman, V. M. (1971). The Herzberg controversy. *Personnel Psychology, 24,* 155–189.

Boehm, V. R. (1980). Research in the "real world"—A conceptual model. *Personnel Psychology, 33,* 495–503.

Borman, W. C., White, L. A., Pulakos, E. D., and Oppler, S. H. (1991). Models of supervisory job performance ratings. *Journal of Applied Psychology, 76,* 863–872.

Boulding, K. (1968). General systems theory—The skeleton of science. In W. Buckley (Ed.), *Modern systems research for the behavioral scientist* (pp. 3–10). Chicago: Aldine.

Bourgeois, V. W., and Pinder, C. C. (1984). *The nonlinearity of progress in organizational science.* Unpublished manuscript, Faculty of Commerce and Business Administration, University of British Columbia, Vancouver, British Columbia, Canada.

Bowen, W. (1979, December 3). Better prospects for our ailing productivity. *Fortune, 3,* 68–70, 74, 77, 80, 83, 86.

Bower, J. L. (1977). Effective public management. *Harvard Business Review, 55*(2), 131–140.

Bowers, K. S. (1973). Situationism in psychology: An analysis and a critique. *Psychological Review, 80,* 307–336.

Branden, N. (1969). *The psychology of self esteem.* Los Angeles: Nash.

Brayfield, A. H., and Crockett, W. H. (1955). Employee attitudes and employee performance. *Psychological Bulletin, 52,* 415–422.

Breaugh, J. A. (1981). Predicting absenteeism from prior absenteeism and work attitudes. *Journal of Applied Psychology, 66,* 555–560.

Brehm, J. W., and Self, E. A. (1989). The intensity of motivation. *Annual Review of Psychology, 40,* 109–131.

Brendl, C. M., and Higgins, E. T. (1996). Principles of judging valence: What makes events positive or negative? In M. P. Zanna (Ed.), *Advances in experimental social psychology* (Vol. 28, pp. 95–160). New York: Academic Press.

Brett, J. M. (1981). The effect of job transfer on employees and their families. In C. L. Cooper and R. Payne (Eds.), *Current concerns in occupational stress.* New York: Wiley.

Bretz, R. D., and Judge, T. A. (1994). Person–environment fit and the theory of work adjustment: Implications for satisfaction, tenure, and career success. *Journal of Vocational Behavior, 44,* 32–54.

Bridges, W. (1994). *Jobshift.* Reading, MA: Addison-Wesley.

Brief, A. P., and Aldag, R. J. (1975). Employee reactions to job characteristics: A constructive replication. *Journal of Applied Psychology, 60,* 182–186.

Brief, A. P., and Aldag, R. J. (1976). Correlates of role indices. *Journal of Applied Psychology, 61,* 468–472.

Brief, A. P., and Dukerich, J. M. (1991). Theory in organizational behavior: Can it be useful? In L. L. Cummings and B. M. Staw (Eds.), *Research in organizational behavior* (Vol. 13, pp. 327–352). Greenwich, CT: JAI Press.

Brief, A. P., and Hollenbeck, J. R. (1985). An exploratory study of self-regulating activities and their effects on job performance. *Journal of Occupational Behavior, 6,* 197–208.

Brief, A. P., and Motowidlo, S. J. (1986). Prosocial organizational behaviors. *Academy of Management Review, 11,* 710–725.

Britton, J., and Gilmour, J. M. (1978). *The weakest link: A technological perspective on Canadian industrial under development.* Ottawa, Ontario, Canada: Science Council of Canada.

Brockner, J. (1988a). The effects of work layoffs on survivors: Research, theory and practice. In B. M. Staw and L. L. Cummings (Eds.), *Research in organizational behavior* (Vol. 10, pp. 213–255). Greenwich, CT: JAI Press.

Brockner, J. (1988b). *Self esteem at work.* Lexington, MA: Lexington Books.

Brockner, J., Grover, S., Reed, T., DeWitt, R., and O'Malley, M. (1987). Survivors' reactions to layoffs: We get by with a little help from our friends. *Administrative Science Quarterly, 32,* 526–541.

Brockner, J., Konovsky, M., Cooper-Schneider, R., Folger, R., Martin, C., and Bies, R. J. (1994). Interactive effects of procedural justice and outcome negativity on victims and survivors of job loss. *Academy of Management Journal, 37,* 397–409.

Brody, N. (1980). Social motivation. *Annual Review of Psychology, 31,* 143–168.

Brooke, P. P., Russell, D. W., and Price, J. L. (1988). Discriminant validation of measures of job satisfaction, job involvement, and organizational commitment. *Journal of Applied Psychology, 73,* 139–145.

Brown, S. P., and Peterson, R. A. (1994). The effect of effort on sales performance and job satisfaction. *Journal of Marketing, 58*(2), 70–80.

Brown, T. J., and Allgeier, E. A. (1996). The impact of participant characteristics, perceived motives, and job behaviors on co-workers' evaluations of workplace romances. *Journal of Applied Social Psychology, 26,* 577–595.

Buchanan, B. (1974). Building organizational commitment: The socialization of managers in work organizations. *Administrative Science Quarterly, 19,* 533–546.

Buck, R. (1985). Prime theory: An integrated view of motivation and emotion. *Psychological Review, 92,* 389–413.

Budd, R. J. (1986). Predicting cigarette use: The need to incorporate measures of salience in the theory of reasoned action. *Journal of Applied Social Psychology, 16,* 663–685.

Burger, J. M. (1992). *Desire for control.* New York: Plenum Press.

Burris, V. (1990). Classes in contemporary capitalist society: Recent Marxist and Weberian perspectives. In S. Clegg (Ed.), *Organization theory and class analysis* (pp. 55–74). New York: Walter de Gruyter.

Buss, A. H. (1983). Social rewards and personality. *Journal of Personality and Social Psychology, 44,* 553–563.

Buss, A. H. (1986). *Social behavior and personality,* Hillsdale, NJ: Lawrence Erlbaum.

Butler, J. K., and Cantrell, R. S. (1989). Extrinsic reward valences and productivity of business faculty: A within- and between-subjects decision modeling experiment. *Psychological Reports, 64,* 343–353.

Byrne, D. (1971). *The attraction paradigm.* New York: Academic Press.

Calder, B. J., and Schurr, P. H. (1981). Attitudinal processes in organizations. In B. M. Staw and L. L. Cummings (Eds.), *Research in organizational behavior* (Vol. 3, pp. 283–302). Greenwich, CT: JAI Press.

Caldwell, D. S., and Ihrke, D. M. (1994). Differentiating between burnout and copout in organizations. *Public Personnel Management, 23,* 77–84.

Cameron, J., and Pierce, W. D. (1994). Reinforcement, reward, and intrinsic motivation: A meta-analysis. *Review of Educational Research, 64,* 363–423.

Campbell, D. J. (1984). The effects of goal-contingent payment on the performance of a complex task. *Personnel Psychology, 37,* 23–40.

Campbell, D. J. (1988). Task complexity: A review and analysis. *Academy of Management Review, 13,* 40–52.

Campbell, D. J., and Gingrich, K. F. (1986). The interactive effects of task complexity and participation on task performance: A field experiment. *Organizational Behavior and Human Decision Processes, 38,* 162–180.

Campbell, D. J., and Ilgen, D. R. (1976). Additive effects of task difficulty and goal setting on subsequent task performance. *Journal of Applied Psychology, 61,* 319–324.

Campbell, J. G. (1983). Equal pay for work of equal value in the federal public service of Canada. *Compensation Review, 15*(3), 42–51.

Campbell, J. P. (1971). Personnel training and development. *Annual Review of Psychology, 22,* 565–602.

Campbell, J. P., Campbell, R. J., and Associates. (1988). *Productivity in organizations: New perspectives from industrial and organizational psychology.* San Francisco: Jossey-Bass.

Campbell, J. P., Dunnette, M. D., Lawler, E. E., III, and Weick, K. E. (1970). *Managerial behavior performance and effectiveness.* New York: McGraw-Hill.

Campbell, J. P., and Pritchard, R. D. (1976). Motivation theory in industrial and organizational psychology. In M. D. Dunnette (Ed.), *Handbook of industrial and organizational psychology* (pp. 63–130). Chicago: Rand McNally.

Campion, M. A., and Lord, R. G. (1982). A control systems conceptualization of the goal setting and changing process. *Organizational Behavior and Human Performance, 30,* 265–287.

Canadian Business. (1991). Unsatisfying work can be a pain. Vol. *64*(4), p. 23.

Caplan, R. D., and Jones, K. W. (1975). Effects of work load role ambiguity and Type A personality on anxiety, depression and heart rate. *Journal of Applied Psychology, 60,* 713–719.

Cappelli, P., and Sherer, P. D. (1991). The missing role of context in OB: The need for a meso-level approach. In B. M. Staw and L. L. Cummings (Eds.), *Research in organizational behavior* (Vol. 13, pp. 55–110). Greenwich, CT: JAI Press.

Carlson, M. (1995, August 28). The louts of discipline. *Time, 146*(9), 35.

Carmen, W. A. (1981). High court fails to address "comparable worth" issue, but opens door a crack. *ABA Banking Journal, 73*(9), 20, 23, 25.

Carrell, M. R., and Dittrich, J. E. (1976). Employee perception of fair treatment. *Personnel Journal, 55,* 523–524.

Carrell, M. R., and Dittrich, J. E. (1978). Equity theory: The recent literature, methodological considerations, and new directions. *Academy of Management Review, 3,* 202–210.

Carroll, S. J., and Tosi, H. (1973). *Management by objectives: Applications and research.* New York: Macmillan.

Cartledge, N. D. (1973). *An experimental study of the relationship between expectancies, goal utility, goals, and task performance.* Ph.D. dissertation, University of Maryland.

Carver, C. S. (1979). A cybernetic model of self-attention processes. *Journal of Personality and Social Psychology, 37,* 1251–1281.

Carver, C. S., and Scheier, M. F. (1981). *Attention and self-regulation: A control-theory approach to human behavior.* New York: Springer-Verlag.

Carver, C. S., and Scheier, M. F. (1982). Control theory: A useful conceptual framework for personality—Social, clinical, and health psychology. *Psychological Bulletin, 92,* 111–135.

Carver, C. S., and Scheier, M. F. (1990a). Origins and functions of positive and negative affect: A control-process view. *Psychological Reports, 97,* 19–35.

Carver, C. S., and Scheier, M. F. (1990b). Principles of self-regulation: Action and emotion. In E. T. Higgins and R. M. Sorrentino (Eds.), *Handbook of motivation and cognition* (pp. 3–52). New York: Guilford Press.

Cascio, W. F. (1987). *Costing human resources: The financial impact of behavior in organizations.* Boston: PWS-Kent.

Cascio, W. F. (1993). Downsizing: What do we know? What have we learned? *Academy of Management Executive, 7*(1), 95–104.

Cash, T. F., Gillen, B., and Burns, D. S. (1977). Sexism and "beautyism" in personnel consultant decision making. *Journal of Applied Psychology, 62,* 301–310.

Caulkins, D. (1974). Job redesign: Pay implications. *Personnel, 51*(3), 29–34.

Chatman, J. A. (1989). Improving interactional organizational research: A model of person–organization fit. *Academy of Management Review, 14,* 333–349.

Cheloha, R. S., and Farr, J. L. (1980). Absenteeism, job involvement, and job satisfaction in an organizational setting. *Journal of Applied Psychology, 65,* 467–473.

Cherrington, D. J., and England, J. L. (1980). The desire for an enriched job as a moderator of the enrichment–satisfaction relationship. *Organizational Behavior and Human Performance, 25,* 139–159.

Chesney, A. A., and Locke, E. A. (1991). Relationships among goal difficulty, business strategies, and performance on a complex management simulation task. *Academy of Management Journal, 34,* 400–424.

Chia, H. (1995). *The effects of assigned goals on goal orientation, learning, and task performance in a new and complex task.* Unpublished doctoral dissertation, University of British Columbia, Vancouver, British Columbia, Canada.

Childers, T. L., Dubinsky, A. J., and Skinner, S. J. (1990). Leadership substitutes as moderators of sales supervisory behavior. *Journal of Business Research, 21,* 363–382.

Chisholm, J. S. (1995). Love's contingencies: The development socioecology of romantic passion. In W. Jankowiak (Ed.), *Romantic passion* (pp. 42–56). New York: Columbia University Press.

Chusmir, L. H. (1982). Job commitment and the organizational woman. *Academy of Management Journal, 7,* 595–602.

Chusmir, L. H. (1985). *Matching individuals to jobs: A motivational answer for personnel and counseling professionals.* New York: AMACOM.

Chusmir, L. H., and Azevedo, A. (1992). Motivation needs of sampled Fortune-500 CEOs: Relations to organizational outcomes. *Perceptual and Motor Skills, 75,* 595–612.

Chusmir, L. H., and Parker, B. (1984). Dimensions of need for power: Personalized vs. socialized power in female and male managers. *Sex Roles, 11*(9/10), 759–769.

Cialdini, R. B. (1993). *Influence: Science and practice* (3rd ed.). New York: Harper Collins.

Cialdini, R. B., Petty, R. E., and Cacioppo, J. T. (1981). Attitude and attitude change. *Annual Review of Psychology, 32,* 357–404.

Clegg, S. (1990). *Organization theory and class analysis.* New York: Walter de Gruyter.

Clore, G. L., and Ortony, A. (1991). What more is there to emotion concepts than prototypes? *Journal of Personality and Social Psychology, 60,* 48–50.

Coch, L., and French, J. R. P. (1984). Overcoming resistance to change. *Human Relations, 1,* 512–532.

Cofer, C. N., and Appley, M. H. (1964). *Motivation theory and research.* New York: Wiley.

Cohen, A. (1993). Organizational commitment and turnover: A meta-analysis. *Academy of Management Journal, 36,* 1140–1157.

Cohen, B. P., and Zhou, X. (1991). Status processes in enduring work groups. *American Sociological Review, 56,* 179–188.

Cohen, R. L. (1990). *Justice, voice and silence.* Paper presented at the International Conference on Social Science and Societal Dilemmas, Utrecht, The Netherlands.

Cohen, R. L. (1991). Justice and negotiation. In R. J. Lewiski, B. H. Sheppard, and M. H. Bagerman (Eds.), *Research on negotiation in organizations* (Vol. 3 pp. 259–282). Greenwich, CT: JAI Press.

Cohen, S., and Wills, T. A. (1985). Stress, social support, and the buffering hypothesis. *Psychological Bulletin, 98,* 310–357.

Cohen, S. L., and Bunker, K. A. (1975). Subtle effects of sex role stereotypes on recruiters' hiring decisions. *Journal of Applied Psychology, 60,* 566–572.

Collins, E. G. C. (1983). Managers and lovers. *Harvard Business Review, 61*(5), 142–153.

Collinson, D. L. (1992). *Managing the shopfloor: Subjectivity, masculinity and workplace culture.* Berlin: Walter de Gruyter.

Colwill, N. L., and Lips, H. M. (1988). Corporate love: The pitfalls of workplace romance. *Business Quarterly, 53*(1), 89–91.

Comer, D. R. (1995). A model of social loafing in real work groups. *Human Relations, 48,* 647–667.

Condry, J. (1975, August). *The role of initial interest and task performance in intrinsic motivation.* Paper presented at the American Psychological Association, Chicago.

Conger, J. A., and Kanungo, R. N. (1988). The empowerment process: Integrating theory and practice. *Academy of Management Review, 13,* 471–482.

Conlon, E. J., and Gallagher, D. G. (1987). Commitment to employer and union: Effects of membership status. *Academy of Management Journal, 30,* 151–162.

Connor, P. E., and Becker, B. W. (1994). Personal values and management: What do we know and why don't we know more? *Journal of Management Inquiry, 3*(1), 67–73.

Cook, S. D. (1972). Coercion and social change. In R. J. Pennock and J. R. Chapman (Eds.), *Coercion* (pp. 107–143). Chicago: Aldine.

Cook, T. D., and Campbell, D. T. (1979). *Quasi-experimentation: Design and analysis issues for field settings.* Boston: Houghton Mifflin.

Cooper, D., and Emory, C. W. (1995). *Business research methods.* Burr Ridge, IL: Irwin.

Cooper, M. R., Morgan, B. S., Foley, P. M., and Kaplan, L. B. (1979). Changing employee values: Deepening discontent? *Harvard Business Review, 57,* 117–125.

Cotton, J. L. (1993). *Employee involvement: Methods for improving performance and work attitudes.* Newbury Park, CA: Sage.

Cotton, J. L., Vollrath, D. A., Froggatt, K. L., Lengnick-Hall, M. L., and Jennings, K. R. (1988). Employee participation: Diverse forms and different outcomes. *Academy of Management Review, 13,* 8–22.

Coulson, R. (1981). *The termination handbook.* New York: Free Press.

Coulter, J. (1979). *The social construction of mind.* London: Macmillan.

Coupland, D. (1991). *Generation X.* New York: St. Martin's.

Covey, S. R. (1989). *The 7 habits of highly effective people.* New York: Simon and Schuster.

Craighead, W. E., Kazdin, A. E., and Mahoney, M. J. (1976). *Behavior modification.* Boston: Houghton Mifflin.

Craik, K. H. (1970). Environmental psychology. In K. H. Craik, B. Kleinmuntz, R. L. Rosnow, R. Rosenthal, J. A. Cheyne, and R. H. Walters (Eds.), *New directions in psychology* (Vol. 4). New York: Holt, Rinehart and Winston.

Craik, K. H. (1977). Multiple scientific paradigms in environmental psychology. *International Journal of Psychology, 12,* 147–157.

Crane, D. P., and Jones, W. A., Jr. (1991). *The public manager.* Atlanta, GA: Georgia State University Press.

Cranny, C. J., Smith, P. C., and Stone, E. F. (Eds.). (1992). *Job satisfaction.* New York: Lexington Books.

Crawford, T. J. and Boyer, R. (1985). Salient consequences, cultural values, and childbearing intentions. *Journal of Applied Social Psychology, 15,* 16–30.

Craychee, G. A. (1987). The psychosocial dimension of professional continuing education: Behavioral intentions. *Radiologic Technology, 58,* 529–535.

Critchlow, B. (1987). A utility analysis of drinking. *Addictive Behaviors, 12,* 269–273.

Cronbach, L. J. (1957). The two disciplines of scientific psychology. *American Psychologist, 12,* 671–684.

Cronbach, L. J. (1970). *Essentials of psychological testing.* New York: Harper and Row.

Cronbach, L. J. (1975). Beyond the two disciplines of scientific psychology. *American Psychologist, 30,* 116–127.

Cronbach, L. J., and Gleser, G. (1965). *Psychological tests and personnel decisions.* Urbana, IL: University of Illinois Press.

Cropanzano, R. (Ed.). (1992). *Justice in the workplace.* Hillsdale, NJ: Lawrence Erlbaum.

Cummings, L. L. (1980). The brother-in-law syndrome: Inequity in everyday life. In L. L. Cummings and R. B. Dunham (Eds.), *Introduction to organizational behavior* (pp. 142–144). Homewood, IL: Irwin.

Cummings, L. L. (1982). Organizational behavior. *Annual Review of Psychology, 33,* 541–579.

Cummings, L. L., and Schwab, D. P. (1973). *Performance in organizations: Determinants and appraisal.* Glenview, IL: Scott, Foresman.

Cummings, T. G., and Molloy, E. S. (Eds.). (1977). *Improving productivity and the quality of everyday work life.* New York: Praeger.

Cummings, T. G., Molloy, E. S., and Glen, R. A. (1977). Methodological critique of fifty-eight selected work experiments. *Human Relations, 30,* 675–708.

Dabbs, J. M. (1992). Testosterone and occupational achievement. *Social Forces, 70,* 813–824.

Dachler, H. P., and Mobley, W. (1973). Construct validation of an instrumentality-expectancy-task-goal model of work motivation: Some theoretical boundary conditions. *Journal of Applied Psychology, 58,* 397–418.

Dachler, H. P., and Wilpert, B. (1978). Conceptual dimensions and boundaries of participation in organizations: A critical evaluation. *Administrative Science Quarterly, 23,* 1–39.

Daft, R. L. (1983). *Organization theory and design.* St. Paul, MN: West.

Dahl, R. A. (1957). The concept of power. *Behavioral Science, 2*(3), 201–215.

Dahl, R. L. (1986). Power as the control of behavior. In S. Lukes (Ed.), *Power* (pp. 37–58). Worcester, England: Basil Blackwell.

Dalton, D. R. (1981). Turnover and absenteeism: Measures of personal effectiveness. In R. S. Schuler, D. R. Dalton, and J. M. McFillen (Eds.), *Applied readings in personnel and human resource management.* St. Paul, MN: West.

Dalton, D. R., and Todor, W. D. (1979). Turnover turned over: An expanded and positive perspective. *Academy of Management Review, 4,* 225–235.

Dalton, D. R., and Todor, W. D. (1982a). Turnover: A lucrative hard dollar phenomenon. *Academy of Management Review, 7,* 212–218.

Dalton, D. R., and Todor, W. D. (1982b). Antecedents of grievance filing behavior: Attitude/behavioral consistency and the union steward. *Academy of Management Journal, 25,* 158–169.

Dalton, M. (1959). *Men who manage: Fusions of feeling and theory in administration.* New York: Wiley.

Damasio, A. R. (1994). *Descartes' error.* New York: Putnam.

Daniels, D., and Mitchell, T. R. (1995). *Differential effects of self-efficacy, goals, and expectations on task performance.* Unpublished manuscript, School of Business Administration, University of Washington at Seattle.

Davidson, D., Suppes, P., and Siegel, S. (1957). *Decision making: An experimental approach.* Stanford, CA: Stanford University Press.

Davis, L. E., and Taylor, J. C. (Eds.). (1979). *Design of jobs.* Santa Monica, CA: Goodyear.

Davis, T. R. V., and Luthans, F. (1980). A social learning approach to organizational behavior. *Academy of Management Review, 5,* 281–290.

Dawes, R. M., and Smith, T. L. (1985). Attitude and opinion measurement. In G. Lindzey and E. Aronson (Eds.), *Handbook of social psychology* (3rd ed., Vol. 1, pp. 509–566). New York: Random House.

Dawis, R., and Lofquist, L. H. (1984). *A psychological theory of work adjustment: An individual differences model and its applications.* Minneapolis, MN: University of Minnesota Press.

de Charms, R. (1968). *Personal causation.* New York: Academic Press.

Deci, E. L. (1971). Effects of externally mediated rewards on intrinsic motivation. *Journal of Personality and Social Psychology, 18,* 105–115.

Deci, E. L. (1972). Intrinsic motivation, extrinsic reinforcement and inequity. *Journal of Personality and Social Psychology, 22,* 113–120.

Deci, E. L. (1975). *Intrinsic motivation.* New York: Plenum Press.

Deci, E. L. (1976). Notes on the theory and metatheory of intrinsic motivation. *Organizational Behavior and Human Performance, 15,* 130–145.

Deci, E. L. (1980). *The psychology of self-determination.* Lexington, MA: D.C. Heath.

Deci, E. L., Connell, J. P., and Ryan, R. M. (1989). Self-determination in a work organization. *Journal of Applied Psychology, 74,* 580–590.

Deci, E. L., and Porac, J. (1978). Cognitive evaluation theory and the study of human motivation. In M. R. Lepper and D. Greene (Eds.), *The hidden costs of reward* (pp. 149–176). Hillsdale, NJ: Lawrence Erlbaum.

Deci, E. L., and Ryan, R. M. (1985). *Intrinsic motivation and self determination in human behavior.* New York: Plenum Press.

Deci, E. L., and Ryan, R. M. (1987). The support of autonomy and the control of behavior. *Journal of Personality and Social Psychology, 53,* 1024–1037.

de Leo, P. J., and Pritchard, R. D. (1974). An examination of some methodological problems in testing expectancy-valence models with survey techniques. *Organizational Behavior and Human Performance, 12,* 143–148.

Dempster, F. N. (1988). The spacing effect. *American Psychologist, 43,* 627–634.

Dempster, F. N. (1989). Spacing effects and their implications for theory and practice. *Educational Psychology Review, 1,* 309–330.

Denny, M., Bernstein, J., Fuss, M., Nakamura, S., and Waverman, L. (1992). Productivity in manufacturing industries, Canada, Japan and the United States, 1953–1986: Was the "productivity slowdown" reversed? *Canadian Journal of Economics, 25,* 584–603.

Derryberry, D., and Tucker, D. M. (1994). Motivating the focus of attention. In P. M. Niedenthal and S. Kitayama (Eds.), *The heart's eye* (pp. 167–196). San Diego, CA: Academic Press.

Dessler, G., and Valenzi, E. R. (1977). Initiation of structure and subordinate satisfaction: A path analysis test of path-goal theory. *Academy of Management Journal, 20,* 251–260.

Dickson, D., Saunders, C., and Stringer, M. (1993). *Rewarding people: The skill of responding positively.* London: Routledge.

Diener, E., Larsen, R., Levine, S., and Emmons, R. A. (1985). Intensity and frequency: Dimensions underlying positive and negative affect. *Journal of Personality and Social Psychology, 48,* 1253–1265.

Digman, J. M. (1990). Personality structure: Emergence of the five-factor model. *Annual Review of Psychology, 41,* 417–440.

Dittrich, J. E., and Carrell, M. R. (1979). Organizational equity perceptions, employee job satisfaction, and departmental absence and turnover rates. *Organizational Behavior and Human Performance, 24,* 29–40.

Dobbins, G. H., and Zaccaro, S. J. (1986). The effects of group cohesion and leader behavior on subordinate satisfaction. *Group and Organization Studies, 11,* 203–219.

Donahue, T. R. (1982). *Labor looks at quality of work life programs.* Keynote address delivered at a conference on labor participation. Amherst, MA: Labor Relations and Research Center, University of Massachusetts.

Dooley, D., and Prause, J. (1995). Effect of unemployment on school leavers' self esteem. *Journal of Occupational Psychology, 68,* 177–192.

Dowling, W. F. (1973a). Job redesign on the assembly line: Farewell to blue-collar blues? *Organizational Dynamics, 2*(1), 51–67.

Dowling, W. F. (1973b). At Emery Air Freight: Positive reinforcement boosts performance. *Organizational Dynamics, 2*(1), 41–50.

Downey, H. K., Hellriegel, D., and Slocum, J. W. (Eds.). (1977). *Organizational behavior: A reader.* St. Paul, MN: West.

Downey, H. K., Sheridan, J. E., and Slocum, J. W. (1976). The path-goal theory of leadership: A longitudinal analysis. *Organizational Behavior and Human Performance, 16,* 156–176.

Drake, J. A. (1974). Planner looks at job enrichment. *Planning Review, 2*(4), 7, 30–31.

Dreher, G. F. (1982). The role of performance in the turnover process. *Academy of Management Journal, 25,* 137–147.

Drever, J. (1952). *A dictionary of psychology.* Harmondsworth, Middlesex, England: Penguin Books.

Driedger, S. D. (1997, April 28). The nurses. *Maclean's, 110*(17), 24–27.

Dubin, R. (1956). Industrial workers' worlds: A study of the central life interests of industrial workers. *Social Problems, 3,* 131–142.

DuBois, P. (1979). *Sabotage in industry.* Harmondsworth, Middlesex, England: Penguin Books.

Dullard, J. P., and Miller, K. I. (1988). Intimate relationships in task environments. In S. W. Duck (Ed.), *Handbook of personal relationships* (pp. 449–466). New York: Wiley.

Dumaine, B. (1993). America's toughest bosses. *Fortune, 128*(9), 38–50.

Duncan, W. J., Smeltzer, L. R., and Leap, T. L. (1990). Humor and work: Applications of joking behavior to management. *Journal of Management, 16,* 255–278.

Dunham, R. B. (1977). Reactions to job characteristics: Moderating effects of the organization. *Academy of Management Journal, 20,* 42–65.

Dunham, R. B., and Smith, F. J. (1979). *Organizational surveys: An internal assessment of organizational health.* Glenview, IL: Scott, Foresman.

Dunnette, M. D. (1963). A modified model for test validation and selection research. *Journal of Applied Psychology, 47,* 317–323.

Dunnette, M. D. (1966). *Personnel selection and placement.* Belmont, CA: Wadsworth.

Dunnette, M. D. (1972). *Performance equals ability and what?* (Tech. Rep. 4009: ONR Contract No. N00014-68-A-0141). Minneapolis, MN, University of Minnesota, Center for the Study of Organizational Performance and Human Effectiveness.

Dunnette, M. D. (1976a). Aptitudes, abilities, and skills. In M. D. Dunnette (Ed.), *Handbook of industrial and organizational psychology* (pp. 473–520). Chicago: Rand McNally.

Dunnette, M. D. (1976b). Mishmash, mush, and milestones in organizational psychology: 1974. In H. Meltzer and F. R. Wickert (Eds.), *Humanizing organizational behavior.* Springfield, IL: Charles C. Thomas.

Dunnette, M. D., Arvey, R. D., and Banas, P. A. (1973, May–June). Why do they leave? *Personnel,* 25–39.

Dunnette, M. D., and Bass, B. M. (1963). Behavioral scientists and personnel management. *Industrial Relations, 2*(3), 115–130.

Dunnette, M. D., and Kirchner, W. K. (1965). *Psychology applied to industry.* New York: Appleton-Century-Crofts.

Dwek, C. S. (1986). Motivational processes affecting learning. *American Psychologist, 41,* 1040–1048.

Dyer, L., and Parker, D. F. (1975). Classifying outcomes in work motivation research: An examination of the intrinsic–extrinsic dichotomy. *Journal of Applied Psychology, 60,* 455–458.

Dyer, L., Schwab, D. P., and Theriault, R. D. (1976). Managerial perceptions regarding salary increase criteria. *Personnel Psychology, 29,* 233–242.

Eagly, A. H., and Chaiken, S. (1993). *The psychology of attitudes.* San Diego, CA: Harcourt Brace Jovanovich.

Eagly, A. H., and Johnson, B. T. (1991). Gender and leadership style: A meta-analysis. *Psychological Bulletin, 108,* 233–256.

Eckblad, G. (1981). *Scheme theory.* New York: Academic Press.

The Economist. (1996, August 24). Undue diligence. *340*(7980), 47–49.

The Economist. (1996, June 8). A wealth of working women. *339*(7969), 27–28.

Eden, D. (1984). Self-fulfilling prophesy as a management tool: Harnessing Pygmalion. *Academy of Management Review, 9,* 64–73.

Eden, D. (1988). Pygmalion, goal setting, and expectancy: Compatible ways to boost productivity. *Academy of Management Review, 13,* 639–652.

Eden, D., and Kinnar, J. (1991). Modeling Galatea: Boosting self-efficacy to increase volunteering. *Journal of Applied Psychology, 76,* 770–780.

Ediger, B. (1991). *Coping with fibromyalgia.* Toronto, Ontario, Canada: LRH.

Edstrom, A., and Galbraith, J. R. (1977). Transfer of managers as a coordination and control strategy in multinational organizations. *Administrative Science Quarterly, 22,* 248–263.

Edwards, J. R. (1994). The study of congruence in organizational behavior research: Critique and proposed alternative. *Organizational Behavior and Human Decision Processes, 58,* 51–100.

Edwards, P. K. (1979). Attachment to work and absence. *Human Relations, 32,* 1065–1080.

Eisenberger, R., and Cameron, J. (1996). Detrimental effects of reward: Reality or myth? *American Psychologist, 51,* 1153–1166.

Eisenhardt, K. M. (1989). Building theories from case study research. *Academy of Management Review, 14,* 532–550.

Ekman, P., and Friesen, W. V. (1975). *Unmasking the face.* Englewood Cliffs, NJ: Prentice Hall.

Elliott, R. H., and Jarrett, D. T. (1994). Violence in the workplace: The role of human resource management. *Public Personnel Management, 23*(2), 287–299.

Encarta. (1993a). *Galatea.* Redmond, WA: Microsoft Corporation.

Encarta. (1993b). *Pygmalion.* Redmond, WA: Microsoft Corporation.

Endler, N. W. (1975). The case for person–situation interactions. *Canadian Psychological Review, 16,* 12–21.

England, G. W. (1991). The meaning of work in the U.S.A.: Recent changes. *European Work and Organizational Psychologist, 1*(2/3), 111–124.

England, P., and McLaughlin, S. D. (1979). Sex segregation of jobs and male–female income differentials. In R. Alvarez and K. G. Lutterman (Eds.), *Discrimination in organizations* (pp. 189–213). San Francisco: Jossey-Bass.

Ephlin, D. F. (1973). The union's role in job enrichment programs. In G. G. Somers (Ed.), *Proceedings of the 26th Annual Winter Meeting.* Madison, WI: Industrial Relations Research Association.

Epstein, C., Olivares, F., Bass, B., Graham, P., Schwartz, F. N., Siegel, M. R., Mansbridge, J., Lloyd, K. R., Wyskocil, P. B., Cohen, A. R., Bradford, D. L., Sonnenfeld, J. A., and Goldberg, C. R. (1991). Ways men and women lead. *Harvard Business Review, 69*(1), 150–160.

Erez, M., and Arad, R. (1986). Participative goal-setting: Social, motivational, and cognitive factors. *Journal of Applied Psychology, 71,* 591–597.

Erez, M., and Kanfer, F. H. (1983). The role of goal acceptance in goal setting and task performance. *Academy of Management Review, 8,* 454–463.

Erikson, K., and Vallas, S. P. (Eds.). (1990). *The nature of work.* New Haven, CT: Yale University Press.

Ettorre, B. (1994). Give me satisfaction. *Management Review, 83*(10), 9.

Evan, W. M., and Simmons, R. G. (1969). Organizational effects of inequitable rewards: Two experiments in status inconsistency. *Administrative Science Quarterly, 14,* 224–237.

Evans, M. G. (1970). The effects of supervisory behavior on the path-goal relationship. *Organizational Behavior and Human Performance, 5,* 277–298.

Evans, M. G. (1974). Extensions of a path-goal theory of motivation. *Journal of Applied Psychology, 59,* 172–178.

Eylon, D. (1994). *Empowerment: A multi-level construct.* Unpublished doctoral dissertation, University of British Columbia, Vancouver, British Columbia, Canada.

Eylon, D., and Pinder, C. C. (1995). *Experimental test of a process model of employee empowerment.* Working paper, Faculty of Commerce and Business Administration, University of British Columbia, Vancouver, British Columbia, Canada.

Faltermayer, E. (1974). Who will do the dirty work tomorrow? *Fortune, 89*(1), 132–138.

Farrell, D. (1983). Exit, voice, loyalty and neglect as responses to job dissatisfaction: A multi-dimensional scaling analysis. *Academy of Management Journal, 26,* 596–607.

Fassel, D. (1992). *Working ourselves to death.* New York: Harper/Collins/Thorsons.

Faunce, W. A. (1982). The relation of status to self esteem: Chain saw sociology at the cutting edge. *Sociological Focus, 15*(3), 163–178.

Faunce, W. A. (1989). Occupational status-assignment systems: The effect of status on self esteem. *American Journal of Sociology, 95,* 378–400.

Fedor, D. B. and Ferris, G. R. (1981). Integrating O.B. mod with cognitive approaches to motivation. *Academy of Management Review, 6,* 115–125.

Fehr, B., and Russell, J. A. (1991). The concept of love viewed from a prototype perspective. *Journal of Personality and Social Psychology, 60,* 425–438.

Fein, M. (1974). Job enrichment: A reevaluation. *Sloan Management Review, 15*(2) 69–88.

Feldman, D. C. (1977). The role of initiation activities in socialization. *Human Relations, 30,* 977–990.

Feldman, D. C. (1981). The multiple socialization of organization members. *Academy of Management Review, 6,* 309–318.

Feldman, D. C., and Brett, J. M. (1983). Coping with new jobs: A comparative study of new hires and job changers. *Academy of Management Journal, 26,* 258–272.

Feldman, D. C., and Leana, C. R. (1989, Summer). Managing layoffs: Experiences at the *Challenger* disaster site and the Pittsburgh steel mills. *Organizational Dynamics, 18*(1), 52–64.

Feldman, J. M., Reitz, H. J., and Hiterman, R. J. (1976). Alternatives to optimization in expectancy theory. *Journal of Applied Psychology, 61,* 712–720.

Fellenz, M. R. (1996). *Control theory in organizational behavior: Review, critique, and prospects.* Unpublished manuscript, University of North Carolina at Chapel Hill.

Fennel, T. (1996, April 15). The high price of salary disclosure. *Maclean's 109*(16), 50.

Festinger, L. A. (1954). A theory of social comparison processes. *Human Relations, 7,* 117–140.

Festinger, L. A. (1957). *A theory of cognitive dissonance.* Evanston, IL: Row, Peterson.

Fichman, M. (1988). Motivational consequences of absence and attendance: Proportional hazard estimation of a dynamic motivation model. *Journal of Applied Psychology, 73,* 119–134.

Fiedler, F. E., and House, R. J. (1988). Leadership theory and research: A report of progress. In C. L. Cooper and I. T. Robertson (Eds.), *International review of industrial and organizational psychology* (pp. 73–92). Chichester, West Sussex, England: Wiley.

Fierman, J. (1990, July 30). Why women still don't hit the top. *Fortune,* 40–62.

Fineman, S. (Ed.). (1993). *Emotion in organizations.* London: Sage.

Fiol, C. M., and Lyles, M. A. (1985). Organizational learning. *Academy of Management Review, 10,* 803–813.

Firebaugh, G., and Harley, B. (1995). Trends in job satisfaction in the United States by race, gender, and type of occupation. In R. L. Simpson and I. H. Simpson (Eds.), *Research in the sociology of work: The meanings of work* (pp. 87–104). Greenwich, CT: JAI Press.

Fischer, A. (1994). Emotion concepts as a function of gender. In J. A. Russell, J. M. Fernandez-Doles, A. S. R. Manstead, and J. C. Wellenkamp (Eds.), *Everyday conceptions of emotions* (pp. 457–474). Dordrecht, The Netherlands: Kluwer.

Fishbein, M. (1967). Attitude and the prediction of behavior. In M. Fishbein (Ed.), *Readings in attitude theory and measurement* (pp. 477–491). New York: Wiley.

Fishbein, M. (1980). A theory of reasoned action: Some applications and implications. In M. M. Page (Ed.), *Nebraska Symposium on Motivation, 1979 BF683,N4.* Lincoln, NE: University of Nebraska Press.

Fishbein, M., and Ajzen, I. (1975). *Belief, attitude, intention and behavior: An introduction to theory and research.* Reading, MA: Addison-Wesley.

Fisher, A. B. (1988, May 23). The downside of downsizing. *Fortune, 117*(11), 42, 46, 48, 50, 52.

Fisher, A. B. (1991, November 18). Morale crisis. *Fortune, 124*(12), 70–80.

Fisher, A. B. (1992, September 21). When will women get to the top? *Fortune,* 44–56.

Fisher, A. B. (1994, October 3). Getting comfortable with couples in the workplace. *Fortune, 130*(7), 138–144.

Fisher, C. D. (1980). On the dubious wisdom of expecting job satisfaction to correlate with performance. *Academy of Management Review, 5,* 607–612.

Fisher, C. D., and Locke, E. A. (1992). The new look in job satisfaction research and theory. In C. U. Cranny, P. C. Smith, and E. F. Stone (Eds.), *Job satisfaction* (pp. 165–194). New York: Lexington Books.

Fisher, H. E. (1992). *The anatomy of love.* New York: Norton.

Fisher, W. A. (1984). Predicting contraceptive behavior among university men: The role of emotions and behavioral intentions. *Journal of Applied Social Psychology, 14,* 104–123.

Fiske, D. W., and Maddi, S. R. (1961). *The functions of a varied experience.* Homewood, IL: Dorsey.

Fiske, S. T. (1993). Social cognition and perception. *Annual Review of Psychology, 44,* 155–194.

Fiske, S. T., and Taylor, S. E. (1991). *Social cognition* (2nd ed.). New York: McGraw-Hill.

Fleischman, E. A. (1958). A relationship between incentive motivation and ability level in psychomotor performance. *Journal of Experimental Psychology, 56,* 78–81.

Florence, S. P. (1975). *Stagflation in Great Britain.* In G. C. Means et al. (Eds.), *The roots of inflation.* New York: Burt Franklin.

Flowers, V. S., and Hughes, C. L. (1973). Why employees stay. *Harvard Business Review, 51*(4), 40–60.

Folger, R. (1986). Rethinking equity theory: A referent cognitions model. In H. W. Bierhoff, R. L., Cohen, and J. Greenberg (Eds.), *Justice in social relations* (pp. 145–162). New York: Plenum Press.

Folger, R. (1993). Reactions to mistreatment at work. In J. K. Murnighan (Ed.), *Social psychology in organizations.* Englewood Cliffs, NJ: Prentice Hall.

Folger, R., and Greenberg, J. (1985). Procedural justice: An interpretative analysis of personnel systems. In K. M. Rowland and G. R. Ferris (Eds.), *Research in personnel and human resources management* (Vol. 3, pp. 141–184). Greenwich, CT: JAI Press.

Ford, C. H. (1979). MBO: An idea whose time has gone? *Business Horizons, 22*(12), 48–55.

Ford, M. E. (1992). *Motivating humans.* Newbury Park, CA: Sage.

Ford, R., and McLaughlin, F. (1987, Summer). Should Cupid come to the workplace? *Personnel Administrator, 53*(1), 100–110.

Ford, R. C., and Fottler, M. D. (1995). Empowerment: A matter of degree. *Academy of Management Executive, 9*(3), 21–29.

Ford, R. N. (1973). Job enrichment lessons from A.T.&T. *Harvard Business Review, 51*(1), 96–106.

Foulkes, F. K. (1980). *Personnel policies in large nonunion companies.* Englewood Cliffs, NJ: Prentice Hall.

Fox, A. C. (1980–1981). Progressive discipline: Policy and process. *EEO Today, 7,* 332–342.

Frayne, C. A., and Geringer, J. M. (1994). A social cognitive approach to examining joint venture general manager performance. *Group and Organization Management, 19,* 240–262.

Frayne, C. A., and Geringer, J. M. (1997). *Self-management training and sales performance: A field experiment.* Paper presented at the meeting of the Western Academy of Management, Squaw Valley, CA.

Frayne, C. A., and Latham, G. P. (1987). Application of social learning theory to employee self-management of attendance. *Journal of Applied Psychology, 72,* 387–392.

Fredericksen, L. W., and Lovett, S. B. (1980). Inside organizational behavior management. *Journal of Organizational Behavior Management, 2,* 193–203.

Fredericksen, N. (1972). Toward a taxonomy of situations. *American Psychologist, 27,* 114–123.

Fredericksen, N., Jensen, O., Beaton, A. E., and Bloxom, B. (1972). *Prediction of organizational behavior.* Elmsford, NY: Pergamon Press.

Freedman, S. J., and Montanari, J. R. (1980). An integrative model of managerial reward allocation. *Academy of Management Review, 5,* 381–390.

Freeman, R. B., and Medoff, J. L. (1984). *What do unions do?* New York: Basic Books.

French, E. G. (1957). Effects of interaction of achievement, motivation, and intelligence on problem solving success. *American Psychologist, 12,* 399–400.

Frese, M., Kring, W., Soose, A., and Zempel, J. (1996). Personal initiative at work: Differences between East and West Germany. *Academy of Management Journal, 39,* 37–63.

Freund, W. C. (1981). Productivity and inflation. *Financial Analysts Journal, 37*(4), 36–39.

Frey, R. (1993). Empowerment or else. *Harvard Business Review, 71*(5), 80–94.

Frijda, N. H. (1986). *The emotions.* Cambridge: Cambridge University Press.

Frijda, N. H., Mesquita, B., Sonnemans, J., and van Goozen, S. (1991). The duration of affective phenomena on emotions, sentiments and passions. In K. T. Strongman (Ed.), *International review of research on emotion* (Vol. 1, pp. 187–225) Chichester, West Sussex, England: Wiley.

Fromm, E., and Xirau, R. (Eds.). (1968). *The nature of man.* New York: Macmillan.

Frone, M. R., Russell, M., and Cooper, M. L. (1994). Relationship between job and family satisfaction: Causal or noncausal covariation? *Journal of Management, 20,* 565–579.

Frone, M. R., Russell, M., and Cooper, M. L. (1995). Job stressors, job involvement and employee health: A test of identity theory. *Journal of Occupational and Organizational Psychology, 68,* 1–11.

Frost, P. J. (1980). Toward a radical framework for practicing organization science. *Academy of Management Review, 5,* 501–507.

Frost, P. J., and Hayes, D. C. (1979). An exploration in two cultures of a model of political behavior in organizations. In G. W. England and B. Wilbert (Eds.), *Organizational functioning in a cross-cultural perspective,* pp. 251–272. Kant, OH: Kent State University.

Frost, P. J., and Jamal, M. (1979). Shift work, attitudes, and reported behavior: Some associations between individual characteristics and hours of work and leisure. *Journal of Applied Psychology, 64,* 77–81.

Frost, P. J., Moore, L. F., Louis, M. R., Lundberg, C. C., and Martin, J. (1991). *Reframing organizational culture.* Newbury Park, CA: Sage.

Fry, L. W., and Smith, D. A. (1987). Congruence, contingency, and theory building. *Academy of Management Review, 12,* 117–132.

Fulmer, W. E., and Casey, A. W. (1990). Employment at will: Options for managers. *Academy of Management Executive, 4*(2), 102–107.

Fusilier, M. R., Ganster, D. C., and Middlemist, R. D. (1984). A within-person test of the expectancy theory model in a choice context. *Organizational Behavior and Human Performance, 34,* 323–342.

Galbraith, J., and Cummings, L. L. (1967). An empirical investigation of the motivational determinants of task performance: Interactive effects between instrumentality-valence and motivation-ability. *Organizational Behavior and Human Performance, 2,* 237–257.

Galsworthy, J. (1927). *The inn of tranquility.* London: William Heinemann.

Gannon, M. J., and Henrickson, D. H. (1973). Career orientation and job satisfaction among working wives. *Journal of Applied Psychology, 57,* 339–340.

Gardner, D. G., and Cummings, L. L. (1988). Activation theory and job design: Review and conceptualization. In B. M. Staw and L. L. Cummings (Eds.), *Research in organizational behavior* (Vol. 10, pp. 81–122). Greenwich, CT: JAI Press.

Garland, H. (1973). Effects of piece rate underpayment and overpayment on job performance: A test of equity theory with a new induction procedure. *Journal of Applied Social Psychology, 57,* 325–334.

Garland, H. (1984). Relation of effort-performance expectancy to performance in goal-setting experiments. *Journal of Applied Psychology, 89,* 79–84.

Garland, H., and Price, K. (1977). Attitudes toward women in management and attributions for their success and failure in a managerial position. *Journal of Applied Psychology, 62,* 29–33.

Garner, W. R. (1972). The acquisition and application of knowledge: A symbiotic relationship. *American Psychologist, 27,* 941–946.

Gay, E. R., Weiss, D. J., Hendel, D. H., Dawis, R. V., and Lofquist, L. H. (1971). *Manual for the Minnesota importance questionnaire.* The Minnesota Studies in Vocational Rehabilitation: XXVIII. Minneapolis, MN.

Gazenboom, H. B. G., De Graf, P. M., De Trieman, D. J., and De Leeuw, J. (1992). A standard international socio-economic index of occupational status. *Social Science Research, 21,* 1–56.

Gecas, V. (1989). The social psychology of self-efficacy. *Annual Review of Sociology, 15,* 291-316.

Geen, R. G. (1991). Social motivation. *Annual Review of Psychology, 42,* 377–399.

George, J. M. (1989). Mood and absence. *Journal of Applied Psychology, 74,* 317–324.

George, J. M. (1991). State or trait: Effects of positive mood on prosocial behaviors at work. *Journal of Applied Psychology, 76,* 299–307.

George, J. M. (1992). The role of personality in organizational life: Issues and evidence. *Journal of Management, 18,* 185–213.

George, J. M., and Brief, A. P. (1992). Feeling good–doing good: A conceptual analysis of the mood at work–organizational spontaneity relationship. *Psychological Bulletin, 112,* 310–329.

George, J. M., and Brief, A. P. (1996). Motivational agendas in the workplace: The effects of feelings on focus of attention and work motivation. In B. M. Staw and L. L. Cummings (Eds.), *Research in organizational behavior* (Vol. 18, pp. 75–110). Greenwich, CT: JAI Press.

George, J. M., and Jones, G. R. (1996). The experience of work and turnover intentions: Interactive effects of value attainment, job satisfaction, and positive mood. *Journal of Applied Psychology, 81,* 318–325.

Georgopoulos, B. C., Mahoney, G. M., and Jones, N. W. (1957). A path-goal approach to productivity. *Journal of Applied Psychology, 41,* 345–353.

Giacalone, R. A., and Greenberg, J. (Eds.). (1997). *Antisocial behavior in organizations.* Thousands Oaks, CA: Sage.

Giles, W. F. (1977). Volunteering for job enrichment: A test of expectancy theory predictions. *Personnel Psychology, 30,* 427–435.

Gioia, D. A., and Pitre, E. (1990). Multiparadigm perspectives on theory building. *Academy of Management Review, 15,* 584–602.

Gist, M. E. (1987). Self-efficacy: Implications for organizational behavior and human resource management. *Academy of Management Review, 12,* 472–485.

Gist, M. E., and Mitchell, T. R. (1992). Self-efficacy: A theoretical analysis of its determinants and malleability. *Academy of Management Review, 17,* 183–211.

Glaser, R. C., and Strauss, A. L. (1967). *The discovery of grounded theory,* Chicago: Aldine.

Gloria, J. da. (1984). Frustration, aggression, and the sense of justice. In A. Mummendey (Ed.), *Social psychology of aggression* (pp. 127–141). Berlin: Springer-Verlag.

Gold, B. (1979). *Productivity, technology, and capital.* Lexington, MA: Lexington Books.

Gold, M. E. (1983). *A dialogue on comparable worth.* Ithaca, NY: ILR Press.

Goleman, D. (1995). *Emotional intelligence.* New York: Bantam Books.

Goodall, K. (1972, November). Shapers at work. *Psychology Today,* pp. 53–132.

Goodman, P. A., and Friedman, A. (1971). An examination of Adams' theory of inequity. *Administrative Science Quarterly, 16,* 271–288.

Goodman, P. S. (1974). An examination of the referents used in the evaluation of pay. *Organizational Behavior and Human Performance, 12,* 170–195.

Goodstadt, B., and Kipnis, D. (1970). Situational influences on the use of power. *Journal of Applied Psychology, 54,* 201–207.

Gordon, M. E., and Johnson, W. A. (1982). Seniority: A review of its legal and scientific standing. *Personnel Psychology, 35,* 255–280.

Gorn, G. J., and Kanungo, R. N. (1980). Job involvement and motivation: Are intrinsically motivated managers more job involved? *Organizational Behavior and Human Performance, 26,* 265–277.

Gouldner, A. W. (1960). The norm of reciprocity: a preliminary statement. *American Sociological Review, 25,* 161–179.

Government Finance Review. (1994, June). Canada's experience with pay equity: National and provincial. Vol. *10*(3), pp. 38–39.

Graen, G. (1969). Instrumentality theory of work motivation: Some experimental results and suggested modifications. *Journal of Applied Psychology Monograph, 53* (2, Pt. 2), 38–39.

Graen, G. (1976). Role making processes within complex organizations. In M. D. Dunnette (Ed.), *Handbook of industrial and organizational psychology* (pp. 1201–1246). Chicago: Rand McNally.

Grams, R., and Schwab, D. P. (1985). An investigation of systematic gender-related error in job evaluation. *Academy of Management Journal, 28,* 279–290.

Grant, D. G., and Wark, J. T. (1995, September 8). Bad pasts haunt good Samaritans. *The Detroit News,* p. 3D.

Gray, J. L. (1979). The myths of the myths about behavior mod in organizations: A reply to Locke's criticisms of behavior modification. *Academy of Management Review, 4,* 121–129.

Greco, P. A., and Woodlock, B. K. (1989, May). Downsizing the organization. *Personnel Administrator, 34* (5), 105–108.

Greenberg, J. (1987). A taxonomy of organizational justice theories. *Academy of Management Review, 12,* 9–22.

Greenberg, J. (1988a). Cultivating an image of justice: Looking fair on the job. *Academy of Management Executive, 2,* 155–158.

Greenberg, J. (1988b). Equity and workplace status: A field experiment. *Journal of Applied Psychology, 73,* 606–613.

Greenberg, J. (1989). Cognitive reevaluation of outcomes in response to underpayment inequity. *Academy of Management Journal, 32,* 174–184.

Greenberg, J. (1990a). Looking fair vs. being fair: Managing impressions of organizational justice. In B. M. Staw and L. L. Cummings (Eds.), *Research in organizational behavior* (Vol. 12, pp. 111–158). Greenwich, CT: JAI Press.

Greenberg, J. (1990b). Employee theft as a reaction to underpayment inequity: The hidden cost of pay cuts. *Journal of Applied Psychology, 75,* 561–568.

Greenberg, J. (1993). Stealing in the name of justice: Informational and interpersonal moderators of theft reactions to underpayment inequity. *Organizational Behavior and Human Decision Processes, 54,* 81–103.

Greenberg, J., and Leventhal, G. S. (1976). Equity and the use of over reward to motivate performance. *Journal of Personality and Social Psychology, 34,* 179–190.

Greenberg, J., and McCarty, (1990). Comparable worth: A matter of justice. In G. R. Ferris and K. M. Rowland (Eds.), *Research in personnel and human resource management* (Vol. 8, pp. 265–301). Greenwich, CT: JAI Press.

Greenberg, J., and Ornstein, S. (1983). High status job title as compensation for underpayment: A test of equity theory. *Journal of Applied Psychology, 68,* 285–297.

Greenberg, J., and Scott, K. S. (1996). Why do workers bite the hand that feeds them? Employee theft as a social exchange process. In B. M. Staw and L. L. Cummings (Eds.), *Research in organizational behavior* (Vol. 18, pp. 111–156). Greenwich, CT: JAI Press.

Greene, C. N. (1979). Questions of causation in the path-goal theory of leadership. *Academy of Management Journal, 22,* 22–41.

Greene, D., and Lepper, M. R. (1974). Effects of extrinsic rewards on children's subsequent intrinsic interest. *Child Development, 45,* 1141–1145.

Greenhaus, J. H., and Parasuraman, S. (1993). Job performance attributions and career advancement prospects: An examination of gender and race effects. *Organizational Behavior and Human Decision Processes, 55,* 273–297.

Greenwald, A. G. (1976). Within-subjects designs: To use or not to use? *Psychological Bulletin, 83,* 314–320.

Greenwood, R. G. (1981). Management by objectives: As developed by Peter Drucker, asisted by Harold Smiddy. *Academy of Management Review, 6,* 225–230.

Gregory, M. S., Silvers, A., and Sutch, D. (Eds.). (1978). *Sociology and human nature.* San Francisco: Jossey-Bass.

Greller, M. M. (1978). The nature of subordinate participation in the appraisal interview. *Academy of Management Journal, 21,* 646–658.

Grey, R. J., and Johnson, G. C. (1988, Winter). Differences between Canadian and American workers. *Canadian Business Review, 15,* 24–27.

Grieff, B. S., and Munter, K. (1980). *Tradeoffs: Executive, family and organizational life.* New York: New American Library.

Griffin, R. W. (1982a). A longitudinal investigation of task characteristics relationships. *Academy of Management Journal, 24,* 99–113.

Griffin, R. W. (1982b). *Task design: An integrative approach.* Glenview, IL: Scott, Foresman.

Griffin, R. W. (1987). Toward an integrated theory of task design. In L. L. Cummings, and B. M. Staw (Eds.), *Research in organizational behavior* (Vol. 9, pp. 79–120). Greenwich, CT: JAI Press.

Griffin, R. W., Bateman, T. S., Wayne, S. J., and Head, T. C. (1987). Objective and social factors as determinants of task perceptions and responses: An integrated perspective and empirical investigation. *Academy of Management Journal, 30,* 501–523.

Griffin, R. W., Welsh, A., and Moorhead, G. (1981). Perceived task characteristics and employee performance: A literature review. *Academy of Management Review, 6,* 655–664.

Grigaliunas, B., and Weiner, Y. (1974). Has the research challenge to motivation-hygiene theory been conclusive? An analysis of critical. *Studies in Human Relations, 27,* 839–871.

Gross, B. (1965). What are your organization's objectives? *Human Relations, 18,* 215.

Guilford, J. P. (1967). *The nature of human intelligence.* New York: McGraw-Hill.

Guion, R. M. (1965). *Personnel testing.* New York: McGraw-Hill.

Guppy, N., and Goyder, C. (1984). Consensus on occupational prestige: A reassessment of the evidence. *Social Forces, 62,* 709–725.

Gutek, B. A., Cohen, A. G., and Konrad, A. M. (1990). Predicting social–sexual behavior at work: A contact hypothesis. *Academy of Management Journal, 33,* 560–577.

Guzzo, R. A. (1979). Types of rewards, cognitions, and work motivation. *Academy of Management Review, 4,* 75–86.

Gyllenhammar, P. G. (1977, July–August). How Volvo adapts work to people. *Harvard Business Review, 55*(4), 102–113.

Hackett, R. D., and Guion, R. M. (1985). A re-evaluation of the absenteeism–job satisfaction relationship. *Organizational Behavior and Human Decision Processes, 35,* 340–381.

Hackman, J. R. (1975). On the coming demise of job enrichment. In E. L. Cass and F. G. Zimmer (Eds.), *Man and work in society.* New York: Van Nostrand Reinhold.

Hackman, J. R. (1977). Work design. In J. R. Hackman and J. L. Suttle (Eds.), *Improving life at work* (pp. 96–159). Santa Monica, CA: Goodyear.

Hackman, J. R., and Lawler, E. E., III. (1971). Employee reactions to job characteristics. *Journal of Applied Psychology, 55,* 259–286.

Hackman, J. R., and Oldham, G. R. (1975). Development of the job diagnostic survey. *Journal of Applied Psychology, 60,* 159–170.

Hackman, J. R., and Oldham, G. R. (1976). Motivation through the design of work: Test of a theory. *Organizational Behavior and Human Performance, 16,* 250–279.

Hackman, J. R., and Oldham, G. R. (1980). *Work redesign.* Reading, MA: Addison-Wesley.

Hackman, J. R., Oldham, G. R., Janson, R., and Purdy, K. A. (1975, Summer). New strategy for job enrichment. *California Management Review, 17* (4), 57–71.

Hall, C. S., and Lindzey, G. (1957). *Theories of personality.* New York: Wiley.

Hall, C. S., and Lindzey, G. (1970). *Theories of personality* (2nd ed.). New York: Wiley.

Hall, D. T. (1976). *Careers in organizations.* Pacific Palisades, CA: Goodyear.

Hall, D. T., and Isabella, L. A. (1985). Downward movement and career development. *Organizational Dynamics, 14*(1), 5–24.

Hall, J. (1994, Winter). Americans know how to be productive if managers will let them. *Organizational Dynamics, 22(1),* 33–46.

Halpern, D., and Osofsky, S. (1990). A dissenting view of MBO. *Public Personnel Management, 19,* 321–330.

Hammer, M., and Champy, J. (1993). *Reengineering the corporation.* New York: Harper Business.

Hammond, K. R., McLelland, G. H., and Mumpower, J. (1980). *Human judgment and decision processes: Theories, methods, and procedures.* New York: Praeger.

Hamner, W. C., and Foster, L. W. (1975). Are intrinsic and extrinsic rewards additive: A test of Deci's cognitive evaluation theory of task motivation. *Organizational Behavior and Human Performance, 14,* 398–415.

Hamner, W. C., and Hamner, E. P. (1976). Behavior modification and the bottom line. *Organizational Dynamics, 4*(4), 3–21.

Hamner, W. C., Ross, J., and Staw, B. M. (1978). Motivation in organizations: The need for a new direction. In D. W. Organ (Ed.), *The applied psychology of work behavior* (pp. 224–250). Dallas, TX: Business Publications.

Hamner, W. C., and Tosi, H. (1974). Relationship of the role conflict and role ambiguity to job involvement measures. *Journal of Applied Psychology, 4,* 497–499.

Hanser, L. M., and Muchinsky, P. M. (1978). Work as an information environment. *Organizational Behavior and Human Performance, 13,* 244–256.

Hanson, R., Porterfield, I. J., and Ames, K. (1995). Employee empowerment at risk: Effects of recent NLRB rulings. *Academy of Management Executive, 9,* 45–54.

Harackiewicz, J. M., and Stone, C. (1991). Goals and intrinsic motivation: You can get there from here. In M. L. Maehr and P. R. Pintrich (Eds.), *Advances in motivation and achievement* (Vol. 7, pp. 21–49). Greenwich, CT: JAI Press.

Harlos, K. P. (1995). *The role of silence in organizational justice and injustice.* Unpublished manuscript, Faculty of Commerce and Business Administration, University of British Columbia, Vancouver, British Columbia, Canada.

Harlow, H. F., Harlow, M. K., and Meyer, D. R. (1950). Learning motivated by a manipulative drive. *Journal of Experimental Psychology, 40,* 228–234.

Harre, R. (1986). An outline of the social constructivist viewpoint. In R. Harre (Ed.), *The social construction of emotions* (pp. 2–14). New York: Basic Blackwell.

Harris, H. (1995). Rethinking heterosexual relationships in Polynesia: A case study of Mangaia, Cook Island. In W. Jankowiak (Ed.), *Romantic passion* (pp. 95–127). New York: Columbia University Press.

Hartnett, J. (1991). A note on the People survey: EEOC data and validation of the honesty scale. *Journal of Psychology, 125,* 489–491.

Harvey, J. B., and Albertson, D. R. (1971). Neurotic organizations: Symptoms, causes, and treatment (Part 1). *Personnel Journal, 50,* 694–699.

Haynes, R. S., Pine, R. C., and Fitch, H. G. (1982). Reducing accident rates with organizational behavior modification. *Academy of Management Journal, 25,* 407–416.

Hebb, D. O. (1955). Drives and the C.N.S. (central nervous system). *Psychological Review, 62,* 243–254.

Heckscher, C. C. (1988). *The new unionism.* New York: Basic Books.

Heilman, M. E., and Guzzo, R. A. (1978). The perceived cause of work success as a mediator of sex discrimination in organizations. *Organizational Behavior and Human Performance, 21,* 346–357.

Heilman, M. E., and Kram, K. E. (1978). Self-derogating behavior in women—fixed or flexible: The effects of co-worker's sex. *Organizational Behavior and Human Performance, 22,* 497–507.

Heiman, G. W. (1975). A note on operant conditioning principles extrapolated to the theory of management. *Organizational Behavior and Human Performance, 13,* 165–170.

Helter, F. (1958). *The psychology of interpersonal relations.* New York: Wiley.

Hendrix, W. H., and Stahl, M. J. (1986). Effects of need for power on job stress for managers and non-managers. *Journal of Social Behavior and Personality, 1*(14), 611–619.

Heneman, H. G., III, and Schwab, D. P. (1972). Evaluation of research on expectancy theory predictions of employee performance. *Psychological Bulletin, 78*(1), 1–9.

Henri, R. (1923). *The art spirit.* Philadelphia: Lippincott.

Henry, R. A. (1994). The effects of choice and incentives on the overestimation of future performance. *Organizational Behavior and Human Decision processes, 57,* 210–225.

Herman, J. B. (1973). Are situational contingencies limiting attitude–job performance relationships? *Organizational Behavior and Human Performance, 10,* 208–224.

Herrnstein, R. J., and Murray, C. (1994). *The bell curve.* New York: Free Press.

Hershey, R. (1973). Coming—A locked in generation of workers. *Personnel, 50*(6), 23–29.

Herzberg, F. (1966). *Work and the nature of man.* Cleveland, OH: World Publishing.

Herzberg, F. (1968). One more time: How do you motivate employees? *Harvard Business Review, 46*(1), 53–62.

Herzberg, F. (1976). Motivational type: Individual differences in motivation. In F. Herzberg (Ed.), *The managerial choice* (pp. 1059–1076). Homewood, IL: Dow Jones–Irwin.

Herzberg, F. (1981). Motivating people. In P. Mali (Ed.), *Management handbook.* New York: Wiley.

Herzberg, F., Mausner, B., Peterson, R. O., and Capwell, D. F. (1957). *Job attitudes: Review of research and opinion.* Pittsburgh, PA: Psychological Service of Pittsburgh.

Herzberg, F., Mausner, B., and Snyderman, B. B. (1959). *The motivation to work.* New York: Wiley.

Hettenhouse, G. W. (9171). Compensation cafeteria for top executives. *Harvard Business Review, 49*(5), 113–119.

Hewstone, M., and Young, L. (1988). Expectancy-value models of attitude: Measurement and combination of evaluations and beliefs. *Journal of Applied Social Psychology, 18,* 958–971.

Hickson, D. J. (1961). Motives of workpeople who restrict their output. *Occupational Psychology, 35,* 111–121.

Hickson, D. J., Hinings, C. R., Lee, C. A., Schneck, R. E., and Pennings, J. M. (1971). A strategic contingencies' theory of intra-organizational power. *Administrative Science Quarterly, 16,* 216–219.

Hill, C. A. (1987a). Affiliation motivation: People who need people . . . but in different ways. *Journal of Personality and Social Psychology, 52,* 1008–1018.

Hill, C. A. (1987b). Social support and health: The role of affiliative need as moderator. *Journal of Research in Personality, 21,* 127–147.

Hill, C. A. (1991). Seeking emotional support: The influence of affiliative need and partner warmth. *Journal of Personality and Social Psychology, 60,* 112–121.

Hinton, B. L., and Barrow, J. C. (1975). The superior's reinforcing behavior as a function of reinforcements received. *Organizational Behavior and Human Performance, 14,* 123–143.

Hirschman, A. O. (1970). *Exit, voice, and loyalty: Response to decline in firms, organizations, and states.* Cambridge, MA: Harvard University Press.

Hitt, W. (1969). Two models of man. *American Psychologist, 24,* 651–658.

Hochschild, A. R. (1983). *The managed heart.* Berkeley, CA: University of California Press.

Hoerr, J. A. (1979, June 4). Warning that worker discontent is rising. *Business Week, 2588,* 152, 156.

Hofstede, G. (1978). The poverty of management control philosophy. *Academy of Management Review, 3,* 450–461.

Hollenbeck, J. R. (1979). A matrix method for expectancy research. *Academy of Management Review, 4,* 579–587.

Hollenbeck, J. R., Williams, C. R., and Klein, H. J. (1989). An empirical examination of commitment to difficult goals. *Journal of Applied Psychology, 74,* 18–23.

Holmes, T. and Rahe, R. H. (1967). The social readjustment rating scale. *Journal of Psychosomatic Research, 12,* 213–218.

Homans, G. C. (1961). *Social behavior: Its elementary forms.* New York: Harcourt, Brace and World.

Hopwood, A. (1976). *Accounting and human behavior.* Englewood Cliffs, NJ: Prentice Hall.

Horn, P. D., and Horn, J. C. (1982). *Sex in the office.* Reading, MA: Addison-Wesley.

Horn, P. W., Katerberg, R., and Hulin, C. L. (1979). Comparative examination of three approaches to the prediction of turnover. *Journal of Applied Psychology, 64,* 280–290.

Horngren, C. T. (1977). *Cost accounting* (4th ed.). Englewood Cliffs, NJ: Prentice Hall.

House, R. J. (1971). A path-goal theory of leadership. *Administrative Science Quarterly, 16,* 321–338.

House, R. J. (1975). The quest for relevance in management education: Some second thoughts and undesired consequences. *Academy of Management Journal, 18,* 323–333.

House, R. J., and Dessler, G. (1974). The path-goal theory of leadership: Some post hoc and a priori tests. In J. G. Hunt (Ed.), *Contingency approaches to leadership.* Carbondale, IL: Southern Illinois University Press.

House, R. J., and Mitchell, T. R. (1974). Path-goal theory of leadership. *Journal of Contemporary Business, 3,* 81–98.

House, R. J., and Rizzo, J. R. (1972). Role conflict and ambiguity as critical variables in a model of organizational behavior. *Organizational Behavior and Human Performance, 7,* 467–505.

House, R. J., Shane, S. A., and Herold, D. M. (1996). Rumors of the death of dispositional research are vastly exaggerated. *Academy of Management Review, 21,* 203–224.

House, R. J., Shapiro, H. J., and Wahba, M. A. (1974). Expectancy theory as a predictor of work behavior and attitude: A reevaluation of empirical evidence. *Decision Sciences, 5,* 481–506.

House, R. J., Spangler, W. D., and Woyke, J. (1991). Personality and charisma in the U.S. presidency: A psychological theory of leader effectiveness. *Administrative Science Quarterly, 36,* 364–396.

House, R. J., and Wigdor, L. A. (1967). Herzberg's dual factor theory of job satisfaction and motivation. *Personnel Psychology, 20,* 369–390.

Hsee, C. K., and Abelson, R. P. (1991). Velocity relation: Satisfaction as a function of the first derivative of outcome over time. *Journal of Personality and Social Psychology, 60,* 341–347.

Huberman, J. (1964). Discipline without punishment. *Harvard Business Review, 42*(4), 62–68.

Hughes, E. C. (1958). *Men and their work.* Glencoe, IL: Free Press.

Hughes, M. A., Price, R. L., and Marrs, D. W. (1986). Linking theory construction and theory testing: Models with multiple indicators of latent variables. *Academy of Management Review, 11,* 128–144.

Hughey, J. B., Sundstrom, E., and Lounsbury, J. W. (1985). Attitudes toward nuclear power: A longitudinal analysis of expectancy-value models. *Basic and Applied Social Psychology, 6,* 75–91.

Huizinga, G. (1970). *Maslow's need hierarchy in the work situation.* Groningen, The Netherlands: Wolters-Noordhoff.

Hulin, C. L. (1990). Adaptation, persistence, and commitment. In M. D. Dunnette, and L. M. Hough (Eds.), *Handbook of industrial and organizational psychology* (2nd ed., Vol. 2) Palo Alto, CA: Consulting Psychologists Press.

Hulin, C. L., and Blood, M. R. (1968). Job enlargement, individual differences, and worker responses. *Psychological Bulletin, 69,* 41–55.

Hull, C. L. (1943). *Principles of behavior.* New York: Appleton-Century-Crofts.

Hunter, J. E., Schmidt, F. L., and Jackson, G. B. (1982). *Meta-analysis: Cumulating research findings across studies.* Beverly Hills, CA: Sage.

Hunt, J. McV. (1965). Intrinsic motivation and its role in psychological development. *Nebraska Symposium on Motivation, 13,* 189–282.

Huseman, R. C., Hatfield, J. D., and Miles, E. W. (1985). Test for individual perceptions of job equity: Some preliminary findings. *Perceptual and Motor Skills, 61,* 1055–1064.

Huseman, R. C., Hatfield, J. D., and Miles, E. W. (1987). A new perspective on equity theory: The equity sensitivity construct. *Academy of Management Review, 12,* 222–234.

Hyland, M. E. (1988). Motivational control theory: An integrative framework. *Journal of Personality and Social Psychology, 55,* 642–651.

Ilardi, B. C., Leone, D., Kasser, T., and Ryan, R. M. (1993, November). Employee and supervisor ratings of motivation: Main effects and discrepancies associated with job satisfaction and adjustment in a factory setting. *Journal of Applied Social Psychology, 23,* 1789–1805.

Ilgen, D. R. (1971). Satisfaction with performance as a function of the initial level of expected performance and the deviation from expectations. *Organizational Behavior and Human Performance, 6,* 345–361.

Ilgen, D. R., Fisher, C., and Taylor, M. (1979). Consequences of individual feedback on behavior in organizations. *Journal of Applied Psychology, 64,* 349–371.

Ilgen, D. R., and Hollenbeck, J. H. (1977). The role of job satisfaction in absence behavior. *Organizational Behavior and Human Performance, 19,* 148–161.

Ilgen, D. R., and Klein, H. J. (1988a). Organizational behavior. *Annual Review of Psychology, 40,* 327–351.

Ilgen, D. R., and Klein, H. J. (1988b). Individual motivation and performance: Cognitive influences on effort and choice. In J. P. Campbell, R. J. Campbell, and Associates (Eds.), *Productivity in organizations* (pp. 143–176). San Francisco: Jossey-Bass.

Ilgen, D. R., Nebeker, D. M., and Pritchard, R. D. (1981). Expectancy theory measures: An empirical comparison in an experimental simulation. *Organizational Behavior and Human Performance, 28,* 189–223.

Ilgen, D. R., and Seely, W. (1974). Realistic expectations as an aid in reducing voluntary resignations. *Journal of Applied Psychology, 59,* 452–455.

Inglehart, R. (1981). Aggregate stability and individual-level flux in mass belief systems: The level of analysis paradox. *American Political Science Review, 79,* 97–116.

Ironson, G. H., Smith, P. C., Brannick, M. T., Gibson, W. M., and Paul, K. B. (1989). Construction of a job in general scale: A comparison of global, composite and specific measures. *Journal of Applied Psychology, 74,* 193–200.

Isen, A. M., and Baron, R. A. (1991). Positive affect as a factor in organizational behavior. In L. L. Cummings and B. M. Staw (Eds.), *Research in organizational behavior* (Vol. 13, pp. 1–54). Greenwich, CT: JAI Press.

Ivancevich, M. J., and Donnelly, J. H., Jr. (1974). A study of role clarity and need for clarity for three occupational groups. *Academy of Management Journal, 17,* 28–36.

Ivancevich, J. M., and McMahon, J. T. (1982). The effects of goal setting, external feedback, and self-generated feedback on outcome variables: A field experiment. *Academy of Management Journal, 25,* 359–372.

Iverson, R. D., Deery, S. J., and Erwin, P. J. (1994). *Absenteeism among health care workers: Causes and intervention strategies.* Paper presented at the 54th Annual Meeting of the Academy of Management, Dallas, TX.

Iverson, R. D., and Erwin, P. J. (1995, August). *Predicting occupational injury: The role of affectivity.* Paper presented at the 55th Annual Meeting of the Academy of Management, Vancouver, British Columbia, Canada.

Jablonsky, S. F., and DeVries, D. L. (1972). Operant conditioning principles extrapolated to the theory of management. *Organizational Behavior and Human Performance, 7,* 340–358.

Jaccard, J. (1981). Attitudes and behaviour: Implications of attitudes toward behavioral alternatives. *Journal of Experimental Social Psychology, 17,* 286–307.

Jaccard, J., King, G. W., and Pomazal, R. (1977). Attitudes and behavior: An analysis of specificity of attitudinal predictors. *Human Relations, 9,* 817–824.

Jackson, J. M., and Harkins, S. G. (1985). Equity in effort: An explanation of the social loafing effect. *Journal of Personality and Social Psychology, 49,* 1199–1206.

Jacobs, J. A., and Powell, B. (1985). Occupational prestige: A sex-neutral concept? *Sex Roles, 12*(9/10), 1061–1071.

Jacques, E. (1961). *Equitable payment.* New York: Wiley.

Jacques, R. (1992). Critique and theory building: Producing knowledge "from the kitchen." *Academy of Management Review, 17,* 582–606.

Jamal, M. (1984). Job stress and job performance controversy. *Organizational Behavior and Human Performance, 33,* 1–21.

Jamal, M., and Mitchell, V. F. (1980). Work, nonwork, and mental health: A model and a test. *Industrial Relations, 19,* 88–93.

James, L. R., and Jones, A. P. (1976). Organizational structure: A review of structural dimensions and their conceptual relationships with individual attitudes and behavior. *Organizational Behavior and Human Performance, 16,* 74–113.

Jamieson, D. (1973). Behavioral problems with management by objectives. *Academy of Management Journal, 16,* 496–505.

Janigan, M. (1995, June 19). Mike the knife: Ontario's new premier has a mandate to cut taxes and slash government. *Maclean's, 108*(25), 10–12, 13, 14–16.

Jankowiak, W. (Ed.). (1995). *Romantic passion.* New York: Columbia University Press.

Jankowiak, W., and Fischer, E. (1992). A cross-cultural perspective on romantic love. *Ethnology, 31*(2), 149–155.

Jansen, E., and Von Glinow, M. A. (1985). Ethical ambivalence and organizational reward systems. *Academy of Management Review, 10,* 814–822.

Janz, T. (1982). Manipulating subjective expectancy through feedback: A laboratory study of the expectancy–performance relationship. *Journal of Applied Psychology, 64,* 480–485.

Jaros, S. J., Jermier, J. M., Koehler, J. W., and Sincich, T. (1993). Effects of continuance, affective, and moral commitment on the withdrawal process: An evaluation of eight structural equation models. *Academy of Management Journal, 36,* 951–995.

Jenkins, D. (1975). Beyond job enrichment. *Working Papers for a New Society, 2,* 51–57.

Jenkins, S. R. (1994). Need for power and women's careers over 14 years: Structural power, job satisfaction, and motive change. *Journal of Personality and Social Psychology, 66,* 155–165.

Jermier, J. M. (1988). Sabotage at work: The rational view. In N. DiTomaso and S. B. Bacharach (Eds.), *Research in the sociology of organizations* (Vol. 6, pp. 101–134). Greenwich, CT: JAI Press.

Joad, C. E. M. (1957). *Guide to philosophy.* New York: Dover.

Johns, G. (1981). Difference score measures of organizational behavior variables: A critique. *Organizational Behavior and Human Performance, 27,* 443–463.

Johns, G. (1991). Substantive and methodological constraints on behavior and attitudes in organizational behavior. *Organizational Behavior and Human Decision Processes, 49,* 80–104.

Johns, G., and Nicholson, N. (1982). The meaning of absence: New strategies for theory and research. In B. M. Staw and L. L. Cummings (Eds.), *Research in organizational behavior* (Vol. 4, pp. 127–172). Greenwich, CT: JAI Press.

Johnson, G. C., and Grey, R. J. (1988a, Spring). Signs of diminishing employee commitment. *Canadian Business Review, 15,* 20–23.

Johnson, G. C., and Grey, R. J. (1988b, Autumn). Employee motivation in high-performance companies. *Canadian Business Review, 15,* 26–29.

Johnson, P. R., and Indvik, J. (1994). Workplace violence: An issue of the nineties. *Public Personnel Management, 23,* 515–523.

Jones, E. E. (1964). *Ingratiation.* New York: Appleton-Century-Crofts.

Jones, M. R. (Ed.). (1955). *Nebraska symposium on motivation.* Lincoln, NE: University of Nebraska Press.

Journal of Vocational Behavior. (1993). Special issue on the theory of work adjustment, *43*(1).

Judge, T. A. (1992). The dispositional perspective in human resource management. In G. R. Ferris and K. M. Rowland (Eds.), *Research in personnel and human resources management* (Vol. 10, pp. 187–232). Greenwich, CT: JAI Press.

Judge, T. A., and Bretz, R. D., Jr. (1992). Effects of work values on job choice decisions. *Journal of Applied Psychology, 77,* 261–271.

Judge, T. A., and Watanabe, S. (1993). Another look at the job satisfaction–life satisfaction relationship. *Journal of Applied Psychology, 78,* 939–948.

Jussim, L. (1986). Self-fulfilling prophesies: A theoretical and integrative review. *Psychological Review, 93,* 429–445.

Kahn, R. F., Wolfe, D. M., Quinn, R. P., Snoek, J. D., and Rosenthal, R. A. (1964). *Organizational stress.* New York: Wiley.

Kahn, W. A. (1989). Toward a sense of organizational humor: Implications for organizational diagnosis and change. *Journal of Applied Behavioral Science, 25*(1), 45–63.

Kahn, W. A. (1990). Psychological conditions of personal engagement and disengagement at work. *Academy of Management Journal, 33,* 692–724.

Kane, K., and Montgomery, K. (1996, April). *A theory of dysempowerment.* Paper presented at the meeting of the Western Academy of Management, Banff, Alberta, Canada.

Kane, K., Montgomery, K., and Vance, C. (1996, April). *A theoretical framework for understanding the empowering and dysempowering nature of social exchanges in employee involvement efforts.* Paper presented at the meeting of the Western Academy of Management, Banff, Alberta, Canada.

Kanfer, F. H. (1970). *Learning foundations of behavior therapy.* New York: Wiley.

Kanfer, F. H. (1971). The maintenance of behavior by self-generated stimuli and reinforcement. In A. Jacobs and L. B. Sachs (Eds.), *The psychology of private events.* New York: Academic Press.

Kanfer, F. H. (1980). Self management methods. In F. H. Kanfer and A. P. Goldstein (Eds.), *Helping people change* (2nd ed., pp. 334–389). New York: Pergamon Press.

Kanfer, R. (1990). Motivation theory in industrial/organizational psychology. In M. D. Dunnette and L. M. Hough (Eds.), *Handbook of industrial and organizational psychology* (2nd ed., Vol. 1, pp. 75-170). Palo Alto, CA: Consulting Psychologists Press.

Kanfer, R., and Ackerman, P. L. (1989). Motivation and cognitive abilities: An integrative/aptitude treatment interaction approach to skill acquisition. *Journal of Applied Psychology, 74,* 657–690.

Kanter, R. M. (1979). Power failure in management circuits. *Harvard Business Review, 57*(4), 65–75.

Karau, S. J., and Williams, K. D. (1993). Social loafing: A meta-analytic review and theoretical integration. *Journal of Personality and Social Psychology, 65,* 681–706.

Karmel, B. (Ed.). (1980). *Point and counterpoint in organizational behavior.* Hillsdale, IL: Dryden Press.

Karoly, P. (1993). Mechanisms of self-regulation: A systems view. *Annual Review of Psychology, 44,* 23–52.

Karp, H. B., and Nickson, J. W. (1973). Motivator-hygiene deprivation as a predictor of job turnover. *Personal Psychology, 26,* 377–384.

Katerberg, R., and Blau, G. J. (1983). An examination of level and direction of effort and job performance. *Academy of Management Journal, 26,* 249–257.

Katz, D. (1964). The motivational basis of organizational behavior. *Behavioral Science, 9,* 131–146.

Katz, D., and Kahn, R. (1966). *The social psychology of organizations.* New York: Wiley.

Katz, D., and Kahn, R. L. (1978). *The social psychology of organizations* (2nd ed.). New York: Wiley.

Katz, R. (1977). Job enrichment: Some career considerations. In J. Van Maanen (Ed.), *Organizational careers* (pp. 133–148). Chichester, West Sussex, England: Wiley.

Katz, R. (1978). Job longevity as situational factor in job satisfaction. *Administrative Science Quarterly, 28,* 204–223.

Katz, R. (1980). Time and work: Toward an integrative perspective. In B. M. Staw and L. L. Cummings (Eds.), *Research in organizational behavior* (Vol. 2, pp. 81–128). Greenwich, CT: JAI Press.

Katzell, R. A., and Thompson, D. E. (1990). Work motivation: Theory and practice. *American Psychologist, 45*(2), 144–153.

Katzell, R. A., Thompson, D. E., and Guzzo, R. A. (1992). How job satisfaction and job performance are and are not linked. In C. J. Cranny, P. C. Smith, and E. F. Stone (Eds.), *Job satisfaction* (pp. 195–217). New York: Lexington Books.

Kavanagh, M. J., Hurst, M. W., and Rose, R. (1981). The relationship between job satisfaction and psychiatric health symptoms for air traffic controllers. *Personnel Psychology, 34,* 691–707.

Kazdin, A. E. (1975). *Behavior modification in applied settings.* Homewood, IL: Dorsey.

Kazdin, A. E. (1978). *History of behavior modification.* Baltimore, MD: University Park Press.

Keeley, M. (1983). Values in organizational theory. *Academy of Management Review, 8,* 376–386.

Keeley, M., and Graham, J. W. (1992). Hirschman's loyalty construct. *Employee Responsibilities and Rights Journal, 5,* 191–200.

Keller, R. T. (1989). A test of the path-goal theory of leadership with need for clarity as a moderator in research and development organizations. *Journal of Applied Psychology, 74,* 208–212.

Kelley, H. H. (1973). Processes of causal attribution. *American Psychologist, 28,* 107–128.

Kelley, H. H., and Michela, J. L. (1980). Attribution theory and research. *Annual Review of Psychology, 31,* 457–501.

Kelly, J. E. (1978). A reappraisal of sociotechnical systems theory. *Human Relations, 31,* 1069–1099.

Kelly, R. M., and Bayes, J. (1988). Comparable worth and pay equity: Issues and trends. In R. M. Kelly and J. Bayes (Eds.), *Comparable worth, pay equity, and public policy.* New York: Greenwood Press.

Kelman, H. C. (1958). Compliance, identification, and internalization: Three processes of attitude change. *Journal of Conflict Resolution, 2,* 51–60.

Kempen, R. W., and Hall, R. V. (1977). Reduction of industrial absenteeism: Results of a behavioral approach. *Journal of Organizational Behavior Management, 1,* 1–21.

Kennedy, M. M. (1992, March). Romance in the office. *Across the Board, 29*(3), 23–27.

Kennedy, C. W., Fossum, J. A., and White, B. J. (1983). An empirical comparison of within-subjects and between-subjects expectancy theory models. *Organizational Behavior and Human Performance, 32,* 124–143.

Kenny, D. A. (1979). *Correlation and causality.* New York: Wiley.

Keren, G. B., and Raaijmakers, J. G. (1988). On between-subjects versus within-subjects comparisons in testing utility theory. *Organizational Behavior and Human Decision Processes, 41,* 233–247.

Kerr, N. L. (1983). Motivation losses in small groups: A social dilemma analysis. *Journal of Personality and Social Psychology, 45,* 819–828.

Kerr, N. L., and Bruun, S. E. (1981). Ringelmann revisited: Alternative explanations for the social loafing effect. *Personality and Social Psychology Bulletin, 7,* 224–231.

Kerr, S. (1975). On the folly of rewarding A, while hoping for B. *Academy of Management Journal, 18,* 769–783.

Kerr, S. (1982). *Some characteristics and consequences of organizational reward systems.* University of Southern California Working Paper.

Kerr, S., and Jermier, J. M. (1978). Substitutes for leadership: Their meaning and measurement. *Organizational Behavior and Human Performance, 22,* 375–403.

Khandwalla, P. N. (1977). *The design of organizations.* New York: Harcourt Brace Jovanovich.

Kidder, L. H., Bellettlrie, G., and Cohn, E. S. (1977). Secret ambitions and public performances: The effects of anonymity on reward allocation made by men and women. *Journal of Experimental Social Psychology, 13,* 70–80.

Kidwell, R. E., and Bennett, N. (1993). Employee propensity to withhold effort: A conceptual model to intersect three avenues of research. *Academy of Management Review, 18,* 429–456.

Killinger, B. (1991). *Workaholics: The respectable addicts.* Toronto, Ontario, Canada: Key Porter Books.

Killingsworth, M. R. (1990). *The economics of comparable worth.* Kalamazoo, MI: W.E. Upjohn Institute for Employment Research.

Kilmann, R. A. (1981). Toward a unique/useful concept of values for interpersonal behaviour: A critical review of the literature on value. *Psychological Reports, 48,* 939–959.

Kim, J. S., and Hamner, W. C. (1976). Effect of performance feedback and goal setting on productivity and satisfaction in an organizational setting. *Journal of Applied Psychology, 61,* 48–57.

King, C. (1993). *Through the glass ceiling.* Newcastle-upon-Tyne, Northumberland, England: Athenaeum Press.

King, N. (1970). Clarification and evaluation of the two-factor theory of job satisfaction. *Psychological Bulletin, 74,* 18–31.

King, W. C., Miles, E. W., and Day, D. D. (1993). A test and refinement of the equity sensitivity construct. *Journal of Organizational Behavior, 14,* 301–317.

Kipnis, D. (1972). Does power corrupt? *Journal of Personality and Social Psychology, 24,* 33–41.

Kipnis, D., Castell, P. J., Gergen, M., and Mauch, D. (1976). Metamorphic effects of power. *Journal of Applied Psychology, 61,* 127–135.

Kitayama, S., and Niedenthal, P. M. (Eds.). (1994). Introduction. In P. M. Niedenthal and S. Kitayama (Eds.), *The heart's eye* (pp. 1–14). San Diego, CA: Academic Press.

Klein, H. J. (1989). An integrated control theory model of work motivation. *Academy of Management Review, 14,* 150–172.

Klein, H. J. (1991a). Further evidence on the relationship between goal setting and expectancy theories. *Organizational Behavior and Human Decision Processes, 49,* 230–257.

Klein, H. J. (1991b). Control theory and understanding motivated behavior: A different conclusion. *Motivation and Emotion, 15,* 29–44.

Kleinbeck, U., Quast, H.-H., Thierry, H., and Hacker, H. (Eds.). (1990). *Work motivation.* Hillsdale, NJ: Lawrence Erlbaum.

Kleinginna, P. R., and Kleinginna, A. M. (1981). A categorized list of motivation definitions with a suggestion for a consensual definition. *Motivation and Emotion,* 263–292.

Klinger, M. R., and Greenwald, A. G. (1994). Preferences need no inferences? The cognitive basis of unconscious mere exposure effects. In P. M. Niedenthal and S. Kitayama (Eds.), *The heart's eye* (pp. 67–85). San Diego, CA: Academic Press.

Knowles, H. P., and Saxberg, B. O. (1967). Human relations and the nature of man. *Harvard Business Review, 45,* 22–24, 28, 30, 32, 34, 36, 38, 40, 172, 174, 176, 178.

Kochan, T. A. (1980). *Collective bargaining and industrial relations.* Homewood, IL: Irwin.

Kohlberg, L. (1981). *The philosophy of moral development.* New York: Harper and Row.

Kohlberg, L. (1984). *The psychology of moral development.* New York: Harper and Row.

Kohn, A. (1993). Why incentive plans cannot work. *Harvard Business Review, 71*(5), 54–63.

Kolb, D. A., and Plovnick, M. S. (1977). The experiential learning theory of career development. In J. Van Maanen (Ed.), *Organizational careers* (pp. 65–88). Chichester, West Sussex, England: Wiley.

Komaki, J., Barwick, K. D., and Scott, L. R. (1978). A behavioral approach to occupational safety pinpointing and reinforcing safe performance in a food processing plant. *Journal of Applied Psychology, 63,* 434–445.

Komaki, J. L. (1986). Applied behavior analysis and organizational behavior: Reciprocal influence of the two fields. In B. M. Staw and L. L. Cummings (Eds.), *Research in organizational behavior* (Vol. 8, pp. 297–334). Greenwich, CT: JAI Press.

Komaki, J. L., Coombs, T., and Schepman, S. (1991). Motivational implications of reinforcement theory. In R. M. Steers and L. W. Porter (Eds.), *Motivation and work behavior* (5th ed., pp. 87–107). New York: McGraw-Hill.

Komaki, J. L., Heinzmann, A. T., and Lawson, L. (1980). Effect of training and feedback: Component analysis of a behavioral safety program. *Journal of Applied Psychology, 65,* 261–270.

Komaki, J. L., Waddell, W. M., and Pearce, M. G. (1977). The applied behavior analysis approach and individual employees: Improving performance in two small businesses. *Organizational Behavior and Human Performance, 19,* 337–352.

Kondrasuk, J. N. (1981). Studies in MBO effectiveness. *Academy of Management Review, 6,* 419–430.

Konrad, A. M., and Langton, N. (1991). Sex differences in job preferences, workplace segregation, and compensating earnings differentials: The case of Stanford MBA's. *Academy of Management Proceedings,* 368–372.

Kopelman, R. E. (1977). Across-individual, within-individual and return on effort. *Decision Sciences, 8,* 651–662.

Kopelman, R. E. (1979). A causal-correlational test of the Porter and Lawler framework. *Human Relations, 32,* 545–556.

Kopelman, R. E. (1986). *Managing productivity in organizations.* New York: McGraw-Hill.

Kopelman, R. E., and Schneller, G. O. (1981). A mixed-consequence system for reducing overtime and unscheduled absences. *Journal of Organizational Behavior Management, 3,* 17–28.

Kopelman, R. E., and Thompson, P. H. (1976). Boundary conditions for expectancy theory predictions of work motivation and job performance. *Academy of Management Journal, 19,* 237–258.

Korman, A. K. (1970). Toward a hypothesis of work behavior. *Journal of Applied Psychology, 54,* 31–41.

Korman, A. K. (1971). *Industrial and organizational psychology.* Englewood Cliffs, NJ: Prentice Hall.

Korman, A. K. (1974). *The psychology of motivation.* Englewood Cliffs, NJ: Prentice Hall.

Korman, A. K. (1976). Hypothesis of work behavior revisited and an extension. *Academy of Management Review, 1,* 50–63.

Kornhauser, A. (1965). *Mental health of the industrial worker.* New York: Wiley.

Kouzes, J. M., and Posner, B. Z. (1995). *The leadership challenge.* San Francisco: Jossey-Bass.

Kovach, K. A. (1987). What motivates employees? Workers and supervisors give different answers. *Business Horizons, 30*(5), 58–64.

Kovach, K. A., and Millspaugh, P. E. (1990). Comparable worth: Canada legislates pay equity. *Academy of Management Executive, 4*(2), 92–101.

Kram, K. E. (1985). *Mentoring at work: Developmental relationships in organizational life.* Glenview, IL: Scott, Foresman.

Kraut, A. I. (1975). Predicting turnover of employees from measured job attitudes. *Organizational Behavior and Human Performance, 13,* 233–243.

Kravitz, D., and Martin, B. (1986). Ringelmann rediscovered: The original article. *Journal of Personality and Social Psychology, 50,* 936–941.

Kreitner, R., and Luthans, F. (1984). A social-leaning approach to behavioral management: Radical behaviorists "mellowing out." *Organizational Dynamics, 13*(2), 47–65.

Kruglanski, A. W., and Mayesless, O. (1990). Classic and current social comparison research: Expanding the perspective. *Psychological Bulletin, 108,* 195–208.

Kuhl, J., and Atkinson, J. W. (1984). Perspectives in human motivational psychology: A new experimental paradigm. In V. Sarris and A. Parducci (Eds.), *Perspective in psychological experimentation: Towards the year 2000* (pp. 235–252). Hillsdale, NJ: Lawrence Erlbaum.

Kuhn, T. (1970). *The structure of scientific revolutions.* Chicago: University of Chicago Press.

Label, S. A., Quinn, R. E., St. Clair, L., and Warfield, A. (1994). Love without sex: The impact of psychological intimacy between men and women at work. *Organizational Dynamics, 23*(1), 5–16.

Lacayo, R. (1995). To hell week and back. *Time, 146*(9), pp. 34–35.

Lakoff, G. (1987). *Women, fire, and dangerous things: What categories reveal about the mind.* Chicago: University of Chicago Press.

Landy, F. J., and Becker, W. S. (1987). Work motivation reconsidered. In L. L. Cummings and B. M. Staw (Eds.), *Research in organizational behavior* (Vol. 9, pp. 1–38). Greenwich, CT: JAI Press.

Lang, P. J. (1988). What are the data of emotion? In V. Hamilton, G. H. Bower, and N. H. Fridja (Eds.), *Cognitive perspectives on emotion and motivation* (pp. 173–191). Dordrecht, The Netherlands: Kluwer.

Lansberg, I. (1984). Hierarchy as a mediator of fairness: A contingency approach to distributive justice in organizations. *Journal of Applied Social Psychology, 14,* 124–135.

La Nuez, D., and Jermier, J. M. (1994). Sabotage by managers and technocrats. In J. M. Jermier, D. Knights, and W. R. Nord (Eds.), *Resistance and power in organizations.* New York: Routledge.

Larwood, L., and Wood, M. M. (1977). *Women in management.* Lexington, MA: Lexington Books.

Latack, J. C., Kiniki, A. J., and Prussia, G. E. (1995). An integrative model of coping with job loss. *Academy of Management Journal, 20,* 311–342.

Latane, B., Williams, K. D., and Harkins, S. G. (1979). Many hands make light the work: The causes and consequences of social loafing. *Journal of Personality and Social Psychology, 37,* 822–832.

Latham, G. P., and Baldes, J. J. (1975). The practical significance of Locke's theory of goal setting. *Journal of Applied Psychology, 60,* 122–124.

Latham, G. P., and Dossett, D. L. (1978). Designing incentive plans for unionized employees: A comparison of continuous and variable ratio reinforcement schedules. *Personnel Psychology, 31,* 47–61.

Latham, G. P., Erez, M., and Locke, E. A. (1988). Resolving scientific dispute by the joint design of crucial experiments by the antagonists: Application to the Erez–Latham dispute regarding participation in goal setting. *Journal of Applied Psychology* [monograph], *73,* 753–772.

Latham, G. P., and Frayne, C. A. (1989). Self-management training for increased job attendance: A follow-up and a replication. *Journal of Applied Psychology, 74,* 411–416.

Latham, G. P., and Kinne, S. B. (1974). Improving job performance through training in goal setting. *Journal of Applied Psychology, 59,* 187–191.

Latham, G. P., and Locke, E. A. (1975). Increasing productivity with decreasing time limits: A field replication of Parkinson's law. *Journal of Applied Psychology, 60,* 524–526.

Latham, G. P., and Locke, E. A. (1991). Self-regulation through goal setting. *Organizational Behavior and Human Decision Processes, 50,* 212–247.

Latham, G. P., Mitchell, T. R., and Dossett, D. L. (1978). Importance of participative goal setting and anticipated rewards on goal difficulty and job performance. *Journal of Applied Psychology, 63,* 163–171.

Latham, G. P., and Saari, L. M. (1979a). The effects of holding goal difficulty constant on assigned and participatively set goals. *Academy of Management Journal, 22,* 163–168.

Latham, G. P., and Saari, L. M. (1979b). Importance of supportive relationships in goal setting. *Journal of Applied Psychology, 64,* 151–156.

Latham, G. P., and Steele, T. P. (1983). The motivational effects of participation versus goal setting on performance. *Academy of Management Journal, 26,* 406–417.

Latham, G. P., Steele, T. P., and Saari, L. M. (1982). The effects of participation and goal difficulty on performance. *Personnel Psychology, 35,* 677–686.

Latham, G. P., and Wexley, K. N. (1981). *Increasing productivity through performance appraisal.* Reading, MA: Addison-Wesley.

Latham, G. P., Winters, D. C., and Locke, E. A. (1994). Cognitive and motivational effects of participation: A mediator study. *Journal of Organizational Behavior, 15,* 49–63.

Latham, G. P., and Yukl, G. (1975). A review of research on the application of goal setting in organizations. *Academy of Management Journal, 18,* 824–845.

Lawler, E. E. (1965). Managers' perception of their subordinates' pay and of their superiors' pay. *Personnel Psychology, 18,* 413–422.

Lawler, E. E. (1966). The mythology of management compensation. *California Management Review, 9,* 11–22.

Lawler, E. E. (1967a). Secrecy about management compensation: Are there hidden costs? *Organizational Behavior and Human Performance, 2,* 182–189.

Lawler, E. E. (1967b). Attitude surveys and job performance. *Personnel Administration, 30(5),* 3–5, 22–24.

Lawler, E. E. (1968). Equity theory as a predictor of productivity and work quality. *Psychological Bulletin, 70,* 596–610.

Lawler, E. E. (1969). Job design and employee motivation. *Personnel Psychology, 22,* 426–435.

Lawler, E. E. (1971). *Pay and organization effectiveness: A psychological view.* New York: McGraw-Hill.

Lawler, E. E. (1972). Secrecy and the need to know. In H. Tosi, R. J. House, and M. D. Dunnette (Eds.), *Managerial motivation and compensation* (pp. 455–476). East Lansing, MI: MSU Business Studies.

Lawler, E. E. (1973). *Motivation in work organizations.* Monterey, CA: Brooks/Cole.

Lawler, E. E. (1976). Individualizing organizations: A needed emphasis in organizational psychology. In H. Meltzer and F. R. Wickert (Eds.), *Humanizing organizational behavior.* Springfield, IL: Charles C. Thomas.

Lawler, E. E. (1992). *The ultimate advantage.* San Francisco: Jossey-Bass.

Lawler, E. E., and Hall, D. T. (1970). Relationship of job characteristics to job involvement, satisfaction, and intrinsic motivation. *Journal of Applied Psychology, 54,* 305–312.

Lawler, E. E., Mohrman, S. A., and Ledford, G. E. (1995). *Creating high performance organizations: Practices and results of employee involvement and total quality management in Fortune 1000 companies.* San Francisco: Jossey-Bass.

Lawler, E. E., and O'Gara, P. W. (1967). Effects of inequity produced by underpayment on work output, work quality, and attitudes toward the work. *Journal of Applied Psychology, 51,* 403–410.

Lawler, E. E., and Porter, L. W. (1967). The effect of performance on job satisfaction. *Industrial Relations, 7,* 20–28.

Lawler, E. E., and Suttle, J. L. (1972). A causal correlational test of the need hierarchy concept. *Organizational Behavior and Human Performance, 7,* 265–287.

Lawler, E. E., and Suttle, J. L. (1973). Expectancy theory and job behavior. *Organizational Behavior and Human Performance, 9,* 482–503.

Lawrence, P. R., and Lorsch, J. (1969). *Organization and environment.* Homewood, IL: Irwin.

Lazarus, R. S. (1984). On the primacy of cognition. *American Psychologist, 39,* 124–129.

Lazarus, R. S. (1991). *Emotion and adaptation.* New York: Oxford University Press.

Lazarus, R. S., and Lazarus, B. N. (1994). *Passion and reason: Making sense of our emotions.* New York: Oxford University Press.

Lazer, R. I. (1979). The "discrimination" danger in performance appraisal. In W. F. Glueck (Ed.), *Personnel: A book of readings* (pp. 188–195). Dallas, TX: Business Publications.

Leacock, E., and Safa, H. I. (1986). *Women's work: Development and the division of labor by gender.* South Hadley, MA: Bergin and Garvey.

Leana, C. R., and Feldman, D. C. (1994). The psychology of job loss. In G. R. Ferris (Ed.), *Research in personnel and human resource management* (Vol. 12, pp. 271–302). Greenwich, CT: JAI Press.

Leck, J., and Saunders, D. (1992). Hirschman's loyalty: Attitude or behavior? *Employee Rights and Responsibilities Journal, 5,* 219–229.

Lee, T. W., Ashford, S. J., Walsh, J. P., and Mowday, R. T. (1992). Commitment propensity, organizational commitment, and voluntary turnover: A longitudinal study of organizational entry processes. *Journal of Management, 18*(1) 15–32.

Lee, T. W., and Mitchell, T. R. (1994). An alternative approach: The unfolding model of employee turnover. *Academy of Management Review, 19,* 51–89.

Lee, T. W., Mitchell, T. R., Wise, L., and Fireman, S. (1996). An unfolding model of voluntary employee turnover. *Academy of Management Journal, 39,* 5–36.

Leon, F. R. (1979). Number of outcomes and accuracy of prediction in expectancy research. *Organizational Behavior and Human Performance, 23,* 251–267.

Leonard, N. H., Beauvais, L. L., and Scholl, R. W. (1995). *A self-concept-based model of work motivation.* Paper presented at the Academy of Management Annual Meeting, Vancouver, British Columbia, Canada.

Lepper, M. R., and Greene, D. (Eds.) (1978). *The hidden costs of reward.* Hillsdale, NJ: Lawrence Erlbaum.

Leventhal, G. S. (1973, August). *Reward allocation by males and females.* Paper presented at the meeting of the American Psychological Association, Montreal, Quebec, Canada.

Leventhal, G. S. (1976). Fairness in social relationships. In J. W. Thibaut, J. T. Spence, and R. C. Carson (Eds.), *Contemporary topics in social psychology* (pp. 211–239). Morristown, NJ: General Learning Press, an imprint of Silver Burdett Company.

Leventhal, G. S. (1980). What should be done with equity theory? In K. J. Gergen, M. S. Greenberg, and R. H. Willis (Eds.), *Social exchange: Advances in theory and research* (pp. 27–55). New York: Plenum Press.

Leventhal, H., and Scherer, K. (1987). The relationship of emotion to cognition: A functional approach to a semantic controversy. *Cognition and Emotion, 1*(1), 3–28.

Leventhal, H., and Tomarken, A. J. (1986). Emotion: Today's problems. *Annual Review of Psychology, 37,* 565–610.

Levin, I., and Stokes, J. P. (1989). Dispositional approach to job satisfaction: Role of negative affectivity. *Journal of Applied Psychology, 74,* 752–758.

Levine, F. M. (Ed.). (1975). *Theoretical readings in motivation.* Chicago: Rand McNally.

Levine, J. M., Resnick, L. B., and Higgins, E. T. (1993). Social foundations of cognition. *Annual Review of Psychology, 44,* 585–612.

Levinson, H. (1970). Management by whose objectives? *Harvard Business Review, 48*(4), 125–134.

Levy, L. H. (1970). *Conceptions of personality.* New York: Random House.

Lewin, K. (1938). The conceptual representation and the measurement of psychological forces. *Contributions to Psychological Theory, 1*(4).

Lewis, C. S. (1960). *The four loves.* New York: Harcourt Brace Jovanovich.

Lewis, H. B. (1992). *Shame: The exposed self.* New York: Free Press.

Lieberman, S. (1956). The effects of changes in roles on the attitudes of role occupants. *Human Relations, 9,* 385–402.

Likert, R. (1961). *New patterns of management.* New York: McGraw-Hill.

Likert, R. (1967). *The human organization: Its management and value.* New York: McGraw-Hill.

Lind, E. A., and Tyler, T. R. (1988). *The social psychology of procedural justice.* New York: Plenum Press.

Lindsley, D. H., Brass, D. J., and Thomas, J. B. (1995). Efficacy–performance spirals: A multi-level perspective. *Academy of Management Review, 20,* 645–678.

Locke, E. A. (1965). Interaction of ability and motivation in performance. *Perceptual and Motor Skills, 21,* 719–725.

Locke, E. A. (1968). Toward a theory of task motives and incentives. *Organizational Behavior and Human Performance, 3,* 157–189.

Locke, E. A. (1969). What is job satisfaction? *Organizational Behavior and Human Performance, 4,* 309–336.

Locke, E. A. (1975). Personnel attitudes and motivation. *Annual Review of Psychology, 26,* 457–480.

Locke, E. A. (1976). The nature and causes of job satisfaction. In M. D. Dunnette (Ed.), *Handbook of industrial and organizational psychology* (pp. 1297–1350). Chicago: Rand McNally.

Locke, E. A. (1977). The myths of behavior mod in organizations. *Academy of Management Review, 2,* 543–553.

Locke, E. A. (1978). The ubiquity of the technique of goal setting in theories of and approaches to employee motivation. *Academy of Management Review, 3,* 594–601.

Locke, E. A. (1979). Myths in the myths of the myths about behavior mod in organizations. *Academy of Management Review, 4,* 131–136.

Locke, E. A. (1980). Latham versus Komaki: A tale of two paradigms. *Journal of Applied Psychology, 65,* 16–23.

Locke, E. A. (1982). The ideas of Frederick W. Taylor: An evaluation. *Academy of Management Review, 7,* 14–24.

Locke, E. A. (1991a). Goal theory vs. control theory: Contrasting approaches to understanding work motivation. *Motivation and Emotion, 15,* 9–28.

Locke, E. A. (1991b). The motivation sequence, the motivation hub, and the motivation core. *Organizational Behavior and Human Decision Processes, 50,* 288–299.

Locke, E. A. (1995). The micro-analysis of job satisfaction: Comments on Taber and Alliger. *Journal of Organizational Behavior, 16,* 123–125.

Locke, E. A. (1996). Motivation through conscious goal setting. *Applied and Preventive Psychology, 5,* 117–124.

Locke, E. A. (in press). The motivation to work: What we know. In P. Pintrich and M. Maehr (Eds.), *Advances in motivation and achievement* (Vol. 10). Greenwich, CT: JAI Press.

Locke, E. A., Alavi, M., and Wagner, J. A. (in press). Participation in decision making: An information exchange perspective. In G. R. Ferris (Ed.), *Research in personnel and human resource management.* Greenwich, CT: JAI Press.

Locke, E. A., Cartledge, N., and Knerr, C. S. (1970). Studies of the relationship between satisfaction, goal setting, and performance. *Organizational Behavior and Human Performance, 5,* 135–158.

Locke, E. A., and Henne, D. (1986). Work motivation theories. In C. L. Cooper and I. Robertson (Eds.), *International review of industrial and organizational psychology 1986* (pp. 1–36). New York: Wiley.

Locke, E. A., and Latham, G. P. (1984). *Goal setting: A motivational technique that works.* Englewood Cliffs, NJ: Prentice Hall.

Locke, E. A., and Latham, G. P. (1990a). *A theory of goal setting and task performance.* Englewood Cliffs, NJ: Prentice Hall.

Locke, E. A., and Latham, G. P. (1990b). Work motivation and satisfaction: Light at the end of the tunnel. *Psychological Science, 1,* 240–246.

Locke, E. A., McClear, K., and Knight, D. (1996). Self esteem and work. In C. L. Cooper and I. T. Robertson (Eds.), *International review of organizational psychology* (Vol. 11, pp. 1–32). New York: Wiley.

Locke, E. A., Shaw, K. N., Saari, L. M., and Latham, G. P. (1981). Goal setting and task performance: 1969–1980. *Psychological Bulletin, 90,* 125–152.

Locke, E. A., Smith, K. G., Erez, M., Chah, D. O., and Schaffer, A. (1994). The effects of intra-individual goal conflict on performance. *Journal of Management, 20,* 67–91.

Lodahl, T., and Kejner, M. (1965). The definition and measurement of job involvement. *Journal of Applied Psychology, 49,* 24–33.

Lofquist, L. H., and Dawis, R. V. (1969). *Adjustment to work.* New York: Appleton-Century-Crofts.

Longenecker, J. G., and Pringle, C. D. (1981). *Management* (5th ed.). Columbus, OH: Charles E. Merrill.

Lord, R. G., and Hanges, P. J. (1987). A control system model of organizational motivation: Theoretical development and applied implications. *Behavioral Science, 32,* 161–178.

Lord, R. G., and Kernan, M. C. (1987). Scripts as determinants of purposeful behavior in organizations. *Academy of Management Review, 12,* 265–277.

Loscocco, K. (1990). Reactions to blue-collar work: A comparison of men and women. *Work and Occupations, 17*(2), 152–177.

Louis, M. R. (1980a). Career transitions: Varieties and commonalities. *Academy of Management Review, 5,* 329–340.

Louis, M. R. (1980b). Surprise and sense making: What newcomers experience in entering unfamiliar organizational settings. *Administrative Science Quarterly, 25,* 226–251.

Luthans, F., and Kreitner, R. (1974). The management of behavioral contingencies. *Personnel, 51,* 7–16.

Luthans, F., and Kreitner, R. (1975). *Organizational behavior modification.* Glenview, IL: Scott, Foresman.

Luthans, F., and Ottemann, R. (1977). Motivation vs. learning approaches to organizational behavior. In F. Luthans (Ed.), *Contemporary readings in organizational behavior* (2nd ed., pp. 266–274). New York: McGraw-Hill.

Luthans, F., and Reif, W. E. (1974). Job enrichment: Long on theory, short on practice. *Organizational Dynamics, 2*(3), 30–37, 43.

Lyons, T. F. (1971). Role clarity, need for clarity satisfaction, tension, and withdrawal. *Organizational Behavior and Human Performance, 6,* 99–110.

MacCorquodale, K., and Meehl, P. E. (1948). On a distinction between hypothetical constructs and intervening variables. *Psychological Review, 55,* 95–107.

Mace, C. A. (1935). *Incentives: Some experimental studies.* Report 72. Industrial Health Research Board (Great Britain).

Machlowitz, M. (1980). *Workaholics: Living with them, working with them.* Reading, MA: Addison-Wesley.

Maddi, S. R. (1976). *Personality theories: A comparative analysis* (3rd ed.). Homewood, IL: Dorsey Press.

Maddi, S. R. (1980). *Personality theories: A comparative analysis* (4th ed.). Homewood, IL: Dorsey Press.

Maehr, M. L. (1987). Managing organizational culture to enhance motivation. In M. L. Maehr and D. A. Kleiber (Eds.), *Advances in motivation and achievement: Vol. 5. Enhancing motivation* (pp. 287–320). Greenwich, CT: JAI Press.

Maehr, M. L., and Braskamp, L. (1986). *The motivation factor: A theory of personal investment.* Lexington, MA: Lexington Books.

Magnet, M. (1993). You don't have to be a workaholic. *Fortune, 128*(3), 64–69.

Magnusson, D., and Endler, N. S. (1977a). Interactional psychology: Present status and future prospects. In D. Magnusson and N. S. Endler (Eds.), *Personality at the crossroads* (pp. 3–36). Hillsdale, NJ: Lawrence Erlbaum.

Magnusson, D., and Endler, N. S. (Eds.). (1977b). *Personality at the crossroads.* Hillsdale, NJ: Lawrence Erlbaum.

Mahoney, M. J. (1974). *Cognition and behavior modification.* Cambridge, MA: Ballinger.

Mahoney, T. A. (1964). Compensation preferences of managers. *Industrial Relations, 3,* 135–144.

Mahoney, T. A. (1979). Another look at job satisfaction and performance. In T. A. Mahoney (Ed.), *Compensation and reward perspectives* (pp. 322–334). Homewood, IL: Irwin.

Mahoney, T. A. (1983). Approaches to the definition of comparable worth. *Academy of Management Review, 8,* 14–22.

Mahoney, T. A. (1987). Understanding comparable worth: A societal and political perspective. In L. L. Cummings and B. M. Staw (Eds.), *Research in organizational behavior* (Vol. 9, pp. 209–246). Greenwich, CT: JAI Press.

Mahoney, T. A. (1988). Productivity defined: The relativity of efficiency, effectiveness, and change. In J. P. Campbell, R. J. Campbell, and Associates (Eds.), *Productivity in organizations: New perspectives from industrial and organizational psychology* (pp. 13–39). San Francisco: Jossey-Bass.

Mahoney, T. A., and Blake, R. H. (1987). Judgements of appropriate pay as influenced by occupational characteristics and sex characteristics. *Applied Psychology: An International Review, 36*(1), 25–38.

Mahoney, T. A., and Weitzel, W. (1978). Secrecy and managerial compensation. *Industrial Relations, 17,* 245–251.

Maier, N. R. F. (1961). Frustration: The study of behavior without a goal. Ann Arbor, MI. The University of Michigan Press.

Main, J. (1981, August 10). Why government works dumb. *Fortune,* pp. 146–148, 152, 155, 156, 158.

Mainiero, L. A. (1986). A review and analysis of power dynamics in organizational romances. *Academy of Management Review, 11,* 750–762.

Mainiero, L. A. (1989). *Office romance: Love, power and sex in the workplace.* New York: Rawson Associates.

Malkiel, B. G. (1979). Productivity: The problem behind the headlines. *Harvard Business Review, 57*(3), 81–90.

Mann, F. C., and Williams, L. K. (1972). Organizational impact of white collar automation. In L. E. Davis and J. C. Taylor (Eds.), *Design of jobs* (pp. 83–90). Harmondsworth, Middlesex, England: Penguin Books.

Manz, C. C. (1986). Self-leadership: Toward an extended theory of self-influence processes in organizations. *Academy of Management Review, 11,* 585–600.

March, J. G., and Simon, H. A. (1958). *Organizations.* New York: Wiley.

Marini, M. M. (1989). Sex differences in earnings in the United States. *Annual Review of Sociology, 15,* 343–380.

Markus, H., and Wurf, E. (1987). The dynamic self-concept: A social psychological perspective. *Annual Review of Psychology, 38,* 299–337.

Martens, M. (1995). *Locating the measurement of emotion.* Unpublished manuscript, Faculty of Commerce and Business Administration, University of British Columbia, Vancouver, British Columbia, Canada.

Martin, J. (1993). Inequality, distributive justice, and organizational legitimacy. In J. K. Murnighan (Ed.), *Social psychology in organizations* (pp. 296–321). Englewood Cliffs, NJ: Prentice Hall.

Martin, L. L., Tesser, A., and McIntosh, J. (1993). Wanting but not having: The effects of unattained goals on thoughts and feelings. In D. M. Wegner and J. W. Pennebaker (Eds.), *Handbook of mental control* (pp. 552–572). Englewood Cliffs, NJ: Prentice Hall.

Martocchio, J. J. (1992). The financial cost of absence decisions. *Journal of Management, 18,* 133–152.

Martocchio, J. J., and Judge, T. A. (1993). A policy-capturing approach to individuals' decisions to be absent. *Organizational Behavior and Human Decision Processes, 57,* 358–386.

Maslach, C. (1982). *Burnout: The cost of caring.* Englewood Cliffs, NJ: Prentice Hall.

Maslow, A. H. (1943). A theory of human motivation. *Psychological Review, 50,* 370–396.

Maslow, A. H. (1954). *Motivation and personality.* New York: Harper and Row.

Maslow, A. H. (1955). Deficiency motivation and growth motivation. In M. R. Jones (Ed.), *Nebraska symposium on motivation.* Lincoln, NE: University of Nebraska Press.

Maslow, A. H. (1962). *Toward a psychology of being.* New York: Van Nostrand Reinhold.

Maslow, A. H. (1968). *Toward a psychology of being* (2nd ed.). New York: Van Nostrand Reinhold.

Massie, J. L. (1965). Management theory. In J. G. March (Ed.), *Handbook of organizations* (pp. 387–422). Chicago: Rand McNally.

Mater, N. R. F. (1973). *Psychology in industrial organizations* (4th ed.). Boston: Houghton Mifflin.

Mathieu, J. E., and Farr, J. L. (1991). Further evidence for the discriminant validity of measures of organizational commitment, job involvement, and job satisfaction. *Journal of Applied Psychology, 76,* 127–133.

Mathieu, J. E., Hofmann, D. A., and Farr, J. L. (1993). Job perception–job satisfaction relations: An empirical comparison of three competing theories. *Organizational Behavior and Human Decision Processes, 56,* 370–387.

Mathieu, J. E., and Zajac, D. M. (1990). A review and meta-analysis of the antecedents, correlates, and consequences of organizational commitment. *Psychological Bulletin, 108,* 171–194.

Matsui, T., Kagawa, M., Nagamatsu, J., and Ohtsuka, Y. (1977). Validity of expectancy theory as a within-person behavioral choice model for sales activities. *Journal of Applied Psychology, 62,* 764–767.

Matsui, T., and Ohtsuka, Y. (1978). Within-person expectancy theory predictions of supervisory consideration and structure behavior. *Journal of Applied Psychology, 63,* 128–131.

Mawhinney, T. C. (1975). Operant terms and concepts in the description of individual work behavior: Some problems of interpretation, application, and evaluation. *Journal of Applied Psychology, 60,* 704–712.

Mawhinney, T. C. (1979). Intrinsic and extrinsic work motivation: Perspectives from behaviorism. *Organizational Behavior and Human Performance, 24,* 411–440.

Mawhinney, T. C. (1990). Decreasing "intrinsic motivation" with extrinsic rewards: Easier said than done. *Journal of Organizational Behavior Management, 11*(1), 175–191.

Mayberry, P. (1985). *Congruencies among organizational components and their relationship to work attitudes.* Unpublished doctoral dissertation, University of Illinois, Urbana.

Mayes, B. T. (1978a). Incorporating time-lag effects into the expectancy model of motivation: A reformulation of the model. *Academy of Management Review, 3,* 374–379.

Mayes, B. T. (1978b). Some boundary conditions in the application of motivation models. *Academy of Management Review, 3,* 51–58.

Mayhew, G. L. (1979). Approaches to employee management: Policies and preferences. *Journal of Organizational Behavior Management, 2,* 103–111.

Mayhew, L. (1971). *Society: Institutions and activity.* Glenview, IL: Scott, Foresman.

Mayo, E. (1933). *The human problems of an industrialized civilization.* New York: Macmillan.

McAdams, D. P. (1988). Personal needs and personal relationships. In S. Duck (Ed.), *Handbook of personal relationships* (pp. 7–22). Chichester, West Sussex, England: Wiley.

McCall, M. W., Jr., Lombardo, M. M., and Morrison, A. M. (1988). *The lessons of experience: How successful executives develop on the job.* Lexington, MA: Lexington Books.

McCaskey, M. B. (1974). A contingency approach to planning: Planning with goals and planning without goals. *Academy of Management Journal, 17,* 281–291.

McClelland, D. C. (1961). *The achieving society.* Princeton, NJ: D. Van Nostrand.

McClelland, D. C. (1962). Business drive and national achievement. *Harvard Business Review, 40,* 99–112.

McClelland, D. C. (1965). Achievement motivation can be developed. *Harvard Business Review, 43,* 6–24, 178.

McClelland, D. C. (1970). The two faces of power. *Journal of International Affairs, 24,* 29–47.

McClelland, D. C. (1975). *Power: The inner experience.* New York: Irvington.

McClelland, D. C., and Boyatzis, R. E. (1982). Leadership motive pattern and long-term success in management. *Journal of Applied Psychology, 67,* 737–743.

McClelland, D. C., and Burnham, D. H. (1976). Power is the great motivator. *Harvard Business Review, 54,* 100–110.

McClelland, D. C., and Winter, D. G. (1969). *Motivating economic achievement.* New York: Free Press.

McConkie, M. L. (1979). A clarification of the goal setting and appraisal processes in MBO. *Academy of Management Review, 4,* 29–40.

McCune, J. T., Beatty, R. W., and Montagno, R. V. (1989). Downsizing: Practices in manufacturing firms. *Human Resource Management, 27*(2), 145–161.

McDonald, L. (1977). Wages of work. In M. Stephenson (Ed.), *Women in Canada* (Rev. ed., pp 181–191). Don Mills, Ontario, Canada: General Publishing.

McDonald, M. (1996, October 28). Cashing out. *Maclean's, 109*(44), 44–50.

McDonald, P., and Gandz, J. (1992). Getting value from shared values. *Organizational Dynamics, 20*(3), 64–77.

McDougall, W. (1923). *Outline of psychology.* New York: Scribner.

McFarlin, D. B., and Rice, R. W. (1992). The role of facet importance as a moderator in job satisfaction processes. *Journal of Organizational Behavior, 13,* 41–54.

McFetridge, D. G. (1981). Research and development expenditures. In G. B. Doern (Ed.), *How Ottawa spends your tax dollars* (pp. 255–279). Toronto, Ontario, Canada: James Lorimer.

McGregor, D. M. (1957a). The human side of enterprise. *Management Review, 46*(11), 22–28, 88–92.

McGregor, D. M. (1957b). An uneasy look at performance appraisal. *Harvard Business Review, 35*(3), 89–94.

McGregor, D. M. (1960). *The human side of enterprise.* New York: McGraw-Hill.

McKelvey, W. W. (1982), *Organizational systematics.* Berkeley, CA: University of California Press.

Mead, M. (1980). A proposal: We need taboos on sex at work. In D. A. Neugarten and J. M. Shaftitz (Eds.), *Sexuality in organizations: Romantic and coercive behaviors at work.* Oak Park, IL: Moore Publishing.

Mento, A. J., Cartledge, N. D., and Locke, E. A. (1980). Maryland vs. Michigan vs. Minnesota: Another look at the relationship of expectancy and goal difficulty to task performance. *Organizational Behavior and Human Performance, 25,* 419–440.

Merrens, M. R., and Garrett, J. B. (1975). The Protestant Ethic Scale as a predictor of repetitive work performance. *Journal of Applied Psychology, 60,* 125–127.

Merton, R. K. (1968). *Social theory and social structure.* New York: Free Press.

Merton, R. K. (1973). *The sociology of science.* Chicago: University of Chicago Press.

Meyer, J. P., and Allen, N. J. (1987). A longitudinal analysis of the early development and consequences of organizational commitment. *Canadian Journal of Behavioral Sciences, 19,* 199–215.

Meyer, J. P., and Allen, N. J. (1988). Links between work experiences and commitment during the first year of employment: A longitudinal analysis. *Journal of Occupational Psychology, 61,* 195–209.

Meyer, J. P., and Allen, N. J. (1991). A three-component conceptualization of organizational commitment. *Human Resource Management Review, 1,* 61–89.

Meyer, J. P., and Allen, N. J. (1997). *Commitment in the workplace.* Thousand Oaks, CA: Sage.

Meyer, J. P., Paunonen, S. V., Gellatly, I. R., Goffin, R. D., and Jackson, D. N. (1989). Organizational commitment and job performance: It's the nature of the commitment that counts. *Journal of Applied Psychology, 74,* 152–156.

Michaels, C. E., and Spector, P. E. (1982). Causes of employee turnover: A test of the Mobley, Griffeth, Hand and Meglino model. *Journal of Applied Psychology, 67,* 53–59.

Middlemist, R. D., and Peterson, R. B. (1976). Test of equity theory by controlling for comparison co-workers' efforts. *Organizational Behavior and Human Performance, 15,* 335–354.

Migliore, R. H. (1977). *MBO: Blue collar to top executive.* Washington, DC: Bureau of National Affairs.

Miles, E. W., Hatfield, J. D., and Huseman, R. C. (1994). Equity sensitivity and outcome importance. *Journal of Organizational Behavior, 15,* 585–596.

Miles, J. A., and Greenberg, J. (1993). Using punishment threats to attenuate social loafing effects among swimmers. *Organizational Behavior and Human Decision Processes, 56,* 246–265.

Miles, R. H. (1976). A comparison of the relative impacts of role perceptions of ambiguity and conflict by role. *Academy of Management Journal, 19,* 25–35.

Miles, R. H., and Perreault, W. D., Jr. (1976). Organizational role conflict: Its antecedents and consequences. *Organizational Behavior and Human Performance, 17,* 19–44.

Miles, R. H., and Petty, M. M. (1975). Relationships between role clarity, need for clarity, and job tension and satisfaction for supervisory and non-supervisory roles. *Academy of Management Journal, 18,* 877–883.

Milkovich, G. T. (1980). Pay inequalities and comparable worth. In B. D. Dennis (Ed.), *Proceedings of the 33rd annual meeting.* Madison, WI: Industrial Relations Research Association.

Milkovich, G. T., and Anderson, P. H. (1972). Management compensation and secrecy policies. *Personnel Psychology, 25,* 293–302.

Miller, G. A., Galanter, E., and Pribram, K. H. (1960). *Plans and the structure of behavior.* New York: Henry Holt.

Miller, J. G. (1978). *Living systems.* New York: McGraw-Hill.

Miller, L. E., and Grush, J. E. (1988). Improving predictions in expectancy theory research: Effects of personality, expectancies, and norms. *Academy of Management Journal, 31,* 107–122.

Miller, L. M. (1977). Improving roles and forecast accuracy in a nationwide sales organization. *Journal of Organizational Behavior Management, 1,* 39–51.

Miller, L. M. (1978). *Behavior management: The new science of managing people at work.* New York: Wiley.

Miller, N. (1993, April). The scales of injustice. *CA Magazine, 126*(4), 28–32.

Miller, V. D., and Jablin, F. M. (1991). Information seeking during organizational entry: Influences, tactics, and a model of the process. *Academy of Management Review, 16,* 92–120.

Mills, P. K. (1983). Self-management: Its control and relationship to other organizational properties. *Academy of Management Review, 3,* 445–453.

Miner, J. B. (1984). The validity and usefulness of theories in an emerging organizational science. *Academy of Management Review, 9,* 296–306.

Miner, M. G. (1974). Pay policies: Secret or open? And why? *Personnel Journal, 53*(2), 110–115.

Miniard, P. W., and Cohen, J. B. (1983). Modeling personal and normative influences on behavior. *Journal of Consumer Research, 10,* 169–180.

Minton, J. W., Lewicki, R. J., and Sheppard, B. H. (1994, November). Unjust dismissal in the context of organizational justice. In S. Henry (Ed.), *The Annals of the American Academy of Political and Social Science: Vol. 536. Employee dismissal: Justice at work* (pp. 135–148). Thousand Oaks, CA: Sage.

Mintzberg, H. (1973). *The nature of managerial work.* New York: Harper and Row.

Mirvis, P., and Lawler, E. E. (1977). Measuring the financial impact of employee attitudes. *Journal of Applied Psychology, 62,* 1–8.

Mischel, W. (1968). *Personality and assessment.* New York: Wiley.

Mitchel, J. O. (1981). The effect of intentions, tenure, personal, and organizational variables on managerial turnover. *Academy of Management Journal, 24,* 742–751.

Mitchell, J. J. (Ed.). (1972). *Human nature: Theories, conjectures, and descriptions.* Metuchen, NJ: Scarecrow Press.

Mitchell, R. (1981, October 5). Boosting productivity of American Express. *Business Week,* No. 2708, pp. 62–64.

Mitchell, T. R. (1973). Motivation and participation: An integration. *Academy of Management Journal, 16,* 670–679.

Mitchell, T. R. (1974). Expectancy models of satisfaction, occupational preference and effort: A theoretical, methodological and empirical appraisal. *Psychological Bulletin, 81,* 1053–1077.

Mitchell, T. R. (1982). Motivation: New directions for theory, research and practice. *Academy of Management Review, 7,* 80–88.

Mitchell, T. R., and Biglan, A. (1971). Instrumentality theories: Current uses in psychology. *Psychological Bulletin, 76,* 432–454.

Mitchell, T. R., Green, S. G., and Wood, R. E. (1981). An attributional model of leadership and the poor performing subordinate: Development and validation. In L. L. Cummings and B. M. Staw (Eds.), *Research in organizational behavior* (Vol. 3, pp. 197–234). Greenwich, CT: JAI Press.

Mitchell, T. R., and James, L. R. (1989). Introduction and background. *Academy of Management Review, 14,* 331–332.

Mitchell, T. R., and Kalb, L. S. (1981). Effects of outcome knowledge and outcome valence on supervisors' evaluations. *Journal of Applied Psychology, 66,* 604–612.

Mitchell, T. R., and Nebeker, D. M. (1973). Expectancy theory, predictions of academic effort and performance. *Journal of Applied Psychology, 37,* 61–67.

Mitchell, T. R., and O'Reilly, C. A. (1983). Managing poor performance and productivity. In K. Rowland and G. R. Ferris (Eds.), *Research in personnel and human resource management* (Vol. 1, pp. 201–223). Greenwich, CT: JAI Press.

Mitchell, V. F., and Moudgill, P. (1976). Measurement of Maslow's need hierarchy. *Organizational Behavior and Human Performance, 16,* 334–349.

Mitroff, I. I. (1983). *Stakeholders of the organizational mind.* San Francisco: Jossey-Bass.

Mobley, W. H. (1982). *Employee turnover: Causes, consequences and control.* Reading, MA: Addison-Wesley.

Mobley, W. H., Griffith, R. W., Hand, H. H., and Meglino, B. M. (1979). Review and conceptual analysis of the employee turnover process. *Psychological Bulletin, 86,* 493–522.

Mobley, W. H., and Meglino, B. M. (1977). A behavioral choice model analysis of the budget allocation behavior of academic deans. *Academy of Management Journal, 20,* 564–572.

Moch, M., and Seashore, S. E. (1981). How norms affect behaviors in and of corporations. In P. C. Nystrom and W. H. Starbuck (Eds.), *Handbook of organizational design* (Vol. 1, pp. 210–237). New York: Oxford University Press.

Mohr, L. (1982). *Understanding organizational behavior.* San Francisco: Jossey-Bass.

Montreal Gazette. (1993, December 24). Woman who quit good job for welfare has no regrets, p. A12.

Moore, L. F., Johns, G., and Pinder, C. C. (1980). Toward middle range theory: An overview and perspective. In C. C. Pinder and L. F. Moore (Eds.), *Middle range theory and the study of organizations* (pp. 1–16). Boston: Martinus Nijhoff.

Moore, M. J., and Abraham, Y. T. (1992). Comparable worth: Is it a moot issue? *Public Personnel Management, 21,* 455–472.

Moore, M. J., and Abraham, Y. T. (1994). Comparable worth: Is it a moot issue? Part II: The legal and judicial posture. *Public Personnel Management, 23,* 263–286.

Morin, W. J., and Yorks, L. (1990). *Dismissal.* New York: Drake Beam Morin.

Morris, J. H., and Sherman, J. D. (1981). Generalizability of an organizational commitment model. *Academy of Management Journal, 24,* 512–526.

Morrison, A. M., White, R. P., Van Velsor, E., and The Center for Creative Leadership. (1987). *Breaking the glass ceiling: Can women reach the top of America's largest corporations?* Reading, MA: Addison-Wesley.

Morrison, E. W. (1993). Newcomer information seeking: Exploring types, modes, sources, and outcomes. *Academy of Management Journal, 36,* 557–589.

Morrow, P. C. (1983). Concept redundancy in organizational research: The case of work commitment. *Academy of Management Review, 8,* 486–500.

Morrow, P. C. (1993). *The theory and measurement of work commitment.* Greenwich, CT: JAI Press.

Mortimer, T. J., and Lorence, J. (1989). Satisfaction and involvement: Disentangling a deceptively simple relationship. *Social Psychology Quarterly, 52,* 249–266.

Mossholder, K. W., Niebuhr, R. E., and Morris, D. R. (1990). Effects of dyadic duration on the relationship between leader behavior perceptions and follower outcomes. *Journal of Organizational Behavior, 11,* 379–388.

Mount, M. K., and Barrick, M. R. (1995). The big five personality dimensions: Implications for research and practice in human resources management. In G. R. Ferris (Ed.), *Research in personnel and human resources management* (Vol. 13, pp. 153–200). Greenwich, CT: JAI Press.

Mowday, R. T. (1991). Equity theory predictions of behavior in organizations. In R. M. Steers and L. W. Porter, (Eds.), *Motivation and work behavior* (5th ed., pp. 111–130). New York: McGraw-Hill.

Mowday, R. T., Porter, L. W., and Steers, R. M. (1982). *Employee–organization linkages.* New York: Academic Press.

Mowday, R. T., Steers, R. M., and Porter, L. W. (1979). The measurement of organizational commitment. *Journal of Vocational Behavior, 14,* 224–227.

Mowday, R. T., and Sutton, R. I. (1993). Organizational behavior: Linking individuals and groups to organizational contexts. *Annual Review of Psychology, 44,* 195–229.

Muchinsky, P. M. (1977). A comparison of within- and across-subjects analyses of the expectancy-valence model for predicting effort. *Academy of Management Journal, 20,* 154–158.

Muczyk, J. P. (1978). A controlled field experiment measuring the impact of MBO on performance data. *Journal of Management Studies, 15*(3), 318–329.

Murphy, G. C., and Remnyi, A. G. (1979). Behavioral analysis and organizational reality: The need for a technology of program implementation. *Journal of Organizational Behavior Management, 2,* 121–131.

Murray, H. (1938). *Explorations in personality.* New York: Oxford University Press.

Murray, H. A., and Kluckhohn, C. (1953). Outline of a conception of personality. In C. Kluckhohn, H. A. Murray, and D. Schneider (Eds.), *Personality and nature, society and culture* (2nd ed.). New York: Knopf.

Murstein, B. (1988). A taxonomy of love. In R. Sternberg and M. Barnes (Eds.), *The psychology of love* (pp. 13–37). New Haven, CT: Yale University Press.

Nadler, D. A. (1977). *Feedback and organization development: Using data-based methods,* Reading, MA: Addison-Wesley.

Naylor, J. D., Pritchard, R. D., and Ilgen, D. R. (1980). *A theory of behavior in organizations.* New York: Academic Press.

Nealey, S. M. (1963). Pay and benefit preference. *Industrial Relations, 3,* 17–28.

Near, J. P., Dworkin, T. M., and Miceli, M. P. (1993). Explaining the whistle-blowing process: Suggestions from power theory and justice theory. *Organization Science, 4,* 393–411.

Nebeker, D. M., and Mitchell, T. R. (1974). Leader behavior: An expectancy theory approach. *Organizational Behavior and Human Performance, 11,* 355–367.

Nehbrass, R. G. (1979). Ideology and the decline of management theory. *Academy of Management Review, 4,* 427–431.

Nelson, B. (1994). *1001 ways to reward employees.* New York: Workman.

Newman, L. (1988, February). Good-bye is not enough. *Personnel Administrator, 33*(2), 84–86.

Newman, W. H., and Wallender, H. W. (1978). Managing not-for-profit enterprises. *Academy of Management Review, 3,* 24–31.

Newton, T., and Keenan, T. (1991). Further analyses of the dispositional argument in organizational behavior. *Journal of Applied Psychology, 76,* 781–787.

Nicholson, N., Wall, T., and Lischeron, J. (1977). The predictability of absence and propensity to leave from employees' job satisfaction and attitudes toward influence in decision making. *Human Relations, 30,* 499–514.

Nickerson, C. A., and McLelland, G. H. (1989). Across-persons versus within-persons tests of expectancy value models: A methodological note. *Journal of Behavioral Decision Making, 2,* 261–270.

Niedenthal, P. M., Setterlund, M. B., and Jones, D. E. (1994). Emotional organization of perceptual memory. In P. M. Niedenthal and S. Kitayama, (Eds.), *The heart's eye* (pp. 87–143). San Diego, CA: Academic Press.

Nisbett, R. E., and Wilson, T. De (1977). Telling more than we can know: Verbal reports on mental processes. *Psychological Review, 84,* 231–259.

Nord, W. R. (1969). Beyond the teaching machine: The neglected area of operant conditioning in the theory and practice of management. *Organizational Behavior and Human Performance, 4,* 375–401.

Nord, W. R. (1970). Improving attendance through rewards. *Personnel Administration, 33*(6), 37–41.

Nord, W. R. (1977). Job satisfaction reconsidered. *American Psychologist, 32,* 1026–1035.

Nord, W. R., Brief, A. P., Atieh, J. M., and Doherty, E. M. (1988). Work values and the conduct of organizational behavior. In B. M. Staw and L. L. Cummings (Eds.), *Research in organizational behavior* (Vol. 10, pp. 1–42). Greenwich, CT: JAI Press.

Nord, W. R., and Durand, D. E. (1975). Beyond resistance to change: Behavioral science on the firing line. *Organizational Dynamics, 4*(2), 2–19.

Nord, W. R., and Durand, D. E. (1978). What's wrong with the human resources approach to management? *Organizational Dynamics, 6*(3), 13–25.

Norman, R. G., and Bahari, S. (1972). *Productivity measurement and incentives.* London: Butterworth.

Northcraft, G. B., and Ashford, S. J. (1990). The preservation of self in everyday life: The effects of performance expectations and feedback inquiry. *Journal of Management, 47,* 42–64.

Notz, W. W. (1975). Work motivation and the negative effects of extrinsic rewards. *American Psychologist, 30,* 884–891.

Nunnally, J. C. W. (1967). *Psychometric theory.* New York: McGraw-Hill.

Oates, W. (1971). *Confessions of a workaholic.* New York: World.

Oatley, K. (1992). *Best laid schemes: The psychology of emotions.* Cambridge: Cambridge University Press.

Oatley, K., and Duncan, E. (1992). Structured diaries for emotions in daily life. In K. T. Strongman (Ed.), *International review of studies on emotion* (Vol. 2). Chichester, West Sussex, England: Wiley.

Oatley, K., and Jenkins, J. M. (1992). Human emotions: Function and dysfunction. *Annual Review of Psychology, 43,* 55–85.

Oatley, K., and Johnson-Laird, P. N. (1987). Towards a cognitive theory of emotions. *Cognition and Emotion, 1*(1), 29–50.

Odiorne, G. S. (1979). *MBO II.* Belmont, CA: Fearon-Pitman.

Offerman, L. R., and Gowing, M. K. (1990). Organizations of the future: Changes and challenges. *American Psychologist, 45,* 95–108.

O'Hara, K., Johnson, C. M., and Beehr, T. A. (1985). Organizational behavior management in the private sector: A review of empirical research and recommendations for further investigation. *Academy of Management Review, 10,* 848–864.

O'Kelly, C. O. (1979). The "impact" of equal employment legislation on women's earnings. *American Journal of Economics and Sociology, 38,* 419–429.

Oldham, G. R., and Cummings, A. (1996). Employee creativity: Personal and contextual factors at work. *Academy of Management Journal, 39,* 604–634.

Oldham, G. R., and Hackman, J. R. (1980). Work design in the organizational context. In. B. M. Staw and L. L. Cummings (Eds.), *Research in organizational behavior* (Vol. 2, 247–278). Greenwich, CT: JAI Press.

Oliver, R. L., and Bearden, W. O. (1985). Crossover effects in the theory of reasoned action: A moderating influence attempt. *Journal of Consumer Research, 12,* 324–340.

Olson, J. M., and Zanna, M. P. (1993). Attitudes and attitude change. *Annual Review of Psychology, 44,* 117–154.

Olson, M. (1965). *The logic of collective action: Public goods and the theory of groups.* Cambridge, MA: Harvard University Press.

Ondrack, D. A. (1974). Defense mechanisms and the Herzberg theory: An alternate test. *Academy of Management Journal, 17,* 79–89.

Oneal, M. (1994, August 1). Managing by values: Is Levi-Strauss's approach visionary—or flaky? *Business Week,* pp. 46–52.

O'Neill, J., and Polachek, S. (1993). Why the gender gap in wages narrowed in the 1980's. *Journal of Labor Economics, 11*(1, Pt. 1), 205–225.

O'Neill, L. (1985). The trend in the male–female wage gap in the United States. *Journal of Labor Economics, 3,* 91–116.

Oppenheimer, V. K. (1968). The sex-labeling of jobs. *Industrial Relations, 7,* 219–234.

Opsahl, R. L., and Dunnette, M. D. (1966). The role of financial compensation in industrial motivation. *Psychological Bulletin, 22,* 94–118.

O'Reilly, C. A. (1990). Organizational behavior: Where we've been, where we're going. *Annual Review of Psychology, 42,* 427–458.

O'Reilly, C. A., and Caldwell, D. F. (1981). The commitment and job tenure of new employees: Some evidence of postdecisional justification. *Administrative Science Quarterly, 26,* 597–616.

O'Reilly, C. A., and Chatman, J. (1986). Organizational commitment and psychological attachment: The effects of compliance, identification, and internalization on prosocial behavior. *Journal of Applied Psychology, 71,* 492–499.

O'Reilly, C. A., and Chatman, J. A. (1994). Working smarter and harder: A longitudinal study of managerial success. *Administrative Science Quarterly, 39,* 603–627.

Organ, D. W. (1977). Inferences about trends in labor force satisfaction: A causal-correlation analysis. *Academy of Management Journal, 20,* 510–519.

Organ, D. W. (1990). The motivational basis of organizational citizenship behavior. In B. M. Staw and L. L. Cummings (Eds.), *Research in organizational behavior* (Vol. 12, 43–72). Greenwich, CT: JAI Press.

Organ, D. W., and Konovsky, M. (1989). Cognitive versus affective determinants of citizenship behavior. *Journal of Applied Psychology, 74,* 157–164.

Organization for Economic Cooperation and Development. (1994). *The OECD economic outlook.* No. 54. Paris: OECD.

Orpen, C. (1978). Effects of bonuses for attendance on the absenteeism of industrial workers. *Journal of Organizational Behavior Management, 1,* 118–124.

Orpen, C. (1979). The effects of job enrichment on employee satisfaction, motivation, involvement, and performance: A field experiment. *Human Relations, 32,* 189–217.

Ostroff, C. (1993). The effects of climate and personal influences on individual behavior and attitudes in organizations. *Organizational Behavior and Human Decision Processes, 56,* 56–90.

O'Toole, J. (1981). *Making America work.* New York: Continuum.

Ouchi, W. G. (1981). *Theory Z.* New York: Avon Books.

Owens, W. A. (1968). Toward one discipline of scientific psychology. *American Psychologist, 23,* 782–785.

Owens, W. A. (1976). Background data. In M. D. Dunnette (Ed.), *Handbook of industrial and organizational psychology* (pp. 609–644). Chicago: Rand McNally.

Oxford English Dictionary. (1961). Oxford: Clarendon Press.

Painter, B., Sutton, A., and Burton, S. (1982). *Provincial worklife survey: A pilot project.* Vancouver, British Columbia, Canada: Socio-technical Systems Group Research.

Parker, D. F., and Dyer, L. (1976). Expectancy theory as a within person behavioral choice model: An empirical test of some conceptual and methodological refinements. *Organizational Behavior and Human Performance, 17,* 97–117.

Parker, S. R. (1981). Industry and social stratification. In S. R. Parker, R. K. Brown, J. Child, and M. A. Smith (Eds.), *The sociology of industry* (pp. 56–64). London: George Allen and Unwin.

Parkinson, C. N. (1957). *Parkinson's law and other studies in administration.* Boston: Houghton Mifflin.

Parks, J. Mc., and Kidder, D. L. (1995). "Till death do us part . . .": Changing work relationships in the 1990's. In C. L. Cooper and D. M. Rousseau (Eds.), *Trends in organizational behavior, 1,* 111–136.

Parmerlee, M., and Schwenk, C. (1979). Radical behaviorism in organizations: Misconceptions in the Locke–Gray debate. *Academy of Management Review, 4,* 601–607.

Parrott, W. G. (1994). The head and the heart. In J. A. Russell, J. M. Fernandez-Doles, A. S. R. Manstead, and J. C. Wellenkamp (Eds.), *Everyday conceptions of emotions* (pp. 73–84). Dordrecht, The Netherlands: Kluwer.

Parsons, T., and Shils, E. A. (Eds.). (1951). *Toward a general theory of action.* Cambridge, MA: Harvard University Press.

Patchen, M. (1961). *The choice of wage comparisons.* Englewood Cliffs, NJ: Prentice Hall.

Patrick, B. C., Skinner, E. A., and Connell, J. P. (1993). What motivates children's behavior and emotion? The joint effects of perceived control and autonomy in the academic domain. *Journal of Personality and Social Psychology, 65,* 781–791.

Paul, W. J., Robertson, K. B., and Herzberg, F. (1969). Job enrichment pays off. *Harvard Business Review, 47*(2), 61–78.

Peak, H. (1955). Attitude and motivation. In M. R. Jones (Ed.) *Nebraska symposium on motivation.* Lincoln, NE: University of Nebraska Press.

Pedalino, E., and Gamboa, V. U. (1974). Behavior modification and absenteeism: Intervention in one industrial setting. *Journal of Applied Psychology, 54,* 694–698.

Pennings, J. H., Barkema, H., and Douma, S. (1994). Organizational learning and diversification. *Academy of Management Journal, 37,* 608–640.

Perrow, C. (1967). A framework for the comparative analysis of organizations. *American Sociological Review, 32*(3), 194–208.

Perry, J. L., and Porter, L. W. (1982). Factors affecting the context for motivation in public organizations. *Academy of Management Review, 7,* 89–98.

Perry, L. S. (1993). Effects of inequity on job satisfaction and self-evaluation in a national sample of African-American workers. *Journal of Social Psychology, 133,* 565–573.

Pervin, L. A. (1968). Performance and satisfaction as a function of individual–environment fit. *Psychological Bulletin, 69,* 56–68.

Pervin, L. A. (1991). Self-regulation and the problem of volition. In M. L. Maehr and P. R. Pintrich (Eds.), *Advances in Motivation and Achievement* (Vol. 7, pp. 1–20). Greenwich, CT: JAI Press.

Peter, L. J., and Hull, R. (1969). *The Peter principle.* New York: Bantam.

Peter, T. J., and Waterman, R. (1982). *In search of excellence.* New York: Harper and Row.

Peters, L. H., and O'Connor, E. J. (1980). Situational constraints and work outcomes: The influences of a frequently overlooked construct. *Academy of Management Review, 3,* 391–397.

Peters, L. H., O'Connor, E. J., and Eulberg, J. R. (1985). Situational constraints: Sources, consequences, and future considerations. In K. R. Rowland and G. R. Ferris (Eds.), *Research in personnel and human resources management* (Vol. 3, pp. 79–114). Greenwich, CT: JAI Press.

Petrie, H. L. (1991). *Motivation: Theory, research, and applications.* Belmont, CA: Wadsworth.

Petrock, F. (1978). Analyzing the balance of consequences for performance improvement. *Journal of Organizational Behavior Management, 1,* 196–205.

Petrock, F., and Gamboa, V. (1976). Expectancy theory and operant conditioning: A conceptual comparison. In W. Nord (Ed.), *Concepts and controversies in organizational behavior* (2nd ed., 175–187). Pacific Palisades, CA: Goodyear.

Pfautz, H. W. (1953). The current literature on social stratification: Critique and bibliography. *American Journal of Sociology, 58,* 391–418.

Pfeffer, J. (1981a). Management as symbolic action: The creation and maintenance of organizational paradigms. In L. L. Cummings and B. M. Staw (Eds.), *Research in organizational behavior* (Vol. 3, pp. 1–52). Greenwich, CT: JAI Press.

Pfeffer, J. (1981b). *Power in organizations.* Marshfield, MA: Pitman.

Pfeffer, J. (1993). Barriers to the advance of organizational science: Paradigm development as a dependent variable. *Academy of Management Review, 18,* 599–620.

Pfeffer, J. (1994). *Competitive advantage through people.* Boston: Harvard University Press.

Pfeffer, J., and Salancik, G. R. (1974). Organizational decision making as a political process: The case of the university budget. *Administrative Science Quarterly, 19,* 135–151.

Phillips, P. L. (1991). Cecil Alec Mace: The life and times of the original goal-setting experimenter. In J. L. Wall and L. R. Jauch (Eds.), *Academy of management proceedings, 51st annual meeting,* Miami Beach, FL, pp. 142–146.

Pierce, J. L., and Dunham, R. B. (1976). Task design: A literature review. *Academy of Management Review, 1*(4), 83–97.

Pierce, J. L., Gardner, D. G., Cummings, L. L., and Dunham, R. B. (1989). Organization-based self-esteem: Construct definition, measurement, and validation. *Academy of Management Journal, 32,* 622–648.

Pieters, R. G. M., and Van Raaij, W. F. (1988). Functions and management of affect: Applications to economic behavior. *Journal of Economic Psychology, 9,* 251–282.

Pinder, C. C. (1976). Additivity versus nonadditivity of intrinsic and extrinsic incentives: Implications for work motivation, performance, and attitudes. *Journal of Applied Psychology, 61,* 693–700.

Pinder, C. C. (1977). Concerning the application of human motivation theories in organizational settings. *Academy of Management Review, 2,* 384–397.

Pinder, C. C. (1978). The marginal utility of the marginal utility criterion: A reply to Bobko. *Academy of Management Review, 3,* 910–913.

Pinder, C. C. (1982). Mutualism between management and behavioral science: The case of motivation theory. In J. Kelly and V. V. Baba (Eds.), *The new management scene: Readings on how managers manage* (133–160). Englewood Cliffs, NJ: Prentice Hall.

Pinder, C. C. (1983). The role of transfers and mobility experiences in employee motivation and control. In H. Meltzer and W. R. Nord (Eds.), *Making organizations humane and productive: A handbook for practitioners* (pp. 281–294). New York: Wiley Interscience.

Pinder, C. C. (1984). *Work motivation: Theory, issues, and applications.* Glenview, IL: Scott, Foresman.

Pinder, C. C. (1989, Spring). The dark side of executive relocation. *Organizational Dynamics, 17* (14), 48–59.

Pinder, C. C., and Das, H. (1979). Hidden costs and benefits of employee transfers. *Human Resource Planning, 2,* 35–145.

Pinder, C. C., and Moore, L. F. (1979). The resurrection of taxonomy to aid the development of middle range theories of organizational behavior. *Administrative Science Quarterly, 24,* 99–118.

Pinder, C. C., and Moore, L. F. (Eds.). (1980). *Middle range theory and the study of organizations.* Boston: Martinus Nijhoff.

Pinder, C. C., Nord, W. R., and Ramirez, C. (1984). *An experimental test of Deci's cognitive evaluation theory.* Unpublished manuscript, Faculty of Commerce and Business Administration, University of British Columbia, Vancouver, British Columbia, Canada.

Pinder, C. C., and Schroeder, K. G. (1987). Time to proficiency following job transfers. *Academy of Management Journal, 30,* 336–353.

Pinder, C. C., Stackman, R. W., and Connor, P. E. (1997). *Values lost: Redirecting research on values in the workplace.* Unpublished manuscript, Faculty of Commerce and Business Administration, University of British Columbia, Vancouver, British Columbia, Canada.

Pinder, C. C., and Walter, G. A. (1984). Personnel transfer and employee development. In K. M. Rowland and G. R. Ferris (Eds.), *Research in personnel and human resource management* (Vol. 2, pp. 187–218). Greenwich, CT: JAI Press.

Pinto, P. R. (1978, October). Your trainers and the law: Are they breaking it in and out of the classroom? *Training: The Magazine of Human Resources Development, 15*(10), 71–76.

Pittman, T. S., and Heller, J. F. (1987). Social motivation. *Annual Review of Psychology, 38,* 461–489.

Podsakoff, P. M., and Williams, L. J. (1986). The relationship between job performance and job satisfaction. In E. A. Locke (Ed.), *Generalizing from laboratory to field settings* (pp. 207–254). Lexington, MA: Lexington Books.

Pondy, L. R., Frost, P. J., Morgan, G., and Dandridge, T. C. (Eds.). (1983). *Organizational symbolism.* Greenwich, CT: JAI Press.

Popper, K. R. (1968). *The logic of scientific discovery* (2nd ed.). New York: Harper Torchbooks.

Popper, K. R. (1976). *Unended quest.* London: Fontana.

Porac, J. F., and Salancik, G. R. (1981). Generic overjustification: The interaction of extrinsic rewards. *Organizational Behavior and Human Performance, 27,* 197–212.

Porter, E. H. (1962). The parable of the spindle. *Harvard Business Review, 40*(3), 58–66.

Porter, L. W. (1962). Job attitudes in management: I. Perceived deficiencies in need fulfillment as a function of job level. *Journal of Applied Psychology, 46,* 375–384.

Porter, L. W. (1963). Job attitudes in management: II. Perceived importance of needs as a function of job level. *Journal of Applied Psychology, 47,* 144–148.

Porter, L. W. (1973). Turning work into nonwork: The rewarding environment. In M. D. Dunnette (Ed.), *Work and nonwork in the year 2001.* Monterey, CA: Brooks/Cole.

Porter, L. W., Crampon, W. J., and Smith, F. J. (1972). *Organizational commitment and managerial turnover: A longitudinal study* (Tech. Rep. 13, Individual–Organization Linkages Research Project). Irvine, CA: University of California.

Porter, L. W., Crampon, W. J., and Smith, F. J. (1976). Organizational commitment and managerial turnover: A longitudinal study. *Organizational Behavior and Human Performance, 15,* 87–98.

Porter, L. W., and Lawler, E. E. (1965). Properties of organizational structure in relation to job attitudes and job behavior. *Psychological Bulletin, 64,* 23–51.

Porter, L. W., and Lawler, E. E. (1968). *Managerial attitudes and performance.* Homewood, IL: Dorsey Press, a division of Richard D. Irwin.

Porter, L. W., Lawler, E. E., and Hackman, J. R. (1975). *Behavior in organizations.* New York: McGraw-Hill.

Porter, L. W., and Steers, R. M. (1973). Organizational, work, and personal factors in employee turnover and absenteeism. *Psychological Bulletin, 80,* 151–176.

Porter, L. W., Steers, R. M., Mowday, R. T., and Boulian, P. V. (1974). Organizational commitment, job satisfaction, and turnover among psychiatric technicians. *Journal of Applied Psychology, 59,* 603–605.

Posner, B. Z., and Munson, J. M. (1979). The importance of values in understanding organizational behaviour. *Human Resource Management, 18*(3), 9–14.

Powell, B., and Jacobs, J. A. (1983). Sex and consensus in occupational prestige ratings. *Sociology and Social Research, 67,* 392–404.

Powell, B., and Jacobs, J. A. (1984). Gender differences in the evaluation of prestige. *The Sociological Quarterly, 25,* 173–190.

Pratkanis, A. R., and Greenwald, A. G. (1989). A sociocognitive model of attitude structure and function. *Advances in Experimental Social Psychology, 22,* 245–285.

Premack, D. (1971). Catching up with common sense or two sides of a generalization: Reinforcement and punishment. In R. Glaser (Ed.), *The nature of reinforcement* (pp. 121–150). New York: Academic Press.

Price, J. L. (1977). *The study of turnover.* Ames, IA: Iowa State University Press.

Pringle, C. D., and Longenecker, J. G. (1982). The ethics of MBO. *Academy of Management Review, 7,* 305–312.

Pritchard, M. (1976). On taking emotions seriously. *Journal for the Theory of Social Behavior, 6*(2), 211–232.

Pritchard, R. D. (1969). Equity theory: A review and critique. *Organizational Behavior and Human Performance, 4,* 176–211.

Pritchard, R. D., Campbell, K. M., and Campbell, D. J. (1977). Effects of extrinsic financial rewards on intrinsic motivation. *Journal of Applied Psychology, 62,* 9–15.

Pritchard, R. D., Dunnette, M. D., and Jorgenson, D. O. (1972). Effects of perceptions of equity and inequity on worker performance and satisfaction. *Journal of Applied Psychology, 56,* 75–94.

Prue, D. M., and Fairbank, J. A. (1980). Performance feedback in organizational behavior management: A review. *Journal of Organizational Behavior Management, 3,* 1–16.

Prussia, G. E., and Kiniki, A. J. (1996). A motivational investigation of group effectiveness using social-cognitive theory. *Journal of Applied Psychology, 81,* 187–198.

Quinn, J. B., and Baily, M. N. (1994). Information technology: Increasing productivity in services. *Academy of Management Executive, 8*(3), 28–48.

Quinn, R. E. (1977). Coping with Cupid: The formation, impact and management of romantic relationships in organizations. *Administrative Science Quarterly, 22,* 30–45.

Rabinowitz, S., and Hall, D. T. (1977). Organizational research on job involvement. *Psychological Bulletin, 84,* 265–288.

Rafaeli, A., and Sutton, R. I. (1987). Expression of emotion as part of the work role. *Academy of Management Review, 12,* 23–37.

Rafaeli, A., and Sutton, R. I. (1989). The expression of emotion in organizational life. In L. L. Cummings and B. M. Staw (Eds.), *Research in organizational behavior* (Vol. 11, pp. 1–42). Greenwich, CT: JAI Press.

Raia, A. (1974). *Managing by objectives.* Glenview, IL: Scott, Foresman.

Ralston, D. A. (1985). Employee ingratiation: The role of management. *Academy of Management Review, 10,* 477–487.

Rand, A. (1943). *The fountainhead.* New York: Bobbs-Merrill.

Rand, A. (1957). *Atlas shrugged.* New York: Signet.

Randall, D. M. (1987). Commitment and the organization: The organization man revisited. *Academy of Management Review, 12,* 460–471.

Rauschenberger, J., Schmitt, N., and Hunter, J. E. (1980). A test of the need hierarchy concept by a Markov model of change in need strength. *Administrative Science Quarterly, 25,* 654–670.

Ravlin, E. C., and Meglino, B. M. (1987a). Effect of values on perception and decision making: A study of alternative work values measures. *Journal of Applied Psychology, 72,* 666–673.

Ravlin, E. C., and Meglino, B. M. (1987b). Issues in work values measurement. In J. E. Post (Ed.), *Research in corporate social performance and policy* (Vol. 9, pp. 153–183). Greenwich, CT: JAI Press.

Ravlin, E. C., and Meglino, B. M. (1989). The transitivity of work values: Hierarchical preference ordering of socially desirable stimuli. *Organizational Behavior and Human Decision Processes, 44,* 494–508.

Reddin, W. J. (1971). *Effective management by objectives.* New York: McGraw-Hill.

Ree, M. J., Earles, J. A., and Teachout, M. S. (1994). Predicting job performance: Not much more than g. *Journal of Applied Psychology, 79*(4), 518–524.

Rees, A. (1980). On interpreting productivity change. In S. Maital and N. M. Meltz (Eds.), *Lagging productivity growth* (pp. 1–6). Cambridge, MA: Ballinger.

Rees, A. (1993). The role of fairness in wage determination. *Journal of Labor Economics, 11*(1 Pt. 1), 243–252.

Reichers, A. E. (1985). A review and reconceptualization of organizational commitment. *Academy of Management Review, 10,* 465–476.

Reif, W. E., and Luthans, F. (1972). Does job enrichment really pay off? *California Management Review, 15*(1), 30–37.

Reilly, B. J., and Fuhr, J. P. (1983). Productivity: An economic and management analysis with a direction towards a new synthesis. *Academy of Management Review, 8,* 108–117.

Reinharth, L., and Wahba, M. A. (1976). A test of alternative models of expectancy theory. *Human Relations, 29,* 257–272.

Repucci, N. D., and Saunders, J. T. (1974). Social psychology of behavior modification: Problems of implementation in natural settings. *American Psychologist, 29,* 649–660.

Reykowski, J. (1982). Social motivation. *Annual Review of Psychology, 33,* 123–154.

Reynolds, G. S. (1975). *A primer of operant conditioning.* Glenview, IL: Scott, Foresman.

Rhodes, S. R., and Steers, R. M. (1981). Conventional vs. worker-owned organizations. *Human Relations, 12,* 1013–1035.

Rice, R. W., Gentile, D. A., and Gentile, D. B. (1991). Facet importance and job satisfaction. *Journal of Applied Psychology, 76,* 31–39.

Rifkin, J. (1995). *The end of work.* New York: Putnam.

Rigby, C. S., Deci, E. L., Patrick, B. C., and Ryan, R. M. (1992). Beyond the intrinsic–extrinsic dichotomy: Self-determination in motivation and learning. *Motivation and Emotion, 16,* 165–185.

Ringelmann, M. (1913). *Reserches sur les moteurs animes: Travail de l'homme [Research on animate sources of power: The work of man].* Annales de l'Institut National Agronomique, 2e serie - tome XII, 1–40.

Ritti, R. R. (1994). *The ropes to skip and the ropes to know* (4th ed.). New York: Wiley.

Ritti, R. R., and Funkhouser, G. R. (1977). *The ropes to skip and the ropes to know.* Columbus, OH: Grid.

Rizzo, J. R., House, R. J., and Lirtzrman, S. E. (1970). Role conflict and ambiguity in complex organizations. *Administrative Science Quarterly, 15,* 150–163.

Roberts, K. H., and Glick, W. (1981). The job characteristics approach to task design: A critical review. *Journal of Applied Psychology, 66,* 193–217.

Robinson, S. L., and Rousseau, D. M. (1994). Violating the psychological contract: Not the exception but the norm. *Journal of Organizational Behavior, 15,* 245–259.

Rodgers, R. (1992). A foundation of good management in government: Managing by objectives. *Public Administration Review, 52*(1), 27–39.

Rodgers, R., and Hunter, J. E. (1991). Impact of management by objectives on organizational productivity. *Journal of Applied Psychology, 76,* 322–336.

Rodgers, R., Hunter, J. E., and Rogers, D. L. (1993). Influence of top management commitment on management program success. *Journal of Applied Psychology, 78,* 151–155.

Roethlisberger, F. J. (1945). The foreman: Master and victim of double-talk. *Harvard Business Review, 23,* 283–298.

Roethlisberger, F. J., and Dickson, W. J. (1939). *Management and the worker.* Cambridge, MA: Harvard University Press.

Rofe, Y., and Lewin, I. (1988). Social comparison or utility: An experimental examination. *Social Behavior and Personality, 16*(1), 5–10.

Rogers, C. R. (1959). A theory of therapy, personality, and interpersonal relationships as developed in the client-centered framework. In S. Koch (Ed.), *Psychology: A study of a science* (Vol. 3, 184–256). New York: McGraw-Hill.

Rogers, C. R., and Skinner, B. F. (1956). Some issues concerning the control of human behavior: A symposium. *Science, 124,* 1057–1066.

Rokeach, M. (1967). *Value survey.* Palo Alto, CA: Consulting Psychologists Press.

Rokeach, M. (1969). *Beliefs, attitudes and values.* San Francisco: Jossey-Bass.

Rokeach, M. (1973). *The nature of human values.* New York: Free Press.

Rokeach, M. (1979). From individual to institutional values: With special reference to the values of science. In M. Rokeach (Ed.), *Understanding human values.* New York: Free Press.

Romzek, B. S. (1989). Personal consequences of organizational commitment. *Academy of Management Journal, 32,* 649–661.

Rose, S. (1977, May). More bang for the buck: The magic of electronic banking. *Fortune,* pp. 202–205, 208, 212, 216, 218, 221, 223, 226.

Rosen, B., and Jerdee, T. H. (1974a). Effects of applicant's sex and difficulty of job on evaluations of candidates for managerial positions. *Journal of Applied Psychology, 59,* 511–512.

Rosen, B., and Jerdee, T. H. (1974b). Influence of sex role stereotypes on personnel decisions. *Journal of Applied Psychology, 59,* 9–14.

Rosen, B., and Jerdee, T. H. (1974c). Factors influencing disciplinary judgments. *Journal of Applied Psychology, 59,* 327–331.

Rosen, B., and Jerdee, T. H. (1976). The influence of age stereotypes on managerial decisions. *Journal of Applied Psychology, 61,* 428–432.

Rosen, B. C., Crockett, H. J., and Nunn, C. Z. (Eds.). (1969). *Achievement in American society.* Cambridge, MA: Schenkman.

Rosenberg, M., Schooler, C., Schoenbach, C., and Rosenberg, F. (1995). Global self-esteem and specific self-esteem: Different concepts, different outcomes. *American Sociological Review, 60,* 141–156.

Rosener, J. B. (1990). Ways women lead. *Harvard Business Review, 68*(6), 119–125.

Rosenthal, R. (1976). *Experimenter effects in behavioral research* (2nd ed.). New York: Wiley.

Ross, A. (1948). *Trade union wage policy.* Berkeley, CA: University of California Press.

Ross, L., and Nisbett, R. E. (1991). *The person and the situation: Perspectives on social psychology.* New York: McGraw-Hill.

Ross, M. (1975). Salience of reward and intrinsic motivation. *Journal of Personality and Social Psychology, 32,* 245–254.

Rotondi, T. (1975). Organizational identification issues and implications. *Organizational Behavior and Human Performance, 13,* 95–109.

Rotter, J. B. (1955). The role of the psychological situation in determining the direction of human behavior. In M. R. Jones (Ed.), *Nebraska symposium on motivation.* Lincoln, NE: University of Nebraska Press.

Rousseau, D. M. (1977). Technological differences in job characteristics, employee satisfaction, and motivation: A synthesis of job design research and sociotechnical systems theory. *Organizational Behavior and Human Performance, 19,* 18–42.

Rousseau, D. M. (1989). Psychological and implied contracts in organizations. *Employee Responsibilities and Rights Journal, 2,* 121–139.

Rousseau, D. M., and Parks, J. M. (1993). The contracts of individuals and organizations. In L. L. Cummings and B. M. Staw (Eds.), *Research in organizational behavior* (Vol. 15, pp. 1–44). Greenwich, CT: JAI Press.

Rowan, R. (1981). Rekindling corporate loyalty. *Fortune, 103*(3), 54–58.

Roy, D. (1952). Quota restriction and gold bricking in a machine shop. *American Journal of Sociology, 57,* 427–442.

Roy, D. (1959–1960). Banana time. *Human Organization, 18*(4), 158–168.

Royce, J. R. (1975). Psychology is multi: Methodological, variate, epistemic, work view, paradigmatic, systemic, theoretic, and disciplinary. In H. E. Howe (Ed.), *Nebraska symposium on motivation* (Vol. 23). Lincoln, NE: University of Nebraska Press.

Runkel, P., and McGrath, J. (1972). *Research on human behavior: A systematic guide to method.* New York: Holt, Rinehart and Winston.

Runnion, A., Johnson, T., and McWhorter, J. (1978). The effects of feedback and reinforcement on truck turnaround time in materials transportation. *Journal of Organizational Behavior Management, 1,* 110–117.

Runnion, A., Watson, J. O., and McWhorter, J. (1978). Energy savings in interstate transportation through feedback and reinforcement. *Journal of Organizational Behavior Management, 1,* 180–191.

Russell, J. A. (1991). In defense of a prototype approach to emotion concepts. *Journal of Personality and Social Psychology, 60,* 337–347.

Russell, J. A., Fernandez-Dols, J.-M., Manstead, A. S. R., and Wellenkamp, J. C. (Eds.). (1994). *Everyday conceptions of emotions.* Dordrecht, The Netherlands: Kluwer.

Russell, J. W., and Ward, L. M. (1982). Environmental psychology. *Annual Review of Psychology, 33,* 651–688.

Ryan, T. A. (1970). *Intentional behavior.* New York: Ronald Press.

Ryan, T. A., and Smith, P. C. (1954). *Principles of industrial psychology.* New York: Ronald Press.

Saari, L. M., and Latham, G. P. (1982). Employee reactions to continuous and variable ratio reinforcement schedules involving a monetary incentive. *Journal of Applied Psychology, 67,* 506–508.

Sackman, S. A. (1992). Culture and subcultures: An analysis of organizational knowledge. *Administrative Science Quarterly, 37,* 140–161.

Sagie, A., and Koslowsky, M. (1994). Organizational attitudes and behaviors as a function of participation in strategic and tactical change decisions: An application of path-goal theory. *Journal of Organizational Behavior, 15,* 37–47.

Salancik, G. (1977). Commitment and the control of organizational behavior and belief. In B. M. Staw and G. R. Salancik (Eds.), *New directions in organizational behavior* (pp. 1–54). Chicago: St. Clair Press.

Salancik, G. R., and Pfeffer, J. (1974). The uses and abuses of power in organizational decision making. *Administrative Science Quarterly, 19,* 453–473.

Salancik, G. R., and Pfeffer, J. (1977). An examination of need satisfaction models of job attitudes. *Administrative Science Quarterly, 22,* 427–456.

Salancik, G. R., and Pfeffer, J. A. (1978). Social information processing approach to job attitudes and task design. *Administrative Science Quarterly, 23,* 224–253.

Saleh, S. D., and Hosek, J. (1976). Job involvement: Concepts and measures. *Academy of Management Journal, 19*(2), 213–224.

Salovey, P. (Ed.). (1991). *The psychology of jealousy and envy,* New York: Guilford Press.

Salovey, P., Hsee, C. K., and Mayer, J. D. (1993). Emotional intelligence and the self-regulation of affect. In D. M. Wegner and J. W. Pennebaker (Eds.), *Handbook of mental control* (pp. 258–277). Englewood Cliffs, NJ: Prentice Hall.

Salovey, P., and Mayer, J. D. (1990). Emotional intelligence. *Imagination, Cognition, and Personality, 9*(3), 185–211.

Sandelands, L. E., and Buckner, G. C. (1989). Of art and work: Aesthetic experience and the psychology of work feelings. In L. L. Cummings and B. M. Staw (Eds.), *Research in organizational behavior* (Vol. 11, pp. 105–132). Greenwich, CT: JAI Press.

Sandler, B. E. (1974). Eclecticism at work: Approaches to job design. *American Psychologist, 29,* 767–773.

Sanna, L. J. (1992). Self-efficacy theory: Implications for social facilitation and social loafing *Journal of Personality and Social Psychology, 62,* 744–786.

Sarason, I. G. (1977). The growth of interactional psychology. In D. Magnusson and N. S. Endler (Eds.), *Personality at the crossroads* (pp. 261–272). Hillsdale, NJ: Lawrence Erlbaum.

Sarbin, T. R. (1986). Emotion and act: Roles and rhetoric. In R. Harre (Ed.), *The social construction of emotions* (pp. 83–97). New York: Basil Blackwell.

Sashkin, M., and Williams, R. L. (1990). Does fairness make a difference? *Organizational Dynamics, 18*(3), 56–71.

Sayles, L., and Strauss, G. (1977). *Managing human resources.* Englewood Cliffs, NJ: Prentice Hall.

Schacter, H. (1996, March). Measure for measure: Does pay equity work? *Chatelaine, 69*(3), 39–43, 78–82.

Schacter, S., and Singer, J. (1962). Cognitive, social, and physiological determinants of emotional states. *Psychological Review, 69,* 379–399.

Schaef, A. W., and Fassel, D. (1988). *The addictive organization.* San Francisco: Harper and Row.

Schein, E. H. (1970). *Organizational psychology* (2nd ed.). Englewood Cliffs, NJ: Prentice Hall.

Schein, E. H. (1978). *Career dynamics.* Reading, MA: Addison-Wesley.

Schein, V. (1973). The relationship between sex role stereotypes and requisite management characteristics. *Journal of Applied Psychology, 57,* 95–100.

Schein, V. (1975). Relationships between sex role stereotypes and requisite management characteristics among female managers. *Journal of Applied Psychology, 60,* 340–344.

Schlenker, B. R., and Leary, M. R. (1982). Social anxiety and self-presentations: A conceptualization and model. *Psychological Bulletin, 92,* 641–669.

Schlesinger, L. A., and Walton, R. E. (1976). Work restructuring in unionized organizations: Risks, opportunities, and impact on collective bargaining. In J. L. Stern and B. D. Dennis (Eds.), *Proceedings of the 29th Annual Winter Meeting.* Madison WI: Industrial Relations Research Association.

Schmidt, F. L. (1973). Implications of a measurement problem for expectancy theory research. *Organizational Behavior and Human Performance, 10,* 243–251.

Schmidt, F. L., and Hunter, J. E. (1977). Development of a general solution to the problem of validity generalization. *Journal of Applied Psychology, 62,* 529–540.

Schmidt, F. L., and Hunter, J. E. (1984). A within-setting empirical test of the situational specificity hypothesis in personnel selection. *Personnel Psychology, 37,* 317–326.

Schmidt, F. L., Law, K., Hunter, J. E., Rothstein, H. R., Perlman, K., and McDaniel, M. (1993) Refinements in validity generalization methods: Implications for the situational specificity hypothesis. *Journal of Applied Psychology, 78,* 3–12.

Schmitt, N., and Bedeian, A. G. (1982). A comparison of LISREL and two-stage least squares analysis of a hypothesized life–job reciprocal relationship. *Journal of Applied Psychology, 67,* 806–817.

Schmitt, N., and McCune, J. T. (1981). The relationship between job attitudes and the decision to retire. *Academy of Management Journal, 24,* 795–802.

Schmitt, N., and Pulakos, E. D. (1985). Predicting job satisfaction from life satisfaction: Is there a general satisfaction factor? *International Journal of Psychology, 20,* 155–167.

Schmitz, L. M., and Heneman, H. G. (1980). Do positive reinforcement programs reduce employee absenteeism? *Personnel Administrator, 25,* 87–93.

Schneider, B. (1976). *Staffing organizations.* Pacific Palisades. CA: Goodyear.

Schneider, B. (1983). Interactional psychology and organizational behavior. In L. L. Cummings and B. M. Staw (Eds.), *Research in organizational behavior* (Vol. 5, pp. 1–32). Greenwich, CT: JAI Press.

Schneier, C. E. (1974). Behavior modification in management: A review and critique. *Academy of Management Journal, 17,* 528–548.

Schoderbek, P. P., and Plambeck, D. L. (1978). The missing link in management by objectives continuing responsibilities. *Public Personnel Management, 7,* 19–25.

Schor, J. B. (1991). *The overworked American.* New York: Basic Books.

Schriesheim, C. A., and De Nisi, A. S. (1981). Task dimensions as moderators of the effects of instrumental leadership: A two-sample replicated test of path-goal leadership theory. *Journal of Applied Psychology, 66,* 589–597.

Schriesheim, C. A., and Von Glinow, M. A. (1977). The path-goal theory of leadership: A theoretical and empirical analysis. *Academy of Management Journal,* 398–405.

Schriesheim, J. F., and Schriesheim, C. A. (1980). A test of the path-goal theory of leadership and some suggested directions for future research. *Personnel Psychology, 33,* 349–370.

Schroeder, K. G. (1988). *Mentoring as work-related support: Relationship with employee outcomes.* Unpublished doctoral dissertation, University of British Columbia, Vancouver, British Columbia, Canada.

Schuler, R. S. (1975). Role perceptions, satisfaction and performance. *Journal of Applied Psychology, 60,* 683–687.

Schuster, F. E., and Kindall, A. S. (1974). Management by objectives: Where we stand—A survey of the Fortune 500. *Human Resource Management, 13*(1), 8–11.

Schuster, J. R. (1969). Another look at compensation preferences. *Industrial Management Review, 10,* 1–18.

Schwab, D. P. (1980). Construct validity in organizational behavior. In B. M. Staw and L. L. Cummings (Eds.), *Research in organizational behavior* (Vol. 2, pp. 3–44). Greenwich, CT: JAI Press.

Schwab, D. P., and Cummings, L. L. (1970). Theories of performance and satisfaction: A review. *Industrial Relations, 9*(4), 408–430.

Schwab, D. P. and Cummings, L. L. (1976). A theoretical analysis of task scope on employee performance. *Academy of Management Review, 1*(2), 23–35.

Schwartz, H., and Davis, S. M. (1981, Summer). Matching corporate culture and business strategy. *Organizational Dynamics,* pp. 30–48.

Schwartz, H. S. (1982). Job involvement as obsession–compulsion. *Academy of Management Review, 7,* 429–432.

Schwartz, S. H. (1992). Universals in the content and structure of values: Theoretical advances and empirical tests in 20 countries. In M. P. Zanna (Ed.), *Advances in experimental social psychology* (Vol. 25, pp. 1–65). New York: Academic Press.

Schwartz, S. H., and Bilsky, W. (1987). Toward a universal psychological structure of human values. *Journal of Applied Psychology, 53,* 550–562.

Schwartz, S. H., and Bilsky, W. (1990). Toward a theory of universal content and structure of values: Extensions and cross-cultural replications. *Journal of Applied* Psychology, 58, 878–891.

Schwartz, S. H., and Tessler, R. C. (1972). A test of a model for reducing measured attitude-behavior discrepancies. *Journal of Personality and Social Psychology, 24,* 225–236.

Schwartzer, R. (Ed.). (1992). *Self-efficacy: Thought control of action,* Bristol, PA: Hemisphere.

Schwarz, H. W. (1981). Budgeting and the managerial process. In H. W. Schwartz, A. Sweeny, and R. Rachlin (Eds.), *Handbook of budgeting.* New York: Wiley.

Schwyhart, W. R., and Smith, P. C. (1972). Factors in the job involvement of middle managers. *Journal of Applied Psychology, 56,* 227–233.

Scott, M. B., and Lyman, S. M. (1968). Accounts. *American Sociological Review, 33,* 46–62.

Scott, W. E., Jr. (1966). Activation theory and task design. *Organizational Behavior and Human Performance, 1,* 3–30.

Scott, W. E., Jr. (1976). The effects of extrinsic rewards on intrinsic motivation: A critique. *Organizational Behavior and Human Performance, 156,* 117–129.

Scott, W. E., Jr., and Podsakoff, P. M. (1983). *Behavioral principles in the practice of management,* New York: Wiley.

Seashore, S. E. (1954). *Group cohesiveness in the industrial work group.* Ann Arbor, MI: University of Michigan, Institute for Social Research Social Research Center.

Senger, J. (1971). Managers' perceptions of subordinates' competence as a function of personal value orientations. *Academy of Management Journal, 14,* 415–423.

Seta, J. J., Caisson, J. E., Seta, C. E., and Wang, M. A. (1989). Task performance and perceptions of anxiety: Averaging and summation in an evaluative setting. *Journal of Personality and Social Psychology, 56,* 387–396.

Settles, M. F. (1988). Humane downsizing: Can it be done? *Journal of Business Ethics, 7,* 961–963.

Seybolt, J. W. (1976). Work satisfaction as a function of the person–environment interaction. *Organizational Behavior and Human Performance, 17,* 66–75.

Shaikh, T., and Kanekar, S. (1994). Attitudinal similarity and affiliation need as determinants of interpersonal attraction. *Journal of Social Psychology, 134*(2), 257–259.

Shepard, H. (1956). Nine dilemmas in industrial research. *Administrative Science Quarterly, 1,* 295–309.

Shepard, J. M., and Houghland, J. G. (1978). Contingency theory: "Complex man" or "complex organization"? *Academy of Management Review, 3,* 413–427.

Sheppard, B. H., Hartwick, J., and Warshaw, P. R. (1988). The theory of reasoned action: A meta-analysis of past research with recommendations for modifications and future research. *Journal of Consumer Research, 15,* 325–343.

Sheppard, B. H., Lewicki, R. J., and Minton, J. W. (1992). *Organizational justice: The search for fairness in the workplace.* New York: Lexington Books.

Shetzer, L. (1993). A social information processing model of employee participation. *Organization Science, 4,* 252–268.

Shimp, T. A., and Kavas, A. (1984). The theory of reasoned action applied to coupon usage. *Journal of Consumer Research, 11,* 795–809.

Shingledecker, P. (1983). *Disciplinary equity: Employee perceptions, evaluations, and reactions.* Dissertation submitted to the University of Houston.

Shipper, F., and Manz, C. C. (1992, Winter). Employee self-management without formally-designated teams: An alternative road to empowerment. *Organizational Dynamics, 20*(3), 48–61.

Shull, F. A., and Cummings, L. L. (1966). Enforcing the rules: How do managers differ? *Personnel, 43*(2), 33–39.

Shumaker, S. A., and Brownell, A. (1984). Toward a theory of social support: Closing the conceptual gaps. *Journal of Social Issues, 40,* 11–36.

Sibson, R. E. (1975, February). The high cost of hiring. *Nation's Business,* pp. 85–88.

Siegel, A., and Ruh, R. A. (1973). Job involvement, participation in decision making, personal background, and job behavior. *Organizational Behavior and Human Performance, 19,* 318–327.

Siegel, P. A., Brockner, J., and Tyler, T. R. (1995, August). *Revisiting the interactive relationship between procedural and distributive justice: The role of trust.* Paper presented at the 55th Annual Meeting of the Academy of Management, Vancouver, British Columbia, Canada.

Sikula, A. F. (1971). Values and value systems: Importance and relationship to managerial and organizational behaviour. *Journal of Psychology, 78,* 277–286.

Simmel, G. (1950). *The sociology of George Simmel* [Trans. K. H. Wolff]. New York: Free Press.

Simon, H. A. (1957). *Administrative behavior* (2nd ed.). New York: Macmillan.

Simon, H. A. (1995). The information-processing theory of mind. *American Psychologist, 50,* 507–508.

Sims, H. P., and Szilagyi, A. D. (1976). Job characteristic relationships: Individual and structural moderators. *Organizational Behavior and Human Performance, 17,* 211–230.

Sirota, D., and Wolfson, A. (1972). Job enrichment: What are the obstacles? *Personnel, 49*(3), 8–17.

Skinner, B. F. (1953). *Science and human behavior.* New York: Macmillan.

Skinner, B. F. (1969). *Contingencies of reinforcement: A theoretical analysis.* New York: Appleton-Century-Crofts.

Skinner, B. F. (1971). *Beyond freedom and dignity.* New York: Knopf.

Skinner, B. F. (1974). *About behaviorism.* New York: Knopf.

Skinner, E. A. (1995). *Perceived control, motivation, and coping.* Thousand Oaks, CA: Sage.

Slicter, S. J., Healy, J. J., and Livernash, E. R. (1960). *The impact of collective bargaining on management.* Washington, DC: Brookings Institution.

Smith, A. (1937). *The wealth of nations: Inquiry into the nature and causes of the wealth of nations* (Canaan ed.). New York: Random House.

Smith, F. J. (1977). Work attitudes as predictors of attendance on a specific day. *Journal of Applied Psychology, 62,* 16–19.

Smith, F. J., Roberts, K. H., and Hulin, C. L. (1976). Ten year job satisfaction trends in a stable organization. *Academy of Management Journal, 19,* 462–469.

Smith, F. J., Scott, K. D., and Hulin, C. L. (1977). Trends in job-related attitudes of managerial and professional employees. *Academy of Management Journal, 20,* 454–460.

Smith, P. C. (1992). In pursuit of happiness: Why study general job satisfaction? In C. J. Cranny, P. C. Smith, and E. F. Stone, (Eds.), *Job satisfaction* (pp. 5–19). New York: Lexington Books.

Smith, P. C., Kendall, L. M., and Hulin, C. L. (1969). *The measurement of satisfaction in work and retirement.* Chicago: Rand McNally.

Smith, R. H. (1991). Envy and the sense of injustice. In P. Salovey (Ed.), *The psychology of jealousy and envy.* New York: Guilford Press.

Snyder, R. A., Howard, A., and Hammer, T. H. (1978). The predictive power of within- versus across-subjects scores in expectancy research. *Journal of Psychology, 100,* 285–292.

Snyder, R. A., and Williams, R. R. (1982). Self theory: An integrative theory of work motivation. *Journal of Occupational Psychology, 55,* 257–267.

Somers, M. J. (1995). Organizational commitment, turnover and absenteeism: An examination of direct and interaction effects. *Journal of Organizational Behavior, 16,* 49–58.

Sorenson, E. (1991). *Exploring the reasons behind the narrowing gender gap in earnings.* Washington, DC: Urban Institute Press.

Sorenson, E. (1994). *Comparable worth: Is it a worthy policy?* Princeton, NJ: Princeton University Press.

Spangler, W. D., and House, R. J. (1991). Presidential effectiveness and the leadership motive profile. *Journal of Personality and Social Psychology, 60,* 439–455.

Spector, P. E. (1978). Organizational frustration: A model art review of the literature. *Personnel Psychology, 31,* 815–829.

Spector, P. E. (1997). The role of frustration in antisocial behavior at work. In R. A. Giacalone and J. Greenberg (Eds.), *Antisocial behavior in organizations* (p. 17). Thousand Oaks, CA: Sage.

Spencer, H. (1870). *The principles of psychology* (Vol. 1, 2nd ed.). New York: Appleton.

Spreitzer, G. M. (1995a). Psychological empowerment in the workplace: Dimensions, measurement, and validation. *Academy of Management Journal, 38,* 1442–1465.

Spreitzer, G. M. (1995b). An empirical test of a comprehensive model of intrapersonal empowerment in the workplace. *American Journal of Community Psychology, 38,* 1442–1465.

Spreitzer, G. M. (1996). Social structural characteristics of psychological empowerment. *Academy of Management Journal, 39,* 483–504.

Stagner, R. (1956). *Psychology of industrial conflict.* New York: Wiley.

Standing, T. E. (1973). Satisfaction with the work itself as a function of cognitive complexity. *Proceedings, 81st Annual Convention,* American Psychological Association, pp. 603–604.

Staw, B. M. (1976). *Intrinsic and extrinsic motivation.* Morristown, NJ: General Learning Press, an imprint of Silver Burdett Company.

Staw, B. M. (1977). Motivation in organizations: Toward synthesis and redirection. In B. M. Staw and G. R. Salancik (Eds.), *New directions in organizational behavior* (pp. 55–96). Chicago: St. Clair Press.

Staw, B. M. (1984). Organizational behavior: A review and reformulation of the field's outcome variables. *Annual Review of Psychology, 35,* 627–666.

Staw, B. M., and Boettger, R. D. (1990). Task revision: A neglected form of work performance. *Academy of Management Journal, 33,* 534–559.

Steers, R. M. (1977). Antecedents and outcomes of organizational commitment. *Administrative Science Quarterly, 22,* 46–56.

Steers, R. M., and Mowday, R. T. (1977). The motivational properties of tasks. *Academy of Management Review, 2,* 645–658.

Steers, R. M., and Porter, L. W. (Eds.). (1975). *Motivation and work behavior.* New York: McGraw-Hill.

Steers, R. M., and Porter, L. W. (Eds.). (1979). *Motivation and work behavior* (2nd ed.). New York: McGraw-Hill.

Steers, R. M., and Porter, L. W. (Eds.). (1991). *Motivation and work behavior* (5th ed.). New York: McGraw-Hill.

Steers, R. M., and Rhodes, S. (1978). Major influences on employee attendance: A process model. *Journal of Applied Psychology, 63,* 391–407.

Stein, A. H., and Bailey, M. M. (1973). The socialization of achievement motivation in females. *Psychological Bulletin, 80,* 345–366.

Stein, C. (1975). Objectives management systems: Two to five years after implementation. *Personnel Journal, 54*(10), 525–528, 548.

Stevens, J. M., Beyer, J. M., and Trice, H. M. (1978). Assessing personal, role and organizational predictors of managerial commitment. *Academy of Management Journal, 21,* 380–396.

Stewart, A. J. (Ed.). (1982). *Motivation and society.* San Francisco: Jossey-Bass.

Stewart, A. J., and Chester, N. L. (1982). Sex differences in human social motives: Achievement, affiliation, and power. In A. Stewart (Ed.), *Motivation and society* (pp. 172–220). San Francisco: Jossey-Bass.

Stockdale, M. S. (Ed.). (1996). *Sexual harassment in the workplace.* Thousand Oaks, CA: Sage.

Stoffman, D. (1991). How to steal from the company. *Canadian Business, 64*(7), 56–60.

Stone, E. F. (1992). A critical analysis of social information processing models of job perceptions and job attitudes. In C. J. Cranny, P. C. Smith, and E. F. Stone (Eds.), *Job satisfaction* (pp. 21–52). New York: Lexington Books.

Strauss, G. (1982). Workers' participation in management: An international perspective. In B. M. Staw and L. L. Cummings (Eds.), *Research in organizational behavior* (Vol. 4, pp. 173–266). Greenwich, CT: JAI Press.

Striker, L. J. (1988). Measuring social status with occupational information: A simple method. *Journal of Applied Social Psychology, 18,* 423–437.

Stuart, P. (1992). Murder on the job. *Personnel Journal, 71*(2), 72–84.

Stumpf, S. A., and Dawley, P. K. (1981). Predicting voluntary and involuntary turnover using absenteeism and performance indices. *Academy of Management Journal, 24,* 148–163.

Sullivan, J. J. (1986). Human nature, organizations, and management theory. *Academy of Management Review, 11,* 534–549.

Sullivan, J. J. (1989). Self theories and employee motivation. *Journal of Management, 15,* 345–363.

Sussman, M., and Vecchio, R. P. (1985). Conceptualizations of valence and instrumentality: A fourfold model. *Organizational Behavior and Human Decision Processes, 36,* 96–112.

Swan, K. P. (1982). Union impact on management of the organization: A legal perspective. In J. Anderson and M. Gunderson (Eds.), *Union–management relations in Canada* (pp. 269–288). Don Mills, Ontario, Canada: Addison-Wesley.

Sweeney, P. D., and McFarlin, D. B. (1993). Workers' evaluations of the "ends" and the "means": An examination of four models of distributive and procedural justice. *Organizational Behavior and Human Decision Processes, 55,* 23–40.

Taber, T. D., and Alliger, G. M. (1995). A task-level assessment of job satisfaction. *Journal of Organizational Behavior, 16,* 101–122.

Tajfel, H., and Turner, J. C. (1985). The social identity theory of intergroup behavior. In S. Worchel and W. G. Austin (Eds.), *Psychology of intergroup relations* (pp. 7–24). Chicago: Nelson-Hall.

Tannenbaum, S. I., Mathieu, J. E., Salas, E., and Cannon-Bowers, J. A. (1991). Meeting trainees' expectations: The influence of training fulfillment on the development of commitment, self-efficacy, and motivation. *Journal of Applied Psychology, 76,* 759–769.

Tausky, C. (1995). The meanings of work. In R. L. Simpson and I. H. Simpson (Eds.), *Research in the sociology of work: The meaning of work* (5th ed., pp. 15–27). Greenwich, CT: JAI Press.

Tavris, C. (1982). *Anger: The misunderstood emotion.* New York: Simon and Schuster.

Taylor E. K., and Griess, T. (1976). The missing middle in validation research. *Personnel Psychology, 29,* 5–11.

Taylor, F. W. (1967). *The principles of scientific management.* New York: Norton (originally published 1911).

Taylor, L., and Watson, P. (1971). Industrial sabotage: Motives and meanings. In S. Cohen (Ed.) *Images of deviance* (pp. 219–245). Harmondsworth, Middlesex, England: Penguin Books.

Tead, O. (1918). *Instincts in industry.* New York: Arno and *The New York Times.*

Tead, O. (1929). *Human nature and management.* New York: McGraw-Hill.

Telly, C. S., French, W. L., and Scott, W. G. (1971). The relationship of inequity to turnover among hourly workers. *Administrative Science Quarterly, 16,* 164–171.

Terborg, J. R. (1977). Validation and extension of an individual differences model of work performance. *Organizational Behavior and Human Performance, 18,* 188–216.

Terborg, J. R., and Ilgen, D. R. (1975). A theoretical approach to sex discrimination in traditionally masculine occupations. *Organizational Behavior and Human Performance, 13,* 352–376.

Terpstra, D. E., and Rozell, E. J. (1994). The relationship of goal setting to organizational profitability. *Group and Organization Management, 19,* 285–294.

Tesser, A., and Shaffer, D. R. (1990). Attitudes and attitude change. *Annual Review of Psychology, 41,* 479–523.

Thibault, J., and Walker, L. (1975). *Procedural justice: A psychological analysis.* Hillsdale, NJ: Lawrence Erlbaum.

Thibault, J., and Walker, L. (1978). A theory of procedure. *California Law Review, 66,* 541–566.

Thierry, H. (1990). Intrinsic motivation reconsidered. In U. Kleinbeck, H. H. Quast, H. Thierry, and H. Hacker (Eds.), *Work motivation* (pp. 67–82). Hillsdale, NJ: Lawrence Erlbaum.

Thomas, C. C., and Ross, T. (1991). Effective leadership: Evaluations of the next generation of workers. *Psychological Reports, 69,* 51–61.

Thomas, J. G., and Griffin, R. W. (1989). The power of social information in the workplace. *Organizational Dynamics, 18*(2), 63–75.

Thomas, K. M., and Mathieu, J. E. (1994). Role of causal attributions in dynamic self-regulation and goal processes. *Journal of Applied Psychology, 79,* 812–818.

Thomas, K. W., and Tymon, W. G., Jr. (1982). Necessary properties of relevant research: Lessons from recent criticisms of the organizational sciences. *Academy of Management Review, 7,* 345–352.

Thomas, K. W., and Velthouse, B. A. (1990). Cognitive elements of empowerment: An "interpretive" model of intrinsic task motivation. *Academy of Management Review, 15,* 666–681.

Thompson, J. D. (1967). *Organizations in action.* New York: McGraw-Hill.

Thomsen, D. (1981). Compensation and benefits. *Personnel Journal, 60*(4), 258–259.

Thoresen, E., and Mahoney, M. (1974). *Behavioral self control.* New York: Holt, Rinehart and Winston.

Thorndike, E. L. (1911). *Animal intelligence.* New York: Macmillan.

Thurow, L. C. (1980). *The zero-sum society.* New York: Penguin Books.

Tice, D. M., and Baumeister, R. F. (1993). Controlling anger: Self-induced emotion change. In D. M. Wegner and J. W. Pennebaker (Eds.), *Handbook of mental control* (pp. 393–409). Englewood Cliffs, NJ: Prentice Hall.

Tien, E., and Frankel, V. (1996). *The I hate my job handbook.* New York: Fawcett Columbine.

Tolman, E. C. (1932). *Purposive behavior in animals and men.* New York: Century.

Tolman, E. C. (1959). Principles of purposive behavior. In S. Koch (Ed.), *Psychology: A study of a science.* (Vol. 2). New York: McGraw-Hill.

Toneatto, T., and Binik, Y. (1987). The role of intentions, social norms, and attitudes in the performance of dental flossing: A test of the theory of reasoned action. *Journal of Applied Social Psychology, 17,* 593–603.

Torbert, W. R. (1994). The good life: Good money, good work, good friends, good questions. *Journal of Management Inquiry, 3*(4), 58–66.

Tornblom, K. Y. (1977). Distributive justice: Typology and propositions. *Human Relations, 30,* 1–25.

Tornow, W. W. (1971). The development and application of an input–outcome moderator test on the perception and reduction of inequity. *Organizational Behavior and Human Performance, 6,* 614–638.

Tosi, H. L. (1977). The human effects of budgeting systems on management. In F. Luthans (Ed.), *Contemporary readings in organizational behavior* (pp. 153–167). New York: McGraw-Hill.

Trevino, L. K. (1992). The social effects of punishment in organizations: A justice perspective. *Academy of Management Review, 17,* 647–676.

Trice, H. M., Belasco, J., and Alutto, J. A. (1969). The role of ceremonials in organizational behavior. *Industrial and Labor Relations Review, 23*(1), 40–51.

Tsui, A. S., and Ashford, S. J. (1994). Adaptive self-regulation: A process view of managerial effectiveness. *Journal of Management, 20,* 93–121.

Tubbs, M. E. (1986). Goal setting: A meta-analytic examination of the empirical evidence. *Journal of Applied Psychology, 71,* 474–483.

Tubbs, M. E. (1993). Commitment as a moderator of the goal-performance relation: A case for clearer construct definition. *Journal of Applied Psychology, 78,* 86–97.

Tubbs, M. E. (1994). Commitment and the role of ability in motivation: Comment on Wright, O'Leary-Kelly, Cortina, Klein, and Hollenbeck. *Journal of Applied Psychology, 79,* 804–811.

Tubbs, M. E., and Ekeberg, S. E. (1991). The role of intentions in work motivation: Implications for goal-setting theory and research. *Academy of Management Journal, 16,* 180–199.

Tuckman, B. W. (1968). Personality and satisfaction with occupational choice: Role of environment as a mediator. *Psychological Reports, 23,* 543–550.

Turner, A. N., and Lawrence, P. R. (1965). *Industrial jobs and the worker.* Boston: Harvard University, School of Business Administration.

Turner, A. N., and Miclette, A. L. (1962). Sources of satisfaction in repetitive work. *Occupational Psychology, 36,* 215–231.

Tyler, L. E. (1965). *The psychology of human differences.* New York: Appleton-Century-Crofts.

Urwick, L. F. (1967). Organization and theories about the nature of man. *Academy of Management Journal, 10,* 9–15.

U.S. Congress, Office of Technology Assessment. (1990, September). *The use of integrity tests for pre-employment screening.* OTA-SET-442. Washington, DC: U.S. Government Printing Office.

U.S. Department of Labor. (1970). *Seniority in promotion and transfer provisions.* Bulletin 1425–11. Washington, DC: Bureau of Labor Statistics.

U.S. Department of Labor, Women's Bureau. (1977). *Brief highlights of major federal laws and order on sex discrimination in employment.* Washington, DC: U.S. Government Printing Office.

Vancouver Province. (1996, June 27). Medal 78 years later. p. A26.

Vancouver Sun. (1993, January 26). In love and work, the labor isn't easy. B1–B2.

Vancouver Sun. (1994, September 19). Toilet toll angers workers as meat plant targets bathroom-break abusers.

Vandenberg, R. J., and Lance, C. E. (1992). Examining the causal order of job satisfaction and organizational commitment. *Journal of Management, 18,* 153–167.

Van Der Merwe, S. (1978). What personal attributes it takes to make it in management. *Business Quarterly, 43*(4), 28–35.

Van de Ven, A. H. (1989). Nothing is quite so practical as a good theory. *Academy of Management Review, 14,* 486–489.

Van Maanen, J. (1977). Experiencing organization notes on the meaning of careers and socialization. In J. Van Maanen (Ed.), *Organizational careers: Some new perspectives* (pp. 15–45). New York: Wiley.

Van Maanen, J., and Kunda, G. (1989). "Real feelings": Emotional expression and organizational culture. In L. L. Cummings and B. M. Staw (Eds.), *Research in organizational behavior* (Vol. 11, pp. 43–104). Greenwich, CT: JAI Press.

Van Sommers, P. (1988). *Jealousy.* London: Penguin Books.

Vannoy, J. S. (1965). Generality of cognitive complexity–simplicity as a personality construct. *Journal of Personality and Social Psychology, 2,* 385–396.

Veale, J. (1993). More men switching loyalties from firms to their families. Reprinted from the *London Observer* as it appeared in the *Vancouver Sun,* July 17, 1993. A9.

Vecchio, R. P. (1995). It's not easy being green: Jealousy and envy in the workplace. In G. R. Ferris (Ed.), *Research in personnel and human resource management* (Vol. 13, pp. 201–244). Greenwich, CT: JAI Press.

Vroom, V. H. (1964). *Work and motivation.* New York: Wiley.

Waele, M. de, Marvel, J., and Sheitoyan, R. G. (1992). *Self management in organizations.* Seattle, WA: Hogrefe and Huber.

Wagner, J. A., III. (1994). Participation's effect on performance and satisfaction: A reconsideration of research evidence. *Academy of Management Journal, 19,* 312–330.

Wahba, M. A., and Bridwell, L. G. (1976). Maslow reconsidered: A review of research on the need hierarchy theory. *Organizational Behavior and Human Performance, 15,* 212–240.

Wall, T. D., and Lischeron, J. A. (1977). *Worker participation.* London: McGraw-Hill.

Wallace, D. (1991, September). The power of goals. *Success, 38*(7), 40–43.

Wallace, M. J. (1988). Methodology, research practice, and progress in personnel and industrial relations. *Academy of Management Review, 8,* 6–13.

Walsh, J. P., and Ungson, G. R. (1991). Organizational memory. *Academy of Management Review, 16,* 92–120.

Walster, E., Berschied, E., and Walster, G. W. (1976). New directions in equity research. In L. Berkowitz and E. Walster (Eds.), *Advances in experimental social psychology* (Vol. 9, 1–38). New York: Academic Press.

Walter, G. A., and Marks, S. E. (1981). *Experimental learning and change.* New York: Wiley.

Walter, G. A., and Pinder, C. C. (1980). Ethical ascendance or backsliding? *American Psychologist, 35,* 936–937.

Walton, R. E. (1975). The diffusion of new work structures: Why success didn't take. *Organizational Dynamics, 3*(3), 2–22.

Waluchow, W. (1988). Pay equity: Equal value to whom? *Journal of Business Ethics, 7,* 185–189.

Wanous, J. P. (1974). Individual differences and reactions to job characteristics. *Journal of Applied Psychology, 59,* 616–622.

Wanous, J. P. (1980). *Organizational entry: Recruitment, selection and socialization of newcomers.* Reading, MA: Addison-Wesley.

Wanous, J. P., Keon, T. L., and Latack, J. C. (1983). Expectancy theory and occupational/organizational choice: A review and test. *Organizational Behavior and Human Performance, 32,* 66–86.

Wanous, J. P., and Lawler, E. E. (1972). Measurement and meaning of job satisfaction *Journal of Applied Psychology, 56,* 95–105.

Ward, L. M. (1977). Multidimensional scaling of the molar physical environment. *Multivariate Behavioral Research, 12,* 23–42.

Ward, L. M., and Porter, C. A. (1980). Age-group differences in cognition of the molar physical environment: A multidimensional scaling approach. *Canadian Journal of Behavioral Science, 12,* 329–346.

Ward, L. M., and Russell, J. A. (1981). The psychological representation of molar physical environments. *Journal of Experimental Psychology, 110,* 121–152.

Warr, P., Barter, J., and Brownbridge, G. (1983). On the independence of positive and negative affect. *Journal of Personality and Social Psychology, 44,* 644–651.

Warr, P., and Conner, M. (1992). Job competence and cognition. In B. M. Staw L. L. Cummings (Eds.), *Research in organizational behavior* (Vol. 14, pp. 91–127). Greenwich, CT: JAI Press.

Watanabe, T. (1996, July 17). Beneath orderly surface, Japanese life turns ugly. *Los Angeles Times,* reported in the *Vancouver Sun,* p. A10.

Watson, D., Clarke, L. A., and Tellegen, A. (1988). Development and validation of brief measures of positive and negative affect: The Panas scales. *Journal of Personality and Social Psychology, 54,* 1063–1070.

Watson, D., and Slack, A. K. (1993). General factors of affective temperament and their relation to job satisfaction over time. *Organizational Behavior and Human Decision Processes, 54,* 181–202.

Watson Wyatt Worldwide. (1995). *Measuring change in the attitudes of the Canadian workforce.* Toronto: WWW.

Webb, E. J., Campbell, D. T., Schwartz, R. D., and Sechrest, L. (1966). *Unobtrusive measures: Nonreactive research in the social sciences.* Chicago: Rand McNally.

Weber, M. (1930). *The Protestant ethic and the spirit of capitalism* [T. Parsons, Trans.]. New York: Scribner.

Weick, K. E. (1967). Dissonance and task enhancement: A problem for compensation theory? *Organizational Behavior and Human Performance, 2,* 189–207.

Weick, K. E. (1969). *The social psychology of organizing.* Reading, MA: Addison-Wesley.

Weick, K. E. (1989). Theory construction as disciplined imagination. *Academy of Management Review, 14,* 516–531.

Weick, K. E. (1995). *Sensemaking in organizations.* Thousand Oaks, CA: Sage.

Weick, K. E., Bougon, M. G., and Maruyama, G. (1976). The equity context. *Organizational Behavior and Human Performance, 15,* 32–65.

Weick, K. E., and Nesset, B. (1968). Preferences among forms of equity. *Organizational Behavior and Human Performance, 3,* 400–416.

Weil, F. A. (1979, December 3). Management's drag on productivity. *Business Week, 2614,* 14.

Weiner, N. (1948). *Cybernetics: Control and communication in the animal and the machine.* Cambridge, MA: MIT Press.

Weiner, Y. (1982). Commitment in organizations: A normative view. *Academy of Management Review, 7,* 48–428.

Weiner, Y., and Vardi, Y. (1980). Relationships between job organization and career commitments and work outcomes—An integrative approach. *Organizational Behavior and Human Performance, 26,* 81–96.

Weiss, H. M., and Cropanzano, R. (1996). Affective events theory: A theoretical discussion of the structure, causes and consequences of affective experiences at work. In B. M. Staw and L. L. Cummings (Eds.), *Research in organizational behavior* (Vol. 18, pp. 1–74). Greenwich, CT: JAI Press.

Wexley, K. N., and Latham, G. P. (1981). *Developing and training human resources in organizations.* Glenview, IL: Scott, Foresman.

Wexley, K. N., and Yukl, G. A. (1977). *Organizational behavior and personnel psychology,* Homewood, IL: Irwin.

Wharton, A. S. (1993). The affective consequences of service work. *Work and Occupations, 20*(2), 205–232.

Wharton, A. S., and Erickson, R. J. (1993). Managing emotions on the job and at home: Understanding the consequences of multiple emotional roles. *Academy of Management Review, 18,* 457–486.

Wheeler, H. (1976). Punishment theory and industrial discipline. *Industrial Relations, 15,* 235–243.

Whetten, D. A. (1989). What constitutes a theoretical contribution? *Academy of Management Review, 14,* 490–495.

White, J. K. (1978a). Individual differences and the job quality–worker response relationship: Review, integration, and comments. *Academy of Management Review, 3,* 267–280.

White, J. K. (1978b). Generalizability of individual difference moderators of the participation in decision-making–employee response relationship. *Academy of Management Journal, 21,* 36–43.

White, R. (1959). Motivation reconsidered: The concept of competence. *Psychological Review, 66,* 297–333.

Whitsett, D. A., and Winslow, E. K. (1967). An analysis of studies critical of the motivation hygiene theory. *Personnel Psychology, 20,* 121–132.

Whyte, W. F. (1948). *Human relations in the restaurant industry.* New York: McGraw-Hill.

Whyte, W. F. (1972). Pigeons, persons and piece rates. *Psychology Today, 5*(11), 66–68, 96, 98, 100.

Whyte, W. H. (1956). *The organization man.* Garden City, NY: Doubleday Anchor Books.

Wiersma, U. J. (1992). The effects of extrinsic rewards in intrinsic motivation: A meta-analysis. *Journal of Occupational and Organizational Psychology, 65,* 101–114.

Wilcoxon, H. C. (1969). Historical introduction to the problem of reinforcement. In J. T. Tapp (Ed.), *Reinforcement and behavior* (pp. 1–46). New York: Academic Press.

Williams, D. E., and Page, M. M. (1989). A multi-dimensional measure of Maslow's hierarchy of needs. *Journal of Research in Personality, 23,* 192–213.

Williams, L. K., Seybolt, J. W., and Pinder, C. C. (1975). On administering questionnaires in organizational settings. *Personnel Psychology, 28,* 93–103.

Wilson, C. B. (1991). U.S. businesses suffer from workplace trauma. *Personnel Journal, 70*(7), 47–50.

Winell, M. (1987). Personal goals: The key to self-direction in adulthood. In M. E. Ford and D. H. Ford (Eds.), *Humans as self-constructing living systems: Putting the framework to work,* (pp. 261–287). Hillsdale, NJ: Lawrence Erlbaum.

Winter, D. G. (1988). The power motive in women—and men. *Journal of Personality and Social Psychology, 54,* 510–519.

Winter, D. G., and Stewart, A. J. (1978). Power-motivated actions in everyday life. In H. London and J. E. Exner, (Eds.), *Dimensions of personality* (pp. 400–412). New York: Wiley.

Winters, D., and Latham, G. P. (1996). The effect of learning versus outcome goals on a simple versus a complex task. *Group and Organization Management, 21,* 236–250.

Wittig, M. A., and Turner, G. (1988). Implementing comparable worth: Some measurement and conceptual issues in job evaluation. In R. M. Kelly and J. Bayes (Eds.), *Comparable worth, pay equity, and public policy* (pp. 143–148). New York: Greenwood Press.

Wofford, J. C. (1994). An examination of the cognitive processes used to handle employee job problems. *Academy of Management Journal, 37,* 180–192.

Wofford, J. C., and Liska, L. Z. (1993). Path–goal theories of leadership: A meta-analysis. *Journal of Management, 19,* 857–876.

Wohlwill, J. F., and Kohn, I. (1976). Dimensionalizing the environmental manifold. In S. Wapner, S. B. Cohen, and B. Kaplan (Eds.), *Experiencing the environment.* New York: Plenum Press.

Wolf, G., and Connolly, T. (1981). Between-subject designs in testing expectancy models: A methodological note. *Decision Sciences, 12,* 39–45.

Wolfe, M. (1994). Dr. Fabrikant's solution. *Saturday Night, 109*(6), 11–13, 16–18, 56–59.

Wollack, S., Goodale, G., Wijting, P., and Smith, P. C. (1971). Development of the survey of work values. *Journal of Applied Psychology, 55,* 331–338.

Wong, P. T. P. (1979). Frustration, exploration, and learning. *Canadian Psychological Review, 20,* 133–144.

Wood, R., and Bailey, T. C. (1985). Some unanswered questions about goal effects: A recommended change in research methods. *Australian Journal of Management, 10,* 61–73.

Wood, R. E., and Bandura, A. (1989). Social-cognitive theory of organizational management. *Academy of Management Review, 14,* 361–384.

Wood, R. E., and Locke, E. A. (1990). Goal setting and strategy effects on complex tasks. In B. M. Staw and L. L. Cummings (Eds.), *Research in organizational behavior* (Vol. 12, pp. 73–109). Greenwich, CT: JAI Press.

Wood, R. E., Mento, A. J., and Locke, E. A. (1987). Task complexity as a moderator of goal effects: A meta-analysis. *Journal of Applied Psychology, 72,* 416–425.

Woodcock, M., and Francis, D. (1989). *Clarifying organizational values.* Aldershot, Hampshire, England: Gower.

Woodworth, R. S. (1918). *Dynamic psychology.* New York: Columbia University Press.

Wortman, C. B., and Linsenmeier, J. A. W. (1977). Interpersonal attraction and techniques of ingratiation in organizational settings. In B. M. Staw and G. R. Salancik (Eds.), *New directions in organizational behavior* (pp. 133–178). Chicago: St. Clair Press.

Wright, L., and Smye, M. (1996). *Corporate abuse.* Toronto, Ontario, Canada: Key Porter.

Wright, P. M., O'Leary-Kelly, A. M., Cortina, J. M., Klein, H. J., and Hollenbeck, J. R. (1994). On the meaning and measurement of goal commitment. *Journal of Applied Psychology, 79,* 795–803.

Wright, T. A., and Bonett, D. G. (1993). Role of employee coping and performance in voluntary employee withdrawal: A research refinement and elaboration. *Journal of Management, 19,* 147–161.

Wright, T. A., and Staw, B. M. (1994). In search of the happy/productive worker: A longitudinal study of affect and performance. *Best Paper Proceedings, 54th Annual Meeting of the Academy of Management,* Dallas, TX.

Yankelovich, D. (1982). The work ethic is underemployed. *Psychology Today, 16*(5), 5, 6, 8.

Yerkes, R. M., and Dodson, J. D. (1908). The relation of strength of stimulus to rapidity of habit formation. *Journal of Comparative and Neurological Psychology, 18,* 459–482.

Yolles, S. F., Carone, P. A., and Krinsky, L. W. (1975). *Absenteeism in industry.* Springfield, IL: Charles C. Thomas.

Yorks, L. (1979). *Job enrichment revisited.* New York: AMACOM.

Youngblood, S. A., and Bierman, L. (1994). Employment-at-will: New developments and research implications. In G. R. Ferris (Ed.), *Research in personnel and human resources management* (Vol. 12, pp. 303–324). Greenwich, CT: JAI Press.

Yukl, G. A., and Latham, G. P. (1975). Consequences of reinforcement schedules and incentive magnitudes for employee performance: Problems encountered in an industrial setting. *Journal of Applied Psychology, 60*(3), 294–298.

Yukl, G. A., Latham, G. P., and Pursell, E. D. (1976). The effectiveness of performance incentives under continuous and variable ratio schedules of reinforcement. *Personnel Psychology, 29,* 221–231.

Yukl, G. A., Wexley, K. N., and Seymore, J. (1972). Effects of pay incentives under variable ratio and continuous reinforcement schedules. *Journal of Applied Psychology, 56,* 19–23.

Zajonc, R. B. (1960). The concepts of balance, congruity, and dissonance. *Public Opinion Quarterly, 24,* 280–296.

Zajonc, R. B. (1965). Social facilitation. *Science, 149,* 269–274.

Zajonc, R. B. (1980). Feeling and thinking: Preferences need no inferences. *American Psychologist, 35,* 151–175.

Zajonc, R. B. (1984). On the primacy of affect. *American Psychologist, 39,* 117–123.

Zalkind, S. S., and Costello, T. W., (1962). Perception: Some recent research and implications on administration. *Administrative Science Quarterly, 7,* 218–235.

Zaltman, G., and Duncan, R. (1977). *Strategies for planned change.* New York: Wiley.

Zedeck, S. (1977). An information processing model and approach to the study of motivation. *Organizational Behavior and Human Performance, 18,* 47–77.

Zeithaml, V. A., Parasuraman, A., and Berry, L. L. (1990). *Delivering quality service: Balancing customer perceptions and expectations.* New York: Free Press.

Zeldich, M. (1968). Social status. In *International encyclopedia of the social sciences* (pp. 250–256). New York: Free Press.

Ziman, J. M. (1987). The problem of "problem choice." *Minerva, 25,* 92–106.

Zoglin, R. (1996, May 27). A question of honor. *Time, 147*(22), 22–24.

Author Index

Subject Index